MW00824526

SIMPLIFIED
COWBOY VERSION

SIMPLIFIED COWBOY VERSION

A Bible Paraphrase
FOR COWBOYS
BY COWBOYS

Save the Cowboy

CONTENTS

INTRODUCTION

Why would someone work 12 years paraphrasing the New Testament in a way that cowboys could really get in to?

Let me tell you why . . .

The first church I pastored had a booth at the local high school rodeo. We were handing out little pocket-sized Bibles to those who wanted one.

A cowboy walked up to the table, picked up one of these and asked, "Is this a cowboy Bible?"

I said, "Well, it's a New International Version® so it's easier to read than some of the other translations out there."

He handed back the Bible and said, "I have all those easy-to-read translations and I still don't really get it. When you have a Bible that is written for a cowboy, I'll take one and read it. Maybe then I'll understand all those others."

Have you ever felt like God just tapped you on the shoulder without saying a word? That's how I felt when that cowboy walked away.

That evening, I sat down at the kitchen table at the ranch, looked at my horses that were eating, said a prayer, and started paraphrasing Matthew. Twelve years later, I finished Revelation.

I have held on to those words for so long and the vision behind this endeavor holds true to what that West Texas cowboy wanted. The word of God in the words of a cowboy. The sole purpose of this work is so that it will inspire a cowboy to pick up the real word of God and study it.

No, I haven't translated the original text. This is not a Bible. It is a Bible paraphrase, or maybe we can say it is a Bible study aid. And that is what I pray you do. Read this and then go see if that's what the real Bible says.

Kevin Weatherby
April 2021

NEW TESTAMENT

MATTHEW

CHAPTER 1

The Family Tree

This is a list of how Jesus came all the way from Abraham and down through King David (because it was said long ago God's Boy would come through David):

² Abraham was Isaac's daddy. Isaac was Jacob's daddy.

Jacob was Judah and his brothers' daddy.

³ Judah was Perez and Zerah's daddy (Tamar was their momma). Perez was Hezron's daddy.

Hezron was Ram's daddy.

⁴ Ram was Amminadab's daddy. Amminadab was Nahshon's daddy. Nahshon was Salmon's daddy.

⁵ Salmon was Boaz's daddy (Rahab was his momma). Boaz was Obed's daddy (Ruth was his momma).

Obed was Jesse's daddy.

⁶ Jesse was King David's daddy.

David was Solomon's daddy (whose momma was Bathsheba, the widow lady of Uriah).

⁷ Solomon was Rehoboam's daddy. Rehoboam was Abijah's daddy.

Abijah was Asa's daddy.

⁸ Asa was Jehoshaphat's daddy. Jehoshaphat was Jehoram's daddy. Jehoram was Uzziah's daddy.

⁹ Uzziah was Jotham's daddy. Jotham was Ahaz's daddy.

Ahaz was Hezekiah's daddy.

¹⁰ Hezekiah was Manasseh's daddy. Manasseh was Amon's daddy.

Amon was Josiah's daddy.

¹¹ Josiah was Jehoiachin and his brothers' daddy.

¹² After the Babylonian boot out:

Jehoiachin was Shealtiel's daddy. Shealtiel was Zerubbabel's daddy. ¹³ Zerubbabel was Abihud's daddy. Abihud was Eliakim's daddy.

Eliakim was Azor's daddy. ¹⁴ Azor was Zadok's daddy. Zadok was Akim's daddy. Akim was Eliud's daddy.

¹⁵ Eliud was Eleazar's daddy. Eleazar was Matthan's daddy. Matthan was Jacob's daddy.

¹⁶ Jacob was Joseph's daddy, and Joseph was hitched to Mary. Mary gave birth to Jesus, who is called the Saving Hero.

¹⁷ So there were fourteen generations from Abraham until David. Then there was another fourteen from David till the time the Jews were taken captive to Babylon, and fourteen from the captivity in Babylon until the Christ.

Joseph and the Birth of Jesus

¹⁸ Before Jesus was born, Joseph had asked for Mary's hand in marriage. Joseph had been honorable toward Mary and she was unspoiled. But before they could get hitched, Mary became pregnant through the power of the Holy Ghost. ¹⁹ In order to avoid an embarrassing shotgun wedding, Joseph was just gonna go away and leave Mary quietly.

²⁰ While Joseph sat ponderin' his options, an angel appeared to him and told him not to run out on Mary. Seems her baby wasn't by any human, but conceived by the Holy Ghost. ²¹ "She's gonna have a son," the angel said. "Be sure and call him Jesus, 'cause he's gonna end up savin' everyone from their sins."

²² This all happened because a prophet had already said, ²³ "A gal that's never been with a man will have her a child and call him Emmanuel"—which is a fancy way of sayin', "God's with us."

²⁴ Joseph went and did just what that angel told him to and tied the knot with Mary. ²⁵ But he didn't never go to her bed like a husband would usually do until after Jesus was born.

CHAPTER 2

Strangers from Afar

After Jesus was born in Bethlehem, while Herod was King, some strangers from the East visited Jerusalem ² and asked, "Where's the little one that's meant to be the King of the Jews? We seen a bright light from way over yonder and we have come to hit a knee before him."

³ King Herod was plumb disturbed, along with all of Jerusalem, at the things the strangers said. ⁴ He gathered up every person who worked around there who had a lick of sense and asked 'em where the Christ was to be born. ⁵ They all told him it was supposed to be in Bethlehem based on what a wise fellow of God had said, ⁶ "Bethlehem ain't no little place among Judah. From you will come a cowboy who will gather all of the herd together and take care of 'em."

⁷ Then Herod asked those strangers when the bright light had appeared in the sky. ⁸ He told 'em to ride for Bethlehem and find this baby they was a lookin' for and send him a message when they did. Herod wanted to come and grab a knee, with his hat in his hands, right along with them.

⁹ The strangers rode hard and followed the light until it stopped over where Jesus was layin'. ¹⁰ When they saw the bright star, they was overcome with happiness. ¹¹ When they got to the house and saw Mary holdin' Jesus, they grabbed a knee and worshiped him. Then they went to their saddlebags and brought out some sure enough nice gifts for the baby. ¹² They rode off at first light, but they didn't return to old Herod. An angel had told them to take another trail and strike a long trot back to where they'd come from.

The Getaway

¹³ After the strangers had lit out, an angel came to Joseph while he was dreamin'. "Saddle up," the angel told him, "ride hard for Egypt and hunker down there until I tell you it's safe. Herod's gonna start killin' all the kids and he's hopin' Jesus is one of 'em."

¹⁴ So Joseph took Mary and Jesus and struck a long lope for Egypt. ¹⁵ He stayed there until Herod had kicked the bucket. This fulfilled a long ago sayin' that said, "My Son's gonna come out of Egypt when I call for him."

¹⁶ When old Herod realized he'd been double-crossed by the strangers, he was spittin' nails. He gave orders to slaughter all the boys in the territory who were two years old or younger. That's the age the strangers had reckoned Jesus to be. ¹⁷ This also brought truth to a long ago foretelling by the prophet Jeremiah, ¹⁸ "There will be wailin' and weepin'. Rachel will cry for her kids and won't take to any comfortin' by anyone because they are all gone."

Headin' Home

¹⁹ When Herod was dead, an angel once again came to Joseph in a dream and ²⁰ told him, "Light out for home. Take Jesus and his momma back. The danger has passed on by."

²¹ So Joseph saddled up and they traveled back to Israel. ²² But when he found out that Archelaus had taken his father Herod's place on the throne, he became scared. Another dream had warned him, so he detoured into Galilee territory, ²³ and made permanent camp in a place called Nazareth. Once again, this made true the old saying, "He's gonna be called a Nazarene."

CHAPTER 3

John the Baptist Blazes a Trail for Jesus

Durin' this time, John the Baptist was preachin' in the dry country of Judea ² and tellin' folks, "Make right your minds, for God's Green Pasture is near." ³ John is who Isaiah was talkin' about when he said, "The dry country will have a voice, 'Blaze a trail for the Lord and make it true and straight.'"

⁴ John's duds were made out of animal hair, and his belt was made of good leather. He made meals out of locusts with wild honey for dessert. ⁵ Cowboys and cowgirls came from all over to see him. ⁶ These cowboys and cowgirls told God about everything they'd done wrong and John baptized them in Jordan Creek.

⁷ When John saw the real religious folks ride over the hill followed by a bunch of no-account politicians, he hollered at them, "You den of rattlesnakes! Who told you to ride as fast as you could from the comin' anger? ⁸ You gotta change the way you live your life if you want what God is offerin' folks here! ⁹ Don't even try to make the excuse that Abraham was your father. God can make these rocks become Abraham's children if that's what he wants to do. It don't mean nothin'. ¹⁰ God's axe is already at the bottom of your tree. If you don't change the way you live your lives, your tree will end up in the BBQ pit.

¹¹ "I dunk folks in water as a symbol that they want to change the way they think and live. But there's a cowboy comin' whose boots I ain't fit for carrying. He's gonna dunk you with the Holy Ghost and flame. ¹² His pitchfork is in his hand and he's gonna separate the good stuff from the moldy. This useless trash will be thrown in the fire that can't go out."

¹³ Then Jesus rode in from Galilee to be dunked in the Jordan by John. ¹⁴ Old John balked at the idea and said, "It's the other way around! I need to be dunked by you."

¹⁵ But Jesus told him, "Nope. This is the way we're gonna do it so everything will be made right with God." John shook his head in disbelief but agreed to do it Jesus's way.

¹⁶ As soon as Jesus had come up out of the creek, heaven's gate was thrown wide open. The Spirit of God came out of that gate in the form of a dove and landed on Jesus. ¹⁷ Out of heaven a voice said, "This is my Son who I love. I am pleased with everything that he is."

CHAPTER 4

The Duel in the Desert

God led Jesus out into the dry country to be tempted by the devil. ² Jesus was famished after not eating for forty days and nights. ³ That old devil rode up and said, "If you're God's Boy, you can easily turn these rocks into bread. What're you waitin' on?"

⁴ Jesus said, "Man don't live on just bread, but on every word that comes out of God's mouth."

⁵ The devil snatched Jesus up and took him to the holy city and they stood at the highest point of the church. ⁶ "If you're God's Boy," the devil said, "bail off of here. 'Cause it's written that,

'God's angels are gonna look out for you. They won't let a scratch of harm come to you.'"

⁷ Jesus answered and said, "It's also said, 'Don't be a fool and try to test God.'"

⁸ The devil whisked him off again and took him to a tall mountain where they could see all of the territories. ⁹ "I'll make a horse trade with you. I'll swap you everything you see below us if you'll take off your hat and call me boss."

¹⁰ Jesus told him, "Get away from me, Satan! It's written that we are to 'Only bow down and call God the boss; him and him only.'"

¹¹ The devil then hightailed it out of there and God sent some angels to take care of his Boy.

Jesus Starts Tellin' Folks the Truth

¹² Jesus heard that his buddy John the Baptist had been thrown in jail so he rode back to Galilee. ¹³ When he left Nazareth, he bunked out in Capernaum ¹⁴ to prove what was once said by Isaiah, ¹⁵ "In the land around Capernaum and along the Jordan, and in Galilee, the land of those who ain't Jews, ¹⁶ the folks livin' in the dark have seen a bright light; those livin' in the land shadowed by death, a great lantern has been lit in the darkness."

¹⁷ From the first time Jesus told folks the truth, he said, "Change the way you think and live, for God's Green Pastures are close."

Some Cowboys Decide to Ride with Jesus

¹⁸ When Jesus was walkin' down by the Sea of Galilee, he saw two cowboys, Peter and his brother Andrew. They were gatherin' some cattle and puttin' 'em in some pens. ¹⁹ "Come and ride with me," Jesus said to 'em, "and help me gather mavericks. I'll make you gatherers of men." ²⁰ They left the herd right there and rode off with him.

²¹ As they rode along, Jesus saw two more cowboys—James and his brother John. They were also gettin' ready to work some cattle. Jesus hollered at them to come on ²² and they immediately dropped what they were doin' and rode off with him.

²³ Jesus traveled everywhere in Galilee. He was teachin', preachin', and healin' all kinds of folks. ²⁴ Word traveled near and far about what he was doin'. People came from everywhere so Jesus could help them. ²⁵ Huge herds of mavericks, from Galilee to the region on the other side of Jordan Creek, began to follow him.

CHAPTER 5

The Message on the Mesa

When Jesus saw the great big herd of mavericks, he rode up on a mesa and hunkered down there. His cowboys grabbed a knee right below him, [2] and he began to tell them, [3] "God takes mighty good care of those folks who don't have anything to depend on except him. [4] God takes mighty good care of those folks who are hurtin' and sad because he's the only one who can offer 'em comfort. [5] God takes mighty good care of those who don't think very highly of themselves and he's gonna give 'em everything one day. [6] God takes mighty good care of those who would rather do what he says than eat or drink, for one day they will never be hungry or thirsty again. [7] God takes mighty good care of those who don't have an ounce of cruelty in 'em, for one day they will be spared. [8] God takes mighty good care of those whose hearts are as pure as spring water, 'cause they will sure enough see God one day. [9] God takes mighty good care of those who don't make trouble for anyone, for he's gonna claim them as his own sons. [10] God takes mighty good care of those who are put down because of their belief in him and the way they live, for their reward is his green, eternal pasture. [11] God's gonna take real special care of those of you who are insulted, spit upon, and talked wrongly about because of me. [12] Just smile and go on because your reward will be more than worth it in heaven. They did the same things to the cowboys who worked for God so many years ago.

Salt and Light

[13] "Y'all are the salt of the earth. If the seasoning loses its flavor, how can it be seasoned again? It ain't good for anything anymore, so it will be thrown out in the backyard to be trampled on by boots and coyotes.

[14] "Y'all are the light of this earth. You can't miss a big city that sits on a hill. [15] And cowboys don't light a lantern and then throw their hat on top of it to keep it from shinin'. [16] Just like that, let your lanterns shine bright before men, so they can see all the good things you do and bow their heads in thanks to the Boss.

Jesus Gives It to 'Em Straight

[17] "Don't think I've come here to take away any of the things the Boss told you to do. I didn't come to take anything away, but to show you the right trail. [18] I ain't lyin' when I say nothing will be changed in what he told you to do until everything is finished. [19] Any cowboy who doesn't do what the Boss says to do, and tries to tell others to act the same way, will not be thought of very highly in heaven, but those cowboys who do what the Boss says to do will be rewarded handsomely in heaven. [20] So listen up, if you can't do better than those fake religious fellows, you won't see hide nor hair of God's Green Pastures.

[21] "You heard that the Boss said long ago, 'Don't kill anyone and if you do, you run the risk of bein' found guilty.' [22] But I'm tellin' you that it's no different if you're even mad at your brother over somethin' stupid. You can still be found just as guilty. Just callin' someone a fool is reason enough to be tried.

[23] "If you're gonna grab a knee and worship God and you realize your brother or amigo is mad at ya, [24] get up and track 'em down and get things right between y'all. Get things straightened out and then come back and offer your prayers.

[25] "If you deal someone from the bottom of the deck and they decide to file charges on you for your wrongdoing, you better make it up to them before you get thrown in jail. [26] I'm tellin' you that you won't get out before every last penny has been repaid.

[27] "Y'all have heard that you shouldn't jack with someone else's Jenny. [28] But I'm tellin' you that even if you look at a girl and think about it, you've done the same thing in your heart. [29] If you think your eye has a mind of its own, then poke it out with a sharp stick. It's better to have one eye than to burn in hell. [30] If your right hand won't listen to you, lop it off with an axe for the very same reason.

[31] "It's been said that, 'If anyone gets a divorce from his wife, he's gotta give her the papers that say so.' [32] But I'm tellin' you that you better stick with her unless she's been sleepin' around. 'Cause if you don't, you're gonna make an adulteress out of her and anyone who marries her is going to be found guilty of adultery.

[33] "If you remember, the Boss told your granddaddies, 'Don't go back on your word, but stand behind everything you say to the Lord.' [34] But I'm tellin' you straight, don't swear at all; either by heaven, for it's the Boss's pasture, [35] or

by the earth, for it's the trap around the head-quarters, or by Jerusalem, for it's the Boss's headquarters. ³⁶ And don't swear by your own abilities. You can't make even one hair on your head become white or black. ³⁷ It's this simple. Let your yes mean yes and your no mean no; anything other than this is the same thing the devil would say.

³⁸ "You've heard again and again, the old sayin', 'An eye for an eye, and a tooth for a tooth.' ³⁹ But I'm tellin' you right now, don't shoot for revenge against anyone. If someone smacks you on the right cheek, let him have an easy shot at the left one too. ⁴⁰ If someone wants to steal your vest, give 'em your coat too. ⁴¹ If someone makes you walk a mile behind their horse, go even further than that. ⁴² Give to those who ask and don't turn anyone away when they ask to borrow something.

⁴³ "You remember that it was said, 'Love your buddies and hate those who hate you.' ⁴⁴ But I tell you, love those who hate you and pray for those who run their mouths about you. ⁴⁵ Then God will claim you as his own son. He makes the sun shine on the good, the bad, and the ugly, and sends 'em all the same rain to boot. ⁴⁶ If you only love those who love you right back, what kind of love are you really showin'? Even politicians do that! ⁴⁷ If you only say hi to your brother and your buddies, do you really think you are doin' somethin' special? Even dogs sniff each other's butts when they recognize each other and growl when a strange dog comes by. ⁴⁸ Be perfect just like the Boss is.

CHAPTER 6

Jesus Continues to Teach

"Don't be a cowboy who only rides his horse in parades so people will notice him. If you do things just so folks will see you, there won't be a reward for you in heaven. ² If you help out a cowboy in need, don't go around telling everyone about it so they will admire you. I'm dead serious when I say you will already have received all the notoriety you will ever get if you act that way. ³ But when you do help someone out, don't let the glove on your left hand know what the glove on your right hand is doin'. ⁴ If you help folks privately, the Boss knows and will reward you himself.

⁵ "If you only take your hat off and pray when other people are watching, their appreciation is all you're gonna get. ⁶ But when you pray, head out to the barn where even the horses can't see you. Then the Boss, who sees and hears everything, will reward you.

⁷ "When you talk to the Boss, don't run your mouth off like an auctioneer who don't know when to say 'Sold!' Just repeatin' the same words over and over and over again don't get your prayers answered. ⁸ Don't be like those kinds of guys, 'cause the Boss knows exactly what you need before you ever open your mouth! ⁹ This is how you should talk to the Boss, 'Our Boss, who owns the heavenly pastures in the sky, may your name be revered above all others. ¹⁰ I hope your pastures come soon and I hope we all do what you want us to down here—just like things are done up there on your spread. ¹¹ Bring us today everything we'll need to get us by, ¹² and look the other way when we fail you. Help us also to look the other way when our partners fail us. ¹³ And don't let us fall into gopher holes that will kill us, but keep us safe and sound from evil.'

¹⁴ "If you look the other way when people do you wrong, the Boss will do the same for you. ¹⁵ But if you hold grudges against your fellow cowboys, the Boss will treat you the same way.

¹⁶ "If you want to show the Boss how much you care for him by goin' without food for a little while, don't go around tellin' everyone what you're doin'. Those who do are lookin' for sympathy and admiration from everyone but the Boss. That's all they'll get out of it, too. ¹⁷ But if you go without food for a while, saddle up and ride just like it's any normal day of work. ¹⁸ Then the Boss will know that the only reason you're doin' it is for him. It's this kind of stuff that he rewards.

¹⁹ "Don't buy a bunch of saddles and tradin' spurs here on earth so that people will think highly of you. The saddles will eventually rot and the spurs will rust if someone doesn't break into your barn and steal 'em first. ²⁰ Shoot for the great things of heaven, where there is no rot and thieves can't break in. ²¹ Whatever you long for the most is where your heart really is.

²² "Your eye is like the lantern of your body. When your eyes are good, your whole body (or the barn in this case) is filled with light.

²³ But when your eyes are bad, the whole barn is filled with darkness. ²⁴ If you mistake darkness for the light, you have a mighty dark barn my friend. You can't live in the dark and the light at the same time. You'll love one and hate the other.

²⁵ "That's why I'm tellin' you not to worry about anything. Don't worry 'bout food or water, or if you will have boots to wear. Isn't this life more than about beef steaks, and isn't your body more than about boots? ²⁶ Look at the birds. They don't have a herd of cattle to butcher for beef or a garden to pick vegetables for canning, but the Boss provides for them every day. You mean a lot more to him than little birds do. ²⁷ Can a little bit of worry really do anything to add a single moment more to your life?

²⁸ "Why worry about your boots and chaps? Even prickly pears have apples and grow strong in the pasture. Cactus don't have to work for these beautiful apples, ²⁹ and even the richest man who ever lived, Solomon, didn't have clothes like a cactus does. ³⁰ And if the Boss cares so much for cactus that are here today and rot tomorrow, he certainly cares for you. Why can't you have a little more faith than that?

³¹ "So don't sit around frettin' all the time, sayin' things like, 'I wonder what we'll eat? Will there be anything to drink? Will I have a neckerchief to keep warm in the winter?' ³² This is the way people think who don't believe in the Boss, but he knows everything you need. ³³ Search out his way before you search for anything else, and be sure and live like he wants you to. Then he will give you everything you need.

³⁴ "Don't fret about tomorrow, for tomorrow will fret about itself. Today's filled with enough frettin' for one day.

CHAPTER 7

Judging Others

"Don't make opinions about what others do, and no opinion will be made about you. ² The way you treat others is the way you will be treated. The judging eye you cast upon others will be the same judging eye that will be cast on you.

³ "Don't criticize your partner's horse for slinging its head when you can't even get on your own horse without gettin' bucked off. ⁴ How can you offer to help your friend out with his horse when you can't even put a saddle on yours? ⁵ That's

just bein' a hypocrite! When you get your horse goin' good and steady, then you can offer to help your partner.

⁶ "Don't give the best of what the Boss has given you to the coyotes. Don't throw pearls into the pig pen just so they will get mashed down in the mud and never be seen again.

How to Talk to the Boss

⁷ "If you need somethin', keep tellin' the Boss about it and you will get it. If you keep lookin' for the cows in the pasture, you will find them if you don't give up. If you keep knockin' on the barn door, he will open it for you. ⁸ If you ask, you will receive. If you knock, the door will be opened. If you look, you will find.

⁹ "If you're a mom or a dad, listen up. If your children are hungry and ask for something to eat, do you hand them a fence post? ¹⁰ If they ask for some macaroni and cheese, do you give them turpentine and taters? Of course you don't! ¹¹ So if you sinners know how to take care of your kids, how much more will the Boss be able to take care of those he thinks of as his own children?

The Rule to Live By

¹² "Work another man's horse the way you want him workin' your best horse. This is what the Rules and the Wise Cowboys were tryin' to teach all those years ago.

The Narrow Sorting Gate

¹³ "You can only enter the Boss's ranch by way of the narrow sortin' gate. The trail to hell is wide open and easy to follow for those who choose it. ¹⁴ But the gate to life is narrow and the trail is rough and steep. Only a few will ever find it or be able to follow it.

The Mesquite Tree and Its Beans

¹⁵ "Look out for the fake fellows who stop by the ranch disguised as harmless sheep but are really rabid coyotes. ¹⁶ You can spot 'em by their beans. Can you pick beans off of tumbleweeds, or taters off of cockleburs? ¹⁷ A good tree produces beans that will feed the animals, but a bad tree produces beans that kill cattle and cowboys. ¹⁸ A good tree can't make bad beans and a bad tree can't make good beans. ¹⁹ So every tree that can't make good beans is cut down and used for firewood. ²⁰ You can spot a tree by its beans, and you can spot people by their ways.

Real Cowboys

²¹ "Not everyone who claims to be a cowboy who works for me will end up on the Boss's ranch. Only those cowboys who do what the Boss wants them to will end up there. ²² On the day of reckonin', many cowboys will claim they worked for me. They will say, 'Lord! Lord! Didn't we ride out and tell people about you and get rid of evil things in your name? Didn't we do things that could only have come from you?' ²³ But I'm gonna tell 'em, 'Maybe so! But we never rode together as partners and amigos. Get out of my sight and off my spread.'

Building a House on Solid Rock

²⁴ "Any cowboy who listens to what I tell them and does it, knows the right trail to take. Just like a cowboy who builds his bunkhouse on solid rock. ²⁵ When the creek rises and the north wind blows like a hurricane, not a thing will happen to it. ²⁶ But anyone who listens to what I'm sayin' and then blows it off is like the cowboy who built his bunkhouse on sand. ²⁷ When the creek rises and the norther starts blowin', his bunkhouse won't last a split second."

²⁸ When Jesus was done talkin', everyone just kind of stood there in awe and wonder. ²⁹ He said things like he knew what he was talkin' about and had the authority to say it—unlike those fake fellas who didn't know nothin' except rules and regulations.

CHAPTER 8

Jesus Heals a Man with Hoof Rot

A ton of people followed Jesus as he came down from the mesa. ² All of a sudden, a man came from the brush and took off his hat and hit a knee right in front of him and said, "Boss, if you want to, you can heal me of this hoof rot." ³ Jesus laid a hand on the guy's shoulder and said, "I sure enough want to. Be healed!" The hoof rot that had covered his body instantly vanished. ⁴ Jesus told him, "Don't say a word about this to anyone. Instead, head to town and let the priest have a look at you. Take something with you so you can offer it to God for healin' you. This is how you will let people know you've been healed."

The Brand Inspector's Faith

⁵ When Jesus went back to Capernaum, a Roman brand inspector came to him and begged him, ⁶ "Lord, my young day worker is paralyzed and in a lot of pain."

⁷ Jesus said, "I'll go with you and make him well."

⁸ But the brand inspector told him, "I'd really rather you not. It's not necessary. All you have to do is say the word and I know the young lad will be healed. ⁹ I know this because I do what my boss tells me to and my cowboys who ride for me do what I tell them to. If I give 'em word to ride hard west, they do it. If I give 'em word to come back, they do it."

¹⁰ Jesus stood there amazed. He turned around and said, "That's the kind of faith I've been lookin' for and I finally found it! ¹¹ And let me tell you something else folks. Cowboys and cowgirls are goin' to come from everywhere and sit down at the Great Campfire in the sky with all the saints. ¹² But a lot of the cowboys from Israel—those the Campfire was made for—will be thrown out in the darkness on their heads, where there will be constant squallin' and grindin' of teeth."

¹³ Then Jesus told the brand inspector, "Go on back to your hacienda. Your young cowboy will be healed because you believed I could do it." Come to find out, the young cowboy was healed at that exact hour.

Jesus Cures Many Folks

¹⁴ When Jesus made it back to Peter's house, Peter's mother-in-law was mighty ill with a burnin' fever. ¹⁵ But when Jesus walked in and touched her on the hand, the fever left her. She felt so good she got up and cooked 'em all some buttermilk biscuits.

¹⁶ That evening while they were sittin' on the porch, a bunch of folks were brought to Jesus who were possessed by devilish spirits. Jesus simply told the spirits to take a hike and the people were cured. Jesus also healed everyone who was sick. ¹⁷ This fulfilled what Isaiah had said about him long ago, "He hauled out our sicknesses and vanquished our diseases."

Following Jesus Has Its Costs

¹⁸ Jesus saw the folks were startin' to crowd around him so he told his cowboys to cross to the other side of the lake.

¹⁹ Then one of the teachers who taught the rules said to him, "Hey, I'll go wherever you go Jesus."

20 But Jesus told him, "Coyotes have dens and birds have nests, but the Boss's Son doesn't have any place to call home."

21 Another fellow said, "My dad died, and as soon as his funeral's over, I'll come with you."

22 Jesus shook his head and said, "If you are really willin' to follow me then do it right now. You can't help anyone who's already dead."

Jesus and the Squall

23 Then Jesus jumped in the boat and they headed for the other side of the lake. 24 All of a sudden, a boat-sinker of a storm blew in. But Jesus had his hat down over his eyes and slept through it. 25 The disciples were frettin' and fearin' that this was gonna be the end of them all. They finally woke Jesus up by shakin' him and saying, "Jesus, save us! We're all gonna drown!"

26 Jesus shook his head patiently and said, "Quit actin' like a bunch of sissies! You ain't got very much faith at all, do you?" Jesus got up, stretched, and told the wind to shut up and the waves to sit down . . . and they did.

27 The hands were shocked, stunned, and amazed and asked, "What kind of hombre is this? Even the wind and the waves listen to him!"

The Demons and the Pigs

28 When he got over to the Gadarene country, two possessed men who came from the cemetery met him. They was so brutal and mean that no one could pass that way. 29 "What does the Boss's Son want with us?" they screamed. "Have you come to kill us before you are supposed to?"

30 There was a herd of pigs feeding in the next pasture. 31 The demons begged and cried out to Jesus, "If you get rid of us, send us into that herd of pigs over there."

32 He told them, "Alright then. Go!" So the demons left the men and went into the herd of pigs. When they possessed the pigs, the four-legged slop-eaters all ran to a cliff and jumped in the water and drowned. 33 The farmers who were tendin' the pigs ran off to town and told everyone what had happened, includin' what had happened to the two demon-possessed men. 34 Everyone got together when they heard the news and went out to confront Jesus. When they saw him, they told him to get the heck out of Dodge.

CHAPTER 9

The Man Who Could Not Move

Jesus got in a boat and headed for the town where he was raised. 2 Some fellows brought him a guy who was paralyzed and could not move, lying on a bedroll. When Jesus saw their faith, he said to the guy on the bedroll, "Don't worry amigo, your sins are forgiven."

3 Some teachers of the Law said to each other, "This fella can't do that and get away with it!"

4 Jesus knew what they were thinking and saying. He said to them, "Why are your minds filled with evil? 5 What's easier for me to say, 'Your sins are forgiven,' or to say, 'Get up and walk?' 6 Just so you know, the Boss's Son can forgive sins here on earth." Then he told the man who couldn't move, "Get up, take your bedroll and mosey on back home." 7 The man did just that. 8 When everyone saw this, they were amazed and praised the Boss, who had given this type of authority and power to men.

Jesus Sups with Sinners

9 When Jesus left there, he saw a guy named Matthew sitting at the tax collector's shack. "Come on," he told him and Matthew left everything right there and went with him.

10 Jesus went to Matthew's house and supped with him. A lot of Matthew's friends, mostly outlaws and politicians who were crooked, came and ate with them and Jesus's hands. 11 When the religious know-it-alls (Pharisees) seen this, they asked Jesus's cowboys, "Why does your trail boss eat with outlaws and no-accounts?"

12 Jesus heard 'em and said, "The healthy cattle don't need a vet, the sick ones do. 13 You need to head off and ponder what this means, 'I want mercy, not sacrifice.' Because I haven't come to round up the gentle cattle, but I have come to gather the mavericks."

Religious Leaders Question Jesus about Fasting

14 John the Baptist's day workers came and questioned Jesus about worshiping God by not eating. They asked, "Why is it that the religious know-it-alls and us fast, but your cowhands don't have to?"

15 Jesus told them, "The folks at a wedding don't get all sad and mopey when the groom is at

the party. There will come a time he has to light out and leave 'em. That's when they will fast.

16 "You don't put an unshrunk cotton patch on a pair of britches that are torn. As soon as you wash them, the patch will shrink and make the tear worse. **17** Neither do cowboys put new wine into an old wineskin. New wine will ferment and expand, stretchin' the leather bag. If the bag has already been stretched, it's just gonna tear. That's why you put new wine into new leather wineskins and old wine into old wineskins. That way, both are still usable."

Jesus Heals a Couple of Girls

18 When Jesus was talking, a man who was in charge of running a church came and got down on his knees in front of him. The man said, "My daughter has just died. But I believe if you come to my house, you can raise her from the dead." **19** Jesus got up immediately and told his hands to come on.

20 Just then, a lady who had been bleeding for twelve years snuck up behind Jesus and touched the edge of his shirt. **21** She told herself, "I know I will be healed if I can touch him. Even if it's the edge of his shirt."

22 Jesus spun around and told her, "Cheer up, daughter," he said, "you've just been healed by your faith." From that very moment, the woman was healed.

23 When Jesus entered the house of the guy whose daughter had died, he saw people cryin' and playin' sad songs on instruments. **24** Jesus told 'em, "This girl ain't dead, she's just asleep." But they all just laughed and mocked him. **25** Jesus told 'em all to get out and when they were all outside, he went into the little girl's bedroom. Jesus went up to her and took her by the hand and she stood up. **26** Word spread around the countryside like wildfire about what had happened.

The Blind and Mute are Healed by Jesus

27 When Jesus left, two blind guys followed him and yelled out to him, "Help us and have mercy on us, Son of David!"

28 He took 'em indoors and asked them, "Do you think I can heal you?"

"Yes, Lord," they said.

29 He reached out and gently touched their eyes and said, "It will be done according to your faith." **30** Just then, their sight was restored. But the first thing they saw was Jesus wagging a stern finger at them. Jesus said, "Don't you tell a soul about this. You understand me?" **31** But them fellows went out and told everyone what had happened to them.

32 When Jesus and his cowhands left, a man who was demon-possessed and couldn't talk was brought to Jesus. **33** Jesus drove the demon out and the man spoke for the first time. Those who were watching stood there with their mouths hanging wide open in astonishment. They said, "No one has ever seen anything as awesome as this in all of Israel!"

34 But the religious know-it-alls said, "He must be working for the devil in order to drive out demons."

Prayer for More Cowboys to Gather Mavericks

35 Jesus went all throughout the country, teaching in their churches, telling the good news of God's Green Pastures and healing every ache and ailment. **36** When he saw all the mavericks, he felt sorry for them because they were shunned and starved, like cattle without a brand and no rancher to take care of 'em. **37** Then he told his cowboys, "The cattle are everywhere, but there just ain't enough cowboys. **38** Ask the Lord of the gathering to send out cowboys into his pastures."

CHAPTER 10

Jesus Sends His Cowboys Out to Gather

Jesus hollered for his cowboys to come over to him. He gave 'em the authority to get rid of evil spirits and to cure ills and ailments.

2 These are the names of the first cowhands (apostles): Peter and his brother Andrew; old Zebedees's sons, James and John; **3** Phillip and Bart (sometimes called Bartholomew); Thomas and the tax collector Matthew; Alphaeus's boy James, and Thad (also called Thaddaeus by his grandma); **4** Simon, who was extremely intense, and Judas Iscariot, who double-crossed Jesus.

5 Jesus sent these twelve cowboys out to gather and laid out for them what he wanted them to do, "Don't go to the pastures that aren't Jewish just yet or any pastures where the cross-bred Samaritans hang out. **6** Go gather the lost cattle of Israel. ⁷ When you're out there, give everyone this message, 'The kingdom of heaven and the Boss's perfect pastures are real close.' ⁸ Doctor anyone who is sick and I'm even givin' you the gift of raisin' up those who are dead. You didn't do anything to deserve any of this and you should give just as I have given you. ⁹ Don't hide any cash or coins in the bottom of your boots; ¹⁰ take no saddle bags or bedrolls, or an extra vest or pair of britches; those you take care of will and should take care of you.

¹¹ "It don't matter whether you're stayin' at a ranch, a town, or a big city, find someone honest and trustworthy and stay at their place until you leave. ¹² When you enter the home, take your hat off to it. ¹³ If the place and its people treat you well and deserves your blessin', give it to 'em. If not, don't feel bad about takin' it with you. ¹⁴ If no one welcomes you in or listens to what you say, shake the dust off your boots and ride away. ¹⁵ I'm tellin' you what, it'll be better for Sodom and Gomorrah on Judgment Day than it will be for that place. ¹⁶ I'm sendin' y'all out like steaks to hungry coyotes. Y'all will need to be savvy as horse traders, but innocent as the day you were born.

Jesus Tells His Cowboys about the Coming Rough Times

¹⁷ "Watch your backs with men. They will hand you over to the local sheriffs and beat you within an inch of your life, right there in the churches. ¹⁸ Because of me, you will be taken before governors, presidents, and later, even to those who aren't Jews, so that you can tell them about who I am. ¹⁹ Don't fret about what you're supposed to say when they arrest you though. When the time comes, I'll give you the words you'll need. ²⁰ It won't be you who'll be talkin' at 'em, it'll be the Spirit of God speakin' through you.

²¹ "Brothers are gonna double-cross each other, and a father will do the same to his kid. Children will buck their parents and turn on 'em, and have 'em put to death. ²² Everyone will hate you because of me, but if you stay in the saddle and ride with me, you will be saved in the end. ²³ When they pester, plague, pick on, and persecute you, just saddle up and ride away to somewhere else. I'm tellin' you honest, you won't even get through the towns of Israel before the Son of Man comes.

²⁴ "A cowhand isn't over the trail boss and a horse isn't above its rider. ²⁵ It's fine for the cowhand to be like the trail boss. If the trail boss has been called Satan, then his crew will be called that more!

²⁶ "So don't fret or be afraid of them. Nothin' will be hidden where you won't see it comin'. ²⁷ What I tell you around the campfire at night, tell everyone else durin' the day. What I whisper to you in private, tell the whole world. ²⁸ Don't be scared of people who can kill your body. They can't kill your soul. Instead, be afraid of the one who can kill your body and soul in hell. ²⁹ You can buy two little birds for a penny, can't you? But not one of them will fall out of the sky without God's permission. ³⁰ He even knows how many hairs you have underneath your hat. ³¹ What I'm sayin' is, don't be afraid of anything. The Boss loves you a lot more than little birds.

³² "If you tell everyone at the livery, the feed store, the cow sale, the boot shop, and anywhere else you go, that you belong to my crew, I will tell God you ride with me. ³³ But if you deny ridin' with me, I'll dang sure deny you before the Boss when you get there.

³⁴ "Don't think I have come to make everyone lovey-dovey and peaceful. I didn't come to bring superficial harmony, but a sword. ³⁵ Because I have come to turn 'a boy against his dad, a girl against her mom, a daughter-in-law against her husband's mother—³⁶ a cowboy's worst enemies will be the folks on his own spread.'

³⁷ "Any cowboy who loves his mom or dad more than me isn't worthy to ride for my outfit. Same goes for anyone who loves their kids more than they love me. ³⁸ Anyone who isn't willin' to take up his own cross and ride with me isn't worthy of me. ³⁹ Anyone who rides for themselves will lose their life, but whoever rides with me and shuns themselves for my sake will find life.

⁴⁰ "He who welcomes and receives you, receives me, and he who receives me, receives the Boss. ⁴¹ Anyone who welcomes one of my cowboys gets the same reward as the cowboy who rides for me and anyone who welcomes an honest man because he is honest will get an honest man's bounty. ⁴² And if someone so much as lifts a finger to help one of my cowboys because they ride for me, I'm tellin' you straight, he will get rewarded."

CHAPTER 11

John's Bout with Doubt

When Jesus got through training his cowboys, he went and trained others who would listen in and around Galilee.

² John the Baptist was stuck in jail and when he heard all the great things Jesus was accomplishin', ³ he sent some of his boys out to ask Jesus, "Are you the real deal or should we be waitin' on someone else?"

⁴ Jesus said, "Go back and tell John what you see and hear, ⁵ the blind have been cured, the lame are walkin' around, those with all sorts of diseases are bein' cured, deaf ears can now hear, folks are comin' back from the dead, and the good news is bein' taught to the poor. ⁶ God will bless those who won't shy away or be ashamed of ridin' with me."

⁷ When John's boys left, Jesus began tellin' everyone who was there about John. "What kind of man did y'all think would be livin' out there in the desert? Someone who resembles a tumbleweed and is just blown around the pasture every time the wind picks up? ⁸ Did you go out there lookin' for a guy in a three-piece suit? Those guys live in fancy houses, not the desert. ⁹ If you went out there lookin' for a prophet, then you sure enough found him. But John was more than just a prophet, ¹⁰ he is the one who they've been talkin' about since before you were born, 'I'm sendin' a cowboy to blaze a trail for you, and he will bust the brush open so you can come through.'

¹¹ "This right here's the truth, no woman has ever given birth to someone greater than John the Baptist. But the sorriest cowboy in God's Green Pastures is greater than John. ¹² From the days of John the Baptist until right now, the Pastures of Heaven have been ridin' this way hard and many ruthless people have been attacking it. ¹³ Until John came, all the world had been waitin' and talkin' and lookin' forward to this time right here. ¹⁴ If you'll open your minds and hearts to understand this, he is just like the great cowboy Elijah, who wasn't scared to tell folks the truth and tell them about me comin'. ¹⁵ If you got a lick of sense you'll be able to understand what I'm tellin' you.

¹⁶ "Let me see if I can explain the folks of this generation. They are like the fans in the stands while the cowboys stand in the arena and talk to them. The cowboys say to them, ¹⁷ 'We rode the rough stock for you and got bucked off, but you didn't cheer because you wanted to see us rope. We roped fast and quick, but you didn't clap because no one got bucked off.'

¹⁸ "John didn't drink alcohol and often went without food so he could pray, but y'all said he was evil. ¹⁹ But then I come, the Son of Man, having a beer with outlaws and whores but y'all say, 'He's a pig and a drunk and he hangs out with lowlifes.' A wise man gets results no matter what."

Rest for the Soul Is Coming

²⁰ Jesus began to criticize the cities where most of his miracles had been done. Even after all he did, they just kept right on with their same old sorry ways instead of ridin' with him. ²¹ "Oh what a heavy price that Chorazin and Bethsaida are gonna have to pay. If the miracles that had been done there had been done in Tyre or Sidon, they would have stopped all their sinning and given glory to God. ²² I'm serious when I say that Tyre and Sidon will be a lot better off on Judgment Day than for y'all. ²³ And don't even get me started on Capernaum! Your trail ain't headed north, it's at a dead run to the south. If the miracles that had been performed for you had been done in Sodom, those cowboys would still be around and ridin' for me. ²⁴ Sodom is gonna fair a lot better on Judgment Day than you are Capernaum."

²⁵ That's when Jesus said, "Thank you God for hiding all these things from the know-it-alls and the pompous wise men, and showin' it all to little kids. ²⁶ Yup! This is the way that you wanted it.

²⁷ "My Father has given me everything. Nobody knows me like my Father does, and nobody knows my Father like I do, except for those cowboys and cowgirls who I choose to show who he really is.

²⁸ "Come and ride with me, all of y'all who are worn smooth out and feel like a miner's old pack mule, and I will take the load off of you and let you lie down in tall green grass. ²⁹ Ride with me and learn what I teach you, 'cause I'm a gentle trail boss and my heart is pure and humble. With me is where you'll find rest for your soul. ³⁰ Ridin' for me is easy, and workin' for me ain't hard either."

CHAPTER 12

Jesus Works on the Day of Rest

Jesus rode through a wheat field on the day God had told everyone to relax and rest. His cowboys were famished and picked some of the grain to eat. ² When the religious know-it-alls saw this, they said to Jesus, "Look at that! Your cowboys are breakin' God's law and workin' on the day he told us to rest."

³ He answered, "Haven't you heard what David did when his crew was hungry? ⁴ He entered God's church, and all of them ate the food that had been left there as offering to God. They weren't supposed to do that. Only the priests are supposed to eat that food. ⁵ When everyone else is supposed to be resting, the priests and preachers are up working and teachin' everyone else, but they are innocent? ⁶ I'm tellin' you that someone better than a church building is standin' right here. ⁷ Religious hypocrites don't ever understand these words, 'I want a relationship, not a religion'. ⁸ The Son of Man is Boss over the day of rest."

⁹ Then Jesus rode up to their church, watered his horse, and went in. ¹⁰ Inside was a fellow who had a deformed hand. Tryin' to catch Jesus in a trap, they asked him, "Is it wrong to heal on the day of rest?"

¹¹ Jesus told 'em, "If you had a baby calf that fell in a wash down by the creek and it couldn't get out, wouldn't you rope it and pull it out even if it was the day of rest? ¹² Cowboys mean a lot more to God than calves do! There ain't nothin' wrong with healin' on the day of rest."

¹³ Then he told the guy with the deformed hand, "Take your hand out of your pocket and hold it over here." The guy did what he was told and Jesus healed it completely. ¹⁴ The religious know-it-alls got so dad-gummed mad at Jesus for doin' this that they started ponderin' how they might take him out.

Folks Flock to Jesus

¹⁵ Jesus knew they was gonna try to take him out, so he left. A huge herd of folks followed him when he left and he healed all who were sick, ¹⁶ but he told 'em all not to tell anyone who did it. ¹⁷ This was because the great cowboy Isaiah had seen the future when he wrote, ¹⁸ "Look here at the guy who works for me, the cowboy who I love and the one I have chosen. I will give my power to him and he will bring justice to the whole world. ¹⁹ He will not squabble or raise his voice in public. ²⁰ He won't ride his horse over the weak and pitiful, nor will he dash the smallest dream until he conquers the world with his final showdown. ²¹ His name will become the hope of the whole world."

²² Then the people brought him a possessed man who couldn't talk or see. Jesus healed him completely so that he was no longer possessed, nor blind or mute. ²³ Everyone was dumbfounded by the things that Jesus did and they asked, "Could this cowboy be the Son of David?"

²⁴ But when the religious know-it-alls heard them ask this, they said, "Jesus can only do this because he has Satan's power!"

²⁵ Jesus knew what they were thinkin' and said, "Any crew that is divided won't be able to get the job done. You can't pull on the reins and spur at the same time and expect to get anywhere. ²⁶ If the devil drives himself out, he won't be able to do his job. ²⁷ If I drive out demons by the devil's power, by what power do y'all drive them out? Y'alls followers are doin' the same thing I am, so what does that say about them? ²⁸ But if I bust demons out of people by the power of God, then that means that God is right here with ya.

²⁹ "Let's go on with this a little longer. How can you take a badger's babies without getting bit? If you shoot the mama, then you'll be able to take her babies.

³⁰ "If you don't ride with me, you are my enemy. If you don't gather with me, then you scatter what I am tryin' to do. ³¹ I'm tellin' you straight that every sin and wrongdoing will be forgiven except sinning against the power of God. ³² You can talk trash about me and it will be forgiven. But if you say that the Spirit of God is just hogwash and you will never want to ride with me or believe in God, for this, you will not be forgiven—in this time, or any time that comes.

³³ "A cow is judged on what kind of calf she throws. Make a cow healthy and she will throw a healthy calf. If a cow is unhealthy or sick, she will have a sick calf. ³⁴ Y'all know-it-alls are a den of snakes! How can a snake tell someone what is good? Whatever is in your heart will spill up and out of your mouth. ³⁵ A good cowboy will bring

good things up out of his good heart without even knowing it, and the evil man will throw up his nastiness on everyone around and not think anything about it. ³⁶ But I'm warnin' you, the next time you let your tongue slip, you will have to explain every single slip and careless word on Judgment Day. ³⁷ Your words today will affect your outcome when you die. They will either get you turned out on perfect pastures or get you shipped off on the killer truck."

Religious Leaders Want a Miracle

³⁸ Some of the know-it-alls and legalistic teachers said to Jesus, "Mr. Teacher, we want to see one of these miracles we keep hearin' about."

³⁹ He answered them, "Only wicked folks who don't believe ask for proof of who I am. The only miracle you will see is the same one that happened to the great godly cowboy Jonah. ⁴⁰ He spent three days and nights in the belly of a big catfish. I will spend three days and nights in the belly of the earth. ⁴¹ When Jonah got out of the fish, he went to Nineveh and told them to quit behavin' like they were or they were goin' to hell. That city listened to him and turned to God. Now standin' before you is a cowboy greater than Jonah and you still don't believe. ⁴² Even the Queen of Sheba, who didn't even know who God was, came and asked Solomon where he got his great wisdom. She listened to him and believed. She will rise up and not speak favorably of all of y'all when Judgment Day comes because you do not believe or change after you've heard the truth. Now one greater and wiser than Solomon is standing here and you still refuse to believe.

⁴³ "When I chase the wolf out of your henhouse, it goes out and searches for another place to eat. ⁴⁴⁻⁴⁵ When it can't find anything to eat, it returns with its whole pack and finds your henhouse standing wide open. This is what happens when men are cleaned up, but don't start ridin' for God. They end up worse than when they started."

Jesus Tells Who His Real Family Is

⁴⁶ While Jesus was still talkin' to folks, his momma and his brothers waited outside to talk to him. ⁴⁷ Someone said, "Hey, your momma and your brothers are waiting outside. They want to talk to you."

⁴⁸ Jesus told him, "Who do you think my momma and brothers are?" ⁴⁹ He turned to his twelve cowboys and said, "My brothers and mother are sittin' right here with me. ⁵⁰ Anyone who rides for my Father's brand is my real family."

CHAPTER 13

Planting Alfalfa

Later on that afternoon, Jesus left the bunkhouse and rode down to the pens. ² There were a bunch of cowboys standing around waitin' on him. He climbed up on the pipe pens where everyone could see him and ³ he started tellin' stories like this one. "There was a big ranch that had their own farmin' operation. ⁴ They planted alfalfa and some of the seed fell on the two-track ranch road. Some blue quail came along and ate it right up. ⁵ Some other seed fell in a rocky area, ⁶ but them rocks acted like ovens and cooked the alfalfa right there on the stalk before it could grow very big. ⁷ Still other seed fell among a prickly pear cactus part of the pasture. That durn cactus choked it out 'fore it ever had a chance. ⁸ But some of that alfalfa seed fell on good, fertile soil. This seed produced about ten tons per acre. ⁹ Is anyone here catchin' what I'm sayin'?"

¹⁰ His cowboys came up to him and asked Jesus, "How come you just tell stories to people?"

¹¹ He nodded in understandin' and said, "You can understand these stories, but some cannot. These stories reveal the true nature of God's Green Pastures. ¹² Cowboys who are willin' to listen and try to understand the real meaning behind the stories will be trusted with secrets that others will not be. But those who won't listen, everything will be taken from 'em. ¹³ I tell these cowboy stories because they see what I do, but they don't really see anything at all. They're lookin', but they don't see. They hear the stories, but they're not even listening. They understand, but they don't savvy. ¹⁴ This is why the great cowboy Isaiah said, 'You hear, but you don't listen. You see, but you don't understand. ¹⁵ The hearts of the cowboys have become calloused. Their ears don't hear and their eyes don't see. Therefore, they can't ride with me and let me fix what ails them.'

¹⁶ "But the blindfold has been taken off of

you and the plugs taken out of your ears. **¹⁷** I'm tellin' you, many a cowboy wished to see what you've seen and hear what you've heard, but they could not.

¹⁸ "Now let me tell you what the alfalfa story really means. **¹⁹** The seed that fell on the ranch road are like those cowboys who hear the good news, but they don't understand it. The Killer then comes and eats the seed away before it can grow in their hearts. **²⁰** The rocky ground is like those cowboys who hear the good news and take it home with them gladly. **²¹** But the first time it gets a little hot around the collar, they wilt. **²²** The seed that fell in the cactus are like those who hear and accept the good news, but then they shove the message out of their lives with the cares of this world and the lure of money. **²³** The good soil is like those cowboys who really accept my words. These cowboys will produce tons of harvest for my sake."

The Registered Cattle and the Cull Bull

²⁴ Here's another cowboy story that Jesus told. "God's Green Pasture is like a rancher that had a herd of registered Angus cattle. **²⁵** But when the cows were all comin' into season, the Counterfeit came and put an old, mangy, ugly, part Holstein, part Watusi, part buffalo bull in the pasture with the registered herd. **²⁶** When calving time came, some of the cows produced fine, pure-bred Angus calves. But some cows produced an ugly, scrawny calf not worth nothing. **²⁷** The cowboys went and told the rancher that another bull must have got to the cows. **²⁸** 'That no-account Counterfeit must have done this to me!' the rancher said.

"'Do you want us to shoot the cross bred calves?' the cowboys asked.

²⁹ "He told them, 'No! You might hit one of the good calves. I've seen your shootin'. **³⁰** Let all of 'em grow up and we'll sort 'em out during shippin' season. That's when I'll tell the sorters to pen them up and burn 'em.'"

The Bull Seed

³¹ Here's another one of Jesus's tales. "God's Green Pasture is like the seed of a bull. **³²** It's so small you can't even see it, but when it is planted in the right spot, it grows and becomes the biggest thing in the pasture one day. It is the protector of the herd and won't let anything harm those it looks after."

The Sourdough Starter

³³ Jesus told 'em this, "The Boss's ranch is like a sourdough starter used by the chuckwagon cook to make biscuits. Even though the starter is the smallest part, it works its way through the flour and other ingredients to make the biscuits what they were meant to be."

³⁴ Jesus constantly used stories like these when he talked to the cowboys and cowgirls. Truth be known, he never spoke to them in any other way. **³⁵** This was because many, many moons ago, it was said, "I will speak to you in cowboy stories. I will explain mysteries hidden since the beginnin' of time."

The Registered Cattle and Cull Bull Explained

³⁶ Jesus left the day workers outside and went into the bunkhouse with his cowboys. They sat down on the bunks and asked him to explain the story about the registered cattle and the cull bull.

³⁷ "All right," he said. "I am the registered bull that makes everything pure. **³⁸** The pasture where the cattle lived is like this old world we're living in right now. The pure-bred calves are like the cowboys who live for the Boss. The cull calves are people who follow the Counterfeit. **³⁹** The enemy who put the cull bull in the pasture is the Devil, or you might know him as Slick, or the Counterfeit one. Shippin' season is when this old world will end. The sorters will be the angels.

⁴⁰ "Just like the cull calves are sorted out and burned, so it will be in the end. **⁴¹** I will send my winged riders to take away anything in my pasture that is not pure and from me. **⁴²** They will throw the culls into the brandin' fire and burn them up. On that day there will be a lot of bawlin' and pain. **⁴³** Then those who are pure because of me will shine like the noon-day sun. If you got ears, ya better listen close to this and understand!

The Unknown Oilfield

⁴⁴ "The Boss's ranch is like a cowboy finding oil comin' up out of the ground in an old useless pasture. In his excitement, the cowboy told no one and went and sold every single thing he owned and bought the property.

The Horse Trader

⁴⁵ "Again, the Boss's ranch is like a horse trader on the lookout for the best horse he could find. **⁴⁶** When he discovered the best filly he had ever seen, he sold all his trucks, trailers, and every horse he owned just to get this one.

The Prescribed Pasture Burn

⁴⁷ "Are you listening yet? Once again, the Boss's ranch is like cowboys gatherin' the cattle before a prescribed pasture burn. ⁴⁸ The cowboys only take the cattle that belong to the rancher and leave everything else. ⁴⁹ This is the way it will be at the end of the world. The winged riders will come down and gather everything that belongs to the Boss and leave everything else. ⁵⁰ Fire will be set to the pasture and everything left will burn. There will be no escape. ⁵¹ Do ya understand what I'm sayin'?"

"Yes sir! We sure enough do," the disciples said.

⁵² Then Jesus said, "Every teacher of the Law who starts ridin' for me is like a cowboy who teaches the old way, but isn't afraid to teach something new."

Jesus Rejected in His Hometown

⁵³ When Jesus had finished telling his tales, he left that part of the country and went back home. ⁵⁴ He returned to Nazareth and did some teachin' in the local church. Everyone kept wondering where he got such great understandin' and how he performed the miracles. ⁵⁵ They said, "He's just a cowboy's son. We know his whole family. ⁵⁶ His sisters live right here in town. What makes him think he's somethin' special?" ⁵⁷ They all got ticked off at Jesus and refused to believe a word he said.

Then Jesus told 'em, "A preacher is honored everywhere except his hometown and by everyone except his family."

⁵⁸ And so Jesus didn't do much around there like he did other places because they didn't believe in him.

CHAPTER 14

When old King Herod heard 'bout Jesus, ² he said, "This must be the ghost of John the Baptist come back to life." ³ Herod's wife had conned the King into throwin' John in the jailhouse. ⁴ John had told the King that it was wrong for him to marry his brother's wife. ⁵ The King would have killed him right away, but he was afraid there might be an uprising against him because John was a prophet.

⁶ At Herod's birthday bash, his wife's daughter danced a jig that really impressed the King. ⁷ Herod told her she could have anything she wanted because she had danced so well. ⁸ At her momma's bidding, she asked the King for the head of John the Baptist.

⁹ Herod was plumb tore up about this and didn't know what to do. He'd given his word and he couldn't back down from that.

¹⁰ So John's head was chopped off ¹¹ and brought on a tray to the daughter who then took it to her momma.

¹² John's crew then came and laid claim to his body and went and buried it on Boot Hill. Then they went and told Jesus what had happened.

¹³ When Jesus heard the news, he rode off out into the pasture to be alone. But a bunch of people saw him ride out and they followed him.

¹⁴ When Jesus got back from his ride, he felt sorry for all those who had gathered and waited on him. He took pity on 'em and healed all who were ailing.

¹⁵ When the sun was goin' down, Jesus's crew came up and told him to send everyone back to town so they could get 'em some supper. ¹⁶ But Jesus said it weren't necessary. "Y'all feed 'em."

¹⁷ They all looked at him like he'd grown donkey ears. "All we got to feed with is five biscuits and two small catfish."

¹⁸ "Bring 'em over here," Jesus said. ¹⁹ He told everyone to hunker down while he said grace over the food. He asked God's blessing over the meager meal and then broke the biscuits apart. The cowboys were told to take some to everybody. ²⁰ By the time everyone was finished eating, they were all layin' up under the mesquites as full as ticks. There was even twelve baskets of food left over. ²¹ Not counting womenfolk and kiddos, there was over five thousand cowboys.

²² Jesus told his cowboys to go load up in a boat and head home while he made sure everyone else made it back to town. ²³ When they had all left, he rode up on a mountain so he could be alone and pray.

²⁴ By this time, the boys were way out in the middle of this huge lake and a big storm had come up. This storm was a poundin' the tar out of everything and the cowboys were scared. ²⁵ A little while later, Jesus came out of the storm walkin' right across the water. ²⁶ The cowboys

saw him and thought for sure a ghost was comin' for 'em. They started screamin' and bellowin' like the end was near.

²⁷ Jesus hollered for 'em to relax and said, "Don't worry fellas! It's me, Jesus. Don't be afraid."

²⁸ Pete hollered back at him, "Jesus, if it's really you, tell me to walk out there on that water and come to you."

²⁹ Jesus smirked and said, "Come on then." Peter stood up and walked right off the boat and strode right out there on the water.

³⁰ But Pete seen the lightning and how the wind was makin' waves and he got scared all over again and began to sink. "Oh, no! Help me Jesus! Help me, I'm a sinkin' down!"

³¹ Jesus walked over to him and grabbed him by the shirt collar and said, "Your faith wouldn't fill a thimble. How come you doubt me?"

³² When Jesus got both of 'em over to the shore, the wind died down and the lightning stopped. ³³ The cowboys huddled underneath a mesquite, got down on their knees, and said, "You are most certainly God's Boy!"

Jesus Heals Some Sick Folks

³⁴ Jesus and his cowboys rode into the town of Gennesaret. ³⁵ The folks found out he was there and sent word to everyone in the county that Jesus and his boys were there. Sick folks came from miles around so Jesus would make 'em better. ³⁶ They begged Jesus to just let 'em touch his boots, and everyone who did was made well.

CHAPTER 15

It was about this time that some religious know-it-alls and some others who taught the same things they did came up from the Jerusalem country. They asked Jesus, ² "Why don't your cowboys do what all of our grandpappies taught us to do? Why, they don't even wash their hands before they eat."

³ Jesus told 'em, "Let me ask you this. Why don't you do what the Boss tells you to do? ⁴ Didn't he tell us to respect our moms and dads? He even said to shoot someone dead if they cussed their parents. ⁵ But y'all let it slide when someone doesn't even help their parents out when they need some help. Y'all tell these kids that it's fine to give money to your organization instead of buying food for their parents. ⁶ Is this the kind of respect you show your mom and dad? You flat out ignore what the Boss says and make up your own rules that will benefit you. ⁷ Y'all ain't nothin' but snake-oil salesmen! Old Isaiah was tellin' the truth when God spoke through him and said, ⁸ 'All of you have real pretty words for me, but I never even cross your mind. ⁹ Don't even bother with your words when all you do is teach rules that you make up.'"

What Really Makes Cowboys Unfit in the Outfit

¹⁰ Jesus hollered for everyone to gather around him. He said, "Y'all listen up and try to follow what I'm sayin'. ¹¹ The food you put in your mouth doesn't make you unfit in the Boss's eye, but the filthy talk that comes out of your mouth sure enough does."

¹² Some of Jesus's cowboys came over to him and whispered, "Do you realize that you put a big burr underneath them hypocritical preacher's saddle blankets by what you just said?"

¹³ Jesus said, "Every animal that doesn't bear the Boss's brand will be shipped off to the slaughterhouse. ¹⁴ Stay away from them hypocritical preachers. They are like blind city slickers leading blind people on blind horses off the edge of a cliff."

¹⁵ Pete asked Jesus, "What was you talkin' about when you said there are things that make a person unfit in the Boss's eyes?"

¹⁶ Jesus told him, "Don't any of you have a clue what I was talkin' about? ¹⁷ Don't you understand that anything you put in your mouth goes into your belly and will eventually find its way out of your body? ¹⁸ But the words that come out of your mouth come from your heart. These words are what will make you unfit accordin' to the Boss. ¹⁹ Out of your heart comes the awful things like killing, cheatin' on your spouse, gross sexual excitement, horse thieving, goin' back on your word, and talkin' crap about other people. ²⁰ These are the things the Boss don't like and these are the things that make you unfit."

Real Faith

²¹ Jesus shucked out and headed for the country around Tyre and Sidon. ²² All of a sudden, a lady from Canaan shouted out, "Jesus, help me! My daughter is full of evil spirits." ²³ Jesus never said a word to her but just kept riding. The lady

wouldn't give up, so the cowboys asked Jesus if he would tell her to shut up and leave.

²⁴ Jesus finally told her, "I was sent only to the cowboys of Israel! They are like a herd of maverick cattle."

²⁵ The lady came up close to his horse and then got down on her knees and begged, "Please, you're the only one who can help my daughter!"

²⁶ Jesus said, "It isn't right to take a horse away from a cowboy and give it to a city slicker."

²⁷ "That is true my Lord," she said, "but even city slickers are given one ride by a gentle cowboy."

²⁸ Jesus smiled and said, "Lady, you've got a passel of faith and you'll be given what you asked for." At that very moment her daughter was made well.

Jesus Keeps On Healing

²⁹ When he left there, Jesus rode along the shore of Lake Galilee. He rode his horse up on top of a hill and sat there. ³⁰ A whole mess of folks came up there where he was and brought with them people who were in bad shape. Some were blind. Some were deaf. Some were paralyzed and others couldn't talk. They brought 'em before Jesus and he fixed 'em all. ³¹ Everyone was shocked by what Jesus was able to do. The paralyzed were walkin' and the mutes were talkin'. Everyone was shoutin' and shootin' up in the air in honor of the Boss.

Jesus Gives Sup to Four Thousand

³² Jesus called his cowboys over to him and said, "I feel sorry for all these people. They have been here with us for three days and some of 'em haven't had anything to eat. If some of 'em leave, they might pass out before they get home."

³³ His cowboys said, "Man, this place is like a barren desert. We could butcher one hundred cows and not have enough food for all these people."

³⁴ Jesus asked 'em what kind of food they had and they showed him seven small biscuits and some sardines.

³⁵ Jesus hollered for everyone to sit down and then ³⁶ he took the seven biscuits and the can of sardines and gave thanks for them. He then broke them and handed 'em to his cowboys so they could pass 'em out to everybody.

³⁷ Everyone ate as much as they wanted and there was enough leftovers to fill seven large Dutch ovens.

³⁸ There were four thousand cowboys who ate, not counting the womenfolk and little ones.

³⁹ After he sent everyone home with their bellies full, Jesus and his crew got on a ferry and went to the other side of the lake near the town of Magadan.

CHAPTER 16

Everyone Wants a Sign

The hypocritical preachers (Pharisees) and cattle barons (Sadducees) came to Jesus askin' for a sign from the Boss.

² He told 'em, "If the sky is red in the evening, you would 'say the weather will be good. ³ But if the sky is red and cloudy in the morning you'd say it was about to rain. You're good at lookin' at the weather by the signs in the sky, but you won't open your eyes to what's happenin' right before your eyes. ⁴ You want proof of the Boss because you are full of evil. The only sign you'll be given is what happened to old Jonah." Then Jesus rode out of town.

The Yeast

⁵ The cowboys had forgotten to bring biscuits when they crossed the lake. ⁶ Jesus warned 'em against the yeast of the hypocritical preachers and the cattle barons.

⁷ The cowboys talked among themselves and said to each other, "He must be sayin' that because we forgot the biscuits."

⁸ Jesus knew what they were thinking and said, "Y'all ain't got a lick of faith do you? Why are you talkin' about not havin' any biscuits? ⁹ Why don't you understand? Did you already forget about those five thousand people and all the leftovers from just five biscuits? ¹⁰ And what about the four thousand cowboys and all the leftovers from just seven pieces of hard tack? ¹¹ Don't you know by now I ain't talkin' about biscuits? Watch out for the yeast of the hypocritical preachers and cattle barons!"

¹² Finally it began to sink in and the cowboys knew what he was talkin' about. He wasn't talkin' about yeast for makin' biscuits, but the things that the hypocritical preachers and cattle barons tried to get people to do.

Who Is Jesus?

¹³ When Jesus and his crew were near the town of Caesarea Philippi, he asked them, "So what do people say about the Son of the Boss?"

¹⁴ The cowboys looked around and said, "Some people say you are John the Baptist or maybe even the great cowboy Elijah. Others say Jeremiah while some just say you're a prophet."

¹⁵ Then Jesus asked, "Who do y'all think I am?"

¹⁶ Pete spoke right up and said, "You are the cowboy we've been waiting on. You're the Boss's Son."

¹⁷ Jesus told him, "Pete, you will be granted favor for your answer. You didn't figure that out on your own. It was shown to you by the Boss. ¹⁸ I'm gonna call you Peter from now on. That means 'rock.' This truth you have been shown is what I will build my ranch on and death itself won't be able to knock down its gates. ¹⁹ I'm gonna give you the key to the gates on this ranch and the Boss will allow in his place whatever you allow outside it. He won't allow anything inside that you don't allow outside."

²⁰ Jesus told all of them not to tell anyone that he was the cowboy everyone had been lookin' for.

Jesus Tells Them He Is Going to Die

²¹ From this point on, Jesus told his cowboys what was gonna happen to him. He said, "Pretty soon, I'm gonna ride up to Jerusalem and all those folks I've warned you about are gonna do some very terrible things to me. In the end, they're gonna string me up. But after three days, I will come back to life."

²² Pete took Jesus a little ways away and said, "The Boss ain't gonna let that happen so you need to quit talkin' nonsense!"

²³ Jesus turned on him and said, "Get away from me Devil! You're standin' in the way because you're acting like everyone else and not like the Boss wants you to."

²⁴ Then Jesus said to all the cowboys, "If y'all want to continue on in this crew, you need to forget about what you want and start focusin' on what the Boss wants. ²⁵ You gotta be willin' to give up your life and ride with me. ²⁶ What will you get if you gain everything this world has to offer and you still lose your soul? What can a man swap that's worth his soul?"

²⁷ "The Boss's Son will soon return with his Dad's crew and reward everyone for the things they do. ²⁸ I'm tellin' you now that some of you who are hunkered down here with me now won't die before you see me comin'."

CHAPTER 17

Jesus then took Pete, James, and John with him up on a mountain. ² It was on this mountain that Jesus was changed completely. His face shone brighter than the noonday sun and his clothes turned bright white. ³ All of a sudden, two great cowboys from the past, Moses and Elijah, stood there with them, visitin' with Jesus.

⁴ Pete told Jesus, "I wouldn't have missed this for the world! I'm gonna put up three tents—one for you, one for Moses, and one for Elijah."

⁵ While Pete was still runnin' his mouth, a big bright cloud surrounded everyone. A voice from the cloud said, "This is my Boy and I sure enough love him and he makes me proud. Listen to every word he says!"

⁶ When Pete, James, and John heard this, they fell flat on the ground and whimpered like weaned pups. ⁷ But Jesus reached down and helped them up and told them, "Don't be scared!"

⁸ When they stood up, Jesus was the only one standin' there.

⁹ As they rode down the mountain, Jesus told them, "Don't say anything about this to anyone until I have been raised from the dead."

¹⁰ They asked him, "Why do the religious teachers say that old cowboy Elijah must come back first?"

¹¹ Jesus said, "Sure enough, a cowboy like Elijah comes and will make all things new. ¹² But here's the thing, a cowboy like Elijah has already come and they didn't even recognize him. They treated him sorry and they will do the same to me." ¹³ The cowboys realized Jesus was talkin' about his buddy John the Baptist.

Jesus Heals a Possessed Kid

¹⁴ They rode up to a crowd of people and a man came and knelt in the dirt before Jesus. ¹⁵ "Lord, please help my boy!" he said. "He has fits and suffers terribly. He falls into the fire and into the water trough. ¹⁶ I took him to some of your cowboys, but they couldn't help him."

¹⁷ Jesus said, "Good grief! Where is all of y'alls faith? How long am I gonna have to stick around

and hold y'alls hands? I don't know how much more I can put up with. Bring that boy over here." **18** Jesus looked at the boy and told the demon that was possessing him to get out. From that moment, the boy was fine.

19 The cowboys asked Jesus, "How come we couldn't rope and drag that ol' demon out?"

20 Jesus said, "Cause you don't have a squirt of faith. With a bit of faith, you could move mountains; anything is possible. **21** But this kind don't shuck loose without prayer and fasting."

22 When all his cowboys had gathered with him near Galilee, he told 'em, "I'm gonna be double-crossed. **23** They're gonna string me up, but on the third day after, I'm gonna be raised from the dead and brought back to life." The cowboys all looked down and some of them cried.

Pete and the Catfish

24 When Jesus and his boys rode into Capernaum, a tax collector pulled Pete aside and asked if Jesus paid the church tax.

25 "Of course he does!" Pete boasted.

When Pete caught up with the others, Jesus asked him, "Pete, do you think the governor of this territory or his family pays taxes for his salary or does he just make other people pay them?"

26 "He don't pay taxes to himself. He just makes others pay them," Pete replied. "Then his sons don't have to pay the taxes either," Jesus said. **27** "I don't want to start any trouble here so I'll pay the tax that keeps my Father's house runnin' even though I don't have to. But I want you to go down to that pond and catch a fish. When you catch that catfish, open its mouth and there will be enough money for my tax and yours. Ride into town and pay it."

CHAPTER 18

The Cowboys Argue about Who Is the Top Hand

The cowboys came up to Jesus and asked him, "Who is the top hand on the Boss's spread?"

2 Jesus hollered for a little cowboy to come over there. He looked down at the small boy and **3** said, "Unless you can change and learn to have the same kind of faith and trust that this little cowboy does, you will never enter the Boss's ranch. **4** A little cowpoke like this com-

pletely depends on those who take care of him and that's what you must do.

5 "When you welcome a little child into your presence, you welcome me. **6** But I don't care who you are, if you make one of these kiddos lose their faith or their trust and cause them to sin, it would be better if you were killed by a pack of coyotes.

Jesus Warns Against Temptation

7 "This whole world is headin' straight for a cliff because of their sins. It's sure enough gonna happen, but I feel sorry for the man who causes one of my little cowboys to sin. **8** If something is causin' you to sin, you better get rid of it. I don't care if it means you have to cut off one of your hands or shoot your best horse, it's better to have eternal life without a hand and a horse than to ride straight to hell with both hands. **9** If you can't even control your own eyes from causin' you to do things the Boss wouldn't approve of, you best get a spoon and gouge 'em out. It's better for you to work for the Boss blind than to see the cliff you are headed for and the hell that awaits you.

Do Not Be Uppity

10 "Don't look down your nose at someone who has faith and trusts in me like a little child. **11** You probably don't realize that these people have winged riders who look upon the face of the Boss every day.

12 "Let me ask you this. If you had a hundred cows, but one of them was missing, wouldn't you go look for it? **13** Wouldn't you be happy when you came over the hill and saw it standing at the bottom? On the Boss's place, finding the one who wandered off is **14** what is important. He don't want a single one lost.

How to Handle Conflict with Other Cowboys

15 "If a cowboy who works for me does something to you that is against one of my rules (not yours), be a man and go talk to him about it. Let it be just between the two of you. Don't go round up all your buddies or even tell them what you're doin'. If he listens to you, y'all will be able to ride together. **16** If he won't listen to you, go ahead and take another cowboy along so that neither side will be able to accuse the other of something that was said. **17** If he still refuses to listen, take it to the men leadin' your crew. If he even refuses to listen to the cowboys I have chosen to be in charge of my outfit, just run him off. Treat him like you would a trespasser and get him off my place.

¹⁸ "Whatever that crew decides is what will happen. The Boss will back them up!

¹⁹ "I'm tellin' you the truth. If two of my cowboys truly seek my guidance and my way, whatever they decide on will be backed up by me. ²⁰ When two or more come to the campfire or anywhere else to be with me, I am there with them."

The Unforgiving Banker

²¹ Then Pete came up to Jesus and asked, "If a cowboy just keeps doing me wrong, how many times do I have to let it go? Seven times?"

²² Jesus replied, "No Pete, not seven times—every time!"

²³ "The Boss's place is like a rancher who had loaned money to some of his cowboys. ²⁴ He wanted to settle up the accounts before winter came on and he talked to a cowboy who owed him ten thousand dollars. ²⁵ The cowboy wasn't able to pay the money so the rancher told his foreman to go and get every horse the cowboy owned, his horse trailer, his saddle, and his truck and sell all of them so he could get his money back.

²⁶ "The cowboy got down on his knees and begged the rancher not to take everything he owned and told him that he would repay every dollar. ²⁷ The rancher felt kind of sorry for the cowboy and decided to cancel the whole debt.

²⁸ "When the cowboy left the headquarters, he ran into a fellow who owed him a hundred dollars. He reached out and grabbed the fellow by the throat and told him he had better pay him his hundred dollars.

²⁹ "The guy told him he didn't have the money right then, but that he would pay back every cent.

³⁰ "But the cowboy would have none of it. He went and took the only horse the man had and sold it for a hundred dollars. ³¹ Some other cowboys saw all of this and they went and told the rancher what had happened.

³² "The rancher called the cowboy in who had all his debt canceled and said, 'You are one sorry son of a gun! I canceled your whole debt of ten thousand dollars even though you had plenty of horses of your own and even a truck and a brand-new trailer. ³³ Then you went out and took a man's only horse from him because he owed you a hundred?!' ³⁴ The rancher then had the guy beaten until he could pay back every cent he owed the rancher.

³⁵ "This is how my Father will run things on his ranch for those who don't let things go when they themselves have been forgiven."

CHAPTER 19

When Jesus finished up talkin' with everyone, he left and went into the territory on the other side of the Jordan Creek. ² Truckloads of people followed him there and he was willin' to help everyone who needed it.

³ Some of the religious know-it-alls tried to corner him with some fancy talkin'. They asked, "Don't you think a man should be able to bust up his marriage for whatever reason he wants?"

⁴ "Don't you remember," he replied, "that the Boss made man and woman and ⁵ said that whenever they get married, they become one. ⁶ So they ain't two people anymore, but rather one. Whatever the Boss brings together no man should separate."

⁷ "Why then," they replied, "did Moses say a man could fill out a piece of paper that busted up the wedlock and then he could send her packin'?"

⁸ Jesus told 'em, "He said y'all could divorce because you are a foolish bunch of people, but that's not the way my Dad planned it. ⁹ I'm tellin' you, if any cowboy sends his bride away for any reason besides cheatin' on him, and marries another gal, he has committed adultery."

¹⁰ The cowboys on his crew said, "Man, if that's the case, we all ought to stay bachelors!"

¹¹ Jesus replied, "Not every cowboy can live up to the Boss's standards on marriage. ¹² Some men have been made into steers by birth and some by the business end of a pocket knife. Other cowboys have not got hitched because of ridin' for me. If this is the case, then all should accept it."

Jesus Blesses the Cowboy Kids

¹³ Then all the little kiddos gathered around Jesus so he could pray for 'em. But as soon as they got close, Jesus's cowboys started tellin' 'em to stand back.

¹⁴ Jesus shushed his boys and said, "Y'all let these little cowboys and cowgirls come and sit with me. Don't ever keep a kid from me because heaven belongs to folks like these." ¹⁵ When he had shook hands with all the kids and blessed 'em, he rode off.

Jesus and the Rich Fellow

¹⁶ A fellow walked up to Jesus and said, "Hey amigo! What kind of good deeds do I have to do to get an eternal job on the Boss's place?"

¹⁷ "Why are you askin' me about good things?" Jesus replied. "There is only One that fits the word good. If you want an eternal place on the ranch, you must hold to all the commandments."

¹⁸ "Which ones in particular?" the fellow asked.

Jesus said, "Don't kill, don't fool around on your spouse, don't rob, don't lie about other folks, ¹⁹ respect your ma and pa, and take care of your neighbors better'n you take care of yourself."

²⁰ "I've done all of these," the rich fellow said. "Is there anything else?"

²¹ Jesus smiled and said, "If you want to get an eternal spot on the ranch, go and give everything you got to those who don't have anything. By givin' everything you have away here, you will receive much more in heaven. Then, when you're done, come and ride with me."

²² When the rich fellow heard this, he hung his head and walked away unwillin' to do as Jesus asked.

²³ Jesus told his cowboys, "It's tough for a rich man to get an eternal spot on the ranch. ²⁴ It's probably easier for a bull to give birth to a coyote than a rich man to enter the Forever Pastures."

²⁵ This spooked the cowboys and they asked, "Who can get in then?"

²⁶ Jesus looked at 'em and said, "Cowboys can't get themselves in, that would be impossible. But with God, all things are possible."

²⁷ Pete said, "We've left everything behind and saddled up with you. What is that gonna get us?"

²⁸ Jesus said, "I'm tellin' you, when all things are made new again and I sit on top of the hill on my Daddy's ranch, you cowboys who have followed me will sit on the twelve hills around me and judge the twelve territories of Israel. ²⁹ And every cowboy or cowgirl who has left their own ranch, or their families, or kids or fields for me will receive a hundred times as much as they left and receive eternal life. ³⁰ But many of the first to ride with me will be the last to come through the gate, and many who are the last to ride with me will be the first ones through the gate.

CHAPTER 20

"The Boss's ranch in heaven is like a ranch owner who went to the feed store early in the morning to hire some day workers to help with brandin' that day. ² He agreed to pay them one hundred dollars for their work that day.

³ "About nine in the morning he went out and saw some other cowboys hanging around the livery stables and not doin' anything. ⁴ He told 'em, 'Y'all head out to my ranch and help with the brandin' and I'll pay you what is right for your time.' ⁵ They saddled up and went. He rode out again at noon and then about three o'clock to look for more cowboys.

⁶ "At about five he rode by the saloon and found some cowboys just sittin' there playin' cards and drinkin' whiskey. The rancher asked them, 'Why have y'all just been sittin' around here not doin' anything all day long?'

⁷ "'Because no one gave us a job today,' they answered.

"He said to them, 'Y'all ride out to the ranch and help them with the brandin'.'

⁸ "When the sun went down that night, the ranch owner called his cattle foreman over to him and said, 'Call these cowboys over and I will pay them. Start with the last ones to ride up and end with the cowboys who have worked all day long in the sun and dirt.'

⁹ "The cowboys who had been playin' cards at the saloon and drinkin' whiskey all day walked over and the rancher paid them one hundred dollars. ¹⁰ When the cowboys who had been there since the sun came up walked over to get their wages, they assumed they would get much more, but they too were given one hundred dollars. ¹¹ When they saw that they had received the same amount for workin' all day as the last cowboys got for workin' an hour, they began to grumble and cuss about the rancher. ¹² 'These cowboys came up and only worked for an hour and barely broke one bead of sweat. You've paid them the same amount as us who've worked all day long in the heat, the sun, and the dirt!'

¹³ "But the rancher said to one of them, 'Cowboy, I ain't cheatin' you out of anything. You agreed to work for me today for one hundred dollars and that's what I paid you. ¹⁴ Take your wages and ride on out of here. I want to give every single cowboy who worked for me today one hundred dollars, regardless of how long they worked. ¹⁵ It is my money, isn't it? I can spend my money however I want. Or do I need to ask you how to spend it? Are you bein' jealous just because I am generous?'

¹⁶ "The last to ride with me will be the first to enter the gate and the first will enter last."

Jesus Talks about Dying

¹⁷ As Jesus was ridin' up toward Jerusalem, he took the twelve cowboys who rode with him to the side and said, ¹⁸ "We are fixin' to get to Jerusalem and the Boss's Son will be double-crossed by one of his own crew and handed over to the hypocritical preachers and legalistic teachers. They are going to sentence him to be strung up ¹⁹ and let those who aren't cowboys beat him and make fun of him and then kill him. On the third day though, he will be brought back from the dead and live!"

Serving Others

²⁰ Then James and John's momma came up to Jesus and kneeled down before him because she thought this might get her what she was fixin' to ask for.

²¹ "What is it you're aimin' to get from me?" Jesus asked.

She said, "When you get control over the Boss's ranch in heaven, I'm askin' that my two boys ride with you and receive special treatment. I want one on the left and one on the right side of you."

²² Jesus answered, "You don't know what you are asking for them. James and John, can you go through the pain and suffering I am going to endure when they beat me and string me up?"

"We can," they told him.

²³ Jesus said, "You will go through some of the same suffering I will, but to ride at my left and right for eternity is not for me to decide. These positions of authority on the Boss's ranch are given by the Boss himself, not granted as favors."

²⁴ When the other ten cowboys heard what James and John were tryin' to get, they got ticked off. ²⁵ Jesus called all of them over to him and said, "You know the governors over the city folk (Gentiles) hold it over their people's heads that they have authority and power. ²⁶ This ain't the way it works with y'all. If any of you want to become a top hand, you must serve and help the other cowboys, not tell them what to do. ²⁷ A top hand is a slave to all the others. ²⁸ The Boss's only Son did not come to tell other cowboys what to do, but to serve them and help them. He came to trade places with y'all and become the Outlaw's hostage to be killed so that y'all and every other person may be set free and live."

The Healing of the Blind

²⁹ When Jesus and his crew were riding away from Jericho, a bunch of people followed them.

³⁰ Two blind men were sittin' by the road, and when they heard it was the Boss's Son who was ridin' by they yelled, "Son of the Boss! Have mercy on us!"

³¹ All the people who followed Jesus yelled at the two blind men and told them to shut up and be quiet, but the men shouted even louder, "Lord, have mercy on us!"

³² Jesus pulled his horse to a stop and said, "What can I do for you?"

³³ "We want to be able to see!" the two men said.

³⁴ Jesus felt sorry for them and climbed down off his horse and touched their eyes.

Immediately they got their sight and they got up and followed him.

CHAPTER 21

Jesus Rides a Burro into Jerusalem

When they got close to Jerusalem, ² he told two of his cowboys, "Go into the village ahead and you will find a burro tied there with her colt standin' next to her. Untie them and bring them to me. ³ If anyone says anything, tell 'em that the Boss's Son needs them."

⁴ This happened to fulfill what had been said long ago, ⁵ "Say to the daughter of Jerusalem, 'Look! Your king comes to you, gentle and ridin' on a donkey, not just any donkey, but the colt of a donkey.'"

⁶ The cowboys went into the village and did just what Jesus told 'em to. ⁷ They brought out

the donkey and her colt, and used their jackets as a saddle blanket for the colt and Jesus got on. [8] A large crowd spread their ponchos, coats, and vests on the road and others cut branches off the trees and covered the ground with them. [9] The crowd of people went ahead of him and shouted, "Yippe-ti-yi-yay, the Boss's Son has come!"

"Great is he who comes from the Lord!"

"Yippe-ti-yi-yo, the Boss's Son has come!"

[10] When Jesus rode into Jerusalem, the whole town was askin', "Who is this cowboy?"

[11] The crowds shouted back, "This is Jesus, the Boss's Son from Nazareth in Galilee."

Jesus Throws People Out of the Church Building

[12] Jesus walked into the church building and started running everyone out who was buying and selling things. He knocked over the money changer's tables and the chairs of those who were selling doves for sacrifices. [13] "It was written long ago," Jesus said, "'My house will be a place where you could talk to me,' but you have made it a 'den of thieves.'"

[14] The blind and the crippled came to Jesus and he healed them all. [15] But when the uppity preachers and the my-way-or-the-highway teachers saw all the great things Jesus was doing and heard the little children shouting, "Yippe-ti-yi-yay to the Boss's Son!" they were mad.

[16] "Do you hear what these kids are shouting?" they asked him.

"You bet I do!" Jesus said. "Have you never read, 'The little cowboys and cowgirls will sing songs of worship?'"

[17] He then left the church and rode out to the small town of Bethany and spent the night there.

Jesus Curses the Fig Tree

[18] The next morning as he was ridin' back to Jerusalem, Jesus wanted somethin' to eat because he was hungry. [19] He saw a fruit tree on the side of the trail and he rode up to it so he could get a piece of fruit, but all he found was leaves. Then he said to the tree, "You look good from a distance, but when I get close to you, I see you don't have any fruit. Because you haven't done what you were made to do, you will never be able to make fruit again!" Just then, the tree withered and died.

[20] When the cowboys saw this, they were astonished. "How come that tree withered and died right before our eyes?" they asked Jesus.

[21] Jesus said, "Listen up and I'll tell you the truth. If you have faith and don't doubt one little bit, not only can you do what I did to this tree, but you could even tell the Rocky Mountains to go jump in the sea and they will do it. [22] If you believe, you will receive what you ask for when you talk to me in prayer."

The Authority of Jesus Is Questioned

[23] Jesus went into the church and started teachin'. The uppity preachers and some old coots came up to him and asked him, "Who told you that you could do these things? And who gave you the authority to do them?"

[24] Jesus told 'em, "First, let me ask you a question. If you can answer mine, I will answer yours. [25] John's baptism, where did it come from? Was it from the Boss or from men?"

They talked about it and finally said among themselves, "If we say that it came from the Boss, then he will say, 'Then how come you didn't believe John?' [26] If we tell him it came from man, then all these cowboys are going to get mad and throw us out because they think he came on the Boss's word."

[27] They finally just threw their hands up and said, "We don't know." Then Jesus said, "Since you didn't answer, neither will I."

The Good Son and the Bad Son

[28] Jesus said, "Let me ask y'all this. There was a cowboy who had two boys. He went to the oldest and said, 'Go check on the cattle in the pasture and make sure they are all there.'

[29] "'I'm not goin' to check on anything,' the boy said, but later he felt bad and went and checked on the cattle.

[30] "Then the cowboy went and told the second boy to do the same thing and go check on the cattle. The boy said, 'Yes sir! I'll go right now,' but the boy never did.

[31] "Which of the two boys did what their dad wanted them to?"

"The first boy," they said.

Jesus told 'em, "Listen to what I say, the bank robbers and the hookers are getting to the Boss's ranch in heaven before you are! [32] John came and showed you how to make things right with the Boss and you shunned his message, but the bank robbers and hookers listened to him. Even after all you have seen, you still don't turn from your sorry way of life or believe him.

³³ "Listen to this story. There was a farmer who planted a field of alfalfa. He fenced it off and even put a lookout tower on the edge of the field. After all the work was done, he rented it out to some other people and went on a long adventure. ³⁴ When it was time for the hay to be baled, the farmer sent some of his employees to collect his part of the hay.

³⁵ "The renters took the employees and beat the snot out of one of 'em and killed two of the others. ³⁶ The farmer then sent some more hired hands and the renters jumped them and did the same thing they had before. ³⁷ Finally, the farmer sent his only son. He thought surely they would respect his son.

³⁸ "The renters saw the son comin' and said to one another, 'Here comes the farmer's boy! If we kill him, then we can have his inheritance and own this place.' ³⁹ So they took the son and strung him up.

⁴⁰ "What do y'all think the farmer is gonna do to these renters?" Jesus asked.

⁴¹ "The farmer is gonna kill them all and take back the field and rent it to some people who will bale the hay like they are supposed to and give the farmer his part," they replied.

⁴² Jesus said to them, "Have you never read the Good Book where it says, 'The perfect calf has been rejected by the cowboys. The Lord has done this and it's amazin' to our eyes.'

⁴³ "The Boss's ranch is going to be taken from the cowboys he entrusted it to and given to those who will work the ranch and give back to him what he is due. ⁴⁴ The cowboy who ignores this Calf and falls over it will be broken, but the cowboy the Calf steps on will be crushed."

⁴⁵ When the uppity preachers and the religious know-it-alls heard this story, they knew that Jesus was talkin' about them. ⁴⁶ They wanted a reason to throw him in jail, but they were afraid because the people thought he was sent from God.

CHAPTER 22

The Wedding BBQ

Jesus told another story and said, ² "The Boss's place is like a big rancher who planned

a BBQ for his son's wedding. ³ He sent some of his cowboys to the other ranches to invite them to the BBQ, but no one came.

⁴ "Then he sent some more cowboys to the neighbors he had invited with the message, 'I've butchered my best steer and the fattest hogs. Y'all be sure and put your cowboy hats on. That's the only thing I ask. Come get the best food in the world and help me celebrate my son's wedding.'

⁵ "But nobody came and they all ignored the invitation. They were too busy for the big rancher. One went and worked his new colt, and another went ropin'. ⁶ The other folks who were invited were just bored so they beat up the big rancher's cowboys and even killed a few of them. ⁷ The big rancher was furious! He sent his hired guns to kill those who had murdered his cowboys and they even burned their ranches to the ground.

⁸ "Then he said to his cowboys, 'The wedding BBQ is ready, but no cowboys wanted to come. ⁹ Go into the city and invite anyone you find. Tell them to put their hats on and come help me celebrate.' ¹⁰ The cowboys went into to the city and invited everyone they saw. It didn't matter if they were good or bad. They invited everyone and the ranch headquarters was packed with people.

¹¹ "But when the big rancher came out of the house, he saw a guy standin' over to one side and he wasn't wearin' a hat. ¹² 'Hey friend,' he said, 'how did you get through the gate without a hat on? That was the only requirement to attend.' The man stood there speechless.

¹³ "The big rancher told some of his cowboys, 'Tie him up and drag him out of here and leave him for the coyotes and buzzards to eat!'

¹⁴ "Many will be invited, but only a few will come."

Taxes

¹⁵ Then the religious know-it-alls tried to trap Jesus with his own words so they could arrest him. ¹⁶ They sent some people to ask him, "We know you're a great cowboy and good teacher of what the Boss wants. You don't care what men think about you or what they say. ¹⁷ Since you don't care, is it right for us to pay taxes to Caesar?"

¹⁸ Jesus knew they were tryin' to trap him with their words and he said, "Why are you dealin'

words off the bottom of the deck and tryin' to trap me with the dead man's hand of aces and eights? ¹⁹ Show me a dollar that you would pay your taxes with." They showed him a silver dollar, ²⁰ and he asked, "Whose picture is stamped on this dollar?"

²¹ "That's Caesar's picture," they said.

Then he told 'em, "If it has his picture on it, then give it back to him. Give to Caesar what belongs to Caesar and give to the Boss what belongs to the Boss."

²² They didn't know what to say to this so they just left.

Being Hitched in Heaven

²³ The cattle barons (Sadducees), who were a group of influential people who didn't believe in life after death, came to Jesus and said, ²⁴ "Moses said that if a man dies without having any kids, the dead cowboy's brother needs to marry his brother's wife, and if they have a son, the son will be considered the dead brother's son. ²⁵ If there were seven brothers and the first one married a gal and died before having a child, and then the ²⁶ second brother married her and the same thing happened, and it went on until the seventh brother married her ²⁷ and she died, ²⁸ who would be married to her in heaven since she was married to all of 'em?"

²⁹ Jesus answered, "Y'all don't know scripture from scribblin'! And you don't know who God is. ³⁰ When God opens the gates of heaven for those who believe in his boy, they won't be hitched to nobody. They'll be like the winged riders who serve him. ³¹ As far as being given eternal life, the Boss was talkin' at you when he said, ³² 'I'm the Boss of Abraham, the first ramrod of my outfit, and of all his sons.' My Dad isn't the Boss of the dead, but of those who are alive!"

³³ The cowboys and cowgirls gathered there stood with their mouths hanging open in surprise at what Jesus was teachin'.

The Greatest Task

³⁴ After Jesus had made the cattle barons look like a bunch of idiots, the hypocritical preachers got together to talk about what he was sayin'. ³⁵ One of them was a know-it-all when it came to the code of Moses and he tried to trap Jesus with a question. He asked Jesus, ³⁶ "What's the most important task in the code of Moses?"

³⁷ Jesus said, "Love the Boss with everything you got and everything you are. ³⁸ This is the first task and it's the most important. ³⁹ The second most important is to love other cowboys and cowgirls as you love yourself. ⁴⁰ Everything in the Code and the writings of the Boss's cowboys (prophets) are based on these two tasks."

The Son of David

⁴¹ While the hypocritical preachers were still standin' there, Jesus asked them,

⁴² "What do y'all think about the One Who Will Save All Cowboys? Where will he come from?" They looked at each other and said, "He will be a son of David."

⁴³ Jesus then asked, "Alright then, if this Savin' Cowboy is David's son, then why did David say this cowboy would be his master? Remember David said, ⁴⁴ 'The Boss said to my Master, "Ride here beside me until I make all your enemies into something that you can rest and prop your boots on."'

⁴⁵ "If David called this cowboy his master, how can this cowboy be a son of King David?"

⁴⁶ No one knew the answer and from that day on, everyone kept their mouths shut and didn't try to trap him with fancy words.

CHAPTER 23

Jesus Puts Down Religious Nonsense

Jesus turned and talked to his cowboys and the rest of the folks who were sittin' around. He said, ² "The hypocritical preachers and the lawyers of the Code are experts in the law of Moses. ³ Y'all need to do what they say, but don't act like they act. They sure as heck don't practice what they preach.

⁴ "They will load y'all down with impossible tasks they wouldn't be willing to bear. ⁵ They have silver on their saddles and jingle bobs on their spurs, just so y'all will think they are important. They are all talk and no action. ⁶ They like the box seats at the rodeo and want to be the first in line at the chuckwagon. ⁷ They care about bein' recognized at the feed store and bein' called by fancy titles.

⁸ "But y'all cowboys who ride for me don't need fancy titles. Y'all have only one Boss and you are all brothers. ⁹ Don't call anyone on earth 'boss' because you only have one Boss and he

is in heaven. ¹⁰ Don't let anyone call you 'teacher' either. You only have one Teacher and he's the Boss's Son. ¹¹ The one who is the top hand among you will be your servant who works like a pack mule. ¹² Whoever tries to rise above others will be thrown down and whoever lowers himself will be raised up.

Jesus Gives It to the Religious Know-It-Alls

¹³ "You hypocritical preachers and lawyers of the Code are going to come to a terrible reckonin'. ¹⁴ You slam the gate to God's Green Pastures in the face of cowboys and cowgirls. Y'all won't ever ride through those gates, nor will you allow anyone else to ride through.

¹⁵ "You hypocritical preachers and lawyers of the Code are going to come to a terrible reckonin'. You ride over mountains and cross great territories to win one cowboy for the Boss, and when he saddles up, you make him twice the son of hell that you are.

¹⁶ "You blind trail guides have a day of reckonin' comin' to you too! You tell folks, 'If you give your word by the church building, it don't mean nothin'; but if you give your word by the gold in the church, you are obligated to keep it.' ¹⁷⁻¹⁹ You blind idiots! Which is more important: the gift, or the means by which the gift is made? ²⁰⁻²¹ Those who give their word by the church do it by the church and everything it stands for. ²² The cowboy who gives his word by heaven gives his word on the Boss's throne and by the one who sits on it.

²³ "You hypocritical preachers and lawyers of the Code are going to come to a terrible reckonin'. Y'all give a tenth of everything from tobacco to toilet paper, but you forget about the important part of the Code: mercy, justice, and faith. You should give a tenth of everything, but don't forget the more important matters. ²⁴ You blind trail guides will pick a piece of dirt out of your coffee, but then eat a mud pie.

²⁵ "You hypocritical preachers and lawyers of the Code are going to come to a terrible reckonin'. You'll wash the dirt off the outside of your coffee cup, but leave the inside full of greed and perversion. ²⁶ If you'll get the inside clean the outside will follow!

²⁷ "You hypocritical preachers and lawyers of the Code are going to come to a terrible recko-

nin'. You are like pretty cedar caskets. You look good on the outside, but on the inside, you are full of rotting flesh and worms. ²⁸ That's the way y'all appear to people. You look good on the outside, but inside you are full of hypocrisy and rebellion.

²⁹ "You hypocritical preachers and lawyers of the Code are going to come to a terrible reckonin'. You carve fancy headstones for the prophets and decorate the graves of those who rode with the Boss. ³⁰ You say, 'If we lived way back then, we wouldn't have been a part of the posse that murdered these great people!' ³¹ But you are proof that you are the sons of those posse riders. ³² Just keep on doin' the same things they did and actin' the way they acted. ³³ You're all coyotes! You're the bastard sons of coyotes! How are you gonna escape the truck that leads to the slaughterhouse? ³⁴ I will send my cowboys and wise foremen and experts in the code of Moses to you. But y'all will string 'em up or nail 'em to a cross or whip 'em away from your meetings or run 'em out of town. ³⁵ That's why you'll be found guilty for every cowboy, starting with Abel. ³⁶ I promise that you people livin' today will be punished for all these things.

Jesus Cries about Jerusalem Again

³⁷ "Oh my town of Jerusalem! You have killed all those I sent to take care of you. I want so bad to take all your children and comfort them like a momma hen comforts her chicks, but you have shunned me. ³⁸ Now your church will be deserted and full of tumbleweeds. ³⁹ You ain't gonna see me again until you say, 'Blessed is the cowboy who comes in the name of the Boss.'"

CHAPTER 24

The Church Building and the Return of Jesus

After Jesus left the church, his cowboys were all gawkin' and talkin' about how big everything was. ² Jesus told 'em, "All this stuff, no matter how big or how nice it is, will be torn down. There won't be one brick that stays where it's at."

³ Later, Jesus was backed up against a tree resting on top of Olive Hill. A few of his cowboys came up and asked, "How will we know when you're ridin' back to get us? Are you gonna give us a whistle or a yell or send us a letter?"

[4] Jesus thought hard and then his eyebrows knitted together as he spoke. "Don't let anyone pull the wool over your eyes. [5] There's gonna be a whole mess of people who claim to be me. They will ride into town and claim to be the cowboy who has come to save you."

[6] "You will hear about wars and battles, but don't fret, this isn't the end. These things must happen, but it ain't the end. [7] Nations and countries will kill each other. Folks will starve to death in their own houses and there will be earthquakes in many different territories. [8] But this is just the birthin' of the problems that will follow.

[9] "Y'all are gonna be beaten and even killed. They will hate you because you ride for me. [10] Folks are gonna start stabbin' each other in the back every day. [11] And a lot of snake-oil salesmen will come and lead many people down the wrong trail. [12] Folks are gonna stop lovin' each other and focus on themselves and the evil that lives there. [13] But if y'all keep your hearts on my message and keep ridin' for me all day, every day, you will be spared and saved. [14] When the good news of my tale has finally been taken to every part of every territory, then the end will come.

The Defecation of Desecration

[15] "One day you will see the most horrible thing in the world. You will see the 'Defecation of Desecration' right there in the church's most holy place. If you've read what Daniel wrote you'll know what I mean when I say that everyone should try real hard to understand. [16] If you're livin' in or around Judea when this happens, saddle up your horse right then, not later, and shuck out for the hills. [17] If you're patchin' some shakes on the roof, don't even go back inside, just ride. [18] If you're muckin' out stalls, don't go back in and change boots. [19] This ride will be double tough on pregnant womenfolk and those with babies who are still on the suck. [20] You ought to pray that this time don't come in the winter or on Sunday, when you're supposed to be restin'. [21] This time is gonna be plumb awful. Nothin' like this has ever been seen or will ever be seen again. [22] If the Boss don't step in with his mighty hand and make this time as short as possible, ain't nobody gonna make it out alive. Nobody! But because God loves the cowboys who ride for

him, he's gonna step in and make sure it don't go on too long.

[23] "People may yell, 'Here's Jesus!' or 'There he is, I see him!' but don't believe them. [24] Jesus impersonators and fake cowboys will come and do amazin' things and fool people. They will even try to fool those cowboys who ride for my Father's brand. [25] I'm readyin' the trail for you and givin' you ample warning ahead of time. [26] If a city slicker tells you that Jesus is out in the desert, don't believe them. If someone tells you that I am in a hidden place and they know where to find me, don't believe their forked tongue. [27] When the Boss's Son returns, you'll know for sure. It'll be like the sky has been cracked open and lightning and thunder have come alive and rode straight from heaven itself. Every cowboy and every city slicker on earth will be able to see and hear it. [28] If you see a crowd of people gathered like buzzards and you don't know what they are lookin' at, it sure enough won't be me. Buzzards circle around the dead, not the Boss's Son.

When the Son Arrives

[29] "After the Boss steps in and all the sufferin' is over, 'The sun will go out and the moon won't shine anymore. The stars will fall and every universe will tremble.'

[30] "When this happens, the Son will ride back. Every person will see it and there will be no doubt. People who have chosen to ride alone or with someone else, instead of with me, will cry and wail in terror when they see me ride out of heaven with all the power of God in my right hand. [31] At the sound of the bugler's charge, the Son will send all the winged riders to gather the faithful who have chosen to ride with him from all over the earth.

[32] "Learn a lesson from a fruit tree. When the branches start buddin' out, you know warmer weather is approachin'. [33] When you see all these things I told you start happenin', you'll know that I am approachin'. [34] I ain't just talkin' to people hundreds of years from now, I'm talkin' right at y'all sitting here too. [35] The rocks imbedded in the deepest mountains and the blue sky over your heads will not last forever, but my word will.

[36] "Nobody but the Boss knows the day or the hour all of this will happen. The winged riders don't know. Your know-it-all neighbor don't

know. Not even the Boss's Son knows. Only the Boss knows. 37 When you see the Boss's Son come back, it will be just like when the rain started fallin' in the time of Noah. 38 Folks were cookin' on the grill and havin' their drink of choice and celebratin' weddings right up to the time that Noah jumped on the big boat. 39 Despite everything that Noah told 'em, they were surprised when the flood came and washed 'em down the gulley. This is exactly how it will be when I come back.

40 "Two cowboys will be gatherin' cattle and one will be taken and the other left right there in the saddle. 41 Two cowgirls will be feedin' horses and one will be taken and the other left standin' right there. 42 Be on the lookout and don't get lax in the saddle. Keep both feet in your stirrups and one eye on the sky. You won't know when I'm comin' back, so be ready. 43 You got to keep a sharp watch. If you knew what time a horse thief was comin', you would be ready with your rifle. 44 Mark my words and be ready for the Son to come ridin' back down.

45 "Who are the top hands and faithful riders of the brand? Who will the Boss choose to make foreman and ramrods? 46 Cowboys who are found doin' their job when the cattle foreman shows up unannounced will be rewarded. 47 If a cowboy does his job the way it's supposed to be done, then he will be promoted on the Boss's spread. 48 But what about the cowboy out there in that far line camp that thinks nobody is watchin'? 49 Suppose he quits checkin' the waters and fails to feed cow cake in the winter. What if he invites all his buddies out to the house and all they do is get drunk and pitch washers instead of what he's supposed to be doing? 50 You can bet that one day the cattle foreman will ride up to the camp without givin' any notice. 51 This cowboy will be thrown off the ranch along with the all the others who pretend to ride for the brand. There they will be exposed to pain and sufferin' like nobody has ever seen.

CHAPTER 25

The Ten Single Gals

"God's Green Pasture is like what happened one night when ten single gals went to meet a famous cowboy. 2 They all took kerosene lanterns because they knew he would be arriving very late. Five of the girls were smart and five of the girls were dumb. 3 The dumb ones took their lanterns, but didn't take any extra oil. 4 The smart ones were prepared for the whole night.

5 "The cowboy was comin' from another ranch and would arrive very late. They waited on him all night to be the first to welcome him. 6 In the middle of the night, someone shouted, 'The cowboy is here! Come and say hello.'

7 "The girls got up and all had left their lanterns burning. 8 The dumb girls said to the others, 'Give us some of your oil. Our lanterns are going out and we won't be able to see.'

9 "The smart cowgirls said, 'There ain't enough for all of us. You'll have to go buy some more.'

10 "While the dumb girls were off buying more oil, the cowboy rode up. The girls with the lit lanterns walked with him to the house where he was stayin'. They went in to visit and the door was closed. 11 Later, the dumb girls got back and knocked on the door and said, 'We want to meet you. Can we come in?'

12 "But the cowboy replied, 'I've never seen y'all before. The girls who wanted to meet me were waiting on me to get here.'

13 "I want y'all who ride with me to pay attention to this story and always be ready. You need to be prepared because you won't know when all this will happen.

The Three Cowboys and Their Talents

14 "The Boss's place is also like a rancher who went away and left three of his cowboys in charge of training the comin' two-year-old colts. 15 He knew what each cowboy was capable of so he gave the first cowboy five colts to break, the second cowboy three colts to break, and one colt to the third.

16 "As soon as the rancher was gone, the first cowboy broke all five of his colts and then swapped them for ten unbroken colts. 17 The cowboy with two colts did the same thing. 18 But the cowboy with one colt was afraid to even work with the horse. He locked it in a stall so nothing would go wrong and the horse would be safe. He didn't ride it or even halter break it.

19 "When the rancher returned, he asked them about the horses he had assigned them. 20 The cowboy who got five horses told about how he had done some horse trading and showed him the ten saddle broke horses. The cowboy said,

'You gave me five horses that couldn't be ridden and now you have ten that you can.'

²¹ "'Great job,' the rancher said, 'I'm gonna make you a full partner on this outfit. I put you in charge of just a little bit, but now I will put you in charge of more. Get your stuff out of the bunkhouse and put it in the big house.'

²² "The cowboy who had been given the two colts walked with the rancher to another set of pens. The cowboy said, 'You gave me two horses that couldn't be ridden and now you have four that can.'

²³ "'Great job,' the rancher said, 'I'm gonna make you a full partner on this outfit. I put you in charge of just a little bit, but now I will put you in charge of more. Get your stuff out of the bunkhouse and put it in the big house.'

²⁴ "The cowboy who had received one colt walked with the rancher over to the stall where he had kept the one horse. The cowboy said, 'I know you're a hard man and don't tolerate excuses or shoddy work. ²⁵ I was afraid that something might happen to this colt so I just kept him in here so he would be safe.'

²⁶ "The rancher was furious and said, 'You know I'm a hard man and I don't tolerate excuses or shoddy work! ²⁷ You could have at least broke this horse so I could use him durin' brandin' season coming up.'

²⁸ "Then the rancher said, 'Take this colt and give it to the cowboy with the ten horses. ²⁹ Everyone who risks everything for me will be given more, but for those who are scared and cautious, all will be taken from them. ³⁰ I know city slickers who are better cowboys than you are. You are gonna be thrown off this ranch where you will suffer in great pain and cry all day and all night.'

The Sheep and the Goats

³¹ "When the Son comes back with all his winged riders and all the power of heaven with him, he will sit upon the highest peak of the ranch. ³² Every territory and every nation will be gathered below him and he will separate the sheep from the goats. ³³ He will put the sheep on his right side and the goats to the left.

³⁴ "Then the Lord of the ranch will say to those sheep on his right, 'Come, all you who are blessed by the Boss, inherit the ranch that was made for you at the beginning of all creation. ³⁵ I was hungry and you fed me. I was thirsty and you watered me. I was a stranger on a lonely road and you welcomed me into your home. ³⁶ I had no chaps to protect me and you gave some to me. I was sick and dyin' and you cared for me. I was locked up in jail and you came to visit me.'

³⁷ "Then these cowboys and cowgirls who had done right in the Lord's eyes will say, 'When did we ever see you like this? ³⁸ When did we give you a room or hand you a pair of batwing leggings? ³⁹ When did we visit you in the jailhouse?'

⁴⁰ "And the Lord will say, 'I'm tellin' it to y'all straight. Every time you did these things for one of the cowboys or cowgirls who rode for my Father's brand, you did them for me too.'

⁴¹ "Then the Lord will turn to the goats on his left and say, 'Get these sorry mongrels off my spread! Put them on the killer trucks and ship them off to the fire that never goes out—the fire that was prepared for the devil and his demons! ⁴² I was hungry and you refused me food. I was thirsty and you laughed. ⁴³ I was a stranger in need and you ignored me. Thorns cut my legs and it made no difference to you. I was sick and in jail and you never visited me.'

⁴⁴ "Then they will cry out, 'Lord, we never saw you hungry, thirsty, or any of those other things. If we would have seen you, we would have done something.'

⁴⁵ "And he will answer, 'Listen to me close. When you refused these things to the cowboys and cowgirls who rode for my Father's brand, you refused them to me!'

⁴⁶ "And then they will be shipped off to the fires of hell, but those cowboys and cowgirls who rode for the Father's brand will be turned out to lush, eternal pasture."

CHAPTER 26

Planning and Plotting to Kill Jesus

When Jesus was done talking, he said to his cowboys, ² "Passover is in a couple of days and it will be then that the Boss's Son will be double-crossed by one of his own and killed."

³ It was at this time that the big wigs of the church were meetin' at the high priest's house and ⁴ tryin' to come up with a plan to kill Jesus. ⁵ "We can't do anything durin' the Passover," they agreed, "or we will have a riot on our hands."

Jesus at Bethany

⁶ Meanwhile, Jesus was hangin' out in the town of Bethany with a fellow named Simon who used to have the bad skin rot. ⁷ While he was there, a woman came in with a jar of very expensive perfume and she used all of it on Jesus. ⁸ The cowboys couldn't believe she had wasted something so valuable by just pourin' it on Jesus. ⁹ "That could have been sold for a bunch of money and given to those who can't buy food or clothes!" they said.

¹⁰ But Jesus got on to them and said, "Wait a minute! Why are y'all criticizin' what this cowgirl has done for me? ¹¹ There will always be poor folks, but I won't always be here like I am now. ¹² She has poured this perfume on me to prepare my body for the grave. ¹³ I'm tellin' you the truth when I say this woman's deed here tonight will be remembered and taught wherever the good news is preached throughout this entire world."

Judas Double-Crosses Jesus

¹⁴ About this time, the dirty double-crosser, Judas Iscariot, one of the cowboys who rode for Jesus, went to the leaders in the church ¹⁵ and asked, "How much will you pay me to double-cross Jesus?" They handed him thirty pieces of silver. ¹⁶ He then began lookin' for a way to ambush Jesus and turn him over to them.

The Last Supper

¹⁷ On the first day of the Feast of the Flatbread, the cowboys who rode for Jesus came up to him and asked, "Where are we supposed to make the biscuits for the Passover supper?"

¹⁸ "When you get to town," Jesus said, "you will see a certain fellow. Tell him, 'The Top Hand says, "My time is up and I will eat the Passover supper at your table with the cowboys who ride for me."'" ¹⁹ The cowboys did what they were told to do and made sup' where they were told to.

²⁰ After the sun had gone down, Jesus sat down at the table with all of his cowboys. ²¹ While they were eatin' he said, "Y'all listen up! One of you is a dirty double-crosser and will betray me."

²² The cowboys couldn't believe their ears and each one asked, "It ain't me, is it Lord?"

²³ He replied, "One of you who is sittin' at this table sharin' biscuits with me is the dirty rat. ²⁴ The Boss's Son must die as it was said long ago in the Good Book. But it's gonna be awfully terrible for the one who snitches him off. It would have been better if he'd never been born."

²⁵ Judas, the one who would do the dirty deed, also asked, "Do you think it's me?" Jesus told him, "You said it, I didn't."

²⁶ As they were eatin', Jesus took a biscuit and blessed it. Then he broke it into some pieces and handed a piece to each cowboy. He said, "Take this and eat it. It represents my body that will be broken for y'all and every other cowboy and cowgirl."

²⁷ Then Jesus took a coffee cup that had wine in it and blessed it. He passed it around the table for everyone to get a drink and said, "Y'all take a swig of this. ²⁸ It represents my blood that my Dad will use to make a new agreement with everyone who believes in me. My blood will be spilt in the dirt as a sacrifice so that the sins of many will be forgiven. ²⁹ I won't drink wine again until the day I drink it with y'all on my Father's spread."

³⁰ They sang a song about God and went to Olive Hill.

Peter Is Gonna Deny Jesus

³¹ As they rode over to Olive Hill, Jesus told them, "Tonight, all of y'all are gonna shuck out on me. The Good Book says, 'The Boss will slay the Trail Guide and the herd will scatter.' ³² But after I come back from the grave, I will meet y'all in Galilee."

³³ Pete said, "I don't care if everyone shucks out for the hills, I ain't leavin' you."

³⁴ "I'm tellin' you the truth, Pete," Jesus said. "Before the sun comes up, you will deny that you ever rode with me three times."

³⁵ Pete stood up and stomped his foot as he said, "Even if I have to die with you to prove it, I will never deny ridin' with you." And all of Jesus's crew made the same vow and waved their hats in the air.

Torture in the Garden

³⁶ Then Jesus and his boys rode over to a place called Gethsemane and he told 'em, "Y'all wait here while I go over yonder and talk to my Dad." ³⁷ He motioned for Pete, James, and John to go with him and Jesus began to get upset and troubled. ³⁸ Then Jesus told the three cowboys, "I feel as if I will be crushed by the pain and sorrow

I'm feelin' right now. I'm worried that it might actually kill me. Y'all wait right here and take first watch while I go and talk to my Dad."

39 Jesus rode a little further and then stepped off and laid face down in the dirt and said, "Daddy, please don't make me go through this cruel deed that is comin'. If it's possible, will you find another way? But if this is the only way and it is your will, then I'll do it."

40 Jesus rode back over to where his boys were keepin' watch and found them fast asleep. "Could y'all not keep watch like I asked you to for even one hour?" he asked Pete. **41** "Say your prayers and keep watch so that you will not fall into temptation again. I know your hearts are willin' to ride with me no matter what, but your bodies are weaker'n pond water."

42 Jesus went away a second time and prayed, "Daddy, if there ain't another way to get this done except by me going through this dastardly deed, then so be it. I just want to please you."

43 When Jesus went back to his boys, he found them asleep again. **44** This time, he didn't say anything, but went back and prayed a third time, sayin' the exact same thing.

45 He finally came back and woke them up by sayin' to them, "Are y'all still sleepin'? Get up, for the hour has come, and the Boss's Son has been double-crossed by one of his own cowboys into the hands of sinners. **46** Get up now! We will go meet them and not let them find us cowerin' in a garden. Here comes my betrayer now!"

Jesus Is Double-Crossed and Arrested

47 While Jesus was sayin' this, Judas, one of the twelve cowboys who rode with Jesus, arrived at the garden. Following Judas was a posse of armed men, sent from the big wigs of the church. **48** Judas told the posse to watch and he would give them a sign as to which man was Jesus. "The one I walk up and shake hands with is Jesus. He's the one to arrest." **49** Judas walked straight up to Jesus and said, "How ya doin', boss!" and shook Jesus's hand.

50 Jesus said, "Alright boys, y'all go ahead and do what you've come to do."

A few guys from the posse stepped forward and grabbed Jesus. **51** Right then, one of Jesus's cowboys pulled a knife out of his boot and cut off the ear of one of the men who had grabbed him.

52 "Put that knife away," Jesus said, "if you pull a knife you will die by the knife. **53** If I wanted to defend myself, I could ask my Father to send twelve thousand winged riders to come and rescue me. **54** But if I did this, how would the things that must be done be fulfilled?"

55 Jesus turned to the posse and asked, "Am I the leader of some outlaw gang? Have I done any violence to anyone that warrants y'all comin' out here to arrest me with all these weapons? Every day I sat in the church teachin' everyone about God and you never arrested me there. **56** But all of this must happen this way in order to fulfill what the great cowboys who rode for my Dad long ago had said would happen." Jesus watched as every one of his cowboys jumped on their horses and loped away in fear.

The Head Honcho of the Church Questions Jesus

57 The posse took Jesus and stood him before Caiaphas, the church's head honcho, and many other big wigs. **58** Pete had been followin' along like a Comanche warrior, at a distance and without bein' seen. He snuck in to the meetin' and sat down in the back to see what the outcome would be.

59 This whole church institution was just lookin' for a way to lie about Jesus so they could sentence him to death. **60** After many attempts and people lyin' on the stand, they couldn't find a reason.

Then two fellows walked in and **61** said, "This cowboy said, 'I will destroy the church and rebuild it in three days.'"

62 The head honcho stood up and asked Jesus, "Are you gonna answer these charges?

What have you got to say about yourself?" **63** But Jesus kept his mouth closed.

The head honcho said, "I dare you to answer this one question, so help you God. Are you the Christ, the Boss's Son?"

64 "Yup," Jesus said, "and I'm tellin' y'all right now that in the future you will see me sittin' right beside the Boss and ridin' back on the clouds of heaven."

65 The head honcho broke into a fit of rage and spit flew from his mouth as he said, "He has called himself God! Why do we need more witnesses? Everyone in here just heard him. What do y'all think we should do now?"

66 "String him up!" they yelled.

[67] Then all the people took turns spittin' on Jesus and hittin' him in the face. All the while they [68] said, "If you're the Son of God, tell us who is hittin' you!"

Pete Denies Riding with Jesus

[69] Now Pete was still there and a young girl came up to him and said, "I know you!

You rode with Jesus didn't you?"

[70] Without skippin' a beat, Pete said, "I ain't got a clue what you're yakkin' about, ma'am."

[71] Pete saddled up and as he rode out of the courtyard, another young lady recognized him and told everyone standin' there, "Hey look! There's one of Jesus's cowboys who rode with him right there."

[72] Pete shook his head and hollered, "Why does everyone keep sayin' that? I ain't never seen that man before in my life."

[73] When things had settled down, some folks who were standin' close to Pete said, "We know you rode with Jesus. We can tell by your accent!"

[74] Then Pete started cussin' himself and everyone else and said, "I ain't never rode with no man named Jesus!"

Immediately, off in the distance, a rooster crowed. [75] Then Pete remembered the words Jesus had spoken to him, "When you hear the cock crow, you will have denied ridin' with me three times." Pete loped away and wept like a child.

CHAPTER 27

Early that morning, the religious institution had decided to put Jesus to death. [2] They tied him up and handed him over to Pilate, the Roman governor.

Judas Kills Himself

[3] When Judas heard they were gonna kill Jesus, his heart was crushed because he was the cause of it all. He went back to the church and gave them the thirty pieces of silver back. [4-5] "I have sinned," he said, "I have double-crossed an innocent man."

"That don't matter to us," they replied. "This innocent blood will be on your hands, not ours!"

Judas threw the money on the floor and went and found a tree and strung himself up by the neck.

[6] The segundos in the church picked up the money and said, "We can't even use this for our church bank account because it's blood money." [7] So they used the money to buy a little plot of land to use as a cemetery for foreigners. [8] That place is still called the field of blood to this day. [9] Then, the words of the great cowboy Jeremiah came true, "They took the thirty pieces of silver, the price of his double cross, [10] and used it to buy the foreigners' field."

Jesus on Trial before Pilate

[11] Meanwhile, Jesus stood before the governor of the territory and the governor asked him, "Are you the Jews' boss?"

"Yup," Jesus replied.

[12] When he was accused by the head honchos of the church, he didn't answer. [13] Then Pilate asked him, "Don't you hear what they are sayin' about you?" [14] But Jesus didn't answer. He didn't say one word about any of the charges. His silence baffled Pilate.

Pilate Signs the Death Warrant

[15] There was an old tradition during this time of the year, to release one prisoner who the crowd chose. [16] There was a ruthless bandito named Barabbas who was in jail at this time. [17] When the crowd gathered around, Pilate asked them, "Which one do you want me to release: Barabbas, or Jesus, who is called the Boss's Son?" [18] He knew that it was out of jealousy that they had shoehorned Jesus and turned him in.

[19] While Pilate was actin' as judge and executioner, his wife sent him a note that said, "Don't have anything to do with that innocent fellow! I have been plagued by awful dreams because of this."

[20] But the head honchos of the church lobbied the crowd and persuaded them to release the bandito and have Jesus strung up.

[21] "Pick your poison and tell me which one you will have turned loose," said the governor.

"Barabbas the Bandito!" they all cried in unison.

[22] "If you choose Barabbas, what do you want done with Jesus?" asked Pilate. They all yelled, "Kill him!"

[23] "Why? What in the world has this man done to deserve this?" asked Pilate. But they got all slobber-mouthed and yelled, "Crucify him!"

[24] When Pilate saw that there was fixin' to be

a riot, he dipped his hands in a horse trough and washed them sayin', "This is y'alls doin', not mine. I'm innocent of this man's blood and I wash my hands of this whole ordeal."

²⁵ The crowd yelled, "Let this killin' fall on our children's souls!"

²⁶ Pilate then ordered the release of the bandito Barabbas and had Jesus horsewhipped before he was to be nailed to the cross.

Jesus Is Mocked and Insulted

²⁷ Pilate's men took Jesus and put about two hundred armed guards around him. ²⁸ They stripped him out of his jeans and shirt and slung a purple horse blanket around him like a robe. ²⁹ Then they wove together a crown of mesquite thorns and shoved it on his head. They gave him a stick to hold like a king's scepter and they knelt down mockingly in front of him sayin', "All hail the boss of the Jews!" ³⁰ They jerked his stick from him and beat him with it as they spit all over him. ³¹ After their sport with him, they took the purple blanket off and dressed him back in his trail gear. Then they tied him up and led him away to be nailed to the cross.

Jesus Is Strung up on the Cross

³² As they traveled to the place where they would kill him, a fellow named Simon was forced to carry the cross-beam Jesus was tryin' to carry. ³³ They came to the place called Golgotha, which means "Skull Hill." ³⁴ They offered Jesus a drink of wine mixed with a narcotic, but he spit it out as soon as he tasted it. ³⁵ When they had strung him up on the cross and nailed him to it to be sure he wouldn't fall off, they rolled dice to see who would get his gear. ³⁶ They all hunkered down to watch him die. ³⁷ Above Jesus's head, they nailed a crudely painted sign that said, "This here's Jesus, the Boss of the Jews." ³⁸ Two bank robbers were strung up beside him, one on his off-side and the other on his left. ³⁹ A bunch of no-accounts rode by and cussed Jesus ⁴⁰ sayin', "You claimed you were gonna destroy the church and rebuild it in three days! If you're the Boss's Son, come down off that cross and prove it, you coward!"

⁴¹ The head honchos of the church acted in the same sorry fashion. They made fun of him and said, ⁴² "He rescued other cowboys, now let's see if he can come down off that cross and rescue himself. If he does, then we'll believe he is who he says he is. ⁴³ He trusts in God. Let the Almighty save him if he really wants him. Jesus said himself, 'I am the Boss's Son.'" ⁴⁴ The bank robbers also talked real bad to him.

Jesus Dies

⁴⁵ From about noon until three, darkness covered the territory. ⁴⁶ About three o'clock, Jesus yelled out, *"Eloi, Eloi, lema sabachthani?"*—which translated into cowboy terms means, "My God, my God, why have you shucked out on me?"

⁴⁷ Some of the fellows standin' nearby said, "He's a hollerin' for Elijah!"

⁴⁸ One of the bystanders ran and filled his hat with soured wine and lifted it up to Jesus so he could get a drink. ⁴⁹ The rest of them said, "Leave him be. Let's see if Elijah will come a ridin' down to get him!"

⁵⁰ Then Jesus gave one last mighty yell and he died.

⁵¹ At that very moment, the drapery in the church that separated man from God was split down the middle startin' at the top and comin' down. The whole earth shook and boulders split wide open like busted watermelons. ⁵² Graves were opened up and a bunch of cowboys who had rode for the brand got up and walked, raised back to life. ⁵³ They rode out of the graveyards, and after Jesus came back to life, they went into Jerusalem and were seen by a lot of folks.

⁵⁴ When the deputy and those who were with him guardin' Jesus saw everything that was happenin', they were terrified and they cried out, "Oh no! He really was the Boss's Son."

⁵⁵ There was a bunch of women watchin' from afar. They had followed Jesus and cooked for him on many occasions. ⁵⁶ Among them were Mary Magdalene, James and Joseph's momma Mary, and the mother of Zebedee's boys.

Jesus Is Buried in a Cave

⁵⁷ When evening' was a comin', a rich fellow named Joseph who had done some studyin' and travelin' with Jesus, ⁵⁸ went to Pilate and asked for Jesus's body. Pilate agreed and gave the order. ⁵⁹ Old Joseph took the body and wrapped it in a clean white sheet and ⁶⁰ put the body in a cave that had been hollowed out of a rock for Joseph when he died. They rolled a boulder in

front of the entrance to keep the two-legged and four-legged coyotes out. ⁶¹ Mary Magdalene and the other Mary were sittin' there watchin' from nearby.

Deputies Guard the Tomb

⁶² The next day, the head honchos of the church and the religious know-it-alls went to Pilate.

⁶³ "Your honor," they said, "whilst that fellow we killed was still alive, he had said he would come back to life three days later. ⁶⁴ We want you to post some deputies at his grave to keep Jesus's cowboys from stealin' the body and claimin' that he come back to life. Jesus deceived many good and honest folks while he was alive, but if they pull this off, it will be worse than the first trick."

⁶⁵ "Take a few deputies," Pilate said. "Do whatever you think you need to do to make the grave secure." ⁶⁶ They went and stretched some rope across the entrance with some mud at each end so's they could tell if it had been messed with. They told the deputies to stand guard and not let anyone mess with the body or the grave.

CHAPTER 28

Jesus Rides Back into Town

After the day of rest, at sunrise of the first day of the week, the two Marys went to visit Jesus's grave.

² All of a sudden there was a violent earthquake. A winged rider from heaven had flown down and rolled the boulder out of the way so they could see inside. ³ This angel looked like he was made of livin' lightnin' and his trail gear was as white as snow. ⁴ The deputies saw him and got so dad-gummed scared that they fell down like dead men.

⁵ The winged rider said, "Y'all don't be scared. I know y'all are lookin' for Jesus who was strung up and killed on that cross. ⁶ But he ain't here! He has ridden back from the dead just like he said he would. Y'all come take a look and see that I ain't pullin' your leg. ⁷ Once yer satisfied that he ain't here, run and tell his cowboys, 'He

has ridden back from the dead and has struck a long trot for Galilee. There is where you'll meet him.' I've said what I came to say."

The Ladies See Jesus

⁸ So the two ladies ran away from the grave. They were afraid, but at the same time they were plumb happy. They ran as fast as they could toward where the cowboys were camped. ⁹ Suddenly they came upon Jesus sittin' there and he said, "Howdy!" They screamed for joy and fell down at his boots and worshiped him. ¹⁰ Then Jesus told 'em, "Don't be scared. Go and tell the boys of my outfit to meet me in Galilee."

The Head Honchos of the Church Bribe the Deputies

¹¹ While the women were goin' to tell Jesus's cowboys about what happened, the deputies rode into town and told the head honchos of the church about the winged rider and everything else that had happened. ¹² The head honchos met together and came up with a devious plan. They gave the deputies a bunch of money and said, ¹³ "Tell people that Jesus's cowboys came in the middle of the night and bushwhacked you and stole Jesus's body. ¹⁴ If this report makes it back to Pilate, he will be fine with it and you won't get in trouble." ¹⁵ So the deputies pocketed their small fortunes and did what they were told to do. This lie has been told all over the place and is still thought to be true today.

Jesus Gives the Great Cow-mission

¹⁶ The eleven remaining cowboys of Jesus's outfit rode out to Galilee to the mountain Jesus had told 'em about. ¹⁷ When they saw him, they took a knee before him and worshiped him, but even then, some of them had doubts. ¹⁸ Then Jesus walked up to 'em and said, "I've been made Boss over heaven's Green Pastures and all the pastures of this world. ¹⁹ Go now and recruit riders for my brand from all over the world, baptize them in the name of the Father and of the Son and of the Holy Ghost, ²⁰ teachin' them to ride the cowboy way I have taught y'all. And remember this, I am always with you, even to the very end of every trail."

MARK

CHAPTER 1

John Blazes the Trail

This ain't about nothing except the good news of a man named Jesus, the Son of God. ² I reckon it all started when one of God's top hands, a fella named Isaiah, wrote this, "God said, 'I got a cowboy coming who is going to show you a new message and a new way of riding for me. ³ He's already shouting from the desert and tellin' y'all to get ready to saddle up for the Lord and ride right straight for him.'"

⁴ So John came out of nowhere, riding for God and baptizing folks. His message was plain and simple, "Quit riding in sin and be baptized and God will turn a blind eye to all the sorry things you've done." ⁵ Folks came from all around the country to hear this cowboy preach. Many a heart turned to God and they told of the sorry things they had done and old John dunked 'em in Jordan Creek.

⁶ John was a different sort of fellow. He wore a vest of camel hair with a stout leather belt holding his jeans up. He didn't waste no time with fancy vittles, but just ate locusts and wild honey. ⁷ He told people time and again, "The Top Hand is coming soon and I ain't worthy enough to pull his boots off after a long ride. ⁸ I dunk y'all in water, but he's gonna dunk you in the Holy Spirit."

The Dunkin' and the Seduction

⁹ It wasn't long before Jesus came riding down from the Nazareth country and told John to baptize him in Jordan Creek. ¹⁰ When Jesus came up out of the water, the sky split plumb apart and you could see right into heaven. And out of heaven come the Spirit of God like a dove and it came right down to him. ¹¹ Then there was a voice from heaven that said, "You are my Boy and that pleases me to no end." ¹² Then the Spirit of God led Jesus out into the wilds and the brush where there were no fences and things were hard to come by. ¹³ Jesus was out there for more'n forty days with nothing to eat and Satan tried to take him out time and again. Jesus spent all those nights surrounded by all sorts of predators, but God sent angels to take care of him.

¹⁴ After all this, old John was thrown in jail and Jesus went into the Galilee country to tell people the good news.

¹⁵ He told 'em, "Y'all been waiting for a long time and the Boss's Green Pasture has made it here. Quit riding in sin and tie hard and fast to the good news."

The First Cowboys

¹⁶ As Jesus rode along telling people this same message over and over, he run into a couple of fellows near the Sea of Galilee. These two cowboys, Simon and Andrew, were gathering some heifers. ¹⁷ Jesus hollered over to 'em and said, "Ride with me and I'll teach you how to gather cowboys." ¹⁸ They immediately coiled their ropes up and loped off after him. ¹⁹ As they were riding, they came upon a cowboy named James and his brother John. ²⁰ They were patching a water trough and Jesus told 'em to saddle up and ride with him. James and John left their old dad sitting there as they rode off with Jesus.

Jesus Whips a Demon

²¹ The cowboys rode all the way to Capernaum. When the day of rest came (the old timers called it the Sabbath), Jesus went up to the church building and began to give all them folks a clinic on what it means to ride for God. ²² These folks couldn't believe what he was teaching them. It was like he knew what he was talking about instead of being like those other preachers who just wanted to hear themselves talk and make up rules.

²³ Just then, a fellow who had an evil way about him shouted out, ²⁴ "You leave us alone Jesus! Have you come here to wipe us out? I know who you really are—God's Top Hand!"

²⁵ But Jesus shushed him with a look and without raising his voice he said, "Be quiet and come out." ²⁶ That fellow fell down like he'd been hit with a whiskey bottle and the evil spirit that had a hold of the him yelped like a whipped pup as it came out of the man.

²⁷ People stood there with their mouths hanging wide open and they turned to each other and said, "Did you see that? This cowboy is teaching us something new. He not only knows what he's doing, but even the evil spirits jump when he says to." ²⁸ Word spread quickly in the country around Galilee about this new cowboy with a new way. ²⁹ When they left the church, they rode over to Simon and Andrew's line camp.

Jesus Fixes a Lot of Folks

James and John were still with them and as they all walked in, ³⁰ it was apparent that Simon's mother-in-law had something bad sick about her. They were asking Jesus what should be done when ³¹ he just pushed passed them, took her by the hand, and helped her stand up. By the time she reached her feet, she was as right as spring rain. She felt so good she went in and fried up some frijoles and tortillas.

³²⁻³³ That evening, people started coming by the line camp and asking Jesus to fix all those people who had an evil way about them or those who were feeling mighty poorly. ³⁴ Jesus fixed ever' single one of 'em. He didn't let any of the demons open their mouths because they knew who he was and Jesus wasn't ready for everyone to know just yet.

Jesus Gathers in Galilee

³⁵ The next morning, Jesus was saddled up way before daylight. He rode a far piece out into the pasture to be alone and pray. ³⁶ Simon and the other cowboys looked and looked for him. ³⁷ When they finally found him, they said, "Everyone is scouring the country for you."

³⁸ Jesus swung up in the saddle and said, "Let's make a big circle into the surrounding country so I can tell people the good news. That's why my Dad sent me." ³⁹ So Jesus and his cowboys rode all through Galilee where Jesus gave clinics in the churches and cast out many a demon along the way.

Jesus Heals a Fella with Rotten Skin

⁴⁰ A man with rotting skin came to Jesus and fell down in front of him, asking him for help. "If you had a mind to, I know you could fix me, Jesus."

⁴¹ Jesus was touched by this man's way of asking and he felt sorry for him. Jesus reached out to the man and touched him, saying, "I am of a mind—be fixed!"

⁴² The rotting skin immediately fell off him and he was clean. ⁴³ But Jesus gave him a stern warning before he let him go, ⁴⁴ "Don't tell anyone what happened here. Just go to the church and show 'em that you're clean. Take along the offering that Moses said to bring for your fixing."

⁴⁵ But that fellow couldn't keep quiet about the great thing Jesus had done for him. Word spread around so quickly that Jesus couldn't even come into town because of the mobs of people that came to him. Because of this, he camped way out where it was hard to find him, but people still came to find him from all parts of the region.

CHAPTER 2

Jesus Fixes a Paralyzed Man

A few days later, Jesus rode back to Capernaum and news spread quickly that he was back in the home country. ² So many people gathered at the house Jesus was at that there was no longer any room to stand, not even by the door. But Jesus preached the good news to all who were there and could hear him. ³ Some people brought a paralyzed fellow to see him, but they couldn't even get in the house. ⁴ These guys were so adamant about getting their friend to Jesus that they climbed up on the roof and dug out the section right above where he was talking.

They lowered their friend on a stretcher right down in front of him. Jesus smiled and admired their boldness and their faith. [5] He said to the paralyzed man, "Your sins have been forgotten."

[6] There were some religious experts watching and they were all thinking, [7] "Who does this cowboy think he is? Only God can forgive sins."

[8] Quick as a cow kick, Jesus knew exactly what these so called "religious experts" were thinking. He decided to clear the air. He asked them, "Why are your thoughts so screwed up with what I just did? [9] Is it easier to say that a man's sins are forgotten or is it easier to tell him to get up and walk? [10] But just so you know that God's Top Hand has the authority on earth to forget sins . . ." He turned to the paralyzed man and said, [11] "Stand up cowboy. Take your bedroll and go home."

[12] Immediately the paralyzed man stood up and did as he was told. He walked out of the house in front of them all. Everyone was slackjawed. They started saying, "We've never seen anything like this!"

Jesus Recruits a Tax Collector

[13] Jesus rode out again along the area close by the sea. A whole crowd came with him and he gave them a clinic on how to ride for God's outfit. [14] As they continued on their travels to spread the good news, he saw a fellow named Levi sitting in a tax collector's booth. "Saddle up, cowboy," he said to him. Levi left everything right there and rode off with them.

[15] They rode over to Levi's place to have some grub and a lot of Levi's friends were there. These fellows were all tax collectors, outcasts, and outlaws. [16] When the religious experts and bigwig preachers saw who Jesus was eating with, they asked his cowboys, "Why does he eat with such lowlifes?"

[17] When Jesus heard their question, he said to them. "Those who are healthy don't need to be doctored, but those who are sick do. I have not come to gather the old pet cows, but the outcasts and outlaws with nines in their tails."

A Talk about Missin' Meals

[18] There was this one time that the guys who rode with John the Baptist, as well as some other goody-goody preachers, were going without food for religious reasons. All these folks came to Jesus and asked, "Why do all those who follow John, and those who follow the Pharisees, go without food in order to get closer to God, but your cowboys don't?"

[19] Jesus smiled a wry smile and said, "If a cowboy invites his buddies over for a BBQ, he doesn't expect them to go hungry, does he? Of course not. As long as the cowboy is cooking, his guests will be eating. [20] There will come a time when the cowboy will no longer be around and that is when they will fast. [21] Besides, you don't put a new patch on old wranglers. If you do, you'll end up with a bigger tear than when you started. [22] Also, you can't put new hooch in an old wineskin. If you do, the new hooch will expand and bust the wineskin open. New wine is poured in a new wineskin."

Discussin' the Day of Rest

[23] A little while after that, Jesus and his cowboys were riding through some grain fields on the day of rest. They got hungry and picked some heads of wheat for a quick snack. [24] Some of those bigwig preachers saw this and accused them of violating the sacred day of rest.

[25] Jesus replied calmly, "Didn't you read where David and his cowboys got hungry and went in and [26] ate the special bread. You all know it is against the Law for anyone to eat it except the priests?" [27] Then he told them, "The day of rest was made for cowboys. Cowboys were not made for the day of rest. God's Top Hand is Boss—even of the day of rest."

CHAPTER 3

Jesus Helps a Fellow on the Day of Rest

Another time, Jesus walked into a church and there was a fellow there with a crippled wing. [2] The bigwig preachers kept an eye on Jesus to see if he would heal the guy on the day of rest. They were always on the lookout for some way to talk bad about him. [3] Jesus said to the guy, "Come up front for a second." [4] Then Jesus turned to all the scowling preachers and said, "Is it against the Law to do something good for someone who is in a bad way?" They sat there and didn't say a word.

[5] Jesus looked hard at them, but he felt sorry for 'em because of their stubbornness and pride. He told the guy with the crippled wing, "Stretch out your hand." He stretched it out and it was

completely normal. ⁶ Them bigwig preachers went straight out and began planning how they could kill Jesus.

Tons of Folks Flock After Jesus

⁷ Then Jesus rode back out toward the Sea of Galilee and a ton of people ⁸ followed after him because of the great things he was doing.

⁹ There were so many people, he told his cowboys to stack some hay up so the crowd wouldn't mash him. ¹⁰ He had healed so many people with various ailments that all kinds of sick people were trying to touch him. ¹¹ But whenever a demon saw him, they would always fall down and holler out, "You are the Son of God, his Top Hand!" ¹² But Jesus always kept the demons from telling anyone who he really was.

Jesus Picks His Twelve Cowboys

¹³ Now Jesus rode up onto the mountain and asked some guys to ride with him. ¹⁴ He chose twelve cowboys to ride with him so he could teach them his ways and they could show others. He also gave them the power to ¹⁵ whip demons that were hurting people. ¹⁶ These are the names of Jesus's twelve cowboys: Simon, who Jesus gave the name of Pete; ¹⁷ James and John, brothers who he called the Sons of Thunder; and the rest were ¹⁸ Andy, Phil, Bart, Matt, Tom, the other James, Thad, Simon the Fanatic, ¹⁹ and Judas, who would double-cross Jesus.

Jesus and the Devil

²⁰ Jesus rode back home and there were so many people needing him that there wasn't even time enough to grab a sandwich. ²¹ When his family heard what was happening, they tried to go get him. They thought he was going crazy. ²² The religious experts came all the way from Jerusalem, but they said he was possessed by the devil and that is how he was able to cast out the demons. ²³ So Jesus called them all around and told them stories. "How can the devil cast out the devil? ²⁴ A cowboy divided against himself ropes no cattle. ²⁵ A person against himself has come to his end. ²⁶ If Satan double-crosses himself, he can't survive. ²⁷ But no one can steal a ranch's cattle unless he first ties up the cowboy watching over it. Then they can rustle anything they find.

²⁸ "I'm telling you straight, every wrong can be forgiven, ²⁹ but anyone who rejects the love of God and attributes the Holy Spirit's work to the devil, that person's sin will not be forgiven." ³⁰ He said all this because they were accusing him of being possessed by a demon.

Jesus Reveals His Real Family

³¹ While all this was happening, Jesus's mom and brothers finally found him. They were standing outside the house where he was and ³² they sent some people in to get him.

Someone in the crowd said, "Hey! Your mom and brothers are outside looking for you."

³³ He shrugged and said, "Who is my mom and who are my brothers?" ³⁴ He motioned toward all the cowboys who were sitting around and learning from him. "Here is my family right here. Whoever rides for the Boss's outfit is my family."

CHAPTER 4

The Farmer and the Field

One day Jesus rode down to the lake. There was such a large crowd that he jumped up on a stack of hay. ² He taught them a lot of things by telling them stories.

He said, ³ "A farmer went out to plant his fields. ⁴ As he planted, some of the seeds fell on the road, and the birds ate it all up. ⁵ Other seeds fell next to some rocks where there wasn't much dirt. The seeds took root quickly in the shallow soil, ⁶ but they withered quickly because there was nowhere for the roots to go. ⁷ Other seeds fell among the cactus and thistles. They sprouted, but were choked out by the thorns. ⁸ And finally, some seeds found good soil and produced a lot of grain. Some of it yielded thirty times as much, some sixty, and still some a hundred times. ⁹ Whoever has ears should be listening."

¹⁰ Later on, when they were alone, some of his cowboys asked about the stories. ¹¹ He told them, "The secret of the Boss's outfit has been given to you. But for the sake of everyone else, I teach with stories ¹² so this old saying would come true, 'They look, but cannot see. They hear, but they cannot understand. If they could see and understand, they would turn to me and be forgiven.'"

¹³ Then Jesus said, "If you can't understand this simple story about the seeds, how are you going to understand all the other stories? ¹⁴ The

farmer spreads God's good news to others. [15] The seed that fell on the road stands for those who hear the good news, but they let Satan take it away before it does anything to them. [16] The seed in the rocks stands for those who love the good news and immediately act like it changes their whole world. [17] But they don't last long because it was all emotion and no faith. They wither quickly when faced with any kind of adversity. [18] The seed that fell among the thorns stands for those who hear God's good news, [19] but the words that could save them are choked out by worry, lusting after money, and the desire for materialistic things. [20] And finally, the seed that found good ground are those people who hear the good news and do something with it. They produce a harvest of thirty, sixty, or even a hundred times as much as has been planted."

A Lamp in a Bedroll

[21] Then Jesus posed a question to them, "Would you light a lamp and then stick it in your bedroll? Of course not. A lamp is lifted up high so its light can shine far. [22] Everything in the dark will eventually be revealed. [23] If you got ears, you'd best use them for listening to what I'm saying."

[24] Then he added, "Don't let what I'm saying go in one ear and out the other. The closer you listen the more you'll start getting—and when you start getting it, you'll be given even more. [25] Those who listen and apply what I say to do, they'll start catching on even more and more. But if you ignore the things I say, you'll end up losing more than you started with."

Story about Growing

[26] Jesus also told them, "God's Green Pasture is like a farmer that plants seeds in a field. [27] Whether he is asleep at night or working a horse in the arena, those seeds are starting to grow. [28] He has no idea how it works, but he knows it does. The earth makes things grow. First, a little green leaf pokes up through the dirt. Then the head of wheat forms. [29] And finally, the grain is ready for harvest. Then the farmer comes and cuts the wheat with a sickle."

Mustard Seeds

[30] Jesus said, "How can I tell you about the Boss's outfit? What kind of cowboy tale will help you understand? [31] It is like a tiny little mustard seed. It may start out tiny, [32] but it grows to be the biggest plant in the garden. It grows large and ends up providing shade and protection."

[33] Jesus used a lot of stories like these in his clinics. [34] Truth be told, he never gave a public clinic without using stories, but later when it was just him and his cowboys, he'd explain everything to them.

Jesus Squelches the Squall

[35] When the sun finally set that day, Jesus told his cowboys, "Let's get our tack and cross the lake to the other side." [36] So they found a boat, leaving all the crowds behind. [37] But soon, after they had bedded down for the night, a terrible storm came upon them. Lightning struck all around and the wind threatened to blow them all away . . . if the waves didn't drown them first.

[38] Jesus was sleeping in his bedroll with his head on his saddle. The cowboys woke him up, yelling, "Boss, don't you care that this storm is going to kill us all?"

[39] Jesus lifted up on one elbow and said to the storm, "Cut it out and be still!" The winds immediately stopped and all the clouds disappeared. It was as calm as if nothing had ever happened. [40] After a second, he said, "Why are y'all so scared? Don't you have faith in me?"

[41] The cowboys looked at each other with wide eyes. "Who are we riding with? Even the wind and lightning give to his hand."

CHAPTER 5

Jesus Throws a Trip on a Demon

The next day, they arrived on the other side of the lake. [2] They had no more than got both feet on the ground when a man possessed by an evil spirit started trotting out of the cemetery toward them. [3] He lived among the tombs and couldn't even be tied up with chains. [4] When he was put in irons, he snapped them like paper. No one was strong enough to subdue him. [5] Night and day he wandered among the dead, howling, and caterwauling, and cutting himself with sharp rocks.

[6] Jesus was still a far piece out when the man had caught sight of him. He ran out and bowed real low in front of Jesus. [7] With an unearthly shriek, he yelled, "Why have you come to stop me, Son of God? By God's good name, please

don't torture me." [8] Jesus had already told the spirit to light out.

[9] Jesus said, "What do they call you?"

[10] "They call me Legion. We are too many to count." [11] He then begged Jesus not to throw a trip on them. [12] There was a herd of pigs grazing nearby and the demonic spirits asked to be sent into the pigs. [13] Jesus told them to go ahead. The evil spirits rushed out and filled the pigs. Then the herd of two thousand pigs stampeded into the lake and drown.

[14] Now the people who had been taking care of that herd of pigs ran off to tell everyone what had happened. [15] People came running and the first thing they saw was Jesus sitting there talking to the man who had been possessed, but this time he was in his right mind. [16] Word spread quickly about what happened and the people were afraid. They [17] begged Jesus to leave the area.

[18] As Jesus threw his saddle back in the boat, the former demon-possessed man asked to ride with him, [19] but Jesus told him to go home. "Tell people what God has done for you and that he had mercy on you." [20] So the guy went off and told everyone his story and all who heard it were amazed.

Faith Heals

[21] When Jesus made it back across the lake, a ton of people gathered around him. [22] All of a sudden, one of the local church leaders named Jairus came up, and when he caught sight of Jesus, he fell at his feet. [23] He pleaded with Jesus, "My daughter is near dead. Come and put your hand on her so she will live." [24] Jesus told him to lead the way and a large crowd followed.

[25] There was also a woman in the crowd who had been bleeding for twelve years. [26] She had suffered a great deal and spent everything she had on people who claimed to have a cure. Yet instead of getting better, everything just made her worse. [27] She'd heard about Jesus and got close enough to touch his vest. She kept telling herself, [28] "I bet if I just touch his clothes, I will be fixed." [29] When she touched his vest, her bleeding immediately stopped and she knew that she'd been healed.

[30] Jesus also knew that healing power had gone out from him. He turned around and asked, "Who touched me?"

[31] His cowboys kind of chuckled and said,

"There's a thousand people within three feet of you and you want to ask, 'Who touched me?'"

[32] But Jesus ignored their jibe and continued to look for whoever had laid a hand on him.

[33] Then the woman came forward, afraid and shaking like a leaf. She fell down on her face before him and explained what, and why, she'd touched him. [34] He said to her, "My daughter, your faith has fixed you. Ride out in peace and be healed."

[35] While he was still talking to the woman, some people came from the church leader's house saying, "Jairus, your daughter is dead. No need to bother Jesus anymore."

[36] But Jesus didn't pay no mind to what the people were saying. He told Jairus, "Don't be scared . . . believe!"

[37] Jesus didn't let anyone go with him except Pete, James, and John. [38] As they neared Jairus's house, there was a terrible commotion of wailing and sobbing coming from inside and out.

[39] When he went in, he asked why everyone was carrying on like that. Jesus told them that she wasn't dead. The girl was just asleep.

[40] They began making fun of him so he put them all out on the porch. He went into the girl's room with her mom and dad, as well as the three cowboys who'd come with him. [41] Jesus gently took the girl by the hand and said, "Get up, sweetie."

[42] The twelve-year-old little girl got up immediately and began to walk around the room like nothing had happened. Everyone was flabbergasted. [43] Jesus told 'em all to keep their traps shut about what had happened. If they wanted to do something, they could get the young girl something to eat.

CHAPTER 6

Shunned at Home

After all those great things were done, Jesus struck a long trot back to his hometown and his cowboys followed him. [2] When the day of rest came, Jesus went and did a little preaching at the local church. People who listened were wondering where he came up with all these different interpretations of God's word. They also wondered where all his wisdom came from and if the miracles he had been performing came from the same place. They all shook their heads and kept asking one another, ³ "Isn't this that carpenter? Isn't this Mary's son? Aren't those his sisters who live near here?" Because of all their questions, they didn't hear him; because of their looking for answers elsewhere they couldn't see him; and they got offended that this ordinary fellow would stand up in front and dare to teach them.

⁴ Then Jesus said to 'em all, "A cowboy who rides for God gets respect for what he does everywhere except his hometown. All the people he grew up with, including his family, think they know who he really is, but they don't."

⁵ Jesus didn't do any miracles there, except to put his hands on a few sick people and heal them. ⁶ He was amazed at how blind all these people he knew so well were. He stayed around that part of the country though and taught among the ranches and cow towns.

Jesus Sends His Cowboys Out to Gather

⁷ One day, Jesus called his cowboys together and sent them out to gather people for his Father's brand two by two. ⁸ He gave them authority over evil spirits and told them to take nothing along on their journey except their saddles. They couldn't fill their saddlebags with money nor morsels of any kind. ⁹ They couldn't even take an extra blue jean jacket.

¹⁰ He told 'em, "When you get to a ranch, stay at their headquarters until you leave that part of the country. ¹¹ If a ranch won't welcome you or listen to the good news, leave that ranch and shake the dust from that place off your boots. That way you will not take any part of an unbelieving outfit with you when you ride off."

¹² So the cowboys set off in pairs to spread the good news and gather people for God's outfit. They told everyone to turn from their wicked ways and start riding for God. ¹³ They cast out many demons that were hurting people and put a little dab of oil on people's heads to show that they ride for God. Many folks were healed.

John the Baptizer's Head is Cut Off

¹⁴ During this, King Herod heard about everything Jesus was doing. Some were telling him John the Baptist had been raised from the dead to do miracles ¹⁵ and others said Jesus was Elijah or a new cowboy of God like there used to be in the olden days. ¹⁶ But when Herod heard all the

rumors he said, "I cut off John the Baptist's head and now he has come back!"

¹⁷ Herod was quite a fright because he had had John arrested and killed because he'd made a promise to his wife. That old gal was a burr under his saddle blanket because she made him kill John. ¹⁸ John had criticized Herod for marrying her in the first place. This wasn't just some gal off the street. She had been married to Herod's brother, Philip. It was against God's law to marry your brother's wife if he was still alive and Philip was still kicking around somewhere.

¹⁹ So Herodias (Herod's no-account wife) held a grudge against John and wanted to kill him, ²⁰ but Herod had kind of taken a liking to a cowboy like John who spoke the truth and rode for God. He didn't really know what to think about the things that John said, but he liked listening to him.

²¹ So on Herod's birthday, he threw himself a party and all the important people in his kingdom came to it. ²²⁻²³ Herodias's daughter came in and danced for the king. He took such a liking to it that he slipped up and said she could have anything she wanted—even up to half of his kingdom! ²⁴⁻²⁵ She went to her mother and asked her what she should request and her mother said, "The head of John the Baptist on a big ol' plate."

²⁶ This shook the king up something fierce, but he'd made a promise in front of a lot of people so he kept it. ²⁷ He sent the executioner to the dungeon in which John was being held and the fellow ²⁸ came back with John's head and presented it to the king's daughter. She took it straight to her mom. ²⁹ When the cowboys who rode alongside John heard that he had been killed, they came and got his body and buried it with the respect he deserved.

Jesus Feeds a Bunch of Folks

³⁰ When all the cowboys got back from their first big gathering for God, they all sat around and told Jesus their stories. ³¹ He told 'em, "Let's go somewhere private so we can all talk and rest up." There were tons of people hanging around and wanting to hear everything Jesus and his cowboys were saying; so much so that they hadn't even had a chance to get a bite to eat.

³² So Jesus and his boys saddled up and headed out, ³³but many saw where they were going

and followed them. ³⁴ When Jesus saw there were so many people wanting to know about riding for God, he felt sorry for them. They were like a stray herd looking for water so Jesus taught them many things. In other words, he watered them. Jesus spent a long time teaching and it got to be very late.

³⁵⁻³⁶ Some of his cowboys came up and told Jesus to send everyone back to town to eat. ³⁷ But he told them, "Y'all get 'em something to eat."

They said, "You want us to ride to town and get all these people something to eat?"

³⁸ Jesus responded, "How many loaves of bread do you have already?"

They went and checked their saddle bags and came back and said, "We've got five loaves of bread and a couple of pieces of fish."

³⁹⁻⁴⁰ Jesus told his cowboys to sit everyone down in groups of fifty and up to one hundred. While this was being done, ⁴¹ Jesus took the five loaves and two pieces of fish, looked up to God and gave thanks, and broke the bread. He gave the pieces of bread and fish to his cowboys to pass out to the hungry crowd. ⁴² There was enough for everybody and no one went away hungry. ⁴³ There was even some for leftovers the next day. ⁴⁴ Jesus fed over five thousand men, not counting all the women and children that were there too.

Jesus Strolls on Water

⁴⁵ Just as soon as they were done, Jesus told his cowboys to get into a nearby boat and go across the sea to Bethsaida. Jesus said goodbye to his boys as the crowd filed away and ⁴⁶ then he went up on a nearby mountain to pray and talk to his Dad.

⁴⁷ Later that evening, a storm caught the cowboys while in their boat. ⁴⁸ Jesus could see his boys straining against the oars as they fought the tumbling sea. When the night was nearly over, he decided to go to Bethsaida and beat them there by walking across the sea as if it were a dry patch of ground. As he was passing them by, ⁴⁹ they saw him and got scared out of their skin. ⁵⁰ They thought he was some sort of ghost and were terrified. But at the height of their fear, he spoke to them and said, "Don't be scared, boys! It's just me." ⁵¹Then he walked over and climbed into the boat with 'em. When he did,

the storm completely stopped. The cowboys couldn't believe what they had just seen. ⁵² Unfortunately, their hearts were hard because they had already forgot about the loaves and the fish earlier in the day.

⁵³ They anchored the boat when they finally got across, and as they came ashore, ⁵⁴ people already started recognizing who they all were. ⁵⁵ The people ran and told everyone around. Sick people started showing up to be healed. ⁵⁶ Wherever Jesus and his cowboys went it was like this. People asked if they could just touch his vest, and all who touched him were healed.

CHAPTER 7

Making up Rules as They Go

Now some of the head honchos of the church, and some religious experts who were from Jerusalem, gathered around Jesus. ² They saw that some of the cowboys were eating before they had washed their hands ³⁻⁴ (it was a religious rule they had made up). ⁵ All these uppity religious fellows asked him, "Why aren't your cowboys keeping the sacred traditions of old? They are eating without washing their hands."

⁶ Jesus calmly replied, "Isaiah foretold the future about you when he said, 'These people will say they ride for me, but it's just all talk. ⁷ What they call church is just teaching a bunch of rules and stuff that they came up with. It's not about me.' ⁸ Y'all don't ride for God. You just make up stuff and say it came from him."

⁹ Jesus kept it up and said, "Y'all conveniently shun the commands from God in order to make up your own sorry rules. ¹⁰ Even the great cowboy, Moses, said, 'Respect your mom and dad,' and, 'Whoever insults his mom or dad must be killed.' ¹¹ But you all tell people that they can get away from helping their parents if they ¹² just say that the money or food is a gift to God. ¹³ You teach people to disobey God's command of honoring your mother and father in the name of greed and tradition. But y'all sure enough don't stop there."

¹⁴ Then Jesus turned away from the religious people and hollered out to the crowd around them, "Listen to me, all of you! ¹⁵ What goes in a person don't make him wrong. It's what comes out of him that does."

Note: Some manuscripts include
the words from 4:23 here.

¹⁷ Jesus rode off and after a long trot, he got to the house he and the cowboys were staying at. As they settled in, some of the cowboys asked him what he meant by his little story about what makes a man wrong in God's eyes. ¹⁸ He asked them, "Are y'all that ignorant? Don't you understand that what goes into a person doesn't defile him? ¹⁹ Whatever goes into a man goes into his stomach, not his heart. And what goes in the stomach, will end up at the bottom of the outhouse eventually. ²⁰ What comes out of a man's heart is what defiles him. ²¹ From the heart comes evil desires, all sorts of gross sexual ideas, theft, killing, cheating on your spouse, ²² greed, deceit, perversion, envy, talking bad about others, gossip, pride, and utter foolishness. ²³ All these evil things don't come from the outside, they come from a person's heart. That is what defiles them."

An Outsider's Faith

²⁴ After Jesus finished everything he was going to do there, he rode off toward the country around Tyre. He tried to keep his presence there a secret, but that was to no avail. ²⁵ A particular woman who had a daughter who was possessed, heard Jesus had come to town and she went and fell at his feet. ²⁶ This lady wasn't a Jew, but a Greek. She asked Jesus to grab the demon and jerk it out of her daughter. ²⁷ Jesus said to her, "A father will feed his own children first. He won't take away their meal and give it to the dogs."

²⁸ She answered, "Yes, my Lord, but even the dogs eat the scraps and crumbs that fall from the father's table."

²⁹ Jesus smiled at that and said, "That's the kind of faith I'm looking for. You go check on your daughter and see that she has been freed from that scoundrel that's been controlling her."

³⁰ When the lady got home, it was just as he'd said. The demon was gone.

The Deaf Hear

³¹ Jesus saddled up again and rode away from the country around Tyre and headed through the area of Sidon on his way to the Sea of Galilee. ³² Some fellows found him and brought along a guy who was deaf and couldn't speak. They asked Jesus to put his hands on him and heal him.

³³ Jesus took him off to the side and put his fingers in the man's ears. Then he spit on his own fingers and touched the mute man's tongue. ³⁴ Jesus looked up to heaven and said quietly, "Open 'em up."

³⁵ Immediately, the man's ears were opened and his tongue was loosened. ³⁶ Jesus asked everyone around not to say anything about this to anyone, but the more he told 'em to keep quiet, the more they told everyone of the great things he was doing.

³⁷ They went around saying, "He ain't no counterfeit. He even makes the deaf hear and the mute speak."

CHAPTER 8

Jesus Feeds a Bunch Again

For at least the second time, there was another large crowd that had gathered for one of Jesus's clinics. ² Jesus called all his cowboys over to him and said, "I feel sorry for all these people here. They've been here with us for three days and most of them haven't even eaten. ³ Some of 'em are so weak they wouldn't even make it home before they fell out."

⁴ A few of his cowboys asked, "Where could we find enough tortillas in this desolate country to feed everyone?"

⁵ Jesus answered 'em, "How many tortillas do y'all have?"

"Seven," they counted.

⁶ Jesus told everyone to take a seat. He took the seven tortillas and tore 'em in half as he gave thanks. He began handing the pieces to the cowboys so they could pass 'em out. ⁷ They also had a few pieces of beef jerky. After giving thanks for these, too, he told the cowboys to pass them out as well. ⁸ Everyone that was there had plenty of tortillas and enough beef jerky to satisfy the lot of 'em. ⁹ There were four thousand people and that was just counting the men.

Jesus immediately sent everyone home and he and his cowboys ¹⁰ struck a long trot for the area around Dalmanutha.

Bigwig Preachers Want a Miracle

¹¹ When he got where he was going, some bigwig preachers started demanding a sign from heaven to test him. ¹² Jesus shook his head in bewilderment and wondered, "Why are y'all always

looking for proof? I'm telling y'all right now that no sign will be given to you." [13] He saddled right back up and rode back the way he'd come.

Yeast and Biscuits

[14] As they were on the trail, they had forgotten to get some provisions and just had one little old loaf of bread. [15] Jesus used it as an illustration and said, "Y'all be careful. Beware of the yeast that infiltrates the biscuits of Herod and all them bigwig preachers."

[16] With that being said, they began to argue about whether or not to eat the bread they had. Jesus shook his head, amazed that they couldn't understand something as simple as what he'd said. [17] So he asked 'em, "Why are you squabblin' over bread? Have any of you been paying attention to what's happened? [18] You have eyes don't you? You have ears don't you? [19] Did any of you see what happened when I fed the five thousand with five loaves? How many baskets of leftovers did y'all pick up?"

"Twelve," they said.

[20] "And when I fed the four thousand with seven tortillas, how many baskets of leftovers did you pick up then?"

"Seven."

[21] "Do you still not see and get it?" Jesus asked.

The Blind See

[22] When they finally reached Bethsaida, a blind man was brought to Jesus for healing. [23] He led the man outside the town, and after spitting in the guy's eyes, Jesus placed his hands on the man's eyes and asked, "What do you see?"

[24] The fellow said, "I see people, but they look like walking bushes."

[25] Jesus placed his hands on the man's eyes again. When the man opened his eyes again, he saw everything the way he should. [26] Jesus sent him home, but told him not to go back to town.

The Word on the Street

[27] Jesus and his cowboys rode off toward Caesarea Philippi. While they were riding along, Jesus asked, "What's the word on the street about me?"

[28] They said, "Some say John the Baptist reborn and others call you Elijah, or some others say a cowboy of God from the old days."

[29] Jesus continued to look ahead and said, "Who do y'all think I am?"

Pete spat his words quickly, "You are the Chosen One. The one God said he'd send to save us all."

[30] After a long silence, Jesus said, "Don't tell anyone else . . . not yet."

Tellin' Them Flat-Out about His Death

[31] Then Jesus told 'em about all the things the Son of Man would go through. He told 'em about all the suffering and rejection he would face from the religious know-it-alls, bigwig preachers, and others. He told 'em flat-out he would die and three days later he would be raised from the dead.

[32] During this conversation, Pete took Jesus aside and tried to scold him about talking about such foolish things.

[33] Jesus wasn't having none of it and said loud enough for everyone to hear, "Get back Satan before I stomp a mud hole in ya. You're only looking at things from a man's perspective and not the ways of God."

[34] About this time, there were a bunch of people around. Jesus stood up in his stirrups and let out a whistle for everyone to pay attention. [35] He told 'em all, "If anyone wants to ride for my outfit, he's gotta give up always looking out for himself. You've got be ready for the world to make fun of you. Be ready to saddle up with me every single day. Any cowboy who rides for himself will end up dead, but anyone who rides only for me and the good news will find true life. [36] What good does owning the whole world do for a cowboy without a soul? [37] What kind of man would trade his soul for a two dollar lie? [38] If any cowboy is ashamed to ride with me down here, that fellow won't find himself riding in the green pastures of heaven with the Boss and his angels."

CHAPTER 9

Jesus kept on a talkin', "There are some cowboys who are right here who will not die before they see the awesome display of God's outfit."

Jesus, Elijah, and Moses

[2] Six days later, Jesus took along Pete, James, and John. They rode up on a high mountain to be alone. As they were sitting there, Jesus's

appearance transformed before their very eyes. ³His clothes became so white they almost blinded 'em.

⁴ Then the great cowboys of old, Elijah and Moses, walked up and started talking to Jesus.

⁵ Pete jumped up quickly and said, "Hey boss! What do you think about us making a memorial about this day? I could make one for you, one for Elijah, and one for old Moses." ⁶ Pete only said this because when he got scared, he usually just ran-off at the mouth. But he wasn't the only one who was scared of what he was seeing.

⁷ Then a cloud seemed to pass over them all and a voice came from it saying, "This is my Boy, the Son who I love. When he says something, you'd all best listen."

⁸ And as quick as that, everyone looked around and Elijah and Moses were gone. Only Jesus and his three cowboys were left.

⁹ As they rode back down, Jesus told 'em not to tell anyone about what they'd seen until he'd been killed and had come back from the dead. ¹⁰ The three cowboys agreed, but from time to time they asked each other what they thought he meant by, "Come back from the dead."

¹¹ The three cowboys questioned Jesus by asking him, "Why do the religious experts say Elijah has to come first?"

¹² He said, "Elijah does come first. He brings everything back and gets everything ready for the Chosen One. ¹³ They treated Elijah poorly and they'll do the same to the Chosen One, who will, according to the word of God, be treated even worse."

Jesus Pulls a Demon Out of a Boy

¹⁴ When they rounded a small hill and trotted up to where the rest of cowboys were, they heard a bunch of people squabblin'. ¹⁵ As soon as they spotted Jesus, they ran to say hello to him.

¹⁶ "What's all the bickerin' about?" Jesus asked while he swung off his horse.

¹⁷ One of the men from the crowd spoke up quickly. "Jesus, I brought my son to be healed by you. He is possessed by an evil spirit that keeps him from talking and every once in a while, ¹⁸ it throws my boy to the ground. It scares the tar out of me because he starts a foamin' at the mouth while gnashing his teeth like a wild hog. He then becomes as rigid as a felled lodgepole

pine. I asked your cowboys for help, but they was useless."

¹⁹ Jesus told all of them, "Do I have to do everything myself? What're y'all gonna do when I'm gone? Bring the boy over here."

²⁰ They brought the boy over and when the devil inside him saw Jesus, it threw the boy on the ground in a violent seizure. The boy was foaming and frothing at the mouth like a rabid coyote.

²¹ "How long has this been going on?" Jesus asked.

The father replied, ²² "Since he was just knee-high, this devil has been throwing my poor son in the water and even in the branding fire a time or two trying to kill him. I can't let him out of my sight and I'm wore plumb out, sir. Will you help us if you can?"

²³ "What do you mean, 'If I can'?" Jesus raised an eyebrow and asked. "Ain't nothin' impossible for a man who believes."

²⁴ The man fell to his knees and sobbed, "I want to believe, but you've got to help me!"

²⁵ Jesus saw that quite a crowd was starting to take notice of what was going on. His words latched onto the evil spirit as he said, "You that is tormenting this boy, I command you to leave and never show your face again."

²⁶ The demon caused the boy to be thrown to the ground one last time as it did as Jesus commanded and hightailed it out of there. The boy lay there still on the ground and many folks started murmuring that he was dead. ²⁷ But Jesus reached down and took hold of the boy's hand and he stood up.

²⁸ Later, when Jesus was alone with his cowboys, they asked him, "Why couldn't we get rid of that demon?"

²⁹ Jesus said, "Prayer is the only thing that will whip those kind."

Jesus Talks about Dying Again

³⁰ Leaving that part of the country, Jesus and his cowboys rode through the area known as Galilee, but he didn't want anyone to know he was there. Jesus wanted as much time alone with his cowboys as he could get so he could ³¹ teach 'em all they would need to know. He told them, "God's Top Hand is going to be double-crossed and handed over to his enemies. They're going to kill him, but he's going to come back from the

dead three days later." [32] None of his cowboys really knew what he was talking about and they were too chicken to ask him.

The Top Hands in the Kingdom

[33] They arrived at Capernaum one evening and as they settled in for the night, Jesus asked his cowboys what they had been discussing on the ride over. [34] None of 'em wanted to say anything because they had all been arguing about which of 'em was the best hand.

[35] He told 'em all to gather 'round, for he had known all along what they had been saying. Jesus said, "Whoever wants to be the top hand in my outfit has to be willing to ride drag and let everyone else go in front of him."

[36] He called a little kid over to him who had been playing nearby. He put the little one on his knee and said, [37] "Whoever is willing to care for the little ones of this world is the one who rides for me. More importantly, he rides for my Dad."

Riding for the Brand

[38] John piped up and said, "Boss, we saw a guy just the other day who was getting rid of evil spirits by using your name. We stopped him because he didn't ride with us."

[39] Jesus put a stop to that foolishness at once, "Why'd you stop him? Ain't no one can use my name for good things and then in the next breath say something bad about me. [40] If someone ain't riding against us, then he is riding for us. [41] Even a person who gives you a drink from their canteen because you ride for God's Top Hand will be rewarded for it. [42] But here's a warning and you better listen close. If anyone causes one of these little ones to abandon their faith and follow the outlaw's trail, well, it would be better for that cowboy if he was tied to an anvil and thrown in the ocean.

[43] "If your hand causes you to sin, then you'd be better off by chopping it off. It'd be better to have one hand in life than both hands in hell. Same way with your feet. [45] If one of your feet takes you someplace you ought not be, it'd be better for you to cut it off than to walk all high and mighty right into hell.

Note: Some manuscripts include the words from verse 48 in verse 44 and 46.

[47] "If your eye keeps looking at things it shouldn't, tear that sucker right out. It's better to ride for God's outfit with a patch over one eye than to see what hell is like with both. [48-50] Here's the skinny of it—everyone will go through a test of fire; will you be refined by it or destroyed by it? My way will refine you and bring you peace. The other way? Not so much."

CHAPTER 10

Getting Unhitched

Then Jesus left and rode off to the region along Jordan Creek. Once again, the crowds of people found him and he taught them about riding for God's outfit.

[2] Some of the bigwig preachers showed their ugly hides and tried to throw a heel trap at him and get him to say something wrong. They asked him, "Is it right for a cowboy to divorce his wife?"

[3] Jesus turned it back on 'em and said, "What did Moses have to say about it?"

[4] They puffed out their chests as they began to show off their scripture knowledge. "Moses said it was fine. All a cowboy has to do is give her a paper that says they are divorced."

[5] But Jesus was already shaking his head. "Yeah, he said that, but only because you are weak and don't understand nothin'. [6] From the beginning, God made cowboys and cowgirls. [7] It's because of this that a cowboy will leave his own parents and unite with a cowgirl and the [8] two will become one. In God's eyes, they are one person. [9] And what God has joined together, what right has anyone else to come and try to sort off one?"

[10] Later on in the house, the cowboys asked Jesus about what he'd said. [11-12] He told them, "Anyone (cowboy or cowgirl) who divorces and marries someone else commits adultery. It's as plain and simple as that."

Jesus and the Kids

[13] In those days, people were always bringing their kids to see Jesus so he could bless 'em. It happened so frequently that the cowboys started trying to keep people from doing it. [14] But when Jesus saw what was happening, he put a stop to it. He said, "Let them kiddos come to me. God's outfit belongs to kiddos like these. [15] I'm telling you straight that anyone who doesn't come to me with the faith and honesty of a little kid has no place on my Dad's ranch." [16] Jesus blessed every kid who ever came to see him.

How to Live Forever

¹⁷ As Jesus rode out one day on his way to Jerusalem, a fellow come running up and got down on his knees in front of him. As he was hunkered over, he asked, "Excuse me good cowboy, but what must I do to live forever?"

¹⁸ Jesus pulled up and asked, "Why do you call me good? No one is good except God himself. Besides that, ¹⁹ you know what the Codes say, 'Don't kill. Don't jack with another man's Jenny. Don't take what ain't yours. Don't say things about others that you know ain't right. Don't talk ill of another man, and hold your mom and dad in high regard.'"

²⁰ The man was smilin' and pattin' himself on the back so hard Jesus was afraid he'd hurt himself. The guy said, "Well I'm as good as gold then. I've done all these things since I was just a little nub."

²¹ As Jesus was looking at him, he felt a tremendous love for the man and so he told him the truth of the matter. "Hang on there, cowboy. One more thing, go and sell every single thing you own and give it to the poor and you will be a rich man in heaven. Once you're done selling, then come and ride for me and I'll take care of you."

²² You would have thought Jesus had just shot the man's favorite dog. The man was wealthy and he wasn't about to sell everything he had and put his life in the hands of someone else, let alone God.

²³ As the man walked away with his tail between his legs, Jesus told his cowboys, "A man who won't let go of the world will never be able to fit through the entrance to God's place."

²⁴ The cowboys all looked at each other in bewilderment at what Jesus had just said. Jesus continued, "I tell you the truth, ²⁵ it'd be easier for a bull to jump through a cinch ring than for a rich man to fit through the gate into heaven."

²⁶ They all started talking at once, but the questions were the same. "Then who can fit through?"

²⁷ Jesus turned to them and said, "A cowboy who thinks he can get there on his own will never make it, but a cowboy who trusts in God and God alone will never miss the gate . . . or anything else."

²⁸ Pete spoke up and said, "Well, we've left everything behind to ride with you."

²⁹ Jesus nodded and added, "Listen, there ain't a cowboy alive who has left their home, their job, their family, or anything, or anyone, in order to ride with me ³⁰ who won't get a hundred times back anything they think they've left. It won't be easy, but it'll all be worth it. But one thing to remember, ³¹ those who ride the longest will be the last to ride through the gate. A good cowboy always makes sure everyone is through the gate before he gets off and shuts it."

Jesus Talks about Dying and Riding Back from the Grave

³² They were still riding for Jerusalem, with Jesus in the lead. The cowboys weren't sure of what was coming so Jesus pulled them aside and told 'em what they should expect. ³³ "This will be the end of the line for me, boys. I'm going to be double-crossed by a pard and the religious institution that claims to serve God. They are going to sentence me to death and hand me over to the Romans. ³⁴ These people are going to mock me, spit on me, beat me nearly to death, and ultimately, kill me. Yet all of this is supposed to happen, because I'm going to come riding back from the dead three days later."

James and John Ask a Favor

³⁵ The brothers, James and John, took Jesus to one side and said, "We'd like for you to do us a favor."

³⁶ "What is it that you want?"

³⁷ They looked at each other and continued, "When you take your spot at the head of the ranch, we want to ride on your right and left. You know, up front with you."

³⁸ But Jesus said, "You don't have any idea what you're asking for. Do you think you will be able to ride the trail that I'm fixing to go down?"

³⁹ "Yes sir!" They exclaimed.

Then he said to them, "Well, in that case, you will travel down the same trail as I do, ⁴⁰ but it ain't for me to decide who rides to my left and my right. These spots are reserved for who my Dad wants there."

⁴¹ Now the other cowboys heard what was happening and they got all frazzled up over the conversation. ⁴² Jesus told 'em all to quiet down and listen to what he had to say. "This outfit don't work the way it does everywhere else. Everyone down here wants titles and positions

so they can tell others what to do and be looked up to like they are something special. **43** But here in this outfit, it works completely opposite. **44** The top hand among you will be the one who puts everyone else first and himself last. **45** For even the Greatest Top Hand did not come down here to ride all high and mighty, but he came to serve others, and to offer his life as a ransom for everyone else."

Jesus Heals a Blind Vagrant

46 They were passing through Jericho and on the outskirts, they ran into a blind beggar named Bartimaeus. He was sitting beside the road. **47** When the blind fellow heard that it was Jesus riding by, he hollered out, "Jesus! Please help me!"

48 A lot of people tried to shut him up because of the racket he was making, but he kept it up. "Jesus, please, please help me!"

49 Jesus reined up and said, "Tell him to come here."

People around him said, "Quick, get up. Jesus is calling you. Don't be scared!" Immediately, like a shot from a gun, **50** he threw off his poncho, jumped up, and ran in the direction of Jesus.

51 Jesus said to him as he got close, "What do you want from me?"

The fellow slid to a stop and said, "Please let me see again."

52 Jesus smiled and said, "Go, your faith has given you back your eyes."

And just like that, the man's sight returned, but he didn't leave . . . he followed Jesus.

CHAPTER 11

They slowed to a walk as they got close to Jerusalem. Jesus sent two of his cowboys ahead to a little cow camp and **2** told them, "When you get there, you will find an unbroke colt tied to the fence. **3** If anyone questions you, just tell them the Lord needs it and will return it shortly."

4 They found the colt and sure enough, **5** some people started asking them where they were taking it. **6** The cowboys told them Jesus needed it and the people said nothing more and let them pass. **7** They brought the colt to Jesus and they threw their coats on its back as saddle blankets and then Jesus hopped up there. **8** Then Jesus started his ride into Jerusalem and people honored him by throwing their own coats on the ground so that even the colt's feet that carried him wouldn't touch the dirt. Some people even cut branches off of nearby trees and laid them down in the road for Jesus's mount to walk on.

9 This was quite a sight to see and people in front of Jesus and behind him were shouting, "The Lord will save us! Here's to the One who rides in the name of the Lord! **10** Here's to the coming of the outfit that our father David talked so much about. Here! Here!"

11 Jesus rode straight to the main church in town to talk to his Daddy in heaven. After he was done, he went out to the little town of Bethany with his twelve cowboys.

Jesus Chews Out the Fig Tree

12 The next morning they got up and rode out of Bethany. Jesus was hungry and **13** he saw a fig tree a little way off the trail. The tree was bright and full of life and leaves, but there were no figs, despite that it was a little early in the season. Jesus rode off from the tree and **14** said loud enough for his cowboys to hear, "May you never make fruit again."

The Robber's Roost

15 When they got to Jerusalem, they went straight to the main church area of town. Jesus jumped off his horse and started throwing the tables of those people who were selling animals for sacrifices across the courtyard. He made quite an impression in the way he handled the money changer's booths. **16** It had become more of a carnival than a place to worship God.

17 He jumped up on a stone and shouted for all to hear, "Everyone listen! Didn't God's writings say, 'My house will be called a house of prayer for the whole world?' But you all here have turned it into a circus and a robber's roost!"

18 When Jesus finished speaking the truth, some religious experts and bigwig preachers immediately started trying to figure out how they could kill this cowboy.

19 Jesus and his cowboys spent all day in town. They left as the sun started to set and they loped off into the darkness.

The Fig Tree Is Dead

20 The next morning, they took the same route as the day before. They passed by that fig tree and many of them noticed it was dead. **21** Pete said, "Look Boss, the fig tree you cursed is dead."

²² Jesus didn't so much as turn his head as he said, "Have faith in God. ²³ This here's the truth, if someone tells a mountain to go jump in the sea, and he does not doubt that God can do it, but believes in the power of God wholeheartedly, then it will happen. ²⁴ This is why I keep telling y'all that when you pray, believe in your hearts that God hears you and has already done what you asked. ²⁵ But don't let anything get in the way of your prayers. If you are holding a grudge or have not done something that someone else asked you for, then go do that so your Boss in heaven will do the same for you."

Note: Some manuscripts include the words from Matthew 6:15.

Jesus Is Accosted

²⁷ They rode into Jerusalem again and headed straight for the main church area. While Jesus was walking amongst the people, some of the bigwigs who ran the place came up to him and asked him, ²⁸ "So just who do you think you are, hotshot? Who gave you the right to come in here like you own this joint?"

²⁹ Jesus turned to them nonchalantly and said, "I'll answer you if you answer me. ³⁰ Did John's authority to baptize come from heaven or did he just make it up on his own? Answer that."

³¹ They huddled together like squabblin' birds at a bird bath. "If we say it was from heaven, he'll ask us why didn't we believe in what John was doing. ³² But if we say it was just his own idea, all these people will get mad because they believe John was a true cowboy of God."

³³ Finally, they turned back to Jesus and said, "We don't know."

Jesus shook his head and then said, "If you don't even know who John was, then I ain't going to tell you who I am or where my authority comes from."

CHAPTER 12

Story about a Leased Ranch

Then Jesus gathered everyone who wanted to learn around him. He taught them with stories they could understand and relate to, "A man started a ranch and strung all the wire and set every post. He even built a big nice entrance with a gate. After that, he leased the ranch on shares to some cowboys who wanted to get started in the business. The rancher moved away to another part of the country, but at the time of shipping calves, ² he sent one of his cowboys back to get the share of his calves for the lease. ³ But the cowboys on the ranch grabbed the cowboy and beat the crap out of him and sent him back without a single calf.

⁴ "The rancher sent another hand over there to get his share of the calves and they beat that fellow also and sent him back empty-handed. ⁵ The next cowboy the rancher sent was even killed. Still, the rancher sent hand after hand to get what was owed and right. They beat or killed every single one.

⁶ "Finally, the rancher was all out of hands and the only one left to send was his only son— the son he loved more than anything else. The rancher finally sent him, thinking, 'Surely they will respect my son.'

"But the evil cowboys saw the son coming and ⁷ said to one another, 'Look, the rancher sends his own son. If we kill him, then the rancher will have no one to leave his ranch to and we will have the boy's inheritance.' ⁸ So they ambushed the rancher's grown son, killed him, and then left his body right outside the front gate."

⁹ Jesus continued the story, "So what do y'all think the rancher will do? He will come back himself and kill those no-account rustlers and give the ranch to other cowboys who will be thankful for the opportunity to ride for him. ¹⁰ Have you not read God's words that say, 'The calf the cowboys culled has now become the sire bull. ¹¹ This is from God and everyone who sees it is amazed?'"

¹² Now this really got them bigwig preacher's feathers ruffled. They wanted to arrest him, but the crowds loved what Jesus was teaching. The bigwigs knew he had just told this story about them, but they just skulked away to scheme against him.

Those Durn Taxes

¹³ Then the bigwigs sent some slick willy politicians, along with some silver-tongued preachers, in an attempt to trap Jesus and make him look bad. ¹⁴ They strolled up to Jesus like they were all friends and said, "Hey there professor, we know you are a straight shooter and don't say things just so people will like you. We know you teach the truth straight from God, but we've got a

question for ya. ¹⁵ Should those of us who follow God really be paying taxes to Caesar?"

But Jesus saw right through their underhanded scheme and said, "Do you think I'm going to fall for your silly games? Bring me one of these coins you use to pay your taxes and let me see it."

¹⁶ One of them pulled a coin out of his pocket and flipped it to Jesus. He held the coin up and asked, "Who's picture is on this coin?"

"Caesar's," they answered.

¹⁷ Jesus nodded his head in agreement and said, "Give Caesar the things that belong to Caesar and give God the things that belong to God." And he tossed the coin back.

Everyone who heard him was amazed.

The Dead Will Ride Again

¹⁸ Some Sadducees (religious politicians who didn't believe in life after death—meaning they tried to get as much out of this life as they could) took their turn trying to trap Jesus. ¹⁹ They asked him, "Sir, Moses told us that God said, 'If a man's brother is married and dies, then the brother is to marry his former sister-in-law and have some kids in memory of his dead brother.' But what about this scenario? ²⁰ Say there were seven brothers and the oldest brother marries a woman, but dies before they have any kids. ²¹ Then the next brother marries her and he dies before they have any kids. ²² This goes on until every brother has married her and died without a single kid being born. Finally, the woman dies too. ²³ If there is life after death, whose wife will she be in heaven?"

²⁴ Jesus said to them, "Y'all ain't got a clue what you're talking about. Y'all don't know God's words from a cow turd. And you certainly don't know anything about the power of God. ²⁵ When people are raised from the dead and enter heaven, none of them will be married to anyone, but rather, they will be like the angels. ²⁶ But, let's cut to the chase here. Y'all are asking me about life after death and you don't even believe in that. Have you not read in Moses's book, in the section about the burning bush, how God said to him, 'I am the God of Abraham, the God of Isaac, and the God of Jacob'? He didn't say he had been the God of those great guys, but that he is the God of them. ²⁷ Those guys are alive with him because he is the God of the living, not

the dead. You boys couldn't find a forty-pound truth if it was hanging off the end of your nose."

²⁸ A religious lawyer had walked up during this debate and was impressed with Jesus's answer. He asked Jesus a question of his own. "Which commandment is the most important one of 'em all?"

²⁹ Jesus turned to him and said, "I'll tell you which one is most important. It's from one of Moses's books, 'Listen up, Israel. Our God is the only God there is. ³⁰ You must ride for God with all your heart, soul, and mind. You've got to ride for him with every ounce of strength you've got.' ³¹ But there is another commandment that is just as important as this one. 'Care about the well-being of others as much as you care about the well-being of yourself.' These two things are more important than all the offerings and sacrifices a person could ever make."

³² "Well said, sir," the lawyer replied. "You speak the truth in that there is one, and only one, God. ³³ To ride for him with all your heart, all your soul, and all your strength, and to love your neighbor as much as you love yourself is more important than all the sacrifices in the world."

³⁴ Jesus saw that the light was starting to come on for this fellow, so he told him, "You are not far from God's outfit right now." After that, no one dared ask any more questions trying to trap him.

³⁵ Later on, Jesus was giving a clinic at the main church in town about how to ride for God. He asked them, "Why do those that stress religious rules claim God's Top Hand will be a son of the great King David? ³⁶ I ask this because even David, in his book, said, 'God told my Boss, "Ride to my right and watch as I trample over all of your enemies and you ride right over them."'

³⁷ "Since David himself called God's Top Hand his Boss, how then can the Chosen One be his son?"

People shook their heads in wonderful amazement at the things Jesus taught.

³⁸ He also taught them, "Keep a sharp lookout for those who teach religious rules! They like to ride around with their fancy tack and hand tooled saddles. ³⁹ They like it when people look up to them like they are all high and mighty. ⁴⁰ But these fellows would cheat a widow out of her last piece of bread and then go and make a long, eloquent prayer at a public gathering.

Because they act like this, they will be punished severely."

The Widow's Donation

41 Jesus rested between his clinics and sat near the offering box in church. He watched as people gave their offering. Many rich people put in a big wad of cash, **42** but then a poor widow came and dropped in two small coins.

43 Jesus immediately got all his cowboy's attention and said, "Did y'all see that? I tell you the truth, that poor lady right there has given more than all the others combined. **44** They gave a little bit of their riches, but she gave everything she had to live on."

CHAPTER 13

Not a Stone Left Standing

As Jesus and his cowboys were leaving the church that day, one of 'em said, "Hey Boss, look at how big and pretty this building is. Isn't it impressive?"

2 Jesus replied, "You got that right. All these buildings are impressive, but not a single one will be left standing. They will all be knocked down."

About the End

3 Later that day, Jesus sat on Olive Hill, across from the main church. Peter, James, John, and Andy came to him and asked, **4** "When will all this stuff you've been talking about happen? Will you give us a whistle, or will there be a signal that the end of time is going to kick off?"

5 Jesus was adamant when he said, "Don't let anyone pull the wool over your eyes. **6** There will be many people claiming to be me, and a lot of people will believe them. **7** There will be wars and threats of wars, but y'all don't have to be afraid. Sure, these things will happen, but just because they happen doesn't mean the end is right around the corner. **8** Nations will go to war against other nations and there will be fighting all over the world. There will be earthquakes and droughts and people will starve, but these things are just the first sharp pain of the birth that will come later.

9 "When you see these things start to happen, be careful, but be ready also. You will be arrested in the towns and beaten right inside the churches. You will stand trial because you ride for me.

This may sound bad, but it is a great opportunity for you to tell others about the free gift I give everyone who rides for me. **10** The good news about what I will do must be spread to everyone in the world. **11** But don't go to worrying about what you will say before you are arrested. When that time comes, God will put the right words in your mouth and the courage in your heart. It won't be you who is talking, it will be the Holy Spirit."

12 Jesus continued, "It's going to get so bad in the end that people will turn against the ones they love the most. They'll turn in their brothers, their kids, their parents, and anyone else for a little reward and these people will be killed because they ride for me. **13** If you ride for me, people are going to hate you and want you dead. But the cowboy who rides all the way to the end for me will be saved.

The Defecation of Desolation

14 "Be ready to hightail it for the hills when you see the Antichrist at the altar of the church. **15** When you see that, you don't even stop to put something in your saddlebags, you just jump on and go. **16** If you are gathering cattle and see it, don't go back for a change of clothes, just whip and spur out of there! **17** It'll be a real bad time for those who are nursing children. **18** Just pray that this hard time don't come in the winter when times are at their hardest. **19** I'm telling y'all, these times will be harder than any other time in history. **20** In fact, the times will be so hard that unless God intervenes, and he will, not a single follower of mine would survive. But for the sake of those who ride for me, God will step in and help.

21 "So if you see anyone who says, 'Look! There is Jesus,' or another says, 'I heard Jesus came back,' don't believe them. **22** There will be many counterfeits who will come and do things that will amaze people. Some who ride for me will be deceived, too. **23** So y'all better watch out. I'm giving you a heads up about these things ahead of time.

God's Top Hand Will Come Ridin'

24 "In the days that follow these hard times, 'The sun will go out and the moon will lose its light. **25** The stars will fall from the skies and the great power in the universe will be shaken.' **26** Then everyone will see the Top Hand riding through the clouds with a power so awesome that it will be undeniable. **27** God's Chosen One, his Son, the Top Hand, will send his angels out to gather all his cowboys and cowgirls who ride for his brand and gather them together from the furthest parts of the earth all the way to heaven. Not one will be left behind."

28 The cowboys sat in awe as he continued, "Learn a lesson from a simple tree. When the leaves start to bud out, you know that spring has arrived and summer is near. **29** In the same way, when you see all these things happening, you know that the Top Hand is riding out of the gate and coming for you. **30** I'm telling you the truth when I say that those who ride for me during that time, not all of them will die before all of this I've told you about happens. **31** The current heaven and the earth you see now will end, but my words will never prove untrue."

32 Jesus held up a cautionary hand, "But no one, and I mean no one—not the angels in heaven, or myself—knows the exact time when this will take place. Only God knows. **33** So keep a sharp lookout and whatever you do, be ready! I can't express enough the need to be ready to ride because you will not know when the time will come. **34** It's kind of like the wagon boss leaving the ranch and telling each of the cowboys what jobs they are supposed to do while he is gone. He even puts one cowboy at the gate to watch for his return. **35** I'm posting y'all at the gate to watch. You don't know if the wagon boss is coming back in the evening, or at noon, or before the rooster crows. **36** You don't want to be caught napping when he arrives. **37** Stay alert and watch like I've told you to do."

CHAPTER 14

The Execution Plan

Two days before the Passover and the Feast of the Flatbread, the bigwig preachers and religious lawmakers were trying to figure out a way to have Jesus killed. They all agreed that they would have to do it before the feast, and **2** before the special Passover celebration, because they didn't want the people to riot.

The Perfume

3 While Jesus was staying in Bethany at the house of a fellow named Simon (who had a terrible skin disease), he relaxed at the table. A woman came by the house and had a small, but extremely expensive jar of aromatic oil. She opened it and poured the whole thing on Jesus's head (this was a great honor she was trying to give him).

4 But some of the people who were there took offense at the gesture. They said, "Why waste such an expensive gift on one person? **5** That could have been sold for three hundred silver pieces and the money could have taken care of many poor people!" Then they all started giving the woman a hard time and scolding her.

6 But Jesus shut them up right quick. "Y'all leave her alone. She hasn't done anything to you, but she has done something extremely nice for me. **7** You will always have the poor to help, but you will not always have me around. She tried to do something special for me and I appreciate it. **8** She has prepared my body for burial before I'm even dead. **9** When my story is told, when the good news is preached all over the world, the story of what she did here today will be told in honor of what she did."

10 While this was going on, Judas Iscariot, one of Jesus's cowboys, rode off to meet with the bigwig preachers and religious lawmakers for the sole purpose of double-crossing his boss. **11** The scoundrels he talked to were tickled pink at the information Judas gave them about Jesus and they promised to reward him handsomely. They all concocted a plan to betray and capture Jesus.

The Flatbread Feast

12 On the first day of the Flatbread Feast is when the Passover lamb is sacrificed. Jesus's cowboys asked him where he wanted to eat the Passover meal. **13** He sent a couple of his cowboys to the city and **14** said, "When you get into town, you'll see a man carrying a canteen. Follow him. When he goes into a house, knock on the door and tell the owner, 'The Boss asks, "Which room shall I stay in and eat the Passover meal with my cowboys?"' **15** He will immediately take you upstairs to a large furnished room. Get everything started and the rest of us will be along shortly."

16 The cowboys rode off and found everything just like Jesus said they would. After it happened just like he said it would, they went upstairs and started cooking. **17** When evening arrived, Jesus arrived at the house with the rest of his men, including Judas the Betrayer. **18** While they were eating, Jesus commented, "One of you eating here with me is a double-crosser."

19 You could have heard a pin drop and then one by one, each cowboy said, "It's not me, Boss!"

20 Jesus had just sat a bowl down that he had passed around and everyone had dipped their bread into. He said, "The double-crosser has just dipped his hand in the same bowl as I did. **21** He will betray me because God said it would happen, but it would be better for the double-crossing cur dog if he'd never been born."

22 While they were eating, he took some bread, gave thanks to God for it, and shared pieces of it with all his cowboys.

After handing some to everyone, he said, "This bread is for y'all and it represents my body that I also give for y'all."

23 He then took his cup, and after giving thanks to God for what was inside it, he shared a little with everyone else. They all drank it and he said, **24** "This is my blood. My blood is the seal on God's new promise. A promise, by my blood that will be shed, for the many. **25** I won't drink another drop of wine until the day when I drink it in my Daddy's place."

26 They all gathered around and sang a few songs and then they struck a long trot for Olive Hill.

When they got there, **27** Jesus said to them, "It's fixing to get real bad, my friends. It was written about long ago when it said, 'God will strike down the Top Hand, and his herd will be scattered.' **28** But after I come riding back from the grave, I will meet you in Galilee."

29 Pete spoke up quickly and said, "All these boys may run off and leave you, but I won't."

30 Jesus replied kindly, "Listen Pete. Today—actually, this very night—before the rooster crows in the morning, you will deny you even know me. Not just once, but three times."

31 Pete shook his head and argued, "Boss, even if I have to die with you, I would never say that I didn't know you."

All the other cowboys agreed and said the same thing.

Gethsemane

32 They all saddled up and rode off toward Gethsemane. When they got there, he told all the cowboys to wait there and pray. **33** He motioned for Pete, James, and John to follow him. Jesus looked worse than they'd ever seen him and **34** he told them, "I want y'all to stay here with me. I'm so full of dread that my heart feels like it's going to stop. Please keep me company. I need y'all right now, pards."

35 Jesus went far enough as to be out of sight and fell down to his knees. He looked up to heaven and said, **36** "Dad, you can find another way—can't you? It doesn't have to happen like this, does it? I sure don't want to drink from this cup of agony that sits before me."

After a moment's pause, he continued, "But you know what, Dad? It's not about what I want. It's about what you want."

37 He got up and went back to where he'd left Pete, James, and John. They were all sound asleep. He woke Pete up and said, "Did you really fall asleep at a time like this? **38** Keep a sharp lookout. Start praying so you will not be ambushed by any sinful temptations. I know you want to do what's right, but talk is cheap."

39 Jesus went back to his prayer spot for a while and then returned only to find them all asleep again. **40** They woke up and just kind of sat there, unsure what to say. They knew they had messed up again.

41 He went away again and came back a third time, only to find them asleep again. He got them up and said, "Y'all rested up now? Enough is enough. The time has come and here is the betrayer bringing the wolves into the sheep pen. **42** Get up, boys. It's time to go. Here comes the double-crossing cur dog now."

43 Just as the words came out of Jesus's mouth, Judas arrived with a crowd of people. Among them were soldiers, religious lawmakers, and bigwig preachers. **44** Judas had told them he would go up and kiss Jesus on the cheek. That way they would know who to grab.

45 Judas sure enough walked right up to Jesus, just like they were good pards, and gave him a kiss on the cheek. **46** The crowd rushed in and grabbed Jesus.

47 Just then, one of Jesus's crew pulled out his castrating blade and took a swing at the main preacher's right-hand man, cutting off his ear.

48 Jesus spoke above the calamity and said, "Am I some vicious outlaw that you come with swords and clubs to arrest me? Why didn't you just take me while I taught in church? **49** I was right there every day and all of you listened to me. But never mind, these things are happening because my Dad said they would."

50 When they took Jesus away, all his cowboys hightailed it out of there, in fear for their lives. **51** One of the cowboys with Jesus was only dressed in overalls. When the mob tried to take him too, **52** he slipped out of the overalls that they had a hold of and ran away buck naked.

Jesus Stands before the Authorities

53 They took Jesus to the main preacher's house where a bunch of the people who had plotted against him were gathered. **54** Pete had circled around and followed them, but at a safe distance. He snuck into the yard and sat down with some of the night guard and warmed himself by the fire like nothing was going on.

55 Inside the house, all the people who had the authority to make decisions were trying to find evidence of guilt so they could kill Jesus. **56** Many people came and made false accusations against him, but they kept contradicting themselves with their testimonies and none of them could be used.

57 Finally, a few men stood up and lied as they said, **58** "We heard Jesus say he would destroy the main church and replace it three days later with one built by God himself." **59** It sounded good, but they couldn't get their facts straight when questioned.

60 The main preacher spoke up and asked Jesus, "What do you have to say about all of this? What do you have to say for yourself?"

61 Jesus stood there, silent and stoic. The preacher then asked, "Are you the Chosen One? Are you the Son of God himself?"

With words that held the power of God, **62** Jesus said, "I AM . . . and you all should know it. Soon, you will see me sitting at the right hand of God himself and riding on the clouds of heaven."

63 That old preacher started frothing at the mouth when he heard Jesus say this. He said, "Why do we need anything more than the filth he just uttered out of his mouth?! **64** You all heard his outright lies. What is your verdict?"

They all responded with a guilty verdict and sentenced him to death.

65 People rushed Jesus and then spit on him. Others blindfolded him and then some took turns sucker punching him. They sneered and asked, "Hey prophet!? Who hit you? Tell us the truth of what you cannot see."

Then Jesus was led away, all the while people took turns punching and slapping him as he went.

Peter Denies He Rode with Jesus

66 While all this was happening inside, Pete was by the fire trying to stay warm. **67** One of the preacher's maids happened to walk by and she suddenly pointed at him and said, "I saw you riding with the one they call Jesus!"

68 Pete looked around like he was shocked. "Who is Jesus? I don't have a clue what you're talking about." He started to walk away as he heard a rooster crow.

69 The young girl followed him and began telling everyone around her, "He's one of Jesus's cowboys. I saw them riding together."

70 Pete shook his head and denied everything.

Word spread through the crowd and many started saying, "You're definitely one of the men who rode with Jesus. You've got that Galilean cowboy look written all over you."

71 Then Pete let out a string of cuss words and he swore in front of everyone, "I do not know this man that y'all are accusing me of riding with. I've never even seen him!"

72 The words were no more out of his mouth when Pete heard a rooster crow for the second time. He remembered what Jesus said to him, "Before a rooster crows twice, you will say you don't know me three times."

Pete broke down and cried.

CHAPTER 15

Very early in the morning, all the religious leaders had made their plan against Jesus. They tied him up and handed him over to Pilate, the local Roman governor in charge.

2 Pilate asked Jesus, "Are you the boss of the Jews?" Jesus replied, "You said it, but I ain't denying it."

3 This got the religious leaders all riled up. They were screaming and yelling accusations at Jesus.

4 Pilate questioned Jesus again, "Are you not going to defend yourself? Listen to everything they are saying about you!"

[5] But Jesus kept his mouth shut and didn't say a word.

Pilate was amazed that a man could keep quiet in the face of so many deadly allegations. [6] During the Feast of Flatbread, and the celebration of Passover, it was a tradition to release one person who was in jail and waiting execution. [7] There was one particularly nasty fellow named Barabbas, who was locked up for murder.

[8] The crowd asked Pilate to release a prisoner and he asked if they would rather release Jesus or Barabbas. [9] Pilate said, "Do you want me to let the Boss of the Jews go?" [10] But he knew the religious leaders were just jealous of Jesus. Pilate was stalling and trying to help him all he could.

[11] The religious leaders stirred up the crowd against Jesus and they lobbied to have Barabbas released instead.

[12] Pilate, still trying to work out a deal, asked, "Then what am I supposed to do with the one who y'all call the Boss of the Jews?"

[13] They shouted, "String him up on the cross!"

[14] Pilate was dismayed and asked, "What has this man done that is so wrong?"

The crowd didn't answer except to chant, "String him up . . . String him up . . . String him up!"

[15] Pilate didn't want a riot on his hands, so he released Barabbas and sent Jesus to be whipped. After that, he would be strung up on the cross.

Jesus Is Made Fun Of

[16] The Roman soldiers led Jesus into the Governor's mansion and gathered everyone around. [17] They put a purple cape on him and wove a crown of thorns that they smashed on his head. The blood ran into Jesus's eyes and down his face.

[18] They paraded mockingly in front of Jesus and saluted him saying, "All hail the Boss of the Jews!"

[19] They repeatedly hit him on the head, and spit on Jesus. They knelt down in fake homage and made fun of him for a long time. [20] Finally, when they'd had their fill of fun, they stripped the purple cape off him and led him away to string him up on the cross.

[21] Jesus was carrying the cross piece he would be nailed to, but could go no further due to his injuries. The soldiers grabbed a guy named Simon and made him carry the cross piece.

They String Jesus Up

[22] They got up to a hill they call Golgotha (which means "Skull Hill"). [23] They offered him a shot of wine with some numbing stuff mixed in, but Jesus refused it. [24] Then they nailed him to the cross and strung him up naked. They gambled and threw dice to see who would get this famous man's clothes. [25] This all happened about nine o'clock in the morning.

[26] They put a sign above Jesus's head that said, "Boss of the Jews" and [27] they strung up two outlaws on crosses on both sides of Jesus.

Note: Some manuscripts include the words from Luke 22:37.

[29] Many who passed by shouted, "You said you could destroy the church building in three days and then rebuild it . . . [30] if you're that powerful, why don't you get yourself off that cross and do it!"

[31] Even the religious leaders made fun of him by saying, "He saved many people, but he can't even save himself. What a joke! [32] If he really is the Chosen One, let him come down off that cross and we'll believe it."

Even those being crucified with him made fun of him.

[33] It was now the midday hour, and when the clock had struck high noon, darkness descended over the entire country for three hours. [34] About three o'clock in the afternoon, Jesus yelled out, *"Eloi, Eloi, lema sabachthani?"* which means, "My God, my God, why have you forgotten about me?"

[35] When some people standing around heard him, they said, "Listen! Jesus is calling out for Elijah!"

[36] Then someone lifted up a sponge soaked with vinegar and gave it to Jesus. Others said, "Leave him alone. Let's see if Elijah does somehow come riding up to save him."

Jesus Breathes His Last

[37] Jesus looked up and cried out with a loud voice and let out his last breath. [38] In the main church, there was a thick curtain that separated God's holy place from the rest of the building. When Jesus died, this curtain was torn in two from the top to the bottom. No longer would God be separated from his people.

[39] One of the soldiers who stood at the foot of the cross saw how Jesus died and said, "I think

we've screwed up boys. This really was God's Son!"

⁴⁰ Also seeing his death were some women watching from a distance. These women included Mary Magdalene, Mary the mother of James, and Salome. ⁴¹ In Galilee, these women had traveled with Jesus and taken care of him. There were other women there also who had gone to Jerusalem with him.

Laid to Rest

⁴² It was the day before the day of rest (the day before the Sabbath Day) and as the sun was setting, ⁴³ a local leader named Joseph of Arimathea and believer of Jesus, went and boldly asked Pilate for the body of Jesus. ⁴⁴ Pilate seemed surprised to find out that Jesus had already died. ⁴⁵ He called for a soldier and asked him if Jesus had indeed already died. When it was confirmed, Pilate gave Joseph permission to take the body.

⁴⁶ Joseph took a fine linen sheet, took the body down and wrapped it up. He placed Jesus's body in a tomb cut into the rock and rolled a large stone in front of the entrance. ⁴⁷ Mary Magdalene and Mary, the mother of Joseph, watched the burial happen.

CHAPTER 16

Jesus Rides Back from the Dead

When the day of rest was over, the women brought spices to embalm Jesus's body. ² It was very early on Sunday morning and ³ they worried about how they were going to move the heavy stone that had been placed in front of the tomb. ⁴ But when they got to the tomb, the stone had already been rolled away.

⁵ They walked into the tomb to take care of Jesus's body, but all they saw was a man sitting to the right of where they had laid him. This shocked them and they didn't know what to do or what to say.

⁶ But the man said to them, "Whoa! Don't be scared ladies. You are looking for Jesus of Nazareth, but he ain't here. This is where his body was placed, but like I said, he ain't here. ⁷ Go tell Jesus's cowboys, especially Pete, that Jesus is heading for Galilee and said to meet him there."

⁸ The ladies hightailed it out of there, not just with a message, but they were scared to death

also. They didn't say anything to anyone because they were so afraid.

Note: The following text does not appear in the earliest manuscripts.

⁹ After Jesus had been raised from the dead, he first appeared to Mary Magdalene, whom he'd cured of seven demons. ¹⁰ She ended up delivering the message to Jesus's cowboys that he was no longer in the tomb. ¹¹ They were still very upset that he had died in the first place and when they heard what she said, they didn't believe a word of it.

¹² Jesus also appeared later to a couple of cowboys who were traveling down the road. ¹³ They went and told Jesus's cowboys that they had seen him, but they didn't believe these two either.

¹⁴ Finally, Jesus appeared to the eleven remaining cowboys himself. He scolded them for not believing everyone who he had sent to tell them the good news of his riding back from the dead.

¹⁵ He told all of 'em, "Y'all get out there and go to every pasture and every place on earth and tell 'em the good news. Tell 'em I've opened the gate to God's outfit and no one ever has to depend on themselves to be perfect, but that I've done it for them. ¹⁶ All they have to do is devote their lives to riding for me and be baptized. Everyone who rides for me will get into heaven and those who don't, won't. ¹⁷ You'll be able to tell who is a cowboy on my Dad's outfit because they will drive out demons and speak in languages no one has heard before. ¹⁸ They will pick up snakes without being bitten and even have poison given to them without it killing 'em. They will place their hands on people and heal them."

¹⁹ After he got done giving them their final instructions, Jesus was whisked up to heaven where he was saddled up at the right hand of God himself.

²⁰ The cowboys went and did exactly what Jesus told 'em to and Jesus was right there in spirit working with them. Everything happened just like Jesus said it would because many miraculous signs happened.

LUKE

CHAPTER 1

The Tale of Jesus

There's a lot of folks who've told the tale of the things that happened. ² These things have been written down and agree with the stories that come from the cowboys who were there. ³ I've studied what was written and talked to many folks. ⁴ I was very careful so that you would know that what I write is the truth.

John the Baptizer's Birth

⁵ When that old rascal Herod was king of Judea, there was a preacher named Zechariah. He belonged to a group called Abijah. He had a wife named Elizabeth and her ancestors come from the line of Aaron. ⁶ Zechariah and Elizabeth were good people. They did everything God ever told 'em to do. ⁷ They were both timeworn, and Elizabeth had never gotten pregnant despite her and her husband's many prayers.

⁸ Zechariah was serving as the preacher for his group because it was their time to serve. ⁹ One preacher was always chosen to carry the incense for the services, and old Zechariah was the one they chose. ¹⁰ When he came in with the incense, there were a ton of people at the church praying. ¹¹ Then an angel appeared right next to the table where Zechariah was offering incense. ¹² The sight of the angel nearly toppled old Zechariah. He started shaking like a leaf. ¹³ But the angel told him, "Whoa, amigo. Don't let me spook ya. I've come to tell ya that God has been listening to your prayers and your wife will give birth to a baby boy. God wants you to name him John. ¹⁴ He's going to make you, and a lot of other peo-

ple, very happy. ¹⁵ He's going to be a top hand for the Lord. He will never let alcohol pass his lips and even before his birth the Holy Spirit will be with him. ¹⁶ John's going to gather a lot of people for God's outfit. ¹⁷ He's going to get everything ready for when the Lord comes. John is going to be as powerful as Elijah and have the same spirit. He will bring families back together and show people who are not riding for God how to change the way they do things."

¹⁸ Zechariah lowered his gaze and asked, "How can I believe this? The wife and I are real long in the tooth."

¹⁹ The angel said, "My name is Gabriel, and I stand before God, always ready to do his, and only his, bidding. He sent me here to bring you this good news. ²⁰ Now you hear me, and you better get used to listening because you're going to be doing a lot of it. You didn't believe what I said, so you are no longer going to be able to speak until all I have told you comes to pass . . . and it will."

²¹ After the church service was over, many people waited on Zechariah to come out. They were wondering why he was taking so long. ²² When he came out, he could not say a word. The people figured out that he'd had a vision because he couldn't speak, but he was trying to communicate with his hands. ²³ He hightailed it home after work.

²⁴ After all this, Elizabeth became pregnant. She kept to herself for about five months. She said a few times, ²⁵ "Just look at what the Lord has done for this old woman. He heard my prayer and now people will stop staring at me like I'm broken."

An Angel Tells of Jesus's Upcoming Birth

26-27 When Elizabeth was six months pregnant, God sent Gabriel to talk to a virgin girl named Mary who lived in Nazareth. She was engaged to a carpenter named Joseph, who descended from David. **28** The angel appeared to her and said, "Mary, you have found favor in the sight of God, and he is with you."

29 Mary was real confused about what any of this meant. **30** The angel said, "Don't be afraid. God is real proud of the lady you've become, and **31** you are going to be pregnant with a son. You will name him Jesus. **32** He is going to the best cowboy ever born. People will call him the Son of God and the Lord will make him like his ancestor David. **33** He's going to rule over the house of Jacob forever; his outfit will never end."

34 Mary sheepishly asked, "How's this going to work since I've never slept with a man?"

35 Gabriel said, "You ain't gotta worry about that part. God will take care of it. This baby is going to be holy, and he is gonna be God's only boy. **36** And here's some more good news, your cousin Elizabeth is going to have a baby in about three months. I know she's old, but this just goes to show you God can and will do whatever he wants with whoever he wants. **37** God can do anything!"

38 Mary sat there a second, thinking about everything Gabriel had told her. Finally, she said, "I'll do whatever God needs me to do." And Gabriel went away.

Mary Pays Elizabeth a Visit

39 Mary gathered up some things and went quickly to a village in the hill country of Judea. **40-41** She showed up at Zechariah's house, and as soon as she said hello to Elizabeth, the soon-to-be born baby jerked inside her. The Holy Spirit filled Elizabeth at her baby's reaction.

42 Elizabeth squealed with excitement as she said to Mary, "God has blessed you more than any other woman in history. And he has blessed your baby. **43** You will be the mother of my Lord, and you've come to my house. I can't believe this is even happening to me! **44** When I heard your voice, my baby jumped for joy inside of me. **45** You are blessed because you believed what God told you."

46 Then Mary humbly said, "I'm happy to give my heart to God. **47** I love that God has saved me. **48** There is nothing special about me, but he has shown his lowly servant just how much he loves me. From this point forward, everyone will remember how much God has shown kindness to me. **49** There's no doubt of the great things our powerful God has done for me. His name is holy and above all others. **50** He shows mercy to those who bow down before him. **51** He stretched out his arm and did miraculous things. He scatters the proud like a heeler dog on new cattle. He doesn't take kindly to people who think they are more important than others. **52** He's brought down kings and raised up the lowly. **53** He's filled the hungry with blessings and left the wealthy with nothing but money. **54** God's given a hand to Israel—the folks he's decided to call his own. He didn't forget his promise to take care of us. **55** He's fulfilled his promise to our ancestors. He made good what he told Abraham and his kids, forever."

56 Mary stayed there with Elizabeth for about three months and then headed back to Nazareth.

57 When the time came, Elizabeth gave birth to a boy. **58** Everyone was happy because of what God had done for her.

59 When the baby was about eight days old, it was time for his pickle to be clipped. Everyone wanted to name him after his daddy, **60** but Elizabeth said his name would be John.

61 A few people spoke up and said, "But why would you name him that? You ain't got a single person in your family named John." **62** Then they turned to Zechariah and used some hand talk to try to ask him what he wanted the baby's name to be.

63 Zechariah motioned for something to write on. Then he wrote, "His name is John." Nobody could believe it. This was highly unusual. **64** Just then, God popped the dally on Zechariah's tongue, and he could talk again. The first thing he did was start praising the Lord. **65** God was doing such great things that it spooked most of the people. In all the hill country of Judea, people were freaking out about the things that had happened. **66** Everyone wondered what this child would become, but there wasn't any doubt that the Lord was with him.

Zechariah Tells of What Is to Come

67 The Holy Spirit filled Zechariah, and he gave everyone a message from God, **68** "Praise be to the Boss of Israel. He's come to lend a hand to his people and freed them in the process. **⁶⁹** He has given us a cowboy from the lineage of David that will save us. **⁷⁰** God's been telling us he was going to do this since he first told the prophets about it. **⁷¹** This cowboy will save us from our enemies. No longer do we have to hunker in the brush afraid. **⁷²** God told us that he would show us mercy, and he has remembered his promise. **⁷³** He gave his word to Abraham **⁷⁴** that he would whip our enemies and allow us to serve him without fear. **⁷⁵** We would serve him by becoming like him and doing things the right way as long as we live. **⁷⁶** And listen, my little child, you will be called a prophet of the Boss. You will blaze a trail for the Top Hand. **⁷⁷** You'll tell them that they will have salvation through the forgiveness of their sins. **⁷⁸** A new day is shining down on us through the mercy of God. **⁷⁹** It'll be a campfire in the darkness. Not even the shadow of death can hide the light that will guide us down the trail that will bring us peace."

⁸⁰ John grew up healthy in body and spirit. When he was older, he lived way out in the country. He stayed there until it was time to tell everyone God's message.

CHAPTER 2

Jesus Is Born

Now it was in this time that Augustus Caesar sent out an order that everyone's name would be on a list. **²** This would be the first census taken while Quirinius was in charge of Syria. **³** Everyone had to ride back to their home place to put their name on the list.

⁴ Joseph left Nazareth, a town in the Galilee area, and headed toward Bethlehem in Judea. Bethlehem was known as the town of David, and that was his hometown. **⁵** Joseph signed the list and included his fiancée Mary. The wedding would be coming up soon. **⁶** While they were there, Mary went into labor. **⁷** She gave birth to a son and wrapped him up in blankets and laid him in a feed trough. They were staying in a barn because there were not any hotel rooms to be found.

Cowboys and Angels

⁸ That night, there were some cowboys on night watch near Bethlehem. **⁹** An angel ap-

peared to them, and they were scared to death. **¹⁰** The angel told them, "Don't be afraid, boys! I've come to give you some great news. **¹¹** Today in the town of David, the cowboy who will save your souls was born. He is God's Top Hand. **¹²** You'll know you've found him when you find a baby wrapped in a horse blanket and lying in a feed trough."

¹³ And just like that, the army of heaven's angels erupted in praise, saying, **¹⁴** "Give God all the glory in heaven, and on earth let there be peace for all the cowboys who ride for the Lord."

¹⁵ Then the angels were gone, and the cowboys said to each other, "Let's head over to Bethlehem and find this little boy the angels told us about."

¹⁶ So they struck a long trot and found Mary and Joseph. And sure enough, there was a baby wrapped in a horse blanket and lying in a feed trough. **¹⁷** When they saw the boy, they told his momma and daddy what the angels had said. **¹⁸** Everyone that night, and later, could hardly believe what the cowboys had to say about that night, **¹⁹** but Mary pondered these things in her heart and tried to sort out everything that had happened. **²⁰** The cowboys headed back out to the herd, giving thanks to God for everything they had seen and heard. It happened just like that angel had told 'em it would.

Jesus Gets Circumcised

²¹ When the baby was eight days old, they clipped his pickle as is the custom. They named the boy Jesus, just like the angel had told 'em.

²² The code of Moses said any first-born baby boy was to be brought to Jerusalem and presented to the Lord. **²³** Moses's code said, "When a momma's first born is a boy, he shall be called 'special for God.'" **²⁴** This code stated that the parents were to sacrifice two doves or two young pigeons.

Simeon Speaks Highly of Baby Jesus

²⁵ There was an old cowboy living in Jerusalem named, Simeon. He was a good fellow, filled with the Holy Spirit, who was all-in for God's outfit. He'd been waiting for the day that God would send his Top Hand. **²⁶** The Holy Spirit had told the old cowboy that he wouldn't die before he had seen God's Top Hand. **²⁷** The Spirit guided old Simeon to the main church in Jerusalem. It was no coincidence because after he had arrived there, Joseph and Mary showed up with Jesus to do what the code of Moses instructed. ²⁸ Simeon took one look at the baby and said, ²⁹ "Now, I can die and go to God in peace. ³⁰ I've done seen with my own eyes how you will save everyone. ³¹ Now everyone will know your plan. ³² This boy will be a light for all men and all nations, and he will bring honor and glory to Israel."

³³ Now Joseph and Mary were stunned by what the old cowboy said. ³⁴ Simeon blessed the parents and then said to Mary, "This boy will be the saving and undoing of many. Not everyone will believe in him. ³⁵ He will reveal the hearts of all people. But I'm telling you that the things that will come will bring you much pain—it'll be like a blade through your heart."

Anna Tells Everyone about Jesus

³⁶ Now there was this lady named, Anna. She was a prophet of God, the daughter of Penuel and from the family of Asher. She was eighty-four years old and ³⁷ had only been married seven years when her husband died. Anna was always at the main church, praying, fasting, and worshiping the Boss. ³⁸ So sure enough, she was there when Mary and Joseph came in with Jesus. She praised God and told everyone there about Jesus and what he was going to do to free Jerusalem.

³⁹ After they had done everything to fulfill the code of Moses, the new parents headed back to Nazareth. ⁴⁰ And Jesus grew up to be a man; he was full of wisdom and it was plain to see God's blessing was on him.

The Twelve-Year-Old Top Hand

⁴¹ Every year, the little family went to Jerusalem to celebrate the Passover. ⁴² When Jesus was about twelve years old, ⁴³ they all left for home after it was over just like they had done every year. But this time, Jesus stayed behind—unknown to his parents. ⁴⁴ Joseph and Mary traveled the whole day, each thinking that Jesus was with the other. When they realized Jesus wasn't with either of them, they began searching for him. ⁴⁵ They searched everywhere. When they couldn't find him, they headed back to Jerusalem.

⁴⁶ After three days of frantically looking, they found him in the main church with the religious teachers, listening and asking questions.

⁴⁷ Everyone who was around was amazed at this young boy's understanding and wisdom concerning the Good Book. ⁴⁸ His parents found him, and they were amazed at his understanding. Mary put all that aside and asked Jesus, "Son, why did you do this to your dad and me? We were going crazy looking for you!"

⁴⁹ Jesus calmly replied, "Why did you look frantically? Didn't you know I would be at my Father's House and learning his work?" ⁵⁰ But Joseph and Mary didn't understand what he had asked them.

⁵¹ Jesus went back to Nazareth with them, but Mary couldn't let go of these thoughts of everything that had happened. ⁵² As he grew in stature, Jesus also grew in wisdom. You could tell God loved him, and so did everyone around him.

CHAPTER 3

John the Baptizer Blazes the Trail for Jesus

Emperor Tiberius had ruled that part of the world for about fifteen years. Pontius Pilate was the governor of Judea, and Herod ruled around the Sea of Galilee. Herod's brother, Philip, ran things around Iturea and Traconitis. Abilene was run by a guy named, Lysanias. ² Annas and Caiaphas were the high preachers of the Jews. It was during this time that God came down and spoke to Zechariah's boy, John. ³ John did what God told him to and went along the Jordan Draw telling people, "Turn your lives back to God and be dunked in water for the forgiveness of your sorry ways."

⁴ Isaiah the prophet was talkin' about John when he said, "There's a fellow shouting from the desert, 'Clear the narrow trail. Get it ready for the Lord. Bust brush straight toward him. ⁵ The draws will be filled and the mountains made flat. Those winding trails will be made straight, and the rough roads become like glass. ⁶ Then there won't be no doubt about how God is going to save us.'"

⁷ Folks from everywhere came to be dunked by John, but he wasn't all lovey-dovey when he said to them, "Y'all are a bunch of snakes in the grass! Who was it that warned you to hightail it out of here before the judgment comes? ⁸ You say that you've turned from your wicked ways?

Well, the proof is in the puddin'. And don't start tellin' me that you're one of Abraham's kids and that's all you have to be. Shoot, God could turn a dog turd into one of Abraham's kids if he wanted to. That don't give you a pass no more. ⁹ There's an axe ready to be swung at any cowboy who don't let his actions speak louder than his words. And if a tree is cut down, it won't be used to build a home, but to stoke the fires of hell."

¹⁰ John was sure enough givin' 'em the what for and they shouted, "Then what should we do?"

¹¹ John said, "It's as simple as this, if you have two slickers, give one to someone who don't have nothin'. If you've got two pieces of jerked beef, give one to someone who has none."

¹² Even those sorry, double-crossing tax collectors came to be dunked by John. They had their tails between their legs and would ask him, "Boss, what are we supposed to do?"

¹³ John said, "Quit greasin' your pockets with other people's money."

¹⁴ Then some soldiers hollered out, "What about us? What are we gonna do?"

John turned and said, "No more extortion. Live on what you make and that's all."

¹⁵ Everyone was jabberin' back and forth, "Is this fellow the one who will save us all?"

¹⁶ John heard them and cut it off quick. "All I'm doing is dunkin' y'all in water. There's a cowboy comin' who I ain't fit to adjust his stirrups. He's gonna dunk you in fire to purify you in the Holy Spirit. ¹⁷ He's got his sortin' stick out and will separate the seed stock from the sorry stock. The sorry stock will be hauled to the butcher and then burned in the fire that never goes out."

¹⁸ John told a bunch of different stories in a bunch of different ways so that people could get the idea about the good news that had arrived. ¹⁹ And John didn't cut old Herod no slack when he said, "And it takes a sorry fella to steal his brother's wife and everything else you've done." ²⁰ Later on, Herod locked John up . . . and this was probably the worst thing he could have done.

Jesus is Dunked

²¹ While everyone was in line to get dunked by John, Jesus came too. After getting dunked, Jesus was praying and the whole sky opened up. ²² The Holy Spirit flew down from heaven in the form of a dove and landed on him. Then from heaven, a voice shook the earth as it said, "You are my boy, and you sure make a Dad proud."

²³ Jesus began giving clinics on how to ride for God when he was about thirty years old. They all thought he was Joseph's son. That family line went something like this starting with Heli: ²⁴ Matthat, Levi, Melki, Jannai, Joseph, ²⁵ Mattathias, Amos, Nahum, Esli, Naggai, ²⁶ Maath, Mattathias, Semein, Josek, Joda, ²⁷ Joanan, Rhesa, Zerubbabel, Shealtiel, Neri, ²⁸ Melki, Addi, Cosam, Elmadam, Er, ²⁹ Joshua, Eliezer, Jorim, Matthat, Levi, ³⁰ Simeon, Judah, Joseph, Jonam, Eliakim, ³¹ Melea, Menna, Mattatha, Nathan, David, ³² Jesse, Obed, Boaz, Salmon, Nahshon, ³³ Amminadab, Admin, Arni, Hezron, Perez, Judah, ³⁴ Jacob, Isaac, Abraham, Terah, Nahor, ³⁵ Serug, Reu, Peleg, Eber, Shelah, ³⁶ Cainan, Arphaxad, Shem, Noah, Lamech, ³⁷ Methuselah, Enoch, Jared, Mahalalel, Kenan, ³⁸ Enosh, and Seth.

So, with that, Jesus went all the way back to Seth's daddy, Adam . . . but more importantly, straight to God.

CHAPTER 4

Jesus Duels the Devil

From the baptism in Jordan Creek, Jesus rode out into the desert where the Spirit led him. ² He stayed there for forty days and was tempted by the devil. He hadn't eaten anything in all those days and he was very weak.

³ That's when that old snake attacked. "If you're God's Boy, make you some bread out of these stones on the ground."

⁴ Jesus said, "The Good Book says, 'Bread alone won't give you life.'"

⁵ Then the devil took him up to a place where they could see all the countries in the world and said, ⁶ "All you see has been given to me and I will give you all its pleasure, all its treasure. ⁷ All you have to do is take a knee before me and kiss my boot."

⁸ Jesus never batted an eye as he said, "The Good Book says, 'Kneel only before God and ride for him only!'"

⁹ Then that old serpent took Jesus to the highest point of the main church and said, ¹⁰ "If you're God's Boy, jump off here and let the angels catch you like your good book says they will. ¹¹ It also says that 'them angels won't even let a pebble strike your heel.'"

¹² But Jesus said, "The Good Book says, 'Don't try God.'"

¹³ The devil snarled and knew he'd been whipped. He slithered off to wait for another opportunity to challenge the Top Hand.

Jesus Starts the Gathering

¹⁴ Then Jesus went back to the area around the Sea of Galilee. The Holy Spirit was ridin' with him like a saddlebag full of dynamite. There was nothing that could stop him. The news about Jesus spread like wildfire through the region. ¹⁵ He gave clinics in the churches and everyone was amazed by him.

¹⁶ Then Jesus rode over the hills and to his old stomping grounds of Nazareth. On the day of rest, he went like always to the local church. ¹⁷ He stood up to read out of the Good Book and turned to Isaiah. He scanned through the verses and then read, ¹⁸ "God's Spirit is riding with me. He has sent me to bring the good news to the poor. I will make a way for those held captive to be let loose, and I will make the blind see. Those who are oppressed will now have a champion. ¹⁹ I will announce that the time is now when the Lord will save his people."

²⁰ Jesus shut the book, handed it back, and sat down. Everyone in church was staring at him and you could've heard a pin drop. With all their eyes locked on him, ²¹ he looked up and said, "All I read has come true today."

²² They all agreed that what Jesus said and did was mighty impressive. They all wondered, "Isn't this Joseph's boy?"

²³ As they were all wonderin', he said, "About now y'all are going to start asking me about that old saying that goes, 'Doctor, cure yourself.' You're also fixing to ask me to start doing some of the things you heard that I had done in Capernaum. ²⁴ But I'm here to tell you that God's top hands are never recognized on the ranch they grew up on. ²⁵ Listen to this, there were many widows in Israel during the time of Elijah. There was no rain for three and a half years and many were starving. ²⁶ But God didn't send Elijah to care for any of the ladies in Israel, only a widow living in Zarephath in Sidon. ²⁷ And not just that, but there was a lot of people who had rotting skin in Israel during the time God put Elisha in charge. But God only allowed him to heal the Syrian guy called, Naaman. Nobody else in Israel was cured."

²⁸ Now this sure got their hackles up. ²⁹ They jumped him and dragged him to a cliff outside of town to pitch him off of it. ³⁰ But right before they succeeded, he just shook his head and walked right out of the middle of them like it was no big deal. He saddled up and rode off.

Jesus Wallops an Evil Spirit

³¹ Jesus rode off to Capernaum and gave a clinic on how to ride for God on the day of rest. ³² Everyone loved his preaching because it sounded like he knew what he was talking about. ³³ While they were in church, a fellow with a demon shouted, ³⁴ "What're you doing here, Jesus of Nazareth? Have you already to come to destroy us? We know who you really are!"

³⁵ Jesus said, "Shut up and get out of that man." The demon threw the man to the ground as it left.

³⁶ Everyone started talking about these things. "What kind of cowboy can whip evil spirits?" ³⁷ Jesus's reputation was starting to travel far and wide.

Jesus Fixes Many People

³⁸ Jesus left the church and walked over to Simon's house. His mother-in-law was there and she was deathly sick. They told Jesus about her and ³⁹ he walked over to her bed. He stood there for a moment and then told the fever to leave. It did and she immediately got up and began to fix everyone some dinner.

⁴⁰ That evening, people came from all over to be healed by Jesus. He touched them all and every one of them was fixed. ⁴¹ He even got rid of demons for many people and every time the demons shrieked, "You are God's Boy!" They knew he was God's Top Hand and he made all of them be quiet.

⁴² At daylight, he rode off into the country. Everyone was searching for him and when they found him, they tried to talk him into staying with them. ⁴³ But he said, "I've got to go tell everyone the good news. That's why my Dad sent me."

⁴⁴ So off he rode to other churches to give clinics on how to truly ride for God's outfit.

CHAPTER 5

The First Cowboys

One day while Jesus was giving a clinic on the bank of the Sea of Galilee, there were so many people that they were crowding in on him. ² He looked around and saw two empty boats docked by the water's edge. The fishermen were cleaning their nets nearby. ³ Jesus went and got into one of these boats and asked the owner, a fellow named Simon, to push it out a little way into the water. He stood and taught right from the boat so everyone could see and hear him.

⁴ When he was done with his clinic, he told Simon to paddle his boat out into the deep water and let down his nets.

⁵ Simon told him, "Sir, we fished out there all night and didn't catch nothing. But if you say so, we'll go out again." ⁶ When they did, they caught so many fish their nets starting tearing apart. ⁷ They hollered for some help and soon other boat's nets were so full that they too began to nearly sink.

⁸ When Simon Peter finally caught on to what was happening, he hit one knee before Jesus and said, "Lord, you've got to ride away from here. I'm not worthy enough to be within your sight." ⁹ His heart was beating fast with amazement at what he'd just experienced. ¹⁰ James and John, his other partners, were also amazed.

Jesus smiled and said, "Don't be afraid of being with me. You're gonna come with me and I'm going to help you go from catching fish to gathering strays." ¹¹ When the boat got back to shore, they saddled up, left everything behind, and rode off with Jesus.

Jesus Fixes a Fella with Skin Rot

¹² Jesus and his new pards rode up to a little village and got off. A fella ran up to them and fell down on his face as he cried, "Lord, I know you can fix me if you're willing to."

¹³ Jesus showed compassion and did something no religious person would ever do, he reached out and touched the man with skin rot as he said, "I'm willing my friend. Be healed!" The man was immediately healed as if nothing had ever been wrong with him. ¹⁴ Jesus then warned him not to tell anyone what happened. He said, "Go let the preacher look at ya and take along the offering as is required by the code of Moses. This is how you will show everyone what has happened."

¹⁵ But that fella couldn't keep his trap shut. People started looking for Jesus everywhere so he could teach 'em to ride for God and cure their poxes and cancers. ¹⁶ Because of this, Jesus often rode off into the wilderness so he could be alone in prayer.

Jesus Fixes a Crippled Man's Legs

¹⁷ One day Jesus was giving a clinic and some religious know-it-alls and some hypocritical code keepers were listening in. They always sent someone to wherever he was giving a clinic. And on this day, just like every other day, the healing power of God was riding with Jesus.

¹⁸ Some fellas showed up with their buddy lying on a homemade stretcher. They were trying to get him to Jesus, but there were just too many people around. ¹⁹ Not to be dissuaded, the cowboys climbed up on the roof and hauled their paralyzed buddy up there with them. Then they tore back part of the roof and sure enough let him down right in front of Jesus by a well rope. ²⁰ Jesus loved their faith and tenacity and said, "Cowboy, your sins are forgiven."

²¹ But that was just what them religious fellows were waiting on. They jumped up and started making a racket saying, "Who does he think he is? This goes against everything God ever said. Only God can forgive sins, not some two-bit cowboy."

²² Jesus already knew what they were thinking so he asked them, "Why are your hearts so bitter? ²³ Is it easier for me to say that his sins are forgiven or to tell him to get up and walk? ²⁴ Just so you know that I have authority to do both, hold my wine and watch this." Jesus then turned back to the crippled cowboy and said, "Get up, go saddle your horse, and head home."

²⁵ And the cowboy did just like the Boss told him to. ²⁶ No one could believe what they'd just seen and heard.

Jesus Wrangles in Levi

²⁷ Later, Jesus was riding out of town and saw a tax collector named Levi sitting in his tax collecting hut. "Ride with me and I'll teach you how to cowboy for the Boss," Jesus said as he rode by. ²⁸ Levi got up, left everything he had in the hut, and saddled up to ride with Jesus.

²⁹ That evening, Levi invited a bunch of other outlaws to his place to meet Jesus. ³⁰ The religious folks got in a tizzy over this and said to Jesus's cowboys, "Why does your boss associate with lowlifes?"

³¹ Jesus heard them and said, "Healthy cattle don't need roped and doctored—sick ones do. ³² I have not come to gather those who think they are show cattle, but the ones who know they are the mavericks, renegades, and strays. I've come to show them a better way of life riding for me."

Jesus Is Asked about Fasting

³³ One day some people asked Jesus, "John the Baptist's boys are always fasting and praying just like the Pharisees students. Why then are your cowboys always eating, drinking, and smiling?" ³⁴ Jesus answered, "If you're invited to a wedding, the groom doesn't ask his guests to go without. ³⁵ But one day the groom will not be there and that is when his guests will fast and pray."

³⁶ Jesus then told them this story so they could understand, "You don't patch a new saddle with old leather. The old leather is dried up and cracked and it will ruin the new saddle."

³⁷ He continued, "And you don't put new hooch in an old wineskin. The new hooch would burst the old skin and you'd lose both. ³⁸ New hooch goes in a new wineskin. ³⁹ So you see, nobody wants anything new, they just want to stay in the old ways. You can have the new, but you can't put it in the old way of thinking."

CHAPTER 6

Jesus Is Lord of the Day of Rest

On one particular day of rest, Jesus was riding through a farmer's field. His cowboys picked some grains of wheat, rubbed their hands together and ate the kernels. ² Some Pharisees said, "Why are you breaking the Law of the day of rest by picking grain?"

³ Jesus answered, "Don't you remember when the guys who were with David got hungry? ⁴ He went into the church and took the holy bread they use for ceremonies. Now you and I both know that the bread can only be eaten by the preachers, but David gave it to his men."

⁵ Then Jesus told 'em, "The Top Hand is the Lord of the day of rest."

⁶ On another day of rest, Jesus was giving a clinic in a church and a man with a crippled hand was there. ⁷ The Code teachers and the Pharisees were watching to see if Jesus would heal this guy. They wanted something to use against Jesus. ⁸ But Jesus knew what they were thinking and so he said to the man, "Stand up, pard." And the guy stood up. ⁹ Then Jesus asked everyone, "What is right on the day of rest? To do good or to do evil? To help someone or just let them suffer?" ¹⁰ Jesus paused for dramatic effect and made sure everyone was watching as he said, "Show me your hand." When the guy raised his hand up, it was healed.

¹¹ But them religious fellas got a burr under their skin about what Jesus had said and done. They all conspired with each other on how they could take him out.

Jesus Chooses His Cowboys

¹² After all this, Jesus rode up into the mountains to pray. He spent the whole night talking to his Dad. ¹³ The next day, he gathered all his followers to him and announced they were going to be his cowboys: ¹⁴ Simon (Jesus changed it to Pete), his brother Andy, James, John, Phil, Bart, ¹⁵ Matt, Tom, Alphaeus's boy James, Simon the Fanatic, ¹⁶ James's boy Judas, and Judas Iscariot, who would later double-cross his Boss.

Some Blessings and Warnings

¹⁷ Jesus and his cowboys came off the mountain and a large group of other people who rode with them were waiting. They were from all over Judea, Jerusalem, Tyre, and Sidon. ¹⁸ They all came to listen to Jesus's clinics on how to ride for God and be healed of the cankers, cancers, and even their demons. ¹⁹ Everyone mashed in trying to touch him because everyone who did was healed.

²⁰ Jesus looked out over the crowd and said, "Everyone who is poor is blessed, because God has given his outfit to you. ²¹ You people who are hungry are blessed, because it is y'all who will be filled. You folks who are crying are blessed, because one day soon you will smile and laugh."

²² Jesus continued, "It's going to be rough going for those of you who ride for me. You'll be hated, insulted, and even shut out because of your decision. But when this happens, you will be blessed. ²³ Even in the darkest of these moments you can smile because your reward in heaven will outweigh any problem down here. And you aren't alone in your trials and trails. They did the same things to God's hands while they rode down here.

²⁴ "But a bad day is comin' for those of you who are rich, because you've had life so easy. ²⁵ A bad day is comin' for those of you who are full, because one day you're going to starve. A bad day is comin' for those who laugh at misery, because one day you will be bawlin' like a baby.

²⁶ "The worst part will be if everyone says only good things about you. False prophets are never criticized.

Love Your Haters

²⁷ "But to those who are actually listening, I tell you to love your haters. Give a hand to those who hate you. ²⁸ Bless those who cuss you. Pray for those who pick on you. ²⁹ If someone slaps you, don't fight back out of anger. If someone steals your jacket, take him your shirt. ³⁰ Give to anyone who asks you, and if someone takes something that ain't theirs, don't go trying to get it back. ³¹ Treat others the way you want God to treat you. ³² If you're only cordial to nice people, you ain't going to get a cookie for good behavior. Even sinners love folks who love them. ³³ If you only help those who help you, what do you expect? Even sinners do that! ³⁴ If you only loan, and never give, what praise do you think you deserve? Even sinners loan stuff out to get something in return. ³⁵ Love your haters, do good to 'em, and lend to 'em without expecting nothin' in return. Then, and only then, will you be gettin' that big reward from God. To those who do this, God will call them his sons because he is kind, even to those who are ungrateful and live in sin. ³⁶ Dole out mercy, just as the Boss is merciful to you.

A Word about Judgin'

³⁷ "Don't judge others harshly, and God won't judge you harshly. If you go around telling others how guilty they are, then God will point out just how guilty you are. Forgive, and you will be forgiven. ³⁸ What you give is what you will receive. But you will receive even more than you give. Your blessings will overflow in your life and run out into your lap. The way you give to others is the way the Boss will give it back to you."

³⁹ Jesus then told 'em this story, "Can the blind lead the blind in canyon country? No! They'll both fall off a cliff. ⁴⁰ A new cowboy is not better than the top hand who teaches him, but the student can eventually become like him. ⁴¹ Why do you laugh at the way a guy rides when you ain't been on a horse in twenty years? ⁴² You think you can give pointers, but it's him that's ridin', not you. Quit being such a hypocrite! Get the log out of your own eye before you worry about the sand in someone else's eye.

Different Fruits

⁴³ "A good tree don't make bad fruit, and a bad tree don't make good fruit. ⁴⁴ You can tell what kind of tree it is by what kind of fruit it bears. You don't gather mangos from mesquite, and you don't get cantaloupes from cactus. ⁴⁵ Good folks share good things from their hearts. Bad folks wreak havoc out of the havoc they have in their hearts. The words you speak tell the truth about your heart.

Two Kinds of Cowboys

⁴⁶ "Why do you call me Boss, but don't do what I tell you to do? ⁴⁷ Listen as I tell you what it's like when someone rides for me and does what I tell him to. ⁴⁸ That person is like a cowboy who cinches his horse down tight. When he ropes a bull and the bull tries to pull him over, his saddle stays put because he cinched down tight like I told him to. ⁴⁹ But the cowboy who hears me, but keeps on riding with a loose cinch will eventually hit the ground. As soon as he ropes something, his saddle is turned and he falls off."

CHAPTER 7

Healing the Marshal's Deputy

When Jesus was done teaching there, he headed back to Capernaum. ² A marshal from Rome had a deputy who he thought a lot of. This deputy had come down with something and was real close to dying. ³ The marshal heard about the things Jesus had done, so he sent some Jewish leaders to see if Jesus would help. ⁴ They came up to Jesus and said, "We're beggin' you to come help the marshal's deputy. ⁵ The marshal has done a lot for our country and he has helped build some of our churches."

⁶ So Jesus rode off with them. When they neared the marshal's place, he sent a messenger out with a message, "Lord, do not come here. I'm not good enough to have you at my place. ⁷ I'm not even good enough to come out and meet you myself. But I know that all you have to do is say the word and my deputy will be healed. ⁸ I work for someone myself and I also

have people who work for me. If I tell someone to do something, they do it. I can tell someone else to go somewhere and they will go. I don't have to go somewhere in order to know my word will be done."

⁹ Jesus was actually a little shocked by this. He turned to a bunch of people who had followed him and said, "I wish the Jews had this much faith." ¹⁰ The messenger went back to the marshal's house and the deputy had been healed.

Jesus Raises a Son from the Dead

¹¹ The next day Jesus rode off to a village called Nain. Many other people rode along with him. ¹² When they got close, there was a dead man being carried out for burial. He was the only son of a widow whose husband had died many years before. Many accompanied the widow in the funeral march. ¹³ When Jesus saw her, he felt real sorry for her so he said, "Don't cry ma'am." ¹⁴ He rode his horse over to the coffin and placed his hand on it as he said, "Listen to me son, get out of that box." ¹⁵ The lid opened and the young man began to speak to everyone. Then Jesus helped him out and walked him to his grieving mom. ¹⁶ Now this spooked everyone pretty good, but they all gave thanks to the Boss. They all said, "God has sent a Top Hand to help his people out. The Boss loves his people!" ¹⁷ News traveled far and wide about the things Jesus was doing.

Jesus and John the Baptizer

¹⁸ The guys who rode with John the Baptizer filled him in on everything that Jesus was doing while John was in prison. ¹⁹ John sent a couple of them to ask Jesus if he was the Top Hand or should they be expecting another cowboy. ²⁰ When the men found Jesus they said, "John the Baptizer sent us to ask if you are the Top Hand or is it someone else?"

²¹ Now when they asked this, Jesus had been busy curing people and whipping demons. He was even healing blind folks. ²² So when Jesus answered them, he said, "Go back and tell John the things you have seen and heard. Tell him the blind are seeing, the crippled are walking, the mute are talking, skin rot is healing, and the dead are being raised back to life. Tell John this is the good news and it is being preached to 'em. ²³ Anyone who has faith in me won't fall off."

²⁴ John's boys left and Jesus began telling the crowds about him. He said, "Why'd y'all go out into the desert? To see a bush blowing in the wind? ²⁵ No? Then what'd you go out there to see? A man in fine britches and sterling silver covered chaps? Those types of folks live in the houses of kings. ²⁶ So what'd you go out to see? One of God's cowboys? Yes, I'm telling you that John wasn't just one of God's cowboys, he was even more than that! ²⁷ This is the cowboy who the Good Book said would come to clear a path for the Top Hand. ²⁸ I'm telling you straight that there is no one greater than John the Baptizer. But here's the thing, the weakest on God's outfit is even greater than he is."

²⁹ All kinds of people who heard what Jesus said had been baptized by John. ³⁰ Well, not all of them. The religious code keepers and teachers heard Jesus but they refused to listen. They wouldn't be baptized by John and so they didn't get the great promise God had planned for them.

³¹ Then Jesus said, "Let me see if I can explain the folks of this generation. ³² They are like the fans in the stands while the cowboys stand in the arena and talk to them. The cowboys say to them, 'We rode the rough stock for you and got bucked off, but you didn't cheer because you wanted to see us rope. We roped fast and quick, but you didn't clap because no one got bucked off.'

³³ "John didn't drink alcohol and often went without food so he could pray, but y'all said he was evil. ³⁴ But then God's Top Hand comes having a beer with outlaws and whores but y'all say, 'He's a pig and a drunk and he hangs out with lowlifes.' ³⁵ Wisdom is found in the truth, not in someone's opinion.

The Pourin' of the Perfume

³⁶ One of the religious know-it-alls invited Jesus to have supper at his house and he accepted. ³⁷ There was a lady from town who wasn't really known for being a "lady." She heard Jesus was eating at the Pharisee's house and so she showed up with an expensive bottle of perfume. ³⁸ She knelt down by his feet and sobbed at the plight of her life. Her tears fell on Jesus's boots and she wiped his boots clean with her hair. She even kissed them as she poured the perfume on them.

³⁹ The religious know-it-all who'd invited Jesus said under his breath, "If this guy was God's Top

Hand, there is no way he'd let that kind of woman touch him with her hair, much less her lips."

⁴⁰ Jesus heard him and said, "Listen to me, Simon."

"I'm listenin'," he answered.

⁴¹ "There was a top hand who was hired by two different ranchers. One ranch owed the cowboy five hundred dollars and the other ranch owed the cowboy fifty dollars. ⁴² Cattle prices were way down and neither rancher could afford to pay the cowboy, so he told them both not to worry about it and take care of their families. Tell me, which one would have the most respect for the cowboy?"

⁴³ Simon said, "I reckon' it would be the rancher who owed him the five hundred dollars."

Jesus said, "You know he would." ⁴⁴ Then Jesus turned to the woman, but spoke to Simon. "You see this girl? I came here as your guest, but you didn't offer me a rag to wipe the trail dust from my boots, but she cleaned them with her tears and her hair. ⁴⁵ You didn't even welcome me with a brotherly hug, yet she has kissed my boots from the time I got here. ⁴⁶ You didn't offer me anything, but she has put special perfume on my feet. ⁴⁷ She loves much because she has been forgiven much. The one who doesn't need forgiving usually doesn't care that much." ⁴⁸ Then Jesus said to the woman, "Your sins are forgiven."

⁴⁹ The other guests that were there started asking, "Who is this guy who thinks he can forgive sins?"

⁵⁰ Jesus continued to speak to the woman and said, "Your faith has saved you from your sins. Now go live in peace, my lady."

CHAPTER 8

Some of the Cowgirls Who Rode with Jesus

After all this, Jesus rode from ranch to ranch and village to village spreading the good news about God's outfit. The twelve appointed cowboys were with him. ² There were also some women with him who had been cured of various ailments. Among them were Mary, sometimes called Magdalene, who was cured of seven demons; ³ Joanna, whose husband Chuza had been a boss for Herod; Susanna; and a few more women. They are the ones who provided the funds for Jesus and his cowboys.

Seed Plantin'

⁴ One day there was such a large crowd that he used this story to teach them. ⁵ "A farmer went out to plant his fields. As he spread the seed, some fell on the road, and the birds ate it all up. ⁶ Other seed fell next to some rocks where there wasn't much dirt. The seed took root quickly in the shallow soil, but they withered quickly because there was nowhere for the roots to go. ⁷ Other seed fell among the cactus and thistles. They sprouted, but were choked out by the thorns. ⁸ And finally, some seed found good soil and produced a lot of grain. Some of it yielded thirty times as much, some sixty, and still some a hundred times. Whoever has ears should be listening."

⁹ Later on, when they were alone, some of his cowboys asked about the stories. ¹⁰ He told them, "The secret of the Boss's outfit has been given to you. But for the sake of everyone else, I teach with stories. They look, but cannot see. They hear, but they cannot understand. If they could see and understand, they would turn to me and be forgiven."

¹¹ Then Jesus said, "This is what that story means. The farmer spreads God's good news to others. ¹² The seed that fell on the road stands for those who hear the good news, but Satan convinces 'em not to listen. ¹³ The seed in the rocks stands for those who love the good news and immediately act like it changes their whole world. But they don't last long because it was all emotion and no faith. They wither quickly when faced with any kind of adversity. ¹⁴ The seed that fell among the thorns stands for those who hear God's good news, but the words that could save them are choked out by worry, lusting after money, and the desire for materialistic things. ¹⁵ And finally, the seed that found good ground are those people who hear the good news and do something with it."

Lamp Lightin'

¹⁶ Then Jesus asked, "Would you light a lamp and then stick it in your bedroll? Of course not. A lamp is lifted up high so that its light can shine far. ¹⁷ Everything in the dark will eventually be revealed."

¹⁸ Then he added, "Don't let what I'm saying go in one ear and out the other. The closer you listen the more you'll start getting—and when

you start getting it, you'll be given even more. But if you ignore the things I say, you'll end up losing more than you started with."

Real Family

¹⁹ Then Jesus's mom and brothers came to see him, but they couldn't get close because of the big crowd. ²⁰ Someone hollered to him and said, "Your mom and brothers are outside and want to talk to you!"

²¹ He answered back, "My real family are those who ride for the Boss and do what he says."

Faith in the Storm

²² One day, Jesus jumped in a boat and they headed for the other side of the lake. ²³ As they sailed, Jesus put his hat down over his eyes and went to sleep. A huge storm swept in and they were about to be capsized. ²⁴ The disciples were frettin' and fearin' that this was gonna be the end of them all. They finally woke Jesus up by shakin' him and saying, "Jesus, save us! We're gonna drown!"

Jesus got up, stretched, and told the wind to shut up and the waves to sit down . . . and they did. ²⁵ He asked them, "Where is your faith during the storm?"

The hands were shocked, stunned, and amazed and asked, "What kind of hombre is this? Even the wind and the waves listen at him!"

Demons and Pigs

²⁶ The next day, they arrived in the region of the Gerasenes on other side of the lake. ²⁷ They had no more than got both feet on the ground when a naked man possessed by an evil spirit started trotting out of the cemetery to go and talk to them. He lived among the tombs because he wouldn't stay in a house. ²⁸ When he saw Jesus, he ran out and bowed real low in front of him. With an unearthly shriek, he yelled, "Why have you come to stop me, Son of God? By God's good name, please don't torture me." ²⁹ Jesus had already told the spirit to leave the man. When he was put in chains and shackles, he snapped them like paper. No one was strong enough to subdue him. Then the demon would force the man into the desert.

³⁰ Jesus asked, "What do they call you?"

The demon responded, "They call me Legion. We are too many to count." ³¹ They begged Jesus not to send them to hell. ³² There was a herd of pigs grazing nearby and the demonic spirits asked to be sent into the pigs. Jesus told them to go ahead. ³³ The evil spirits rushed in and filled the pigs. Then the herd of two thousand pigs rushed off the bank into the lake and drowned.

³⁴ Now the people who had been taking care of that herd of pigs ran off to tell everyone what had happened. ³⁵ People came running and the first thing they saw was Jesus sitting there talking to the now clothed man who had been possessed, but this time he was in his right mind. ³⁶ Word spread quickly around the Gerasenes about what happened, but the people were afraid and begged Jesus to leave the area.

³⁷ As Jesus threw his saddle back in the boat, ³⁸ the former demon-possessed man asked to ride with him, but Jesus told him to go home. ³⁹ "Go home to your family and tell them what God has done for you today." Off the guy went, telling everyone what Jesus had done for him.

A Church Leader and a Bleeder

⁴⁰ When Jesus returned, a big crowd was waiting on him. ⁴¹ A local church leader named Jairus came up and bowed down in front of Jesus. He begged Jesus to come to his home. ⁴² His twelve-year-old daughter was dying. Jesus left with him at once and was followed by a lot of folks.

⁴³ In the crowd following Jesus was a woman who'd been bleeding for nearly twelve years and no one had been able to help her. ⁴⁴ She came up behind Jesus and touched his vest. Immediately her bleeding stopped.

⁴⁵ Jesus turned and asked, "Who touched me?"

Everyone turned around all innocent like and then Pete said, "Boss, there's a bunch of people. Maybe someone accidentally bumped ya."

⁴⁶ But Jesus replied, "I felt the healing power leave me. Someone touched me on purpose."

⁴⁷ The woman was real scared now and she trembled as she took a knee before Jesus. She then explained why she had touched his vest and how she had immediately been cured.

⁴⁸ Jesus smiled kindly at her and said, "Daughter, your faith in me has healed you. Go in peace!"

⁴⁹ While Jesus was still talking to her, someone came running up from the church leader's home and told Jairus, "Your daughter is dead. No need to bring Jesus anymore."

⁵⁰ When Jesus heard the man, he told Jairus, "It's never too late to believe that she will get better." ⁵¹ They went to the house and Jesus didn't let anyone go in except the girl's parents, Pete, John, and James. ⁵² Everyone was bawling and squalling, but Jesus said, "Why are y'all carryin' on like this? She's just sleeping."

⁵³ This was the last straw for some of these people. They all started mocking him and laughing at him because they knew she was dead. ⁵⁴ But Jesus had the last laugh when he walked over, held her hand, and said, "Get up, little lady."

⁵⁵ She opened up her eyes and got up at once. Jesus told her parents to get her something to eat. ⁵⁶ They just stood there for a second with a dumbfounded look, but Jesus told them not to tell anyone what happened as he walked out the door.

CHAPTER 9

Jesus Sends His Hands to Gather

Jesus called his twelve cowboys to him and told 'em to listen up. He gave 'em all power to whip demons and cure cankers and cancers. ² He then sent them out to tell everyone the good news about God's outfit. ³ He told 'em, "Just take what you need and nothing else. Don't take a pack horse or even saddle bags. Don't stick any money into the bottom of your boots for emergency and don't even take your slicker. ⁴ When people are glad to see you, stay at their place until you leave. ⁵ If people are unfriendly toward you, then leave that ranch and shake the dust off your boots, so you don't spread their hate around."

⁶ So Jesus dropped 'em off at different points on the first gatherin', and they gave clinics on the good news and how to ride in God's outfit. The cowboys healed folks from all over.

Herod's Question

⁷ When Herod, the fellow who ran the area of Galilee, heard about all these things that were happening, he started getting a sinking feeling because folks were saying that John the Baptizer had come back to life. ⁸ Still other rumors were saying that Elijah had returned. The stories also included that it was another long-dead cowboy of God who was doing all of this. ⁹ When receiving a report one day, Herod stated, "I cut the Baptizer's head off. But if it ain't him doing all these miracles, then who could it be?" And Herod wanted to see for himself this man named Jesus.

The Five Thousand Feeding

¹⁰ The cowboys all returned and were telling the tales of the trail. They rode off by themselves to a place near Bethsaida so Jesus could talk to 'em. ¹¹ Word got around that Jesus and his boys were out there and a whole mess of people showed up. Jesus welcomed them and gave them some clinics on how to ride for God. He even healed a bunch of the sick.

¹² Late in the evening, the twelve cowboys came up to Jesus and said, "Send these people home so they can get some vittles. There ain't nothing to eat around here."

¹³ But Jesus said, "Y'all feed them."

The twelve cowboys all looked at each other, and one of them said, "All we got is five biscuits and two pieces of fish. You want us to lope into town and grab about five thousand cans of beans or what? ¹⁴ That's how many it'll take to feed all these folks."

Jesus smiled and said, "Have folks sit down in bunches of about fifty."

¹⁵ The cowboys tallied the groups and did as the Boss said. ¹⁶ When this was done, Jesus took the five biscuits and two pieces of fish and looked up to heaven as he said grace. He then tore them all apart, and the twelve cowboys put the pieces in their hats to pass around. ¹⁷ Them hats never run out of vittles, and everyone had their fill. When they got done, the twelve hats were still full.

Pete's Right Response

¹⁸ On another occasion, the twelve cowboys came to Jesus as he prayed alone. When they walked up, he asked them, "Who does everyone think I am?"

¹⁹ "Some say you are John the Baptizer," one of 'em said. "Others claim you are Elijah or one of the other great cowboys of God from long ago."

²⁰ "What about y'all?" he asked them. "Who do you think I am?"

Pete said, "You are God's Top Hand. The one who will gather us and save us from the coming brush fire."

Jesus Tells 'Em about His Death

²¹ Jesus told all of 'em not to tell anyone what Pete had just said. ²² He then told 'em, "God's Top Hand will suffer terribly at the hands of the religious institution. They will kill him, but three days later he will come over the hill, riding back from the dead."

²³ And then he spoke up for all to hear. "If you want to ride with me, you've got to quit riding for yourself, sacrifice your own desires, and follow me. ²⁴ If you try to protect your own life, you'll lose it, but if you are willing to lose your life for me, you will find it. ²⁵ What does a man gain if he has everything in the world, but loses himself in the process? ²⁶ If you are ashamed of my brand, then God's Top Hand will shut the gate to God's outfit on you. ²⁷ I'm telling you straight that there are some here now who will not die before they have seen God's outfit."

The Top Hand Is Revealed

²⁸ About a week later, Jesus took Pete, James, and John up on a hill to pray. ²⁹ While he was praying, Jesus's face and clothes became whiter than the sun. ³⁰ All of a sudden, Moses and Elijah were there talking to Jesus. ³¹ They were as bright as Jesus, and they talked with him about God's plan for him to die in Jerusalem. ³² Pete and the other two had been napping while Jesus was praying. When they woke up and saw what was happening, ³³ Pete said, "Boss, we're all tickled pink about being here on this special day. We will build three campfires: one for you, one for Moses, and one for Elijah." (Pete tended to spout off at the mouth when he didn't know what to say or do.)

³⁴ While his mouth was still moving, a cloud came across and cast its shadow on everyone. It was ominous looking, and ³⁵ a voice came from the cloud saying, "This is my boy who I have chosen—listen to him."

³⁶ Then all was silent and it was just Jesus and his three cowboys. The boys didn't tell anyone what they had seen until much later.

Jesus and the Demon-Possessed Boy

³⁷ The next day, they rode up to a crowd of people, and ³⁸ a man hollered out to Jesus, "Lord, please help my boy!" he said. ³⁹ "A spirit has attacked him, and he has fits and suffers terribly. He falls into the fire and the water trough.

⁴⁰ I took him to some of your cowboys, but they couldn't help him."

⁴¹ Jesus said, "Good grief! Where is all of y'alls faith? How long am I gonna have to stick around and hold your hands? I don't know how much more I can tolerate. Bring that boy over here."

⁴² Jesus looked at the boy and told the demon that was possessing him to get out. The demon knocked the boy down one final time and then it was gone. From that moment, the boy was fine. ⁴³ Everyone was amazed at the power of God.

Jesus Talks about His Death

Everyone was still jabbering about the things Jesus was doing when he said to his cowboys, ⁴⁴ "Don't forget what I'm about to say. The Top Hand is going to be betrayed and given over to the religious institution." ⁴⁵ They all looked at each other questioningly, but nobody said anything. God didn't want them to understand it yet, and so they were afraid to ask him what he meant.

Who's the Best

⁴⁶ Later, a squabble broke out amongst the twelve cowboys about who was the best hand in their crew. ⁴⁷ Jesus heard them, and called a little kid over next to him and ⁴⁸ said, "Whoever loves a child like this loves me. And if you love me, you love the Boss who sent me. The best hand among you will be the one who thinks of themselves the least."

⁴⁹ Then John spoke up, "Boss, we seen a fellow driving demons out in your name, but we put a stop to that because he doesn't ride in our crew."

⁵⁰ "Don't do that," Jesus said. "If they ain't riding against us then they are riding for us."

The Crossbred Samaritans Refuse Jesus

⁵¹ Now the time was gettin' close to when Jesus would be taken up to heaven, and they headed out for the final showdown in Jerusalem. ⁵² He sent some folks on ahead to a village in Samaria to get a room for the night. ⁵³ But when the village heard Jesus's destination was Jerusalem, they refused him service. ⁵⁴ After hearing this, James and John asked Jesus, "Boss, do you want us to call down fire from heaven and wipe these sorry people from the face of the earth?"

⁵⁵ Jesus told them to quit their foolish thinking. ⁵⁶ They just rode on by and stayed at another village.

Ridin' for the Brand

[57] As they were headed for Jerusalem, a cowboy came running up and said, "I'll ride with you wherever you go, Boss!"

[58] Jesus looked down from his mount and said, "Coyotes have dens and birds have nests, but the Boss's Son doesn't have any place to call home." [59] Jesus looked at another cowboy standing nearby and said, "What about you? You want to ride for the brand?"

But the man said, "As soon as my father dies, I will ride with you wherever you go."

[60] Jesus told him, "Let the dead bury the dead. You ride out and gather folks for the brand."

[61] Still someone else hollered out, "I'll ride for ya Boss! Let me go tell my family goodbye, and I'll be right back."

[62] Jesus shook his head sadly, "Anyone who saddles up, but looks back at what they are leaving, is not fit to ride for the brand."

CHAPTER 10

Jesus Sends Out the Day Workers

Then Jesus found seventy other day workers willing to ride for him and sent them out in pairs to prepare all the places he would go. [2] He told them, "There's plenty of strays to be gathered, but there ain't many cowboys. Pray to the Lord of the roundup for cowboys to come help. [3] Go now and ride, but understand, I am sending y'all out like sheep among the wolves. [4] Don't take a money pouch, no saddlebags, no extra boots, and don't talk to anyone on the road. [5] When you get to a house, first say, 'May peace fill this place.' [6] If someone who wants that too lives there, then it will happen. If not, then your gift will be returned, and peace will leave with you. [7] Stay there until you finish your job. Let them take care of you because the worker deserves his wages. Don't be moving around to other houses. [8] If you head into a town, and they welcome you, then eat the vittles they provide. [9] Heal all the people who are sick and tell them, 'God's outfit is close!'

[10] "But if someone doesn't want you in their town, then walk right out in the street and say, [11] 'We are shaking your dust off our boots because y'all didn't welcome us. Your fate is in your hands now. God's outfit is right outside the gates.' [12] I'm telling y'all that even Sodom will be better off when Judgment Day arrives than these towns that do not welcome you.

[13] "You're gonna regret your choices, you cities of Chorazin and Bethsaida. If I'd done the miracles I did for you in Tyre or Sidon, they would have changed their sorry ways and already be saddled up and riding for God's outfit. They would be wearing burlap, and ashes would cover their heads in remorse for their wicked ways. [14] I'm being honest! Tyre and Sidon, cities that ain't even in Israel, will be better off than some of our own. [15] And don't think I didn't notice you Capernaum. Will you get buckles in heaven? Nope! Most will end up in the trash fire."

[16] Then Jesus said to his crew of seventy cowboys, "If they listen to you, then they will listen to me. If they shun you, then they will shun me, too. And if they shun me, then they shun the Boss who sent me to save everyone."

[17] When the seventy day workers got back, they were all happy and said, "Boss, even the demons did what we said in your name."

[18] "Yep," Jesus said. "I watched when Satan fell from heaven. It was like a lightning bolt from the sky! [19] But listen close, I have given you authority over all the powers of darkness. You can even trample over snakes and scorpions without injury. [20] But don't pat yourselves on the back because of these things, be happy that you are in God's tally book."

Jesus Offers up Thanks

[21] At that moment, the Holy Spirit filled Jesus with joy, and he prayed, "Boss, you're Lord over heaven and this big ball of dirt and water. Thank you for hiding the truth from those who think they are smart and showing it to those who have a childlike faith in you. I know this was your plan, Dad, and I know you like it."

[22] Then Jesus turned his attention back to everyone and said, "My Dad has given me everything. No one knows him but me and those cowboys who I choose to reveal him to."

[23] Later on when they were all alone, he told his twelve cowboys, "If only others were as blessed as y'all to see the things that you've seen. [24] Even the old-time prophets and kings wished they could have seen just a smidge of what y'all have laid eyes on. They dreamed of hearing the things that y'alls ears have heard."

The Good Deed of the Half-Breed

25 One day, a religious expert tried to test Jesus with this question, "Boss, what'll I have to do to live forever?"

26 Jesus replied, "What does the code of Moses say? What's your take on it?"

27 They guy answered, "Love the Boss with all your heart, strength, mind, and soul. And also take care of your neighbor better than you take care of yourself."

28 Jesus said, "Well done! There, you have your answer."

29 But that fellow was up to no good and asked, "But who is my neighbor?"

30 Jesus sat down and began a story, "A Jewish fellow was riding down the trail from Jerusalem to Jericho and was bushwhacked by outlaws. They stripped all his clothes, beat him nearly to death, and left him for the buzzards beside the trail.

31 "Then a Jewish preacher rode by and saw the plight of the man and instead of helping him, he just side passed his pony to the other side of the trail and rode on. **32** Then a church worker rode by and stopped and looked, but kept right on riding.

33 "Then one of those despised half-breed Jews saw the man and felt sorry for him. **34** The Samaritan covered him and did what he could for his wounds. He then lifted the guy onto his horse and took him to a hotel. The Samaritan stayed in the room with him and cared for him. **35** The next day, he went downstairs and handed the hotel manager two silver coins and said, 'Take care of the fellow in my room. If his tab runs over, I'll come back and pay it.'

36 "Now which of the three people who rode by the fellow was the neighbor?" Jesus asked sternly.

37 The guy replied, "The one who took care of him."

Jesus said, "You do the same."

The Difference in Mary and Martha

38 Jesus and his twelve cowboys rode along and finally stopped in a village. A lady named Martha invited him to her house. **39** She had a sister named Mary who sat at the feet of Jesus and drank in every word as he talked.

40 But Martha worked herself into a tizzy and went and asked Jesus, "Do you even care that I'm bustin' my butt for y'all and Mary is just sitting there? Tell her to get up and help."

41 But Jesus said, "Whoa, Martha! Quit worrying and fussin'. **42** Mary is the one who is making the better choice right now, and I'm sure not going to take that away from her."

CHAPTER 11

The Top Hand's Prayer

Jesus was praying one day, and one of the twelve cowboys came up and asked him to teach them how to pray.

2 Jesus said, "This is how you should pray, 'Dad, there is no name like yours. **3** Let your outfit get here soon. Give us what we need to eat and **4** forgive us of our sorry ways. We will also forgive others who are sorry toward us. And keep us from hanging up in the stirrup of temptation.'"

5-7 Then he gave them a clinic on prayer and said, "Let's say you eat the last of the food you have in your house and some company shows up. You run over to the neighboring ranch and knock on the door. A cowboy opens it and asks what you want so late, and you ask to borrow a bag of beans to feed your visitor. He shuts the door in your face and tells you to leave because everyone is asleep. **8** But I'll say this, if you keep knocking on that door, he will give you a bag of beans just to make you go away. Persistence and boldness are the keys to prayer.

9 "So I'm telling you to knock on the Boss's door until he answers and don't go away until he gives you what you need. **10** Everyone who asks will get it, and everyone who knows where to look will find it. You knock, and the Boss will answer the door.

11 "If you're a dad and your son asks for some jerky, are you going to hand him a live rattlesnake? **12** If your kid asks for eggs in his sandwich are you going to put a scorpion in there? **13** You see, evil and selfish hearts control y'all, but you still know how to take care of your kids. If this is so, how much will your actual Dad in heaven take care of his kids with the Holy Spirit when they need help?"

Jesus Accused of Ridin' for the Enemy

14 One day Jesus was kickin' a demon out of a guy, and when it was gone, he began to talk. **15** Some folks started a rumor that said, "He can kick demons out of people because he rides for the devil." [16] Many folks wanted more proof and more miracles to prove Jesus had come from God.

[17] Jesus was not oblivious to their thinking. He told 'em, "Any outfit that can't get along will fail. A crew that fights will fall apart. [18] You say I ride for the devil, but if I'm fightin' the one I ride for, how can his crew succeed? [19] And if I'm ridin' for Satan, then what about your people who cast out demons too? Are they ridin' for the devil also? If they hear what you're saying they ain't gonna like it much, [20] but if I am working for the Boss in heaven, then his outfit has arrived on earth. [21] When a cowboy rides shotgun over his herd, everything is safe. [22] That is until someone sneaks up on him and takes his weapon, his horse, and all his herd.

[23] "Anyone who doesn't ride for me is against me. If you don't gather with me, then you are scattering it.

[24] "When an evil spirit leaves someone, it goes out searching for someone else in the desert. [25] If it finds no one, it will come back to the one it left. [26] When it finds him, if he is not riding for the Boss, the evil spirit will bring seven more, and they will possess him again. He'll be worse off than he was before."

[27] While he was talkin', a lady hollered out, "Bless your momma and the breasts that fed you!"

[28] Jesus replied, "But even more blessed is the one who listens to what I say and does it."

Jonah's Miracle

[29] More and more folks crowded around Jesus as he talked, "All those ridin' for themselves keep asking me to do more and more miracles. But the only miracle they will see will be the same one the Boss did for Jonah. [30] He was dead three days and then came back. This miracle was to prove to the evil people in Nineveh that Jonah came from the Boss. God will do the same thing for his Top Hand. [31] The Queen of Sheba traveled all the way from her foreign land to listen to the wisdom of Solomon. On Judgment Day, she will condemn y'all because now there is one even wiser than he was. [32] Even the people of Nineveh will talk bad about y'all on Judgment Day. They listened and did what Jonah told them to, but there is someone greater than even Jonah here, but y'all won't turn from your sorry ways.

Shine a Light

[33] "No one lights an oil lamp at night and then puts a hat over it. They will put it on a high shelf so that it can shine for everyone to see.

[34] "Your eye is the oil lamp for your body. When your eyes are open to the truth, your whole body shines with light. [35] But if you are only looking for the ways of the world to please you, then your eye is squeezed shut, and no light is within you. [36] If your body is full of light, your whole life will shine bright and be blessed."

Jesus Sets Religious Leaders Straight

[37] After Jesus was gone, a religious leader invited him over to his house for lunch. Jesus accepted the invite and went with him. [38] When they walked in, the Pharisee was surprised that Jesus didn't wash his hands before eating.

[39] Jesus knew what the man was thinking and said, "You religious leaders make sure you look squeaky clean on the outside, but inside you are full of greed and wickedness. [40] You're all a bunch of fools. If the Boss made the outside, didn't he make the inside too? [41] Clean up the inside by giving yourself in service to the poor and the outside will match.

[42] "Y'all religious people are going to get what's coming to you. Y'all make sure and tithe even the money that comes from your herb patches, but you don't even realize that sticking up for the less fortunate and loving God are just as important. Don't pick and choose what you are supposed to do. Do it all.

[43] "Y'all religious people are going to get what's coming to you. Y'all sure like the box seats at the rodeo and for everyone to know your name at the feed store. [44] Y'all religious people are going to get what's coming to you. Y'all are like septic tanks in the ground. There's green grass on top that people admire, but they don't know the filth that lies underneath."

[45] One expert on the code of Moses said, "When you talk like this, you are insulting us too!"

[46] "Y'all experts on the code of Moses will get what's coming to you too! You are good at pointing fingers, but you won't lift a finger to help anyone. [47] You're gonna get what's coming to ya! You build statues honoring the cowboys of God from the past, but you act like your ancestors who killed them in the first place. [48] By acting

like them, you agree with what they did. **49** This is why our wise Boss said, 'I'll send them cowboys and guides, but the people will just hurt them and even kill them.' **50-51** So all the people living now will be held responsible for all the murders of all the prophets from Zechariah to Abel. Yep, this generation will certainly pay the fiddler.

52 "Y'all experts on the code of Moses will get what's coming to you! You took the key to knowledge and hid it so no one else could get it, not even yourselves."

53 When Jesus walked away, the religious leaders and the experts on the code of Moses tried to get under his skin with questions and accusations. **54** They wanted to trap him, but he didn't take the bait.

CHAPTER 12

A Heed against Hypocrisy

While all this was happening, many thousands of people had shown up to see and hear Jesus. There were so many people around that some were getting crushed. Jesus spoke to his twelve cowboys amidst the throng of folks saying, "Watch out for the religious leader's hypocrisy· **2** It's like yeast in the dinner rolls. The time is coming when there will be no more secrets. **3** Things whispered behind the hay will be shouted in the streets. Things mumbled under your breath will be blasted from the rooftops.

4 "My friends, don't be afraid of those who can kill your body. When you die, it is over in a second. **5** But listen, be afraid of the One who has power over your soul. We should fear the Boss because he is the only one who has the authority and power to throw you in the trash fire which is forever. He's the One you should be bowing down to.

6 "But before you start thinking the Boss is against you, consider this, what do a few birds cost—two cents at the most? But God doesn't even forget about these little birds. **7** The Boss has numbered the hairs on your head, so you don't have to be afraid. You are worth more than all the birds in the world. **8** I'm telling you the truth. If you ride for me in public down here, I will show the angels in heaven that you have eternal life in God's outfit because you are in my tally book. **9** But if you shun me down here, I'm going to shun you in heaven. **10** I will forgive everyone

and everything except the person who denies me and the power of the Holy Spirit.

11 "And when you are arrested or put on trial, don't try to work up a defense strategy. **12** When the time comes for you to speak, the Holy Spirit will give you the words to say."

The Folly of Material Wealth

13 Someone in the crowd hollered out, "Boss, tell my brother to split the cow herd with me that our father left us!"

14 Jesus turned to him and said, "I'm not here to settle your petty disputes." **15** Then he said to everyone, "Beware of the greed of material wealth. True life cannot be measured by what you have in your pastures."

16 Then he told them a story, "A rich man had a fine ranch that produced fine cattle. **17** He thought to himself, 'I don't have enough grass for all my cows. I wonder what I should do?' **18** Then he thought, 'I know! I'll sell this small ranch and buy a bigger one. Then I will be the biggest rancher around. **19** I'll be able to sit back and admire all the things I have accomplished and obtained! I'll spend my days with wine, women, and song.

20 "But God said to the rancher, 'You've been a fool, cowboy! You're gonna die tonight, and someone else will get everything you've worked so hard for.' **21** So the moral of the story is not to waste your life on things, but store up treasure in heaven by a genuine ride with the Boss."

Quit Frettin'

22 Then Jesus spoke again to his twelve cowboys, "So don't fret about what you will eat or wear. **23** True life is more than feeding your stomach and clothing your body. **24** Look at the crows. They don't farm or ranch. They don't even have a barn to store their grain in, but the Boss still gives them food. And you are more loved than crows. **25** Can frettin' about something add even one minute to a day? **26** And if frettin' can't even fix a small problem, why are you wastin' all that time frettin' about the big stuff? **27** Think about the flowers you see while ridin' through your pastures. They don't do anything to clothe themselves in such beauty. But I'm telling you the truth that even the wise King Solomon could not spend all the money in the world and dress as beautiful as they. **28** So if the Boss takes such care with flowers that are here one day and gone the next, how much more will he care for you? Why do you doubt God so much?

²⁹ "Don't worry about where your food and drink comes from. These things are trivial compared to the more important things in life. ³⁰ People who don't know or trust in God worry and fret about things like these. But the Boss already knows all your needs and will provide for you. ³¹ You just saddle up and ride for him, and he will take care of all your needs. ³² Don't worry, cowboys. The Boss wants to take care of you.

³³ "Sell everything you own and give the money to those who need it more. This way you will be investing in your eternal future. This type of investment will never lose its value or fall out of a hole in your pocket. Down here, money can be stolen and even lost, ³⁴ but wherever you keep your treasure, that's where your heart will remain.

Don't Let Your Guard Down

³⁵ "Keep your britches on and your boots by your bed. Keep a light burning in the barn so you can catch your horse at a moment's notice. ³⁶ You need to be ready when the Boss calls. ³⁷ The cowboys who are waiting on his return will receive a magnificent reward. I'm telling you the truth when I say that the Boss will give the cowboys new clothes, sit them down at the big table, and give them food to eat. ³⁸ Now the Boss might get back in the middle of the night or just before daylight, but when most everyone has given up, that's when the Boss will return. A reward will be waiting on the cowboy who is ready to ride.

³⁹ "I mean, if you knew someone was going to steal your saddle, you would wait up and keep him from taking it. You wouldn't just let him grab your rig! ⁴⁰ But you must also keep this same diligence when waiting on the Boss, for God's Top Hand will come when you least expect him."

⁴¹ Pete asked, "Are you talking about everyone being ready or just us?"

⁴² Jesus said, "A top hand is a cowboy who has shown himself to be faithful in the little things as well as the big. The boss is always looking for top hands to lead and teach other cowboys. ⁴³ A top hand will get an excellent reward for the integrity he shows while the boss is away. ⁴⁴ If he does well, the boss will put him in charge of the whole ranch. ⁴⁵ A cowboy who thinks he is top

hand material, but mistreats other people and then thinks about nothing except eating, drinking, and getting drunk, ⁴⁶ this cowboy will be punished severely when the boss returns. He'll be thrown off the ranch and told never to return.

⁴⁷ "And the cowboy who knows what he should be doing, but isn't prepared or ready to do the job will also be punished. ⁴⁸ Now if someone doesn't know what they are supposed to do, but makes a mistake anyway, they will just be talked to. Top notch work will be required from top hands. And when more is given, more will be expected."

Jesus Will Split the Herd

⁴⁹ Jesus said, "I have come to start the prescribed burn over the dead patches of this world. ⁵⁰ My upcoming baptism will not be in cool water, but I will suffer a terrible agony until I have paid the price for all. ⁵¹ Did you think that I came to bring peace? No, I have come to split the herd and reveal people's true hearts. ⁵² Now families will be torn apart because of me. ⁵³ Fathers will be against sons and mothers will be against their daughters. Children will rebel against their parents and in-laws will all hate each other—all on account of some riding for me and others choosing not to."

⁵⁴ Then Jesus turned to the crowd of people and said, "When you see the clouds building, you know there is rain coming. And you are right. ⁵⁵ When the south wind starts howling, you know it's gonna be hot. And it will be. ⁵⁶ So how can you be so foolish as to not see what is happening right here in front of you? You can see the signs and make accurate predictions, but in this instance, you are all as blind as bats. ⁵⁷ Why can't you see what is right in front of you? ⁵⁸ I mean, if someone is trying to take you to court because you did something wrong, wouldn't it be better to try to make amends before the court hearing? If you don't, you will be found guilty and thrown in jail. ⁵⁹ When that happens, you won't get out until all restitution has been paid in full."

CHAPTER 13

Changing Who You Ride For

About this time, some people asked Jesus if it was because of sin that God had allowed Pilate to kill some people from Galilee who were making sacrifices at the main church in Jerusalem. ² Jesus answered, "Do you think they were allowed to die because their sin was greater than someone else's? ³ Absolutely not! I guarantee you that was not the case. But if you don't quit riding for yourselves and start riding for the Boss, y'all will die too. ⁴ What about all those people who tragically died when the tower in Siloam fell on them? Was it because of their sin that they died? ⁵ No, it wasn't. But if you don't change your sorry ways, you too will all die."

⁶ Then Jesus told 'em this tale, "A rancher had a cow in his herd that hadn't calved in three years. ⁷ He told the top hand, 'For three years now I've let this cow stay on the ranch, but she hasn't calved yet. Ship her off. Why should she eat green grass and not give anything in return?'

⁸ "The top hand replied, 'Boss, give her one more year. I'll check her teeth and give her some vitamins and do everything I can to be sure she is healthy. ⁹ Maybe next year she will calve. Don't give up on her yet, but if she still hasn't calved by next year, we will sell her off.'"

Jesus Fixes the Crippled

¹⁰ Not long after, Jesus was giving a clinic in one of the churches. This particular day was the day of rest. ¹¹ A woman who was possessed by an evil spirit was there. This spirit had her hunched over for nearly twenty years. The poor lady couldn't stand up straight. ¹² Jesus saw her and felt sorry for her condition. He told her to come to him and said, "My dear, I am setting you free." ¹³ Jesus placed his hands on her, and she immediately stood up straight and gave thanks to the Boss.

¹⁴ The church leader stood up and clearly had his phylacteries in a wad. He said, "There are six days when you can come for healing. Come on one of those days, not the day of rest. It is a holy day, and no work should be done, not even healing."

¹⁵ Then Jesus fired back, "You sir are nothing but a no-good hypocrite. Don't you unhalter your horse or let the milk cow out to graze of the day of rest? Don't you water your animals? ¹⁶ Here stands one of Abraham's children who Satan has been tormenting for eighteen years. Why is she less than animals? Shouldn't she be set free also—even on the day of rest?"

¹⁷ The crowd that had gathered erupted in applause, and the hypocritical church leader and his minions skulked away in shame.

Mustard and Sourdough

¹⁸ Then Jesus asked, "What's God's outfit like? How can I explain it to you? ¹⁹ It's like a tiny mustard seed that someone plants in a garden and then it grows to become a nice big tree that the birds use for nesting."

²⁰ Again he asked, "What is God's outfit really like? ²¹ It's like a little sourdough starter that works its way through the dough to make it better than before."

The Ranch Gate

²² Jesus continued teaching in villages and cow camps on his way to Jerusalem. ²³ Someone once asked him, "How many will end up on God's ranch?"

He replied, ²⁴ "You need to try hard to get on with God's outfit before it's too late. Many will want on, but only a few will be chosen. ²⁵ When the boss shuts the gate, it will be too late. You will stand outside and beg and plead, but the boss will say, 'I will not. You're not one of my cowboys.'

²⁶ "Then you'll say, 'But I went to one of your clinics and even ate with your cowboys.'

²⁷ "And he will say, 'Get away from me. I offered you a place a long time ago, and you refused. The gate has been open all this time for anyone who wanted to come in, but now it's too late. Get away from here and get away from me.' ²⁸ When you finally realize the ranch you will spend eternity on, you will be in such severe pain that you will cry out and gnash your teeth as you suffer endlessly. You'll look across the fence and see Abraham, Isaac, and Jacob, and all of the old cowboys who rode for God. They'll be happy on God's outfit, but you'll never step foot on it. ²⁹ People from all over the world will be on God's outfit. ³⁰ But understand this, the cowboys who showed up last will be the first to see God and the ones who came in first will be riding drag."

Jerusalem Beware

³¹ As this was happening, some Pharisees told him, "You better lope on out of here if you want to live. Herod Antipas has put a bounty on your head."

³² Jesus said, "Go tell that old fox that I will

keep on whipping demons and healing people as I head toward Jerusalem. [33] None of y'all will stop me from doing what the Boss has sent me to do. Besides, Jerusalem is where God's cowboys go to die."

[34] "Jerusalem, old Jerusalem. She is the city that kills God's cowboys and his messengers. I've wanted to put her calves in one pen and protect them, but you are not willing. [35] Your house is forgotten, and you won't see me until you say, 'Here comes God's Top Hand who comes in the name of the Boss.'"

CHAPTER 14

Jesus Riles up the Religious

On one of the Days of Rest, Jesus went to eat at the home of one the leaders of the Pharisees. Many people were watching him closely to see what Jesus would do. [2] A man approached Jesus who had arms and legs that were swollen up like a bloated cow. [3] Jesus asked the religious leaders and teachers of Moses's code, "Does the code of Moses allow healing on the day of rest or not?"

[4] Everyone was scared to answer. Jesus shook his head and then healed the man and sent him away. [5] Then he turned back to them and said, "If any of you had a child who fell into a well, wouldn't you get them out—even if it was on the day of rest? Wouldn't you do it even if it was a donkey?"

[6] But nobody said a word.

Cowboy Manners

[7] As people were sitting down to eat, Jesus noticed how everyone was trying to get the best spots near the head of the table. Jesus said, [8-10] "When you are eating at a branding and lunch is served, don't run in and try to sit at the table with the rancher. You take your plate and go outside to eat. It would be much better for you to have the rancher come outside and insist that you sit with him rather than him have to ask you to go sit outside. Then you'd be all kinds of embarrassed and you'd have brought it on yourself. [11] A wannabe who tries to pass himself off as a top hand will be humiliated, but the top hand who doesn't mind sitting outside will be given a place of honor."

[12] Jesus then turned to the host and said, "When you have a BBQ, don't invite those who you know can do something for you. Don't invite your friends or relatives who will return the favor. [13] Instead, invite the less fortunate. Invite the poor, hungry, crippled, and blind. [14] Then you will know that when the Boss picks his crew, you will be rewarded for inviting those who couldn't do anything for you."

The Great Big BBQ

[15] While listening to Jesus, a man hollered out, "It sure would be a blessing to attend a BBQ at the Big Boss's place!"

[16] Jesus said, "There was once a rancher who was having a great big BBQ. [17] When everything was ready, he sent his cowboy to town and invited all the people from church. [18] But they all had an excuse as to why they couldn't come. One church guy said, 'I just bought some land and need to go check it out. Please offer my apologies.'

[19] "Another church guy said, 'I just bought a team of horses, and I want to try them out on my wagon. Tell him thanks anyway for the invite.'

[20] "And still another said, 'I just got married, and we have plans. Please accept our apologies.'

[21] "The cowboy went back to the ranch with all the denials and excuses from the church people. The rancher was furious and said, 'Go get the rough cowboys and the crippled. Gather up the lame, the blind, and the poor.'

[22] "The cowboy went out and did like the boss told him. He came back and said, 'I did what you said, but we've still got food left.'

[23] "So the rancher said, 'Bring the mavericks and the mistresses, the whores, and the harlots. Tell the outlaws and rabble-rousers they are welcome. I want their bellies, and my ranch, full. [24] All those I initially invited are no longer welcome and will not taste the food I have to offer.'"

The Cost of the Ride

[25] One day, Jesus was riding along, and a large group of people were following. He turned around and said, [26] "If y'all want to ride with me, you must prove you love me more than your mother, your father, your wife, and even your children. And most of all? You must love me more than your own life. If you don't, you can't saddle up with my crew and me. [27] You've

got to be willing to die for the brand if you're gonna ride for the brand.

²⁸ "But don't say you will ride for me until you've tallied the toll it will take on you. I mean, you're not going to buy a bunch of cattle that you don't have grass for. ²⁹ Otherwise your cattle will starve, and people will laugh at you. ³⁰ They would say, 'There goes that greenhorn who doesn't know cows from caterpillars!'

³¹ "Or what general would go to war without sitting down to figure out if his ten thousand men could beat the army of twenty thousand he would be fighting? ³² If he sees that he can't win, wouldn't he try to negotiate peace before the war begins? ³³ You best realize that I am asking for everything when you ride for me, not just your weekends or a little of your wages. I require everything. Anything less than that and you'll never make it.

³⁴ "A salty cowboy is one who isn't afraid to go after rank cattle. But if he loses his salt and becomes lazy and only thinks about himself, then he is no longer good for the ranch. ³⁵ If he won't do the job, then he will be fired and kicked out. If you've got ears, you better be using them to listen."

CHAPTER 15

The Lost Calf

One day Jesus was talkin' to a bunch of tax collectors and outcasts. ² The religious know-it-alls and teachers of Moses's code started complaining, "This man would rather hang out with lowlifes than good folk!"

³ So Jesus said, ⁴ "If a cowboy has a hundred head of cattle and one calf goes missing, what would he do? Wouldn't he leave the ninety-nine and go find the one that was lost? ⁵ And when he finds it, won't he pull it up into the saddle with him and carry it home? ⁶ When he gets home, he will tell all the other cowboys that he found it and everyone will be relieved and glad. ⁷ In the same way, there is more happiness in heaven about the Top Hand bringing in one stray than there is about the ninety-nine that were already there.

The Lost Coin

⁸ "Or suppose a lady only had ten silver coins to her name, and she lost one. Wouldn't she search all over the house until she found it?

Wouldn't she continue to look until it was found? ⁹ Then when she found it, she would tell all her family that she'd found it and they would celebrate with her. ¹⁰ In the same way, there is happiness in heaven when one that is lost is found."

The Lost Son

¹¹ Jesus continued with his examples, "Suppose a rancher had two sons. ¹² The younger cowboy told his dad, 'Give me my share of the ranch now. I don't want to wait around for you to die.' The rancher did as the son asked and gave him what his half was worth. ¹³ A few days later, the son saddled up and left the ranch and moved to town. He spent all his money on booze, drugs, and wild women. ¹⁴ About the time all his money ran out, a depression hit the country, and there were no jobs or food to be found. ¹⁵ The young cowboy persuaded a farmer to let him take care of his pigs. ¹⁶ The boy was so hungry that even the pig's food looked appetizing because he was starving to death. ¹⁷ Finally, the young cowboy came to his senses, and he said to himself, 'All my dad's workers have more than they can even eat and here I am starving to death. ¹⁸ I'll show up and say, 'Dad, I've made a terrible mistake. I messed up my life and my relationship with you! ¹⁹ I'm not worthy to be called your son, but would you hire me on as a worker?'

²⁰ "So the boy headed for home, and while he was still a long way off, his dad spotted him walking up the road. His dad was nothing but relieved and happy at the sight of his boy coming back. He bolted out of the house and ran toward his son. The dad wrapped him in his arms and kissed him on his cheek. ²¹ The boy said, 'Dad, I have sinned against heaven and you. I'm unfit to be called your boy.'

²² "But the dad hollered to the cowboys who were working near the barn, 'Hey! Someone grab my best coat out of the house and put it on my son. Get a ring for his finger and boots for his feet. ²³ Butcher the grain-fed steer and get ready for a party. ²⁴ We are going to celebrate the return of my son to the ranch. He was once dead to us, but now he has returned to life! He was lost, but now he has been found!' Everyone started getting ready for the celebration to begin.

²⁵ "In the meantime, the older son was out in the pastures doctoring yearlings. When he got back to the house, there was music and dancing

in the barn. ²⁶ He stopped his horse and asked one of the other cowboys what was going on. ²⁷ 'Your brother has returned,' he said, 'and your dad has butchered the grain-fed steer and we are all celebrating his return.'

²⁸ "The older brother was angrier than a mad momma cow. He refused to join the celebration. The father came out to talk him into coming in, but he said, ²⁹ 'I've worked for you all my life. I've done everything you've ever asked of me. Not one single time have you ever even given me a goat to BBQ with my friends. ³⁰ But let this whelp disrespect you, take all your money and spend it on whores, and you celebrate his return by killing and eating the grain-fed calf—that I've been feeding!'

³¹ "His dad looked at him kindly and said, 'Son, listen to me. I didn't give you any of that because they were already yours. You didn't have to ask me. Everything I have is yours. ³² But this day is a cause for celebration. Your brother was dead in his sins, and now he has come back to life! He was lost, but he has been found.'"

CHAPTER 16

The Wily Bean Counter

Jesus told his twelve cowboys this story, "There was a rich rancher who hired a bean counter to manage his properties. One day, the rancher was informed that the bean counter was wasting a lot of money. ² The rancher called him in and said, 'I've heard a lot about what you've been doing with my money and property. Give me the books and get out of here. You're fired.'

³ "The bean counter was beside himself with worry. He said to himself, 'My boss is firing me, and I don't know what to do. I'm not strong enough to be a cowboy, and I've got too much pride to beg. ⁴ I know what I'll do! I'll make some quick friends by using the rancher's business so I can call in some favors after I'm fired.'

⁵ "So he called in everyone who owed the rancher anything and made them a deal to reduce their debt. He asked the first one, 'How much do you owe my boss?'

⁶ "'One hundred barrels of olive oil,' the man answered.

"'I'll reduce that debt by half if you can pay it now.' ⁷ Then he called another guy and asked, 'How much do you owe my boss?'

"The guy said, 'One thousand bushels of wheat.'

"The bean counter said, 'I'll reduce that to only eight hundred if you can pay it now.'

⁸ "After all of this, the rancher still fired the bean counter, but he admired the way he collected the debts and set himself up for the future. ⁹ So here's what I'm trying to tell you, use any earthly gain you have to help people. And when you have nothing left, God will welcome you in.

¹⁰ "If you can be trusted with little things, more will be trusted to you. If you cannot be trusted with small tasks, you cannot be trusted with bigger ones. ¹¹ If you are untrustworthy with things of this world, do you think God is going to trust you with the secrets of heaven? ¹² If you can't take care of other people's things, why should you be given more things of your own?

¹³ "No cowboy can ride for two outfits, for he will favor one over the other. He will be loyal to one and learn to hate the other. You cannot ride for God if you are a slave to money."

¹⁴ When the Pharisees heard this, they started making fun of Jesus. They loved their money and did everything they could to discredit him. ¹⁵ Jesus told 'em, "Y'all are the ones who try to look so good in other people's eyes, but the Boss knows what kind of leather you're made of. The things you and the world hold in high regard are useless in the eyes of the Boss.

¹⁶ "Everything that was written by Moses and the other prophets was the contract to God's outfit. But ever since John the Baptizer started spreading the good news, everyone has been trying to force their way in to God's outfit. ¹⁷ The original contract won't be torn up, it will be paid off. Heaven and earth could be moved easier than removing one dot over one "i" in the contract.

¹⁸ "Let me give you an example. The Code says you can divorce a woman for adultery and marry another. But I'm telling you that anyone that marries a divorced person has already committed adultery in the eyes of God."

Lazarus and the Rich Guy

¹⁹ Jesus then said, "There was a rich guy who dressed in expensive clothes and lived in absolute luxury. ²⁰ There was also a poor beggar named Lazarus who was covered in sores. People would bring Lazarus to the rich man's gate

entrance to beg. ²¹ Lazarus prayed for just a small scrap from the rich guy's table, but all he could settle for were dogs to lick his rotting flesh.

²² "Finally, old Lazarus gave up the ghost, and the angels carried him to sit beside Abraham at the great banquet in heaven. ²³ Coincidentally, the rich guy died at the same time, but he ended up in hell. While his flesh burned, he saw the beggar Lazarus sitting with Abraham in heaven.

²⁴ "The rich man hollered, 'Abraham! My ancestor, please help me! Send Lazarus with just a drip of water to drop on my tongue. I am burning alive, and I cannot stand the pain of the flames.'

²⁵ "But Abraham said, 'Son, remember that while you were living, you had everything and Lazarus had nothing. You never lifted a finger for him, so why should he dip his finger in the water for you. He will now be comforted, and you will feel his pain. ²⁶ And besides that, there is a canyon between us that you cannot cross and neither can we. What's done is done.'

²⁷ "Then the rich guy begged, 'Then please, Abraham, send someone to my father's house and ²⁸ tell my brothers what waits for them if they are selfish as I was. I don't want them to end up in this torment with me.'

²⁹ "Abraham said, 'Moses and the rest of the old cowboy prophets have warned them. All they have to do is read what they wrote.'

³⁰ "The rich man said, 'That's not enough Abraham! If someone from here could go back and tell them, then they would turn from their selfishness and ride for God!'

³¹ "But Abraham replied, 'If they wouldn't listen and heed the warning of Moses and the old cowboy prophets, then they won't listen to anyone else, even if someone were to rise from the dead and tell them.'"

CHAPTER 17

Faith and Forgivin'

One day Jesus spoke to his twelve cowboys, "Folks will always be inclined to sin, but it is sure going to turn out bad for someone who talks another person into it. ² It'd be better for that person if an anvil was tied around their neck and they were thrown into the sea. You don't want to be the person who tries to lure the Boss's kids away from him. ³ And I ain't talkin' about other people. I'm talking to you.

"If a cowboy on God's crew starts sinning, talk to him about it and warn him. If he listens and gets back on the right trail, then forgive him. ⁴ Even if this happens over and over and over, if they turn from their sorry ways, you must forgive."

⁵ Then the twelve cowboys said, "Show us how to have more faith!"

⁶ Jesus answered, "If you had the faith of an alfalfa seed, you could tell that oak tree, 'Climb out of the ground and go plant yourself in the bottom of the ocean,' and it would do what you said. ⁷ When a cowboy comes in from checking fence, does the ranch owner tell him, 'Let me unsaddle your horse and rub it down while you go in and get something to eat?' ⁸ No, he tells him, 'Go milk the cow and bring it to me while I eat supper. After that, then you can go eat.' ⁹ Does the ranch owner praise the cowboy for doing his job? Of course not. ¹⁰ In the same way, when you ride for me you should say, 'We're just happy to ride for you and do what you tell us to do.'"

Ten Townspeople Healed

¹¹ Jesus continued riding toward Jerusalem. When he reached the border between Galilee and Samaria, ¹² he rode through a village. Ten townspeople stood at a distance ¹³ and hollered out to Jesus, "Jesus, Boss, help us, please!"

¹⁴ He looked over at them and said, "Go show yourselves to the preachers." And as they went in faith, they were healed.

¹⁵ One of these who was healed came back and said to Jesus, "Praise the Boss!" ¹⁶ He then got down on one knee in front of Jesus and thanked him for what he'd done. This man wasn't even Jewish, he was a half-breed Samaritan.

¹⁷ Jesus asked, "Where are the other nine that I healed? ¹⁸ Has not one of the Boss's kids from Israel returned to give glory to God? Is this foreigner the only one?" ¹⁹ Then Jesus said to him, "You may stand and go. Your faith in me has healed you."

God's Outfit Is Comin'

²⁰ One day the Pharisees asked Jesus, "When will the Boss's outfit get here?"

Jesus said, "You won't be able to see it with your eyes. ²¹ You won't be able to say, 'Ah, there it is!' or 'I found it. It's right here!' For the Boss's outfit is inside of you."

²² Then he told his twelve cowboys, "There will come a day when you wish the Top Hand would come back, but you won't see it happen. ²³ There will be people saying, 'Look, over there! or, 'Here he is over here!' But don't believe those people. ²⁴ Just like lightning will light up the sky from horizon to horizon, so it will be when the Top Hand comes ridin' back on his horse.

²⁵ "But before all that, the Top Hand must suffer the humiliation and rejection of his own people. ²⁶ When the Top Hand returns, it will be like in the days of Noah. ²⁷ People paid no mind to God and only cared about eating and drinking and taking care of themselves. They were all still doing this when Noah entered his boat and sealed up the door. Then the flood came, and everyone else was destroyed. ²⁸ It'll be a repeat of the time of Lot. Everyone was just doing their own thing, not worried about anyone else besides their own sin and pleasure. ²⁹ They didn't even notice the day Lot left Sodom and fire and brimstone rained down and destroyed everyone. ³⁰ This is how it will be on the day the Top Hand returns.

³¹ "On that day, a cowboy repairing the roof of a barn shouldn't even go back to the bunkhouse to pack a bag. A person gathering cattle in the field shouldn't even return home. ³² Don't forget what happened to Lot's wife when she turned around to look at what she was leaving! ³³ If you try to go back for anything, you will lose your life. But if you give everything up for me, then you will live. ³⁴ That night, there will be two people sleeping in the bunkhouse. One will be taken, and the other left behind. ³⁵ Two ladies will be fixing grub. One will be taken, and the other left behind."

Note: Some manuscripts include the words from Matthew 24:40.

³⁷ "Where will this happen, Boss?" the cowboys asked him.

Jesus said, "Just like buzzards gather around the dead, these signs will gather when the end is close."

CHAPTER 18

The Widow Who Never Gave Up

One day Jesus told a story to his twelve cowboys to teach them about prayer and never givin' up. ² He said, "There was a judge in a town, and this fellow didn't like God or people. ³ But there was this one lady who felt like she had been wronged who came to him every day and asked for justice to be done for her. ⁴ For a while, he brushed her off with a gruff rebuttal and sent her on her way, but this woman wouldn't give up. ⁵ Finally, just to be rid of her, the judge did what she wanted because he was tired of seeing and hearing from her every single day."

⁶ And then Jesus said, "See what a godless judge will do for those who never give up? ⁷ So if even a no-good sorry judge will dispense justice, how much more will our loving God hear our pleas that we cry out for day and night? Will he just turn a blind eye to his kids? ⁸ God is going to help his kids right away. But when the Top Hand comes riding into town, will he find anyone with faith?"

The Crooked Brand Inspector and the Religious Fellow

⁹ Then Jesus told 'em this story of a guy who depended on his own goodness and shunned everyone else, ¹⁰ "Two guys went into the church to pray. One was a religious fellow, and the other was a brand inspector. ¹¹ The religious fellow thought he was better than other people, so he stayed away from everyone else and prayed, 'Thank you, God, for not making me like the lowlife cheaters, sinners, and fornicators. And a special thank you for not making me like that crooked brand inspector over there. ¹² God, I go without food twice a week, and I tithe religiously.'

¹³ "But the crooked brand inspector stood a far piece away from everyone else because he didn't feel worthy. He wouldn't even look at heaven as he prayed. Instead, he dug his fingernails into his palm as he prayed, 'God, I'm a sorry piece of work. Please take me onto your outfit even though we both know I don't deserve it.'"

Jesus continued, ¹⁴ "I'm telling you the truth cowboys, this crooked brand inspector was right in God's eyes, not that religious fellow. Those who pat themselves on their back will end up flat on their back. And those who cry out to God with their face down in sorrow will be lifted up to heaven."

Jesus and Some Kids

¹⁵ One day some parents brought their kids to see Jesus so he could bless them. As they all

huddled around Jesus, his twelve cowboys started trying to shoo everyone away.

¹⁶ Then Jesus said, "Whoa, what do y'all think you are doing? Kids are always welcome on my Daddy's outfit. It belongs to children like these. ¹⁷ I'm telling you the truth. Unless you can have the faith of a little kid, you'll never end up on my spread."

You Can't Buy or Earn God's Outfit

¹⁸ A religious leader once asked Jesus, "Hey Good Cowboy, how could I live forever?"

¹⁹ "What makes you think I'm good?" Jesus asked. "Only the Boss is truly good. ²⁰ But to answer your question, you know what the Code says, 'Don't jack with another man's Jenny. Don't murder people in cold blood. Don't be a thief. Don't slander anyone. And do what your ma and pa tell you to.'"

²¹ The guy puffed out his chest in self-congratulations and said, "Been there. Done that. Got the t-shirt."

²² When Jesus saw his actions and heard his words, he said, "But you've got one thing left to do to secure your spot in God's outfit. Give everything you have to the poor and then come and ride for me. Then you will have treasure in heaven."

²³ But when the fellow heard this, his shoulders sank low. He was a rich guy, and he knew he wasn't about to give away all of his wealth for any reason.

²⁴ Jesus saw what was happening and said, "It's going to be nearly impossible for a rich guy to get into heaven. ²⁵ As a matter of fact, it'd be easier for a Charolais bull to fit through a cinch ring than for a rich man to squeeze into God's outfit."

²⁶ Everyone around him gasped, and they all asked, "Then who will get in?"

²⁷ Jesus said, "It is impossible for man to get in on his own, but all things are possible with God."

²⁸ Then Pete spoke up and said, "We've left everything behind to ride for you."

²⁹ Jesus said, "Here's a guarantee for y'all, there ain't a single person who will give up a ranch, wife, brothers, parents, or children in order to saddle up and ride for God's outfit ³⁰ that won't get back much, much more in return in this life and the next."

Jesus Talks about His Death—Again

³¹ Jesus rode off a little ways with his twelve cowboys and said, "Listen, we're getting close to Jerusalem. Everything that the old cowboys of God talked about concerning the Top Hand are fixing to come true. ³² He will be double-crossed by one of his cowboys and handed over to the Romans where ³³ they will beat him, spit on him, make fun of him, whip him, and ultimately kill him. But three days later, he's going to come riding back into town."

³⁴ But the cowboys didn't understand what he was talking about. Jesus's words were hidden from them. His words went in one ear and right out the other.

Fixin' the Blind

³⁵ As Jesus was ridin' into Jericho, a blind beggar was sitting beside the trail. ³⁶ When he heard many people passing by, he hollered out and asked what was going on. ³⁷ They told him Jesus was coming into town. ³⁸ He jumped up and started waving his arms and yelling, "Jesus, Son of David, show me your mercy. I beg you!"

³⁹ Now this fellow was causing a ruckus. People around him told him to sit down and shut up. But the guy only yelled louder and louder.

⁴⁰ Jesus pulled up to a stop and turned around. He told some people to bring the blind man to him. When they did, Jesus looked down and said, ⁴¹ "What do you want me to do for you?"

"Lord," he said, "will you fix my eyes?"

⁴² And Jesus said, "Your eyes have been fixed. Your faith has fixed you." ⁴³ Immediately, the blind guy could see again. He followed behind Jesus, praising God just as loud as he had cried for help. And everyone who saw this, their eyes were opened too.

CHAPTER 19

Jesus and Zacc

Jesus finally got into Jericho and rode through town. ² There was a fellow who lived there named Zacc. He was the head brand inspector for the area and had become rich off of the fees he charged. ³ He wanted to see the man that everyone was talking about, but he couldn't see over the throng of people because he was a short fellow. ⁴ So he did the only thing he knew to do. He climbed a tree nearby. He knew Jesus would come right by there and he would get a good look.

⁵ Sure enough, Jesus rode right by the tree. But instead of passing by, Jesus pulled up and

looked up and said, "Zacc, climb down from there. I'm going to stay with you while I'm here. Let's go to your place."

⁶ Zacc scurried down the tree and led the way to his place. His face had a smile a mile wide because Jesus was going to be staying with him. ⁷ But the other folks sure didn't like it much. They said, "Of all the people he could stay with, why did he choose the sorriest one in Jericho?"

⁸ Later that evening during dinner, Zacc stood up in front of Jesus and said, "I am going to give half my wealth to the poor. I will also give back four times as much to all those I cheated on their brand inspections."

⁹ Jesus smiled and said, "Eternal life has come to this ranch today. This guy has shown himself a true cowboy and son of Abraham. ¹⁰ The Top Hand has come to doctor the sick and bring back the strays."

The Hard Cow Boss

¹¹ Everyone was listening to everything Jesus was saying. He told them a story because everyone was thinking that God's outfit was coming very soon. ¹² He said, "A hard cow boss was summoned to the ranch owner's house far away to be made the ranch manager. ¹³ Before he left, he called together ten cowboys and gave them each a young colt to work with while he was gone. ¹⁴ But many people who worked on the big ranch hated the cow boss and didn't want him to be the ranch manager.

¹⁵ "After he was made the ranch manager, he returned to his ranch and called in all the cowboys he'd given colts to. He wanted to see what they'd done with the horses. ¹⁶ The first cowboy said, 'Hey boss. I started your colt, and now you can rope off him, cut cattle, and even throw a little kid up on him if you're of a mind to.'

¹⁷ "'Great job, cowboy!' the new ranch manager said. 'You've done well. You were given a little and returned it to me better. I'm going to make you the new cow boss.'

¹⁸ "The next cowboy said, 'Here you go boss. I've started your colt, and you can drag calves off of him. He's moving real good off your feet, too.'

¹⁹ "'You too did a great job, cowboy!' the ranch manager said. 'I'm going to make you the wagon boss of this outfit.'

²⁰ "But the third cowboy walked up with his horse and handed it back to the ranch manager.

The cowboy said, 'I kept him safe for you. I was afraid to do anything with him for fear he'd get hurt, and you'd get mad. ²¹ I didn't want to make you mad because you take credit for what you didn't do and ride horses that you didn't start.'

²² "'You're a sorry excuse for a cowboy!' the new ranch manager roared. 'You've nailed shut your own coffin. If you knew I was a hard man to work for, ²³ at least you could've broke the horse to a saddle or picked up his feet so I could trim him.'

²⁴ "Then the ranch manager handed the horse to another cowboy and said, 'Give this horse to the cow boss.'

²⁵ "'But, sir,' the cowboy said, 'he already has the best horse here. Why does he get two?'

²⁶ "'Because I reward those who do something with a little. But to those who do nothing with a little, everything will be taken from them. ²⁷ And everyone who spoke against me being the new ranch manager, bring them here and kill them in front of me. Every single one of them.'

The Top Hand Rides into Jerusalem

²⁸ After he finished with his story, Jesus struck a long trot for Jerusalem. His twelve cowboys lined up behind him and followed. ²⁹ When they neared Bethphage and Bethany at the Olive Hill, he sent two cowboys ahead. ³⁰ "Go over there and you will find a young donkey that has never been ridden tied up next to a tree. Bring it to me. ³¹ And if anyone asks what you are doing, say, 'The Top Hand needs it.'"

³² So the cowboys rode ahead, and everything was just as Jesus had said. ³³ Even when they untied the colt, the owners asked them what they were doing.

³⁴ The two cowboys said, "The Top Hand needs it for a little while." ³⁵ They brought the colt to Jesus and threw a saddle blanket on it for him to sit on.

³⁶ As he rode into Jerusalem, people laid their coats down on the ground in front of him. ³⁷ When he turned down the road leading down from Olive Hill, all of the people following him began praising God for sending the Top Hand and all the miracles he had done.

³⁸ They hollered, "Let's hear it for the Top Hand who has been sent by the Boss to save us! Peace in heaven, and give all the praise to the highest parts of heaven!"

39 But some of the religious leaders in the crowd said to Jesus, "Hey, tell your followers to quit saying things like that!"

40 He replied, "If they didn't say it, the stones in the road would sing out."

41 When Jesus got closer to the city, his eyes filled with tears. 42 He said, "You, Jerusalem, have cried out to God for help and he has answered your prayers. But now it is too late, and you cannot see the gift you've been given. 43 It won't be long before your enemies destroy you. 44 They will muck you out like a mad mama cow and do the same to your kids. They won't leave one stone standing on top of another because you were too blind to see when God stood among you."

Jesus Clears Out the Sacrifice Salesmen

45 Then Jesus walked into the main church area and began driving out those who were selling animals for sacrifices. 46 He said, "The Good Book said, 'My House will be one of prayer,' but you have turned it into a carnival booth."

47 After that, he taught every day in the main church, but the preachers, teachers of Moses's code, and other religious leaders didn't like him and started plotting how they could kill him. 48 They argued and fought, but they couldn't come up with anything because everyone loved him so much and listened to everything Jesus said.

CHAPTER 20

Jesus Is Challenged

One day Jesus was teaching in the main church and telling folks about the good news. Many church leaders and preachers came up to him and asked, 2 "Who said you could teach in here?"

3 Jesus said, "Well, let me ask you this first, 4 did John baptize because the Boss told him to or was it just something he came up with on his own?"

5 They talked it over for a second. "If we say the Boss told him to, he'll ask us why we didn't believe John. 6 But if we say he came up with it on his own, everyone will get mad because they all believe John was sent from the Boss." 7 Finally, they told Jesus they didn't know the answer.

8 So Jesus said, "If you won't answer, then neither will I."

Story about the Murderous Cowboys

9 Jesus told the people listening, "A man leased his ranch and cattle to some cowboys and went on a long journey.

10 "When calving season was done, he sent one of his own cowboys to collect his share of the calves, but the cowboys who leased the ranch beat him up and sent him back with nothing. 11 So the owner sent another cowboy to try and collect what was due. The sorry thieves did the same thing and sent him back with nothing. 12 Then the owner sent a third cowboy, but they beat this one nearly to death and sent him back with nothing.

13 "The owner wondered what he could do. He said, 'Maybe if I send my son, my only son, with a stern warning, they will listen to him.'

14 "But when the outlaw cowboys saw the ranch owner's son coming up, they said to each other, 'Alright boys! Here's the chance we've been waiting on. We'll kill the rancher's only son and then there will be no one to inherit the ranch, and it will be ours!' 15 So they grabbed the son when he rode through the gate and strung him up and killed him.

"What do you think the ranch owner will do to those boys who killed his son?" Jesus asked. 16 "Let me tell you. He will come with a terrible vengeance and wipe them off the face of the earth. Then he will give his ranch to cowboys who will take care of it and appreciate it."

Everyone who was listening cried out, "Let's hope nothing like that ever happens around here!"

17 So Jesus asked them, "Then what do y'all think these words from the Good Book mean? 'The calf the cowboys rejected has now become the sire bull.'

18 "Everyone who does not recognize the bull will be trampled by it. It will crush those who oppose it."

19 Now the religious leaders and preachers wanted Jesus arrested immediately because they knew he was comparing them to the sorry cowboys who killed the rancher's son. They knew what Jesus was saying, but they were afraid of the crowds who seemed to love him.

Tax Questions

20 So they conspired against Jesus and sent some of them in regular clothes to try and

trap Jesus. They wanted him to say something against Rome so he could be arrested. ²¹ They said, "Hey boss, we can tell that you ain't afraid to tell it like it is. ²² So tell us truthfully, should God's people pay taxes to Caesar or not?"

²³ But Jesus saw through their treachery and said, ²⁴ "Show me a coin and tell me whose picture is on it."

"Caesar's picture is on it," they said.

²⁵ "Well then, if his picture is on it then he must own it. Give to Caesar what is his and give God what belongs to God."

²⁶ They stood there with stupid looks on their faces. They were amazed by his wisdom and his answers. They shut their mouths and left.

A Discussion about the Dead

²⁷ Then a group of people called the Sadducees came to talk to Jesus. They were religious leaders who did not believe in life after death. ²⁸ They asked Jesus this question, "Boss, Moses said in his Code that if a man dies, leaving his wife behind without a child, then the man's brother should marry her and give her a child to carry on his brother's name. ²⁹⁻³¹ Suppose this happens every time, and the woman goes through seven brothers, all of them dying before she has a child. ³² Finally, the woman dies too. ³³ Tell us, whose wife will she be if there is life after death? All of the brothers were married to her at some point."

³⁴ Jesus said, "Marriage is just for down here. ³⁵ In heaven, people will not be married to each other. ³⁶ Not only will they not be married, but they will live forever—just like the angels. They are God's children, and they will be brought back to life."

³⁷ Jesus continued, "But this isn't a question about marriage, but one about life after death. Even Moses proved this when he wrote about his experience with the burning bush. Way after Abraham, Isaac, and Jacob had died, Moses referred to God as 'the Boss of Abraham, the Boss of Isaac, and the Boss of Jacob.' ³⁸ If death was the end, and there was no more, then dead people don't need a God. The Boss is God over the living, not the dead. These three great cowboys are alive with God today, not dead."

³⁹ "Very well said, cowboy," said some of the people standing around. ⁴⁰ And no one dared to ask him any more stupid questions meant to trap him.

Whose Son Is the Top Hand?

⁴¹ Then Jesus posed his own question, "Why does everyone think the Top Hand who will save everyone is David's son? ⁴² Think about it. David himself wrote in the book of Psalms, 'God said to the Top Hand, Son, ride here in the place of honor to my right. ⁴³ I will destroy your enemies and make them nothing more than a heap of dirt to rest your feet on at night.'"

⁴⁴ "If the Top Hand is God's Son, how can he be David's?"

⁴⁵ While everyone was watching and listening, Jesus turned to his twelve cowboys nearby and said, ⁴⁶ "Beware of these preachers and teachers of Moses's code. They like the honor their positions bring, ⁴⁷ but they steal from widows with the same hands they fold for their long public prayers. They will get what's coming to them. I will see to that."

CHAPTER 21

The Widow's Great Gift

While Jesus was sitting in the main church, he watched as rich folks came in and made a flourish of dropping large bills and gold coins into the offering box. ² Then a little old lady came by and dropped in two small copper coins.

³ Jesus said, "Did y'all see that? That little old widow lady just put in more than all those rich people combined. ⁴ They gave a microscopic amount of their wealth and she gave everything she had."

Jesus Predicts the Future

⁵ Some of the twelve cowboys began pointing out the magnificent stonework in the main church walls. Jesus saw their wonder and he said, ⁶ "Not too long from now, every one of these stones will be torn down. Not a single wall will be left."

⁷ "Boss," they asked, "when will it happen? What will set it off so we can know what to look for?"

⁸ Jesus replied, "Don't be fooled by imitations. Many people will come bearing what appears to be my name. They will say, 'I am the Top Hand who will save you' and also things like, 'Now is the time that God foretold!' But don't believe a word of it. ⁹ And when wars and rebellions

happen, don't worry. Sure, these things will take place, but the end will still be a ways off."

¹⁰ Then Jesus said, "Nations will fight nations and ranches will fight ranches. ¹¹ The ground will shake, and people will go hungry. Plagues will break out, and there will be both terrors from below and miracles from above.

¹² "But before any of this happens, there will be a great persecution of those who ride for God. His cowboys will be sent to prisons and punished in the churches. They will stand trial before national leaders just because they ride for me. ¹³ But all of this will happen so you can tell them about me. ¹⁴ So don't fret about the charges or how you will answer. ¹⁵ When the time comes, I will give you the words to say and everyone will be astounded by my answers. ¹⁶ Also know this, those closest to you will double-cross you and stab you in the back. They will even have some of you murdered. ¹⁷ Everyone will hate you because you ride for my brand. ¹⁸ But I will not allow a single hair on your head to perish. ¹⁹ By your courage down here, you will receive the greatest reward for your souls in heaven.

²⁰ "You'll know everything is about to be destroyed when you see Jerusalem's enemies camped outside the gates. ²¹ Those who live in Judea will need to lope out of town and into the hills. Those who live in Jerusalem better hightail it out of there if they know what's good for 'em. ²² Those will be the days of God's wrath, and the words of his great cowboys will come true. ²³ Those are going to be hard days for nursing mothers. The days will be filled with pain and anguish. ²⁴ They will be impaled with swords or sold as slaves to other countries. And Jerusalem? It will be walked on by foreigners until the time when God's people return.

²⁵ "Signs will appear in the sky that are beyond comprehension. The sea will swell and roll in turmoil. There will be roaring waves and strange tides. ²⁶ Everyone will be confused as to what is happening. ²⁷ Then folks will see the Top Hand, riding through the clouds with great power and God's glory. ²⁸ When these things happen, you can be confident and know the time is close for your victory."

²⁹ Then he said, "All you have to do is see that a cow bags up and ³⁰ you'll know her time to calve is close. ³¹ In the same way, you can see the signs that God's outfit is close at hand. ³² I'm speaking the truth when I say that the people now will not die until all these things happen. ³³ Heaven, and even this earth will disappear, but my words will live forever.

³⁴ "Be careful! Worrying about life is as bad as partying all night and coming home drunk. Don't let any of these happen to you. ³⁵ These things will trap you as quick as a coyote in a snare. You'll be as surprised as the coyote when it happens, and your end will be the same. ³⁶ Stay vigilant as a cowboy on night duty in outlaw country. Say a prayer to the Boss that you'll be strong enough to make it through and join the Top Hand on my Daddy's outfit."

³⁷ Every day Jesus went to the main church to teach. Every evening he went back to Olive Hill to spend the night. ³⁸ People came from all over to hear him teach at the main church.

CHAPTER 22

Double-Crossin' Coward

The festival that celebrates Passover was coming up soon. ² The head preachers and keepers of the code of Moses were trying to figure out a way to kill Jesus. They went over many scenarios, but they were afraid that all their options would cause a riot.

³ Then Satan took control of Judas Iscariot, one of Jesus's twelve cowboys. ⁴ Judas went to the preachers and teachers and agreed to double-cross his boss. ⁵ They liked Judas's idea and decided to pay him for his betrayal. ⁶ He told them he would look for a time and place where they could arrest him without a bunch of people around.

The Final Meal

⁷ The day finally arrived to celebrate the Passover. On that day, a lamb is sacrificed ⁸ and Jesus sent Pete and John ahead to find the place where they would share the Passover meal together.

⁹ "Where do you want to eat?" they asked.

¹⁰ Jesus said, "When you get into Jerusalem, you'll find a guy carrying a pitcher of water. Follow him to his house. ¹¹ When you get there, tell him the Top Hand asks, 'Where can I eat the Passover meal with my cowboys?' ¹² He will take you upstairs, and you will find a large room filled with all we need. Get things ready."

¹³ Pete and John left, and everything happened just like Jesus said it would.

¹⁴ When the time came to eat the Passover meal, Jesus and his cowboys were sitting at the table. ¹⁵ Jesus told them, "I couldn't wait to share this meal with y'all before I suffer the things that are about to take place. ¹⁶ The next time I eat, everything that this meal symbolizes will have taken place on God's outfit." ¹⁷ Then he took a cup, gave thanks to the Boss for it and said, "Everyone get a drink. ¹⁸ I will not drink wine again until God's outfit has arrived."

¹⁹ Then Jesus took some bread, gave thanks to the Boss for it and broke it in pieces. He gave a piece to all his cowboys and said, "This is a symbol of my body, which will be sacrificed for you. When you eat it, remember what I did."

²⁰ After the meal, he took another cup of wine and said, "This cup symbolizes a new agreement between y'all and God. The agreement will be signed in my blood. It will be poured out as a sacrifice for all of you.

²¹ "But there is a friend sitting here with us who will double-cross the man who loves him the most. He will betray me. ²² My fate has been sealed. The Top Hand must die, but hell's comin' for the cuss who would give up his Boss." ²³ Talk erupted around the table at how anyone could ever do such a thing.

²⁴ This set off an argument about who was the best cowboy in their crew. ²⁵ Jesus said, "The way this world works, the people in power make people do whatever they want, yet they call themselves, 'a friend of the good folks.' ²⁶ But y'all better not act like that. The best of you will be the ones who give the most of themselves away for my sake. The best will be thought of the least, and the least will be thought of most by God. ²⁷ You think about it. Who is more important, the boss or the servant? The boss is most important, but I didn't come here to boss people around. I came to show you how to serve.

²⁸ "Y'all have ridden with me during the good times and bad. ²⁹ And just like the Boss has granted me the keys to his outfit, ³⁰ I now give you a place at my table there. You will sit on the finest horses and be the boss over the twelve family houses of Israel.

Pete's Denial

³¹ "Pete, listen close. Satan has asked to rope and drag you to the fire. ³² But I have talked to my Dad about you so that he will strengthen you in the days to come and you will be filled with courage after you fail. When you come back to me, be there for your brothers who you ride with and encourage them."

³³ Pete said, "Boss, I'd stand in front of a stampede for you."

³⁴ But Jesus replied, "Pete, listen close. Before the cock crows in the morning, there will be three times you deny riding with me. You'll even say you don't even know me."

³⁵ Then Jesus turned to all the twelve cowboys and said, "When I sent all y'all out to gather and spread the good news of God's outfit, you did not take anything extra with you. You didn't take any extra money or clothes or anything else. During this time, did you ever need anything or go without?"

"No, sir," they all said.

³⁶ "But now," Jesus said, "grab some extra money and take your bedrolls. And if you don't have a sword, sell whatever you have and buy one. ³⁷ The time has come for this old saying to be fulfilled, 'He was deemed an outlaw.' Yep, everything that's ever been written about me will come true."

³⁸ "Look, Boss," they said, "we have two swords."

"That should do," he said.

Jesus Prays on Olive Hill

³⁹ Jesus left then, and his cowboys went with him to Olive Hill. ⁴⁰ When they got there, Jesus said, "Y'all better get to prayin', or temptation's going to sneak up and get ya."

⁴¹ He walked a little ways away from everybody else and knelt down to pray. ⁴² "Dad, if there is another way, can we find it? But it's not what I want that's important, it's what you want." ⁴³ Then an angel showed up and strengthened his body for what was to come. ⁴⁴ Jesus started praying some more. He prayed so hard that his sweat turned to blood and fell to the ground.

⁴⁵ Jesus finished praying and got up to go to where his cowboys were waiting. They weren't praying, but snoring softly. Their slumber made Jesus sorrowful, and ⁴⁶ he said as he woke them, "If you knew what was fixing to happen, you would be praying instead of sleeping. Start praying that you won't give into temptation."

Jesus is Double-Crossed

47 As Jesus was talking, a bunch of people walked up, led by the double-crossing cuss, Judas. Judas walked over to Jesus and kissed him on the cheek in greeting. **48** Jesus said stoically, "Judas, you picked a hell of a way to double-cross the Top Hand. You chose a kiss?"

49 The cowboys saw what was happening and yelled, "Boss! Do we fight them all? We brought the swords!" **50** Before Jesus could answer, one of the cowboys cut off the ear of the high preacher's servant.

51 But Jesus said, "Everyone stop! No more." He reached down and healed the man's ear.

52 Then Jesus said to the preachers, church marshals, and religious leaders, "Have you come to arrest an outlaw? Did you bring your swords and clubs because I am dangerous? **53** I taught right beside you in the church courtyard, and you did nothing. I know why, though. This is your time and place because your hearts are as dark as night."

54 They arrested Jesus and took him straight to the high preacher's house.

Pete Denies His Boss

Pete followed at a distance, trying to see where they would take Jesus. **55** Some men had started a fire in the yard of the high preacher's place and were warming themselves. Pete joined them around the fire but said nothing. **56** A maid who worked for the high preacher saw him and said, "That cowboy right there rides with Jesus."

57 But Pete shook his head and said, "I don't even know who you are talking about, lady."

58 A little while later, someone else recognized him and said, "You are one of Jesus's cowboys aren't you?"

But Pete said, "No! Why would you think such a stupid thing?"

59 About an hour later, another person said, "This guy rode with Jesus. Anyone could tell he's from Galilee."

60 But Pete again said, "Why does everyone keep saying I know this man? I don't!"

Just then, while the words were still tumbling from his mouth, a rooster crowed. **61** Jesus turned and looked directly at Pete from across the yard. Pete then remembered what Jesus had said, "Before the cock crows in the morning, there will be three times that you deny riding with me."

62 Pete ran out of the yard and cried like he'd never cried before.

Jesus's Trial in Front of the Jews

63 The church marshals who were guarding Jesus beat him up and made fun of him. **64** They would blindfold him and then hit him. They would say, "If you know everything, then tell us who hit you!" **65** They didn't stop there. They did many other insulting things to him.

66 When the sun rose, the council of leaders, head preachers, and experts on the code of Moses, gathered together for Jesus's trial. They brought Jesus in front of them and questioned him, **67** "Answer the council this, are you the Top Hand who will save us all?"

Jesus replied, "You wouldn't be able to see the truth if it was standing right in front of you. **68** If I asked y'all that same question about me, you wouldn't answer it either. **69** But from here on out, the Top Hand will be riding at the right hand of God himself."

70 They all looked around at each other and then asked, "So you're saying that you are the Son of God?"

Jesus said, "You said it right. I AM."

71 "Why do we need anybody else to testify?" they asked. "We just heard everything we need to string him up."

CHAPTER 23

Then they gathered Jesus up and marched him out to meet the Roman governor, Pilate. **2** When they arrived, they told Pilate, "This man is trying to claim he is the true king of this land and he tells people not to pay taxes to Rome."

3 Pilate looked down at Jesus and said, "Are you the king of these Jews?"

Jesus looked him in the eye and said, "You spoke the words."

4 Pilate turned to the religious rioters and said, "This man has done nothing wrong."

5 The uproar got even louder as they all shouted, "He causes problems everywhere he goes. He is insolent to our teachings. He started in Galilee and has worked his way here."

6-7 "If he's from Galilee, send him to Herod. He's in town. This man is his problem, not mine." Pilate said.

8 Now Herod was glad to meet the man he'd heard so much about. He wanted to see a miracle.

⁹ But when he questioned him, Jesus stood stoically and never opened his mouth. ¹⁰ The religious rabble stood by and yelled their accusations at Jesus and tried to get Herod riled up. ¹¹ It worked. Herod and his soldiers started making fun of Jesus. Finally, they mocked him by putting a purple robe (the color of royalty) on him and sent him back to Pilate. ¹² Now Pilate and Herod had never got along, but they became friends that day.

¹³ So Pilate got everyone who was trying to have Jesus killed ¹⁴ and said to them, "You brought me a man and accused him of inciting riots, but from what I see, he has done nothing wrong. ¹⁵ And for that matter, even your own ruler Herod has found nothing to warrant his death. ¹⁶ I'll punish him for you, but then I'm letting him go."

Note: Some manuscripts include the words from Matthew 27:15 and Mark 15:6.

¹⁸ But the crowd rebelled and said, "Kill Jesus and release Barabbas." ¹⁹ (Barabbas had been found guilty of rebellion and murder.)

²⁰ Pilate couldn't believe what he was hearing and tried to talk sense into them. ²¹ But the kept yelling, "String him up! String him up!"

²² For the third time, Pilate appealed to them, "What for? Look at him! He has done nothing. I will have him whipped, but then I'm releasing him."

²³ But the frenzied mob pushed closer and got louder and louder. They yelled for Jesus's death. ²⁴ Finally, fearing that things might get out of hand, Pilate agreed to kill Jesus as they demanded. ²⁵ He released Barabbas and turned Jesus over to them.

They String Jesus Up

²⁶ After everything had been done, they led Jesus out of town to be crucified on a cross. A cowboy named Simon had come to town from his ranch. The Roman soldiers grabbed him and made him carry the cross piece because they were afraid Jesus might die before they got him to the cross. ²⁷ Many people followed them out of town. This included many women who cried for what was happening to Jesus. ²⁸ But he turned to them and said, "Cowgirls of Jerusalem, don't cry for me. Cry for yourselves and your children. ²⁹ There is going to come a day when they will say, 'God has blessed those women who have no child and those who have never fed from their breasts.' ³⁰ The time will come that will be so hard that folks will beg the mountains to fall on them and the hills to bury them. ³¹ If the things that are being done to me happen in the day, how much worse will they be for others when the night comes? And the night is indeed coming."

³² Two other outlaws were being led out with Jesus to be killed. ³³ When they got to Skull Hill, they nailed Jesus to a cross and lifted him up for all to see. The outlaws were also put on crosses—one on the left and one on Jesus's right.

³⁴ Jesus said, "Dad, don't hold this against them. They have no idea what they are truly doing." Below him, the Roman soldiers were betting on his clothes by rolling dice.

³⁵ As the crowds watched, some of the religious leaders laughed and yelled, "If he is God's Son, if he is God's Top Hand, if he can save others, let's see him get himself off that cross!" ³⁶ The soldiers also made fun of him by offering him some sour wine like they were his servants and he was a king. ³⁷ Many called out to Jesus saying, "If you are the King of the Jews, prove it by saving yourself!" ³⁸ Someone had placed a handwritten plaque above Jesus's head that said, "King of the Jews."

³⁹ One of the outlaws next to him said, "Show 'em all who is Boss. Save yourself and take us with you."

⁴⁰ But the other outlaw shushed him and said, "Don't you see? We're fixing to meet our Maker, and ⁴¹ we deserve what we're gettin'. But this man," he shook his head sadly as he looked at Jesus, "but this man has done nothing. ⁴² Jesus? Will you remember me when you ride into your Daddy's outfit today?"

⁴³ And Jesus turned his head and said, "I promise you. You will ride with me through the gate today."

Jesus Breathes His Last

⁴⁴ Now the sun was standing directly overhead, but a darkness descended over the land for about three hours. ⁴⁵ The sun seemed to have lost its light. At the same time, the curtain that symbolized the separation of God from man, which hung in the main church, was torn from the top to the bottom. ⁴⁶ With the last of his strength, Jesus said, "Dad, I give my life into your hands." When he'd spoke these words, his final breath left his body.

⁴⁷ When the Roman officer in charge of the execution saw this, he fell down on his knees and cried out, "This man was indeed innocent of any crimes we've punished him for." ⁴⁸ Everyone who had witnessed the execution went away with many tears in their eyes. ⁴⁹ But those who knew him, including the women from Galilee, stood at a far distance watching everything that happened.

Jesus Is Buried

⁵⁰ Now there was a good cowboy named Joseph. He'd been a part of the same group that had Jesus killed, ⁵¹ but he didn't agree with anything they had done. He was from a town called Arimathea in Judea. He had spent his whole life waiting on God's outfit to get here. ⁵² This cowboy went to Pilate and asked if he could take down Jesus's body and bury it. ⁵³ When he got the approval, he wrapped the body in a long piece of cloth and laid it in a new tomb carved out of the rock. ⁵⁴ He had to do it quickly because it was late in the day on Friday and the day of rest was about to begin at sundown.

⁵⁵ The ladies from Galilee had stood watching all of this and saw where Joseph laid the body. ⁵⁶ After this was done, they went home to prepare spices and perfumes for Jesus's body. They wouldn't be able to go and put them on him until after the day of rest was over.

CHAPTER 24

Jesus Comes Riding Back

Very early on Sunday morning, the women went to the tomb to prepare Jesus's body. ² The stone that blocked the entrance had been pushed aside, ³ so they went in, but Jesus wasn't there. ⁴ As they stood in the tomb, two cowboys appeared to them. The two men shone so brightly they had to squint their eyes.

⁵ The women came close to freakin' out, and they hit the ground and bowed low before the two cowboys. One of the men asked, "Why do you search a tomb for one who is alive? ⁶ The one you look for isn't here. He has ridden back from the dead. He told y'all this would happen, ⁷ 'Sinners will double-cross God's Top Hand and be strung up, but he will come riding back on the third day.'"

⁸ When the man said this, all the things Jesus had said started to make sense. ⁹ The women ran back to tell everyone, including the remaining eleven cowboys, what had happened. ¹⁰ Mary Magdalene, Joanna, James's momma Mary, and several others described to the cowboys what had happened at the tomb. ¹¹ The cowboys scoffed at the idea of such a thing and didn't believe a word of it. ¹² But Pete had to see for himself. He ran to the tomb and looked. All that was inside was the linen cloth. He went back and wondered what had happened to Jesus.

The Emmaus Trail

¹³ The same day, two of the cowboys who rode with Jesus were riding down the seven-mile trail from Jerusalem to Emmaus. ¹⁴ They talked about everything that had happened that weekend. ¹⁵ As they were talking, a cowboy came up and rode beside them. ¹⁶ God kept the two from recognizing Jesus.

¹⁷ He said, "Y'all seem to be in a deep discussion. What're y'all talking about?"

They reined up, and he could see the sadness in their eyes. ¹⁸ Cleopas said, "Are you the only one around here who hasn't heard what happened?"

¹⁹ "What happened to cause such a stir?" Jesus asked.

"Jesus, the cowboy from Nazareth, the one who did so many miracles, the one who taught us so many things . . . he's what happened. ²⁰ The religious leaders had him killed. ²¹ We all thought he was the Top Hand who would come and rescue God's people from the Romans. But he died three days ago."

²² "Some women who have been with us who rode with Jesus went to the tomb this morning to prepare his body, but they came back with a tale too hard to believe. ²³ They said Jesus was not there and two angels told them he had ridden back from the dead. ²⁴ Some of the cowboys went to the tomb, and they verified that Jesus's body was indeed gone."

²⁵ Then Jesus said, "Why is it so hard to believe and so easy to be foolish? ²⁶ Didn't the Good Book clearly say the Top Hand would suffer many things before he rode into God's outfit and took his place at his Dad's right hand?" ²⁷ Then Jesus took them on the journey through the scriptures that told of what had just happened.

²⁸ Jesus finished about the time they got to Emmaus, but he acted like he was going to ride on. ²⁹ The two cowboys begged him, "It's getting late. Stay here with us tonight and let's talk more!" So, he went in with them. ³⁰ When they sat down to eat, Jesus took the bread and gave thanks to God for it. He broke it and handed it out. ³¹ When this happened, the two cowboys were allowed to recognize him for who he was and then he disappeared!

³² The two cowboys sat there slack-jawed and with tears in their eyes. They said, "Couldn't you feel the truth burn inside you as he explained the Scriptures to us?" ³³ They wasted no time and saddled back up to head to Jerusalem. When they got there, all eleven of the remaining cowboys were there. They rushed in ³⁴ and said, "It's all true! Jesus has ridden back into town. Ask Pete, he has seen him!"

Jesus Shows Up

³⁵ As the two from Emmaus were explaining how Jesus had ridden with them and taught them. They told the tale of not recognizing him until Jesus had broken the bread and handed it to them. ³⁶ And at that moment, Jesus was suddenly in the room and said, "Howdy, boys. Peace be with y'all." ³⁷ But the boys didn't have peace, they were scared out of their minds. They thought a ghost had shown up.

³⁸ "Why are y'all afraid?" Jesus asked. "I can see doubts in your hearts. ³⁹ Look at my hands and feet where the nails were. It's me, boys. Touch me, I ain't no ghost. You can't feel a spirit, but you can touch me." ⁴⁰ Jesus held out his hands and put his foot out so they could see.

⁴¹ No one said a word. The cowboys stood there frozen in shock, fear, and disbelieving wonder. Then Jesus looked around and said, "Y'all got any vittles?" ⁴² Someone handed him a piece of jerky, and ⁴³ they watched as he ate.

⁴⁴ Then he said, "You know? I told all y'all this would have to happen. Everything that Moses said, everything the old cowboy prophets said, everything the Psalms said, all of it had to happen." ⁴⁵ Then he unlocked the understanding in their minds, and everything made sense. ⁴⁶ He continued, "It's been in the Good Book all along that the Top Hand would suffer, be killed, and come riding back on the third day. ⁴⁷ It also said that if anyone would turn from sin and ride for me, I would forgive their sins. This good news has started in Jerusalem and will go out to every nation on earth. ⁴⁸ Y'all are witnesses that everything is just as I've said. ⁴⁹ I'm going to send you a helper to accomplish all of this. My Dad promised you this gift but stay here until you receive it. You'll know you have it when power from heaven clothes you."

⁵⁰ Later on, Jesus led them out near Bethany. He lifted his hands and blessed his cowboys. ⁵¹ While he was doing this, he was lifted into the air and taken up to heaven. ⁵² They stayed there for a while and worshiped him. Then they returned to Jerusalem, and their hearts were full of joy. ⁵³ And for a long time, they stayed at the main church. They continually thanked God for all he had done.

JOHN

CHAPTER 1

God's Word Becomes a Real Person

Before anything else, the Word existed. The Word was right there with God and not just that, but the Word was God. ² He rode with God at the start of all things. ³ When God opened his mouth, it was the Word that spoke and made all things. Nothing is made without the Word of God. ⁴ All life began through the speaking of God's Word. That spark of life has been given to everyone. ⁵ This light that comes from the Word shines brightly in the darkness. No matter how dark it is, the light will prevail.

⁶ God sent a cowboy named John to tell us about this light. ⁷ God gave John a message to give to everyone else so that they would become believers. ⁸ Now John was not the light, but his message was to give everyone the truth about who the light is.

⁹ At this time, the real light was riding down from heaven to join us here on earth. ¹⁰ He had come down to ride in the pastures that he had made. But the world he created did not recognize him. ¹¹ He rode straight to his people, but they shunned him and turned him away. ¹² But because of his love, he offered the chance for every cowboy and cowgirl to become one of God's kids just by believing in him. ¹³ When a cowboy becomes one of God's kids, nothing really happens to them physically. The transformation occurs in their soul. They are branded and marked for eternity by God himself.

¹⁴ So the Word of God put on a human body and rode among us. We saw his magnificence. This bright light that shone from him, a light that only the soul can see, was a gift from the Father to his only Boy. God's Son rode with a love that wouldn't quit and a faithfulness that could not be snuffed out.

¹⁵ John told everyone, "This is the one I was telling y'all about! There's a cowboy riding down here who is greater than me. He's been around forever."

¹⁶ This cowboy, the Word, is the source of all good things that are given to us. ¹⁷ The Code we cannot fully obey was given through Moses, but grace and truth came through Jesus Christ. ¹⁸ No one has ever laid eyes on God, but his Top Hand, who is God himself, has seen him and knows him. And it's Jesus who has shown us who God really is.

John the Baptizer

¹⁹ When the Jewish leaders sent some preachers and others from Jerusalem to ask John who he was, ²⁰ John flat out told them, "I am not the Top Hand. I cannot save you."

²¹ They asked him, "Well, are you Elijah who has come riding back?"

He said, "Nope."

Then they asked, "Are you the prophet who we've been waiting on?"

"Nope."

²² "Then who are you? We've got to go back and tell the leaders who you are. Just tell us."

²³ John quoted words from the Good Book of Isaiah, "I'm a voice hollerin' from the back side of the pasture, 'Get out of the way because the Top Hand is ridin' into town.'"

²⁴ Then these religious know-it-alls ²⁵ asked him, "If you aren't the Top Hand, or Elijah, or the Prophet, then how come you think you can baptize folks?"

²⁶ John said, "I just baptize with water. But look around, someone is standing right here that you do not recognize. ²⁷ Though his ministry will come after mine, I'm not worthy to pull his boots off after a long day of gatherin'."

²⁸ This exchange between John and the Pharisees took place at a place called Bethany, east of Jordan Creek. It's where John did his baptizing.

John Calls Jesus the Lamb of God

²⁹ The next day John saw Jesus riding toward him. John yelled out, "Will everyone just look at that! Here is the Lamb of God who will be sacrificed for the forgiveness of all the world's sins. ³⁰ This is the cowboy who I was telling y'all about. Remember when I said, 'He will follow after me, but he existed before I was ever made.' ³¹ I didn't know who he was until now. But I've been baptizin' with water so I could point him out to the folks of Israel."

³² John said, "I saw the Holy Spirit in the shape of a dove come and rest upon him. ³³ I didn't know who he was at the time. But God told me, 'when you see the Spirit of God come down from heaven and rest on a cowboy, that is who will baptize with the Holy Spirit.' ³⁴ I saw with my own eyes that this happened to Jesus. I'm tellin' y'all he is the Top Hand who will gather everyone and save them."

The First Twelve Cowboys

³⁵ The next day John was standing with two of the guys who rode with him. ³⁶ When Jesus walked by, John said, "Look, boys! Right there is the Lamb of God—the final sacrifice to save all mankind." ³⁷ When the two men heard what John said, they followed him.

³⁸ Jesus knew he was being tailed so he asked, "What can I do for y'all, cowboys?"

They replied, "Hey Boss, where are you stayin'?"

³⁹ Jesus didn't answer, but said, "Ride with me, and you will see." Now it was about four o'clock when they rode with him to where he was staying. They stayed there with him the rest of the day.

⁴⁰ Andy, Simon Pete's brother, was one of these cowboys who had heard what John said and followed after Jesus. ⁴¹ Andy went and found his brother and told him, "I have found the Top Hand who will save us all! I have found the Christ!"

⁴² Then Andy brought Pete to meet Jesus. Jesus looked at him and said, "Your name is Simon, John's boy—but I'm going to call you Cephas" (which just means "Pete").

⁴³ The following day Jesus decided to ride out for Galilee. He saw a cowboy named Phil and told him, "Come and ride with me." ⁴⁴ Phil was from Bethsaida, the same hometown as Andy and Pete.

⁴⁵ Phil went and found Nate and told him, "We've found the cowboy who Moses and the other prophets talked about. He is Joseph's son, Jesus. He is from Nazareth!"

⁴⁶ "Nazareth?" Nate said doubtfully. "Has there ever been anything good that came from Nazareth?"

Phil waved him on and said, "Come, and you will see for yourself!"

⁴⁷ When they rode up, Jesus said, "Now there is an authentic cowboy from Israel—honest, sincere, and full of integrity."

⁴⁸ Nate looked questioningly at Jesus and asked, "How would you know anything about me?"

Jesus smiled and said, "Because I saw you sittin' underneath that fig tree right before Phil found you."

⁴⁹ Then Nate said with wide eyes, "Boss, you really are God's Son. You are the Top Hand of Israel!"

⁵⁰ Jesus again smiled and said, "You believe in who I am because I said I saw you sittin' underneath that tree. But you will see many greater things than that when you ride for me. I'm tellin' you straight. You are going to see right into heaven and watch as angels come down and talk to me and go back up. I am the bridge between heaven and earth."

CHAPTER 2

Water into Wine

The next day, Jesus attended a wedding in Cana with his mom. ² Jesus's twelve cowboys were also invited to the party. ³ The celebration ran out of wine before the party was over and Jesus's mom said, "They've run out of wine."

⁴ "That ain't none of my business," Jesus replied. "I'm staying out of the limelight for now, but my time will come."

⁵ But Mary was undaunted, and she told the serving staff, "Do whatever he tells you to do."

⁶ There were six water barrels nearby that the Jews used for their ritual washing. Each barrel could hold about thirty gallons. ⁷ Jesus told the serving staff, "Fill those barrels with water." After this was done, ⁸ he said, "Take some out and give it to the person in charge of the party." The staff hurried and did as instructed.

⁹ The fellow in charge had no idea where the wine had come from, but the servants knew. The guy called the groom over to him and said, ¹⁰ "Most people serve the best wine first. After everyone is drunk, then they bring out the cheap stuff. But you did so differently. You saved the best wine for last."

¹¹ This was Jesus's first miracle, and his cowboys believed in him because of what they had seen.

¹² Later, Jesus and his cowboys rode to Capernaum for a spell. His mother and brothers rode along also.

Jesus Clears the Church

¹³ It was gettin' close to the big Passover celebration, so Jesus went to Jerusalem. ¹⁴ When he got to the main church, he saw people making a mockery of the sacrificial system by selling cattle, sheep, and doves. There were also people making a fortune off of exchanging money for foreigners. ¹⁵ Jesus sat down and braided a bullwhip out of some rope and sent all those scoundrels runnin' for the fences. He drove out all the stock and flipped over the tables of the money exchangers. ¹⁶ He stopped in front of the dove salesmen and said, "Get out and take all these doves with you. My Daddy's house isn't a shopping center." ¹⁷ His cowboys remembered that it had been written long ago, "I'll protect my Daddy's place at all cost."

¹⁸ But Jesus's actions stirred up the Jewish leaders. They asked him, "Who do you think you are? If God gave you authority to do this, then give us a sign to prove it, cowboy."

¹⁹ Jesus said, "Knock this church down, and I'll rebuild it in three days."

²⁰ They scoffed at him, "It took forty-six years to build this church. You think you could rebuild

it in three days?" ²¹ But they didn't realize that when he said "this church," he was talking about his body. ²² After he had died and then come riding back into town, Jesus's cowboys remembered what he said this day and they believed everything about him the Good Book had said.

²³ While Jesus was in Jerusalem for the Passover celebration, a lot of people saw and heard what he was doing and believed in him. ²⁴ But Jesus never let his guard down because he knew their sorry tendencies. ²⁵ He didn't need anyone telling him they couldn't be trusted. He already knew their hearts.

CHAPTER 3

Jesus and Nick

There was a Jewish leader and Pharisee named, Nicodemus, or Nick for short. ² He didn't want anyone to see him talking to Jesus, so one evening after dark, he sought him out and said, "Hey boss, we all know you are from God because of the miracles you can do."

³ But Jesus said, "I'm telling you the truth, unless you are born again, you will never see the inside of God's ranch."

⁴ "What in the world are you talking about?" Nick exclaimed. "How can a grown man go back to the womb and be born again?"

⁵ Jesus said, "I promise you, no one can get on God's outfit unless they are born of water and Spirit. ⁶ Humans can only make humans, but the Holy Spirit can give birth to spiritual life. ⁷ So don't think it strange when I say, 'You've gotta be born again.' ⁸ Let me explain it this way, you can hear the wind, but can't tell where it comes from. It goes wherever it wants, but you can't explain it. Same thing goes for the Holy Spirit."

⁹ "How can this happen though?" Nick asked.

¹⁰ Jesus said, "Aren't you one of Israel's teachers? How is it that you cannot understand something as simple as this? ¹¹ We tell you the things we have seen and done, but y'all don't believe a word we say. ¹² And if you won't believe me about things you can touch and feel, how are you going to believe me about spiritual things? ¹³ Nobody has ever gone to heaven and come back, but the Top Hand rode down from heaven to help y'all. ¹⁴ And just like Moses lifted up that bronze snake on a pole to heal everyone, so the Top Hand will be strung up also. ¹⁵ And everyone

who sees and believes in him will live forever on God's outfit."

¹⁶ "This is how much the Boss loves his hands, he sent his only Son, the Top Hand, that everyone who believes in him shall not perish, but live forever on God's outfit. ¹⁷ For the Boss didn't send the Top Hand to point out people's faults, but to save them from their sins. ¹⁸ Nothing will be held against a cowboy who believes, but the one who doesn't, everything will be held against him. ¹⁹ And this is why they will be judged harshly, God shined a light down into this dark world to show people the way to him, but people were more interested in the dark than the light. They like things that happen in the dark. ²⁰ Sorry people hate the light because they are afraid that people will see them for who they really are. ²¹ But those who want to ride the right way are not afraid to come into the light."

John the Baptizer Talks More about Jesus

²² Then Jesus and his cowboys left Jerusalem and went out into the countryside. Jesus stuck around there for a while baptizing people. ²³ John was out near Aenon doing his baptizing. He was there because there was plenty of water to baptize. ²⁴ (This was before John was thrown in the slammer.) ²⁵ Some of John's crew and some Jews got to squabblin' over being religiously clean. ²⁶ They went to John and said, "Boss, the guy you pointed out as the Top Hand is now baptizing people like you did. Folks are going to him instead of coming to us."

²⁷ John replied, "No one has anything unless God gives it to 'em. ²⁸ Don't forget that I told y'all that I ain't the Top Hand. I'm just bustin' a trail for him. ²⁹ When a man gets married, the best man isn't offended when everyone goes to talk to the groom. He's just happy to stand up with him and hear the vows that are made. I'm very happy for his success and now my life has been made complete. ³⁰ It's his time to shine, and time for me to saddle up and ride away. My job is done. ³¹ He's rode down from heaven and is greater than anyone else that has ever stepped foot on this earth. ³² He tells folks what he knows, but nobody listens or believes him. ³³ Anyone who believes what he says knows God's truth. ³⁴ That's because God sent him and he speaks with God's words. The Top Hand is given the Spirit without any limitations. ³⁵ The Boss loves the Top Hand, who is his only son, and has put him in charge of everything. ³⁶ Whoever believes in God's Son will live forever. And anyone who doesn't do what the Top Hand says, will never make it onto God's outfit. Those who do not choose God's outfit choose a forever death instead of eternal life."

CHAPTER 4

Now Jesus knew that the Pharisees had their tally books out and were keeping count of the baptisms that he and John did. ² (Well, Jesus didn't do the baptizing, his cowboys did.) ³ So he rode out of Judea and off toward Galilee.

Jesus and the Samaritan Lady

⁴ Jesus was riding through Samaria and ⁵ came to a town called Sychar. It was right by a ranchito that Jacob had given his son Joseph. ⁶ Jacob's well was near this small plot of land. Jesus dismounted and stretched his legs next to the well. He'd come a far piece for it just being noon and he was tired. ⁷ About this time, a Samaritan woman came by to get some water and Jesus asked her, "Would you fetch me a drink, ma'am?" ⁸ None of his cowboys were there because they'd gone into town to get some food.

⁹ She nearly fell down when he asked her because Jews don't talk to Samaritans. She said, "Is there something wrong with you? Jews don't talk to Samaritans, and you're asking me to give you a drink?"

¹⁰ Jesus replied, "If you had an inkling of the gift God has given, you would ask me for a drink, and I would give you living water."

¹¹ "Well, that might prove a tad difficult for you, sir. You don't even have a rope or a bucket. This well is very deep. So where are you going to get this living water? ¹² Do you think your water is better than our ancestor Jacob's? He drank from it himself, and it has sustained us and our livestock for generations."

¹³ Jesus smiled as he kneeled down by the well and said, "Anyone who drinks this water will eventually get thirsty again. ¹⁴ But the water I give is a fountain of youth and gives eternal life."

¹⁵ The woman quickly said, "I would take your water in a heartbeat. That way I wouldn't have to walk all the way out here to get water every day."

¹⁶ "Go get your husband," Jesus told her.

¹⁷ "I don't have one," the woman replied sheepishly.

Jesus said, "I think you're putting lipstick on a pig. ¹⁸ Truth is, you have had five husbands and the man you live with now ain't one of them. So, you're right. You don't have a husband."

¹⁹ "Sir," she replied in reverence, "I can see you're one of God's cowboys. ²⁰ Tell me why you Jews say you can only worship God in Jerusalem, but our ancestors have always worshiped here."

²¹ "Believe me, ma'am," Jesus replied, "the time is fast approaching when it won't matter where you worship God. ²² You Samaritans don't know who you are worshiping. Y'all wander around like cowboys trying to gather black cattle at night, but the Jews have the light of day to gather by. God's outfit and eternal life comes from the light of day that the Jews have. ²³ But the time is coming—indeed the clock has already struck noon—when real cowboys will ride for a real God. A real ride with God will come from your soul and be true, not from a building. ²⁴ God is real, and those who ride for him must worship him for real also."

²⁵ The lady said, "I know God's Top Hand will come and tell us everything we need to know."

²⁶ Jesus stood up and said, "I AM God's Top Hand."

²⁷ It was then that Jesus's cowboys rode back up with the vittles. They saw that he was talking to a Samaritan lady, but none of them had the nerve to ask why. ²⁸ The lady left all of her stuff there and ran back to the village. She excitedly told the story of what had just occurred to everyone she met along the way. ²⁹ "Quick, come see the cowboy who could read my mind and see into my soul! Go and see for yourself. I think he is God's Top Hand . . . I believe he is the Messiah!"

³⁰ They all looked his way and started heading toward the well.

³¹ Meanwhile, the cowboys were telling Jesus, "Hey Boss, you need to eat something."

³² But Jesus replied, "I already have food that you cannot fathom."

³³ The cowboys began asking each other if maybe someone had already brought him a biscuit or something.

³⁴ Jesus sighed and said, "My strength comes not from the food that goes in your mouth, but by doing what my Father tells me to do. My nourishment is finishing what he has sent me to do. ³⁵ There's a saying, 'In a few months after the calves are born, there will be a branding.' But I'm telling y'all to open your eyes right here. These calves are ready to brand now. ³⁶ The branding crew will be paid good wages, and the calves they brand will be those who will spend eternity on God's outfit. There will be a fine reward for those who did the calving and the branding when the time comes. ³⁷ You know that saying that goes, 'One cowboy calves 'em out and another brands 'em.' And that is the truth. ³⁸ I sent y'all to brand where you did not calve. Other cowboys had already finished that hard job. Now you get to do the fun stuff and brand 'em."

Many Samaritans Saddle up with Jesus

³⁹ Now many Samaritans believed Jesus was the Top Hand because she had said, "He could see inside my soul and knew everything I had ever done." ⁴⁰ When they went to the well to talk to him, they begged him to stay for a while. He gave a two-day clinic at that little ranchito. He taught them who God was and how to ride for him. ⁴¹ And because of this, many people were saved. ⁴² The villagers said to the woman, "Now we believe, not because of what you said, but because of what he said. He truly is the Savior of the world."

Jesus Heals a Government Worker's Son

⁴³ After he'd finished his two-day clinic, Jesus continued toward Galilee. ⁴⁴ He had already said that God's cowboys would be respected everywhere except his hometown, ⁴⁵ but the folks in Galilee were accommodating. They had been in Jerusalem during the Passover and seen everything he did there.

⁴⁶ He rode through Cana where he'd first turned water into wine. ⁴⁷ A government worker heard Jesus was there and rushed in to talk to him. His son was sick in nearby Capernaum, and the man begged Jesus to come and heal him before he died.

⁴⁸ Jesus said, "Y'all only believe when you see wondrous things."

⁴⁹ The government worker hit his knees and pleaded, "Boss, you're the only one who can help my son. Please come before it's too late."

50 Jesus put a reassuring hand on the man's shoulder and said, "Go home. Your son will be fine." The man believed him and headed out at once.

51 While he was heading back, he ran into one of his servants who had been caring for the boy. The servant told him that his son was alive and well. **52** He asked him when he had recovered and he said that it had been the day before at about one in the afternoon. **53** The man knew that was the time when Jesus had said his son would be okay. Because of this, everyone in the government officials house believed in Jesus.

54 This was the second miracle Jesus had done since coming in from Judea.

CHAPTER 5

No Need for a Bedroll

Later on, Jesus went back to Jerusalem for another Jewish festival. **2** When you go in the Sheep Gate in Jerusalem, there is a pool called Bethesda. Around the water are five covered porches. **3** Under these porch coverings lay the blind, lame, and paralyzed. **4** Every once in a while, an angel would ride down and stir up the water. When this happened, the first one to get in the water would be healed.

Note: This verse is not included in the earliest manuscripts.

5 One man had been lying there sick for thirty-eight years. **6** Someone told Jesus about the man. Jesus went over to him and asked the man, "How would you like to be made well?"

7 "Sir, when the angel stirs the water, the first one in is healed, but someone always gets there before me."

8 Jesus said to him, "Get up, take your bedroll and walk out of here."

9 The man was instantly healed. He rolled up his bedroll and began walking around. This all happened on the day of rest, **10** so the Jewish leaders weren't too happy about it. They approached the man and said, "You can't be carrying your bedroll around on the day of rest. That is against our laws."

11 The man shot back, "That fellow who healed me told me to, so that's what I'm going to do."

12 "What fellow told you that?" they shouted.

13 The healed guy looked around, but couldn't find Jesus. He had slipped away in all the commotion. **14** Later on, the healed guy ran into Jesus in the temple. Jesus told him, "Now that you are healed, stop sinning or you'll end up in wire worse than just being sick." **15** The man went back and told the leaders that it was Jesus who had healed him.

Jesus Tells Them He Is the Son of God

16 So the Jewish leaders started nit-picking Jesus about healing a man on the day of rest. **17** Jesus told them, "When your Father is out working, you go and work with him. My Dad is working today and I am too." **18** Now this really kicked the hornet's nest, and the leaders tried to find a way to get rid of Jesus for good. Not only had Jesus broke the Law by working on the day of rest, when he called God his Father, he was saying that he was equal with God.

19 So Jesus tried to explain himself to the knotheads. "The Son doesn't do anything on his own. He only works beside his Dad and does the things he does. **20** The Father loves his Son and teaches him all things and shows him everything he is doing. The truth is, the Father is going to show the Son how to do greater things than just healing a sick dude. If that blew your mind, you ain't going to believe what's coming next. **21** The Father can bring the dead back to life, and in the same way, the Son can give life to anyone he chooses.

22 "And besides that, the Father has turned all his operations over to the Son, who now has the final say in all matters. **23** If you don't show respect to the Son, then you are disrespecting the Father. He's the one who sent the Son to you.

24 "Listen carefully to what I'm fixing to tell you. Those who believe what I am telling you right now, and believe that the God has sent me, that person will live forever in heaven. No sin will be held against a cowboy who believes in me. That cowboy has walked from the land of the dead and crossed the cattle guard to saddle up for eternal life.

25 "Don't miss what I'm saying. A time is coming—right now as a matter of fact—when dead men will hear my words and come alive. **26** Only the Father has the power to give life, and he has given that power to the Son. **27** And with this power comes the authority to judge every cowboy because he is the Son of Man.

²⁸ "And don't let all this surprise you. There will be time for amazement when those who are dead hear the Son's voice and ²⁹ rise from their graves. Those who believe will go on to do good things and experience eternal life, but those who dismiss this message will only ride for themselves and continue to live evil lives. These will experience judgment for their sins. ³⁰ But I do not judge unfairly. I only judge as God tells me. Therefore, my judgment is fair, and they will get what they deserve. I only carry out the will of my Father who sent me, not my own.

³¹ "You know, I'm not telling you anything you haven't heard about me already. I didn't just come up with this on my own. ³² There is someone else who has already said all of this is true. ³³ In fact, y'all sent people to listen to John the Baptizer, and everything he said was the truth. ³⁴ To be honest though, I don't even need someone else to verify what I tell you is the truth. I tell you the truth because I want you to be saved. ³⁵ John was a campfire that shined bright in this dark world and y'all enjoyed the warmth of his message for a while. ³⁶ But I have something that verifies me even more than what John said. My teachings and the miracles I do prove that my Father has sent me. ³⁷ My words and my miracles are the testimony of God that I AM who I say I AM. Y'all have never seen God face to voice or heard his voice with your own ears, ³⁸ therefore you do not understand his message. You cannot understand his message because you do not believe his messenger—who he sent to you today. ³⁹ You pat yourselves on the back for memorizing all the scriptures that describe me, but you are too blind to see that I stand here before you. ⁴⁰ If you were not blind, you would not refuse the life that only I can give.

⁴¹ "Make no mistake, your approval means diddly-squat to me. ⁴² I see into your hearts and know that you do not ride for God. ⁴³ I have been sent by my Father and you turn me away. I have come saying, 'Look at God' and you reject me. Others have come saying, 'Look at me' and you welcome them. ⁴⁴ No wonder y'all can't believe. You're too busy standing in a big circle patting each other on the back. You seek glory from each other instead of from God.

⁴⁵ "But it isn't me who will criticize you in front of God. Moses is going to do that, not me. Yes, the same Moses you put so much hope in. ⁴⁶ If you put so much stock in what Moses said, you would believe me because he wrote about me. ⁴⁷ But since you won't even believe what he wrote, how will you believe what I say?"

CHAPTER 6

Supper for Five Thousand

Sometime after, Jesus rode to the far side of the Sea of Galilee (also known as Lake Tiberias). ² Huge crowds followed him because they had seen many of the miracles he'd done on the sick and dying. ³ Then Jesus rode up on a hill and got off to rest. He sat with his cowboys around him. ⁴ The Jewish Passover festival was getting close. ⁵ The crowd finally made it up the hill so Jesus said to Phil, "Where can we get food for all these folks?" ⁶ Jesus wasn't asking a question but teaching them all a lesson.

⁷ Phil said, "It'd take a year's wages to buy all these people one piece of jerky, Boss! We don't have anything even close to that."

⁸ Then Andy, Pete's brother, chuckled and said, ⁹ "Is this boy's five biscuits and two pieces of jerky close, Phil?"

¹⁰ "Have everyone sit down," Jesus said. So about five thousand men (not counting women and children) all sat down on the grassy slope. ¹¹ Then Jesus lifted up the biscuits and thanked God for them and put them in a few different baskets to hand out to everyone. Everyone had as many biscuits as they could eat. He did the same thing with the jerky, and everyone got full. ¹² After everyone had eaten their fill, Jesus told his cowboys, "Gather up the leftovers so that nothing goes to waste." ¹³ They did as they were instructed and needed twelve baskets to get it all. The leftovers were more than they had started with.

¹⁴ Everyone who was there began saying, "This has to be the Top Hand we've been waiting on." ¹⁵ Jesus knew they were fixing to try to make him their king, so while they talked, he rode off into the hills by himself.

Walking on Water

¹⁶ That evening, Jesus's cowboy rode down to the water's edge to wait for their boss. ¹⁷ When he didn't show up, they got on a boat and headed across the lake toward Capernaum. ¹⁸ Soon

a storm swept in, and the water started pitching like a rank bronc. **19** The cowboys had rowed about three of four miles when they saw Jesus walking casually toward them on the water. This scared the tar out of 'em all. **20** When he got close, he said, "It's me, boys. Don't be scared." **21** Then they reached out and gave him a hand as he climbed into the boat. His second foot had no more touched the floor of the boat than they felt the bottom scrape land. In the blink of an eye, they had miraculously arrived at their destination.

The Bread of Life

22 The next day, the crowd noticed the cowboys had only taken one boat and they knew Jesus hadn't been with them. **23** Several boats from the town of Tiberias had arrived where Jesus had fed everyone. **24** When everyone realized that Jesus and his cowboys were not around, they got in the boats to go look for him. **25** They found him in Capernaum and asked, "Hey Boss, when did you get here?"

26 Jesus said to them, "Y'all aren't here to ride for God. You're here because I filled your bellies and now you're hungry and wanting another free meal. **27** Quit chasing meaningless stuff like food and start longing for eternal life by riding for the Top Hand. For God has approved of him by giving him the key to the ranch."

28 They all replied, "We want to rope, ride, and brand for God's outfit too. What do we have to do first to saddle up with ya?"

29 Jesus said, "There is only one thing you have to do. Give your whole life to the Top Hand that God has sent ya."

30 They pondered this for a second and then someone shouted out, "Well, show us a miracle so that we know you are the Top Hand. We want to see what you can do. I mean, our ancestors got to eat bread from heaven while they rode across the desert. **31** The Good Book says, 'Moses gave 'em biscuits from heaven to eat.'"

32 Jesus shot back, "The truth is, Moses didn't give nobody nothin'. My Father did. And now he is offerin' y'all the real bread from heaven. **33** The real bread of God gives life, not full bellies."

34 "Well," they replied, "give us this bread every day like our ancestors had, and we'll eat it."

35 Jesus said, "I am the bread of life. Whoever rides for me will never be hungry again. Whoever gives his life to me will never be thirsty. **36** I'm standing right here in front of you, but you still don't believe I am who I say I am. **37** My Father will send the true cowboys to me, and I will never turn them away. **38** I didn't ride all the way down here from heaven to do what I want, but only what my Father tells me to do. **39-40** And this is what he has told me to do, 'Give eternal life in paradise to the real cowboys that I send you. Bring the dead back to life on the last day.'"

41 Then some arguing started breaking out because he had said, "I am the bread of life who rode down from heaven." **42**

They said, "Isn't this the boy they call Jesus. Isn't this Joseph's son? We know both his parents. How can he say that he 'rode down from heaven'?"

43 "Quit your bickerin'," Jesus said. **44** "You can't decide who rides for me and who doesn't. You can't ride for me unless my Father sends you. And only those who my Father sends me will be raised up to life on the last day. **45** That's why the Scriptures say, 'God will personally teach them how to ride for the brand.' You see? God ain't going to send nobody to me who hasn't listened and done what he told them to do. **46** Not that any of you has seen God. Only the one sent from God has seen him.

47 "Listen to the truth. Anyone who rides for me has eternal life. **48** I am the bread of life. **49** Your ancestors ate manna from heaven in the desert, but they all died. **50** Anyone who eats the bread from heaven will never die. **51** Remember, I am the living bread that rode down from heaven. Anyone who eats this bread will live forever. This bread I offer the world is my flesh."

52 When Jesus said this, the place erupted in arguments. "How can this man cut his flesh off and feed us all? This is preposterous!"

53 Jesus stared at them and said, "I'm telling you the truth. Unless you eat my flesh and drink my blood, you are already dead. **54** But any cowboy who eats my flesh and drinks my blood has eternal life, and I will pull him up out of the grave on the last day. **55** My flesh is the real food you need, and my blood is the real drink you crave. **56** Those who ride for me will eat my flesh and drink my blood. I will live in him, and he will live in me. **57** The Father gave me life, and I will give that same life to the cowboy who rides for me.

⁵⁸ I am the real bread that rode down from heaven. Anyone who eats this bread will not die in the wilderness like your ancestors did (even though they did eat manna) but will live for eternity."

⁵⁹ He said all this while teaching in the church at Capernaum.

Cowboys Start Quitting Left and Right

⁶⁰ On hearing all of this, many of the day workers who followed him around said, "I quit. He's gone too far this time."

⁶¹ Jesus knew what they were thinking and said, "Is this too much for you? ⁶² If this is too much, then what would you think if you saw the Top Hand ride back into heaven with your own eyes? ⁶³ Your real life is a spiritual one that comes from the Spirit of God. You think life is what you can see and touch, but it's not. Your flesh is like the color of a horse. It's nothing but decoration. My words are not decoration. They are the foundation of Spirit and the foundation of life. ⁶⁴ Even now, there are some of you who do not believe what I tell you."

Jesus had known from day one that some of these who claimed to ride for him were counterfeits. They would be the ones who quit when the going got tough. ⁶⁵ Then he added, "That's why I told you that you wouldn't be able to ride for me unless God sent you."

⁶⁶ When the words had come out of his mouth, many of the day workers who had been trying to get on with Jesus walked out. ⁶⁷ Then Jesus turned to the twelve cowboys who rode for him and asked, "Are y'all going to quit, too?"

⁶⁸ Pete replied, "Lord, where would we go? You are the only one who holds the keys to God's ranch. Only your words give life to sorry cowboys. ⁶⁹ We believe what you said and we know with all our heart that you are the Holy One of God."

⁷⁰ Then Jesus said, "I picked y'all, but one of you has made a deal with the devil." He was talking about Judas Iscariot, one of the original twelve, who would double-cross him later.

CHAPTER 7

Unbelieving Brothers

Jesus later traveled throughout the land of Galilee. He stayed out of Judea because the Jews wanted to string him up. ² Then the time came for the Jewish Festival of Tents, and ³ Jesus's brothers poked fun at him saying, "Leave Galilee and go to Judea. Your cowboys need to see what you can really do. ⁴ If you want people to follow you, you can't hide out in the country where no one can see your great power. Since you are so powerful, go show yourself to the world." ⁵ Obviously his brothers didn't even believe in who he was at this time.

⁶ Jesus replied, "My time to go to Judea isn't right now, but you can leave if you want to. ⁷ This world won't turn against you, but it has already turned against me because I tell it like it is—this world is full of evil people. ⁸ So, y'all go ahead and go to the festival, but I won't go before my time." ⁹ When he was done, he rode off to another ranch in the Galilee area.

Jesus Preaches at the Temple

¹⁰ After his brothers had left for Jerusalem, Jesus headed there at a long trot, too. But he went in secret. ¹¹ At the festival the Jewish leaders were all asking where Jesus was, but no one had seen him. ¹² There were a lot of rumors flying around about him. Some people said he was a good man and others called him a fraud. ¹³ The only thing not said in public was anything in support of him. Everyone was afraid of getting in trouble with the Jewish leaders who opposed him.

¹⁴ About halfway through the festival, Jesus stood up in the main church and began to preach. ¹⁵ The people listening marveled at his knowledge and wondered where he came by such wisdom without having attended seminary.

¹⁶ Jesus knew their questions and said, "My teaching does not come from me. It comes from God who sent me. ¹⁷ Anyone who rides for God will be able to tell if my teaching is from him or it is merely my own. ¹⁸ Those who speak on their own are after personal glory, but the cowboy who seeks glory only for God is a man of truth. There will be nothing false about him. ¹⁹ Moses gave y'all the Law. There are a lot of teachers and preachers of the Law, but not one of you obeys it. Not only that, but you are trying to kill me."

²⁰ This riled everyone up, and people started yelling, "A demon has you hog-tied! Who is trying to kill you?"

²¹ Jesus said, "I showed y'all one miracle, and you were astonished. ²² But I'm not the only one who did work on the day of rest. Y'all do too when you circumcise a boy on the Sabbath. (Actually,

circumcision came from our ancestors and not Moses.) ²³ You say that you circumcise on the Sabbath so that the child will follow the teachings of Moses, but then you get mad at me for healing a man's whole body on the same day. You cut off a piece of man on the Sabbath and call it holy, but I make them whole, and you call me possessed. ²⁴ If you're going to judge correctly, you've got to do it with more than what you see on the surface."

A Split in the Herd

²⁵ Some of the people in Jerusalem started wondering, "Isn't this the cowboy they want to kill? ²⁶ He's standing right here, so why aren't they doing something? Maybe it's because he is the Top Hand? ²⁷ But how can that be? We know this cowboy and where he comes from. The Messiah is supposed to show up, but nobody will know where he came from."

²⁸ Jesus was still teaching in the main church while they were talking and he addressed them, "Yeah, you know who I am and where I came from. I didn't come here by myself. I was sent here by the one who is Truth. You don't know him, ²⁹ but I do. And he sent me here to you." ³⁰ At this they tried to arrest him, but he just walked out like nothing had happened.

³¹ Still, there were a lot of cowboys who had been listening and started to believe in him. They said to others, "He's doing everything the Good Book said the Messiah, or God's Top Hand, would do."

³² The religious know-it-alls heard what the crowds were saying and finally sent the church police to arrest Jesus. ³³ When they found him said, "I won't be here for long. Then I'll be going back to where I'm from. ³⁴ You'll think you know where that is, but you don't. And you cannot go where I am headed back to."

³⁵ The Jewish leaders didn't know what to make of his comments. They thought he must be leaving the country or something. ³⁶ They kept wondering what Jesus meant when he said, "You cannot go where I'm headed."

The Well Won't Run Dry

³⁷ On the last and most important day of the festival, Jesus stood in the main church courtyard and shouted to the people, "If you're thirsty, come to me. ³⁸ Just like the Good Book says, 'A fountain of youth will flow from within the cowboy who believes in me.'" ³⁹ Jesus was talking about the Holy Spirit, who would be given to the believers later on.

Split and Divided

⁴⁰ When people heard this, they were saying, "This must be the cowboy we've heard about and been waiting on." ⁴¹ Others went further and said, "Let's just call it like it is, he is the Messiah, the Christ." But there were still those who argued and said, "I'm sorry, but he just can't be. There is no way our Savior can come from a Podunk place like Galilee. ⁴² The Good Book clearly says that the Savior will be of the royal lineage of David." ⁴³ So the crowd was split and divided about who Jesus really was. ⁴⁴ Many still wanted him arrested, but nobody could lay a hand on him.

⁴⁵ When the church police came back without Jesus, the Pharisees and priests demanded, "Why did you not bring him in!?"

⁴⁶ "We have never in our lives heard someone speak like that," the policemen reported.

⁴⁷ "Have y'all fallen in love with him, too?" the Pharisees said in a mocking tone. ⁴⁸ "Is there a single one of us leaders who have fallen for his lies? Is there even one of us who believes in him? ⁴⁹ The crowds follow him because they are just ignorant farmers, ranchers, and day trash. They are dirty and uneducated, unlike us. They are ignorant of the Law. God will curse them all."

⁵⁰ Then Nicodemus, the Pharisee who had met with Jesus before, spoke up and asked, ⁵¹ "Does our Law convict a man before his side of the story is told?"

⁵² They laughed at him and said, "Are you a Podunk from Galilee, too? Search the Good Book, and you will see that no prophet ever comes from Galilee."

Note: The most ancient documents do not include John 7:53-8:11. There are a few manuscripts that have some of the verses, but each one places them somewhere else.

⁵³ Then the meeting was closed, and everyone went home.

CHAPTER 8

Caught Red-Handed

Jesus went to Olive Hill, ² but was back at the main church early the next morning. He drew quite a crowd. He sat them all down and taught them how to ride for God's outfit. ³ As he was teaching, some seminary professors and a Pharisee brought a woman who had just been caught having sex with a married man. They stood her up in front of the gawking crowd.

⁴ "Oh great teacher," they chided, "we caught this woman having sex with a married man. ⁵ The code of Moses says to kill her with stones. What say you?"

⁶ Jesus knew they were trying to trap him. He said nothing, but stooped down and started writing something in the dust with his finger. ⁷ They kept hounding him for an answer, but when he stood up, he said, "Stone her. But only the man who has never sinned, not even once in his entire life, may throw a stone." ⁸ He knelt back down and continued writing in the dirt.

⁹ The oldest of the woman's accusers walked off first, but soon all of them had gone. Now it was just Jesus and woman standing among the crowd. ¹⁰ He finally stood up and looked around. "Where are all your accusers, my lady? Is there no one here to accuse you?"

¹¹ "There are none, my Lord," she said.

"Then I will not accuse you either," Jesus said. "Go now and live your life the right way. Do not sin anymore."

The Light of the World

¹² Jesus turned back to the crowd and said, "I am the light of the world. Those who ride with me will never ride in the dark. They will live in the light."

¹³ Some Pharisees challenged him, "You can't claim that about yourself without a witness to back it up."

¹⁴ Jesus replied, "I don't have to have a witness because I know who I am and where I came from. Just because you don't know these things doesn't make what I said untrue. ¹⁵ You only judge by human standards, but I judge no one. ¹⁶ And even if I did, my judgment would be absolutely correct every single time because I am not alone. I ride with my Father who sent me to you. ¹⁷ Your own code says that the testimony of two witnesses makes something true. ¹⁸ Well, the first witness is me, and the second is my Father who sent me."

¹⁹ "Where is your father then?" they replied. "Let's hear what he has to say."

Jesus said, "If you don't recognize who I am, how can you recognize who my Father is? If you knew me, you would know him." ²⁰ Jesus was standing near the offering table when he said all this. No one tried to arrest him because his time had not yet come . . . but it would.

People Keep Arguing about Jesus

²¹ Jesus repeated himself later, "I am leaving soon. You will look for me, but you'll only find death when your sins catch up to you. You can't find me because you can't go where I am headed."

²² The people started wondering if Jesus meant he was going to kill himself.

²³ Jesus continued, "You live in what you can see, hear, feel, and touch. I come from beyond such human standards. You are hobbled to this world. I am not. ²⁴ This is why I said that you would die when your sins catch up to you. Nothing of this world can save you from your sins. I AM the only one who can save you and you must believe that with all of your soul. If you don't, you are already dead."

²⁵ The Jews said to him, "Then tell us who you really are."

Jesus replied, "I've already told you, but you don't listen. ²⁶ There is a lot I could say about each of you. I could start listing off your sins one by one, but I won't. I only say what the one who sent me tells me to say. And everything he tells me is entirely true." ²⁷ They still didn't understand that he was talking about his Father.

²⁸ So Jesus finally said, "When you have finally strung me up on the cross, then you will know that I AM he. I only do what my Father says for me to do. ²⁹ The One who sent me rides with me now, for he has not left my side. For I always do what is pleasing to him." ³⁰ As he spoke, many people began to believe.

The Devil's Kids

³¹ Jesus spoke then to those who believed. "You ride for me if you do what I tell you to do. ³² Only then will you know the truth, and the truth will set you free."

³³ "But we have never been a slave to anyone," they answered. "We are all descendants of Abraham. If we are not slaves, then how can we be 'set free'?"

³⁴⁻³⁶ Jesus replied, "Anyone who has sinned is a slave to sin. A slave can belong to no family,

but if the Son sets you free, you are truly free. ³⁷ I know you are descendants of Abraham, but I also know that some of you are trying to kill me. There's no room in your dead hearts for my life-giving message. ³⁸ I am acting like my Father and y'all are behaving like yours."

³⁹ "Our father is Abraham," they yelled.

"No, he's not," Jesus replied. "If he were your father then you would do as he did. ⁴⁰ Abraham wouldn't be standing here trying to plot my murder, but y'all are. ⁴¹ You all are acting like your real father."

They yelled back, "We are not bastard children! God is our real father."

⁴² Jesus said, "If that were true, then you would love me. I have been sent by God. I have never said that I came on my own. ⁴³ Why do y'all not understand this? Am I speaking a foreign language that you've never heard? ⁴⁴ No, the reason you don't understand me is because your real father is the devil. He wants to kill me and so do y'all. He was a murderer in the beginning, and his bastard children act just like him. He has always despised the truth because he couldn't handle it. He lies because it's who he is. He is the father of lies. ⁴⁵ When I tell y'all the truth, you can't handle it either, so you don't believe me. ⁴⁶ Which of you has ever seen me commit an actual sin? If I'm telling the truth, why can't you believe it? ⁴⁷ A child of God understands what God says. You don't understand because you are not a child of God."

⁴⁸ The people began shouting, "Well, you're actually a Samaritan and possessed by a demon."

⁴⁹ Jesus said, "I'm not possessed by a demon. I bring honor to my Father, and you bring dishonor to his Son. ⁵⁰ I'm not looking for honor though, but there is one who wants it, and I give it to him. He is the judge of all things. ⁵¹ I ain't lying when I promise you that whoever rides for me and does what I do will never see death."

⁵² The unbelievers said, "Now there is no doubt that you have a demon inside you. Even Abraham died, and so did the prophets. But you are telling us now that if we do what you say, we won't ever die? ⁵³ You think you are greater than Abraham? You think you are better than the prophets? Who do you think you are?"

⁵⁴ Jesus continued, "If I am seeking my own glory then all I've said doesn't mean anything. I do not seek glory, but my Father will give it to me. ⁵⁵ You claim that he is your God, but you wouldn't know it if he was standing here talking to you. I know who God is. If I said I didn't, I would be a liar like y'all. But I do know God, and I obey him completely. ⁵⁶ Did you know that Abraham was allowed to see what I would do and he absolutely rejoiced at the sight?"

⁵⁷ "You are less than fifty years old," they sneered. "How could you have seen Abraham?"

⁵⁸ "Listen to me close," Jesus said. "Before Abraham was born, I AM!" ⁵⁹ They screamed in rage and picked up stones to kill him, but Jesus slipped away from the main church grounds.

CHAPTER 9

What God Can Do

As they rode along, Jesus saw a man who had been blind his whole life. ² "Boss," his cowboys asked, "why is this man blind? Did his daddy commit some kind of sin that made God mad or something?"

³ "Neither of his parents did anything to make this happen," Jesus said as he dismounted. "This happened so God could show y'all what he can do. ⁴ While the sun is shining, the Son will be out shinin': ropin', gatherin', doctorin', and brandin'. It's what my Daddy sent me to do. But it'll be dark soon, and no one will be able to work. ⁵ While I am here, I am the light that lets people see."

⁶ After this, Jesus spat on the ground and made a little mud. He put the mud on that blind fellow's eyes ⁷ and said to him, "Go wash this mud off in Siloam Pond." (Siloam means "sent.") The guy felt his way there and did as he was told. He came back with eyes better'n a bald eagle.

⁸ All his neighbors and those who had known him when he was blind couldn't believe their own eyes. They asked, "Isn't this the beggar who we used to help because he was blind?"

⁹ Some of the folks thought it was him and others thought it must be someone else. But the guy kept telling them, "Yeah, that was me. I am the one."

¹⁰ So they asked him how he got his eyes back to workin' condition.

¹¹ He said, "The cowboy they call Jesus spat in the dirt and made a mud pie to go on my eyes.

He then told me to wash it off in Siloam Pond. When I did, I could see."

¹² They asked, "Where is this Jesus fellow?" The man answered, "I ain't got no idea. I ain't his keeper."

¹³ So some people took the guy to the Pharisees. ¹⁴ Jesus had healed him on the day of rest, ¹⁵ and they asked him about how it was done. Once again, he told the story.

¹⁶ Some of the Pharisees said, "This guy isn't a man of God. If he were, he wouldn't have done work on the day of rest."

Another Pharisee stood up and asked, "If he is not, then how can a sinner perform such a good work as this?" A squabble broke out among these religious know-it-alls.

¹⁷ So they turned back to the man and asked, "What do you say about the man who healed you?"

"I think he's one of God's cowboys. I believe he's a prophet," the man quickly answered.

¹⁸ The discussion then turned to wondering if the guy had been born blind or if someone was trying to pull a fast one. So, they sent for the man's parents and ¹⁹ asked them, "Is this your son? Has he been blind his whole life? How is it that he can now see?"

²⁰ His parents knew they were in a sticky situation and said, "This is our boy, and yes, he was born blind as a bat. ²¹ We have no idea how he can see now. Ask him that question. He's old enough to speak for himself." ²² His parents were evasive because the church leaders had already made it public that if you support Jesus, you would be thrown out of the church. ²³ That's why they said, "Ask him. He's a full-grown man."

²⁴ So the Pharisees called the healed man back in and said, "Give God the credit for your eyes, not this sinner who claims to have cured you. He was just a swindler prayin' on helpless folks."

²⁵ The man said, "Whether Jesus is some kind of swindler, I do not know. But I'll tell you what I do know. I once was blind, but now I see!"

²⁶ They asked him, "Then what did he do? How did you get your sight back?"

²⁷ The guy threw his hands in the air and said, "I might've been blind, but I'm startin' to wonder if y'all are all deaf. I have already told you how it happened. Are y'all tryin' to figure out how to find Jesus so you can ride with him, too?"

²⁸ Then all hell broke loose at the meeting. They yelled at him, "You ride for him! We only follow Moses! ²⁹ We know he was a man of God, but we don't have any idea where this Jesus fellow came from."

³⁰ The man held his ground and said, "Oh, really? You don't know where he's from, but he healed my eyes. ³¹ You may not know him, but this we do know, We know God don't cotton to sinners, nor does he answer their prayers. God answers the prayers of people who ride only for him. ³² There has never been an instance of a blind man being given back his sight, yet here I stand. ³³ If Jesus wasn't from God, he couldn't have done that and y'all know it."

³⁴ The Jews attacked him again and said, "You were blind because of your sin. Who do you think you are that you can teach us anything about God?" Then they threw him out of the church and told him never to come back.

Setting the Record Straight

³⁵ Jesus heard about what happened and went and found the man. He asked him, "Do you believe in the Top Hand?"

³⁶ The man replied, "Tell me who he is and show him to me so that I can ride for him."

³⁷ Jesus said, "You're looking at him, cowboy."

³⁸ The man kneeled and said, "I believe it is you, Lord."

³⁹ Then Jesus put his hand on the man's shoulder and said to everyone watching, "I have come into this world to set the record straight. Those who thought they were blind will now realize they can see. And those who thought they could see everything will now find out they were the ones who were blind."

⁴⁰ Some Pharisees spoke up and said, "We know you're talking about us. Set the record straight, cowboy. Are you calling us blind?"

⁴¹ Jesus replied, "If you were blind, you wouldn't be guilty of leading people astray. But since you claim to see clearly, you will be held responsible for your sins."

CHAPTER 10

Cattle Rustlers and Cowboys

Jesus said, "All y'all Pharisees better listen up. A fellow who goes over the fence and starts walking through the cows on foot must be a cattle rustler. ² But the one who rides through the gate on horseback is the cowboy. ³ The cow boss tells him what gate to go through to get to the pasture the cows are in, and the cattle recognize the cowboy's voice. The cowboy knows each cow by number and leads them to tall grass and clean water. ⁴ When he gets them all out of the pasture, he doesn't have to push because they will follow. ⁵ They won't follow a stranger. They'll get boogered and run off when someone is walking through 'em on foot. They only recognize a cowboy who sits tall in the saddle and takes care of 'em." ⁶ Jesus told this story, but the Pharisees didn't understand what he meant.

⁷ Jesus explained to them, "Listen up! I am the gate for the cattle. ⁸ Any person who tries to get to the cattle in any way except through me are liars and cattle rustlers. The cattle will spook if they come near. ⁹ I am the gate. Through me, everyone will be saved. I lead to tall grass and clean water. ¹⁰ A cattle rustler only comes to steal, kill, and destroy. I have come that my cattle will have tall grass and clean water . . . and have a bunch of it.

¹¹ "I am the good cowboy. The good cowboy will die for his cattle. ¹² The day worker is not the cowboy and does not own the cattle. If a day worker sees a wolf or a rustler, he's not going to defend the cattle with his life. He will hightail it out of there. Then the herd is run through the fence and scattered. ¹³ The day worker isn't going to put his life on the line.

¹⁴ "I am the good cowboy. I know my cattle and my cattle know me, ¹⁵ just like the Father knows me, and I know the Father. I will lay down my life for my cattle. ¹⁶ But this isn't the only herd I care for. I have been given other herds that aren't in this pasture. I will gather them together too. They will listen and follow me also. Eventually, there will be one herd, taken care of by one cowboy.

¹⁷ "My Father loves me because I am willing to give my life and take it back. ¹⁸ No one can take my life from me, but it is my choice to give it. I have the authority to lay down my life and to get it back. This is the job my Father gave me to do."

¹⁹ The Jews who heard this were divided once again. ²⁰ Some said, "This guy is a total nutjob. Why are we even listening to this?"

²¹ But others disagreed, "Nutjobs don't speak with this kind of wisdom, nor do they heal the blind."

The Jews Toss Jesus Aside

²² It was now winter, and Jesus was at the Festival of Dedication of the Temple, or Hanukkah, in Jerusalem. ²³ Jesus was walking along Solomon's Porch in the church courtyard.

²⁴ Some Jews surrounded him and asked, "How long are you going to keep up this ruse? If you are the Top Hand, tell us straight right now."

²⁵ Jesus said, "I've already told you, but you won't believe me. The things I do, and the fact that I only give God the credit, tells all you should need to know. ²⁶ But you don't believe me because y'all are not my cattle. You were another outfit's brand. ²⁷ My cattle know me, and I know them. They go where I lead them. ²⁸ The pasture I lead them to is eternal life. I'll never lose a single one, and no one can take a single one from me. ²⁹ My Father gave me each one. He is greater than everyone else, and no one could stand against Him and be able to steal one. ³⁰ My Father and I ride together."

³¹ The Jews got so mad that they picked up rocks to stone him, ³² but Jesus said, "I have done great things that my Father sent me to do. For which of these great acts of kindness to you want to kill me?"

³³ They spat back, "We're not killing you for good works. We're gonna kill you for claiming that you are God."

³⁴ Jesus calmly replied, "God himself said to some of your ancestors, 'I call y'all gods!' ³⁵ Now you know the Good Book never lies. So, if God himself called some of his Cowboys 'gods', ³⁶ why is it so bad that I call myself the 'Son of God'? After all, God sorted me off and sent me down here to y'all. ³⁷ I wouldn't believe me either unless I had seen the great things God has done through me. ³⁸ But God has done great things through me. If you don't believe in me, at least recognize the great things God is doing. If you did see these things and knew they were from Him, then you would believe that God and I are one."

³⁹ This set them off again, and they attacked Jesus, but no one laid a hand on him. He left like a boss—because he was.

⁴⁰ Then Jesus loped out across Jordan Creek where John the Baptizer had done all his work in the early days. He stayed there for a while, and many people came out to see him. ⁴¹ A lot of folks

said, "John never performed a miracle, but everything he said about Jesus is true." [42] A whole mess of folks there started believing in who Jesus was.

CHAPTER 11

Lazarus Has Taken the Long Sleep

There was a man named Lazarus from a little town called Bethany. Lazarus was sick. He was the brother of Mary and Martha. [2] (Mary was that gal who poured perfume on Jesus and cleaned his feet with her hair.) [3] The two sisters sent a message to Jesus telling him of their brother's deathly illness.

[4] When Jesus got the message, he said, "This sickness will not result in death, but it will lead to glory for the Son of God—the Top Hand." [5] Now Jesus loved Mary and Martha like sisters. He loved Lazarus like a brother. [6] So when he heard the news, he stayed put for two days before he left. [7] When the time was right, he told his cowboys to saddle up. "Let's strike a long trot for Judea," he said.

[8] "Hey Boss, you do remember they are trying to kill you, don't you?" they said.

[9] Jesus looked over his shoulder as he rode off, "We're burning daylight. No one stumbles while the sun is out, [10] but at night it is easy to trip and fall. [11] Our pard, Lazarus, has fallen asleep, but I'm going to go get him up."

[12] The cowboys looked at each other in confusion and said, "If he's asleep now, he'll probably be awake by the time we get there." [13] They didn't realize Jesus was saying Lazarus was dead.

[14] So then he told 'em, "Lazarus has taken the long sleep, [15] and it's a good thing I wasn't there, or you wouldn't be about to see something amazing. Let's go, boys!"

[16] Then Tom, whose nickname was the Twin, said, "Yeah, boys. Let's go, it should be fun. They're just going to try to kill us when we get there, but we've got his back."

Jesus and the Sisters

[17] When he got there, Jesus discovered Lazarus had been buried in a cave for four days. [18] Now Bethany was just a couple of miles outside of Jerusalem, [19] and many Jews had come out to be with the family in their time of mourning. [20] When Martha heard Jesus was there, she ran out to meet him. Mary stayed inside.

[21] "Boss," Martha said. "if you'd been here, this tragedy would never have happened. [22] But that is irrelevant now. I know God will do whatever you ask."

[23] Jesus said, "Your brother will live again, Martha."

[24] "Yes," she said, "I know he will come back to life on the last day."

[25] Jesus replied, "I am the giver of life. Anyone who believes this will live, even if they are dead. [26] Anyone who rides for me will never die. Do you believe this Martha?"

[27] "Yes, Lord," she said, "I have always believed you are the Messiah, God's Son, the Top Hand who has come to the world to save it." [28] Then she went back in the house and told her sister that Jesus had arrived and he wanted to see her. [29] Mary got up at once and went outside.

[30] Jesus was still there. [31] When the people saw Mary rush out, they had assumed she was going to the grave to mourn. They followed her out to offer comfort. [32] When Mary got to Jesus, she fell at his feet once again and said, "You could have kept him from dying if you'd been here, Lord."

[33] When Jesus saw her and the rest of the people crying, a deep anger rose up within him. He didn't like to see his nation hurting. He asked, [34] "Where is he?"

When they showed him the grave, [35] Jesus cried.

[36] The people could see just how much Jesus loved his friend, [37] but some people said it was his fault Lazarus had died. Some of them said, "If he could heal the blind, he could have healed his friend if he cared that much."

[38] Despite his tears, Jesus was still angry and said, [39] "Roll this rock out of the way."

But Martha said, "Lord, he's been in there for four days. It's going to smell like the south end of a rancid goat."

[40] But Jesus responded, "Didn't you hear me say that if you believed you would see the glory of God?" [41] So they rolled the stone aside, and Jesus looked into heaven and said, [42] "Dad, thank you for always hearing me when I call. I don't have to talk out loud for you to hear me, but I say this for the benefit of all who are listening. I want them to believe in you and me."

[43] Then Jesus stated in a commanding voice, "Lazarus, come here!" [44] And the dead guy

walked out of the tomb. He was still wrapped in the burial cloth. Jesus told those standing nearby, "Take off his grave clothes. He won't need them anymore."

The Plot to Ambush Jesus

45 There was a whole mess of folks who saw this and started believing in Jesus. **46** But some of them went away and snitched Jesus out to the Pharisees. **47** A meeting was called of the Jewish rulers to try to figure out what to do about Jesus.

"What are we going to do about him," some of them said. "There is no doubt he can do amazing things. **48** If we let this continue, everyone will believe in him, and we will be out of power. If we aren't in power, then Rome will come in and destroy the main church and everyone with it."

49 The High Preacher, Caiaphas, spoke up, "Y'all are idiots if **50** you don't see what we should do. It is better that one man dies rather than everyone else." **51** Now he didn't come up with on his own. God had spoken through him sometime before and said that Jesus would die for **52** everyone so that the scattered herd might be brought back together. **53** From the time Caiaphas had said this, they had been plotting to ambush Jesus.

54 But Jesus knew their plans and stayed out of public sight. We went and stayed at a place called Ephraim with all his cowboys.

55 When it was nearly time for Passover, people from all over the country went to Jerusalem to be ceremonially washed. **56** Jesus was the talk of the town and people watched for him everywhere. Everyone kept asking, "Do you think he'll be here? He wouldn't miss the Passover, would he?" **57** But the bigwig preachers had issued orders that Jesus was to be arrested if he was seen.

CHAPTER 12

Jesus Won't Be around Long

Six days before the Passover party, Jesus rode up to Bethany to visit Lazarus and his sisters. **2** A meal was prepared in Jesus's honor. **3** Then Mary got a bottle of priceless perfume and poured it on Jesus's feet. She wiped his feet with her hair. The house was filled with a pleasing aroma.

4 But Judas Iscariot, the cowboy who would later double-cross Jesus, said, **5** "Why is she wasting that perfume? We could've sold that

and given money to the poor. That cost a year's wages." **6** He didn't care about the poor. He was the treasurer of the ministry and dipped his hand into the cookie jar all the time.

7 "Let her alone," Jesus said. "She's preparing my body for the day of my death. **8** The poor will always be around, but I won't."

9 When word got out that Jesus was in town, people came from all around to see him and the man who had come back from the dead. **10** Lazarus's fame had him on the radar of the church's head honchos. They planned to kill him too. **11** Too many people believed in Jesus when they saw Lazarus.

Jesus Comes in Like a Boss

12 Word spread like wildfire the next day Jesus was in town. **13** Folks gathered up palm branches to lay in the road when he arrived. They were all shouting, "Hear, hear for God! May he bless the Boss. All hail the Boss, the King of Israel."

14 Jesus found an unbroke colt and rode into Jerusalem on it. This fulfilled a prophecy that said, **15** "Don't be scared Jerusalem. Look, your king is coming down the road on an unbroke colt."

16 His cowboys didn't see the relevance of all this, but after he had gone back to heaven, they put the pieces together, and it made sense.

17 Most of the crowd had seen what Jesus did with Lazarus. They were telling everybody around about the cool things Jesus was doing. **18** More and more people were signing up to ride with him. **19** The Pharisees said to one another, "This is getting out of hand! Look at how everyone is flocking to him."

Jesus Speaks of His Coming Demise

20 There were some people from Greece who were in town for the Passover party. **21** They found Phil, who was from Bethsaida in Galilee, and said, "Can we meet your Boss?" **22** Phil told Andy about it, and they went to see if Jesus would meet them.

23 Jesus said, "My time is at hand. I'll soon get the glory my Father has promised. **24** I'm telling you straight, unless a seed is buried in the dirt and dies, it cannot produce new plants. But its death and burial will produce a great harvest of new life. **25** Those who protect their lives at all cost will lose their life. But those who will give up their life will find eternity. **26** If you want to ride for me, you must ride where I go. And my Father will honor any man who does.

²⁷ "Right now I feel like I'm hung up in the stirrup, but do you think I'm going to whine about it and say, 'Make it stop, Dad'? No, this is what I came to do. ²⁸ God, all this glory is yours!"

Then a mighty voice came from heaven, "I have shown my power, and I will do so again." ²⁹ Everyone was looking around to see where the voice came from. Some said it was thunder and others said an angel had spoken.

³⁰ Then Jesus said, "God let you hear him for your benefit, not mine. ³¹ The time for the showdown has arrived. I will meet the devil, the ruler of this world, in the street and when the clock strikes, I will be faster. ³² I will be lifted up for all the world to see, and I will gather the herd to me." ³³ He was telling them how he was going to die.

³⁴ People started shouting questions at him, saying, "We read the Good Book. The Top Hand, the Messiah, is supposed to live forever. Why do you say now that you will die and be lifted up, but still be faster and win? Who is this 'Top Hand'?"

³⁵ Jesus said, "While I'm here, walk in the light and find your way. Get there quick before the darkness overtakes you. ³⁶ Trust what I, the light, show you. Don't waste any time. Then you will be children of the light."

After he had said this, he was gone.

Nobody Believes

³⁷ Despite everything Jesus had done, people still didn't believe in him. ³⁸ Of course, the great cowboy Isaiah had already said many moons before, "Lord, no one believes what we tell them. Has anyone recognized God's arm that is about ready to strike?"

³⁹ But folks didn't believe, because Isaiah had also said, ⁴⁰ "He has blinded 'em and made 'em hard. They can't see with their eyes or feel with their hearts. They cannot turn to me and let me doctor them."

⁴¹ Isaiah had been talking about Jesus because he'd seen the future and jotted down what he saw. ⁴² Now many people did believe in him, including some of the Jewish leaders. But these fellows kept their beliefs to themselves for fear that they would be run out of the church. ⁴³ Even though they believed, they still cared more about what other people thought than standing up for what was true.

⁴⁴ Jesus shouted out to the crowds, "If you trust God, trust in me too. He's the one who is orchestrating these things you see. ⁴⁵ When you look at me, you are looking at God who sent me. ⁴⁶ I have been sent to light the path so that no one rides off the cliff in the darkness. ⁴⁷ I'm not here to judge those who won't do what I say. I came to save the world, not judge it. ⁴⁸ But there will be a judge for those who shun me and my message. They will be condemned on the last day. ⁴⁹ My message is not my own, but the one God told me to say. ⁵⁰ His message is right and guarantees eternal life. I say whatever he tells me to say and that is all."

CHAPTER 13

Feet Washin'

Before the Passover party, Jesus knew his time was short for this world. He knew he was leaving to go be with his Dad. But Jesus loved his cowboys up until the very end.

² They were eating the evening meal, and Judas had already made his deal with the devil. The plan was already in motion to double-cross Jesus. ³ God had put everything in Jesus's command, and he knew it. He also knew he'd come from God and was fixing to go back. ⁴ Jesus got up from the table, took off his clothes, and wrapped a towel around his waist. ⁵ He poured water in a big bowl and started washing his cowboy's feet. He dried their feet with the towel he had wrapped around his waist.

⁶ When he got to Pete, Pete said, "I ain't gonna let you lower yourself on my account. You ain't washin' my feet, Boss."

⁷ Jesus looked up and said, "You don't understand what I'm doing right now, but one day you will."

⁸ "It ain't gonna happen." Pete said, "I won't let you touch my nasty feet."

Then Jesus said, "Then you don't ride for me."

⁹ Pete changed his tone quickly and said, "Then start at my feet and then wash my hands and head!"

¹⁰ Jesus said, "Those who shower in the morning don't need a bath in the evening. They just need their feet cleaned. This is about godliness, Pete, not grime. Everyone here is clean except for one." ¹¹ Jesus knew exactly who the doublecrossing cur dog was.

¹² When he was done, he put his clothes back and sat down at the table. "Do y'all know what just happened?" he asked. ¹³ "Y'all call me 'Boss' and 'Lord,' and that's what I am. ¹⁴ A good cowboy watches the Boss and does what he does. If he ain't above washin' someone's feet, then neither are y'all. ¹⁵ I have just handed you directions on how to gather the pastures. So do what I have done to you. ¹⁶ I'm telling you that the cows ain't better than the cowboys, and cowboys ain't better than the jigger boss. ¹⁷ Now that you know the circle, go ride it and gather and the Boss will bless your socks off."

Jesus Discusses His Double-Crossin'

¹⁸ "I'm not talking to all of y'all though. I know which ones of y'all are my true cowboys. What's happening right now is because the Good Book already said, 'He supped with me and then shot me in the back.' ¹⁹ I'm not telling y'all this to hear myself talk. I'm telling y'all this so that later you will understand that I predicted it and that I really am the Top Hand. I AM the Messiah—the cowboy who will save the world. ²⁰ I tell you the truth, anyone who welcomes a cowboy that I send welcomes me. If they welcome me, then they welcome the Father too."

²¹ Jesus got real quiet then, and a troubled look came over his face. He looked around and said, "It's a fact, one of you is about to shoot me in the back."

²² All the cowboys looked around at each other. You could've heard a pin drop. ²³ The cowboy who Jesus loved scooted over real close to Jesus and held on to him. ²⁴ Pete caught the cowboy's eye and mouthed, "Ask who the double-crosser is."

²⁵ The cowboy nodded his head and turned to Jesus and asked quietly, "Which one is it, Boss?"

²⁶ Jesus said, "The one I hand this dipped bread to." He dipped the bread in a dish and handed it to Judas Iscariot. ²⁷ When Judas took the bread, Satan took control of him. Jesus looked him in the eye and said, "What are you waitin' on? Pull the trigger you dog." ²⁸ None of the other cowboys caught on to what was taking place. ²⁹ They thought Jesus was tellin' his treasurer to go pay for the meal or something. ³⁰ Judas, with murder in his eyes and a piece of bread in his hand, scurried out the door and into the darkness.

Jesus Predicts Pete's Denial

³¹ When Judas left, Jesus said, "It's time for the Top Hand to be honored and God is honored because of him. ³² And since God receives all the honor the Top Hand brings, he will honor his Son. He won't waste any time doing so either. ³³ Boys, my time here is shorter than a piggin' string now. When I'm gone, y'all are going to look for me. But like I told the Jews, you can't follow me this time."

³⁴ "I'm going to give you a new rule. Love each other as I have loved you. ³⁵ Anyone can claim to be one of my cowboys. This will be the proof. If you don't love each other, then you're a counterfeit cowboy."

³⁶ Pete asked, "Boss, where are you ridin' off to?"

Jesus replied, "I'm going somewhere you can't go. But later you will."

³⁷ Pete asked, "I don't understand why you won't let me come. I'd ride right through death's doorstep at a high lope for you."

³⁸ Then Jesus said, "That's big talk, Pete. Would you really die for me? Because you wait and see, before the cock crows at sunrise, you'll bail on me three times."

CHAPTER 14

Gettin' the Ranch Ready

"Don't let this get you down. Trust God and trust me. ² My Father's outfit has many ranches. If that wasn't the case, would I have told you I'm going to prepare one for you? ³ If I go to get your ranch ready, I'll come back and get you when the time is right. Then you'll be with me forever. ⁴ Y'all know the trail that leads where I'm headed."

⁵ Tom said, "Boss, we ain't sure where you're going. So how can we know which trail to take?"

⁶ Jesus said, "I am the Trail, the Truth, and the Life. No one gets to God without going through me. ⁷ If you know me, you know my Dad. Not only that, but if you've seen me, you've seen him."

⁸ Phil said, "Just give us a glimpse of God. That's all we ask."

⁹ Jesus replied, "Don't you know me, Phil? Have you not ridden right beside me all this time? If you've seen me, you've seen God. Why in the world would you say, 'Give us a glimpse of God'? ¹⁰ Me and my Daddy are spitting images

of each other, heart and soul. I don't pull these words out of my pocket. I only say what my Father tells me to. When you hear me, you're listenin' to him. [11] Believe me when I tell you that I am in him and he is in me. At the very least believe in what you've seen. [12] The truth is, the cowboy who rides for me will do the same miracles I have done. Better yet, they will do things greater than these because I'm going home to my Father. [13] If you need me to do something for you that will bring honor to my Father and me, [14] all you have to do is ask, and it'll be done.

Never Fail or Get Lost

[15] "If you love me, you'll ride for me. If you truly ride for me, you'll do like I've taught you. [16] I'm going to talk to my Dad and he's going to send you someone to give you a hand. And this Hand will be with you forever. [17] This Hand is the Essence of Truth. This world cannot believe in him because it can neither see the Truth nor know him. You'll know him because he's gonna live right inside you.

[18] "I ain't gonna run off and leave you like a dogie calf. I'll come get you. [19] Soon this old world won't be able to see me, but you will. If I'm alive, you're gonna be alive. [20] When the time comes, there won't be any doubt that my Father and I are one. [21] The cowboy who loves me is the one who knows my ways and follows 'em. Those who love me will be loved by my Father. And I too will love that cowboy and show myself to him."

[22] Judas (not the double-crosser) asked Jesus, "Why are you keeping this just between you and us? Why not show the world who you really are?"

[23] Jesus replied, "Because the world does not love me. You've gotta love me to be part of my crew. Anyone who is a part of my crew will do what I've told them to do. [24] People who don't love me won't do what I've told them to do. This is what God says, not me.

[25] "I'm tellin' y'all this while I'm still here. [26] However, the Pard, the Holy Spirit, will be sent by my Dad to help you with all of this. He'll show you the way and remind you of the things you need to do. He's going to back you up so that you never fail or get lost.

[27] "Everything is going to be alright. That's my gift to you. You have peace if you want it. This ain't the same kind of peace the world promises. The world's peace is an empty promise. Mine is a rock-solid guarantee. Listen real close, you do not have to be afraid. [28] Remember, I'm heading out, but I will come back. If you love me, you'll be happy that I'm going to see my Dad. There is no one greater than him. [29] I'm telling you this so when it happens, you'll understand. [30] I'm not going to be saying much else. The king of this world has me in his sights and is about to pull the trigger. Despite what you see and hear, he has no control over me. [31] The job my Father gave me is about to start. I do it so that the world will know I love my Dad."

Jesus opened the door and said, "Saddle up, boys. Let's ride!"

CHAPTER 15

No Longer Hired Hands

Then Jesus said, "I am the Top Hand, and my Father is the ranch owner. He's the one who cares for everything on the ranch. [2] He'll fire every cowboy who doesn't do what a real cowboy should do. As to those who do their jobs well, he will push them harder and harder to make them better and better. [3] Y'all are pretty good already because of my message that you have believed. [4] Stay with me, and I'll stay with you. You can't do what I've asked you to do without me. As a matter of fact, you can't do anything of value without me there with you.

[5] "I am the Top Hand, and you are my cowboys. If you ride with me, then I will ride with you, and you'll do great things. Without me, you won't accomplish anything. [6] Anyone who rides without me will find himself in a box canyon during a brush fire. There will be no escape. [7] If you ride with me, and I ride with you, I'll help you with anything you ask. [8] You bring honor to my Father's outfit when you do great things for those less fortunate.

[9] "I've loved you the way my Daddy loves me. My love is like a campfire on a cold night. Stay close and stay safe. [10] If you do what I tell you to do, you'll remain within my love. If you remain in my love, then you remain within God's love. [11] I've told you these things so you might be overflowing with joy. These things are what your soul longs for, and the world tries to keep you away from. [12] Take care of others like I am taking care of you. That is my command. [13] The greatest love is to die for your friends. [14] My friends

are those who do the things I tell them to do. ¹⁵ I don't call y'all hired hands anymore. Hired hands don't know the ranch's business, but I've told y'all everything my Daddy told me. ¹⁶ Y'all didn't come and find me, I came and found you. I taught y'all how to make a difference in the world . . . a difference that will last. Anything y'all need will be given to you if you ask. ¹⁷ Don't forget what I've told you to do—love each other.

The World Hates Real Cowboys

¹⁸ "When people start hating you, remember that they hated me first. ¹⁹ The world loves only those who belong to it, but you no longer ride for the world. Y'all ride for me. I have called you to ride for me, and the world hates you for it. ²⁰ Remember when I told you 'a cow isn't greater than the cowboy'? If they attack me, they will attack you. If they would have listened to me, they would have listened to you. ²¹ They'll hate you because they hate me. They have rejected the one person who could save them. By rejecting me, they have rejected God too. ²² Ignorance isn't bad unless you've been told the truth. Now they are no longer ignorant, but they are now condemned because they do not believe the truth. They are out of excuses. ²³ If anyone hates me, they hate my Father. ²⁴ They saw everything I did and still chose to hate my Dad and me. ²⁵ The Good Book even said it would happen like this when it said, 'They hated me with no cause.'

²⁶ "But I will send the cowboy to you. He is the Spirit of Truth. He'll come from my Father and tell y'all the truth about me. ²⁷ And you must also tell others the truth about me because y'all have ridden with me since the beginning.

CHAPTER 16

"I'm telling you these things so you don't get pitched off into the cactus and lose your faith. ² You're gonna be kicked out of churches. There'll even come a point when they'll kill you and think they are doing the right thing. ³ They won't know what they're doing because they don't follow my Father or me. ⁴ I'm saying this to prepare you for what is coming. There was no point in telling you before, but now you need to know.

The Work of the Trail Guide

⁵ "But now I'm about to head out. Every one of you is missing the point about where I'm going.

⁶ If you understood, you would be happy, but yet you do nothing except hang your heads. ⁷ Truth is, it's a good thing I'm going. The Trail Guide can't come and help you until I'm gone. ⁸ When he gets here, he's gonna show people three things: sin, being right with God, and the judgment that waits for unbelievers. ⁹ The world's greatest sin is that they do not believe in who I am. ¹⁰ Y'all are going to be made right with God when I get to him. I won't be around anymore, but I'll still be with you. ¹¹ Judgment awaits those who follow the world because its ruler has already been judged.

¹² "Now there is much more I could tell you, but it would be too much to handle. ¹³ But when the Trail Guide comes, he will lead you to all truths. He will not speak anything that he has not heard. He's going to guide you in all things to come. ¹⁴ He's going to bring me honor because he's going to get all his information straight from me. ¹⁵ Everything God possesses has been given to me. That's why the Trail Guide will tell you only what he gets from me.

Switchin' Leads

¹⁶ "In a little while, I'll be gone. But I'm going to come riding back very soon."

¹⁷ Some of the cowboys started questioning each other, "What does he mean 'be gone'? What is he talkin' about when he said, 'You won't see me, but then you will later' and 'I'm headed out to see my Daddy'? ¹⁸ And what is 'a little while'? We don't understand any of this."

¹⁹ Jesus knew they had questions, but were afraid to ask. He said, "Y'all are looking a little bewildered. Y'all look like a calf that doesn't know whether to run through the fence or head back. ²⁰ The truth is, y'all are going to cry when you see what happens to me. Y'all will cry, and the world will laugh and cheer. But then I'm going to switch leads on you. Y'all will laugh and cheer, and the world will bawl and squall. ²¹ A woman will cry out in pain as she gives birth, but her tears will turn to smiles once she brings new life into the world. ²² Y'all will go through the same range of emotions. Soon you will cry, but your tears will turn to joy. And no one will be able to take your joy away. ²³ When that joy arrives, you will have no more uncertain questions to ask. You will be asking for my help and I'll give it you so that you can accomplish your task. ²⁴ Until now, you haven't really needed anything, but

the time is going to come when you will have a need, and I'm going to give it to you.

²⁵ "I have used many illustrations to try to teach you the truth, but a time is coming when we will no longer need such things. We will be able to speak plainly. ²⁶ By asking in my name, that doesn't mean I will ask my Father on your behalf. It means you will be able to ask him yourself. ²⁷ The whole point of all of this is to bring you close to God because he loves you so much. ²⁸ I came from my Father and now I'm fixing to go back to him."

²⁹ The cowboys slapped their legs and said, "Now we can understand you, ³⁰ there's no need to ask a bunch of questions because the only thing that is important is that you came from God and we believe it."

³¹ Jesus asked, "You say you believe now, ³² but the time is nearly here when all of you will scatter into the brush to save your hides. You'll leave me high and dry, but I won't be alone. My Father will be there with me. ³³ I've told you all of this so you will be able to be calm. While you ride for me, you'll have plenty of trouble, but keep your chin up! I have conquered this world."

CHAPTER 17

The Time Has Come

After he'd finished saying all of this, Jesus looked up and said, "Dad, the time has come. Bring honor to your Son so he can bring honor to you. ² You've given your Boy all authority over everyone. If you bring 'em to the Son, he will give them eternal life. ³ Eternal life is simply knowing you, the true God, and Jesus Christ, the one you sent to save 'em. ⁴ I've honored you by finishing the work you gave me to do. ⁵ Now, Father, clothe me in the glory I had before the world began.

Jesus Prays for His Cowboys

⁶ "God, I have shown you to the cowboys you brought me. They were yours and you gave them to me. They have kept their word and ride only for you. ⁷ They finally understand that everything I've given them has come from you. ⁸ I only gave them words you gave me, and they believed. They know I came from you and you sent me. ⁹ I pray for them, Dad. I ain't praying for those of the world, but only for those you've given me. I pray for 'em because they are yours.

¹⁰ Everything I have is yours, and everything you have is mine. These cowboys have honored me. ¹¹ I'm headed home, but they will be stuck here for a while longer. Holy Father, keep them safe by the power of your name, and the power of the name you gave me. That way they can be as close as me and you. ¹² I've been watching over them, and I didn't lose a single one. None has been lost except the one who was destined for destruction. It had to happen that way to fulfill the things written long ago in the Good Book.

¹³ "I'm headed your way, but I say these things while I'm still here. I want them to feel the same way about you as I do. They need to feel that kind of joy. ¹⁴ I've given them your Word, but the world hates them because of it. They stand out now just as I did. ¹⁵ I'm not asking you to remove them from this world, but to protect them from the devil. ¹⁶ They don't belong to him any more than I did.

¹⁷ "Use the truth to make them holy like you. Your word is the truth. ¹⁸ I've given them a mission just like you gave me. ¹⁹ I'm offering myself as a holy sacrifice so that they may be made holy by your word.

Jesus Prays for All Who Believe

²⁰ "This prayer isn't just for them. I also pray for all of those who will ride for me because of my cowboys' work. ²¹ I want them to be as close to us as you and I are to each other. I want them to know us so completely that the world will believe you sent me. ²² I'm giving them the same honor and glory you gave me. I did this so we could all be united in love and purpose. ²³ I am with them, and you are with me. We are all together now. Since we are one, the world will finally realize you sent me and you love them just as you have loved me.

²⁴ "Dad, I want all those who ride for me to be where I am. Only when they are with me will they be able to see the glory you gave me. Only then can they see that you have loved me since before the world was made. ²⁵ Dad, you have done everything right, the world still doesn't know you, but I do. My cowboys know you too. They know that you sent me down here to save them. ²⁶ I have shown them who you are and will continue to do so. I want them to know you so that the love you have for me will be experienced by them. They will experience the love I have experienced."

CHAPTER 18

After praying, Jesus rode across Kidron Draw with his cowboys and entered an olive grove.

Jesus Is Arrested

² Now the double-crosser, Judas, knew the place well. Jesus had taken his cowboys there often. ³ Judas led the way to the olive grove. He brought with him some church mercenaries and church leaders. There were even a few Pharisees who tagged along. A long line of torches, swords, and lanterns made their way through the trees.

⁴ Jesus, knowing what was about to happen, walked out to meet them. He said, "Who are y'all looking for?"

⁵ "Jesus of Nazareth," one of the mercenaries said.

⁶ Jesus looked at the traitor Judas and said, "I AM he." They all drew back and fell down at the power of his words.

⁷ He asked them again, "Who are you looking for?"

"Jesus of Nazareth," they said again.

⁸ Jesus said, "I already told you that I AM he. I've asked you twice who you are looking for. You are looking for one man. Let the rest of these cowboys go." ⁹ This happened because Jesus had said, "I will not lose a single one you have given me."

¹⁰ Then Pete swung into action. He drew his sword and cut off the ear of Malchus, the head preacher's slave. ¹¹ But Jesus hollered at Pete and said, "Holster your weapon, cowboy. I have to finish the job my Father gave me. Even the suffering that goes with it."

¹² So the mercenaries, their commanding officer, and the church police arrested Jesus and handcuffed him. ¹³ They took him first to Annas, the father-in-law of Caiaphas, the head preacher at that time. ¹⁴ Caiaphas is the one who said, "It's better that one man should die rather than all of them."

Pete Bails Out on Jesus for the First Time

¹⁵ Pete and another cowboy followed at a distance. The other cowboy knew the head preacher and was allowed to enter the courtyard with Jesus. ¹⁶ Pete waited outside. The other cowboy spoke to the girl working the gate and Pete was allowed in. ¹⁷ As they walked in, the girl working the gate asked, "Wait a minute. Aren't you one of the cowboys who ride for the man they just arrested?"

"Nope," Pete said. "Don't know who you're talking about."

¹⁸ The night was cold, and the servants had made a fire in the courtyard. Pete stood with them warming himself.

The Interrogation of Jesus

¹⁹ Inside the house, Annas started asking Jesus about his message and what he taught his cowboys.

²⁰ Jesus said, "I don't need to repeat myself. Y'all have heard everything I've said in the churches and the main church courtyard where all the Jews hang out. I haven't been secretive about one thing. ²¹ Why ask me what I said? Ask those that heard me."

²² The final word had barely come out of Jesus's mouth when a guard standing close by slapped him in the face and said, "That ain't no way to talk to the head preacher."

²³ Jesus looked at him and said, "Tell me what I said wrong. But if I've only told the truth, then why do you hit me?"

²⁴ Annas sent Jesus to the head preacher, Caiaphas. Jesus was still bound up tight like a criminal.

Pete Bails on Jesus Two More Times

²⁵ Meanwhile, Pete still stood by the fire. One of the men standing there asked him, "Aren't you one of the cowboys who rode with Jesus?"

Pete said, "Nope."

²⁶ There was a relative of the man whose ear Pete had cut off, and he said, "I'm pretty sure I saw you in that grove of olive trees with Jesus." ²⁷ Pete denied knowing Jesus a third time. At that moment, a rooster began to crow.

Pilate Interrogates Jesus

²⁸ Jesus was then dragged from Caiaphas's house to the Roman mansion to see the governor. It was early in the morning, and to avoid being disqualified from the Passover meal, no one entered the Roman mansion. ²⁹ Pilate came outside and asked, "What are the charges against this man?"

³⁰ The Jews said, "He is a criminal. Why else would we have brought him to you?"

³¹ Pilate shook his head and said, "Then take

him back and deal with him yourselves according to your own law."

"But we can't execute anyone," they exclaimed. ³² (This fulfilled Jesus's words about how he would die.)

³³ Pilate walked back inside to his office and ordered Jesus brought in. "Are you the king of the Jews?"

³⁴ Jesus replied, "Where did you hear that?"

³⁵ "Do I look like a Jew to you?" Pilate spat back. "Your own people brought you to me. What have you done?"

³⁶ Jesus said, "My kingdom is not here. If it were, you wouldn't be able to take me. My cowboys would keep me safe from the Jewish leaders. My kingdom is not in this world."

³⁷ "Then you are a king!" said Pilate.

Jesus said, "You said it, I didn't. I was born to tell people the truth. The seekers of truth listen to me."

³⁸ "What is truth?" Pilate said sorrowfully. He then went out and tried to dismiss the charges against Jesus. ³⁹ Then Pilate said, "Jesus is in my custody, and I always release one prisoner to you at Passover. Do you want me to release this 'king of the Jews'?"

⁴⁰ "No," the screamed. "Give us Barabbas!" Barabbas had fought against the Romans.

CHAPTER 19

String Him Up

Then Pilate had Jesus beaten with a whip. ² The Roman soldiers made a crown of thorns and put it on Jesus's head. They threw a purple robe around him ³ and made fun of him saying, "All hail the king of the Jews!" Then they would slap him on the face.

⁴ Pilate went outside again and said, "I've done my part. I'm telling you now that I find no basis for the charges brought against him." ⁵ The soldiers brought Jesus out with the crown of thorns and the purple robe. Pilate said, "Look, here he is."

⁶ As soon as he said this, the crowd exploded. "String him up! String him up!"

But Pilate said, "You do it. I can find no wrong in him."

⁷ The Jews pressured him and said, "Our law states that any man who claims to be the Son of God must die."

⁸ When Pilate heard this, he started getting worried. ⁹ He brought Jesus with him back into the mansion and asked him, "Where are you from?" But Jesus said nothing.

¹⁰ Pilate continued, "Will you say nothing in your defense? On my authority, I can have you freed or killed."

¹¹ Jesus then spoke up and said, "The only authority over me that you have is the authority that my Father gives you. The man who double-crossed me has committed a far greater sin."

¹² Pilate again tried to release Jesus, but the Jewish leader yelled, "This man is claiming to be above Caesar. That makes him a rebel and you just as bad for allowing it."

¹³ Pilate brought Jesus back out and sat down in the judge's chair (in Aramaic, it's called Gabbatha). ¹⁴ It was now about noon on the day of preparation of the Passover.

"Here is your king," Pilate announced.

¹⁵ But the crowd erupted and said, "Take him out and string him up. Kill him!"

"You want me to kill your king?" Pilate asked incredulously.

"Our king is Caesar," the head preachers yelled.

¹⁶ Finally, Pilate gave the order to string Jesus up.

Jesus Is Crucified

Jesus was then led away. ¹⁷ He carried his own cross to the place called the Skull (in Aramaic, it's called Golgotha). ¹⁸ The Romans strung him up between two thieves.

¹⁹ Pilate had the last word and had a sign posted on Jesus's cross that said, "Jesus of Nazareth, King of the Jews." ²⁰ The killing spot was near the city, and many people saw the sign. It was even posted in three languages: Hebrew, Latin, and Greek.

²¹ The religious leaders objected and asked the sign be changed to, "He said he was the king of the Jews."

²² But Pilate replied, "What's written is written."

²³ After Jesus was strung up, the soldiers took his clothes and divided the spoils among the four of them. The only thing that was left was his robe and they didn't want to tear it. ²⁴ The soldiers said, "Let's roll dice to see who gets the best part." This happened because the Good

Book said, "They divided my clothes among themselves. They gambled for my garments." And this is what happened.

²⁵ Near the foot of the cross stood Jesus's momma, his momma's sister, Mary the bride of Clopas, and Mary Magdalene. ²⁶ When Jesus saw his momma, standing there with the cowboy who he loved so much, he said, "Momma, here is your son," ²⁷ and to the cowboy he said, "Here is your momma." That cowboy took care of her the rest of her life.

Jesus Dies

²⁸ After this, when everything had nearly been accomplished, Jesus said, "I'm so thirsty." He said this to fulfill the Good Book's final prophecy about his death. ²⁹ A jar of sour wine was nearby. The soldiers dipped a sponge in the vinegar and held it up for him to drink. ³⁰ He drank some and said, "It is done." And his last breath left his body with his spirit.

³¹ All this happened on Friday. The next day was a very special day of rest and the Jews didn't want any bodies hanging around. They asked Pilate if he would break the legs of those on the crosses so they would die faster and their bodies could be removed. ³² Pilate agreed, and the soldiers broke the legs of the two men on either side of Jesus. ³³ When the soldiers saw Jesus had already died, they didn't break his legs. ³⁴ They did stab him in the side with a spear. Blood and water poured out. ³⁵ The cowboy who saw it is giving an eyewitness account so that you may believe. ³⁶ These things happened to fulfill the scripture that said, "No bone will be broken," ³⁷ and another that said, "They will look at the one who has been stabbed."

Jesus Is Buried

³⁸ Later, Joseph from Arimathea asked Pilate if he could have Jesus's body. Joseph was a secret rider for Jesus because he was afraid of the Jews. With Pilate's permission, he took Jesus's body away. ³⁹ Nicodemus, the fellow who had visited Jesus under the cover of darkness, gave him a hand. He brought some stuff to put on Jesus's body for burial. ⁴⁰ They followed the Jewish custom and wrapped Jesus in a long linen cloth. ⁴¹⁻⁴² There was a new tomb near the place where Jesus died and they laid him in it because of the Day of Preparation.

CHAPTER 20

Jesus Comes Riding Back from the Grave

Early Sunday morning before sunrise, Mary Magdalene went to Jesus's grave and saw that the big stone had been rolled away. ² She came running back to Pete and the cowboy who Jesus loved, and said, "Jesus has been taken. We don't know where he is."

³ So Pete and the other cowboy headed out toward the grave at a high lope. ⁴ Pete was still on his way when the other cowboy stuck his head in the tomb. ⁵ Inside he could see the grave linens, but he didn't go in. ⁶ Pete got there at this point and barreled right by him and went in. He saw the grave linens lying there, ⁷ as well as the cloth that had been wrapped around Jesus's head. The cloth was laying there right where Jesus's head should have been. ⁸ Finally, the other cowboy joined Pete inside. He saw what had happened and believed. ⁹ Until now, they hadn't understood that Jesus would come riding back from the grave. ¹⁰ Then they went back to the house.

Jesus Talks to Mary Magdalene

¹¹ Mary had been standing outside crying. After they left, she looked in the tomb ¹² and saw two angels sittin' where Jesus's body should have been. ¹³ "My dear," they said, "why are you crying?"

"Because my Lord is missing. We don't know where he is," she said.

¹⁴ She turned around to leave and Jesus was standing there, but she didn't recognize him. ¹⁵ "My dear," he said, "why are you crying? Who are you looking for?"

She thought Jesus was the gardener and said, "Have you taken the body away? Please tell me where you have put him."

¹⁶ "Mary," Jesus said.

She then recognized him and cried out, "Rabboni!" (which means "Teacher" in Aramaic).

¹⁷ Jesus then said, "Don't hold on to me, for I haven't yet gone to my Father. Go tell my cowboys, 'I am going to our Father, and to our God.'"

¹⁸ Mary found the cowboys and said, "I have seen the Lord!" Then she told them what he'd said.

Jesus Appears to His Cowboys

¹⁹ That Sunday evening, the cowboys were sitting around with each other. They were keeping

out of sight because they were afraid of the Jewish leaders. All of a sudden, Jesus was in the room with them. "Peace be with y'all," he said. ²⁰ He showed them the nail scars and the one in his side. They were filled with happiness at seeing him alive. ²¹ He told them again, "Peace be with y'all. Like the Father sent me, it's time for me to send y'all." ²² Then he breathed the Holy Spirit, the Trail Guide, into them saying, ²³ "If you forgive, they are forgiven. If not, then they are not."

Jesus Shows Himself to Tom

²⁴ One of the cowboys, Tom (nicknamed the Twin), had not been there when Jesus showed up. ²⁵ They told him, "The Lord was here!"

But Tom said, "I won't believe a word of it until I put my fingers in the nail holes and place my hand in his side."

²⁶ About a week later, all the cowboys were together—including Tom. The doors were locked and all of a sudden, Jesus was there with them. Jesus said, "Peace be with y'all!" ²⁷ Then he turned to Tom and said, "Put your finger in the nail holes. Place your hand in my side. Stop doubting and just believe."

²⁸ Tom bowed his head and said, "My Lord and my God!"

²⁹ Jesus replied, "You say that now that you've seen me. Better blessings await the cowboy who believes without seeing."

John's Reason for Writing His Book

³⁰ Jesus did a whole bunch of other things while he was with his cowboys. Things that are not recorded in this book. ³¹ But I've written these things down that you may believe that Jesus was the Son of God, the Messiah, the Top Hand, and that by believing these things, you would have eternal life.

CHAPTER 21

Jesus Cooks 'Em Breakfast

Later on, Jesus appeared once again to his cowboys by the Sea of Galilee. ² It happened like this. Pete, Tom, Nate, James, and John, and two other cowboys were together. ³ Pete said, "I'm going fishin'," and the others said they wanted to go too. So, they all jumped in a boat, but they didn't catch anything all night long.

⁴ Early the next morning, Jesus stood on the shore, but the cowboys couldn't tell who it was.

⁵ Jesus hollered out to them, "Hey, amigos. Did y'all catch anything?"

"Nope," they answered.

⁶ Jesus hollered back, "Cast your net on the right side of the boat and I bet you'll catch something." When they did, their nets started to break because of all the fish.

⁷ Then the cowboy who Jesus loved said to Pete, "Hey, it's the Lord!" Pete barely registered the words before he threw his clothes on and jumped out of the boat and swam to shore. ⁸ The others hauled the fish in and headed back to shore. ⁹ When they got there, they found breakfast was waiting. Jesus had cooked them some biscuits and fish.

¹⁰ Jesus said, "Bring some of the fish over here." ¹¹ Pete climbed back into the boat and pulled the massive net of fish ashore. There were 153 large fish in the net, but it wasn't torn. ¹² Jesus said to all the cowboys, "Come get y'all some grub." None of the cowboys asked who he was because they knew it was the Lord. ¹³ Jesus handed them all some biscuits and some fish. ¹⁴ This was the third time that Jesus had appeared to his cowboys after coming back from the grave.

Jesus Makes It Right with Pete

¹⁵ When they'd finished eating, Jesus asked Pete, "Do you love me more than the rest of the cowboys do?"

"Absolutely, Lord," he said. "You know that."

Jesus said, "Feed my cattle."

¹⁶ Again, Jesus asked Pete, "Do you love me?"

He answered, "Yes, Lord. You know that I do."

Jesus said, "Take care of my cattle."

¹⁷ Then a third time Jesus asked, "Pete, do you love me?"

Pete's feelings were hurt because Jesus kept asking him the same question over and over as if Pete didn't love him. Pete said, "Lord, you know all things. So, you know that I do love you."

Jesus said, "Feed my cattle."

¹⁸ "Let me tell you something Pete," Jesus said. "When you were young, you got to make your own choices and do what you wanted. But there will come a day when you are old that someone else will stretch out your hands, dress you, and lead you somewhere you do not want to go." ¹⁹ Jesus was telling him about the way he would die and bring honor to God. Then he said, "Come with me, my friend."

²⁰ Pete turned and saw the cowboy who Jesus loved was walking up. (This is the same cowboy who was sitting next to Jesus that last night and had asked him who the double-crosser was.) ²¹ When Pete saw him, he asked, "What about this cowboy? What will happen to him, Lord?"

²² Jesus said, "If I want to keep him alive until the day I return, it is none of your business. You just follow me and don't worry about anything else." ²³ Because Jesus said this, rumors spread that this particular cowboy would never die. But Jesus never said that. He only said, "If I want to keep him alive until the day I return, it is none of your business."

²⁴ This is the cowboy who was an eyewitness and wrote everything down. We know that what he said was true.

²⁵ Jesus did a lot more things as well. If every single thing were written down, I'm not sure the whole world could contain the books it would take to document them all.

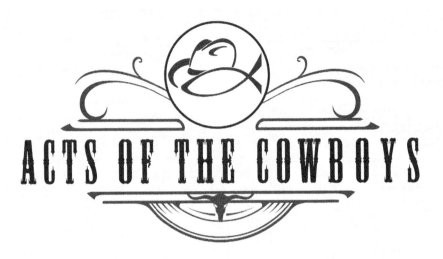

ACTS OF THE COWBOYS

CHAPTER 1

Dear Theophilus, in the last book I wrote you, I told you of all the things Jesus did and what he taught. [2] The book ended with Jesus going to heaven after giving instructions through the Trail Guide, or Holy Spirit, to his cowboys. [3] During those forty days between his riding back into town and heading over the hill to go be with his Father, Jesus left no doubt he had ridden back from the dead and was indeed alive. [4] At one point, Jesus told all of 'em, "Don't leave Jerusalem until my Dad has given you the gift he promised. [5] John the Baptizer used water, but in a few days you'll be baptized with the Holy Spirit."

Jesus Heads North

[6] The cowboys gathered around him and asked, "Boss, are you fixin' to free Israel and give us a king again?"

[7] He replied, "That ain't for y'all to know. [8] But I will let y'all in on this, when the Holy Ghost fills you up, y'all will ride to the far ends of the world to tell folks about me."

[9] After saying this, he was taken up to heaven, and a cloud moved in between the cowboys and Jesus. [10] As they stood there trying to keep him in view, two cowboys on white horses suddenly stood in their presence. [11] "Cowboys," they said, "why are y'all standing around gawking at the sky? Jesus has been taken to heaven, but one day he will return in the same fashion."

A New Cowboy Is Chosen

[12] The cowboys then made the short ride from Olive Hill back into Jerusalem. [13] They unsaddled and went to the upstairs room of the house they

were staying in. The cowboys who were there were Pete, John, James, Bart, Matt, Alpheus's son James, Simon, and the other Judas (James's boy). [14] They all made a pact that they were going to see their mission through to the end. They prayed together along with Jesus's momma, Mary, and several other women. Jesus's brothers were there, too.

[15] At this time, there were about 120 people in the room. [16] Pete stood up and said, "Pards, the double-crossing that Judas did on our Boss was predicted a long time ago by David. [17] Judas gathered right alongside of us in this ministry."

[18] With the money he got for stabbing Jesus in the back, Judas bought some acreage outside of town. He got yard-darted out there, and when he hit the ground, his intestines spilled out of his body like a gut-shot animal. [19] Everyone heard about what had happened, and the acreage got the nickname of "Akeldama," which means "Blood Field."

[20] Pete continued, "What Judas did was written in the Book of Psalms and says, 'Let his land be barren. Let no one make a home there.' It also says, 'Find a good cowboy to fill the gap.'

[21] "So now we have to find a new cowboy to take his place. This cowboy must have ridden with us the entire time we rode with the Lord. [22] He needs to have been there from the time Jesus was baptized by John until the day he died. This cowboy will help us spread the news that Jesus came ridin' back from the dead."

[23] Two cowboys who fit the criteria were nominated: Justus, aka Joseph Barsabbas, and Matthias. [24] Then all the people prayed, "God,

you know all of us inside and out. Pick which of these two men you would have ²⁵ on your crew to replace Judas. That counterfeit Judas got just what he deserved and is now in the place he belongs." ²⁶ The two cowboys drew straws and Matthias was chosen to ride with the other eleven cowboys.

CHAPTER 2

On the day of Pentecost, all the cowboys and others were together. ² Suddenly a sound like a tornado tearin' through a hay pasture filled the whole house where they were staying. ³ Something like fire spread among them. ⁴ All of 'em were filled with the Holy Spirit and began to speak in other languages without any effort or knowledge from the cowboy talkin'.

⁵ People from all over the world were in Jerusalem and ⁶ when they heard the sound, they followed it to its source. When they arrived where the sound came from, they were astonished because every person heard the cowboys speaking in their native language.

⁷ The people were flabbergasted and wondered, "How is this possible? These cowboys are all from Galilee. ⁸ How can they speak our languages? ⁹ The people here are Parthians, Medes, Elamites, Mesopotamians, Judeans, Cappadocians, Pontus, and Asians. ¹⁰ There are also people from Phrygia, Pamphylia, Egypt, and the country around Libya and Cyrene, folks from Rome ¹¹(both Jews and Jewish converts), Cretans, and Arabs. And all of these are hearing twelve cowboys speak in the people's native language about the great things God has done!" ¹² They all stood listening with their jaws on the floor. Many wondered, "What can this mean?"

¹³ But some in the crowd didn't believe. They yelled, "These cowboys have just been on the whiskey, that's all."

Pete Talks to Everyone

¹⁴ Then Pete stood up and said, "Listen up, all of you! Don't doubt what's happening here. ¹⁵ These cowboys ain't drunk. Shoot, it's too early for that even for cowboys. ¹⁶ No, what you are seeing here today is what the great cowboy Joel had predicted when God said through him, ¹⁷ 'Near the end, I will fill all kinds of folks with my Spirit. Sons and daughters will prophesy. Young men will have visions, and your old cowhands

will dream dreams. ¹⁸ My hands, both cowboys and cowgirls, will be filled with my Power and they will also prophesy. ¹⁹ I will put on a show in the heavens and do mighty things on the earth below. There will be blood and fire and clouds of smoke. ²⁰ The sun will shut off, and the moon will turn red when the Lord comes back. ²¹ But everyone who asks Jesus to save them will be saved.'

²² "My fellow Israelites, God himself acknowledged the truth of Jesus Christ with miracles, signs, and wonders like this world has never seen. ²³ He knew y'all would hand his boy over to evil people and they would have Jesus killed. ²⁴ But God brought him back from the dead, setting him free from the agony of the grave. Death could not hold the Top Hand. ²⁵ David had even said, 'I always see the Lord in front of me as I ride. I will be unshakeable because he is at my right side. ²⁶ Is it a wonder that my heart should be filled with such joy? Is there any doubt why my mouth shouts praises to Him? My body is at peace with the hope that is in Him. ²⁷ He will never leave me alone and let me rot in a grave. Your Top Hand will not see maggots or worms. ²⁸ You have shown me the trail and filled me with joy and happiness that can only come from you.'

²⁹ "Listen up my countrymen! I can tell you our ancestor David is dead and buried. You can visit his grave, ³⁰ but God had told him one of his descendants would sit on the throne. ³¹ David had seen a glimpse of the future and was talking about Jesus riding back from the grave after getting killed. He was saying God wouldn't allow the Top Hand to rot in the grave and be a snack for maggots.

³² "God has brought Jesus back to life, and we saw it all. ³³ Now he sits in the place of honor at God's right hand. And God has given him the Holy Spirit, the Trail Guide, to give us this gift you have seen today. ³⁴ Even David hadn't gone to heaven when he said, 'God said to my Boss, "Ride here to the right of me, in the place of honor for the Top Hand. ³⁵ I will humble those who hate you, and you'll be able to use them as a footstool."'"

³⁶ Pete continued, "So be sure, and tell everyone else too, that God has made Jesus, who was killed, our Lord and Savior!"

³⁷ Pete's words cut to the quick, and they all asked, "How do we ride for Jesus?"

[38] Pete replied, "All of you must stop ridin' in sin and start ridin' for God. Then you need to get baptized in the name of Jesus for the forgiveness of your sorry ways. Then God will give you the Trail Guide like he's given us. [39] This promise is for all of you and your children. It's for anyone who is called to ride for the Lord." [40] Then Pete started preachin' and teachin' for a long time. He told everyone, "Save yourselves from getting hung up in this crooked world we live in."

[41] About three thousand people started ridin' for God that day and were baptized.

All the Believers Form a Crew

[42] After this, all those who believed devoted themselves to the cowboy's teachings and to being neighborly. They shared grub (including the Boss's supper) and prayed with each other. [43] Crazy, wonderful things filled all their lives, and the cowboys did many miracles and wonders. [44] This new crew worked well together and took care of each other. [45] They sold what they didn't need and helped those who were in need. [46] They met every day to worship God. They ate together often, and their hearts were filled to overflowing. [47] The crew praised God, and God turned around and blessed their socks off. He brought them new cowboys every single day to add to the outfit of those who were being saved.

CHAPTER 3

Pete and John showed up at the main church one day for the three o'clock prayer. [2] They got there at the same time a lame fellow was being helped in. People put him at the Beautiful Gate every day to beg. [3] When Pete and John came by, the fellow asked them for some money.

[4] Pete and John stared a hole through this guy, and then Pete said, "Look at us!" [5] The man looked up, obviously expecting a handout. [6] But Pete said, "I don't have any money for you, but I'll give you something better. In the name of Jesus Christ, get up and walk."

[7] Pete helped the guy to his feet. As the man got up, his feet and ankles became strong and were healed. [8] The man jumped up and began to walk around. Once he got used to the sensation, he started jumpin' around like a young foal turned out to pasture. He went around praising God, and then went into the Church with Pete and John.

[9] Everyone was staring at what had just happened. [10] When they realized it was that beggar by the Beautiful Gate who had been healed, they couldn't believe their eyes. [11] People filed out onto Solomon's Porch to see what was happening and saw the man with his arms around Pete and John.

Pete Preaches

[12] Pete took this opportunity and said, "My friends, why are you astonished by this? Do you stare at us because you think we had something to do with it? It was not our power that healed this man, but the power of God. [13] The same God who Abraham, Isaac, and Jacob served has now brought honor and glory to his Son, Jesus Christ. This is the same Jesus who you had killed. The same one you shunned in front of Pilate. [14] You double-crossed God's Top Hand and chose instead to release a murderer. [15] You killed the One who spoke us into existence, but God brought him back from the grave. We saw it happen. [16] By faith in Jesus this man has been healed. See it for yourself."

[17] Pete continued, "My fellow countrymen, I know you thought you were doing the right thing. I know your leaders thought the same thing. [18] But all of it had to happen because God had predicted a long time ago that the Top Hand would suffer. [19] Turn away from your sin, and turn back to God. If you do, your sins will be blown away like a feed sack in a windstorm. [20] A time is comin' fast where you will get your second wind in the presence of the Lord, and God is going to send him back to gather all his cowboys up and take them home with him. [21] The Top Hand has to stay in heaven until that time comes just like the old prophets said. [22] Remember when Moses said, 'God's gonna send someone to help y'all, like he did me, so y'all best listen to him. [23] Anyone who doesn't will be cut out of the herd and shipped to the killers.'

[24] "Samuel started it, and all the prophets have repeated him about the days to come. [25] Y'all come from these men, and y'all share in the same promise they had. God said to Abraham, 'Through your kids, many generations from now, the whole world will be blessed.' [26] When God sent the Top Hand, he sent him to y'all first. Turn from your wicked ways and be blessed."

CHAPTER 4

While Pete and John were talking to the people, they were accosted by some preachers, church police, and some of the Sadducees. ² They were fit to be tied because these two cowboys were telling people that everyone can be raised from the dead through faith in Jesus. ³ They grabbed the cowboys and threw them in jail overnight. ⁴ That didn't stop the number of believers from growing to about five thousand.

⁵ The next day, all the church decision makers met in Jerusalem. ⁶ Annas, the Head Preacher, was in attendance as well as Caiaphas, John, Alex, and others of the Head Preacher's family. ⁷ They brought Pete and John into the meeting and asked them, "How did you do this? What name did you call down from heaven?"

⁸ Pete, who was filled with the Holy Spirit, said, "Y'all head honchos listen up! ⁹ If y'all are here today to punish us for committing a great act of kindness on a fellow who was lame, and you want to know how he was healed, ¹⁰ then you need to understand one thing first. The power and the name are from Jesus Christ of Nazareth. Y'all remember him don't you—the one you killed, but God brought him back from the grave? It is because of him that the fellow was healed. ¹¹ Jesus even said, 'The bull the ranchers sorted out has now become the sire bull.' ¹² You can't be saved and get to heaven by no other means than faith in Jesus Christ. There is no other name or method that can do that job."

¹³ Pete and John's courage amazed the decision makers. These two cowboys were obviously uneducated and crude, but there was no doubt they had ridden with Jesus. ¹⁴ The decision makers wanted to do a lot of things, but the fact that the man who'd once been lame was standing right there was hard to argue with. ¹⁵ They told the police to escort the cowboys out of the room, and then they conferred with each other saying, ¹⁶ "What are we going to do? We can't hide what they've done. Everyone has seen it. ¹⁷ Let's just tell them they can't do it anymore and see if that works."

¹⁸ So they called the cowboys back in and told them not to do anything like that ever again. They commanded Pete and John not to preach about Jesus or even say anything about him. ¹⁹ But the two cowboys asked, "Which should we do—obey the Boss, or you? What do y'all think is the right answer? ²⁰ As for us, you couldn't shut us up if you tried."

²¹ A few more threats were made and then the cowboys were let go. The decision makers couldn't have them punished because everyone was celebrating the miracle the cowboys had done. ²² Everyone was praising God that a man who had been lame for over forty years had been healed.

Courage for the Cowboys

²³ As soon as they were bonded out, Pete and John went back and told all the other riders what the preachers and elders had said. ²⁴ When they'd heard what happened, everyone began to pray, "Our Mighty Master, the One who made it all, ²⁵ you used the Holy Spirit to talk to David, your cowboy, saying, 'Why is everyone so angry? Why do they think their plans will work? ²⁶ The cattle barons of the earth prepare for war, and the governors gather to fight the Lord and his Top Hand.'

²⁷ "Truth is, this has already happened. Right here in Jerusalem. Herod Antipas, Pilate, and all the folks in Israel plotted against Jesus, your holy cowboy, who you set apart to save us all. ²⁸ But you knew all of that would happen. ²⁹ And now, Boss, give us courage in the face of these threats. Give us boldness to preach your word. ³⁰ Give us a hand with your healing power so we can do great things in the name of your holy cowboy Jesus."

³¹ When they said, "Amen," the place shook violently, and all who were there praying were filled with the Holy Spirit. They all went out and preached with courage and conviction in the face of imminent danger.

Everyone Lends a Hand

³² All the cowboys and riders for the brand were together with one heart and one mind. No one looked at their possessions as their own. If someone needed something, someone gave it to them. ³³ The cowboys talked all the time about how Jesus had ridden back from the dead and God blessed everyone who listened. ³⁴ There was no one there who did without. If someone had some land or a house, they sold it to help others. ³⁵ The money would be brought to the cowboys to give out to those in need.

36 For example, there was this rider named Joseph, who the cowboys nicknamed Barney (meaning "Encourager"). He was from Levi's clan and came from Cyprus. **37** He sold a ranch he had and brought all the money to the cowboys.

CHAPTER 5

Now there was a married couple who promised to sell a piece of property to raise money for Pete, John, and the rest of the cowboys. **2** Ananias and Sapphira did sell the property, but instead of giving all the money to the cause, they kept back a sizable amount for themselves.

3 Then Pete said, "Ananias, I thought you were more of a man than that. You didn't just lie to us. You lied to God. You told him you'd sell that property and give all the money to help us spread the word. **4** The property belonged to you to do as you wanted. You could have sold it and kept all the money, but you said you'd donate it all. You didn't just lie to us. You lied to God."

5 When Ananias heard what Pete said, he collapsed and died. Everyone who heard about what happened was scared to death. **6** Some younger men who were there when it happened got up and took care of the body and buried him.

7 About three hours later, Sapphira came walking in, unaware of what had happened. **8** Pete showed her the money Ananias had given him and asked, "Is this the price y'all got for the land?"

"Yes, sir," she said quickly.

9 Pete said, "How is it that you thought you could pull a fast one on God? The footsteps you hear behind you are the feet of the men who just buried your husband, and they will bury you too."

10 She was dead before she hit the floor. The young men came back in and found another dead body. They went back out and buried her next to her husband. **11** Word spread quickly that the new church wasn't one to be trifled with. No longer could you say one thing and do another. God was to be respected.

The Cowboys Cure Many

12 The cowboys were healing folks right and left. They performed miracles and other great things that many people saw. Everyone who believed in what the cowboys said met on the porch at the main church. This porch was named

after Solomon. **13** But the bad thing was no one else would join them there in public. Fear of persecution and other things made folks wary. But one thing was true, the cowboys and those who followed their teachings were well respected. **14** Yet more and more cowboys started to ride for the Lord. Some of the greatest of these new cowboys were women. **15** As a result of the cowboy's work and message, sick folks were laid out in the street in the hope that Pete's shadow might fall across them when he walked by and the sick would be healed. **16** Loads and loads of the sick, hurting, and possessed were brought to the cowboys, and all of them were healed.

The Cowboys Are Opposed

17 The head preacher and his cronies, who belonged the Sadducees, were jealous and completely frustrated because of what these cowboys were doing. **18** They arrested the cowboys and threw them in jail. **19** But God sent an angel that night to open the prison doors and set the cowboys free. The angel told them, **20** "Go to the main church and give people the good news about the new life that is available to all."

21 The cowboys rode through the gates of the main church at daylight and spoke loud and clear for all to hear.

When the head preacher and his cronies arrived at work that day, they called for an emergency meeting of all the bigwig rulers of Israel. They told the guards to bring the cowboys in for a hearing. **22** But when the church police went to get them, they found the guards still there and all the doors locked, but no one was inside. They ran back to the meeting and said, **23** "The doors are locked and the guards are there, but the ones who ain't there are the cowboys. They've vanished!" **24** Everyone looked around trying to figure out what had happened and who could be blamed for their escape.

25 Then someone busted in and said, "Look out the window! Those cowboys we arrested are out there in front of the main church teaching again." **26** The church police captain went out there and asked them nicely to come talk to the bigwigs. The captain didn't cause a scene and asked nicely because he was afraid of all the people. The last thing he wanted was to get stoned to death.

27 The cowboys went in and stood before all

the bigwigs and were questioned by the main preacher. [28] "We gave y'all strict orders not to teach about Jesus. You have caused everyone to believe we were responsible for his death."

[29] Pete and some of the other cowboys said, "We don't take orders from y'all. We obey God. [30] The God of all our granddaddies raised Jesus from the grave—the same grave y'all put him in when you strung him up on that cross. [31] God raised him from the dead and gave him the best seat in his house. He made him Prince of the kingdom and Savior of all cowboys. Why would he do this, you ask? God did it so the people of Israel would turn from their sins and be forgiven. [32] We saw all this with our own two eyes, and so did the Holy Ghost. The Holy Ghost is the power of God given to those who obey him."

[33] When they heard this, the bigwigs gnashed their teeth like rabid coyotes and wanted to kill them on the spot. [34] But one of the members of the ruling party, Gamaliel, who was a teacher of the Code and very well respected, stood up and sent the cowboys outside for a minute. [35] Then he turned to the other bigwigs and said, "Listen closely, men. Consider very carefully what course of action you will take. [36] Do y'all remember when Theudas was claiming to be someone important? He had about four hundred followers, but he and all his men were killed. It turned out they were nothing. [37] A little while later, that guy named Judas from Galilee came riding out during the census making a big ruckus, but he and his men were also killed. Everything they claimed they rode for came to nothing. [38] So this is what I'm saying, leave these cowboys be. Just leave them alone. If they are charlatans, their human efforts will fail. [39] But if they are riding for God, then you will be opposing the Lord himself."

[40] Gamaliel's speech convinced them. They called the cowboys back into the meeting and had them flogged with a bullwhip and then released. As the cowboys left, the bigwigs once again ordered them not to preach about Jesus.

[41] The cowboys left in a good mood. They felt honored that they had been bullwhipped and got to suffer for the name of Jesus. [42] Day in and day out, the cowboys rode the countryside. They went from house to house and from ranch to ranch telling people the good news of Jesus Christ. They never stopped.

CHAPTER 6

In the days that followed, more and more people saddled up to ride for God's outfit. But things weren't always rosy in the crew. The cowboys from Greece complained about the cowboys from Israel, saying the Greek widows were being left out of the food distribution. [2] The twelve cowboys gathered everyone together and said, "We are not going to stop traveling around and preaching the good news so we might wait tables for the poor. [3] But, it is vitally important to care for the needy and so we are going to find seven cowboys who are known to have the Holy Ghost in their life and have them be responsible for caring for the poor. [4] We will then be able to focus on prayer and gathering the lost."

[5] Everyone thought this was a great plan. They chose the following cowboys: Steve (a cowboy full of faith and the Holy Ghost), Phil, Procorus, Nic, Tim, Parmenas, and Nick of Antioch (who had converted to the Jewish faith earlier). [6] These seven men presented themselves to the cowboys and the cowboys blessed them.

[7] So the word of God spread like wildfire through the countryside. The number of cowboys riding for the brand in Jerusalem swelled every day. Even a large number of Jewish priests saddled up too.

Steve Is Arrested

[8] Steve, a cowboy full of the grace of God and full of God's power, did amazing miracles for the people. [9] But one day some fellows from the Freed-Slave Church started a fight with him. They were Jews from Cyrene, Alexandria, Cicilia, and Asia. [10] They tried to trap Steve with fancy words and accusations, but they were no match for the wisdom from the Holy Ghost with which Steve spoke.

[11] When they couldn't beat him, they had some scoundrels lie and say they heard Steve talk crap about Moses, and even God. [12] This riled up the people who heard it and word got back to bigwigs. They sent some deputies to arrest Steve and bring him before the council.

[13] The liars said, "This man is always talking crap about Moses and those in the church. [14] We heard him say Jesus of Nazareth was going to tear the church down and change the Code Moses gave us."

[15] No one said a word because they were all looking at Steve, whose face was shining as bright as an angel's.

CHAPTER 7

Then the head preacher asked Steve, "What have you got to say about this?"

[2] This is what he said, "Listen to me, all of you. God, in all his glory, showed himself to our greatest of granddaddies, Abe. He did this while Abe still lived in Mesopotamia, before he moved to Haran. [3] God said to him, 'Leave your ranch behind and strike a long trot toward the place I've shown ya.' [4] So Abe did just that and stayed in Haran until his daddy had died. Then God led him to the land where we now live.

[5] "But God didn't give him the land. Not even a small water lot to keep his horses. But God did say he would give all the land to Abe's descendants. This was ironic because Abe and his wife couldn't have kids. [6] God also told Abe his descendants would be in a foreign country as slaves for four hundred years. [7] God said, 'But I'll pay back that country for all the abuse they'll give your family. When all is said and done, they will leave that country and come back here to worship me.'

[8] "God also taught Abe the pickle-clippin' promise. When Abe's son, Isaac, was born, he clipped his little boy's pickle on the eighth day just like God told him to. The ceremony continued with Isaac's boy, Jake, and on down the line to his boys. And it is Jake's boys who would become the twelve patriarchs of Israel.

[9] "Now these patriarchs were jealous of one of their brothers. They ended up selling their brother Joseph to some slavers from Egypt. But God was takin' care of Joseph [10] and saved his hide from a bunch of troubles down there. God helped Joseph become the second most powerful man in Egypt behind Pharaoh.

[11] "But a drought struck the area of Egypt and Canaan. A lot of people died when the food ran out. [12] Jake heard there was still some food down in Egypt, so he sent his sons down there to trade for some. [13] They made two trips, and on the second trip, Joseph told his brothers who he was. Pharaoh even learned about Joseph's family and their struggles. [14] Joseph told his brothers to go and fetch the whole family—seventy-five in all.

[15] Jake made the journey to Egypt and ended up staying there until he and the rest of our ancestors died. [16] They were all eventually brought back to Shechem and buried in the graveyard Abe had bought while he was still alive.

[17] "When the time got close to fulfill his promise to Abe about freeing all his descendants from slavery, there was a whole herd of people. [18] Then Egypt got a new king and he didn't know anything about Joseph or the fact that all these foreigners were his family. [19] He was a wicked hombre and made them throw away their firstborn kids.

[20] "At this time, a boy named Moses was born. But this wasn't no ordinary kiddo. His momma raised him for about three months and then she had to throw him away. [21] She put him in a basket in the river and arranged for the new Pharaoh's daughter to find him. She did and raised Moses like he was her own. [22] Moses was raised as an Egyptian and learned all their ways and all their wisdom. He turned out to be quite the cowboy.

[23] "When Moses was about forty, he rode down to meet some of his real kin. [24] He saw how cruel they were being treated and ended up killing an Egyptian in defense of one of his people. [25] Moses thought the Israelites would see how much he was willing to fight for them, but they could not see how God was using him. [26] The next day, Moses came across two Israelite men who were fighting. He broke it up and said, 'Men, why do y'all try to hurt each other? Y'all are brothers and should be looking out for each other.'

[27] "But the Israelite who had started the fight said, 'Who made you the cow boss over this outfit? [28] You gonna kill me like you killed that Egyptian yesterday?' [29] Moses never looked back and struck a high-lope for the land of Midian. He lived as a foreigner in this land and even got married and had two sons.

[30] "Forty years later, an angel showed himself to Moses in the form of a burning bush. This was in the desert country near Mount Sinai. [31] Moses couldn't believe his eyes and went over to get a better look. When he got close, God said, [32] 'I am the God of all your daddies. I am the God of Abe, Isaac, and Jake.' Moses was shakin' like a newborn calf in a snowstorm and didn't even dare look.

33 "Then God said to him, 'Take your boots off, cowboy. The land you are standin' on is holy. 34 I've seen what the Egyptians have been doing to my kids. I have heard their cries for help, and I'm coming. I'm coming to rescue them by ridin' with you. Now head back to Egypt.'

35 "Now this is the same Moses who the Israelites had mocked by asking him, 'Who made you cow boss of this outfit?' He was sent back by God to be their cow boss and rescuer. 36 It's a long story, but God did many miraculous things through Moses as he led all his people out of Egypt by way of the Red Sea and the barren wilderness.

37 "This is the same Moses who told the Israelites, 'God is going to send another cow boss and rescuer like me from your own people.' 38 Now these words didn't come from himself, but from an angel who'd given them to him. The angel didn't just give Moses the words to give to our ancestors, but to us today, too.

39 "But those Israelites he was leadin' turned their back on Moses. They wanted to go back to Egypt and be slaves. 40 They told Aaron, 'Build us a god we can see and touch that will lead us back to Egypt. Moses has shucked out on us, and nobody has seen him in days.' 41 So they made the statue of a calf and worshiped it like it was a god. They made sacrifices to it and made idiots of themselves. 42 Because of this, God turned his back on all those folks. He let them worship the sun, the moon, and the stars. But these things couldn't do anything for them. This is why the Good Book said, 'Did y'all bring me offerings and sacrifices during the forty years in the wilderness? 43 No, you didn't. Y'all were too busy cavorting with battle gods and slutty goddesses. Y'all worshiped them with all of your might. That's why I will send y'all to Babylon.'

44 "Our ancestors had a tent to worship the true God in while they were in the wilderness. It wasn't that the tent was where God was, it was the fact that God was with his people where they were. God had even told Moses how to set it up and where. 45 Many years later, when Josh battled against the people who were in the land God had given the Israelites, the tent was there with them. It stayed in the land until the time of David. 46 God loved David, especially when David asked to build God a permanent place to be worshiped. 47 God didn't let David build it, but he did let his son Solomon complete the church.

48 "But listen close, guys. God doesn't live in a barn made by humans. Remember that prophet who said, 49 'Heaven is my throne, and the earth is my footstool. Can you humans build something worthy like that for me? Could you even envision such a thing for me to rest my feet? 50 Don't you remember it was my hands that created all the heavens and the entire earth?'

Steve Seals His Fate

51 "You boneheaded people! Y'all have the hearts of heathens and deaf ears to the truth. Y'all sit right here on your comfy seats and deny the power of the Holy Spirit. But y'all weren't the only ones to do it. Your ancestors did it, too. 52 Name one of the prophets your ancestors didn't try to kill or punish. They even killed the ones who said the Top Hand was coming. If that wasn't bad enough, you even killed the Top Hand himself. You murdered God's own Son. 53 You shunned God's code deliberately, even though it was given to you from the very hands of angels."

54 When Steve finished, all hell broke loose. 55 But Steve remained calm and looked up. He saw right into heaven and the glory of God with Jesus standing at his right hand. 56 Steve said, "Look right there, boys! I can see right into heaven. God's sitting there and Jesus is standing at his right hand."

57 This was the final straw. They covered their ears as to not hear the truth and bull rushed Steve. 58 They dragged him out of the city like a calf to the fire and started killing him with rocks. The leaders of the vigilante mob took off their coats and handed them to a young man named Saul.

59 While they were killing him, Steve prayed, "Lord Jesus, open the gate. I'm coming home." 60 Then he fell to his knees and cried out his last words, "Lord, please don't hold this against them." After he'd said this, he fell asleep.

CHAPTER 8

Saul smiled as Steve was killed.

The Church is Scattered

The day Steve was killed began a great day of persecution in the early church. It swept through the believers in Jerusalem and most of them, except for the twelve cowboys, were scattered throughout the region. ² Some brave men came and got Steve's body and buried it. He was mourned greatly. ³ But Saul didn't care. He went from ranch to ranch, from house to house, and dragged men and women who believed in Jesus off to prison.

Phil in Samaria

⁴ Now just because the believers were scattered didn't mean they weren't preaching wherever they went. ⁵ Phil, one of the men who had been in charge of the food distribution, went into Samaria and told them about the Top Hand. ⁶ When people saw what he could do and heard the words he said, they paid close attention. ⁷ He cast out demons who shrieked at their defeat and many paralyzed people were healed. ⁸ A time of great joy had come to that part of the country.

Simon the Voodoo Priest

⁹ Now there was a guy named Simon who had been practicing voodoo around there and had amazed many people with his feats. He never neglected to tell people how great he was. ¹⁰ People of all walks of life agreed and said, "This man's name should be God's Great Power." ¹¹ They had great admiration for Simon because of his magic. ¹² But when Phil came to town, he told them the good news about God's outfit. People heard the message and were baptized. ¹³ Even that voodoo priest, Simon, was baptized. Simon followed Phil around everywhere he went. He was amazed at what Phil could do.

¹⁴ When the twelve cowboys in Jerusalem heard the Samaritans had accepted the good news, Pete and John headed that way. ¹⁵ When they rode in, the first thing they did was pray that the Holy Spirit might be given to all the new believers. ¹⁶ The Holy Spirit hadn't yet come on any of them because they'd only been baptized in the name of Jesus. ¹⁷ Then Pete and John placed their hands on the people, and the Holy Spirit filled the new believer's lives.

¹⁸ When Simon, the voodoo priest, saw what was happening, he asked them how much they charged to get this new power. He said, ¹⁹ "I will pay whatever the price to be able to give the Holy Spirit to others."

²⁰ But Pete answered, "To hell with you and your money. You can't buy this. ²¹ You can't buy your way onto God's outfit like it was a carnival ride. You'll never have a spot on his outfit because your heart is not right. ²² You better change your ways if you don't want to end up in the fire. Pray that God forgives you. What you did is worse than riding in front of the boss. ²³ You are full of sin, and I can see your god is money."

²⁴ Simon retreated quickly, "Please, cowboy. Pray for me that none of what you said will happen to me!"

²⁵ Pete and John stayed a while longer and answered questions about Jesus and God's outfit. When they headed back to Jerusalem, they preached in every Samaritan town they came to.

Phil and the Ethiopian

²⁶ Then an angel said to Phil, "Saddle up and head along the desert road that leads from Jerusalem to Gaza." ²⁷

So he started that way and met a government banker from Ethiopia. This man had been gelded and was held in high regard under Kandake, the queen of Ethiopia. The man had been in Jerusalem to worship, ²⁸ and was headed back home. He sat in his chariot as it bounced along the road and read aloud from the book of Isaiah. ²⁹ The Holy Spirit told Phil, "Ride up beside that chariot and stay there."

³⁰ When Phil got close, he heard what the man was reading and asked, "You got any idea what that means?"

³¹ "Honestly, I don't have a clue," the man said. "I've never had anybody to explain it to me." He invited Phil to sit with him.

³² The passage the man was reading was this, "As he was led to slaughter, like a lamb to the shearing table, he did not make a sound. ³³ They humiliated him and gave him a fake trial. But who is his kin? He has none since his life was taken from him."

³⁴ The gelded man asked Phil, "Who in the world is Isaiah talking about? Is he talking about himself or someone else?" ³⁵ So, Phil started right there in that passage and told him the good news of Jesus Christ.

³⁶ They had traveled a far piece when they happened alongside some water. The man exclaimed, "Look, here is some water. Is there any reason I may not be baptized?" ³⁷⁻³⁸ The

chariot was ordered to stop. Phil and the man went down to the water, and Phil baptized him. [39] When the man came up out of the water, the Holy Spirit whisked Phil away, and the man never saw him again. But the man did rejoice at what had happened. [40] Phil later appeared at Azotus and stopped at every ranch and village to tell them about Jesus. He preached all the way to Caesarea.

CHAPTER 9

Meanwhile, Saul was in a blood rage. He threatened to kill every cowboy who rode for Jesus. He went to the head preacher [2] and asked for a warrant he could take to the churches in Damascus. The order would seek the church's cooperation in ferreting out those who rode for the Way. He wanted to round them up and bring them back to Jerusalem in shackles.

[3] He got the warrant and was riding fast toward Damascus when a bright light consumed him on the trail. [4] He hit the ground hard and heard a voice saying, "Saul! Saul! Why are you hell-bent on trying to destroy me?"

[5] Saul's voice shook as he said, "Who are you, Lord?"

The voice said, "It's me, Jesus. The one you are out to get. [6] Now get back on and go to the city. Wait there, and you'll be told what to do."

[7] The men riding with Saul couldn't believe what was happening. They heard a voice but saw nothing other than Saul falling to the ground. [8] Saul got up, but when he opened his eyes, he was blind. His friends led his horse all the way to Damascus. [9] He stayed there three days without eating or drinking anything.

[10] There was a rider for the Way living in Damascus named, Ananias. The Lord spoke to him in a dream and said, "Ananias!"

"I'm here," said the man.

[11] "Head over to a place on Straight Road where Judas lives. When you get there, ask for a fellow called Saul of Tarsus. He is there praying to me right now. [12] I have given him a vision of a cowboy named Ananias who will come in and lay his hands on him so he can see again."

[13] "Whoa, wait just a minute, Lord." Ananias said. "This guy is bad news to those of us who ride for you. [14] He has a warrant out for every cowboy who follows you."

[15] But Jesus said, "Head out. I've chosen Saul to be my cowboy to the Gentiles, kings, as well as the people of Israel. [16] I'm going to show him how hard it is to be one of my cowboys."

[17] Ananias saddled up and went and found Saul. He put his hands on him and said, "Saul, my new brother, the Lord Jesus showed himself to you on the trail and sent me here to heal your eyes. You will also be filled with the Holy Ghost." [18] Right then Saul's eyes were opened, and something like scales fell from them. He got up and immediately got baptized. [19] Afterward he got him some grub and got his strength back.

Saul Is Hunted

Saul hunkered down with some cowboys of the Way in Damascus for a while. [20] He didn't waste any time telling folks anywhere and everywhere that Jesus was the Son of God.

[21] No one could believe what they were hearing from him. "Isn't this the guy who'd waged war on Jesus's cowboys in Jerusalem?" they asked. "I thought he'd got a warrant to roundup anyone who believed in Jesus and take them back to Jerusalem in shackles?" [22] But all this controversy just strengthened Saul's message, and he showed them God was with him by proving to a bunch of Jews living in Damascus that Jesus was the Top Hand everyone had been waiting on.

[23] This sure enough stirred up the hornet's nest and the Jews began to plan Saul's assassination. [24] They waited in ambush at the city gates, but Saul found out about it. [25] Some guys who rode for the brand helped Saul out of the city by lowering him in a basket over the wall.

[26] He hightailed it for Jerusalem to meet with the twelve cowboys, but they were all afraid of him. They didn't really believe he had been converted, but that it was a plot to have them arrested. [27] But Barnabas helped him out and took him to the cowboys. He told the men how Saul had come face to face with Jesus on the road to Damascus and he'd had to escape the city in secret because of his preaching about Jesus being the Top Hand. Barnabas told them about Saul's fearlessness in preaching. [28] So the cowboys let him stay with them. Saul went all throughout Jerusalem and preached boldly in the name of the Lord. [29] He got into it with some Jews from Greece, and they tried to kill him over

it. ³⁰ When the believers found out, they smuggled him to Caesarea and sent him off to Tarsus.

³¹ During this time, God's outfit grew in number because folks lived in fear of the Lord and they were all being led by the Holy Ghost.

Pete Heals and Brings Back the Dead

³² Pete took the outside circle and traveled around. He came to a town called Lydda and hung out with some believers there. ³³ He met a man named, Aeneas, who'd been crippled and in bed for eight years. ³⁴ Pete said to him, "Get up, cowboy. Jesus Christ has healed you. Roll up your bedroll and get on with life." Instantly, the man was healed. ³⁵ When the good people around the area saw Aeneas walking around, they all came to be believers and ride for the Lord.

³⁶ There was a good lady named Tabitha who lived in nearby Joppa. She was always helping the poor and doing kind things. ³⁷ About then, she got sick and died. Her body was prepared for the funeral and she was held in an upstairs room. ³⁸ When some folks who rode for the Lord heard Pete was in the area, they sent for him to come immediately.

³⁹ Pete showed up and they took him upstairs where Tabitha was. The room was like a set of shipping pens filled with cattle. But it was folks who were all mourning the loss of a great woman. They cried and showed Pete the clothes and coats Tabitha had made for them. ⁴⁰ Pete opened the door and asked them all to wait outside. When they were gone, he went to his knees and prayed. Turning his gaze upon Tabitha's body, he said, "Get up, sweetheart." Her eyes opened and she turned toward Pete. When she saw him, she sat up. ⁴¹ He gave her a hand and she swung her legs over the edge of the table. Pete then went to the door and invited all the mourners inside. He nodded toward her and nobody could believe what they saw.

⁴² Now this news spread fast throughout the whole countryside. Folks were giving their lives to the Lord left and right. ⁴³ Pete stayed in Joppa a long time with a cowboy named Simon, who was a hide tanner.

CHAPTER 10

In Caesarea, there was a Roman Regiment Captain named Cornelius. ² He followed God and so did all his family. He prayed every day and helped the poor as much as he could. ³ One afternoon, an angel visited him and said, "Hey, Cornelius!"

⁴ Cornelius was spooked something awful, but he managed to ask, "Yes, sir?"

The angel said, "Listen, buddy. God has seen what you've been doing and he thinks it's awesome. ⁵ Send some of your men over to Joppa and tell them to bring Pete to you. ⁶ He's staying with a fellow named Simon near the sea."

⁷ The angel left and Cornelius immediately called for two of his servants and one of his most loyal soldiers. ⁸ He filled them in on what had just happened and sent them to Joppa to fetch Pete.

Pete's Confusing Vision

⁹ It was the following day when Cornelius's men were getting close to Joppa. About this time, Pete went up on the roof to pray. It was about noon and ¹⁰ he was getting hungry. Food was being prepared in the kitchen and Pete suddenly fell into a trance. ¹¹ The sky was folded back and something like a large tarp was being lowered by the four corners. ¹² Inside the tarp was all kinds of birds, reptiles, and animals. ¹³ Then he heard a voice say, "Get up, Pete. Kill something and eat it."

¹⁴ "No way, Lord," Pete said. "I've never eaten anything the Jewish Code says is unclean and I'm not going to start now."

¹⁵ But the voice was adamant and said, "It ain't your job to declare something clean or not. If God says to eat it, then it is clean and you can eat it." ¹⁶ This same vision happened about three more times and then the tarp was yanked back into heaven.

¹⁷ Pete was shaking his head in confusion at what he'd just seen. Just then, the men who Cornelius had sent showed up at the house. They were standing near the front gate ¹⁸ and asked for Pete.

¹⁹ While Pete was still ponderin' the dream, the Holy Ghost said, "There's some boys here to get you. ²⁰ Go ahead and go with them. Don't fret. I'm the one who sent them."

²¹ Pete went downstairs and said, "I'm Pete. What can I do for y'all, gents?"

²² One of them said, "Our boss, Cornelius, a Roman officer, sent us to fetch ya. He's well

respected and rides for God. An angel told him to send for ya and we're here to take you back so you can give him your message." ²³ Pete invited everyone to spend the night so they could ride out at sunrise the next day. They left out at daylight for Caesarea and some boys from Joppa rode with them.

²⁴ When they arrived a day later, Cornelius was waiting on them. He gathered his whole family and some good buddies to listen to what Pete had to say. ²⁵ When Pete arrived, Cornelius fell down at his feet and worshiped him. ²⁶ But Pete lifted him up and said, "Whoa, cowboy. I'm just a man like you." ²⁷ They talked for a second and then went inside where many people were waiting.

²⁸ The first thing Pete said was, "Now y'all know it is against the Jewish Code for me to walk in someone's house who ain't Jewish. But God showed me yesterday that things have changed. No one is unclean in his eyes anymore. ²⁹ So this is a first for me and I'm here without complaint. What can I do for you?"

³⁰ Cornelius said, "Four days ago, I was praying about three o'clock in the afternoon and all of a sudden, there was a cowboy in dazzling garments standing in front of me. ³¹ He told me, 'Listen, buddy. God has seen what you've been doing and he thinks it's awesome. ³² Send some of your men over to Joppa and tell them to bring Pete to you. He's staying with a fellow named Simon near the sea.' ³³ So I sent my men to fetch you and I appreciate you coming. Now, let's hear what God has to say through you."

³⁴ Then Pete said, "God ain't got no favorites anymore. ³⁵ He'll take in any stray who fears him and does what is right. ³⁶ This is the good news for the people of Israel. We can all get a spot on God's outfit through his Son, Jesus Christ. ³⁷ I'm sure y'all have heard everything that happened. It started in Galilee when John started preachin' and baptizin' folks. ³⁸ And you probably heard the Boss blessed Jesus of Nazareth with the power of the Holy Ghost. Then Jesus rode the countryside doing amazing things like healing people and whipping those demons that were possessing folks. There wasn't any doubt God was with him.

³⁹ "And we cowboys saw nearly everything he did in Judea and Jerusalem. They killed him by stringin' him up on a cross, ⁴⁰ but God brought him back to life three days later. God let him appear, ⁴¹ not to everyone, but to the cowboys who rode for his Son. We ate and drank with him after he came ridin' back from the grave. ⁴² He told us to go out and tell folks God has made him judge over the living and the dead. ⁴³ All the old cowboy prophets talked about Jesus and the fact that all who believe in him will be forgiven of their sins."

⁴⁴ While Pete was talkin', the Holy Ghost filled everyone in the room who was listening. ⁴⁵ The Jews who had ridden with Pete from Joppa couldn't believe the Holy Ghost was being given to people who were not Jewish. ⁴⁶ But sure enough, these Gentiles were speaking in languages they didn't know and praising the Boss.

Then Pete said, ⁴⁷ "Is anyone against baptizin' these kind folks? They've got the Ghost just like we do." ⁴⁸ So Pete had them baptized in Jesus's name. Afterwards, they asked Pete to stay a couple of days with them.

CHAPTER 11

It wasn't long before the word got out that outsiders had been invited into God's outfit. ² But when Pete got back to Jerusalem, some of the boys who rode for God tried to get on his case. ³ "What do you think you are doing going in a Gentile's house?" they accused.

⁴ Pete was upfront with them about what had happened. ⁵ "I was staying in Joppa," he said. "I had been up on the roof doin' some talkin' to God, and he gave me a vision. A tarp come down out of heaven right in front of me. ⁶ Inside the tarp was all kinds of animals, birds, and reptiles. ⁷ There was a voice that said, 'Stand up, Pete. Kill something and eat it.'

⁸ "'I can't do it,' I said to the Lord. 'I ain't never eaten unclean stuff and I'm not gonna start now.'

⁹ "But then the voice said, 'It ain't your job to declare something clean or not. If God says to eat it, then it is clean and you can eat it.' ¹⁰ This happened about three times, and then the tarp was hauled back into heaven.

¹¹ "It was at this moment that three men from Caesarea arrived to fetch me. ¹² The Holy Ghost told me to go with 'em even though they were Gentile outsiders. I took these six cowboys with me, and we did go in the house of the man who'd

sent for me. [13] He told us about how an angel had visited with him and said, 'Send some men to fetch Pete from Joppa. [14] He'll tell you how you and everyone else can be saved.'

[15] "When I opened my mouth to talk," Pete continued, "the Holy Ghost filled 'em like it had done when it first filled us. [16] Then I recalled what Jesus said, 'John baptized with water, but I'm gonna dunk y'all with the Holy Ghost.' [17] It was God who did the givin', not me. And if God is givin' outsiders the same thing he gave insiders, then who am I to question that?"

[18] This shut everyone up, but for just a second. After that, everyone began praising God. Many people agreed, "God has now given outsiders a chance to come onto the ranch and live forever!"

The Antioch Church

[19] Now there were many cowboys who had scattered when Steve was killed. They went to Phoenicia, Cyprus, and Antioch in Syria. They stuck to tellin' Jewish folks about Jesus. [20] But there were some of them, particularly some cowboys from Cyprus and Cyrene, who started telling Greeks about the good news of Jesus Christ. [21] God was with them, and many folks started riding for the Lord.

[22] News got back to Jerusalem about what was happening. Barnabas was sent to check things out in Antioch. [23] When he got there, he beheld quite a sight. He encouraged all the new cowboys to remain true to the brand and ride for the Lord with all their hearts. [24] Barnabas was a good cowboy who was filled with the Holy Ghost and full of faith. He showed many people how to ride for God's outfit.

[25] Barnabas struck a long trot for Tarsus to find Saul. [26] When he found him, they both went back to Antioch. For an entire year, these two cowboys met with all the cowboys in Antioch and taught them how to ride for Jesus. This was the first place the term "Christian" was used to describe a cowboy ridin' for the Lord.

[27] During this time, some prophets came up from Jerusalem. [28] One of them, Agabus, relayed a message he'd got from the Holy Ghost that there was going to be a severe famine. It ended up happening during the reign of Claudius. [29] So the cowboys in Antioch got together a bunch of stuff that would help out the other cowboys living in Judea during the famine. They all gave as much as they could. [30] Barnabas and Saul took the gifts back to Jerusalem to the leaders of God's outfit there.

CHAPTER 12

It was at this time that King Herod Agrippa began to cause problems in the church. [2] He had James killed with a sword. James was one of the twelve original cowboys (the brother of John). [3] When he saw how much the Jewish people liked this, he went and had Pete arrested too. This happened during the Passover celebration. [4] The king had Pete thrown in prison with four squads of police watching him. Herod was going to wait for Passover to end and then have a public trial for Pete. [5] But while Pete was locked up, everyone who rode for the Lord prayed for him constantly.

Pete's Escape

[6] Pete was asleep the night before his trial. He was locked up with two chains between two policemen. The other guards were at the door. [7] All of a sudden, there was a bright light, and an angel stood there in front of Pete. The angel kicked him and told him, "Get up and be quick about it!" When Pete stood up, the chains fell off. [8] The angel then said, "Put your boots on and get dressed. Get your coat and let's go."

[9] The angel led Pete out of the cell, but Pete didn't realize this was happening. He thought it was a vision the whole time. [10] They passed by the other guards and came to the door that led into the city. When they approached, the door opened like magic. They walked out into the street and then Pete was alone.

[11] Pete finally shook the cobwebs out of his brain and realized an angel had saved him. He said, "The Lord has saved me from Herod and the other Jewish leaders. He has foiled their plans."

[12] He went off toward the home of Mary, the mother of John Mark. When he arrived, there was a bunch of people there praying. [13] He knocked on the door. A servant girl named Rhoda asked who was there. [14] She recognized Pete's voice and got so excited she left him outside the door and ran to tell everyone else, "Pete's at the door!"

[15] "You're crazy!" everyone said. But when she was adamant, they said, "It must be Pete's angel with a message."

[16] Pete was still standing outside knocking. Then someone else opened the door and couldn't believe their eyes. [17] Pete put a finger to his lips and told everyone to be quiet. He told them the tale of the angel rescuing him. Pete then said, "Tell the Lord's brother, James, and the other cowboys what happened." Then Pete slipped out and went off into the darkness.

[18] When the sun came up, the prison was stirred up like a mound of ants. Everyone was wondering how Pete had escaped. [19] Herod Agrippa ordered soldiers and police to search for him everywhere, but he couldn't be found. The king had the guards questioned and then killed them. Herod and his entourage headed off for Caesarea.

Herod Agrippa's Death

[20] Now Herod wasn't none too happy with the towns of Tyre and Sidon. These cities sent some representatives to the king to try to make amends. These cities were very dependent on Herod for food. These reps got in good with Herod's personal assistant, Blastus. [21] This guy got them a meeting with the king. When the time came, Herod dressed in his royal outfit and made a great speech. [22] People applauded and cheered, "This is not a man talking, but a god!" [23] Right then, an angel of God came down and struck Herod down with a sickness. Herod had accepted the worship of these people and God showed him what happens to people who think they are equal to him. Herod fell down in front of everyone and was eaten by worms as they watched.

[24] In the meantime, the word of God continued to spread throughout the country and many people started riding for the Lord. [25] When Barnabas and Saul had made their delivery to Jerusalem, they headed back and took John Mark with them.

CHAPTER 13

Now there were some top hands at the church in Antioch of Syria. There was Barnabas, Simeon (nicknamed Blackie), Lucius from Cyrene, Manaen (who'd been brought up in the palace with King Herod Antipas), and Saul. [2] One day these cowboys were all fasting and praising God, and the Holy Spirit said, "Turn loose Barnabas and Saul. I got something special for them to do."

[3] They all did more fasting and praying. Then the other cowboys laid their hands on the two men and sent them out to gather remnants for God.

Paul's First Cattle Drive

[4] The two cowboys, guided by the Holy Spirit, long trotted to Seleucia, and then sailed from there to Cyprus. [5] When they got to Salamis, they headed to the local Jewish church and started telling them about Jesus. A young cowboy named John Mark was with 'em.

[6] They trotted the whole island until they reached Paphos. It was there they ran into a Jewish witch doctor named Bar-Jesus. [7] This fellow rode for the local governor there, a man named Sergius Paulus. The governor was a sharp man, and he sent for these two cowboys who were gathering remnants on the island. He wanted to hear what they were telling everyone about God. [8] But Elymas, the witch doctor (that's what his name means in the plain tongue), rode right in front of the two cowboys and tried to cut them off before the governor could talk to them. He urged his boss not to listen to the cowboy's nonsense. He knew he'd be ruined if the governor started believing in God.

[9] Saul, who most people know as Paul, was filled with the Holy Ghost and looked that old witch doctor right in the eye and said, [10] "You no-account, devil-riddled, son of a gun! You think you can ride in and scatter this gathering? [11] Watch what's fixing to happen to you. The Lord is fixing to show you who's boss. He's jerking the sight right out of your head, and you won't even be able to see the sun for a while." Right then, something like a dark fog enveloped him, and he couldn't see. He started screaming and feeling around for someone to help him. [12] When the governor seen what happened, he became a believer in God right there. He couldn't get enough of the teaching about God.

Paul Gathers in Antioch of Pisidia

[13] Paul and the other two cowboys sailed out of Paphos for Pamphylia. They arrived in the port of Perga. When they got there, John Mark turned yellow and quit the crew and returned to Jerusalem. [14] Paul and Barnabas struck a long trot inland for Antioch of Pisidia. On the day of rest, they went to the local Jewish church for the services. [15] After the usual readings from the Good

Book of Moses, the preachers invited Paul and Barnabas saying, "If y'all cowboys got a word from the Lord, we'd love to hear it."

[16] So Paul got up and motioned for everyone to quiet down. He said, "Listen up you cowboys from Israel and you God-fearing mavericks. [17] The God of Israel chose our granddaddies over everyone else. He even strengthened them while they were slaves in Egypt and [18] he was with 'em during the forty years in the wilderness after he set 'em free. [19] He led the charge and defeat of seven mighty nations in Canaan so his kids could have the country he promised 'em. [20] Everything I've just said took about four hundred and fifty years. After this, God gave Israel some cowboys he called Judges to lead the nation. This went on until the time of Samuel the prophet. [21] Then the people were crying out for a king and God gave 'em Saul, son of Kish. This cowboy was from the Benjamin outfit and he ruled for forty years. [22] After God got rid of Saul, he made David the king. God said this about David, 'I have found this buckaroo, David, son of Jesse, to be a man after my own heart. He will do everything I tell him to do.'

[23] "From David descendants, God gave us the Top Hand who would save Israel from their sins just like he promised to. [24] Before Jesus came, the great cowboy named John preached a message of radically changing your life to ride for God and being dunked in water. He told his message to all the cowboys in Israel. [25] When John's gathering was just about finished he said, 'Who do y'all think I am? It ain't me who will save you from the killer-buyer. There's another cowboy coming who I ain't fit to pull the boots off of after a long day's ride.'

[26] "Listen to me all you Jewish cowboys and all y'all God-fearing mavericks. This message on how to be saved has been sent directly to you. [27-28] The people of Jerusalem and the head honchos of the church didn't recognize Jesus for the cowboy he really was and had him strung up and killed without cause. But this had to happen to fulfill all the things in the Good Book that had been predicted. [29] When everything had been done to him, they took him off the cross and laid him in a tomb. [30] But God reached down and snatched him from the grave, [31] and for a while he was seen by many who'd rode with him from Galilee to Jerusalem. They are the ones who give our people an eyewitness account of these great things.

[32] "This is the good news we tell you, God promised our ancestors a cowboy who would save us all. [33] He has fulfilled that promise to us, their children, by raising up Jesus from the dead. It's even written in the Good Book of Psalms, 'You're my boy, and today I have become your daddy.' [34] God had said he wouldn't leave his boy in a grave on boot hill to rot. He said, 'I'm passing along to you the blessings I promised to David.' [35] It's also written in another place, 'You won't let your holy one be eaten by worms.'

[36] "When David's ride for God was done, he fell asleep and was buried with his granddaddies. His body has decayed. [37] But the cowboy who came riding back from the dead did not decay.

[38] "Ok, here's the point I've been getting at, it is through Jesus all your sins will be forgiven and you'll be saved from the kill truck. [39] Any cowboy who believes in Jesus will be in good standing with God. This is something the code of Moses could never accomplish. [40] But watch for badger holes! Don't let the prophets' words apply to you when they said, [41] 'All y'all who made fun of me, the true God, better look out because you're being loaded on the kill truck. I am doing things that are amazing, and most people wouldn't even believe it if someone told them it was happening.'"

[42] When Paul and Barnabas left that day, people were begging them to come back next week and tell them more. [43] There were a lot of Jews and Jewish converts who believed what they said and became believers. The two cowboys urged all of 'em to continue to ride and rely on the grace of God.

Paul Gathers the Mavericks

[44] That following week, the whole area turned out to listen to the word of the Lord. [45] But when some of the Jews saw how many people turned out, they became jealous. They started talking crap about Paul and argued with him over anything he said.

[46] Paul and Barnabas didn't cut them any slack and said, "We've done our part and told you Jews about Jesus first. But since y'all won't listen, and therefore loaded yourselves on the

kill truck, then we will offer this gift to the un-branded mavericks. **47** The Lord gave us these orders, 'Y'all are a campfire in the night for all the mavericks to come to. Y'all will help bring salvation to the far corners of the world.'"

48 When the mavericks (anyone not Jewish) heard this, they whooped and hollered with joy. Everyone who believed in the brand would now be saved. **49** The Lord's good news spread throughout the whole countryside.

50 Then the Jews stirred up the prominent women of the area, and those busy bodies incited a riot against the two cowboys. They chased them out of town. **51** Paul and Barnabas shook the dust off their boots as a sign of rejection and loped off toward Iconium. **52** And all the believers around there were filled with the Holy Ghost.

CHAPTER 14

Just like before, Paul and Barnabas went to the Jewish church in Iconium, and God spoke through them so powerfully that many Jews and Greeks became believers. **2** But there were some hard-headed Jews who refused to believe and they riled up some of the mavericks in the area and poisoned their minds against the two cow-boys. **3** So Paul and Barnabas camped there for quite some time. They preached boldly about how to ride for God's outfit, and God proved what they were saying was right by allowing them to do some great signs and amazing feats. **4** The whole town was split in two. Half sided with the hard-headed scoffers and the other half with the cowboys. **5** There was even an assassination plot by some unbelieving Jews and mavericks to stone them to death. **6** They caught wind of it though and hightailed it south down to Lystra and Derbe and the surrounding ranches. **7** It was there they preached the good news.

Derbe and Lystra

8 While in Lystra, Paul and Barnabas found a man who had been crippled since birth and had never been able to walk. He was sitting there **9** and listening to some mighty good preaching and Paul saw the man had faith enough to be healed. **10** So Paul hollered at him and told him to get up. The man jumped to his feet and started walking for the first time.

11 Now, this sure started a ruckus. The people there were amazed and started shouting, "These are gods in the form of cowboys!" **12** They reckoned Barnabas was the Greek god Zeus and Paul was Hermes since he's the one who did most of the talking. **13** The temple of Zeus was just outside of town. The priests there got some bulls and flowers and started preparing a sacrifice and a shindig in honor of the two cowboys.

14 But when the cowboys, Paul and Barnabas, realized what was happening, they tore their hats from their heads, threw them down, and said, **15** "Amigos! What in the world are y'all doing? We ain't gods. We're just a couple of cowboys sent to gather the strays for the Boss with the good news. Quit paying attention to statues made by human hands and bow down and worship the living God. He made the heavens and the seas and everything in 'em. **16** Up until recently, God had let folks go their own ways, **17** but he never did so without showing them how much he loved them. He sent down the rain for crops, cattle for food, and smiles for your ugly mugs." **18** Even with these words, Paul and Barnabas had a heck of a time turning the stampede that wanted to sacrifice to them.

19 Then some Jews came from Antioch and Iconium and talked the crowd into turning on Paul. They pelted him with rocks until they thought he was dead and then drug him outside the city like a dog that had been run over in the street. **20** All the believers gathered around him after the crowd left and Paul got to his feet and went right back in the city like a boss. The next day, Paul and Barnabas struck a long trot for Derbe.

Headed Back to Antioch in Syria

21 After gathering many strays in Derbe, Paul and Barnabas headed back the way they'd come. They went back to Lystra, Iconium, and Antioch in Pisidia. **22** On their way through, they stopped and checked with all the cowboys who had started riding for God. They encouraged them to be strong and faithful. They reminded them it ain't easy to cowboy for God's outfit and there would be hard times gathering remnants out of the brush. **23** Paul and Barnabas appointed some jigger bosses over every group of believers to help them and guide them. They all prayed so hard they didn't eat and then turned the jigger bosses over to the Lord's guidance. **24** With a wave goodbye, they continued down the trail through Pisidia to Pamphylia. **25** They did some gathering in Perga and then headed down to Attalia.

²⁶ Finally, they got on a boat and headed back to Antioch in Syria where they'd first began their journey. The believers in Antioch had trusted these two cowboys to go out and gather remnants and lean on the grace of God. ²⁷ When they got back to Antioch, they called all the cowboys in the outfit there together and told them about everything that had happened. They were especially excited about telling them how God opened the gate to his outfit and let mavericks in too. ²⁸ And they put their saddles in the tack room and stayed there a long time.

CHAPTER 15

While Paul and Barnabas were still in Antioch in Syria, some cowboys showed up from the country around Jerusalem. These cowboys began giving clinics on how to ride for God, but they were telling people, "You've got to have the tip of your pickle clipped like the code of Moses says if you want to be saved. If you ain't got a clipped pickle, then you ain't saved." ² Paul and Barnabas lit into them and argued sternly with 'em. Finally, the local outfit decided to send Paul and Barnabas, along with a few other cowboys, to Jerusalem to see what the cowboys who rode with Jesus had to say about it. ³ The cowboys saddled up and headed for Jerusalem. They stopped in Phoenicia and Samaria to visit those who had previously been gathered and were now cowboying for God's outfit. They told them, much to everyone gladness, the unbranded mavericks were also being allowed to ride for God and were being saved.

⁴ When they got to Jerusalem, they were warmly welcomed by the whole outfit there. The jigger bosses and cowboys who personally rode with Jesus also showed up to welcome them. The cowboys from Antioch excitedly told all the Jerusalem outfit what had been happening. ⁵ But then some Pharisees, who believed in Jesus while also wanting to follow the code of Moses, stood up and said, "The Gentiles, or mavericks as you call them, must be circumcised and follow the code of Moses if they want to be saved."

⁶ So the jigger bosses, along with Jesus's handpicked cowboys, met together to come up with a decision on the matter. ⁷ Everyone spoke

for a long time and then Pete stood up and said, "Brothers, you all know God chose me a long time ago to go out and gather the unbranded Gentiles. He was pulling them into his herd, and they believed in him. ⁸ God knows all people's hearts, and he branded these mavericks with the Holy Spirit just like he did us. ⁹ He didn't check their pickles, just their faith . . . and he washed 'em clean of their sins. ¹⁰ So here's my question, cowboys. Why are y'all now bucking the way God does things and putting a load on the new cowboys' backs that we couldn't carry ourselves? We couldn't follow the code of Moses either, but you want these new cowboys to do what can't be done? That's insane! ¹¹ We are saved by what Jesus did, not by what we do. That's the grace of God. And we are all saved the same way."

¹² You could have heard a pin drop as Paul and Barnabas talked about the miracles God had performed while they were gathering mavericks up north.

¹³ When they were done, Jesus's brother James stood up and said, "Listen to me, boys. ¹⁴ Pete talked to you about how God first decided he was going to bring the unbranded mavericks into his herd for himself. ¹⁵ Gathering and branding these unbranded mavericks is exactly what the Good Book predicted when it said, ¹⁶ 'After this I'm going to come back and rebuild the ranch David started. I'll fix the fences and get the windmills going. ¹⁷ That way, all of mankind will have a place, even the unbranded mavericks who will now be part of the herd. Everyone will have a place who wants it,' says the Lord, who knows all and does all ¹⁸ things like he knew he would."

¹⁹ James continued, "This is what we're going to do. We ain't gonna make it hard for the mavericks to be a part of God's outfit. ²⁰ We're just gonna tell them they should not eat meat that has been sacrificed to false gods. They should keep away from all sexual perversions. They should also avoid eating meat from strangled animals, and never consume blood. ²¹ This is all wisdom from Moses that has been taught for centuries. It would be harder to change it than follow it. And following these doesn't hurt anyone."

The Letter to the Mavericks

²² Then Jesus's handpicked cowboys and the church jigger bosses, as well as the rest of the outfit, chose some cowboys to represent them

and sent them back to Antioch in Syria with a letter about their decision. They all traveled back with Paul and Barnabas. The two cowboys chosen as representatives were a couple of the church bosses, Judas (called Barsabbas) and Silas.

²³ The letter said, "This letter is from Jesus's handpicked cowboys and jigger bosses from the church in Jerusalem. It is written to the maverick believers in Antioch, Syria, and Cilicia. Howdy, boys! ²⁴ We heard some cowboys from Jerusalem have been saying some troubling things to y'all. They've been teaching some wrong stuff, but understand that we did not send them to you. ²⁵ We've all got together and came up with a decision about what they were teaching. We've sent some representatives back with Paul and Barnabas, ²⁶ who have risked their lives for Jesus Christ, so you will know this is from us. ²⁷ Judas and Silas will confirm what we've come up with regarding those other fellow's wrong teachings. ²⁸ It seemed like the right thing to do, and we believe the Holy Spirit agrees we should not make y'all do anything burdensome besides these few things, ²⁹ Don't eat meat from sacrificed animals. Don't consume blood or the meat of strangled animals. And stay away from sexual perversions. If you do this, you will be riding good. Adios, amigos!"

³⁰ The messengers struck a long trot toward Antioch with the letter. As soon as they arrived, they gathered in all the cowboys who were riding for God and read them the letter. ³¹ People were whooping and hollering and waving their hats in the air at the good news.

³² Then Judas and Silas, both being top hands, talked with all the cowboys. They encouraged them and told them to be strong and keep the faith. ³³ These two top hands stuck around for a while and then they headed back to Jerusalem with a blessing of peace riding with 'em.

Note: Here, some manuscripts include ³⁴ *But Silas decided to remain there.*

³⁵ Paul and Barnabas stayed in Antioch and taught folks how to ride for the Lord.

Paul and Barnabas Split Ways

³⁶ After quite a while, Paul told Barnabas, "Let's head back to all those churches we started and see how them outfits are doing."

³⁷ Barnabas totally agreed and wanted to take John Mark with them again, ³⁸ but Paul didn't want to have anything to do with him after he'd turned his back on them the last time. ³⁹ They argued fiercely and they decided to go different ways. Barnabas took John Mark and went to Cyprus. ⁴⁰ Paul chose Silas, and with the blessing of the outfit there in Syria, ⁴¹ they headed out through Syria and Cilicia. They strengthened all the outfits they went through that were riding and gathering for the Lord.

CHAPTER 16

Paul headed north to Derbe and then on to nearby Lystra. There was a young cowboy there named, Timothy. His momma was a Jewish believer, but his daddy was a Greek. ² Timothy was quickly becoming a hand, and everyone thought very highly of him in Lystra and Iconium. ³ Paul saw something in the young man too and invited Timothy to saddle up and ride with them. Paul took Timothy aside and told him they would be around a lot of Jews, and it would probably be better if Timothy had his pickle clipped. This wasn't for salvation, but to be able to reach more people who might be narrow-minded at first because of his daddy being Greek. ⁴ As they rode from place to place, they delivered the message from the main church in Jerusalem. ⁵ All of the churches, or outfits, they went to became larger in size and stronger in faith.

The Macedonia Dream

⁶ Then Paul and his little crew worked through all the countryside of Phrygia and Galatia. They would have kept going, but the Holy Spirit kept them from heading into Asia. ⁷ When the reined up at the border of Mysia, they wanted to continue north and go into Bithynia, but once again the Holy Spirit kept them from going. ⁸ With all their ways seemingly blocked, they headed west to the port at Troas. ⁹ That night Paul had a dream of a man from northern Greece standing there and begging him saying, "We need you in Macedonia. Help us, cowboy!" ¹⁰ So we boarded a ship to leave for Macedonia right away. We knew this was God telling us to take the good news to new places.

Lady Lydia Believes in Jesus

¹¹ We got on the boat at Troas and sailed quickly to the island of Samothrace. The next

day we reached Neapolis. ¹² We saddled up there and rode for the big town of Philippi. It was a Roman colony, and we stayed there for several days. ¹³ On the day of rest, we trotted out to a river where we thought some people might be meeting for prayer. Sure enough, there was a group of ladies there, and we walked up and introduced ourselves. ¹⁴ One of them was Lady Lydia from Thyatira. She was a peddler of fine purple cloth and a believer in God. She listened to what we had to say, and God opened her heart to believe in Jesus. ¹⁵ She was baptized along with her whole household. Then she insisted we stay at her ranchito. She said, "If you believe I am a believer like y'all, then you must be my guests." This little lady wouldn't take no for an answer.

Paul and Silas in the Jailhouse

¹⁶ One day we were walking along, headed to a place where everyone gathered to pray, and we ran into a slave girl who was possessed. Her demon helped her tell people's fortunes, and her masters made a lot of money off of her. ¹⁷ She followed along behind us and shouted, "These men are cowboys who gather for the Most High God. They are here to tell you how to be saved!" ¹⁸ This went on every single day, and finally, Paul got sick of it. As we were walking and she was shouting, he turned to the spirit and said, "In the name of Jesus Christ, I'm telling you to get out of her and skedaddle." Instantly the demon was gone.

¹⁹ When her masters realized what Paul had done, they were furious. They grabbed Paul and Silas and drug 'em to the courthouse. ²⁰ There, they told the authorities, "These men are troublemakers! They have the whole town in an uproar. ²¹ They are telling everyone to rebel against the Roman way of doing things."

²² Things got nasty really quick. Paul and Silas were arrested, stripped naked, and beaten with axe handles. ²³ After they were severely beaten, they were thrown in the jailhouse. The jailer was told not to let them escape or he would pay the price. ²⁴ So the jailer put them in the basement cell and even locked them in stocks.

²⁵ It was the middle of the night, and Paul and Silas were praying and singing hymns to God. Other prisoners couldn't help but listen to them. ²⁶ Suddenly, the ground started shaking

something fierce, and the whole jail seemed to be coming apart. But the only things that came apart were every prisoner's chains and all the doors to the cells. ²⁷ All the commotion woke the jailer. He stumbled downstairs and saw all the doors were open. He assumed everyone had fled and he took out his knife to slit his throat. ²⁸ But out of the darkness, Paul yelled, "Whoa, fellow! Put the blade away. We're still here."

²⁹ The jailer grabbed a torch and raced into the cells. He fell down in front of Paul and Silas, shaking like a leaf. ³⁰ He then led them out of the stinking cell and asked, "I nearly died tonight. What must I do to be saved?" ³¹ They put a reassuring hand on his shoulder and said, "Believe in Jesus who died in your place. Then you and your whole family will be saved." ³² Then they told him, and all of his family who had gathered there also, the story of Jesus. ³³ Even though it was the middle of the night, the jailer cleaned up their wounds. Then the jailer and his whole family were baptized. ³⁴ The jailer invited them into his house, which was part of the jail, and laid before them a fine feast of a meal. This was the best day of the man's life because he and his whole family were now saved and believed in God.

³⁵ The next morning, the authorities sent word to the jailer saying, "Go ahead and let those two cowboys out." ³⁶ The jailer told Paul, "They said you and Silas are free to go. Go in peace, cowboys!"

³⁷ But Paul wasn't having any of it. He said, "We were beaten and imprisoned without a trial. We are Roman citizens and what happened here is against the law. And now they want us to just go away like nothing happened? I don't think so! Let them come here and release us themselves."

³⁸ When this message was taken to the city officials, they got scared. They had no idea Paul and Silas were Roman citizens. ³⁹ So the city officials all went to the jailhouse and apologized for what had happened. They led Paul and Silas outside and begged them to saddle up and leave the city. ⁴⁰ The two cowboys didn't say anything but headed straight for Lady Lydia's house. They met with everyone who had believed in Jesus and encouraged them to never give up the faith. Then they saddled up and rode away.

CHAPTER 17

Paul and his crew passed through the towns of Amphipolis and Apollonia before arriving in Thessalonica. There was a Jewish church there, so they stopped to say hello. [2] Like he did all the time, Paul went to the church to preach on the day of rest for three weeks. He used the Good Book to reason with people. [3] He explained what the Good Book had predicted about how the Top Hand must have the roughest ride anyone ever had, then die, and then come riding back from the grave three days later. Paul told 'em, "This cowboy, Jesus, is the Top Hand." [4] A few Jews dared to join Paul and Silas. There were many Greeks who believed along with a quite a few well-to-do ladies.

[5] But there were those hard-hearted Jews who wouldn't believe. They became so jealous of Paul that they rounded up some shady characters and convinced them to run through town and shoot out the lights and windows. These fellows tore up the town and then headed toward the home of Jason. They kicked the door down looking for Paul and Silas in order to lynch them. [6] Since they weren't there, they settled on Jason. The angry mob dragged him, and some other believers to the city council and said, "Paul and Silas have stirred up trouble all over the world, and now they've got their sights on our little town. [7] This cowboy here, Jason, has welcomed them into his home and wants to help them destroy us. They are all guilty of treason against Rome. They tell everyone not to listen to Caesar, but worship a cowboy named Jesus." [8] With these words, the city council and all those who had come to see this circus act were instantly thrown into mayhem. [9] The city council made Jason and the others post a heavy bail, and they let them go.

Paul and Silas Head for Berea

[10] That night, under cover of darkness, Paul and Silas slipped out of town and headed southwest to Berea. Once again, they went to the local Jewish church. [11] But the folks in this town were different than those in Thessalonica. They listened to what Paul had to say. But the best part was that they themselves looked at the passages in the Good Book to see if what Paul and Silas said was the truth. [12] As a result, a whole herd of Jews, as well as many well-off Greek men and women, started believing in Jesus.

[13] But as luck would have it, the Jews in Thessalonica heard Paul and Silas were in Berea preaching the good word. They rounded up a lynch mob and thundered down there with blood in their eyes. [14] The new Berean cowboys smuggled Paul to the coast, but Silas and Timothy stayed behind. [15] The good-hearted believers traveled with Paul all the way to Athens and then rode back with instructions for Silas and Timothy to join him there.

Paul Preaches in Athens

[16] Paul waited on his pards to get to Athens. He strolled the city and was torn-up inside with all the idols of other gods he saw there. [17] He went to the local Jewish church to try to talk some sense into the Jews and God-following mavericks. He even preached in the town square to anyone who would listen.

[18] Now Greece was known for its philosophers, and Paul talked at length with them; ones who followed the Epicurean style as well as the Stoic ones. Some of them rolled their eyes at him, and others acted all high and mighty, saying, "Let us listen to him. He is teaching us about some foreign gods."

[19] Then they invited him to come speak at the courthouse square. They introduced Paul by saying, "We would like to hear more about this new teaching you bring. [20] Gods walking around like humans and coming back from the dead seem mighty strange, and we'd like to know more." [21] (The cool thing to do in Athens was to sit around and discuss news and the latest ideas.)

[22] Paul stood up and said, "People of Athens, I have walked through your city, and I can see you are a very religious bunch. [23] As I walked, I saw many statues and idols that y'all worship. There was even an altar with an inscription that said, 'To the Unknown God.' Y'all don't even know the God you worship, but I'm fixing to introduce you to him. He has a name.

[24] "He is the God who made everything, including the dirt you stand on now. He's not a God who needs a barn to live in. [25] As a matter of fact, he doesn't need us for anything. But here's the cool part, he doesn't need anything from us, yet he gives us the air we breathe and the heart that beats in our chest. [26] He started

this world with one cowboy. It was through this cowboy that every ranch and every cowpoke who ever pushed a cow came to be. God decided the boundaries and how good the grass would be on each of them. He determined long ago when each would rise and fall.

²⁷ "The only thing God wants is for all cowboys to find the trail that leads to him and follow it. It ain't a hard trail to follow if a cowboy has the right heart. ²⁸ Listen, we owe everything to him. Even some of your own bards have said, 'We are his kiddos.' ²⁹ And since all this is the truth, we really can't expect God to be some chainsaw carving or a sculpted bronze idol made by mortal hands.

³⁰ "But man can be pretty ignorant sometimes and choose things like idols over the real God. He let y'all get away with this for a while, but he's finally said enough is enough. He is telling you right now to turn from your sorry ways and set your eyes on him and only him. ³¹ God has marked his calendar with the day he will judge the world. The man God raised from the dead on the third day is going to return with justice in his eyes."

³² When Paul talked about people being raised from the dead, that's when some people started making fun of him. But a few said, "Tell us more, later." ³³ The discussion had reached its end, ³⁴ but some folks saddled up to ride for Jesus. Among these new cowboys were Dionysius (a fellow with some clout in the city), a lady named Damaris, and a few others.

CHAPTER 18

Paul saddled up, left Athens, and headed for Corinth. ² He ran into a fellow named Aquila from Pontus along with his wife, Priscilla. This cowboy and his wife were from Italy and had lit out of there when Claudius Caesar had kicked all the Jews out of Rome. ³ Paul stayed with them in Athens and helped them make cowboy tents, because that was his trade.

⁴ But on the day of rest, Paul could be found down at the Jewish church in town. He did everything he could to recruit riders for Jesus's outfit. ⁵ When Silas and Timothy got there from Macedonia, Paul spent all his time preaching about Jesus. He told everyone who would listen that Jesus was the Top Hand who would save them

all. ⁶ Most folks would listen for a spell and then make fun of him or just argue. Paul would then shrug his shoulders and say, "Y'all go ahead and try to save yourselves. Your deaths will be long, hard, and your fault. I'm headed out to gather the unbranded mavericks. At least they'll listen."

⁷ He headed over to Titius Justus's place. This cowboy had once been an unbranded maverick, but now he wore the brand of Jesus proudly. Ol' Titius's place was right next door to the Jewish church. ⁸ But not everyone had shunned Paul's message. Crispus, the head honcho at the church, believed in Jesus along with his whole family and household staff. There were quite a few others who also became believers and were baptized with the brand of Jesus on their hearts.

⁹ Paul was laying in his bedroll one night, and the Lord said to him, "Don't weaken, cowboy. Don't let people bully you into silence. ¹⁰ I'm behind you so speak out boldly. No one's going to lay a finger on ya. There's more folks who ride for me here than you know about." ¹¹ So Paul stuck around there for about eighteen months teaching and preaching about Jesus.

¹² But then a fellow named Gallio rose to power in Achaia. Some Jews got together and started a ruckus about Paul. They hauled him in before the new governor and demanded a trial. ¹³ They said Paul was "Splitting God's herd with his teachings and making a mockery of our code."

¹⁴ Paul was about to respond to the allegations when Gallio stood up and said to the Jews, "If this man had shot someone or rustled some cattle, I'd listen to the case. ¹⁵ But this all boils down to him saying something y'all don't like. Quit wasting my time over arguments about words and take care of it yourselves. I'm not going to listen to any more of this nonsense from y'all." ¹⁶ And then he threw them all out of the courtroom.

¹⁷ As they were leaving, the Jews grabbed a guy named Sosthenes (the new leader of the Jewish church and a believer in Jesus) and beat him mercilessly. Gallio rolled his eyes and said nothing.

Paul Heads Back to Antioch in Syria

¹⁸ Paul hung around Corinth for a little while longer and then said his goodbyes as he headed out for Cenchreae. While there, he shaved his head according to Jewish custom when a

vow you have made has been completed. Then he grabbed his saddle and other tack, got on a boat with Aquila and Priscilla, and sailed for Syria.

¹⁹ The boat stopped at the port of Ephesus and Paul left his two companions there. While he was there, he once again went to the Jewish church to try to talk some sense into them. ²⁰ They asked him to stick around a while, but he told them he couldn't. ²¹ But Paul did say, "I'll come back here if God lets me. You can count on that." Then he boarded the boat, and they sailed away from Ephesus. ²² The next stop was the port of Caesarea. Since he was close by, he rode over to Jerusalem and met with the cowboys there before heading back north to Antioch in Syria. ²³ After spending some time with the cowboys in Antioch, Paul saddled up and went back down the trail through Galatia and Phrygia. He stopped and visited with every cowboy he came across who was a believer and urged them to keep riding hard for the brand.

Apollos is Schooled in Ephesus

²⁴ Meanwhile, there was a great speaker named Apollos who'd arrived in Ephesus from Alexandria in Egypt. This cowboy knew quite a bit about the Good Book. ²⁵ He was really good at gathering folks to ride for the brand of Jesus. But he only went as far as the baptism of John because that's all he knew. ²⁶ When Aquila and Priscilla heard him preach in the Jewish church, they mentored him and explained Jesus's way even more to him.

²⁷ Apollos told them he'd been thinking of heading over to Achaia. All the believers in Ephesus encouraged him to head out. They even sent word to the believers over there to welcome him and listen to what he had to say. He proved to be quite a hand to the believers around Achaia. ²⁸ He stood up to the Jews lofty arguments in public meetings. He used the Good Book to prove Jesus was the Top Hand who would save all those who rode for him.

CHAPTER 19

While Apollos was working in Corinth, Paul left Antioch in Syria and made his way through the mountains. His westerly travel finally brought him to Ephesus on the coast of the Aegean Sea. There he found some cowboys riding for the Lord

and ² he asked them, "Did y'all boys get the Holy Spirit when you started riding for the Lord?"

They said, "We've never even heard about a Holy Spirit."

³ Paul inquired, "What type of baptism did you have?"

"John's baptism," they responded.

⁴ "I see," said Paul. "John was baptizing folks to get 'em ready to ride for the Top Hand. John's baptism taught folks to turn away from their wicked ways and be ready to saddle up for the Boss." ⁵ When they heard this, they were all baptized in the name of Jesus. ⁶ Paul put his hands on them and the Holy Spirit filled their lives. They instantly began to preach and speak in languages they didn't know before. ⁷ There were around twelve cowboys who saddled up for the Lord that day.

⁸ While in Ephesus, Paul once again went to the Jewish church and talked convincingly to them about God's outfit for about three months. ⁹ Despite his great arguments, some of the folks there spurned his message and spoke out publicly against Paul and the cowboy he rode for. So, Paul washed his hands of the Jewish church there and left, taking the believers with him. They moved their talks to a big room at Tyrannus. ¹⁰ Paul taught there for about two years. Everyone in the province of Asia (Greeks and Jews) who wanted to hear about God's outfit had an opportunity to hear what Paul had to say.

¹¹ God did some mighty powerful things through Paul while he was there. ¹² If a wild rag or even a scarf touched Paul, they could take that item and heal the sick with it. These items Paul touched also had the power to kick demons out of good folks.

¹³ A group of Jewish gypsies was going from town to town and claiming to cast demons out of people. They tried to imitate Paul in their little show and said, "By the power of Jesus, who Paul talks about, I'm ordering you to shuck out." ¹⁴ These gypsies were the seven sons of a Jewish preacher named Sceva. ¹⁵ One time while they were doing their little song and dance, a demon spoke back to them and said, "I know Jesus. I've even heard of this cowboy named Paul. But you are neither of these!" ¹⁶ The demon-possessed man then lit into all seven of the men and whipped them like puppies. They barely es-

caped. They got out with their lives, but not with their clothes.

¹⁷ Word of this spread like wildfire. Everyone living in Ephesus got real nervous, but the name of Jesus was held in high regard after that. ¹⁸ A whole herd of folks who believed came forward and confessed their sins. They had finally realized this wasn't a game. ¹⁹ Even some people who'd practiced witchcraft came forward and burned all their scrolls and books. The value of all the burned books and scrolls was several million dollars. ²⁰ Because of this, God's message spread to the far corners of every pasture around there.

²¹ The Holy Spirit then told Paul to head off for Macedonia and Achaia on his way to Jerusalem. "That's where I'm headed," Paul said, "and then I'm off to Rome." ²² He told his two most trusted cowboys, Timothy and Erastus, to head to Macedonia and he'd join them shortly.

The Brawl in Ephesus

²³ About this time, tempers began to flare about the cowboys who rode for the Way. ²⁴ A blacksmith who made silver idols of the Greek goddess Artemis had hired a bunch of craftsmen and Paul's message had been bad for business. ²⁵ The blacksmith got everyone together and said, "Y'all know this is how we make our living. You also know how profitable making these idols are. ²⁶ You also know this cowboy named Paul has been taking customers away from us. And he ain't just doing it here in Ephesus, but the whole province of Asia. He convinces folks that man-made idols are worthless. ²⁷ If we don't do something, our business is going to dry up and our great Artemis is going get a bad name. Folks will stop worshiping her and we will lose everything."

²⁸ Now, this really got 'em riled up. They all began chanting, "Artemis! Artemis! Artemis!" ²⁹ The chant spread throughout the city of Ephesus. The chant turned to violence as Paul's buddies from Macedonia, Gaius and Aristarchus, were grabbed and taken to the stadium. ³⁰ Paul wanted to go and save them, but the cowboys with him kept him from rushing in there. ³¹ There were even city officials who were friends of Paul who sent him a message to stay away from the stadium or he would likely be killed.

³² Inside the stadium, people were in a frenzy. Everyone was shouting something different and confusion reigned. Most people had just been caught up in action and didn't know why they were even there. ³³ The Jews pushed Alexander to the stage and he got everyone quieted down for just a second. ³⁴ But when they realized Alexander was a Jew, the Greeks started their chant up again. "Artemis! Artemis! Artemis!" This went on for nearly two hours.

³⁵ Finally, the mayor of Ephesus was able to get them under control for just a second as he spoke, "Good folks of Ephesus," he said. "Everyone knows Ephesus is the home of the great goddess Artemis. Her image came down to us from heaven itself. ³⁶ No one can dispute this fact. So why are you worked up so much? ³⁷ These boys you brought in have not stolen, damaged, or spoke against Artemis."

³⁸ The mayor continued, "If Demetrius and his workers have something against them, let it be settled in the courts like civilized men. Let them file their complaint and state their case. ³⁹ If there are other matters as well, let us handle them like adults. ⁴⁰ Because if we don't, then Rome is going to think we are rioting and we'll be in a real mess then." ⁴¹ The mayor asked them all to go home and the crowd went away in grumbling agreement.

CHAPTER 20

When the dust had settled, Paul said his goodbyes and struck a long trot for Macedonia. ² He stopped at ranches along the way and spread the word to anyone who would listen. He finally made his way all the way down to Greece. ³ He stayed there about three months doing what God had called him to do for so long. He was about to board a ship for Syria when he heard of a plot by some Jews. So, Paul doubled back and gave them the slip as we went back the way he'd come through Macedonia. ⁴ Seven cowboys rode with him: Pyrrhus's boy Sopater from Berea, Aristarchus and Secundus from Thessalonica, Gaius from Derbe, Timothy, and finally Tychicus and Trophimus from Asia. ⁵ These cowboys scouted ahead and waited for us in Troas. ⁶ We stuck around for the Passover week at Philippi and then took a boat five days later to Troas. There we camped out for seven days.

A Young Cowpuncher Is Raised from the Dead

⁷ We all met together on Sunday morning for a time of worship and the Lord's Supper. Paul planned on heading out the next day, so he taught all day long and well into the night. ⁸ There were a lot of oil lamps in the upstairs room where Paul was teaching. ⁹ Sitting on the sill of an open window, a young cowpuncher named Eutychus began to nod off. He grew so tired that he fell asleep and then fell out of the third story window. He was dead when he hit the ground. ¹⁰ Paul raced down the stairs and upon reaching the young cowpuncher, he threw himself on top of Eutychus and hugged him. Paul shouted, "Everything's going to be fine! He will live." ¹¹ Then they all went back upstairs and had the Lord's Supper. Paul continued to teach about Jesus until the sun came up and then he rode off. ¹² The folks who were there took the young cowpuncher home and he was fit as a fiddle; as was everyone else who had been there.

¹³ The rest of us got on a boat and sailed to Assos to wait for Paul. He wanted to go by land by himself. ¹⁴ When he finally arrived, we all got back on a boat and sailed to Mitylene. ¹⁵ The next day we set sail again and arrived at Chios. We continued sailing to Samos and then on to Miletus. ¹⁶ Paul wanted to bypass Ephesus this time because he wanted to get to Jerusalem by Pentecost.

Paul's Adios

¹⁷ But while at Miletus, Paul sent a letter to the church leaders at Ephesus asking them to come talk to him. ¹⁸ When they rode up, he said, "Y'all saw everything I did while I was with you. You know what I did from the first time my boot hit the ground in the province of Asia. ¹⁹ I rode for the Lord in humility, and sometimes with tears, while my Jewish brothers tried to stab me in the back. ²⁰ I held nothing back in teaching y'all how to ride for the Lord. I went from house to house telling folks the good news. ²¹ I left no one out. I spoke the truth to both Jews and Greeks. I told them how they were to turn to God and quit their sorry ways and have faith in Jesus.

²² "Now, I'm headed for Jerusalem. I'm not sure what's going to happen there, ²³ but God has told me it ain't gonna be skittles and rainbows. It's going to be rough and rank from here on out. ²⁴ But none of that worries me. My only thoughts are to finish the job. Jesus told me to tell everyone about the grace of God through his Son, Jesus Christ. This is the good news that I've told everyone I could.

²⁵ "So, this is where I tell y'all, 'Adios.' We won't ever see each other again in this life. I have told y'all everything I could about God's outfit. ²⁶ I've done my part and what you do with it will be on your heads. ²⁷ Not once did I hold anything back from you about what God wants. ²⁸ Take care of yourselves and watch over the herd God put you in charge of. Be good cowboys who watch over God's herd day and night. Take your jobs seriously because he bought that herd with his own blood. ²⁹ When I leave, wolves are coming, and they will go after the herd. ³⁰ Some of these wolves will be cowboys you thought you could trust, but they will twist the truth in an attempt to lure the weak ones away. ³¹ Keep your eyes open! Don't forget I warned you about this for three years straight. Don't let your guard down.

³² "And now I'm turning y'all loose on your own to follow God. He will take great care of you and make you into the cowboys you could never become on your own. He's going to make y'all strong, and to the strong, he will give an inheritance that cannot be measured. This is the reward to all those who faithfully served him. ³³ I've not lusted after anyone's vest, vittles, or dinero. ³⁴ Y'all know this because I've provided for myself and my cowboys with my own two hands. ³⁵ I made no bones about the value of hard work. I showed you myself that we are to help those less fortunate. We remember the words of the Lord when he said, 'You'll get more by giving than getting.'"

³⁶ Then Paul motioned for them to get out the saddle and they all took a knee in prayer. ³⁷ Tears were shed, and when they were done praying, they all shook hands with Paul. But no one had the right words. ³⁸ Paul's words echoed in their ears that they would never see him again. The range bosses from Ephesus escorted him to the boat, tipped their hats, and went out to do the job God had given them.

CHAPTER 21

We watched the range bosses from Ephesus ride away and then boarded a ship for Kos. We went from there to Rhodes and then on to Patara.

² We switched ships there and then went to Phoenicia. ³ We passed to the south of Cyprus and continued on to Syria. We unloaded at Tyre ⁴ and found some cowboys who rode for the Lord. We stayed at their place for about a week. The Holy Spirit filled these cowboys in on what was going to happen to Paul. They pleaded with him not to go to Jerusalem. ⁵ When it was time to leave, these cowboys and their families followed us out of the city and then prayed with all of us. ⁶ We told them, "Adios," and then got on another ship.

⁷ It wasn't a long ride to Ptolemais. We stayed with some believers there for a day. ⁸ We reached Caesarea the following day and stayed with Philip the Evangelist, who was one of "the Seven." ⁹ He had four virgin daughters who also spoke the word of the Lord.

¹⁰ We stayed with Philip a few days and then a prophet named Agabus rode up from Judea. ¹¹ He walked right up to Paul, took Paul's belt, and made a noose out of it while placing it over his head. With the leather noose around his neck, he said, "Listen to what the Holy Spirit has to say. 'This is the fate of the owner of this belt when he gets to Jerusalem. They are going to sort him out and hand him over to the mavericks.'"

¹² When we heard this, we all began telling Paul not to go to Jerusalem. ¹³ Paul smiled and shook his head saying, "Why are y'all making this worse for me? I'm ready for whatever they dish out, even if it's death. It's not about what they can do to me. It's about what God will do through me that matters." ¹⁴ When it was clear Paul wouldn't change his mind, we gave in and said, "The Lord do with you as he will."

Paul Trots into Jerusalem

¹⁵ We packed up our gear and headed for Jerusalem then. ¹⁶ Some of the cowboys from Caesarea went with us and introduced us to a man named Mnason. He was originally from Cyprus and one of the first cowboys to ride for the Lord. ¹⁷ When we trotted into Jerusalem, the cowboys and cowgirls welcomed us warmly.

¹⁸ After a good night's rest, we went the next day with Paul to meet with James and all the other range bosses at the church in Jerusalem. ¹⁹ After handshakes and pats on the shoulder, Paul told them his tale of the things that had happened among the mavericks.

²⁰ After listening to his story, they said, "It's been the same here, too. Thousands of Jews now believe in Jesus, but they still hold tight to the code of Moses. ²¹ Rumors are spreading, Paul, that you are teaching the mavericks that they don't have to have their pickles clipped or follow any other of the Jewish customs. ²² What should we do? They will know soon enough you are here. And there's liable to be a squabble. ²³ But listen to our plan and see if you like it. There are four men here who have completed a vow they made and now need to go get purified at the main church by getting their heads shaved. But these men don't have the money for it. ²⁴ Join them, and then everyone will see you still hold to the Jewish laws. ²⁵ But we still believe what we told the mavericks still applies to them—stay away from blood, animals sacrificed to idols, meat from strangled animals, and all forms of sexual perversions."

²⁶ The next day, Paul and the four other cowboys went to the main church to be purified. Paul gave the church all the requirements and payments for the purification.

Paul Is Ambushed

²⁷ The required seven days had nearly passed without incident until one day some Jews from the province of Asia saw Paul at the main church. They riled a bunch of folks up, and they went and ambushed Paul. As they grabbed him, ²⁸ they yelled, "All men of Israel, help us! This is the cowboy who is telling the whole world to shun our ways and our code. He encourages people to turn from our ways and our customs. He even brings shame on the main church just by being here today! He has brought in mavericks to this holy place." ²⁹ They said this because one time in Ephesus they saw him with a Gentile and had just assumed he had brought him to the main church.

³⁰ All of Jerusalem looked like an anthill that had been stomped by a herd of Corriente cattle. Paul was walloped and drug out of the church. ³¹ They were just about to kill him when the commander of the Roman army in Jerusalem heard about a riot happening. ³² He immediately sent soldiers to find out what was going on. When the rioters saw the soldiers coming, they all stood very still.

³³ The commander then arrested Paul and had him double chained. The commander asked the

crowd who Paul was and why they were beating him. ³⁴ A hundred different answers were shouted out, and it was clear most of the people had no idea who Paul was or why he was being beaten. So the commander ordered that Paul be taken to the garrison to be questioned. ³⁵ As they were leaving, the mob rose up again and the soldiers had to lift Paul onto their shoulders to keep him from being killed. ³⁶ The crowd followed in a bloodlust shouting, "String him up! String him up!"

Paul's Request to Speak

³⁷ As Paul was about to be taken inside the garrison, he asked the commander, "May I talk to you for a second?"

"You can talk Greek?" the commander asked in surprise. ³⁸ "Aren't you that Egyptian fellow who led a rebellion from out in the desert?"

³⁹ "No, sir," said Paul. "I'm a Jew from the important city of Tarsus in Cilicia. Please give me just a moment to talk to all these folks." ⁴⁰ The commander shrugged his shoulders and motioned for him to speak. Paul stood up and got everyone's attention. You could have heard a pin drop when Paul started speaking to them in their own language of Aramaic.

CHAPTER 22

"Listen to me all y'all cowboys and old-timers," Paul said. "Let me tell y'all what really happened." ² When they heard Paul talking in their language, it got real quiet.

³ Paul waited a moment and then spoke. "I'm a Jew, just like you. Born in Tarsus and went to school here in Jerusalem. Y'all all know Gamaliel. He was my teacher. He taught me all the Jewish ways and codes. I followed all of these to a T. No one was better at it than me. ⁴ I even hunted down Jesus's followers and either killed 'em or locked 'em up. It didn't matter if they were men or women, I hounded them day and night. ⁵ The head preacher and all the church bigwigs can attest to these truths. I even had letters from them to the head honchos in Damascus authorizing me to bring the Cowboys of the Way back to Jerusalem dead or alive.

⁶ "As we were getting close to Damascus, the time was around noon if I recollect, a ray of light came down from heaven and hit me square in the chest. ⁷ I fell off my horse and heard a voice say, 'Saul, why are you hell-bent on destroying what was heaven-sent?'

⁸ "'Who are you, Boss?' I asked shakily.

"'I'm Jesus from Nazareth. I'm the one you're hunting down and trying to kill.' ⁹ The people with me saw the light, but didn't hear the voice talking to me.

¹⁰ "I asked, 'What do you want from me, Lord?'

"The Lord said to me, 'Get up off the ground and head into Damascus. Then you will be given further orders.'

¹¹ "Now y'all have to understand, that light had completely blinded me. I couldn't have seen the sun if I was four inches from it. My companions had to lead me into Damascus like a donkey. ¹²⁻¹³ A cowboy named Ananias lived there and came out to meet us. He was a godly man and was devoted to the Code. He was a popular fellow there. When he came up to me, he said, 'Open your eyes and see for the first time.' And right then, my vision returned.

¹⁴ "Then Ananias said, 'God himself has handpicked you for an important mission. He let you see and hear from the Top Hand himself. ¹⁵ You are going to tell everyone what you've seen and heard. This is your mission. ¹⁶ So quit lollygagging around and get to it. It's time to be baptized and get your sins washed away by the Top Hand.'

¹⁷ "I did all that and then returned to Jerusalem. One day I was praying in the Big Church and fell into some sort of trance. ¹⁸ Jesus, the Top Hand, was standing in front of me and said, 'Get out of here now. Folks in Jerusalem aren't going to believe what you say about me.'

¹⁹ "'But, Boss,' I said, 'I'm the best cowboy for the job. All these people know I hunted your followers like coyotes. ²⁰ And when your cowboy Steve was killed, I held the jackets of the assassins and cheered them on. When they see my turn around, won't they see the truth?'

²¹ "But Jesus said, 'Saddle up and go. Your job isn't to ride pens at the headquarters. You're headed out to gather mavericks in the rough country.'"

²² Everyone was listening intently up until Paul said he was to go gather mavericks. All hell broke loose, and everyone started yelling for his death. ²³ Everyone was screaming, taking off their coats, and slinging dirt in the air.

Paul Tells about His Citizenship

²⁴ The commander grabbed Paul and took him inside where the soldiers were commanded to lash Paul until he confessed his crimes. The commander figured Paul must be guilty of something for all those folks to act like that. ²⁵ They had just tied Paul down when he said, "Do you think it's a good idea to whip a Roman citizen without a trial?"

²⁶ This rattled the centurion and he went and asked the commander, "Did you know this guy is a Roman citizen?"

²⁷ The commander told them to hold up and went over to Paul and asked, "Are you a Roman citizen?"

"Yes, sir," Paul said matter-of-factly.

²⁸ "I am, too," the commander said. "My citizenship cost me everything I had. How much did it cost you?"

Paul said, "Nothing. I was born a Roman citizen."

²⁹ Everyone backed away from Paul. None of the soldiers wanted to be blamed for whipping a Roman citizen without a trial. The commander's face went white because he'd come close to making a fatal mistake.

Paul Stands in Front of the Bigwigs

³⁰ The next day, the commander wanted to get to the bottom of all this. He ordered the Jewish High Council to have a meeting and he took Paul to stand up in front of them.

CHAPTER 23

Paul stood with his shoulders back and his head high as he said, "Brothers, I stand before God and y'all with a clear conscience."

² When these words had come out of Paul's mouth, Ananias (the high priest) nodded his head at a man close to Paul. Immediately, Paul was rocked by an open-handed slap across the face. ³ Paul shot back with ferocity at Ananias, "You will be slapped down by God himself you two-faced hypocrite! You judge me by the Code and then break it yourself by having me slapped like a mongrel dog!"

⁴ Some people standing near gasped, "How dare you speak to the high priest like that?!"

⁵ Paul took a deep breath and then said, "I didn't know he was the high priest. He sure doesn't act like one. But that doesn't matter.

The Good Book says to treat your rulers with respect."

⁶ Paul saw that some of the high council were of the Sadducee clan and others were Pharisees. He used this to his advantage and said, "Y'all know me. I am a Pharisee just like all my granddaddies were. I'm not standing here today for any other reason than I believe we will be raised from the dead."

⁷ And just like that, the High Council was split in two like a bronc through a branding crew. The Sadducees on one side and the Pharisees on the other. ⁸ The Sadducees didn't believe in life after death (or angels or spirits), and the Pharisees did. ⁹ People were on their feet and screaming at each other like the Hatfields and McCoys. Then some influential Pharisees shouted over the ruckus, "He hasn't said anything wrong! What if it was an angel who spoke to him? What if God is behind all of this?" ¹⁰ This brought even more conflict to the council. Finally, the commander sent some soldiers to get Paul before they all turned on him. Paul was then taken back to the garrison.

¹¹ That night, Jesus appeared in front of Paul and said, "You done good cowboy. You've accomplished what I wanted you to here in Jerusalem. You've told everyone about me. Now I'm sending you to Rome to do the same thing."

¹² The next morning a group of Jewish rabble-rousers got together and made a promise that they wouldn't eat or drink until they killed Paul. ¹³ Over forty people made this pledge. ¹⁴ They went to the Jewish movers and shakers and told them of their vow. They said, "We've made an oath not to eat or drink until the outlaw Paul is dead. ¹⁵ We need you to talk to the Roman commander and have him bring Paul back for some more questioning. We will ambush Paul while he is being transferred. He won't live another day."

¹⁶ But Paul's nephew on his sister's side heard the plot and went to the garrison to tell Paul about the plan to ambush and kill him. ¹⁷ Paul asked to speak to one of the officers and said, "It's extremely important that this young man be allowed to speak to the commander. It's a matter of life and death."

¹⁸ The officer took the young boy to the commander and the officer whispered in the

commander's ear, "Paul, the prisoner, said it was a life and death matter that this boy be allowed to speak to you."

¹⁹ The commander looked around and then took the boy by the shoulder and led him a little way away and said, "What is it, son?"

²⁰ Paul's nephew said, "The Jews are going to ask you to bring my uncle back to them for some more questioning. ²¹ But this is all a ruse, sir. There are forty people lined up along the street who are going to ambush Paul and kill him. They've even taken a vow not to eat or drink until he is dead. I believe they've already made the request for tomorrow. They're just waiting for you to agree."

²² "Tell no one about this," the commander said in a stern voice.

Paul is Transferred to Caesarea

²³ Then the commander called over two officers and said, "Y'all gather up two hundred soldiers and take Paul to Caesarea tonight at nine o'clock. Take no chances either. Take two hundred men with spears and seventy mounted cavalry, as well. ²⁴ Give Paul his own horse and get him to Governor Felix." ²⁵

Then the commander wrote this letter to the governor, ²⁶ "From Claudius Lysias, to the great Governor Felix, Greetings Sir! ²⁷ This guy was about to be killed by the Jews, but when I learned he was a Roman citizen, I had him rescued. ²⁸ I escorted him to their High Council to find out why they had a burr under their saddle about him. ²⁹ They were all mad over something that has to do with their religion. No charges were brought up against him, but they were sure enough fixing to kill him. ³⁰ Then I found out they were planning on asking me for another meeting with him and then they were going to ambush him and kill him on the streets. That's when I decided to send him to you. I told his accusers they would have to talk to you about the man now."

³¹ That night, the soldiers escorted Paul as far as Antipatris. ³² The next morning, the cavalry took him the rest of the way to Caesarea. ³³ When they got there, they gave Felix the commander's letter. ³⁴ Felix read it carefully and then looked at Paul and asked him what province he was from. "Cilicia," Paul said.

³⁵ "I'll preside over your trial myself when your accusers arrive," Felix said. Then Paul was ordered to be put in the jail at Herod's headquarters.

CHAPTER 24

About five days later, Ananias, the high priest, showed up with some bigwigs and a hot-shot trial lawyer named, Tertullus. They were ready to present their case against Paul. ² When Paul got to the courtroom, Tertullus presented the charges in a highfalutin address.

He said to the governor, "You've treated us with honor and respect your Excellency. You have led us with wisdom and great foresight. ³ We are humbled by your prowess in government. ⁴ But I will make this short because I know you are a busy man and have better things to do. ⁵ This guy we charge before you is nothing but a troublemaker. Everywhere he goes, all over the world in fact, he leaves a wake of discontent within the Jewish cities. He is one of the jigger bosses in a cult of no-accounts subversives called the Nazarenes. ⁶ We barely managed to catch him this time before he desecrated our most holy place, the main church.

Note: The earliest manuscripts do not have verse 7.

⁸ "You'll quickly come to find upon examining him that all we've said is the absolute truth." ⁹ All across the courtroom, cheers and jeers filled the air attesting to the truth of what Tertullus had said.

¹⁰ The governor raised an eyebrow and motioned for Paul to rise and speak. Paul said, "Your reputation precedes you, sir. I asked to come here and present my case to you because I know for a fact you have been impartial in Jewish affairs before. ¹¹ It is no secret I arrived in Jerusalem about twelve days ago. I merely went to the main church to worship as I have done my whole life. ¹² These people talk about facts, but none of them can produce a shred of evidence that I was inciting a riot or riling anyone up. I didn't do anything wrong in a church building or even a street corner. ¹³ They have nothing but words as proof of their accusations."

¹⁴ Paul continued, "But I stand here today and tell you plainly that I am a cowboy riding for the Way. They call it a cult, but it is the furthest thing from it. I worship the same God they do and believe everything in the Code and what the

prophets said. ¹⁵ My accusers and I both share the hope that God will raise the dead . . . the good, the bad, and the ugly. ¹⁶ Because of this, I watch everything I say and do. My conscience is absolutely clear before God and man.

¹⁷ "I had been away for a couple of years and just returned with money to help my people and to offer sacrifices to God. ¹⁸ They did find me in the main church as they said, but all I was doing was completing a purification ceremony. No one was around me, and there was certainly no riot. ¹⁹ But here's what really happened, some Jews from the province of Asia saw me there. And might I add, they should be the ones here making the accusations, not these folks. ²⁰ Better yet, the high council in Jerusalem didn't even find me guilty of anything ²¹ except for the one time I shouted, 'I'm only on trial because I believe God will raise the dead!'"

²² Felix finally held a hand up. He was quite familiar with the cowboys who rode for the Way. Felix then said, "I've sent for Lysias, the garrison commander. I will hear his testimony and then make a decision." ²³ He adjourned the court and ordered Paul to be kept in custody, but he was free to come and go as he pleased. Felix also allowed Paul's friends to come and see him and care for his needs.

²⁴ A few days later, Felix, along with his Jewish wife, Drusilla, sent for Paul. They asked him in private about his faith in Jesus. ²⁵ Paul held nothing back. He told them the only way to be right with God was through Jesus. Paul also spoke of self-control and the day of judgment that would come for every man. This boogered Felix. He said to Paul, "That's enough for today. If I want more, I'll send for you." ²⁶ He sent for Paul quite a few times, but it wasn't always because he wanted to hear what the cowboy had to say. Felix was secretly hoping Paul would offer a bribe to let him go.

²⁷ Two years went by, and Felix was finally replaced with Porcius Festus. Felix hadn't wanted the Jews to say anything bad about him, so he'd left Paul locked up the whole time.

CHAPTER 25

Festus had been in the country for three days and headed to Jerusalem. ² When he got there, the main preachers and head honchos brought up the charges against Paul. ³ With silver tongues, they graciously asked that Paul be returned to them for a trial. Of course, they were still going to ambush him and kill him before any trial took place. ⁴ But Festus said, "Paul is in Caesarea. That's where I'm heading. ⁵ If you want a trial, bring your accusations there and I'll listen."

⁶ About a week and a half later, Festus arrived in Caesarea. The next day, he took his seat in the courtroom and ordered for Paul to be brought in. ⁷ When Paul was in place, the dog and pony show began again. The Jewish leaders made lots of accusations and had no evidence whatsoever.

⁸ When Paul was allowed to speak, he said, "I ain't wronged nobody, not the Jewish Code, not the main church, or the Roman Government."

⁹ Festus was trying to please the Jews when he said, "Then why don't you go back to Jerusalem and stand trial before them if you've done nothing wrong?"

¹⁰ Paul shook his head and said, "Absolutely not! This is the Roman court right here. You know good and well they have no evidence against me. I didn't hurt anyone. ¹¹ If I deserve to be strung up, I wouldn't argue at all. I'd tell you if I'd done something wrong. But if I'm innocent, why send me to another trial. If you turn me over to these people, they will kill me. So, I invoke my Roman right! I appeal my case to Caesar himself!"

¹² There was quite a commotion and Festus hunkered behind closed doors to talk to his advisors. Finally, he came out and said, "Then it's settled. You asked for Caesar? You'll get Caesar."

¹³ A few days later, King Agrippa stopped by with his sister Bernice to pay respects to the new Roman governor. ¹⁴ While they were there, Festus told him about his Paul problem. Festus said, "There's a cowboy I have locked up here. Felix left me to deal with him. ¹⁵ When I first got here, I went to Jerusalem. One of the first things that came up was this fellow, Paul. He'd sure put a burr underneath the saddle blanket of the church leaders. They pressed charges and asked me to have him strung up. ¹⁶ I told them Roman law doesn't put people to death without a trial. The two sides must have an opportunity to accuse and defend in the presence of each other. ¹⁷ When the plaintiffs arrived in Caesarea, I wasted no time in starting the trial. ¹⁸ But honestly, I was surprised. The accusations were nothing

like I thought they'd be. ¹⁹ All the talk was about their religion and whether or not some cowboy named Jesus was alive like Paul said he was. ²⁰ How're you supposed to investigate that? I asked Paul if he'd like to go back to Jerusalem and stand trial. ²¹ But Paul was adamant and asked that he appear before Caesar. So, I locked Paul back up until I could arrange to have him transferred to Rome."

²² Agrippa sat silent for a moment and then said, "Do you think I could hear Paul's story for myself?"

Festus said, "You bet. I'll send for him tomorrow."

Paul with Agrippa

²³ The next day, Agrippa and Bernice strolled into the auditorium followed by military leaders and other prominent citizens. After they were seated, Festus sent for Paul. ²⁴ Festus rose and said, "King Agrippa and all you fine people! I bring you the man that Jews from here to Jerusalem want strung up by his neck until he is dead. ²⁵ It is my opinion that Paul has done nothing to warrant the death penalty. But Paul asked to bring his case before Caesar, and I will be sending him to Rome as soon as I can. ²⁶ But the question is this, what am I supposed to tell the emperor? What charge am I supposed to bring that will be both the truth and one that won't make me look like an idiot for sending him all the way to Rome? So I let you hear his story, King Agrippa. Maybe after you hear it, you can tell me how to proceed. ²⁷ I can't send him without a viable charge."

CHAPTER 26

Agrippa turned to Paul and said, "Tell me your side of the story, cowboy. Tell it plain and true."

Paul began his story, ² "King Agrippa, I'm glad I am still alive to tell you my story and defend my good name against these baseless accusations. ³ You, as well as anyone, can understand the Jewish ways and customs, even our controversies. Please sit back and listen as I tell you my tale.

⁴ "It is no secret the way I have lived my life. From the time I was just a speck of a boy in my own country until the time I became a man in Jerusalem. ⁵ I am no stranger to anyone. They all know I followed the Code to a T. I am a Pharisee through and through. ⁶ And I am standing here today for one simple fact, I believe God will keep his promise he made to our ancestors. ⁷ It's why all of us worship God day and night. We all have the same hope in God. And this hope is why I am on trial. Nothing else. ⁸ Why is so hard to believe God can bring someone dead back to life?

⁹ "Listen, I once led the fight against Jesus of Nazareth. ¹⁰ That was my job in Jerusalem. With authority given to me by the church, I arrested every believer I could find and threw them in prison. When it came time to sentence them to death for their belief, I cast my vote to have them killed. ¹¹ I went so far as to torture them in the churches just to get them to curse his name. I chased them down like the dogs I thought they were, even to foreign cities!

¹² "I was headed to Damascus on one of these missions. I was armed with the authority and commission of the church. ¹³ It was about noon and we were riding down the road. All of a sudden, there was a light around me brighter than the sun. ¹⁴ My companions and I all fell to the ground. I raised my head and heard a voice speak to me in Aramaic, 'Saul, Saul, why are you hell-bent on destroying me?'

¹⁵ "'Who are you?' I asked.

"And the voice replied, 'It's me. Jesus. The one you are out to get. ¹⁶ Get up! I'm making you switch sides. You're gonna ride for me now. You will tell people about me and tell them the truths I will reveal to you in the future. ¹⁷ I'm going to keep you safe from your own people and the mavericks. Yep, I'm sending you to save the mavericks, too. ¹⁸ You will help them see with open eyes so they will no longer walk in darkness, but the light. You will help them turn from Satan and ride for God. Then they will be forgiven for their sorry ways and have a spot on God's outfit. And the only way you get there is through me.'

¹⁹ "King Agrippa, I have obeyed everything I was told to do when heaven opened up and talked to me. ²⁰ I preached first to those in the Damascus area. Then I preached in Jerusalem and all of Judea. Then I went to the mavericks, or Gentiles, so all would turn from their sorry ways and ride for God. And the proof of this change was the good things they did. ²¹ All these problems we are gathered here for is a result of me telling this story to everyone. Some Jews arrested me in the main church for telling my tale. And they did

all they could to kill me, ²² but God has protected me. He protected me so all might hear the truth. Folks from the greatest to the least have heard it. And the crazy thing is I only preach what Moses and the other great prophets said would happen. ²³ They all said the Top Hand would suffer greatly and then be the first one raised from the dead. And this resurrection was God's way of showing Jews and mavericks his love."

²⁴ Festus then hollered out, "Give us a break, Paul. You've had your nose in a book so long you will believe anything. You've driven yourself mad, sir!"

²⁵ Paul shook his head and said, "No sir, I ain't been in the locoweed. Everything I've said is true. ²⁶ King Agrippa is familiar with everything I've said. Why would I be so bold as to risk my life for a fable? These things didn't take place in a dark alley, but right out in the open for everyone to see. ²⁷ King Agrippa, do you believe what the Good Book and prophets said? I know you believe, Sir!"

²⁸ Agrippa shot back angrily, "Do you think I'm some tavern girl who can be persuaded with a nice tale of adventure? Do you think I will just become a Christian in the blink of an eye?"

²⁹ Paul shrugged his shoulders and said, "I care not if it is today or tomorrow. I just pray to God you and everyone else here might become like me . . . except for the chains that lay heavy upon me."

³⁰ Agrippa, Bernice, and Festus left, followed by everyone else. ³¹ They talked on the way out and agreed Paul had not done anything to deserve the death penalty.

³² Then Agrippa shook his head and said to Festus, "He'd be a free man right now if he hadn't insisted on taking his case before Caesar."

CHAPTER 27

When the time came to send Paul to Rome, he and some other prisoners were transferred to a centurion of the Imperial Regiment named, Julius. ² We got on a boat at Adramyttium and readied to sail for ports along the coast and in the Asia province. Then we were off. Aristarchus of Macedonia accompanied us.

³ We docked at Sidon the next day, and Julius was kind enough to let Paul go see some friends and let them tend to him while they were there.

⁴ Back out at sea again, we had a headwind that made the going rough. The captain took us north of Cyprus between the island and the coast of Asia. ⁵ We were way out at sea, but passed by where Cilicia and Pamphylia were. We finally landed at Myra, in the province of Lycia. ⁶ The commanding officer found a boat from Egypt that was headed to Rome, and we boarded that and set sail.

⁷ The winds were not favorable, and we made slow progress. After what seemed like forever, we made it close to Cnidus. But once again the winds were against us. The captain took us across to Crete and along the easier sailing coast, past the edge of Salmone. ⁸ Like a cow in a bog, we trudged our way along, finally landing at Fair Havens, near Lasea. ⁹ A lot of time had been lost and Paul spoke to the ship's captain about how dangerous the seas were. It had become late in the fall and treacherous.

¹⁰ Paul said, "Guys, listen! I truly believe if we continue on there will be nothing but loss and danger." ¹¹ But the officer in charge of Paul turned a deaf ear to him, and the ship's captain and the owner decided to head for Phoenix. ¹² It had a better port than Fair Havens. They would spend the winter in Phoenix.

¹³ A light wind came up and the crew pulled up the anchor quick. They sailed close to the shore and made good time. ¹⁴ But all of sudden, the weather turned on them like a mad momma cow. A storm close to a hurricane came across the land and blew us out to sea. ¹⁵ The ship couldn't be turned in such a strong wind and so the sailors just shucked the reins and let her run.

¹⁶ We got to one side of the small island of Cauda and pulled the lifeboat in we'd been dragging behind us. ¹⁷ The sailors also lashed the ship with ropes to give it more strength in the high seas. They were afraid of sandbars off the coast of Africa if the wind kept pushing us that way.

¹⁸ The storm continued on to the next day. That's when the crew started throwing cargo overboard. ¹⁹ The next day, they started throwing nonessential gear overboard as well. ²⁰ The storm continued until all were afraid this would be the end of everyone.

²¹ No one had eaten anything in a couple of days when Paul gathered everyone together. He

said to everyone, "Y'all should have listened to me and not left Crete. If you'd listened, none of this would be happening. ²² But listen close and have hope. No one will die, but the ship will sink. ²³ An angel of the Lord appeared to me last night and stood beside my bunk. ²⁴ The angel said to me, 'Do not fear, Paul. You will stand before Caesar. And because of you, God is going to save everyone on the ship.' ²⁵ So take courage, men! God will do what he says he will do. ²⁶ But we will be shipwrecked on an island."

Shipwrecked

²⁷ It was the fourteenth consecutive day of stormy weather. We were still being driven across the Adriatic Sea, and at about midnight, the sailors knew we were close to land. ²⁸ They measured the water depth and is was about 120 feet deep. A short time later, it was thirty feet shallower. ²⁹ They dropped all four anchors to keep themselves from being dashed on the rocks below and everyone prayed for the day to come. ³⁰ Some of the sailors decided to make a run in the only lifeboat. ³¹ Paul told the centurion and the soldiers, "If they leave, you will die too." ³² The soldiers ran and cut the ropes before the sailors could climb down and make their getaway.

³³ Right before sunrise, Paul urged everyone to eat, saying, "No one has eaten, and we've been living on the edge of our seats. ³⁴ Eat something now. You'll need it to survive the coming days. But remember, no one is going to die." ³⁵ Paul then took some bread, broke it, gave thanks to God, and began to eat. ³⁶ This got everyone else to eating, and the mood brightened a little. ³⁷ There were 276 people who ate that early morning. ³⁸ When everyone had finished, they threw the rest of the grain into the sea to lighten the load on the ship.

³⁹ When daylight came, no one recognized the land around them. But they did see a sandy beach and decided to run the ship aground there. ⁴⁰ The anchors were cut loose and the rudder was untied. They raised the mainsail and made out like a bandit for the safety of the beach. ⁴¹ But before they could get there, the ship struck a sandbar and the waves started smashing the ship to pieces.

⁴² The soldiers were just going to kill all the prisoners to keep them from escaping, ⁴³ but the centurion kept them from killing Paul. The centurion ordered everyone to abandon ship and swim for the shore. ⁴⁴ Anyone who couldn't swim was handed pieces of the wood to hold onto. Everyone reached the shore safely.

CHAPTER 28

Once everyone was accounted for, we found out we had crash-landed on the island of Malta. ² The people there were incredibly kind to us all. They built a large fire and insisted we all warm ourselves. ³ Paul was helping gather firewood. He carried it over to the fire and threw it on. A rattlesnake had been in the wood, and it slithered out quickly and bit Paul on the hand. It held on like a pit bull. ⁴ The people from Malta saw what happened and some of them said, "He must be guilty. The sea didn't take him so the land will. Justice will be served." ⁵ But Paul pulled the snake off his hand and threw it in the fire. He kept working like nothing ever happened. ⁶ The people changed their mind about him then and thought he was a god.

⁷ There was a large ranch nearby that belonged to one of the head honchos of the island named Publius. He welcomed everyone to stay there and took care of everyone for three days. ⁸ The ranch owner's father was sick in bed. He had a bad case of the scours and a fever that wouldn't break. Paul went in to see him and put his hands on the sick man in prayer. Then the old boy got up as if nothing had ever been wrong. ⁹ Word got out and all the sick came to Paul. All were healed. ¹⁰ Because of this, everyone who had been on the ship was treated with great honor. When the time came to leave, they provisioned us with all we needed.

¹¹ We had stayed in Malta for three months before we began our journey again. We were given a ship with two gods on the figurehead. ¹² We reached Syracuse and stayed there three days. ¹³ From there we sailed to Rhegium. The next day there was a favorable wind and we made it all the way to Puteoli. ¹⁴ We ran into some cowboys of the Way, and they invited us to spend a week with them. And then we went toward Rome. ¹⁵ The believers there had heard we were coming and came out to meet us. The sight of the cowboys riding and waving filled Paul with thanks to God. ¹⁶ When we finally got to Rome, Paul was given

a place to live all by himself, but a guard was placed at his door.

¹⁷ Three days later, Paul called all the local Jewish leaders together for a meeting. He quieted everyone down and then said, "I have done nothing against any Jewish law or custom. But despite this, they arrested me in Jerusalem and handed me over the Romans for execution. ¹⁸ After a trial, the Romans found me not guilty. ¹⁹ But the Jews objected and kept up their pressure on the local Roman government. I was forced to appeal to Caesar. My hand was forced even though I never wanted to bring any charges against my own people. ²⁰ I invited y'all here today so I could explain myself. And also explain that I believe the hope of all our ancestors—the Top Hand—has already come to save us all."

²¹ They all looked a little perplexed and said, "We haven't heard from anyone in Jerusalem and have not heard anything bad about you. ²² But we have heard about those who ride for the Way. We'd like to hear more about this because some of the things we've heard haven't been all that great."

²³ They all agreed on a time to meet again. Every single time they met, more and more people came to hear what Paul had to say. He preached and taught about Jesus all day long and often into the night. He brought everything together from the code of Moses to the Prophets and even to God's outfit. He held nothing about Jesus back from them. ²⁴ A few came to see the truth, but others were too stubborn to turn from their ways. ²⁵ They argued amongst themselves and began to leave when Paul finished saying, "It was the Holy Spirit who told the truth to Isaiah and said, ²⁶ 'Go tell 'em this, "You'll hear, but you won't listen; you'll see, but you won't notice what it is. ²⁷ For these people's hearts are like a blacksmith's callused hands. They don't hear with their ears. They have sown their own eyes shut. If not, they would see with their eyes, hear with their ears, understand with their hearts, And if all of this happened, I would heal them.'"

²⁸ "You've heard the truth now and what you do with it is your business. But God now offers eternity to the mavericks . . . and they listen and receive it gladly!"

Note: Some manuscripts include
²⁹ *After he said this, the Jews left, arguing vigorously among themselves.*

³⁰ For two years, Paul taught out of his little rented shack. He welcomed any who came and never turned anyone away. ³¹ He taught about God's outfit and showed people how to ride for Jesus. He did so boldly and wouldn't let anyone stop him . . . as a real man should.

ROMANS

CHAPTER 1

From Paul, a hand for Christ, picked and commanded to spread the good news of God.

² Long ago, God had promised the good news through the Good Book and the cowboys who wrote it. ³ The good news is all about Jesus, God's own son. He comes from the family of David if we're talking about human things. ⁴ But in truth, he was said and proved to be the Son of God. Nothing else needs said about it because he came back to life after being in the grave for three days. ⁵ Everything we've got and everything we ride for comes from God through Jesus Christ. He gives us the opportunity to cowboy for him and gather the herd from all the nations who've said they believe in Him. We do it, not for ourselves or to say look at me, but only to bring honor to his name. ⁶ And guess what? Y'all have been chosen to ride as cowhands for Christ as well.

⁷ This letter is to all in Rome who God loves and has called to ride for him.

May your water be clean and your horse never stumble as you ride in grace and peace that comes from God.

The Good News Is the Best News

⁸ First off, I want to thank God for all of ya. The things y'all are doing in faith is spreading like a brushfire in a stiff wind. ⁹ I serve God by spreading the good news of his son everywhere I ride. God knows y'all are ¹⁰ in my prayers every single day. I know God is going to make a way for me to finally ride out and see y'all. ¹¹ It'll be good for everyone's spirit when this happens. ¹² Faith and courage are as contagious as hoof and mouth.

¹³ Listen, I've been wanting to ride out to see y'all for a long time now. But up until now, it hasn't been possible. What I want is for us to ride together. I've ridden with others and worked for Christ alongside them. I want the same with you. ¹⁴ I've been called to ride with real hands and city slickers, smart people and not so smart people. ¹⁵ But I can't wait to get to y'all and tell y'all what I know of the good news.

¹⁶ I am not ashamed of the good news. I wear its brand upon my heart with pride. It's the power of God by which all those who ride for God are saved—first the Jews, and then the rest of them. ¹⁷ The good news shows us how God makes us all right with him. It's nothing but faith from nose to tail. It's nothing more than faith, but nothing less either. The Good Book says, "It's faith that makes us right with God, nothing else."

God Don't Like Sin

¹⁸ God don't like sin because sorry people use it to cover up the truth about him. ¹⁹ God is going to give these evil folks what's coming to them. They try to say there is no God, but God ain't going to be hearing this excuse. He's made himself plain to see for the whole world. ²⁰ God made the world and that ain't hard to see. It didn't happen by chance. Because of this fact, people have no excuse at all for not believing in God. ²¹ They know him, they just deny him. They take credit for his great work. Their thoughts are worthless and their minds filled with nonsense. ²² They brag about their wisdom, but they are fools. ²³ They worship things that look like people, animals, birds, or snakes instead of worshiping the one true God.

[24] And so God has let them throw their souls into the pig pen of their nasty desires. The wallow around on each other like flies on crap. [25] They'd rather tell a lie than hear the truth. They worship the things God has made instead of the one who made them. Only he is to be worshiped. Amen.

[26] Because of their filth, God has turned 'em loose to do what they want, even though they bring shame upon themselves by it. Women use their natural sex appeal to do the appalling. [27] Guys have even traded Eve for Steve. They do vile and unnatural acts with each other and burn their own souls away in the process.

[28] Since no one would listen to God's truth or his warnings, he finally turned these hooligans loose with their own depravity. [29] They are filled up to the brim on all kinds of trash, wickedness, evil, greed, and hate; they are full of jealousy, killing, fighting, lies, and bad attitudes. They talk trash [30] and speak out against each other. They hate God and everyone else. They are backstabbers, insolent, proud, and braggarts. They sit around and make up new ways to sin and defile themselves and others. They disrespect their parents. [31] They refuse to listen, go back on their word, and not only are they heartless, they have no pity for anyone. [32] They know this type of life leads to death, but they continue on like it's a joke. The only people they like are the ones who go with them toward the cliff.

CHAPTER 2

God Don't Play Favorites

Do you look down your nose at the way other cowboys ride? There's no excuse for judgin' another cowboy. When you do, it ain't nothing but the pot calling the kettle black. When you condemn others, you are really condemning yourself. [2] Don't think you can hide your sins by pointing out someone else's. God cannot be fooled by such feebleness. [3] So when you, a human cowpuncher, judge another fella, but do the same things he does, what makes you think God sees his sin, but not yours? [4] These kinds of cowboys throw their nose up at God's kindness, tolerance, and patience. They don't realize it's these things that God uses to turn your life around.

[5] But because you're stubborn as a mule and won't quit doin' things you ought not be doing, you're just piling up judgment on yourself. If you keep it up, God's gonna have to call you to the carpet for 'em. [6] God's going to give you what you've been striving for. [7] If you've been strivin' to bring glory and honor to God, he will give you glory and honor. [8] But to those who have been strivin' for sin that destroys the body, he will let sin destroy their body forever in hell. [9] Those who bring pain and suffering will end up with pain and suffering for eternity. It won't matter if you're a Jew or not a Jew. [10] But God takes his hat off to all those who do what's right. Those cowboys will be rewarded with glory and honor, first for the Jews who do right, and then for everyone else who does. [11] God don't play favorites.

[12] Ignorance is no longer an excuse. Sin is sin and will be judged accordingly. [13] You don't get credit for knowing what the Code says. You only get credit for doing what the Code said to do. [14] Some cowpunchers have never heard the Code, but God has spoken to their hearts and they know the right things to do. [15] This proves they're being guided by something deep down inside 'em that is good. There's also something deep down that urges them to do wrong. Whichever one the cowboy decides to follow will show whether they are forgiven or condemned. [16] My message on this has always been plain as a sorrel horse. God will look at who someone really is and judge them accordingly through Christ Jesus.

Don't Be Counterfeit

[17] Some of you claim to be some of God's original cowboys, the Jews. You claim to follow the Code and boast about your ride with God. [18] You say you know what God wants and that the Code guides your every loop. [19] You think you're a trail guide for the blind and a campfire for those ridin' in the dark. [20] You say you're a clinician who can teach fools and a top hand the young'uns can follow. You are absolutely certain the Code contains the full measure of knowledge and truth that there is. [21] But how can you teach others when you refuse to learn? You claim it is wrong to steal, but you steal anyway. [22] You say to remain faithful in marriage, but your thoughts betray your preachin'. You say to stay away from idols, but your saddlebags are piled full of them. [23] You take pride in the Code, but then you turn your back on it every time it suits you. You don't

bring honor to God, but shame. ²⁴ That's why the Good Book says, "Y'all Jews didn't gather the lost, you've run 'em off by giving God a bad name."

²⁵ Havin' your pickle clipped is great if you're following the Code, but if you ain't, you're missing more than just a piece of yourself. ²⁶ If an outsider (someone who's not a Jew) follows the Code, but doesn't have his pickle clipped, don't you realize God will regard him as if he were circumcised? ²⁷ You Jews are being put to shame by the outsiders. You have the Code written down and your pickle clipped, but they are the ones doing what the Code says even though they are not circumcised. You've got to walk the walk, not just talk the talk.

²⁸ Birth and circumcision doesn't make you a real Jew. ²⁹ To be one of God's original cowboys, you must obey the Code. Real circumcision happens in your heart, not your pants. What motivates you? What God thinks? Or what man thinks?

CHAPTER 3

God Ain't Gonna Quit Ya

What's so great about bein' a Jew and having your pickle clipped? ² Well, more than you might think! First off, God trusted them with his story. ³ Now some of them didn't believe his story. But just because some of them turned their backs on God, doesn't mean he's gonna turn his back on us. ⁴ God never screws up like we do. He don't screw up at all. The Good Book says, "You and truth are tied hard and fast. You are unfazed by rejection."

⁵ But if our sorry ways go to show just how good God is, why would God punish us for making him look good? (That's just the cowpuncher in me talkin'.) ⁶ That's foolish talk. God is completely fair and the only one qualified to judge the whole world. ⁷ Still others will argue, "If my lies reveal God's honesty, what is wrong with that?" ⁸ Others have gone on to twist our words and tell people we have said the more you sin the better it is for God. Those counterfeits will get what's comin' to 'em.

Ain't No One Perfect

⁹ Is it safe to say the Jews are better off than everyone else? Nope! Jews and outsiders (those who were not born Jews) are all under the power of sin. ¹⁰ The Good Book says, "No one is good enough for God—not one single cowboy. ¹¹ Nobody is really wise; no one is even looking for God. ¹² They've all dropped their ropes; everyone is useless. Nobody is doing anything good, not a single one. ¹³ Gross things come from their mouth, like the smell from a rotting corpse. Their tongues are addicted to lies. Venom slips from their lips. ¹⁴ Their mouths curse and complain. ¹⁵ They are hotheaded and violent without cause. ¹⁶ Pain and tears follow their every move. ¹⁷ They've given up looking for peace. ¹⁸ They fear a rock in their boot more than they fear God."

¹⁹ The Code was given in the Good Book, not for others, but us. The Code doesn't tell us how to be perfect, it shows us that we are not and cannot be. ²⁰ No one is made right with God by following rules.

Right with God, Right in Faith

²¹ But God hasn't shunned us. He showed us a way to be right with him that wasn't keeping the requirements of the Code. ²² The only way we can be made right with God is by believing in his boy, Jesus Christ. This is for everyone.

²³ For all have been bucked off and fallen short of the glory of God. ²⁴ But God, because he loves us, makes us right in his eyes. He does this through his son, Jesus, who paid the price for our sins on the cross. ²⁵ God accepted Jesus's death on the cross as the perfect sacrifice for every cowboy's sin. The only way to be made right with God is to believe Jesus died for your sins. God showed he was being fair when he withheld the punishment for those in the past who had sinned. ²⁶ God knew what he was going to do with his son. That sacrifice covered everyone before and after. God did this to show he does the right thing every time. He makes even sorry cowboys flawless in his sight when they believe in Jesus.

²⁷ So do we have any bragging rights about being made right with God? Shoot no, we were made right because of what Jesus did, not because we followed the Code. ²⁸ Let me say this plain, you are made right with God through faith, not by obeying rules.

²⁹ Is God only a God of the Jews? Isn't he the God of the outsiders and day trash too? You know the answer is yes. ³⁰ There's only one God

and only one way to be made right with him—faith in Jesus. And it doesn't matter if they are Jews, Gentiles, cowpunchers, or day trash. ³¹ Do we throw the Code away when we have faith? Not one bit. The Code shows us we need God to make us right with him. We can't do it on our own. That's why our faith makes the Code even more powerful.

CHAPTER 4

Abraham's Trust

Let's talk about Abraham, the sire of the Jewish people. What was it God saw in him? Was it the things he did? ² If it was, he'd have plenty to brag about. But that's not what God saw in him. ³ The Good Book says, "Abraham trusted God, and because of this faith, God saw him as righteous." ⁴ Think about it this way, a fellow that day works is owed a wage because of his work. It ain't a gift. ⁵ But what God offers can't be earned, only gifted. And this gift comes through faith and trust in God. ⁶ Old David even talked about it long ago when he spoke of the happiness of the cowboys who God had chosen, not because they were Top Hands, but because they had top faith. They got all of this without toeing a stirrup. He said, ⁷ "Blessed are them whose screwups are forgotten, whose sins are forgiven. ⁸ Blessed is the cowboy whose sins the Boss won't never hold against him."

⁹ So is David saying these gifts only belong to those who've had their pickles clipped? Absolutely not! It belongs to anyone with faith and pickles don't have nothing to do with it. We've already said, "Abraham trusted God, and because of this faith, God saw him as righteous." ¹⁰ But many asked if God said this before or after Abraham's pickle was clipped. Let me tell you. God said it before it happened, not after. ¹¹ Yes, he did have his pickle clipped to show a sign of his faith and that God had accepted him because of the trust. We might say Abraham is the ramrod of all who are accepted by God through faith, regardless of pickles. ¹² But he is also the ramrod of those who are circumcised and live a life of faith like he did before he was cut.

¹³ God's promise to give the whole world to Abraham's line was not based on how well rules were followed, but on a right relationship with God through faith and trust. ¹⁴ If God only did this for those who obeyed the Code, the faith would be useless. ¹⁵ The Code is only to show you that you can't be perfect and must depend on faith and trust in God to save you.

¹⁶ The promise of God is a free gift we get for having faith. We know this gift is guaranteed through faith, regardless of whether we follow the code of Moses or not. It's about having faith, not following rules. Abraham had this kind of faith and so can we. That's why he is the sire of God's people. ¹⁷ That's what the Good Book means when it says, "I have made you the sire of my people, the first of many that will come." Abraham received this blessing because he believed in God who could bring the dead back to life and whose word brings something from nothing.

¹⁸ With the deck seemingly stacked against him, Abraham kept trusting God—believing he would be the sire of a many nations. God had said to him, "Your offspring and theirs will be more than the number of stars in the sky." ¹⁹⁻²⁰ Abraham was nearly one hundred years old and his wife was barren, but still he believed in what God told him about being the sire of many nations. ²¹ He was absolutely positive God wouldn't go back on his word. ²² Because of this confidence, God looked at him as righteous. ²³ But this isn't just reserved for Abraham and his kin. ²⁴ It's also for every cowboy who has bent the knee and knows God raised Jesus from the dead. ²⁵ He took our place in the firing line and died. Then his daddy raised him from the dead so we could be raised too.

CHAPTER 5

Pards with God

Faith makes us right with God and this is the way to have peace in your life. ² We ride in grace and we live to ride for Him.

³ We don't shy away from wrecks. We know getting through them gives us endurance. ⁴ Endurance gives us an authentic cowboy character, and this character gives us the strength to trust in the hope of salvation. ⁵ Hope in God doesn't disappoint. We can be sure he loves us because he sent the Holy Ghost as our guide to his love.

⁶ When we were hung up in the stirrup of sin, Christ came at just the right time and saved us by dying for our sins. ⁷ It's one thing for someone to

die for a good person or an innocent child, **8** but God sent his son to die for us and we were no good at all. **9** God has accepted us because of his Son's blood, we no longer have to fear God's anger. **10** Since we have been made pards with God by Jesus's death, even though at the time we were not friends of God, we will most certainly be saved through his perfect life. **11** This new relationship with God is something we should celebrate daily. Jesus has made us pards with God.

Adam's Sin and Christ's Perfection

12 When Adam sinned, he doomed us all. Adam's sin brought death and no one escapes it because everyone sins. **13** Yes, there was sin in the world before God spelled it out in the Code. It wasn't counted as sin, but it was there. **14** The result was the same though—sin leads to death and everyone dies. Adam was a glimpse of things to come from Jesus. **15** Adam doomed everyone and Christ saves everyone who believes in him. This is God's wonderful grace. **16** The result of sin is very different from the result of grace. One led to condemnation and the other leads to forgiveness. **17** Adam's sin caused death. God's wonderful grace causes life. All who receive this grace will ride triumphantly forever through the one man, Jesus Christ.

18 I'm going to keep harping on this. Adam's one sin leads to death, Christ's death leads to life by being pards with God. **19** One person disobeyed God and we all become sinners. Another cowboy obeyed God and many will be made right with God because of it.

20 God's code was just to show everyone how many sins they had. But God was better at forgiving than we are at sinning. **21** Yes, sin ruled people's lives and it brought death, but now God's grace rules instead. We can stand with God now instead of against him. We now have eternal life because of the life, death, and resurrection of Jesus Christ our Lord.

CHAPTER 6

Done with Sin

What's up, then? Should we keep on sinning so God's goodness can shine brighter? **2** No, that's stupid. We have died to sin. If something is dead, how can it go on living and flourishing?

3 When we were dunked in baptism, we joined Jesus in his life and death. **4** Baptism means we share his death, burial, and his resurrection.

5 When we share in his death, we get to share in his life as well. **6** Our old self is being put to death on the cross so the power of sin can be destroyed. We no longer ride in sin, but in salvation. **7** Our living-death sets us free from the power of sin. **8** When we die with Christ, we will be raised to life with him as well. **9** Jesus was brought back to life, never to die again. Death doesn't have the reins to his life. **10** Sin has no power over those who have died. Jesus now rides with God. **11** Now we do the same. We have died to our old selves and our old sin and now ride with God.

12 Don't let sin have the reins of your life. Don't give in to those sinful desires you'll regret later. **13** Don't let any part of you be used for evil purposes. Give yourself over to God like you know you should. Surrender yourself to him. **14** Sin must not be your boss. You do not live under the Code, but under grace.

15 So, since we don't live by the Code, does that mean we can do whatever we want? It don't work that way, cowboy. **16** Don't you know that when ya hire onto an outfit, ya gotta do things the way they do 'em—whether ya hire onto sin's outfit, which leads to death, or ya sign on to ride for the Lord, which leads to life. **17** Thank God that even though ya used to ride for sin's outfit, ya took ahold of the things you've been taught. **18** Ya don't work for sin no more. Now you're one of the Lord's hands. **19** I'm using cowboy lingo because I don't want you to say fancy words tripped you up. At one point, we were all hands in sin's outfit. But now, we ride for the Lord and are slaves of his for his good purposes.

20 When you rode for sin, it didn't matter how things were done on God's outfit. **21** What good did you get out of doin' the stuff that now you wish you wouldn't have done? Livin' that way is a trail straight to hell! **22** But since you don't ride for sin's outfit no more and now you ride for God, the good you get puts you on a trail to bein' more like Jesus and the trail ends with livin' forever in heaven. **23** Workin' for sin's outfit pays ya in death, but God offers ya eternal life through Jesus.

CHAPTER 7

Listen close, cowboys. I know you've heard about the Code. It only applies to people who are alive. [2] Another way to say this is if a woman is married, she is married as long as her husband lives. If he dies, she is no longer married. [3] If she shacks up with another man while her husband is alive, then she is a cheater. Now, if her husband were to die, she is free to marry another without being an adulterer. [4] So, let's see how you're following along. You have died with Christ and so you are no longer under the Code. [5] When we lived however, we wanted according to our sinful desires, the Code showed us how wrong we were and deserving of punishment. [6] But we have died with Christ and are no longer bound by the Code that shows our sinfulness. Now we can ride for God, not in sin, but in the new life with Jesus.

The Code and Sin

[7] So, does all of this mean the Code is sinful? Of course not! It was the Code that showed me my sins. If the Code had not said, "Don't jack with another man's Jenny," I wouldn't have known this was a sin. [8] But when I read the commandment, I realized just how much I lusted after other men's possessions. [9] The Code didn't make me sin, it just made me realize how much sin lived within me. [10] This, and other sins, only lead to death. The Code that should have brought me life only showed me how much I deserved death. [11] Sin found a weakness in me and used something great from God against me.

[12] There is nothing wrong with the Code. It is good and holy. [13] Am I saying something good and holy caused death to come upon me? Absolutely not! That was sin working in me, not God's goodness. The Code merely revealed what was really ruling my life.

The Fight Within

[14] The problem ain't with the Code. It is good. [15] The problem is that I don't know why I do the things I do. I don't do what I know I should and I tie hard and fast to things I know aren't good for me. [16] If I know what I'm doing is wrong, then that shows the Code is good. [17] It's not really me doing these things wrong, it is the sin that still lives within me.

[18] I finally realize there is nothing good that lives within me. At least as far as my natural desires go. No matter how much I want to do the right thing, I rarely get it done. [19] I don't do the right thing. I usually do the wrong thing. [20] If I do something I don't want to do, this means I am not the one who does it. It's the sin that lives within me.

[21] Unfortunately, I have found this true of my life—when I want to do what is right, I inevitably do what is wrong. [22] I love God's code with all my heart. [23] But there's another power within me that is at war with my heart. This power makes me a slave to sin. [24] Oh, what a sorry cowboy I am. Who can set me free from this power that dominates my life and leads to eternal death? [25] Thanks to God that the answer is Jesus Christ.

In summary, I want to follow God's code, but because of my human nature I am a slave to sin.

CHAPTER 8

There is no black cloud of judgement for those who ride with Christ Jesus. [2] Because you ride with him, the power of life he offers trumps the power of death sin offers. [3] No one could follow the code of Moses. The Code couldn't save us because we are sinners by nature and unable to follow the Code no matter how hard we try. God did for us what the Code could not. He sent his son to live a perfect life for us and then be sacrificed as the last and final sin offering. [4] Jesus followed the Code perfectly and then passed that perfection on to us. The Code was fulfilled for us. We now have a choice to ride in sin and death or ride in life with Jesus.

[5] Do you think more about sin or the things that please the Holy Ghost? That's how you know which of these you ride for. [6] Letting sin fill your head like an overflowing water trough will be the end of you. But if you fill your mind with the Holy Ghost, you will find life and inner peace. [7] Our sinful nature is an enemy of God. [8] An enemy of God can never please him.

[9] But that can't be you. You are not controlled by sin any longer. You are controlled by the Spirit of God. Those who are not controlled by the Spirit of Christ do not ride for him. [10] When you ride for Jesus, your body will die, but your spirit will live because you've been made right with God. [11] The same power that raised Jesus from the grave will raise you on the last day.

¹² Listen cowboys, just because you think about sin doesn't mean you have to follow those sinful urges. ¹³ If you ride for sin, you'll die in it. But if you ride for the Lord, you will live. ¹⁴ Those who ride for God are children of God.

¹⁵ The spirit you've been given doesn't make scared slaves. The Spirit was given to you when he adopted you as one of his own kiddos. That's why we call him, "Abba, Daddy." ¹⁶ When his spirit ties hard and fast to ours, we know we are God's kids. ¹⁷ If we are his kids, then we are his heirs. Together with Jesus, we will inherit God's glory. But if you want the glory, you'll have to share in the suffering.

The Glory to Come

¹⁸ The suffering will seem like a lot, but only until we receive the glory . . . then it will all have been worth it. ¹⁹ Everything on earth burns with anticipation when God will open the book and read the names written in it. ²⁰ God has a tight rein on all of creation as everything waits for that hopeful day. ²¹ Even creation longs for the day when all of God's kids will join it, free from death and decay. ²² All of creation has been in pain like a mother awaiting the birth of a child. ²³ We who ride for God also suffer in pain as we wait for the future glory that is to come. We wait to be freed from sin and suffering. ²⁴ We long to be given our inheritance as children of God. We will have new bodies and a new life free of pain and suffering. Those who ride for him hold onto this hope since it was given to us when we saddled up for him. We need this hope because we don't have what God promised us yet. ²⁵ If we had it already, we wouldn't be waiting for it so calmly and patiently.

²⁶ When our feet slip in the stirrups, the Holy Ghost is there to help us. Think about this, we don't really even know what to pray for, but the Holy Ghost prays for us with words and sounds we don't understand. ²⁷ We may not understand it, but God does, and he likes it. ²⁸ We have no doubt God will take the reins and lead all us cowboys and cowgirls who have answered his call to green pastures. ²⁹ God knows who will ride for him. He chose them to ride for his Son and become like him. Jesus would be the firstborn of God's line of kids. ³⁰ Since he chose them, he calls them by name to come to him. When they answer, he made them right with himself.

Since they have been made right with God, he gave them his glory.

Nothing Can Get in the Way of God's Love

³¹ So, what can we say about all of this good news? If God rides with us, who do we need to fear? ³² If God were willing to give his son as a sacrifice for you, do you think he would hold other things from us? ³³⁻³⁴ Who thinks they can accuse one of God's kids? No one can. Jesus died for us and will raise us to life. He sits at the right hand of God pleading for us.

³⁵ Can we do anything to make Jesus throw rocks at us and run us off? Does it mean he has given up on us if we go through hard times, or we are hungry, or near death, or even threatened with death? ³⁶ Even the Good Book says, "For the sake of the brand, we ride in danger every single day. We are being butchered like sheep." ³⁷ But, despite all these things, victory is guaranteed for us who ride for the Lord.

³⁸ I'm plumb certain that neither livin' nor dyin', neither the angels from heaven nor the boogers from brush, neither the right now's nor the will be's, nor any force on earth or heaven can get in the way of God lovin' us. ³⁹ There ain't no fence, no gate, nor any mountain or problem that will be able to keep us from the love of God that is found in his only Son.

CHAPTER 9

God Chooses His People to Work His Pastures

I'm not blowing smoke and Jesus knows it . . . the Holy Spirit has my back in this. ² I'm torn plumb in two ³ because of my kin, the Jews. I'd ride right through the gates of hell and spend eternity there away from Christ if it meant they would be saved. ⁴ God chose these people to work his pastures and be his own adopted kids. God showed himself to them. He made promises to them and told them what it'd take to receive those promises. He allowed them to worship him and come right into his presence. ⁵ Abe, Isaac, and Jake are their ancestors, and Jesus himself was an Israelite by all human standards and nature. But he wasn't just any ordinary human. He was God himself and rules over all of God's spread.

⁶ But just because all the Jews won't be saved doesn't mean God has crawfished on

his promise to his kids. 7 Bloodline and papers don't make you Abe's kids. The Good Book says, "Isaac is the one whose kids will be counted." 8 Remember, Abe (or Abraham as he's known in the old ways) had other kids too. 9 God had promised, "I'll ride back in a about a year and Sarah will have a boy."

10 That boy she had is Isaac, our ancestor. He married Rebekah and they had twins. 11 But before she even gave birth, before the twins took a breath or made a mistake, Rebekah got a message from God. 12 This shows God cannot be backed into a corner by religious doctrine and will choose who he wants regardless of good or bad works. 13 In the words of the Good Book, "I loved Jake, but didn't cotton to Esau."

14 Does that make God unfair? Absolutely not! 15 God said to Moses, "I'll show mercy to whoever I want. I'll give compassion to anyone I choose."

16 It's God's mercy to give and he'll give it the way he chooses. We can't choose for him nor can we be good enough to get it.

17 The Good Book says God told Pharaoh, "I've picked you as a character on the stage to reveal my fame and power." 18 You ain't got to like it, but the truth is that God gets to choose who he will save and whose hearts will be hardened against him.

19 I've heard all the arguments. One might say, "Then why does God blame us for not riding for him? If he's in charge, then it ain't our responsibility."

20 My answer is who do you think you are? You think you are better at making decisions than God? Should the created second-guess the creator who is perfect? 21 When a cowboy tools leather, doesn't he have the right to keep some and throw the rest away regardless of who likes it or disagrees with it? 22 That's how it is with God. He is the master tooler and can choose to do what he likes with his mercy and his anger. 23 He does this to show his power and his glory to those who he has called, who were prepared before the dawn of time. 24 We are some of those he has called, both Jews and outsiders.

25 Old Hosea spoke of the outsiders when he said, "Those who weren't my people I will call to ride for my brand. I will shower them with love, unlike I did before."

26 Furthermore, he said, "At the place where I once rejected them, that is where I call them my kids now."

27 As for Israel, Old Isaiah hollered out, "There's more people of Israel than blades of grass in the pastures, but only a few will be rescued. 28 The Lord will come quickly and with finality."

29 Still, Isaiah said the same thing later, "If the Lord hadn't kept some replacement stock, we would have ended up like Sodom and Gomorrah."

An Unbelieving Lot

30 So, what does all this mean? Even though the outsiders were not following God's code, he still brought them in and made them right with him. It wasn't by following a code. It was by faith. 31 But Israel couldn't wrap their heads around it. They wanted the Code, not mercy. They were an unbelieving lot and never succeeded in becoming right with him. 32 You wonder why? Because they wanted rules instead of faith. They tripped over the great rock in the trail. 33 And don't feel sorry for them. God warned them when he said, "I'm setting a rock in the middle of Jerusalem that will make them stumble and fall. But those who trust solely in me will never be turned away."

CHAPTER 10

Hardheaded Israel

Dear cowboys and cowgirls, what I want more than anything, the thing I pray about every day is for Israel to be saved. 2 They have a lot of enthusiasm, but it is totally misdirected. They are like a Blue Heeler that constantly works the horses instead of the cattle. 3 They refuse to accept God's new way of making people right with him. They are hardheaded and tie hard and fast to keeping the Code. 4 Christ did for us what we couldn't— he kept the Code and was sacrificed for us. The end result is that all who believe in this with a life-changing attitude are made right with God.

5 Moses said you had to keep the Code to be made right with God. 6 But faith's method of getting right with God says, "Don't say, 'Who will go to heaven? 7 Who will go to hell?'"

8 What faith really says is, "The Word that will save you is right here—close as the tongue

between your teeth and the heart between your ribs."

It's this message of faith that we talk about everywhere. [9] If you speak with your mouth and believe in your heart that Jesus is Lord and God brought him back from the dead, you'll be saved. [10] It's all about believing with a soft heart and proclaiming your faith out loud that you are saved.

[11] The Good Book tells us, "Anyone who trusts in him will not have the gate shut on them." [12] This is for Jews and outsiders. They have only one God who doles out a heaping of blessings on all who come to him and ask. [13] Everyone who cries out to God will be saved.

[14] But here's the sticker, how can they cry out to him unless they believe in him? How can they believe in him if no one has ever heard about him? How can anyone hear of him if no one talks about him? [15] And how will anyone go talk about him unless they are sent? That is why the Good Book says, "Look at those who aren't afraid to ride out and gather!"

[16] But not everyone is happy to hear the good news. Isaiah said, "Lord, who's believed what we've said?" [17] Faith comes from hearing and listening to the good news about what Jesus did for us.

[18] But I often wonder, have the folks of Israel heard the good news? Of course they have, "The message has struck a lope throughout the earth, spoken to the whole world."

[19] But did they really understand? I believe they did, for even when Moses was riding for the brand, God said, "You will become jealous of those you think are below you, Israel. You'll throw a fit when I give my grace and mercy to those who were not even looking for me."

[20] Later on, Isaiah said, "People came across me who weren't even looking for me. I showed myself to those looking for other things."

[21] God said about Israel, "I sounded the siren for them to come to me all day long and they ignored me because they are rebellious and disobedient."

CHAPTER 11

Seven Thousand Who Still Ride

So, do you think God has somehow double-crossed his own people? That's foolishness! I'm

an Israelite, an ancestor of Abraham and part of the Benjamite Crew.

[2] God didn't double-cross his own people. He chose them from the get-go. Have you not studied the Good Book? Elijah complained to God about his own people when he said, [3] "Lord, they've ambushed and killed all of your true followers and torn down your special places. I'm all that's left and I'm being hunted like wolves after a rabbit."

[4] Don't forget God's reply. "Don't think for a minute you know what's happening Elijah. I still have over seven thousand cowboys who haven't bent the knee to Baal!"

[5] Not much has changed since then. There are a few Israelites who have remained faithful to the brand. This brand is based on grace and kindness from God, [6] not following rules and regulations. If it was about the latter, then God's grace wouldn't have the power it does. It is free and totally undeserved.

[7] So, here's the deal amigos, most folks ain't come to God for the life they've been prowling the brush for. There have been a few, but those are the ones he has chosen. The rest of their hearts have become hardened. [8] The Good Book says, "After all God did for them, he finally turned 'em loose to their own devices. He shut their eyes like the blind and closed their ears like the deaf."

[9] Even David said, "Let all you've done be their undoing. Let them trip over your blessings and think they are getting somewhere. [10] Shield your glory from their eyes and let their backs break for all time."

[11] So, has God totally given up on them? Again, no! Sure, they've been trying it their own way, but all that got them was God inviting the outsiders to his table. It wasn't that he shunned his people, it was so they might become jealous of the favor he granted the outsiders and come back to Him. [12] If God would give so much to outsiders, think about how much he would give his own people.

[13] I'm not blowing smoke, I'm talking to you outsiders now. God has given me the responsibility to go out and gather your pastures for his brand. I've got a good motive, too! [14] I want the people of Israel to become green with envy over y'alls relationship with God. I hope this will

spur some of them to change their ways. **15** They turned their backs on God's grace so he turned toward y'all outsiders. But how much better would it be if God's own people would come back to Him? It would be like bringing the dead back to life. **16** Since Abe and the other patriarchs were holy, surely there is some holy fruit left. If the roots are holy, the branches can be, too.

17 But some of these branches have been broken off. You outsiders have been grafted in like an apple branch grafted on a pear tree. So, now you get all the benefits that have been long reserved for only Israel. **18** But don't go spoutin' off at the mouth. You're a grafted branch, not the roots of the tree.

19 Some might be saying, "Well, those branches were broken off so we could squeeze in." **20** While that's true, remember you are there because of your faith in Christ. They were broken off because they rejected him. Instead of bragging about this, switch to just being thankful you haven't been broken off and thrown in the fire. **21** If God didn't hesitate to cut his own people off, don't think you are somehow immune if you turn your back.

22 God is both dangerous and kind. He is dangerous to the disobedient, but kind to those who seek his guidance through Christ. But if you turn your back, the axe is coming out. **23** If Israel will come back, they will be welcomed back. But it will be on God's terms, not theirs. **24** You outsiders were like a wild branch cut from the wilderness and grafted in God's orchard. If he did this for you, do not think he would hesitate to bring his own people back.

Mercy for the Multitudes

25 I know this is hard to understand, like a mystery, but do not start thinking too highly of yourselves. Yes, some of the Israel's cowboys have hard hearts, but this is only until the right number of outsiders have been brought into the herd through Jesus. **26** And then, Israel will come back and be rescued from the fire. The Good Book says, "The cowboy who can save will come from Jerusalem and save Israel from the quicksand of ungodliness. **27** I've made a promise to them to take away their sins."

28 Israel has become an enemy of the good news. But their loss is your gain for now. Yet, God still loves them because of the grandpap-

pies Abe, Isaac, and Jake. **29** God's gifts and his calling can never be thrown away. **30** Once, you outsiders were enemies of God and Israel wasn't. **31** Now, y'all have swapped sides. **32** Everyone has turned their back on God, but his mercy is greater.

33 There is nothing better than God's riches and his wisdom. There ain't no way we can ever truly understand his ways or his reasonings. **34** Who knows what he's thinking? Who thinks they can offer advice? **35** Has anyone given so much that God owes them something back?

36 There's nothing we have that he didn't make or have a hand in. It's not for our personal glory, but only his. Give him the glory forever! Amen.

CHAPTER 12

Offer up Your Life for His Outfit

I'm saying this as if the God of mercy himself were standing right here. I urge each of you to offer up your lives into his outfit—this is how you really worship God. **2** Quit tryin' to fit into the sorry ways of the world, but be made new by changing the way you think. Only then will you find the trail that the Boss wants you to ride.

3 Because of my position in this gathering, the Boss has given me the authority to pass along this warning. Don't look down your nose at anyone. You worry about you and the faith you have. **4** Just like a saddle has many parts, each serves its own function. Some parts can be seen and some can't. **5** It's the same way with the body of Christ. We are many parts with many functions, but we all belong together and for each other.

6 Because of his grace, God gave us different specialties for doing things well. If God gave you the specialty of speaking his truth, do it with as much faith as God has given you. **7** If your gift is helping others, ride for them just like you do for Him. If you're a clinician, teach it God's way. **8** If your gift is to lift others up, lift them up high. If it is donating, do it to the max. If it is being a ramrod, take your responsibility with all the seriousness of the job. And finally, if you have the specialty of kindness, do it without complaint.

9 But above all, don't just pretend like you love others. Really love 'em. Shun all wrongdoing and tie hard and fast to what is good and holy. **10** Let there be no deception in your love for others.

Be authentic like cowboys should. [11] Don't be a recliner cowboy. Work hard at what the Lord calls you to do. [12] Keep your eye on our hope that God sent. Be patient during the pitching, and keep on praying. [13] Be ready to snub for those in need. Don't turn anyone away from your table.

[14] Bless those who talk crap about you. Don't cuss 'em, but pray God will bless 'em. [15] Give a smile to those with a smile and shed a tear with those shedding tears. [16] Get along with each other like a cowboy with his best mount. Don't be too proud to sit at the fire with greenhorns. And whatever you do, don't ever think you know it all.

[17] Never pay someone back for something evil they did. Be the bigger man so others will see the honor with which you live. [18] Get along with everyone better than you think you can.

[19] Never seek revenge or retaliation. Leave paybacks to God. Even the Good Book says, "Revenge is mine. I've reserved the paybacks for myself," says the Lord.

[20] "Instead, if your enemy is hungry, give them your freshest biscuit. If they're thirsty, give them the rest of your water. In doing so, you will shame them with God's love and pour coals over their heads."

[21] Don't give in to evil. If you want to come out on top, conquer evil with all things good.

CHAPTER 13

Respect for the Cow Bosses

Y'all have to do what the cow bosses tell you to. All authority is given by God and God alone and you don't get to second-guess his decisions. [2] Be a good hand whether or not you have a good boss. Otherwise, you are going against God himself. Don't take a chapping from God because of your pride. [3] If you do what is right, you have nothing to be afraid of. Wouldn't you like to ride without fear of a surly cow boss? Make a hand and that will make you stand out. [4] All who have authority over you are God's servants in one way or another. If you screw up, then you should be scared because they have the power to throw you off the ranch. These authority figures in various shapes and sizes are sent to make you better and punish you if you screw up. [5] Let go of your pride and do your job, not just to keep your butt out of trouble, but also so you can lay your head down at night with a clear conscience.

[6] Pay your taxes as well. I say this for the same reasons I just got through talking about. Even government officials need grub to eat. They are riding for God whether they know it or not. [7] Don't shuck your obligations in any form, monetarily or otherwise.

Love Is the Cinch That Holds Everything Tight

[8] Don't owe anyone anything—except that you are willing to love each other. Loving your neighbor is the cinch that holds you tight to God. It's not part of what he wants you to do. It's everything. [9] Even the mighty regulations God passed down to us said, "Don't jack with another man's Jenny. Don't murder or be a thief. Don't hanker for something that ain't yours." These things, as well as other things, can be summed up as, "Love your neighbor as if he was you." [10] Love doesn't wrong others and so it fulfills all God asked us to do.

[11] Don't kick your leg over the saddle and think you've reached the end of the drive. The hour is growing late and you've still got a far piece to go. Put your feet back in the stirrups and strike a long trot. Eternal life is waiting and the time is drawing near. [12] Dawn approaches, which means the day of redemption is close at hand. Shuck all your foul deeds just like dirty clothes. Put on the leather chaps of who you were meant to be. [13] We're not made for the night, but to be seen in the daylight and bring glory to God. Ride way around orgies and drunken parties. Go out of your way to avoid sexual promiscuity and all other types of rotten living, which includes envy and nit-picking. [14] Instead, outfit yourself in the presence of Jesus and turn your mind away from counterfeit desires.

CHAPTER 14

Breeding Good Relationships

Quit arguing with those with a weaker faith than you. [2] Let me explain, one might think it's okay to eat anything and another is a vegan. [3] You worry about you and let others make their own decisions. Quit condemning others because they don't act like you do, this goes both ways. God accepts all kinds based on their heart. [4] Who are you to condemn another ranch's hands? The Boss will judge whether they ride through the gate or get yard-darted before they get there. If they're following the Lord, they'll make it.

⁵ Quit bickering over which day is holy. You do what you feel God has led you to do and let that be enough. Again, you worry about you. ⁶ If they are honoring the Lord, he doesn't really care what day it is on the calendar. If two people honor the Lord with two different diets, that's okay too. ⁷ We don't live or die for ourselves, but for our Lord. ⁸ We live to honor God. We die to honor God. So, it doesn't matter whether we are living or dying, to it all for the Lord. ⁹ Jesus died and rose again for this very matter—to be the Lord of both the living and the dead.

¹⁰ So why do you keep quarreling with others who ride for God? What gives you the right to look down your nose at them? We will all stand in front of the Boss one day to be judged. ¹¹ The Good Book says, "'As much as I am alive, every soul will bend the knee and every mouth shall pledge themselves to me,' says the Lord."

¹² Ain't nobody going to be standing there making excuses for your life in front of God. ¹³ Don't get caught with your pants down over petty squabbling. Ride in a way that you don't get others bucked off.

¹⁴ I'm a hundred percent positive the Lord doesn't care what you eat. But if one person thinks it's wrong to eat something, then it is wrong for them to eat it. ¹⁵ If someone thinks it's wrong to eat something, don't try to serve it to them. That ain't loving 'em. Don't let something as good as food turn y'all against each other. Christ died for both of y'all. ¹⁶ You'll be blameless if you act this way. ¹⁷ God's outfit is not about what you eat or drink, but living the honorable life of a cowboy who rides for the brand. You live this way by following the Holy Spirit. ¹⁸ Ride for Christ with an attitude like this and God will be pleased. Not only that, but you'll gain the respect of others. ¹⁹ Ride as one and help each other out in order to build the crew up.

²⁰ Don't tear the crew apart over beans or bacon. They are both fine as long as it doesn't cause another man to fall from the saddle. ²¹ It is better to stay away from meat or wine if it causes the other person to question their beliefs. ²² You can do that later on your own as long as you don't go overboard with either, but keep it between yourself and God. Don't feel guilty about doing something you feel is right as long as it doesn't harm others in your vicinity. ²³ But a word of caution, if you're unsure whether or not something is wrong, stay away from it. It would be a sin then. You do what God leads you to do. If you do anything you don't believe is right then that is sin.

CHAPTER 15

Ride for Others

Top hands must be considerate to beginners in things such as these. Life ain't about just riding for yourself, but take others into consideration as well. ² Build each other up and help them to become top hands as well. ³ Jesus didn't even live only for himself. The Good Book says, "I've stepped in front of the insults meant for you, God." ⁴ These things were written for our benefit to show us the right trail. This trail doesn't lead to disappointment even though it gets rough at times. There is hope waiting on the promises of God.

⁵ God's the one who doles out patience and encouragement for those who use them to build a crew that works well together. This is how Jesus wants his crew to operate. ⁶ This life sends one voice up to heaven glorifying God, the Daddy of our Lord Jesus Christ.

⁷ If you want God to accept you and all your mistakes, do the same for others. ⁸ Jesus was a servant of the Jews to fulfill the promises God made to their ancestors. ⁹ He also came that the promises would be extended to the outsiders. The Psalms speak of this when they say, "Because of who you are, I will praise you among the outsiders. I will sing of your mighty name."

¹⁰ Another place it is written, "Insiders and outsiders, sing together to the same God!"

¹¹ And still again, "Everyone sing praises to God. Everyone of the earth, lift him up."

¹² Even Isaiah stated, "The descendant of David's crown will come and rule over the outsiders. They will give their faith and hope to him."

¹³ God is the only source of hope and my prayer at the campfire each night is that you are filled with joy and peace by trusting in his power instead of your own. I pray that this filling will be like a trough overflowing through the Holy Ghost.

Paul Ain't Saying This to Hear Himself Talk

14 I've got no doubt, cowboys and cowgirls, that you have a heapin' of goodness inside all of ya. You can show others how to ride for the Lord. **15** I haven't said these things to hear myself to talk, but to remind you of these things because you'll be needin' 'em. It is by God's mercy **16** that I am a hand for God tasked with gathering y'all remnants. I bring you good news, not bad news. **17** This is an acceptable offering to God by the Holy Ghost. **18** But you ain't going to hear me bragging on anything but God and what he's done through me. I've rode with the outsiders and they now ride for God. **19** They witnessed great things done by God and they fully believe. I've presented the good news to all the pastures from Jerusalem to Illyricum.

20 My sole purpose is to bring the good news to those who have never heard it. I didn't go to the churches, I went into the brush. **21** I've been following the trail talked about in the Good Book where it says, "The wild cattle that have never seen a cowboy will come across one and they will hear and understand."

22 I haven't made it to y'all yet because I've been so busy doing these things and riding these pastures and canyons.

Paul's Plans

23 But I can say that I'm done here. I'm certainly ready to see all of y'all after years of riding the rough brush and the rough stock. **24** I'm going to go to Spain and I'll stop in Rome to see y'all. I'll stay with y'all a while so you can offer me some much needed rest before I head out again.

25 But first, I have to ride over to Jerusalem to give the offerings I've collected to the hands there. **26** The cowboys who ride for the Lord in Macedonia and Achaia took it upon themselves to gather some money for the poor in Jerusalem. **27** They did this willingly out of the goodness in their hearts. These outsiders are thankful for the spiritual blessing that was brought to them from Jerusalem. The least they can do is help out. That's what real hands do. **28** When I'm done paying it forward, I'm coming your way. **29** I know God is going to bless our time together.

30 Cowboys, I'm sure enough counting on all of y'all to join with me in the struggle that comes with riding for Christ. Keep me in your prayers and I know God will answer them. Y'all care about me because the Holy Ghost is in your hearts. **31** Pray that God will protect me from those in Judea who don't want this message spread to the world. Also pray that the gifts I take to Jerusalem will be accepted with the same heart they were given. **32** Again, I long to see your faces and shake your hands. We will strengthen each other.

33 Now let God, who doesn't hold back anything, give us peace. Amen.

CHAPTER 16

I am recommending to y'all a cowgirl named Phoebe. She is instrumental in the church in Cenchreae. **2** Treat her like you would me. Help with whatever she may need. She's done the same for me many times over.

3 Say hello to Priscilla and Aquila for me. I consider both of them my pards in riding for the Lord. **4** They've put their necks on the line for me more than once. Every church filled with outsiders knows of them and how thankful I am for them both. **5** Say hello to all who meet at their house to learn about the Lord.

Give a shout out to my friend Epenetus. He was the first Outsider I gathered in the province of Asia. **6** Give a hug for me to Mary who has done so much for all of us. **7** Also do the same for Andronicus and Junia. They are Jews who spent time in jail with me. They came to Christ before I did and are much respected with the Apostles. **8** I don't want to forget Ampliatus. He is a true friend in Christ. **9** Tell Urbanus, a hand for the brand, I said hello, also, to my friend Stachys.

10 Greet Apelles, a good hand who Jesus is proud of. Give my greetings to all the cowboys and cowgirls staying with Aristobulus. **11** Say hello for me to Herodion, a Jew as well. The same goes for all those with Narcissus. **12** A special hello goes out Tryphena and Tryphosa, who ride hard for the Lord, and to Persis, who is the first to step up and the last to quit. **13** Say hello to Rufus. Jesus picked him personally, as well as his momma, who has been like a second mom to me.

14 Hello to Asyncritus, Phelgon, Hermes, Patrobas, Hermas, and all who meet at their place. **15** Hello to Philologus, Julia, Nereus and his hermana, as well as Olympas and all they watch out for.

¹⁶ Give them all a hug and a hand shake. All the outfits I've started send their best.

A Final Order

¹⁷ Let me say one last thing. Watch out for the herd splitters. They'll try to teach things other than what I've taught you. Stay clear of them. ¹⁸ These cowboys ain't riding for the Lord. They do these things for personal interest and gain. They talk good, but their message is rotten . . . and people fall for it. ¹⁹ Everyone knows y'all know the truth and ride for the Lord with all your heart. This makes me so proud. I want you to be wise in doing good things and innocent of wrong things. ²⁰ Satan will be crushed by God soon. Let the grace of God guide you.

²¹ Timothy, my saddle pard, sends his hellos along with Lucius, Jason, and Sosipater—my fellow Jews.

²² I, Tertius, am writing this for Paul. I send my greetings as well.

²³ Gaius said to tell y'all hi. I'm staying with him and our outfit meets at his place. Erastus, the city's bean-counter, along with Quartus, send their regards.

Note: Some manuscripts include ²⁴ *May the grace of Jesus Christ ride with ya. Amen.*

²⁵ Finally, all glory to God, who builds us up strong, just like the good news says. This message about Jesus has shown you God's plan for all the outsiders. This plan has been kept secret since the beginning, but now it is revealed. ²⁶ All the prophets hinted about it, but now the message has been made known to all outsiders. May they believe and follow Jesus completely as they ride for God. ²⁷ Once again, all glory goes to God, through Christ Jesus, forever and ever. Amen.

1 CORINTHIANS

CHAPTER 1

Hey, fellas. This is Paul, chosen by God to ride for the brand of Jesus Christ. My amigo Sosthenes is with me, too.

² I'm writing to God's outfit in Corinth. I'm writing to those God has chosen to be his cowboys. He has straightened your lives out through his son, Jesus, and given y'all the job of gathering and tending the herd. But this is not just your job, but the job of every cowboy who has called on the name of the Lord Jesus Christ.

³ Here's to God giving you everything he has, that you don't deserve.

Being Grateful

⁴ When I'm riding along, my thoughts often wander to you and all the benefits of riding for the brand. This brand is Jesus's brand, but he lets us ride for him. ⁵ You all have more now, through him, than you ever had before. Words can't describe, nor can the mind fathom, what you have now. ⁶ I told y'all this would happen and now you know I was speaking the truth. ⁷ You've been given every cowboy gift you need to ride for the Lord until he comes riding back. ⁸ He's going to keep you strong in the saddle and on the day of his return, he's going to vouch for you before God. ⁹ All of this is what God promised, and he don't ever crawfish on a promise. He's made us a partner with Jesus on his outfit.

Quit Squabblin'

¹⁰ But let me tell you something, cowboys. I'm passing this on to you from the Top Hand himself. Y'all need to get along with each other. Y'all quit your squabbling and bickering. God's cowboys work together, not against each other. ¹¹ Some of Chloe's kin came to me and told me y'all are nit-picking each other like five-year-olds. ¹² I was told some of y'all are thinking you're better than others. Some of you say, "Well, Paul taught me to ride." Others say, "I ride like Apollos does," or "Pete and I ride together," or "Well, I only ride for the Top Hand."

¹³ Has Jesus started playin' favorites? Was Paul hung on a cross to die for you? Quit being silly! ¹⁴ Now, I'm glad I didn't baptize any of y'all except for Crispus and Gaius. ¹⁵ That way, none of y'all can say you were dunked in my name. ¹⁶ But come to think of it, I did baptize everyone at Stephanas's, but no one else. ¹⁷ God didn't send me to see how many people I could baptize. He sent me to preach the good news. And I don't do it with clever words or speeches. Jesus's strength don't lie in fancy tongue talk.

God's Wisdom

¹⁸ Jesus's message from the cross is folly to those heading for the kill-truck. But those of us who will ride in the green grass forever, we know the cross is the power of God. ¹⁹ Even the Good Books says, "I'll show the wise what wisdom really looks like; the know-it-alls will become know-nothings."

²⁰ This begs the question, can wisdom be found here on earth? Let me answer—it cannot! Because God has turned conventional thinking on its head like a forefooted runaway steer. ²¹ God made sure he couldn't be found with the scientific method or fancy philosophy. In his wisdom,

he has used simple cowboy preaching, the type the "wise" have scoffed at, to save those people who choose to believe. ²² The Jews want their miracles and the Greeks their lofty philosophies, so they both turn up their noses at our foolishness. ²³ When we preach that Jesus was killed, the Jews get butthurt, and the Gentiles just roll their eyes.

²⁴ But to those who have been saved, they understand Jesus is the power of God and the wisdom of God. ²⁵ This foolish plan of God's is wiser than the wisest, stronger than the strongest, and better than the best.

²⁶ Don't forget cowboys, there were very few of you who were considered wise by worldly standards or thought to be rich and powerful. But then God got ahold of you. ²⁷ God chose the lowest of us to shame those on high. He personally chose nobodies to show the somebodies what he could do. He chose the weak to put the powerful in their place. ²⁸ God chose those looked down upon to shame those who turn their nose up. ²⁹ He did all this to humble every single one of us. Ain't none of us can stand before him and brag about who we are.

³⁰ God used his Son to bring us together and make a crew out of us. God made pure wisdom into a man and called him his Son. His Son vouched for us and made us right with God; he freed us from the slavery of sin. ³¹ That's why the Good Book says, "If you're gonna brag, brag about what God has done."

CHAPTER 2

When I rode into town, I didn't use riddles and fancy speeches to reveal God's secret plan. ² I spoke as plainly as the nose on your face. I told you who Jesus was and what he did for all of us when he was strung up on the cross. ³ You didn't hear this from some cocky roper, but from one who didn't feel worthy of the words he said. Quite frankly, I was scared out of my gourd. ⁴ But as I said, the message you heard was a plain and simple one. I didn't rely on practiced sermons, but on the power of the Holy Ghost. ⁵ God wanted it like this because he wants you to trust in his abilities, not in men's words.

⁶ But don't get me wrong, when I'm with top hands I can give them wisdom that can even make them better hands. But this knowledge isn't one you can hear from blowhards and braggarts. ⁷ Nope, this wisdom comes from the mystery of God himself. This secret has been hidden from the world for a long time but was finally revealed for our glory and his honor. ⁸ But the folks who run this world had no idea. If they'd even suspected, they would have never crucified Jesus and unleashed God's power on the world. ⁹ This is what the Good Book meant when it said, "No eye has seen, nor any ear has heard; no mind could even imagine what God has in store for those who ride for him."

¹⁰ God told us the secret through the Holy Ghost. His Spirit is the one who guides us on the trail and reveals the mysteries of God. ¹¹⁻¹³ When a cowboy rides the pastures, only his soul hears his secret thoughts. It's the same way with God. The Holy Spirit is the soul of God and it knows God's thoughts and explains them to us. ¹⁴ And just like a city fellow can't know what it's like to ride for the brand, neither can an unbeliever know what God's thoughts are. They think all this stuff about God is just myth and folly. But it's no surprise to us, is it? A cowboy's secrets can't be explained to a tenderfoot. They'd never understand the life or the code of the West. ¹⁵ Those who ride for the brand are made aware of all things. Now that we know the truth, we pay little attention to those who criticize us for following it. ¹⁶ Even the great cowboy Isaiah, said, "Who knows what the Boss is up to? Who thinks they can tell him a better way to run the ranch?"

We understand what he's doing because we ride the trail with the Top Hand, Jesus.

CHAPTER 3

Listen cowboys and cowgirls, when I was with you, I had to talk to y'all like the greenhorns you were. You knew nothing of riding for God. You only knew how to ride for yourselves. You were like little kids. ² You couldn't handle anything more than a slow walk around the pasture being led every step. And the sad part is, you've still got both hands wrapped around the saddle horn like gunsels. You still aren't ready to walk by yourselves, much less ride. ³ Why? Because you are still being controlled by sin and emotions. You're all looking to one-up each other and you squabble like a pen full of squealin' mares. You see? You're acting just like the rest of the world does. ⁴ When y'all say things like, "I ride with

Paul," and someone else shoots back, "Well, I ride with Apollos," can't you see y'all sound like gunsels?

⁵ Besides, who is Apollos? Who is this Paul you speak of? We're just cowboys who had the job of telling y'all the good news. We ain't special. We were just doing what the Good Lord told us to. ⁶ I did the groundwork with you. Apollos started you under saddle, but it was God who was doing the growin' inside ya. ⁷ The one who does the groundwork and the one who starts you under saddle both are working toward the same goal. ⁸ Each will be rewarded for their work in the process. One cowboy ain't more important than the next. ⁹ Both of us are just cowboys in God's outfit. We are gatherin' his pastures and you are these pastures.

¹⁰ Because of the grace of God, I have laid the foundations of a ranch like a top-notch cowman. Now others are working its pastures, but they must be very careful. ¹¹ Do not be misled! This foundation can only be the one that has been there since the beginning—Jesus Christ. ¹² Listen, everyone who works here will build their legacy with different materials—silver, gold, stone, wood, or straw. ¹³ But there will come a day of judgment through fire. This fire will reveal who took pride in what they built. ¹⁴ If their work survives, then that cowboy will be shown as a top hand. ¹⁵ But if their work falls apart, that cowboy will end up flat on his back. He will still be saved, but just barely . . . like a cowboy who survived being run over by a stampede.

¹⁶ Come on, cowboys, don't y'all realize God's outfit is all of you put together? Don't you realize the Holy Ghost lives inside ya? ¹⁷ God will destroy anyone who tries to destroy his outfit. God's outfit is holy, and y'all are his outfit.

¹⁸ So don't be pulling the wool over your own eyes. Wisdom doesn't come from clever ideas or fancy words. If this is your wisdom then you should try to become fools. Only then will you know what it takes to become wise. ¹⁹ What's considered wisdom down here is malarkey to God. Remember when the Good Book says, "He ropes the wise with their own reata," ²⁰ and another time when it says, "The Boss knows the thoughts of the wise and laughs at their stupidity." ²¹ So, no more big-talking and name-dropping. You don't need any human to gain all things because they already belong to you. ²² It don't matter if you ride with Paul, Apollos, or even Pete himself, you already have everything. You have the world, the past, the future, and even this present age. You've already been given everything ²³ and you belong to Christ, and Christ belongs to God.

CHAPTER 4

So, don't look at Apollos and me as anything more than cowboys who've been put in charge of teaching you the mystery of how to ride for God. ² Now when a cowboy is put in charge of something, he must be faithful to the brand. ³ But as for me, I don't give two shakes whether you like me or agree with what I do or say. I ain't gonna let you judge me. I won't even judge myself. ⁴ My conscience is clear. Now I ain't saying I'm perfect, but the One who will judge me is, and I trust him with my soul.

⁵ So don't go making judgments about yourselves or others. If there's breath left in either, there's time to make things right. The only judgment that matters will happen when the Lord rides back through the main gate. Like a light in a pitch-dark tack room, he will reveal our darkest secrets and our secret prayers. Then, if there's attaboys to be given, God will do the givin'.

⁶ Now, cowboys and cowgirls, this is how Apollos and I ride for the Lord. We do this so you can see God's way in action. That's what the Good Book means when it says, "Don't do more'n what you're told." If you follow this, you won't be bragging about riding with any cowboy except Jesus. ⁷ So don't go making judgments about the way other cowboys do things. What gives you the right? What do you have that didn't come from God? And if you answer that everything is from God, then why brag like you're better than the next cowboy?

⁸ I've already said you have everything you need already. As a matter of fact, you have more access to God than you know what to do with. You're like a little kid with a champion cutting horse, but you've never straddled a saddle. But I wish you were already champions in your own rights. If you were, then we would be too. ⁹ Instead, it seems as if God has put us cowboys on display to the movers and shakers of this world to be made fun of. We are on display for men and

angels alike to gawk at. We walk and there are whispers. We talk and eyes roll in disgust. We ride and folks throw rocks and laugh. [10] Our dedication to the brand of Christ makes us look like fools, but y'all flounce around like you're better than others. Y'all ride with your chests puffed out like you're at a parade, but we are out there in the sun and rain, looking like misfits riding the grub line. [11] Even now we are hungry and don't have a piece of jerky to calm the growl of our bellies. We're thirsty, hungry, and our clothes won't turn away the chill. We're beaten in public and don't even have a campfire by which to lick our wounds. [12] We daywork to earn a living. We bless those who cuss us and we let it slide when we are abused. [13] When people talk crap about us, we repay it with a gentle answer. We have become the laughingstock of the world and the scum of the earth. This is true at this very moment.

[14] But don't think I'm trying to make you feel bad about yourselves. I'm warning you what real cowboying for the Lord is like. [15] I'm writing to you like a father would to his kids. Many will come and tell you what you did wrong, but I'm the only one who will take you under his wing and guide you. [16] So watch me carefully and do what I do. [17] That's the reason I've sent you Timothy. He is like a son to me and I've taught him nearly everything I know. He will help you ride for Christ while I'm out teaching others to do the same.

[18] But some of you have become full of yourselves. Like a bully at the playground, you think the teacher is gone, [19] but I'm right around the corner and coming soon if the Lord lets me. When I get there, we will see who the big dogs are and who the little yappers are. [20] God's outfit ain't about big talk, but a big walk. Big talkers rely on their power, but cowboys rely on God's power. [21] So I guess y'all have a decision to make. Do you want me to come back with a quirt or with love?

CHAPTER 5

Spiritual Pride and Sexual Perverts

And another thing, I've heard there are perverts in your outfit there. There is dirty stuff going on there that even sinners would frown on. Please tell me there isn't a man sleeping with his stepmom! [2] Y'all walk around proud like banty roosters, but you should be bawling your eyes out for letting this happen in your outfit. Some real men should take this fellow and send him down the road. [3-4] I may not be riding with you in person, but I'm still a part of your outfit and in the name of the Lord, I pass judgment on this no-account scoundrel. Call a meeting between all the cowboys and know I'm there with you in spirit. [5] Then send this man down the road and let him ride with the devil so his evil ways will be destroyed. Hopefully, he will be saved when the Lord comes riding back.

[6] I can't get over why y'all would be proud to still be riding with this cowboy. Don't y'all know even a little sin will spread through your outfit like tick fever? [7] Get rid of the tick and you get rid of the fever. Then you will go from mangy to magnificent, which is what you really are. Our Passover Lamb, Christ, has been killed. [8] Now that judgment has passed us over, let us celebrate with honor and glory, not horny and gory.

[9] In my last letter, I told y'all not to ride with sexual deviants. [10] Now, just to be clear, I wasn't talking about unbelievers who give into sexual sins, or those who are greedy, or those who put a foot on the scale at shipping time, or those who bow down to things other than God. You'd have to leave this world to keep from riding next to one of these every once in a while. [11] What I meant was you are not to ride in the same outfit as a believer who is a sexual deviant, or one who lusts after money, or drunks, or bullies, or horse thieves. Don't even sit at the same campfire as a believer who acts like this.

[12] It ain't my job to judge outsiders, but I can sure pass judgment on those who ride for God's outfit. [13] God will take care of the outsiders, but the Good Book says, "If you find an outlaw in your outfit, send him down the road to keep your camp clean."

CHAPTER 6

Avoiding Squabbles Between Cowboys

Listen up, when you have a squabble with another of God's cowboys, why in the world would you go to an outsider to judge who is right? That's like letting a city slicker judge the rodeo. [2] Don't you know God's cowboys will get to judge the world when the time comes? If God is going to let you judge the world, can't you handle a little squabble between two cowboys? ³ Did you not know we will even judge angels? If you can ride that bronc, can't you handle a little crow-hop between cowboys? ⁴ When these little squabbles come up, I don't understand why you'd trust outsiders with knowing what is right or wrong when they don't even know where right and wrong comes from. ⁵ Y'all should be hanging your heads in shame! Isn't there one cowboy who is wise enough to decide on these issues? ⁶ I guess not! One of God's cowboys are squabbling with another of God's cowboys right out in the open—right in front of unbelievers. That makes our outfit look good doesn't it?

⁷ But the fact y'all are even squabblin' means you've failed. It'd be better to be wronged than to fail. Shoot, it'd be better to be cheated than fail on purpose. ⁸ Instead, y'all are out there cheating and stealing among yourselves and others.

⁹ Are y'all so dense that you haven't figured out that cowboys who act like that won't get through the narrow gate when their ride is done? You've got your hats pulled down over your eyes if you think perverts, idol worshipers, adulterers, gigolos, gays, ¹⁰ thieves, money lusters, drunks, bullies, or cheats will get through the narrow gate onto God's outfit. ¹¹ I know some of you used to do those things, but you sit in a new saddle now. It's been oiled and washed clean and so have you. Y'all are holy now. You've been made right with God by asking to ride for Jesus Christ and be guided by the Holy Ghost.

Shucking Sexual Sin

¹² I know some of you are already saying, "But I am set free and can do anything I want." Yeah, you can. But just because you can doesn't mean you should. You are free and can do anything you want, but don't become a slave once again to sin. ¹³ I know some of you are thinking, "Food was made for the stomach and the stomach was made for food." But just because this is true doesn't mean you should stuff yourselves like gluttons or use your body for sexual things God never intended. Don't use your bodies for your own pleasure, but for the will of God. He gave you your body so give your body to him. ¹⁴ God raised Jesus's body from the grave and he will do the same for you if you ride for him the way Jesus did.

¹⁵ Don't you realize your body is part of the body of Christ? If Jesus wouldn't join his body to a harlot then you shouldn't either. ¹⁶ Did you not know that when you sleep with a prostitute, you become part of her and she becomes part of you. The Good Book says, "Two will be joined together forever." ¹⁷ But the one who rides with the Lord is one with him.

¹⁸ Don't just avoid sexual sin, run from it like your butt is on fire. This kind of sin affects you much differently than the others. It is a sin against your own body and your body should belong to the Lord. ¹⁹ Don't you know your body is the saddlebag for the Holy Ghost? You wouldn't throw God's great gift in the dirt and stomp on it, so don't do it to yourself either. ²⁰ God paid too much for you to use your body like trash. You honor or dishonor him with every action.

CHAPTER 7

Stuff about Marriage

Now, let's talk about some questions you had in your letter. You asked if cowboys should stay away from sex. Listen, there ain't nothing wrong with sex if it is in the right context. And God is the one who decides the context, not you. ² I'd say stay away from it completely, but if you cannot, get married and have sex like God intended— each man with his own wife, and each woman with her own husband.

³ A real cowboy will take care of his wife's sexual needs, and the wife should take care of her cowboy. ⁴ The wife gives her body to her husband, and the husband gives his body to his wife.

⁵ Don't be using sex like a bargaining chip. If y'all are going to quit having sex, then it should be a mutual agreement. Use the free time to be in prayer. But when your prayers are done, get back at it or the devil will get a foothold in the bedroom door. ⁶ I say these things, not as a command from God, but as a permission from him. ⁷ But I'm telling you the truth, it'd be better if y'all were just single like me. It'd save you a whole lot of discomfort. But being single is a special gift from God, no more or less than the other gifts he gives.

⁸ That's why I tell people who aren't married, and to widows, that it'd be better to stay unmarried like me. ⁹ But if you run too hot in the loins,

then go ahead and get married. It's better to be married than burn with passion that leads to sin.

¹⁰ To all y'all married folks, I have something the Lord wanted me to tell you. A wife shouldn't run out on her husband. ¹¹ But if she does, she needs to stay single or go back to him. And husbands shouldn't divorce their wives.

¹² To the rest of you, God hasn't given me anything explicit to pass on, but it's safe to say that if a cowboy who rides for the Lord has a wife who doesn't believe, he must not divorce her if she's willing to stay married. ¹³ And if a cowgirl who rides for the Lord is married to an unbeliever, she needs to stay married if he's willing. ¹⁴ The unbelieving husband will be looked favorably upon to an extent by God because of the believing wife. And the unbelieving wife will be looked favorably upon to an extent by God because of the believing husband. If this wasn't the case, then their kids would be like outsiders to God, but that ain't the case. God loves them and looks favorably on his kids. ¹⁵ But if the one who does not believe wants out, let 'em out. In this case, the believer is free and not bound by marriage anymore. Do it this way because God has called us to live in peace, not conflict. ¹⁶ Don't forget though that an unbelieving husband might be saved because of the believing wife and vice versa.

Live How God Has You

¹⁷ Don't be wishing things were different for you. Don't wish you were with someone else or that you lived someplace else. Live how God has you right now. ¹⁸ If a cowboy had his pickle clipped long ago and becomes a believer, he shouldn't be trying to glue anything back on. But if a fellow is uncircumcised, he shouldn't get his pickle clipped when he becomes a believer. ¹⁹ Clipped pickles don't make a cowboy for God. Doing what the Boss says is what makes a cowboy of God. ²⁰ Each one should remain as they were when they gave their lives to the brand. ²¹ If you were a slave, don't fret about remaining so . . . but if you get the chance to be free, take it. ²² Look at it this way, if you were a slave before Jesus, you are now free. But if you were free before Jesus, you are a slave to him now. ²³ God paid a terrible price for you, so don't tie-on to the world's ways. ²⁴ All of you should stay like you were when God came for you.

Virgins and Widows

²⁵ Now, let's talk about your question about virgins. God hasn't told me anything specific, but he has given me mercy and wisdom that can be trusted. This is what I have to say about them. ²⁶ Because life is so hard and temptations are so strong, I think it is best to remain a virgin your entire life. ²⁷ If you have a wife, don't try to get a divorce. If you don't have a wife, don't go looking for one. ²⁸ But getting married isn't a sin. If a young lady gets married, it isn't a sin for her to lose her virginity. However, those who are married will have a lot tougher time than those who are not.

²⁹⁻³¹ There ain't a whole lot of time left. Don't concern yourselves too much with things that are not eternal: marriage, sadness, happiness, shopping, etc. This world and the things in it will not be here much longer. Don't complicate your life with temporary thoughts, feelings, and actions.

³² I don't want you to worry all the time. A single cowboy only cares about riding for the Lord and doing the Lord's work. ³³ But a married fellow has to worry about supporting his family and his wife, not to mention worrying about if she's happy or not. ³⁴ Do you see how he is trying to do two things at once? He's trying to ride for the Lord and take care of his family. The same goes for a widow or a virgin. They concern themselves only with the Lord's work because they are dedicated in body and soul. But a married woman has to worry about worldly matters and pleasing her husband. ³⁵ Don't get me wrong, I'm trying to help, not make things harder. I want you to do what is right and that is giving yourselves completely to riding for the brand without reservation or hesitation.

³⁶ Let's look at this situation, a cowboy has a girlfriend, but they don't intend to get married. If they think they might get sexual with each other, then they should get married before that happens. Then there is no sin. ³⁷ But if he can control himself and they decide not to get married, that would be better. ³⁸ So the fellow who marries his girlfriend, and the guy who doesn't, are both good with God.

³⁹ A wife belongs to her husband as long as he lives. If he dies, she can marry another, but only if he is a cowboy for the Lord. ⁴⁰ But honestly it

would be better if she just stayed single. God didn't say it, but it still is wise counsel.

CHAPTER 8

Responsible Freedoms

I know there's been a lot of talk about what to do about food that's been sacrificed to idols. Everyone seems to have a different "right" answer. Thinking you are right might make you feel like a big shot, but it is loving each other that makes us strong. ² And besides, a fellow who claims to know everything doesn't know very much at all. ³ The true measure of a man is in how much he loves God and how much he understands how much God loves him.

⁴ So let us answer the question about eating meat that has been sacrificed to idols once and for all. An idol is not a god because there is only one true God. ⁵ Who cares if someone says a rock or a stick is a god? You can call a horse a cow, but that don't make it true. People use the words "god" and "lord" all the time, but those are just made up words when used incorrectly. ⁶ As for us, there is only one God, and he's our Father. Everything came from him and belongs to him. And there is only one Lord, Jesus Christ.

⁷ But not everyone knows this. Some folks still think sticks are gods. They think food offered to idols is a real thing instead of just a bunch of chanting and waving arms in front of a rock. These folks feel guilty when they eat meat that has been through these rituals. ⁸ But listen close, food doesn't have anything to do with faith. Eating something doesn't bring you closer to God or vice versa.

⁹ But just because you are free to eat what you want doesn't mean you should intentionally flaunt your freedom at a weaker person's expense. ¹⁰ It might not be good to express your freedom by going and eating a steak in an idol's temple just because you can. Someone might be watching, and even though you don't struggle with this dilemma, he might. ¹¹ This might set the weaker cowboy on a path away from God. Just because you understand the truth doesn't mean everyone else does. ¹² If a cowboy with a weaker faith thinks something is wrong, and you intentionally encourage him to do it anyway, that is a sin. It's not just a sin against him, but again Jesus. ¹³ So if eating a steak causes a cowboy

to sin, I'll never touch another one. I will not be responsible for another cowboy's sin.

CHAPTER 9

Rights and Refusal to Use Them

I am a free cowboy. I have been personally chosen by Jesus Christ whom I have seen. I am responsible for you being a part of God's outfit here on earth and in heaven. ² Others can think what they want about these things, but Jesus chose me to be a ramrod, or an apostle to you. Y'all are proof of this.

³ This is my answer to my critics and those who judge me. ⁴ A ramrod has the right to eat and drink, doesn't he? ⁵ He can bring a believing wife on his travels, can't he? The other ramrods (Pete and the Lord's brothers) do this. ⁶ Are Barnabas and I the only ones who have to daywork for our meals? ⁷ A soldier in the army doesn't have to have a side job to pay for his meals. A farmer eats his own vegetables. A dairyman drinks the milk from his own cows.

⁸ I'm not saying these things because it fits my agenda. God's code says the same thing. ⁹ The code of Moses says, "When an ox is treading grain, don't keep it from eating as it works." Are oxen worth more to God than we are? ¹⁰ Wasn't this an illustration about us? Yes, it was. The cowboys all get a share of the meat regardless if they do the calving, the gathering, or the roping and doctoring.

¹¹ Since we are the ones who gathered you and brought you onto God's outfit, shouldn't we be entitled to sustenance? ¹² If y'all support cowboys who come in and preach, shouldn't we get at least the same support, maybe even more? But we've never used this right. We'd rather be dog-tired from working all day rather than be a burr in the good news about Jesus.

¹³ Did you not know that those who work in the temple get their meals and salary from what is brought in as offerings? Those who work at the altar get a piece of the meat. ¹⁴ In the same way, Jesus said that those who preach the good news should be taken care of by those who benefit from it. ¹⁵ But I've never used this "ace in the hole" even though I could. And I'm not going to start using it because I've been called to something different than the rest of them. I preach without pay and I can brag about it. ¹⁶ But don't

mistake what I'm saying. I ain't bragging about preaching the good news. That's what God has called me to do. I can't imagine my life any other way. **17** If I had decided on my own to preach, then I'd accept my wages for it, but Jesus appeared to me himself and gave me my duty. **18** So what is my wage for working? My reward is telling people the good news for free and not using the rights I'm entitled to.

19 Even though I don't owe any man anything, I have made myself a slave to all men in hopes to bring them to Christ. **20** When I was with the Jews, I acted like a Jew to show them Jesus. I lived under the Law when I was with those living under the Law. I know I don't have to, but I do it anyway in order to bring them to Christ. **21** When I'm with the Gentile outsiders, I live like they do in order to show them how they too can live for Jesus. It's not about disobeying the law of God, it's about following the code of Jesus. **22** To the weak, I became weak to help save them. I have become all things to all people in order to save them by any means possible. **23** This is about the good news being known. I do what I do for the glory of God and his good news.

24 You know that in a roping, all the ropers rope, but only one team gets the buckle. Rope to win! **25** All who rope put in a lot of practice in order to win. But the things these cowboys win will not last. However, our prize will last forever. **26** So, I rope like I'm gonna win. I train for the real deal, not just so I can be good on a dummy. **27** I train my body every single day to make it do what I want, when I want. I can talk all I want, but I want the prize for myself. I don't just talk a good game, I rope it, too.

CHAPTER 10

Lessons Learned

Listen to me, cowboys and cowgirls. Let's not forget the lessons we learned from our ancestors who came out of Egypt with Moses. Their trail guide through the wilderness was a cloud in the sky and they all walked across a sea on dry ground. **2** This was their baptism as they followed Moses. **3** They all ate the same food from heaven **4** and drank the same spiritual water. They drank from the rock that traveled with them and that rock was Jesus. **5** Despite all they saw and experienced, God was not pleased with them.

As a result, their bodies are strewn all through the wilderness.

6 Learning from our mistakes might be good, but learning from their mistakes is even better. We should stay away from the things that resulted in their deaths. **7** Don't do like they did and worship idols or anything other than God. The Good Book says, "The cowboys and cowgirls sat by the fire and ate and drank, and then had a wild party." **8** We should not commit the same sexual sins as they did during their parties. Because of this, twenty-three thousand people died in one day. **9** Some of them even decided to test Christ and died because of snake bites. **10** You might be saying to yourself, "I would never do anything like that," but remember that the angel of death came in and killed. Why? Because of their complaining and grumbling.

11 Don't make the same mistakes they did! These things were even written down so you'd pay attention and not make the same foolish mistakes they did. These warnings apply to us today. **12** So, anyone who thinks they are doing just fine ought to get off and check their cinch. **13** You have the same temptation today that they had long ago. But you can trust God to help you. He will not let you be tempted beyond what you are capable of handling. There is never a temptation God hasn't already provided a way of escaping. With God's help, you will succeed. Without it, you will fail.

14 So stay away from worshiping idols. **15** I'm not talking to a bunch of dummies. Y'all know what I am saying is true. **16** When we bless the cup during the Lord's Supper, aren't we sharing the blood of Christ? And when we bless the bread, aren't we sharing the body of Christ, too? **17** We all eat from the same loaf because we are all of the same body. **18** It's no different than the people of Israel eating food sacrificed on the altar.

19 Am I saying that food sacrificed on the altar at the main church is the same as food sacrificed to idols? No! An idol is a stick or a rock or a demon, not God. **20** Have nothing to do with anything sacrificed to demons. **21** You cannot drink from the cup of Jesus and from the cup of demons, too. You cannot share the table of Jesus and the table of demons. **22** This ain't going to do nothing but make the Big Man upset. You don't want to do that, do you? He doesn't share his table with demons.

Use Your Freedom for God

[23] Y'all keep saying, "I'm allowed to do whatever I want." But I'm telling you that just because you can doesn't mean you should. Some things don't help people, and that's our main mission. [24] We need to be doing what's good for others, not just the stuff that's good for us.

[25] If you go to the butcher, just get the cut of meat you want and eat with a good conscience. You don't have to grill the guy about where it come from. [26] If God made it and it's meant for eating, you can.

[27] An outsider might invite you over for sup one night. Don't worry about what you are served. You can eat it with a clean conscience. Don't question where it came from. [28] Now if someone else comes and tells you it came from an idol sacrifice, then don't touch it. The person telling you might think it's wrong to eat food sacrificed to idols. [29] You'll just be looking out for the other person when you do it like this. That's the only reason to keep from eating it. Don't freak out and worry about what everyone else is thinking about what you're doing. You know what is right and what is not. [30] I eat everything with a thankful heart, so I'm not going to let someone criticize me for being thankful.

[31] I don't care if you're eating or drinking, do it for the glory of God. [32] Be mindful of your reputation with Jews, Gentiles, and anyone else for that matter. [33] I do this, too. I try to respect everyone in every way. I'm not just looking out for myself. I am trying to do what is best for every individual I come into contact with so they too can be saved.

CHAPTER 11

Y'all just watch what I'm doing because I'm watching what Christ does.

Worshiping with Others

[2] I'm sure glad y'all keep me in your prayers. I'm also glad y'all are doing things the way I told you to do 'em. [3] But listen to this so there's no confusion—when you ride out in your pasture, God is the Boss, Jesus follows him, man follows Jesus, and woman follows man. [4] A man who rides in front of Jesus, even when praying to God, dishonors the one with authority over him. [5] A woman who rides in front of a man, even if she is praying to God, dishonors the man who has authority over her. [6] That's like if she were to cut off all her hair and try to be a man. She is denying the wonderful person God made her to be.

[7] A man should remove his hat when praying, for he was made in the image of God and God's glory shines through him. A woman reflects a man's glory in the same way. Now everyone is shining when we do things the way God says to do 'em. [8] God didn't make a man from a woman, he made a woman from a man. [9] In the same way, a man wasn't made to help a woman, but a woman was made to help man. [10] For this reason, and even the angels are watching to see if we do this, a woman shouldn't ride in front of a man because he was given authority over her.

[11] But we are all working the same pastures together. Men ain't better than women and women ain't better than men. [12] Even though the first woman came from a man, every man after that came from a woman. So, if you want to get all technical about it, everything and everyone came from God . . . and that's what's important.

[13] See if this ain't right, a woman shouldn't be going to God in prayer or say she rides for the brand without doing things the way God said to do 'em. [14] Same thing goes for a man. It's obvious a man who prays to God should do things the way God tells him to do it. It's a disgrace if a man prays one way and acts another. [15] A woman's beauty is a reflection of who God made her to be and she should not dishonor that. [16] You can argue and throw a hissy fit about this if you want to, but this is the way God said to run his churches.

The Lord's Supper

[17] I've patted y'all on the back for a lot of things, but in this next thing, there ain't no praise. Y'all are worse off after meeting together to worship than you were before you started. [18] First of all, I've heard y'all are dividing people up according to who you think they are. You're putting gunsels on one side, city slickers on the other, top hands in the front, and weekend cowboys in the back. And you know what? I can see y'all doing this. [19] Every man should be tested to make sure he walks the walk instead of just talks the talk, but don't take that to such an extreme where you become judgmental and divided.

²⁰ Y'all are not getting together for the Lord's Supper, you just use that as an excuse to eat a good meal. ²¹ How do I know? Y'all don't even wait on each other before you start. The first ones in line get all they want and those at the end don't have much, if anything. ²² If you're starving, eat at your own hacienda. God's house is for everyone and everyone should be thinking about his fellow man. You think I'm going to pat you on the back for being a disgrace? I don't think so!

²³ You listen to what I'm telling you because Jesus himself told it to me. On the night Jesus was double-crossed, the Lord Jesus took some bread ²⁴ and thanked God for it. Then he tore it up and said, "This is my body and my body is given for you. When you eat it, remember what I did." ²⁵ After supper, he took a cup of wine and said, "This cup is the new contract between God and his cowboys. It is signed in my blood. Anytime you drink it, remember what I did." ²⁶ Every single time you eat bread or drink wine, you are remembering what Jesus did and announcing to the world that you eagerly wait for him to ride back over the hill to get us.

²⁷ Those who eat this bread or drink the cup of the Lord in a manner that does bring glory to God are like the ones who spit on Jesus at his death. ²⁸ Before you do this sacred ritual, you'd best really examine how you've been living and what you've been saying. ²⁹ If you eat and drink without thought for your fellow cowboys, who are the body of Christ, you aren't receiving a blessing from God, but his judgment. ³⁰ That's why a lot of you are sickly and weak. Shoot, some have died because of their irreverence.

³¹ All you have to do is judge yourself, and then God doesn't have to. ³² But if the Lord does judge us, it's like a butt chewin' to get us back on the right trail. If we ain't on the right trail, we will be like the rest of the world that is headed for the brush fire that never goes out.

³³ Here, let me summarize this for you. When you gather together for the Lord's Supper, wait on each other to eat. ³⁴ If you are starving to death, get you something to eat at the house before you arrive. Otherwise, you will bring God's judgment on yourselves. I'll give you some more instructions about the other stuff when I get there.

CHAPTER 12

Special Abilities

Alright, cowboys and cowgirls, let's talk about the special abilities God gives his hands who are riding for the brand. I don't want there to be any confusion about these great gifts from the Holy Ghost. ² There was a time, before you were one of God's cowboys, that you followed your own desires and worshiped rocks and sticks and other people. ³ One of God's cowboys wouldn't curse Jesus. In the same manner, no cowboy would be inclined to say Jesus is Lord without the Holy Ghost's prompting.

⁴ There are different kinds of special abilities, but they all come from the same God. ⁵ There are different kinds of jobs, but they all serve the same Lord. ⁶ God works in different people in different ways, but it is the same God doing the work in all of us.

⁷ Listen close and don't let your mind get to wanderin' off. Special abilities we have are for the benefit of others, not yourself. ⁸ If you're given wisdom, it's so you can give others good advice. Someone else might be given the ability to talk with supernatural knowledge. ⁹ To one, the gift of faith is given and to another it is the gift of healing others. ¹⁰ The Holy Ghost might give the ability for one cowboy to do miracles and another to prophecy, and still another might have the ability to tell if something is from God or not. The Holy Ghost gives one person the ability to speak in other languages, and still another cowboy will be able to understand it. ¹¹ But don't forget, all of these different things come from just one God. And it is the One True God, and only God, who decides who gets what.

One Body, Many Parts

¹² Your body is made up of a bunch of different parts that do different things. The same thing applies to the church, or what we like to call, "The Body of Christ." ¹³ Some of us were born Jews, others were born outsiders. Some of us are free, and others are slaves. Some are cowpunchers and some are buckaroos, but we have all been baptized into the body of Christ and we share the same Spirit.

¹⁴ Our bodies have many different parts and God made each part for a specific and grand purpose. ¹⁵ Just because your foot can't swing

a loop doesn't mean it's not part of your body. [16] And just because you can't see out of your ear doesn't mean it's not just as useful to the body. [17] If the whole body were an eye, how would you listen? If your whole body were an ear, how would you smell the steak cooking?

[18] I'm going on and on so you will understand that the church, or the Body of Christ, is made up of vastly different parts, doing vastly different things, but all for the same Lord. [19] If your body wouldn't function with just one part, how do you expect the church to function with just one part? [20] There are many different parts in the church, but only one body. [21] Your eye cannot say to the hand, "I'm more important and I don't need you." Your head cannot say to the to the feet, "I'm more important and you don't serve any purpose."

[22] In fact, some parts of the body that seem unimportant and unnecessary are really the most needed. [23] Have you ever noticed the parts we don't think are worth very much are the parts we care the most about? How much do we strive to cover the parts we don't think anyone would find beautiful? [24] But there are other parts that are just as important that we never cover up. God put this whole body together, and while some parts are more visible, the entire body should be honored. [25] God did this so our body would not be divided. God wants us to care for the entire body, not just the visible parts. [26] If one part of the body suffers, then all the others will suffer as well. If one part is honored, then that honor is shared through the entire body.

[27] All of you are part of the body of Christ. Each and every one of you serves a great part of that body. [28] And in the church, or the body, God has given special appointments. First are the apostles, second is the prophets, and third are the teachers. Then there are the special appointments of miracle workers, healers, helpers, leaders, and finally those who speak in different kinds of languages. [29] Now listen, not everyone is an apostle, or a prophet, or a teacher. Not everyone can do miracles [30] or is able to heal. Not everyone will be able to speak in unknown languages or be able to interpret those languages. [31] Some of you desire the abilities you think are most important, but you should be glad with what God has given you, not what you think is better.

Now let me show you a way of life that tops everything else.

CHAPTER 13

A Top Hand Loves

If I could speak every language on earth and even knew how to speak the angel's tongue, but I didn't have love . . . then I'm just yappin' like a coyote in the desert. [2] If I had the power of God, could speak mighty words with supernatural knowledge, and had faith that could make mountains march, but if I didn't show love to others, I'm worthless. [3] If I gave all my tack, horses, bits, and bridles, and everything else to the poor and even sacrificed my body to be burned up, I would be able to brag about it; but if I didn't love others, I have done nothing in God's eyes.

[4] Love is kind and never gets in a rush. Love ain't jealous, arrogant, or proud. [5] Love ain't rude, selfish, nor does it fly off the handle. Love don't keep a tally book of wrongs against it. [6] Love don't condone injustice, but celebrates truth. [7] Love never gives up, always gets back on, never turns loose of faith, is forever hopeful, and never, ever, quits.

[8] Preaching, prophecy, and even praying in tongues will one day be useless, but love is forever. [9] We don't know everything, and even prophecy reveals only so much, [10] but when we are made perfect, these other things won't be needed.

[11] When I was just a little tike, I acted like a little tike. But when I grew up, I quit acting like a child. [12] Right now it's like we are looking at God in a dirty mirror, but one day everything will be washed away and we will see him clearly. We can't see the whole trail right now, but one day we will reach the end and God will be there to show us everything.

[13] There's a lot of stuff that will end up tromped in the dirt, but these three things will endure forever: faith, hope, and love. And the best of 'em is love.

CHAPTER 14

Using Your Special Abilities for the Church

Love should be your highest achievement, but I ain't saying you shouldn't want some of these other special abilities the Holy Ghost gives—especially the gift of telling folks the truth. ² You can have the ability to speak in unknown languages, but the only one who will be able to understand you is God. It's a special ability, but only to you. No one else will know what you are saying. ³ But the fellow who is gifted with speaking God's truth does so to strengthen, encourage, and comfort others. ⁴ A cowboy speaking in tongues helps themselves, but no one else. But those who hand out God's truth, they are helping everyone.

⁵ Now, don't get me wrong. I hope all of you can speak in tongues. But what I hope for more is that you can all speak God's truth. The truth is more important than tongues unless they can interpret them also. If everyone understands and benefits, then it's good.

⁶ Listen cowboys and cowgirls, is it really doing you any good if I come and talk to you in a language you don't understand? Nope! The only good that can come from talkin' is talkin' that can be understood. ⁷ Even when a melody is played clear on the guitar, people can recognize the tune. If the notes aren't clear and orderly, then you might as well be hitting the guitar up against a wall. ⁸ If a bugler can't play the notes to attack, how will the soldiers know when to charge?

⁹ Y'all should be able to understand all this. If someone can't understand you, what's the point in opening your mouth?

¹⁰ There's a bunch of different languages out there, and every one of them has meaning. ¹¹ But if no one speaks that language, then there is no meaning. The person who doesn't understand will feel like a foreigner in a strange land or ¹² vice versa. If you're wanting a special ability, ask for those who strengthen the whole church, not just one cowboy.

¹³ If you're gonna pray for the ability to speak in tongues, pray also for the ability to interpret them. ¹⁴ Praying in tongues is your spirit praying, not your conscious mind. ¹⁵ So what's a cowboy to do? I'll pray with my soul, but pray with my mind, too. I'll sing with my spirit, but I'll sing with my mind as well. ¹⁶ You might be saying something profound in the spirit, but if no one understands you, how can they say, "Amen"? ¹⁷ You might be saying a thousand thanks to God, but not a single person will understand it.

If they don't understand it, they ain't helped by your words.

¹⁸ No one talks in tongues more than me. ¹⁹ But when I'm with others, I'd rather say five things everyone can understand rather than a thousand words they can't. I can't teach if they can't understand.

²⁰ Listen, amigos. Don't get all childish on me. You can be as innocent as a newborn baby and still think like a grown man. ²¹ It's even written in the Good Book, "I'll speak strange languages with the lips of strangers. I'll try to get through to these folks, but that doesn't mean they'll listen." That's what the Lord says.

²² Speaking in tongues isn't for those in God's outfit, it is for the others. ²³ Think about what you'll look like if an outsider comes into your church and sees you going on and on like it's gibberish. They don't understand and they never will because they'll be headed for the door. ²⁴ But if they come in and hear the word of God and understand it, then they will be convicted of their sin. They will have no excuse except to know the truth or deny him. ²⁵ Their secrets will be laid bare as they fall to their knees and worship the Most High, saying, "God is truly here with us."

Worship That Helps Everyone

²⁶ Here's the problem, one fellow wants to sing a song. Another says he has a truth to reveal. Still another guy starts talking in a language only one other person can understand and he interprets it. The point to worshiping with others is so everyone benefits. When everyone benefits, then everyone grows in faith. ²⁷ If someone starts speaking in tongues, and understanding that there should always be an interpreter, only let two or three at the most have their turn. Don't everyone start praying in the spirit out loud at the same time. ²⁸ If there isn't an interpreter, there isn't speaking in tongues. Got it? They can still speak in tongues, but only to themselves.

²⁹ The same goes for preaching. Only let two or three people have a turn. That way there is time to ponder on their message and see if it lines up with scripture. ³⁰ And don't talk over each other. If someone who is sitting down has a message from the Lord, the one standing up and speaking should let the other give God's word. ³¹ Take turns. It ain't a competition between two

preachers, it's for the benefit of all in attendance. Everyone should be taught and inspired while they are there. ³² Even when a prophet gets a word from the Lord, he can hold it until it's his turn. ³³ God does not create confusion when his cowboys and cowgirls gather together. His goal is peace and unity.

³⁴⁻³⁵ Ladies shouldn't interrupt a church meeting with needless talking. If they have a question, they should ask their husbands at home. God's word guides the rituals and customs here, not personal want or belief.

³⁶ Do you think everything revolves around you? Are y'all the only one who received the truth? ³⁷ If you think God has a message through you or God has a mission for you to go on, pay close attention to the things I've said. ³⁸ If you go against these things, it just proves the message or mission you claim to have isn't from God. Sorry, Charlie.

³⁹ Let me say this and then I'm done. Pay attention to good preaching, and don't stop someone from praying in tongues ⁴⁰ as long as it's done the right way. And the right way is courteous, considerate, and proper.

CHAPTER 15

The Good News

Now boys, y'all don't go forgettin' what I've told y'all about the good news. I know y'all have tied hard and fast to this message and it changed your lives. ² This good news I gave you is the only way you'll be saved, but you can't go lettin' your cinch get loose. You've got to stay pulled down to the message or all of this has been in vain.

³ I was given the truth and I've told it to you plain and straight. Christ died for our sins just like the Good Book said he would. ⁴ He was buried in a tomb for three days and then walked out like nothin' ever happened, just like the Good Book said he would. ⁵ He went and talked to Pete and the other twelve cowboys. ⁶ But he didn't stop there. He later showed himself to more'n five hundred other riders of the brand all at the same time. Most of 'em are still around today, although a few have gone over the final hill. ⁷ He was then seen by James and again by the cowboys. ⁸ Last and least of all, Jesus showed himself to me. I felt like a cowboy who had been born a hundred years too late, but been given the chance to ride in the old ways.

⁹ But I am a gunsel compared to those other cowboys that he chose. Why? Because I used to hunt cowboys down and kill 'em. Even though I now ride for Jesus, I ain't worthy to be called one of his cowboys. ¹⁰ It's only because of his grace that I know I really am a cowboy. And you know what? I didn't waste the grace. I ride harder and further, taking the outside in this big gathering of the lost and those who have strayed away. (But it's not really me riding. It's God's grace working through me that allows me to do what I do.) ¹¹ So it don't really matter who gave you the good news. All the cowboys spread the same good news and this is what is important.

Coming Back from the Dead

¹² We tell everyone that Christ came back from the dead. If that was what we told you, why are some of y'all telling folks they won't come back from the dead too? ¹³ If we ain't gonna be raised from the grave, then Jesus wasn't either. ¹⁴ And if he didn't come back, then everything we've told you is a farce . . . and so is your faith. ¹⁵ And not just that, we'd be guilty of lying about God because we've told everyone it was God who raised him back to life. If God doesn't raise us up after we die, then he didn't raise Christ up either. ¹⁶ Let me repeat, if those cowboys who die aren't going to be raised up, then Jesus wasn't either. ¹⁷ And if Jesus is still dead, then so is our faith. If Jesus is still dead, then we are still guilty of our sins and will pay for them in full. ¹⁸ All those cowboys who rode for Christ would be lost if he wasn't alive today. ¹⁹ And if all we get for riding for the brand is a little bit of inspiration in this life, then we are a sorry lot.

²⁰ But Christ did ride back from the grave. He was the first and the rest of his cowboys will follow. ²¹ Through a single man, death came for us all. Likewise, through a single man, life is available for all. ²² I'm talking about how sin entered the world through Adam, and now, eternal life is waiting on us all through Jesus Christ. ²³ But we ain't gettin' in ahead of the boss. Jesus was brought back to life first. Then, when he comes back to get us, those who've ridden for him will be raised to life again as well. ²⁴ That's when everything as we know it will end. The prescribed burn will destroy all earthly rulers, governments,

and powers. Then, Jesus is going to give the keys of the ranch to God the Father.

²⁵ Christ will rule until all his enemies have been crushed. ²⁶ The last enemy to fall will be death. ²⁷ Like the Good Book says, "God has given him control over everything." When it says "everything" is under his control, it goes without saying that Jesus does not control God. God is the one giving Jesus the authority. ²⁸ When Jesus has conquered everything, he is going to turn around and hand everything over to God so that God will be the one and only ruler.

²⁹ If there is no hope for coming back from the dead, why then do some people go as far as trying to be baptized for those who have already died? Without hope, everything is in vain.

³⁰ And what can we say about ourselves? We ride treacherous country trying to save the lost. Why would we risk our lives for nothing? ³¹ I look death in the face every single day. I'm able to because I'm convinced of my resurrection and yours through Jesus Christ. ³² What would I have gained fighting those people in Ephesus, who were as crazy as wild beasts, if I had been killed with no hope of eternal life? Only those with no hope live by the motto, "Eat and drink today; die tomorrow!"

³³ Don't be a fool. "Bad friends ruin a good ride." ³⁴ Get back in the middle of your saddle and get both feet in the stirrups. You need to think right and quit all that sinning you know is wrong. Some of you don't even know who God is because you'd rather live a life of sin rather than one that's eternal. And to that, it's your own fault and you'll get what you deserve.

The New Skin

³⁵ Some have wondered, "How are we brought back from the grave? What will our bodies look like?" ³⁶ There's no such thing as a stupid question, but these come close. A plant cannot grow unless it is buried in the ground. ³⁷ But what you plant isn't the same as what comes up. One is a seed and what comes up is a new plant. ³⁸ God gives each seed the body he wants to see. ³⁹ Just think about how different life is here on earth. People have one type of body, animals another, and still birds have something completely different just like the fish have something different. ⁴⁰ Well, there are heavenly bodies and earthly bodies. Both

are beautiful, but both are different from the other. ⁴¹ The sun is beautiful in one way and the moon just as much in another. The stars shine differently and their beauty is different.

⁴² It's going to be the same when the dead are raised again. The body is planted like a seed, but it will be raised as something brand new, something that cannot see death, decay, or destruction. ⁴³ When our bodies are planted, it is with sin and decay. But what we are raised to will be glorious and powerful. ⁴⁴ The body that is planted will be a physical body, but the body that is raised will be a spiritual one. We have physical bodies and spiritual bodies.

⁴⁵ The Good Book tells us, "Adam, the first man, became a living being." But the last Adam—Jesus Christ—is a Spirit who brings life instead of death. ⁴⁶ First is the physical body, then the spiritual body comes later. ⁴⁷ The first man came from dirt. The second man came from heaven. ⁴⁸ Earthly folks are like the first, but heavenly people are like the second. ⁴⁹ We all may be like Adam now, but a few of us will be like Jesus one day.

⁵⁰ Let me make this clear, cowboys. Our physical bodies can't inherit the kingdom of God. These bodies have to die so that we can have bodies that can last forever.

⁵¹ But listen to this! Here's a secret, not all of us will die, but we will all be changed. ⁵² It'll happen in a split-second. When the last trumpet sounds, we cowboys will be changed. Those who rode for God and died will be raised to new life and live forever. ⁵³ Our dying bodies must be transformed into ones that will never die. The mortal must give way to the immortal. ⁵⁴ So this body that is so full of death and disease will be swapped out for one of power and immortality. This will fulfill what was written in the Good Book. "Death has been swallowed in victory. Death, where is your victory? ⁵⁵ O death, where is your power to sting?"

⁵⁶ Death's power to sting is sin, and the power of sin is the code. ⁵⁷ But we are thankful God has already given us victory and power through our Lord Jesus Christ!

⁵⁸ So, cowboys, sit tall in the saddle. Don't ever quit riding for the brand because your work down here makes a difference.

CHAPTER 16

Passing the Hat

Now, let's talk straight about taking up a collection for God's people in Jerusalem. I'm going to tell y'all the same as I told the church in Galatia. ² On the first day of every week, put some money in a jar and keep it safe. Save up as much as you possibly can from what you've been blessed with. Then, when I come see you, everything will be ready and you won't have to scramble around and dig through your saddle bags for crumbs. ³ When I get there, I will send some cowboys to deliver the money to the Jerusalem church. I'll send the ones you suggested with a letter of introduction. ⁴ If God wills it, I will even accompany them there.

Paul's Plan

⁵ I'm thinking about going through Macedonia and then on to y'all. ⁶ I hope to stay with y'all for a while, maybe all winter. Then y'all can help me on my trip, wherever God decides to send me. ⁷ I wish I could come now, but then I wouldn't be able to stay long as I've got other things to do. I want to get them out of the way so I can stay with y'all longer if God says it's okay. ⁸ I'm probably going to hang out here in Ephesus until Pentecost. ⁹ We've got something real good started here, but there are a lot of enemies I must deal with before I leave.

¹⁰ Timothy might be stopping by soon. Make him feel at home because he's working for God as hard as I am. ¹¹ Don't let me hear of anyone turning him away or shunning him in any way. Help him out with anything he needs so he may return to me in peace and safety. Don't delay in this. I'm waiting on him and the others who are riding with him.

¹² Let me tell you about a cowboy named Apollos, I told him and those riding with him to come see y'all. I don't think he's coming any time soon, but he said he would come later when he had the opportunity.

Final Words

¹³ Stay alert and keep both feet deep in the stirrups. Tie hard and fast to your faith. Be courageous and be strong. ¹⁴ Do nothing without love.

¹⁵ I hope you have heard of Stephanus and his family. They were among the first cowboys to ride for the Lord in Greece. They have devoted their lives in service of God's people. I urge y'all ¹⁶ to follow their example and their leadership. Such devoted cowboys and cowgirls are rare.

¹⁷ It is of my good fortune that Stephanas, Fortunatus, and Achaicus are here. I wish y'all were too, but they have helped fill the gap. ¹⁸ They've done nothing except offer me encouragement and they do the same for y'all. If y'all don't see the value in cowboys such as these, then y'all are blind.

¹⁹ All the churches in the province of Asia said to tell y'all hello. Aquila and Priscilla, and all the others who meet in their homes for church, also send their greetings. ²⁰ Everyone here says hello and offer a hearty handshake. Be sure and greet each other with sacred affection.

²¹ Here's my hello in my own handwriting—Paul.

²² If anyone chooses to shun God's love, then let that person be forever separated from him. Let them be lost forever.

Get ready! The Boss is coming soon!

²³ May God's grace—Jesus Christ—lead, guide, and love you.

²⁴ My love also rides with you in Christ Jesus.

2 CORINTHIANS

CHAPTER 1

Howdy, boys! It's me, Paul. I'm one of the cowboys God chose to lead this gathering because I reckon it's what he wanted. Timothy says howdy, also.

I'm writing to the big gatherin' of cowboys and cowgirls who make up the church in Corinth as well as all those scattered throughout Achaia taking the outside for God.

² Here's to grace and peace and may they overflow your coffee cup in the name of our Father and of Jesus Christ.

Hung up in the Stirrup

³ If there's praise to be doled out, let us praise God, the Father of our Lord Jesus Christ. God shows us more mercy than we deserve, and comforts us in the hard times. ⁴ He gives us comfort for ourselves, but also so we can comfort others when they get hung up in the stirrup of life. ⁵ If we ride for Jesus, we're gonna experience the same suffering he did during his ride. But his daddy comforted him and he will do the same for us. ⁶ If times are hard on us, it means you're being saved and comforted. If God comforts us, it is so we can pass it along to you. That way, you know you aren't alone when you go through the mesquite and suffer as we do. ⁷ We have high hopes for y'all. We want y'all to share in the suffering because if you share in the suffering, you'll get to share in the comfort that can only come from God himself.

⁸ Listen cowboys and cowgirls, let me tell you a little about the wreck that happened in Asia. It was so rank at times that we just wanted to die. ⁹ We truly felt like God was preparing us for death. It was that bad. But God had another plan. He let us suffer that bad to show us how often we depended on our own strength instead of his. He raises the dead and sometimes we couldn't even raise our heads. ¹⁰ But he pulled our foot out of the stirrup at the last minute before we were dragged to death. He saved us and he will continue to save us until our circle is complete. ¹¹ When y'all pray for us, it helps us! Then we will be able to tell others of how God so graciously saved us and answered your prayers.

Paul's Plans Change

¹² If I can say I'm proud of something we've done, it's been that everything we've done has been with a pure and honest heart. We've put our faith in God's grace, not human understanding. You saw this first hand when we met y'all. ¹³ The letters you've received from us have been straight-shooting and uncompromising. One day, I hope y'all understand, ¹⁴ even if what we say seems like it's coming from left field sometimes. When Jesus comes riding back to get all of us, we hope that y'all can be as proud of us as we have been of you.

¹⁵ I was sure y'all would understand. That's why I planned on stopping by to bless y'all twice. ¹⁶ I'd planned to visit on my way to Macedonia and then when I came back headed for Judea. ¹⁷ Well, we both know it didn't work out that way. But I am wondering if you all think I make plans frivolously or without thought? Do y'all think I make promises and then act like folks who don't keep their word?

¹⁸ Just like you can trust in what God says, you can trust our word as well. ¹⁹ Jesus never seesawed with his yes's and no's. Jesus is the one Silas, Timothy, and I talked to you so much about. Jesus is the "yes" in God's greatest promise. ²⁰ As a matter of fact, Jesus is the fulfillment of all of God's promises. If you're wondering, this is why we say "amen" (which means "yes") after we hear something great about God. Jesus is the trail that takes our prayers straight to the Boss.

²¹ It is God who makes all of us strong and gives us the will and want to ride hard for Jesus. He chose us for this task. ²² He branded us as his own by giving us the Holy Spirit to ride with us and in us. The Holy Spirit was the down payment on all the great things he has promised his cowboys.

²³ Now, with God as my witness, I'm telling y'all that the reason I didn't come back to Corinth was to save y'all from a bad scoldin'. ²⁴ We ain't out to micromanage your faith or be overly critical. We are flanking each other in this gathering. We will be victorious because we work together, not because we work the same.

CHAPTER 2

So, I decided not to come just to be the bearer of bad news. ² My goal is not to scold, but to bring joy. If all I did was scold y'all, who would be able to bring me joy then? It's sure not going to be the one who just took a bad butt chewin'! ³ That's why I decided to just write y'all a letter. That way, there'd be time for hard growing and when I got there, it would be a joyous time instead of a hard time. If y'all are hurting, then you can bet I'm hurting. If y'all are glad, then I'm glad, too. ⁴ When I sat down to write that letter to you, it felt like a knife in my gut. Tears spilled out of me like a waterfall because of what I had to say for your benefit. I didn't want to say anything hurtful, but I loved y'all enough to tell you the truth.

Forgiveness Time

⁵ That fellow you all know about sure caused a lot of trouble—not for me, but for you. ⁶ I know most of you stood up to him and I think that was probably punishment enough. ⁷ I think the time has come for everyone to forgive him and let bygones be bygones. If you don't, he might sink into such a despair that he won't be able to find his way back. ⁸ Lift your chins and put your pride in your pocket and go get the guy and tell him y'all love him. ⁹ One of the reasons I wrote you a letter was to see if y'all would do what you were told to do. ¹⁰ If you'll forgive him, so will I. And if I'm willing to forgive someone, I do so with the authority of Jesus himself. ¹¹ When we don't forgive folks, that leaves the door ajar for the devil to sneak through. And that old serpent don't need much of an opening to create pure chaos.

¹² When I arrived in Troas, Jesus gave me a great opportunity to preach the good news. ¹³ But I was restless because my pard, Titus, hadn't showed up yet. So I saddled up and headed for Macedonia to find him.

Overcoming Obstacles

¹⁴ But I tip my hat to God! He has put his word in our hearts and we spread the good news like a sweet perfume everywhere we go. ¹⁵ Our very lives are a pleasing scent to God. You know how a feedlot smells great to a cowboy, but it stinks to everyone else. This is how the Christ-like fragrance of God is to others. ¹⁶ To those headed for hell, we stink. But to those who are being saved, our smell is beautiful. Who can be trusted with work such as this?

¹⁷ You see, we ain't preaching for profit. We only preach for the glory of God and with the authority of Jesus. We know God's watching and we must answer to him.

CHAPTER 3

Does it seem like we are tooting our own horns so that y'all will believe we are who we say we are? Do we really need some letter of introduction or endorsement concerning the things we've done? ² Nope! Y'all are our letter of recognition that has been read by everyone. ³ That's right, y'all are a living letter, written not with quill and ink, but with the Holy Spirit. This new letter wasn't written on stone tablets like the first one, but rather on human hearts by the Spirit of God.

⁴ We can say this proudly because of our never-ending trust in God through Jesus Christ. ⁵ Now we know we ain't qualified or worthy of this task, but we tell you it is God working through us that allows all these good works. ⁶ He signed us up as day hands of a new agreement from himself to his cowboys. This new agreement, or code, is

not a set of written rules, but a written promise on our soul by the Spirit.

The Good News of the New Code

7 The old agreement was a code of condemnation that brought death. This code was written on stone tablets and shone with the glory of God, but just like how Moses's face shone the same way, it was already fading away. At first, the people of Israel couldn't even look at Moses. 8 If the old code shined bright with God's glory but faded, how much more will the new one shine even brighter. 9 What I mean is, the old agreement was a code of condemnation that judged people guilty of sin and brought death. Even so, it was filled with God's glory. So surely this new agreement, a code of confirmation that forgives people of sin and brings life, has even more glory from God. 10 In fact, the old code's glory is really nothing compared the new code's magnificent glory. 11 Since the code of condemnation that was brought to an end came with glory, then surely the code of confirmation that brings life, forgiveness, and never ends, has more glory by far.

12 We can talk openly about this new hope without being ashamed. In fact, it gives us confidence and boldness we never had before. 13 We aren't like Moses, who hid his face with a wild rag when he came off the mountain. He didn't want them to see the glory that had already started to fade away. 14 But the people didn't notice because their hearts were hard like stone. Even today when the old code of condemnation is read, it covers their minds where they cannot see or understand the truth. This covering can only be removed by believing in Jesus, who brought the new code of confirmation with him. 15 Yep, even today when the code of Moses is read, hearts and minds are covered and they cannot understand. 16 But when someone changes and believes in the Lord and decides once and for all to ride for him, that covering is stripped away. 17 The Lord is the Spirit, and where the Spirit is, there is freedom. 18 Our faces don't hide behind wild rags to keep people from seeing the glory of God. We show the Lord's glory, not in our faces, but in our hearts and in our lives that are being changed to be like his. As we change more and more, there is more and more glory that belongs only to the Lord—who is the Spirit.

CHAPTER 4

Treasure in Clay Canteens

God has mercifully given us a spot on his outfit. He assigned us this work to do and we never give up. 2 But we have given up on our old shameful deeds and underhanded way of living. We don't try to trick people or distort the word of God. We explain the truth in a way you can understand it, and those who are honest know it. 3 If the good news seems too hard to understand to some folks, it because those people are lost and don't know God. 4 That old devil has put blinders on those who don't believe. They just can't see the good news. They have chosen to live in darkness with the devil rather than live in the light with God. 5 We can tell you stories about ourselves, but it's only to point you toward God. We don't preach about ourselves. We preach that Jesus is the boss and we are his cowboys who ride for his brand. 6 God once said, "Let a light shine in the darkness." This light has come on inside our hearts and it is the glory of God which is Christ Jesus.

7 It's true! This light shines in our hearts, but this gift is like a treasure in an old worn out feed sack that could tear open at any moment. God did this on purpose to show it's his power that sustains us, not what we can accomplish. 8 We are surrounded by things that could kill us, but we ain't even been whipped yet. We may not know what we're doing, but we know better than to give up. 9 People are always out to get us, but God never leaves our side. We might get knocked down, but we always get up. 10 When we suffer, we share what Jesus went through and that makes us more like him. 11 We live with the constant threat of death, which proves we truly do ride for him. 12 We go through the worst so you can have the best—eternal life.

13 The Good Book once stated, "I said it because I believed it." That pretty much sums up our faith. 14 God brought Jesus back from the dead and he will do the same for us. We will all be gathered together one day to stand before him. 15 All of this is for y'all. Everything we do, everything we say, everything we go through, is for y'all. And God's grace is reaching more and more cowboys every single day. One day, there will be a great celebration and God will receive the glory he is due.

Living Faithfully

¹⁶ That's why we bear down and never give up. Our bodies are growing older and weaker, but our spirits are getting stronger and stronger. ¹⁷ Sure, we've got troubles, but they are preparing us for something much better to come. ¹⁸ So we don't even acknowledge the problems we have now, but we set our sights on things that can't be seen. The things we can see now are temporary and will soon be gone, but the things we can't see will be forever.

CHAPTER 5

This wall tent we live in here will one day be taken down and put away. What we will get is a brand-new body in heaven that won't flap, sag, or tear. God is going to do us up just right. ² Sure, we get tired of living in these earthly bodies and long for the new one that we know is waiting on us. ³ Don't let anyone tell you differently, we will have bodies in heaven. We ain't gonna be like ghosts just floating around like a fog. ⁴ These tents we live in here groan, sigh, and complain, but we ain't trying to shuck 'em before God is through with us. We know the times coming and we can't wait to put on our new duds. ⁵ Having something made specifically for us from God is something special. We know it's waiting on us because the Holy Spirit was the guarantee sent to us as a promise of what's to come.

⁶ So we can walk with our head high even though we know as long as we are down here, we are away from the Lord. ⁷ What we believe will happen guides us and keeps us confident, not what we might be seeing right now. ⁸ Yep, we ride with our shoulders back and head high. There's nothing that can happen to these bodies we don't long for so we can be with the Lord. ⁹ So, here's the secret, if we are here or there, the goal is to please God. ¹⁰ We're all going to stand in front of Jesus and give an account of the things we did on his spread. We will then receive our reward or our damnation based on what we did down here.

We Represent the Brand

¹¹ Since we know what we do down here has eternal consequence, we are vigilant in our responsibilities to the Lord. He knows how hard we work and hopefully you can see it, too. ¹² We ain't bragging about ourselves, but we do hope you are glad we ride with you. We aren't like those other cowboys who are all hat and no cattle. We'd rather have a good heart than a fancy ministry. ¹³ If you thought we were genuinely crazy, it is for the glory of God. But if you thought we were sane, it was for you. ¹⁴ But neither really matters. It's Jesus who we follow every single day. We follow him because he died for us and we are willing to die for him. ¹⁵ When anyone believes his death was for their life, they begin to live for something other than themselves. When they start riding for the brand, they will live for Christ, who died and was raised back to life just like we will be.

¹⁶ It's because of this that we no longer judge people by their looks or their breeding. Shoot, there was a time not too long ago when we judged Jesus by human standards, too. But now we know he was one with God. ¹⁷ This means that anyone who rides for the Lord has become a brand-new cowboy. The old city life is gone and new life of purpose has begun.

¹⁸ All of this is God's gift to us. Jesus opened the gate to the ranch so all of us could come in and be a part of the greatest crew the world has ever known. And our job is to gather the strays and show 'em where the gate is. ¹⁹ God was working through Jesus when he had him die for our sins and the narrow gate was flung open. This wonderful message has the power to change our relationship with God from being an enemy to a son. ²⁰ We represent the brand in all we say and do. God is spreading his message through his cowboys. We tell it just like Jesus told us to when we say, "Quit your sorry ways and come back to God!" ²¹ God swapped his perfect son for our sorry ways so we could be right with him through what Jesus did for us.

CHAPTER 6

Riding Our Country

Don't you realize the gift you've been given to be able to cowboy for God? Don't waste your new opportunity by living like you used to. ² God said, "Just in the nick of time, I heard you cry out for help and I saved you."

Now is the time to listen. Today is the day to be saved.

³ We never ride in a way that would cause someone else to doubt who we are. We don't

ride in front of anyone or do anything that would make someone question who we were. ⁴ In every single thing we do, we prove that we ride for the brand. Shoot, we don't even whine or complain about the hardships of the riding in the saddle. ⁵ We've been beaten and thrown into prison. We've faced down vigilante groups hell-bent on killing us. We've worked to sheer exhaustion and not slept a wink at night. And there's been many a day we didn't even have a piece of beef jerky to eat. ⁶ We prove we are cowboys by our pure lives, our knowledge and understanding of gathering strays, our patience in times of trouble, our kindness in times of strife, by the Holy Spirit riding with us, and by the way we love others. ⁷ We speak nothing but the truth and depend a hundred percent on God's power instead of our own. When you live this way—like a cowboy should—you are prepared for any kind of attack. ⁸ We ride for the brand whether people are pattin' us on the back or spittin' in our face. We are nothing but honest, but folks call us crooked horse traders peddlin' lies. ⁹ We are shunned everywhere we go. They act like they don't know us, but they do. We ride the canyon edge of death every single day, but nonetheless, here we are. They've stomped a mud hole in us, but they ain't been able to kill us yet. ¹⁰ Our hearts are broken, yet we are filled with joy. We have nothing anyone has, but everything they want.

¹¹ Won't all you cowboys in Corinth listen? I have spoken plainly with an open heart. ¹² We have given y'all our lives, but yet y'all hold back. We've given everything and y'all have given nothing. ¹³ I feel like a father who has given everything to his kids, but they show no gratitude or love. Pop your dallies on whatever is holding you back and open your hearts to us.

God's Casa

¹⁴ You aren't like the unbelievers who carry runnin' irons in their bags. If you ain't like 'em, quit ridin' with 'em. Real top hands don't ride with wannabe gunsels with a bad streak. Light cannot live in darkness. ¹⁵ Jesus and the devil ain't pards, so how can you still ride with someone who sneers at God and his ways. ¹⁶ You wouldn't find Greek idols in God's casa, would you? Well, then why do you have idols. Don't you know you are God's casa now?

Remember, the Boss said, "I'm gonna live in 'em and ride among them. I'm gonna be their God and they're gonna be my cowboys. ¹⁷ So separate yourselves from the unbelieving gunsels. Just ride off and leave 'em behind. Don't touch their filthy ways and you'll always have a spot at my fire. ¹⁸ Then I will be your Father and you'll by my sons and daughters, says the Lord Almighty."

CHAPTER 7

Listen to me, cowboys. We have these amazing promises from God so we should always do the best we can to stay away from things he tells us to stay away from. If you truly respect the brand, then you will strive to live holy lives.

Paul's Passion

² I'm going to ask y'all again, open your hearts to us! We've done no wrong to anyone. We haven't talked anyone into doing something they shouldn't or cheated anyone out of something they have. ³ But don't think I'm accusing y'all of any of this. I've told you more'n a few times that we love y'all. We'd stand in front of a mad momma cow for y'all. ⁴ In fact, we are very proud of the cowboys y'all have become. Y'all have encouraged me immensely, even during all my troubles.

⁵ When we rode into Macedonia, it was constant mayhem. We were attacked from every direction. The battle against evil on the outside wasn't any harder than the battle against fear on the inside. ⁶ But God, who always lifts up those who've been knocked down, sure helped us out when he sent Titus to us. ⁷ It was great to see another cowboy, but it was even greater to hear how y'all had encouraged him to ride with faith and courage. He passed along what y'all said about wanting to see me again. He also told me how sorry y'all were for the things you'd done. And finally, he told me y'all are really ready to ride for the brand now and help me in this gathering. When I heard this, I was ecstatic.

⁸ Even if my last letter got you down a little bit, I'm not sorry for the things I said. I know it hurt to hear some of those things and that was not my intention. But I'm glad y'all didn't stay hurt for long. ⁹ Now, I'm happy. Not because you were hurt, but because of your pain you decided to change. ¹⁰ God will allow a little bit of pain that will produce a whole lot of change. God wants you to have sorrow that will help you turn away

from sin and turn to him. And when we turn to him, then we are saved. But beware of worldly sorrow! Worldly sorrow is pain without repentance and that results in death.

¹¹ Godly sorrow on the other hand, results in focus. It made you want to clear your name. It opened your eyes. It made you want to see me. It made you long for the right way of doing things. You've shown you know how to do the hard things that are necessary. ¹² So, don't get me wrong. My first letter's purpose wasn't to chastise the one who was doing things wrong. It wasn't even to make the one who was hurt feel better. I wrote to you so we would be a crew again, riding together for the brand. ¹³ And God allowed that to happen. For that, I am greatly encouraged.

Not only that, but we were also thrilled to see how happy y'all made Titus. ¹⁴ I'd bragged on y'all a lot and you didn't disappoint me. I've always told the truth and y'all didn't make a liar out of me. ¹⁵ He's always talking about how much y'all want to learn and ride for the Lord. He was happy to teach cowboys who want to learn and know what respect is. ¹⁶ My confidence in y'all is now complete.

CHAPTER 8

Going from Greedy to Generous

Now listen to this, cowboys. Y'all ain't going to believe what God has done for all the outfits in Macedonia. ² These cowboys have been tested to the limit. They were in one wreck after another. These cowboys didn't have two halters between them, but they were happy riding for the brand. This type of elation led them to go from greedy to generous. ³ They didn't just give a little of what they had. They gave more'n what they could actually afford. It wasn't because anyone asked them to do it, either. It was their idea and the result was astonishing joy on their part. ⁴ They rode up to me every single day and asked—they actually begged me to take their offering so it could help others ride for the brand. ⁵ But the most astonishing part wasn't the money. Before they gave the money, they gave themselves wholeheartedly. If you're looking for what God wants from his cowboys, this is it!

⁶ So we've sent Titus back to you to give you a hand in this. He's the one who taught y'all about

the need for giving and he'll help you finish your training by going out and doing it. ⁷ Y'all are top hands in many ways—faith, speaking, knowledge, being neighborly, and loving folks. Now I want you to become top hands in giving.

⁸ This ain't a command from me. It's a test. Money is usually the last thing people will part with and I want to see if y'all are as good at giving as the other outfits are. They give eagerly, not with some sort of forced obedience. ⁹ Not that I need to remind you, but Jesus gave us his riches and became poor for your sake. He gave up everything he had so you could have it instead.

¹⁰ Here's what I think, y'all need to finish what you started last year. Y'all were the first to talk about taking up an offering. ¹¹ Now, finish what you started. Don't be all talk and no walk. Y'all said you were eager to give, now prove it. ¹² The amount doesn't matter as much as the willingness to, but be sure you are giving in proportion to what you have. The trick is to concentrate on how much you have to give, not how much you'll have left after you do. ¹³ Your gifts aren't supposed to make your life hard and other cowboy's lives easier. It's a way of offering a leg up to someone in need and you know that one day the tables might be turned. ¹⁴ I know right now you've got some cash laying around you could help with. Who knows? One day it might be you who's in need. ¹⁵ Remember, the Good Book says, "Those who hoarded had nothing, but those who gathered just what they needed had enough."

Titus and His Pards

¹⁶ I'm thankful God put y'all on Titus's heart just like y'all are on mine. ¹⁷ I talked to him about what I'm asking for and he's agreed to come help. He wants to see y'all again. ¹⁸ We are sending a top hand with Titus to help. He's known to all the outfits and is always eager to share the good news while serving in any way he can. ¹⁹ He will also be riding with us when we deliver your offering to Jerusalem. This will bring glory to God and show how much we want to help others.

²⁰ We aren't going to take any chances with our reputation regarding the money. ²¹ We will do what is right. We will do what the Lord says is right. And we will do what the people say is right. ²² There will be another cowboy who rides with

us also. He's also a top hand and wants to serve God and y'all. This fellow has proven himself time and time again. When he heard what y'all were going to do, he wanted in.

²³ If anyone has any questions about Titus, you tell him he's my pard. He's working right alongside me in this mission to help you. The other boys are sent from the other outfits and they bring honor to Christ with them. ²⁴ Show these guys your love and prove to the other outfits that you'll do what you said you would do.

CHAPTER 9

Passing the Hat

I don't need to keep going on and on about lending a hand to the cowboys in Jerusalem. ² I know y'all are on board. I've been bragging about y'all to all the outfits in Macedonia. I told everyone the outfit in Greece was ready to send an offering over a year ago. This has stoked the fire and now others want to give because of y'all. ³ I'm sending these cowboys to be sure y'all have passed the hat and are ready to send your offering. I hope I wasn't wrong about y'all. ⁴ It would be an embarrassment to all of us if I showed up with some cowboys from Macedonia and y'all weren't ready after all. ⁵ That's why I'm sending y'all the help before I get there to ensure that doesn't happen. The only thing I'm concerned about is y'all will give your gift grudgingly instead of willingly. Everyone talks big about giving while the money is still in their pocket.

⁶ Don't forget, a farmer who only plants a few seeds only reaps a small harvest. But the farmer who plants a bunch harvests a bunch. ⁷ Each of you should give what you know you should. Don't give anything if you don't want to. God will bless giving made generously. ⁸ And God won't forget what you give. He will bless you so that your giving will result in you having plenty left over to do other good works. ⁹ The Good Books says, "The cowboys gave what they had to those who didn't have anything. Their deeds will be remembered forever."

¹⁰ Did the farmer make the seeds himself? No, they came from God in the first place. We just use them to make bread for food. He is going to give you more and more so you can give more and more away. He is planting a harvest of generosity in you! ¹¹ God will make you rich in more

ways than just money so you will always be able to give. When we show up with your gift, people will thank God because of you.

¹² What you are doing for those folks will really help them with their needs, but that ain't all. It makes people give thanks to God. ¹³ Y'all don't have any idea of the impact this will have on people . . . and God will get the glory! This will prove to everyone that y'all ride for the brand in deed, not just in hats. ¹⁴ Prayers will be sent up with tears flowing because of the grace that God has given you. ¹⁵ All the thanks for all our lives goes to God and his wonderful gift. The gift that words cannot describe.

CHAPTER 10

Paul Sets 'Em Straight

Listen boys, I'm writing to you with all the kindness Jesus has given me. Some of y'all think I talk big in letters and small in person, but that ain't the case at all. ² I sure hope the ones who think this reconsider their opinion before I get there. I don't want to have to use this type of boldness in person if I don't have to. We don't do what we do for worldly gain.

³ We are just cowboys, but we don't fight our battles like the rest of the world does. ⁴ We use weapons from God to destroy the enemy fortresses and obliterate people's best arguments against God. ⁵ We smash every proud opinion that is contrary to the knowledge of God. We rope every thought and break it to lead by obeying Christ. ⁶ We won't hesitate to punish anyone who tries to do their own thing in this outfit. That ain't what we want though. We want you to ride for the brand and follow Jesus.

⁷ Look at the facts instead of just listening to roosters crowing. If someone says they ride for the brand, then we do the same. There is only one brand. ⁸ Some might think we brag too much about the authority Jesus gave us. But this authority is only used to make y'all better cowboys, not hurt you. ⁹ I'm not trying to be a bully with my letters. ¹⁰ I've heard that people say, "Paul can write a powerful letter and seems strong, but when he's here, he's kind of a sissy." ¹¹ When I get there, I will show these people how much of a sissy I am . . . and they won't like it.

¹² We don't compare ourselves with self-important cowboys. When you make yourself the

standard, it ain't hard to live up to it. When you make the rules, it's not hard to abide by them. These people ain't important. They're fools and know nothing.

13 But we ain't going to brag about anything more than the job Jesus gave us to do. He gave us some country to gather and we are proud of the job we've done. Y'all are part of this country we've gathered. **14** We ain't bragging about something we haven't done. We were the first to travel all the way to Corinth and bring y'all the good news.

15 We don't include another cowboy's work in our tally book. We stand on what we've done. What we want is your faith to grow so our gathering will grow as well. **16** When we get new country to ride in, we will be able to gather new cowboys for the brand. We don't want someone else's country that has already been picked through. We want raw, untamed, wild country to ride in. Then no one can say we bragged about what someone else did. **17** Remember, the Good Book says, "If you're gonna brag, brag about the Lord."

18 Patting yourself on the back don't count for nothing. Ride in a way where God will do the pattin'.

CHAPTER 11

Paul and the Wannabe Cowboys

What I need from y'all right now though is a little patience for a cowboy who has been on the trail for a long time. **2** You see, I've promised you to Jesus like a father promising his virgin daughter to a king. **3** But I think y'all are anything but pure. Y'all have passed yourselves around like a bad cold. Your loyalty to the brand has been corrupted. Y'all have been seduced like Eve was in the beginning. **4** There are wannabe cowboys showing up preaching a different Jesus than we did. Instead of running them off, y'all invite them in, listen, and pat them on the back. Can you not see the truth or can you not tell the difference between a drugstore cowboy and a real hand preaching the truth?

5 But I don't think I'm any less of a cowboy than those other "top hands." **6** I may not be a great speaker, but that don't mean the knowledge I have isn't valuable. This has been clear to y'all from the start.

7 I brought y'all the good news like a neighbor at branding time. I came to serve and did so without pay. I did the hard work and never complained or demanded to rope. Do you think I should have done something different? **8** Sure, I accepted some pay from some other outfits, but that was just so I could get to y'all and help out. **9** When my groceries ran out, I didn't come and bother y'all with it. I was never a burden on anyone. The cowboys who came from Macedonia gave me everything I needed, not y'all. I refused to be a burden to y'all. **10** As surely as Jesus is Lord and lives in me, no one will ever keep me from bragging about how I worked for y'all. **11** Why did I do it? Why did I work so hard without being a burden? Do you think it's because I don't care about y'all? Only God knows how much I love y'all.

12 I'm going to continue to ride for y'all this way. That way you will be able to tell the difference in a real cowboy and one who comes riding in with shiny silver on his saddle and fancy words on his tongue. These charlatans say they do the same things we do, but you'll be able to spot the difference a mile away. **13** They are wannabe cowboys, charlatans and gunsels, all hat and no cattle! They only pretend to ride for the brand. **14** Of course, this is of no surprise to us. Even the devil likes to dress up like an angel. **15** If he does that, of course his servants will play dress up as well. But when the big sorting arrives, we will see who is sorted in and out of the narrow gate.

Paul's Rough Ride

16 I ain't no fool, but if that's what you think, then bear with this foolish cowboy a little longer. That way I can brag a little bit. **17** And when I do, I'm not talking like the Boss would talk. You see? I am a fool. **18** Other cowboys are bragging about their wild rides so I will too. **19** Y'all are the wise ones, so put up with me for a little spell. **20** I'm only talking like this to show y'all that you are constantly putting up with fools. You welcome those who use you and force y'all into doing things you know ain't right. Y'all put up with smooth-talking drugstore cowboys, those who take advantage of you, control the things you say and do, and even those who push you around like they own you or something. **21** I guess I should say that if you think that's what strength is, then my crew is just a bunch of pansies. We'd never treat y'all like that.

But whatever they can brag about, I can brag about too! (I'm talking facetiously again if you haven't caught on yet.) **22** They say they are Hebrew? Me too! They say they are Israelites? Me too! They are descendants of Abraham? Me too! **23** Do they ride for the brand? Even talking like this to make a point makes me throw up a little bit, but I've ridden for Jesus much longer and much harder than they have. I've been thrown in jail, bullwhipped more times than I can count, and faced death time and time again.

24 Five different times, the Jews have given me the maximum punishment of thirty-nine lashes with a stock whip. **25** Three times I was beaten with axe handles. Once, they hurled big rocks down on me until they thought I was dead. Three different times I have survived ship wrecks and once spent an entire night and day drifting on a piece of wood at sea. **26** I've taken the outside in this gathering and rode at a long trot on many perilous journeys. I've faced raging rivers and bloodthirsty bandits. I've had showdowns in the street with my own people, the Jews, as well as from the outsider Gentiles. I've ridden through hell in cities, deserts, and even on the open sea. I've gone toe to toe with cowboys who pretended to ride for the brand, but really were trying to get close enough to stab me in the back.

27 I have ridden the rough string and the rough trails. Most of the time I got little sleep. Many times I had no food or water. I've been in bad cold weather without a coat. **28** And of all the problems I have, the main one is how much I care about all the outfits. I worry about these crews of believers every single day. **29** I feel the desperation when someone reaches the end of their rope. It kills me every time a cowboy rides back to a life of sin.

30 But if I'm going to brag, it's going to be about the things I am weak at. **31** God knows I'm telling the truth. He's Jesus's daddy and the only one worthy of praise. **32** When I was in Damascus, the governor posted spies at all the gates so they could find me and arrest me. **33** But some friends put me in a trunk and lowered me down the outside wall of the city. That's the only way I made it out alive.

CHAPTER 12

A Mesquite Thorn in the Hide

Ok, that's enough of that. I could go on and on, but I guess I need to tell y'all about what God showed me and told me. **2** I was swept from the saddle and taken far beyond the earth fourteen years ago. Now, whether this was done in spirit or my actual body, only God knows. **3** Listen close, I don't know if my body made the trip or just my mind. Like I said, only God knows. **4** But I was taken to a place of paradise. I heard things that are too much to repeat and saw things that no words can describe. These were things I'm not allowed to share.

5 I wish I could brag about the things I heard and saw, but I'm not going to. I'm only going to brag about my weaknesses. **6** Understand though, it ain't bragging if it happened and I wouldn't be a fool for telling y'all the truth. But the reason I ain't going to tell y'all is because I don't want credit for something I only saw and heard. I only want credit for what y'all have seen me do. **7** It'd be way too easy for me to brag about what I saw, but I really had no part in it. I can't take credit for a gift like I'd earned it or something. And just to make sure I remember, I was given a mesquite thorn in my hide to remind me of just how weak I really am. **8** I prayed and asked Jesus to remove this thorn three times. **9** But the Lord told me, "My grace is the only thing you need. Only in your weakness can you receive the power you need to accomplish the tasks I've set before you." This is why I will only brag about my weaknesses. When I am weak, Jesus's power is working through me. **10** As a matter of fact, I'm proud of these weaknesses. I don't even care when I'm insulted or when there are rough trails. I look forward to being persecuted and having problems, because it is in these times that I am the weakest. And it is only then that I am at my most powerful.

Paul's Care for the Corinthian Outfit

11 I know I've been talking foolish, but y'all made me do it. Y'all are the ones who should be bragging about me, not me having to brag about myself. I know I am nothing, but those "super cowboys" aren't any handier than I am. **12** When I was with y'all, I showed y'all how handy I was. I proved I was a cowboy with signs, wonders, and miracles that could only come from God. **¹³** The only thing I didn't give y'all was the opportunity to support me financially. I think this is the only way I've wronged y'all. Please forgive me for not allowing y'all to help me.

¹⁴ I'm going to come see y'all for the third time. And like the last times, I will not be a burden. I don't want what you have—I just want you riding for the brand. Children shouldn't be the ones providing for the parent when they are able to provide for themselves. It's the other way around. **¹⁵** I'll give everything I have for y'all. But I'll be honest, it seems like the more I care for y'all, the less you care about me.

¹⁶ Y'all know I didn't ask for anything while I was there. Yet, some of you still think I somehow tricked y'all into doing something you didn't want to do. **¹⁷** Do y'all think I cheated you? Did the cowboys I send to y'all take advantage of you somehow? **¹⁸** Did Titus pull a fast one over on you? I know that's not true! He's my pard and we ride the same trail and do things the exact same way.

¹⁹ Do you think we are just being defensive? No, we are talking plain to y'all and we'd say the same things if Jesus was standing right here. We care about y'all and push y'all every day to be better cowboys. **²⁰** I'm pushing y'all hard because I'm afraid that when I get there, y'all won't even be able to swing a rope. I'm afraid all my work has been for nothing and y'all haven't practiced or taken anything seriously. I'm worried that when I get there I'm going to find bickering, jealousy, anger, gossip, arrogance, and wrong living. **²¹** I really am afraid that when I get there, God is going to humble me because y'all have done nothing you were supposed to. My tears will flow down my cheeks because you have given up your ride for the brand for a life of sin again. You have not rode off from your evil lies, sexual immorality, and sorry ways. I'm afraid you just hid them in a closet, not repented and rode off from them.

CHAPTER 13

A Final Word

This will be my third time coming to see y'all. Don't forget, if someone has a complaint about someone else, there's got to be at least two or three other cowboys who can testify to the truth of it. **²** When I was there before, I warned those who were still sinning. I may not be there yet, but let me offer another warning to stop before I arrive. If it is still happening when I get there, they will be dealt with accordingly. **³** If you need proof that Jesus speaks through me, you'll get it when he deals with you when I arrive. You'll sure enough see his power then. **⁴** He might have been nailed to a cross while he was weak, but now he rides with the full power of God. We are not different. We may be weak now, but when it comes to dealing with y'all, we will have God's full power at our disposal.

⁵ So I suggest you test yourselves to see if your faith is true. If you don't realize Jesus lives in you now then you have failed the test. **⁶** While you reflect on your own lives, notice that we have not failed the test. Jesus does live in us and our actions prove it.

⁷ We pray that y'all will not refuse correction. I hope we have no need to exercise the authority we've been given when we get there. Please, do the right thing and fix what needs fixing so we don't have to when we arrive. I don't even care if it looks like we failed. If it gets fixed, that's all that matters. **⁸** We can't go against what is true. We stick to the truth, that's all. **⁹** We'll gladly appear weak if it makes y'all strong. Your growth is all we care about.

¹⁰ Again, I'm writing all of this before I get there so y'all will have time to fix things. I don't want to get there and immediately start punishing people. I have the authority, but I want to use it to make you better cowboys, not tear you down. But the choice is yours, not mine.

¹¹ Now, listen cowboys and cowgirls, I want y'all to be joyful. I want you to become the best cowboys and cowgirls you can be. Encourage each other and don't let each other down. Get along with each other. Then God will send his peace and love to ride with you.

¹² Greet each other with a hearty handshake or a kiss.

¹³ All of the cowboys here send their best to y'all.

¹⁴ May the grace of Jesus, the love of God, and the togetherness of the Holy Spirit ride with you down every trail.

GALATIANS

CHAPTER 1

This letter is from Paul, a cowboy for Jesus. I was chosen to be a cowboy, but not by anyone here on earth. The authority I've been given came from Jesus himself and his Dad, who raised his boy up from the dead. ² All the other cowboys in my outfit send howdies as well.

To the cowboys in God's outfits in Galatia:

³ I hope y'all are filled with grace and peace that comes from riding for the brand. This doesn't come from what we do, it comes from God through our ride with Jesus. ⁴ Jesus set us free from sin when he died on that cross. As hard as it is to believe, this was God's plan all along. ⁵ And we thank him for that precious act. Thank you, God!

The Only Good News

⁶ Not too long ago, God called you to ride for his outfit through his son, Jesus. I'm appalled you are now riding for another brand. There is only one good news message, but y'all have jumped the fence and are chasing something else. ⁷ Let me be clear, there is only one good news message, but some people have convinced y'all otherwise. They're doing everything they can to change the message. ⁸ Don't let anyone tell y'all something different than what we passed along to you. Anyone who says differently than we did should be shunned—even if it was an angel or one of us. ⁹ I've said this before and I'll say it again. You've already believed the good news and are riding for the brand. Anyone who tries to tell you differently is a counterfeit and should be cursed.

¹⁰ If you think I ride for the brand so people will like me, you've got things all twisted up. God is the only one I aim to please. If I wanted people to like me, I wouldn't be riding for the Lord.

Jesus Gave Paul the Message

¹¹ Cowboys and cowgirls, I want you to understand I didn't come up with the good news on my own. It didn't come from human reasoning. ¹² Men didn't teach me what to say, Jesus himself did.

¹³ The way I used to be isn't a secret. When I rode for the Jews, I carried a running iron and tried to wipe out Jesus's brand. I wanted to wipe it off the face of the earth. ¹⁴ I was one of the top Jews in the country. Very few could best me in anything religious. I was bought in, entered up, and tied hard and fast to the religion of my ancestors.

¹⁵ Little did I know though, before I was even born, God had chosen me to ride for his brand. I didn't deserve this kind of grace, but God was pleased ¹⁶ to show me his son and recruit me to ride for his brand. Now my life is all about gathering strays and telling outsiders the good news.

When God showed me his son, I didn't run out to find a human teacher to answer my questions. ¹⁷ I didn't even run up to Jerusalem to talk with the cowboys who rode with Jesus. Instead, I rode off to Arabia and later rode back to Damascus.

¹⁸ Three years later, I rode to Jerusalem to meet Pete. I stayed at his place for about two weeks. ¹⁹ The only other cowboy I met while there was Jesus's brother, James. ²⁰ This here is the truth and you can set it in stone.

²¹ After that, I rode north into Syria and Cilicia, ²² but none of the outfits in Judea knew me. ²³ The only thing they knew about me was I was the one who would go to any length to wipe out the name of Jesus, but now I ride for Jesus's brand. ²⁴ Because of this, cowboys from all over Judea praised God that the great enemy of the brand was now its greatest ally.

CHAPTER 2

The Other Cowboys Accept Paul

Fourteen years later, I rode back to Jerusalem with Barnabas and Titus. ² I went there because God told me to. I met in private with the leaders of the outfit in Jerusalem and told them the same message I'd been giving to the outsiders. I wanted to be sure everyone agreed on the same message. I didn't want my past or future endeavors to be wasted.

³ They all agreed with me. They didn't even ask Titus, who was a Gentile outsider, to have his pickle clipped. ⁴ This was a topic of discussion though. It seemed some wolves dressed in cowboy clothes had come into the outfits and were spying on us. They wanted to take away all the freedom Jesus gave us. They wanted us to go back to following all the Jewish rules and codes. ⁵ Not only did we refuse, we didn't make one single compromise. The truth we gave you is the truth and it is the only truth that will save you.

⁶ Even those cowboys who were running the outfit couldn't think of a single thing to add to what I'd been telling folks. (Not that it would have mattered if they were running things or not. God doesn't have favorites.) ⁷ Instead, these leaders saw me as a cowboy who God had given the responsibility of taking the outside in this great gathering of souls. I was tasked with gathering the Gentile outsiders just like Pete had been called to gather the Jews. ⁸ The same Boss who worked through Pete is the same Boss who worked through me.

⁹ James, Pete, and John, who were looked at as the ramrods of the outfit in Jerusalem, recognized God's brand on my heart. They accepted Barnabas and I as cowboys equal to them. They told us to keep gathering the Gentile outsiders and they'd keep working on the Jews. ¹⁰ The only suggestion they made was that we keep looking after the poor. But we were already doing that and weren't going to stop.

Paul Chastises Pete

¹¹ But Pete messed up real bad when he came up to Antioch. I confronted him face to face like a man. ¹² When he first got there, he'd eat with everyone, even those without their pickles clipped. But some friends of James showed up and Pete wouldn't eat with the outsiders anymore. He didn't want to rock the boat with those who believed circumcision was necessary for salvation. ¹³ This kind of hypocrisy spread like a wildfire in dry grass. Even my buddy Barnabas started siding with these Jewish cowboys.

¹⁴ When I saw what was going on, I told Pete in front of everyone, "You were born a Jew and followed their ways, but now you ride for the brand and live like an outsider. Why then are you trying to get the outsiders to act like Jews and follow all their rules?

¹⁵ "Me and you were born Jews. The Jews like to say anyone not born a Jew is a sinner. Neither of us were born sinners. ¹⁶ We both know a cowboy is made right with God by his faith in Jesus, not by following the code of Moses. Both of us believe in Jesus and are right with God because of it, not by following the Code. You can't be right with God by following rules.

¹⁷ "So if we try to be right with God through faith in Jesus, and on the day of judgment we find out we should have obeyed the Code, would that mean Jesus caused us to sin? That's the dumbest thing I've ever heard! ¹⁸ I'd really be a sinner if I tried to make people do the things that I gave up when I signed on to ride for Jesus. ¹⁹ When I tried to keep the Code, I was condemned because I couldn't do it. So, I gave it all up and trusted Jesus did for me what I couldn't do for myself. Instead of being condemned by the code of Moses, I now live for the brand of God. ²⁰ My old life has been nailed to the cross with Jesus. I no longer live, but Christ lives within me. This earthly body only lives by trusting in the man who died to save me. ²¹ And I don't take the grace of God lightly. If we could be right with God by following rules, there'd be no use for Jesus."

CHAPTER 3

The Code and Faith

You folks in Galatia are a bunch of gunsels. Why? Why Jesus died on the cross is as clear as the nose on your face. [2] Let me explain. Did you get the Holy Spirit by obeying the code of Moses? Of course you didn't. You got the Holy Ghost by believing the story of Jesus. [3] But here's the part I don't understand, after getting into God's outfit by believing in Jesus, why are you now trying to be perfect by your own works? [4] Was everything you heard and saw a waste? I hope it wasn't all in vain.

[5] Let me ask you again, is the Holy Ghost a gift from God for obeying rules or believing in Jesus? I think y'all know the answer. It's because you believed in Jesus and signed up to be a part of his crew.

[6] Think about it! Abraham believed in God. He and God were tight because of that, not because he was good at following rules. It was because of his faith. [7] Abraham's real descendants are those who have faith in God, not rules.

[8] Not only that, but the Good Book told us what was going to happen. It said all people, not just Jews, would be made right with God through faith. God told Abraham this good news when he said, "All cowboys will be blessed because of you." [9] So every cowboy who has faith in God shares the same blessing as Abraham did.

[10] But those who trust in rules to make 'em right with God are cursed. The Good Book says, "Cursed is the cowboy who doesn't follow all the rules and obey them completely." [11] This means no one is right with God by following rules. The Good Books also says, "It is by faith that a cowboy rides the right trail with God." [12] This is a lot different than when the Code says, "It is only by following the Code that one will find life."

[13] But Jesus saved us from this curse of following a code that can't be followed. When he was strung up on that cross, he took this curse for us and suffered our consequences. The Good Book said, "Cursed is the one who is strung up on a tree." [14] Because of Jesus, even Gentile outsiders can share the same blessing promised to Abraham. Those who ride for the brand will get the Holy Ghost through faith.

The Code and the Promise

[15] Here's something that will maybe help you understand this better. When a contract is drawn up and agreed to by both sides and signed by a judge, you have to go by it. You can't be adding to or taking away from it just because you changed your mind for a minute. [16] God made a promise to Abraham and his child. I want you to notice that it didn't say, "and his children." The promise was made to Abraham and God's Boy, Jesus. [17] God made that promise 430 years before the Law was given to Moses. The Law didn't cancel God's promise. Nothing can cancel a promise from God. [18] Think about this, can following a set of rules bless us? If it could, then we wouldn't need God's promise, just good rule-following ability. But God blessed Abraham because of his faith, not because he followed rules. We have the same promise made to us.

[19] So, what good was the Code? It was to show us how often we do wrong things. These rules would continue until the special cowboy came along—the child of Abraham. The Code was given through angels to Moses. And Moses was the middleman between God and his people. [20] A middleman is needed when two sides must reach an agreement. But remember, God didn't use a middleman when he gave his promise to Abraham.

[21] So, is it possible things don't line up between the code God gave and the promise he gave to Abraham? Absolutely not! If the Code could grant us eternal life, then we would have it by being good at following rules. [22] But the Good Book says we are all slaves to sin. We are only freed from sin by our faith in Jesus, not by following rules.

God's Kids

[23] Before Jesus came to set us free, we had a strict nanny called the code of Moses. It was for our protection until Jesus came.

[24] Here's another way of looking at it. The Law was like a prison guard until Jesus came. It kept us safe, but locked away until Jesus could make us right with God and set us free. [25] Now that Jesus came, we don't need a prison guard anymore.

[26] Every single one of us is one of God's kids if we believe in Jesus and ride for his brand. [27] Every cowboy who has been dunked in baptism is riding with Christ. It's a new way of life. A life we

couldn't get on our own. [28] There are no more labels like Jew or Gentile. There are no more prisoners or free men. There isn't even male or female in God's eyes. We are all equal in the sight of God through his son. [29] And now that you ride for the brand, you are the real children of Abraham. You are his heirs and Abraham's inheritance belongs to you too.

CHAPTER 4

It's like this, if a dad dies and leaves an inheritance to his kids, they're not much better off until they grow up. They may own what their dad had, but it's not really theirs until they grow up. [2] They have to do what the nanny says until they reach the age their dad had set for them to receive the inheritance. [3] That's what it was like before Jesus came. We were like children. We were subject to the ways of this world until he came.

[4] But at just the right moment, God sent his only boy, born to a virgin, and under the same set of rules as everyone else. [5] God sent his boy to buy our freedom so he could adopt us as his very own. [6] And since we are his kids, God sent the Spirit of his Son into our hearts. Now we call out, "Abba, Daddy!" [7] You are no longer a child slave of sin, but one of God's own children—with an inheritance that will come as well.

Paul Cares for the Galatians

[8] It wasn't long ago that you didn't know God. Y'all were slaves to false gods. [9] But now you know the one and only God. But to be honest, it is God who knows us, not the other way around. [10] Just look at y'all now though. You are trying to make God happy by celebrating certain days or months or seasons or years. [11] I feel sorry for you. Maybe all my hard work was for nothing. [12] Listen close! I want y'all to ride with the same kind of freedom I do. I don't want you to be slaves of the Law. In that respect, I am like the outsiders. I am free of the prison of the Law.

Y'all were real good to me the first time we met. [13] Remember, I was so sick when I brought y'all the good news. [14] Even though it was hard on y'all, you didn't turn me away. You welcomed me as if I were an angel sent by God. You treated me as if I were Jesus himself. [15] I remember the smiles on your faces. Where did those smiles go? I know y'all would've done anything for me if I'd asked. If I'd needed eyes, y'all would've given me your own. I know you would have. [16] But what has changed? Am I now your arch enemy just because I told you the truth?

[17] Don't listen to those people. They are trying very hard to turn you away from riding for the brand. They want y'all to ride for them and work hard for them, not Jesus. [18] Now y'all know working hard is good for you. Y'all should be working hard regardless of whether I am there or not. [19] Listen, I'm hurting bad for y'all. I hurt as bad as a mom watching her son get in a horse wreck. I will feel like this until people can look at y'all and see Jesus. [20] I wish I were there so I could help y'all. But as it is now, this is all I can do.

Abraham's Two Kids

[21] Some of you folks want to live under the Code, but do you really know what is says? [22] Abraham had two sons. The first son was from a slave woman and the second was from a free woman. [23] His first son was born like any other kid. But his second son wasn't the result of normal human birth. Isaac was the result of a promise from God.

[24] This is an illustration of the two agreements between God and his people. One agreement was made on Sinai Mountain. This agreement was the Code that enslaved people, just like Hagar was a slave to Abraham. [25] Jerusalem is no better off. It is a city that has been enslaved to the Code. She and her children live in slavery to a set of rules. [26] But the other wife, Sarah, is like the Jerusalem that will come down from heaven. She is a free woman and this new city will be like our mother.

[27] Isaiah even said, "Put a grin on your face, O dry woman, who has never given birth! Break into a dance for you've never gone through labor. The woman who'd never had kids now has more than the lady who lives with her husband!"

[28] You cowboys and cowgirls are promised children, just like Isaac was. [29] But Abraham's other boy, Ishmael, the one born normal, caused a lot of problems for the promised child, Isaac. The same thing is happening today. [30] But don't go forgetting what the Good Book said, "Sort out the slave woman and her child. The son of the free lady will receive all his daddy's inheritance. The slave woman's son will receive nothing." [31] So, cowboys and cowgirls, we ain't kids of the slave, we are children of the free.

CHAPTER 5

Freedom

Jesus has taken the hobbles off us! You are free and no longer hobbled to the Law.

² Listen to me! If you think clipping your pickles is going to make God like you better, then you must not need Jesus. ³ I've said it once and I'll say it again, any cowboy who tries to go by one part of the Law must obey every part of the Law—every twist, turn, nook, and cranny. ⁴ Those of you wanting to reinstitute the old code have quit on Jesus. When you ain't got him, you ain't got God's grace anymore either. ⁵ But those of us who ride with the power of the Holy Ghost are waitin' on God to make us right through our faith in his boy. ⁶ It don't make no difference at all if you are clipped or not when you ride with Jesus. The important thing is that you have faith in God and love for others.

⁷ Man, y'all were doing so good! What on earth made y'all sidestep the truth? What did that fellow say to y'all to make you turn away from Jesus? ⁸ You can't say, "That's what God said," because God ain't gonna make you quit on his boy. ⁹ The lies these people are spreadin' is like foot-and-mouth disease in cattle. It infects one and then fatally spreads to others. ¹⁰ You ain't going to get infected or infect anyone else if you keep to the truth. I'm confident all of y'all are true riders of the brand. These lies might find your ears, but don't let 'em get to your heart or your mouth. God will deal with these liars one day and it ain't gonna be pretty.

¹¹ Do y'all really think the Jews are after me because I'm trying to convince everyone to get their pickles clipped? If I were doing that, nobody would bother me at all! If I went back to telling people they could be saved by following rules instead of trustin' in the cross, my problems would all go away. ¹² I wish these people who keep harassing you about circumcision would just try to be an example and go all the way. Why stop at the tip? Let 'em castrate themselves, too. Maybe then their lies wouldn't reproduce.

¹³ As for y'all though, you were called to ride free. But this freedom doesn't mean you are free to follow every dirty thought that crosses your mind. Use your freedom to serve others, not satisfy yourselves. ¹⁴ Even the old code of Moses can be summed up in one sentence, "Love yourself and others the same." ¹⁵ But if y'all act like a bunch of hungry coyotes who are constantly biting and snarling at each other, don't be surprised when y'all are all chewed to pieces.

Enemies

¹⁶ You can either follow the Holy Ghost or you can follow your human nature. You'll have to pick one because you can't ride for both. ¹⁷ What the Spirit wants for us and what our human nature wants are two opposite things. Trying to do both is like straddlin' a barbed wire fence. You don't get anywhere and it hurts real bad. ¹⁸ And when you choose to ride with the Holy Ghost, you are under no obligation whatsoever to follow the code of Moses.

¹⁹ The trail of sinful nature is easy to follow. It's marked plain with immoral sexuality, unclean acts, dirty pleasures, ²⁰ worshiping things other than God, witchcraft, getting mad all the time, picking fights, being jealous, throwin' fits, thinking only of yourself, blaming others for everything, picking sides, ²¹ wanting what another man has, staying drunk every weekend, having orgies, and other sins like these. I've warned you before and I'll warn you again, anyone living intentionally like this won't have no part in God's outfit.

²² But riding with the Holy Ghost makes a man be able to love and have things like joy, peace, patience, kindness, goodness, faithfulness, ²³ humility, and self-control. There's no code against such things. ²⁴ And those who ride for Christ have nailed their sinful human natures to the cross. All the dirty passions and nasty desires are dead. ²⁵ Our new life comes from the Holy Spirit and so we must give him the reins. ²⁶ Do not be proud, irritating, or jealous of one another.

CHAPTER 6

Help a Fellow Up

Cowboys, if you catch someone doing something they shouldn't, you should love 'em enough to set 'em back on the right path; but do it gently. And another thing, watch what you're doing, too. Don't be a hypocrite and point out people's faults while you're neck deep in the same mud. ² We should get off and help people up who've been bucked off hard. I mean, this is essentially everything Jesus told us to do. ³ But if you think you're too good to get off and lend a hand to a broken fellow, you show just how small a man you really are. You can talk a big game all you want, but the only one who believes your lies is you. ⁴ You should take a good, long, hard look at your motives every single day. If everything is good, then you can be proud of yourself. A cowboy who looks to better himself every day doesn't feel the need to compare himself to others. ⁵ We all have to ride our own broncs.

⁶ If you're riding for God, you should take care of those who are mentorin' you and making you a top hand.

⁷ Don't be a durn fool. You can't pull the wool over God's eyes. He knows if you really tried or you were just faking. All of us will get out of it what we truly put into it. ⁸ If your ride was only about pleasing yourself, then you'll have an eternity to ride in death and decay. But those who only ride to please the Holy Ghost will have an eternity to ride in green pastures on perfect horses with ropes that ain't got a miss in 'em. ⁹ So don't give up doing the right thing. If you keep to the right trail, you're gonna find the narrow gate that leads to everything you never dreamed possible. ¹⁰ So every chance we get, let's help others out, especially those who ride for the brand.

The Last Word

¹¹ See these big letters I'm writing to you with my own hand! ¹² Those who are trying to get y'all to clip your pickles are only doing it to look good in front of others. They don't want the Jews on their case by saying Jesus is the only way to be saved. ¹³ Even those who circumcise don't follow the whole Code. They are just picking and choosing stuff to make themselves appear holy. If they get you to do it too, then they get to brag and put another notch in their pickle holster.

¹⁴ But me, I'm only going to brag about what Jesus did on the cross. My petty wants in this world died with him there. As a matter of fact, I did too. ¹⁵ It don't matter if your pickle is clipped. It matters if you're a new man. ¹⁶ May peace and mercy ride with you every step of your journey with God.

¹⁷ Finally, don't let anyone trouble y'all anymore about this foolishness. I have the scars that show I ride for the brand.

¹⁸ Cowboys and cowgirls, may the grace of Jesus be your guide. Amen.

EPHESIANS

CHAPTER 1

Howdy, Boys! It's me, Paul. I was handpicked by God himself to be a cowboy for Jesus Christ. I'm writing to all the other cowboys and cowgirls in Ephesus who ride for the brand and follow Christ. ² Here's hoping that God doles out a mess of grace and peace on all of ya through Jesus.

Blessings of the Spiritual Kind

³ Let's all take our hats off in thanks to everything God has given us through his son, Jesus. By riding with him, we have already received every spiritual blessing in heaven. ⁴ Even before God built the place we call home, he had chosen us to ride for his brand. By doing so, we became holy and in us he finds no fault. Not because we are perfect, but because he loves us. ⁵ He knew from the beginning he would bring us into his outfit through his son. We don't just work for God, we are now his kids because of what Jesus did. He did all this on purpose because it pleased him to do so. ⁶ Now, we give him praise for what he did in giving us his son. Shoot, he gave us the blessing his son deserved. ⁷ But this blessing came at a terrible price! We got this blessing through Jesus's blood. He shed his blood so we wouldn't have to. Now our sins are forgiven, having been paid in full by Christ. We got a blessing we didn't deserve. That is the grace of God. ⁸ And you know what? He don't ever hold grace over our heads. He gives it to us without measure.

With wisdom we can neither know nor understand, ⁹ God did something we never saw coming. He'd planned it from the very beginning. It all hinged on the life, death, and resurrection of his only boy. ¹⁰ But that plan ain't done yet! When the right time comes, everything will be brought together under the brand of Jesus. Everything in heaven and everything on earth will wear Christ's brand.

¹¹ Because we ride for this brand already, we've received an inheritance from God. He chose us before we were born and everything works according to his plan.

¹² Some of us Jews were the first to ride for the brand and bring glory and honor to God. ¹³ Now, even outsiders are allowed into God's crew. This doesn't happen because they are top hands, it's because they believed the good news. And when you believe the good news, the Holy Ghost comes in and rides with you. This was a promise God made to us long ago. ¹⁴ The Holy Ghost is God's guarantee he will keep his promise and we will inherit everything he said we would. He paid a terrible price to give us such a wonderful gift. The least we can do is praise and honor him.

Paul's Prayer

¹⁵ Ever since I heard y'all had saddled up to ride for the brand, ¹⁶ I have been thanking God for bringing you in. I'm always praying for y'all. ¹⁷ I ride right up to the big boss, Jesus's daddy, and ask him to give y'all the Holy Ghost. When the Spirit rides with you, you'll get wisdom and knowledge that can't be found anywhere else. And we use this to grow closer to God. Nothing trumps the need to know him better. ¹⁸ My prayer is that God will light a fire in your hearts so you can understand just how much he loves

you. When you can tie onto this, your hope will outweigh everything else. He's called y'all to be his cowboys, and a great inheritance waits for each of us who ride for the brand.

¹⁹ But it's not just a future inheritance we can hope for. He's also given us great power. The same power ²⁰ that brought Jesus back from the coffin is the one that's camped inside us right now. It's the same power that made a place for him at the right hand of God. ²¹ We follow a man who God gave all authority in heaven and earth to. ²² There's no stick, rock, or cowboy who don't fall under the authority of Jesus. God made Jesus the ramrod of his outfit. Or, in other words, Jesus is the head of the church. ²³ And the cowboys who ride for the brand serve as Jesus's body on earth, doing great things in great ways just as if Jesus were doing them himself.

CHAPTER 2

It wasn't long ago that you were hung up in the stirrup of sin because you wouldn't live the way the Boss told you to. ² You weren't just hung up, you were being dragged to death just like the rest of the world. You didn't listen to God, you flat-out followed the devil himself into every bedroom and bottle you could find. He ain't no outlaw to be trifled with. He's the leader of hell itself and you were riding for him. ³ But the truth is, all of us used to act like that. We only followed what felt good at the moment. We thought we were doing what we wanted, but we were being guided by the devil. Because of this, it's no wonder we were destined to be punished by God.

⁴ But we are thankful that the Boss is a merciful God. His mercy don't ever run dry either, and neither does his love. ⁵ Get this, boys! We were dead because we were hung up in the stirrup of sin, but when God brought his son back to life, he grabbed us by the belt and lifted us back in the saddle with a new purpose. It's God's grace that saved us, cowboys! ⁶ God raised Jesus up from the dead and gave him a place of honor in heaven. And we get to go with him because we are part of his crew! ⁷ People will look back and see the extraordinary gift that is available to everyone who rides for the brand. We've got a spot in God's crew because of his grace through Jesus, not because we are top hands.

⁸ It's our faith in God's love for us that does the saving—and this is not from our rope, or our hand, or our horse, it is the gift of the Almighty. ⁹ No matter how tough you think you are, you can't save your own hide. You can't toot your own horn about something you can't do on your own. ¹⁰ Like the greatest saddle maker ever, we were tooled by God himself, created in Christ Jesus to do good things God prepared for us before we even got here.

One in Our Ride with Christ

¹¹ Don't forget that those of you who were not Jews used to be outsiders. The Jews even called y'all, "unclipped outlaws." They were proud of their clipped pickles, but they didn't realize it only affected their body, not their heart. ¹² Back in them days, y'all didn't have a spot with Jesus on the ranch. Y'all had no part in the promise of God because you weren't his people. You rode through this world without God and without hope. ¹³ But now you ride for the brand and have been made one with Christ. There was a time you didn't even know God and now he lives inside you through the blood of Jesus.

¹⁴ Now there is peace throughout the land. Jesus has united the outsiders and the Jews together into one people. He broke down the barbed wire fence that separated us with his own body on the cross. ¹⁵ He ended the Code, with all its rules and regulations, and made one crew out of two groups of people. ¹⁶ Jesus's death on the cross made us right with God and allowed two enemies to ride for one brand.

¹⁷ He rode out and delivered the good news to the outsiders who were far away, but on his way, he gave the same good news to the Jews. ¹⁸ Now we ride right beside God and can ask him anything through the Holy Ghost. All of this is possible because of what Jesus did for us.

A Headquarters for the Lord

¹⁹ So now you Gentiles are no longer outsiders. You are part of the crew along with all of God's other cowboys. Even more than that, you are part of God's family. ²⁰ Together, we are his headquarters. It's built on the foundation laid by the handpicked cowboys and the prophets. The cornerstone of the headquarters is Christ Jesus himself. ²¹ He's the one who everything is measured off of. We are joined together with him to make a holy place for God. ²² It's because of

him you outsiders are now brought in and made a part of the place where God resides through his Spirit.

CHAPTER 3

God's Crazy Plan

It's because of this that I, Paul, who is a prisoner of Christ Jesus for the sake of the outsiders, pray to God. ² Surely, you've heard that God picked me to saddle up and ride out to bring his grace to y'all. ³ As I've written before, God yanked me out of the saddle and showed me his crazy plan. ⁴ If you'll go back and read what I said, you'll understand God's crazy plan and how it hinged on Christ. ⁵ The plan was always in place, but it wasn't until now that he has unveiled it to his holy cowboys and prophets.

⁶ This is his crazy plan, both the Jews and the outsiders who believe the good news will be God's children and share in a rich inheritance. Both are part of the same crew and will receive the same blessing because they ride for Christ Jesus. ⁷ It's by God's grace and power that I get to go out and gather his crew by spreading this good news.

⁸ Although I am the least qualified cowboy of all, God gave me the privilege of telling the outsiders about the great treasures they could have in Christ. ⁹ I am the cowboy he chose to tell everyone about his crazy plan. He'd kept this crazy plan secret since he sunk the first H-brace in this dirt we call home. ¹⁰ God's plan was to use his crew of cowboys to reveal all his wisdom. Everybody is watching and listening . . . even the angels in heaven. ¹¹ Using regular cowboys was part of God's crazy plan. And he's carrying out his plan through Christ Jesus our Lord.

¹² Because of what Jesus did for us, we can ride with God boldly and confidently. ¹³ Even though I am suffering greatly, don't lose heart. I suffer so y'all don't have to.

Becoming Top Hands

¹⁴ When I ponder on all this, I always end up on my knees and praying to the Boss. ¹⁵ He is the Creator of all things in heaven and on earth. ¹⁶ God's resources don't ever run out and I ask him to give you overflowing strength through the Holy Ghost. ¹⁷ Then Christ will put his bedroll down next to you and stay with you forever.

All you have to do is trust in him. ¹⁸ As you ride with him every day, you will become a strong top hand. A top hand has the power to understand just how much God loves us. ¹⁹ Your ride with Christ will let you experience this love, but to be honest, it's too great to fully understand. Only through this process will you be made a complete hand, with all the fullness of life and power that comes with it.

²⁰ There ain't nothin' God can't do, no matter what we think we can ask for or imagine. For his glory, his spirit is workin' inside of us nonstop. ²¹ All the glory goes first to God and then to his crew who ride for Jesus forever. Amen!

CHAPTER 4

A Crew That Works Together

Even though I am in chains behind bars for gatherin' for Christ, y'all need to get out there and ride the thick brush and draws looking for strays like you're supposed to. ² Don't look down your nose and help anyone who needs it or asks for it. Don't nitpick each other, ³ but work together like a crew of top hands. ⁴ There is just one body of Christ and one Spirit, there ain't no room for a show-off.

⁵ There is only one Lord, one faith, and one dunkin', ⁶ one God and Dad of all, who is the Boss of all, in all, and living through all.

⁷ But, he has given each of us special abilities through his generousness. ⁸ The Good Book says, "He scaled the unscalable mountain and rescued the prisoners, plundering the treasure and handing it out to his riders."

⁹ Notice that it says, "he scaled." Well, you can't scale a mountain if you don't start at the bottom. That means God came down to our sorry world. ¹⁰ This same one who did all of this is the one who scaled to the top of the heavens and filled the universe with his glory.

¹¹ Here are the gifts he gave to his outfits: the twelve cowboys, the old wise cow bosses, the gatherers, the grow yard bosses, and the clinicians. ¹² Their jobs are to make top hands in all the outfits, which is the body of Christ. ¹³ We will all work hard until we reach top hand status in Christ's eyes, not our own.

¹⁴ Then we will no longer be immature like wannabe cowboys. We won't fall for every gimmick and charade that comes along. ¹⁵ We will

ride in truth, love, and growth in Christ every single day we saddle up with the morning sun. ⁱ⁶ Jesus fits all of us together perfectly. We each have a part to play and a pasture to gather. By doing our part, we fill in the gaps until the body is whole.

Shun Your Old Ways

¹⁷ Jesus told me to pass this along to y'all. Don't live like the outsiders do, for they are kicking and pulling on the reins at the same time. ¹⁸ Their minds are as foggy as a humid valley morning. They don't know sic 'em from come here. They have shut their eyes and ears and now their hearts are like stone against him. ¹⁹ They justify everything they do without shame. Lust is their life and their hunger is for rotten things that destroy the soul.

²⁰ But that isn't what Jesus taught us. ²¹ He's the one who showed us the way to live and ride. ²² Shun your old ways that were full of lies and lust. ²³ Instead, let the Holy Ghost give you better thoughts and ways. ²⁴ Put on your new nature like a new pair of chaps that allow you to ride for our Holy God.

²⁵ Quit your lying ways. Speak the truth and the truth alone. ²⁶ Don't let anger control you. Don't let the sun set while you are fuming or bitter. ²⁷ This is the door that lets the devil in.

²⁸ Don't be a thief. Use what you know for good work and give generously to those in need. ²⁹ Watch your mouth, too. Let all you say be truthful, honest, inspiring, necessary, and kind.

³⁰ Don't let the way you live make God regret that you ride for him. If you ride for him, he's guaranteeing you will be saved—act like it.

³¹ There's no place in your saddlebags for backbiting, rage, gossip, harsh talk, or anything else that will bring dishonor to God. ³² There is a place though for being kind, gentle, and forgiving, just as God has forgiven you through Jesus.

CHAPTER 5

Live in Light, Not Darkness

Do what God does because you are now his cowboys. ² Live a life of love like Jesus did. He loved us even though we didn't deserve it and willingly died for those who don't even appreciate him by the way they live their lives.

³ Shun lust, promiscuity, and all your jealous hankerin'. That ain't the way God's cowboys live or ride. ⁴ Dirty stories, foolish talk, and crude jokes are not the ways of God or you. If you're wondering what to do then, learn to just be thankful. ⁵ There ain't a place on God's outfit for the immoral or greedy. A greedy cowboy makes a god out of what he wants, not the one who saved him.

⁶ Don't be one of these who justify sin by saying, "God made me this way." God will give a good chappin' to any cowboy who does this. ⁷ Don't ride like the no-account counterfeit cowboys who surround you. ⁸ You were once just like them, but now you live in the light, not the darkness. ⁹ This light that lives within you will work good in you if you just let it and listen to it, but it ain't going to make you do it.

¹⁰ Every day, ask yourself this question, does this make God happy? ¹¹ Don't waste your energy on the things that will destroy you. ¹² I don't even want to mention the things ungodly men do in secret. ¹³ But just because they think these things are secret, they will be exposed one day when the light of God reveals all. ¹⁴ No one can hide from God's light. This is why this was spoken, "Get up sleeper, rise from your grave, and Christ will light your way."

Ride with the Holy Ghost

¹⁵ Be careful how you ride. Don't ride like fools, but like top hands. ¹⁶ Pay attention to every single opportunity to do good, even though the days are evil. ¹⁷ Don't ride with your head in the clouds. ¹⁸ Stay away from the whiskey. You think you can control it, but it's the other way around. Instead, let the Holy Ghost guide your every waking moment. ¹⁹ Write a campfire song that honors God. Sing 'em together to settle the herd and your hearts. ²⁰ Be thankful every moment of every day.

Godly Marriage

²¹ Be honorable and reverent to each other out of your love for Christ.

²² Wives, be honorable and reverent to your husbands just like you are to the Lord. ²³ A husband is the head of his family as Jesus is head of his outfit. He is the savior of his outfit. ²⁴ As the outfit is honorable and reverent of Christ, so you wives must be honorable and reverent to your husbands in everything.

²⁵ Husbands, love your wives as much as Christ loves his outfit (the church). Jesus gave his life up for it and you husbands must love your wives just as much. ²⁶ He did this to make us holy and clean. We've been washed in the cleansing river of God's word. ²⁷ Jesus did this so his outfit would be worthy of his love. He has made us without spot, wrinkle, or liver spot. His outfit will be perfect and without fault. ²⁸ Husbands must do the same for their wives. Loving his wife shows that he loves himself. ²⁹ No one should hate their own body, but feed it good food and care for it, just like Jesus does for his outfit. ³⁰ And we ride for his outfit.

³¹ The Good Book says, "A man rides off from his mom and pop and makes a new life with his wife. The two of them become like one." ³² This is hard to understand, but it's another way of saying Jesus and his outfit are one. ³³ Again, let me say that each cowboy should love his wife, and the wife must honor and be reverent of her husband.

CHAPTER 6

Kids and Parents

Kids, listen to your parents because you ride for the Lord. This is right in the eyes of God. ² "Honor your father and mother." This is the first rule that has a promise attached to it. ³ If you honor your father and mother, "you'll make it to the end of the trail in one piece after a good, long life."

⁴ Dads, don't be too hard on your kids. Raise 'em up with discipline and love for the Lord and what he says to do.

Slaves and Bosses

⁵ Slaves, do what your bosses tell you to do. If you have to, just think of it like you are serving Christ. ⁶ Do what you're supposed to do at all times, not just when they are keeping an eye on you. We are all slaves to Christ and should do this. ⁷ Work hard, just as if it were Jesus standing there telling you what to do. ⁸ In the end, we will

all receive the reward for the work we've done, regardless if we are slaves or not.

⁹ Bosses, treat your slaves in the same manner. Don't threaten 'em. You may be the boss, but you and your slave serve the same master in heaven. Remember, he doesn't play favorites.

The Get-up of God

¹⁰ Finally, be strong like God made you to be. ¹¹ Put on the get-up of God so you will be protected from the devil and his devilish ways. ¹² We ain't fighting a battle against men, but evil in all its forms and places.

¹³ Put on every piece of God's get-up so you will be kept safe. After the battle, you may be bloody, but you will still be standing. ¹⁴ Stand your ground with the belt of truth and the armor of God's goodness. ¹⁵ Put on boots that will carry the good news to the furthest pastures. ¹⁶ Put on the chaps of faith that will protect you from the arrows of fire the devil launches. ¹⁷ Put on the felt hat of salvation and strap on the sword of God's word.

¹⁸ Be in prayer at all times and all occasions. Stay alert and sober for any ambush. Pray for all the cowboys who ride for the brand, no matter where they are.

¹⁹ And don't forget to include me in your prayers. Ask God to give me the things he wants me to say that reveal his great mystery, which is the good news for everyone. ²⁰ I'm locked up in chains right now, but I'm still spreading the word. Pray that I will continue to live courageously for Christ.

Adios

²¹ Just so you know, Tychicus will tell you everything that has been going on with me. I love him like a brother. ²² I'm sending him to you to tell you everything. I hope you will all be encouraged.

²³ Ride in peace, pards. Take the love and faith God offers us through Christ Jesus. ²⁴ May the grace of God keep you in the saddle until Jesus comes back.

PHILIPPIANS

CHAPTER 1

Hey, boys! It's me, Paul. I've got Timothy with me and he says to tell y'all hello as well.

I'm reaching out to all of God's cowboys around Philippi who ride for Christ Jesus. This includes the church jigger and wagon bosses.

² Here's hoping all of y'all are riding with grace and peace that comes from God the Father and his son Jesus Christ.

Doling Out Prayers and Thanks

³ Every time y'all cross my mind I give thanks to God. ⁴ When I'm praying, I ask God to take care of y'all and my heart is filled with gladness. ⁵ Y'all have been cowboying with me since you first heard the good news of Jesus Christ. ⁶ And there ain't no doubt God is going to make top hands out of all of y'all. He ain't gonna quit growing you until his work is finished and Jesus comes riding back over the hill to get us all.

⁷ This is the way any cowboy should feel about his crew. I care about y'all deeply because y'all have been with me through thick and thin, through brush and plains, through sunshine and chains. We have special favor from God while we spread the good news and gather the strays. ⁸ Only God could tell you how much I long to ride with y'all again.

⁹ My prayer for y'all is this, y'all keep growing, knowing, and understanding. ¹⁰ Y'all have to do this so you'll be able to know what is truly important in this life. Only by doing this will you be able to sit tall in the saddle when Jesus comes riding back. Then you will be able to show you are pure and blameless. ¹¹ I pray y'all reap the benefits of what Jesus did for you by becoming the cowboys who Jesus called you to be. This will bring God much praise and glory.

Paul's Pain Paves the Way

¹² Y'all need to understand that everything that has happened to me has paved the way for the good news to spread like a wildfire through old grass. ¹³ Everyone here knows I am in chains because I ride for the brand that belongs to Christ Jesus. The whole palace guard knows it too. ¹⁴ Because I am in chains, most of the other cowboys didn't become cowards, they became courageous. They are bolder now spreading the Gospel than they ever were before. These are real men and women riding for the Lord.

¹⁵ Now, it is true that some want fame and glory for preaching, but just because there are a few like that, it doesn't mean they all are. ¹⁶ The ones who ride for the right reason do so because they have the love of God in their heart. They know the only reason I'm here is because I'm a cowboy for God. ¹⁷ Those others who preach for the wrong reasons, they do so to make trouble for me. They are cowards who talk big when I'm in jail and cannot get to them. ¹⁸ But that doesn't matter! The only thing that matters is that Jesus Christ is preached. It doesn't matter if a person's motives are true or false. If Jesus is preached, that's all that matters. This fact gives me peace and a smile on my face.

And there ain't no one who can keep the smile off my face. ¹⁹ I know y'all are praying for me and God is going to take care of everything one way or another through Jesus Christ. ²⁰ You want to know what I think about while in prison? It's not getting out. It's that I will not be ashamed of Jesus. I pray every day that I will have the right amount of courage. So that when the time comes, it won't matter if I'm to live or die. I will do so courageously. ²¹ To me, living means I get to keep riding for Jesus, but dying means I get to go be with him . . . and that is even better. ²² If I live, I'll keep riding and gathering every single day. Come to think of it, I want both of these! I want to ride for Jesus and be with him. Which one should I choose? ²³ I'm torn between the two. I want to die so I can be with Jesus, which is far better as you all know. ²⁴ But honestly, it'd be better for all of y'all if I were to remain here and help y'all out in any way I can. ²⁵ I've realized the harder way is the right way. I am convinced I will stick around and give y'all a hand. ²⁶ And when I get back, y'all will have even more reasons to ride with pride in Christ Jesus because of what he has done through me.

A Ride Worthy of the Gospel

²⁷ Whatever happens, ride in a manner worthy of the Gospel of Christ. Then, whether I get to come see y'all or not, there won't be any doubt y'all are riding for the brand. Y'all will be riding together through the Holy Spirit, sharing the same faith, and helping each other. ²⁸ Only in this way will you be able to keep from being afraid of all of those who will oppose you. This courage that will be instilled in you will be a clear message to them that they will be destroyed and you will be saved by God. ²⁹ To cowboy for God, you've got to understand you've been called to believe in him, but also suffer for him. ³⁰ We are all in this together. Y'all have seen how much I have struggled, but I'm still in the saddle.

CHAPTER 2

It Ain't about You

If you are really riding for Jesus, if you've really received his love, if you've been riding together like Jesus told you to, if any of this has changed your attitude, ² then make me happy by being an outfit that works well together. Love each other and let no selfish ambition take a hold of you. Ride as if all of y'all are one. ³ Do nothing out of pride or conceit. A top hand is humble and puts others before himself. ⁴ Look out for others, not yourself.

⁵ Ride with the same attitude Christ rode with. ⁶ Although he rode with God, he didn't ride in front of him or even beside him. ⁷ Instead of using his privilege, he got off and opened all the gates. He put himself at the bottom instead of thinking of himself as the boss. ⁸ He humbled himself in obedience to God and rode all the way to the cross. He died like a criminal so you could live like a king. ⁹ Because of this, God made him the boss over everything. God honored him above every man and his name is above all other names. ¹⁰ At the name of Jesus, every knee will bow in heaven and on earth. ¹¹ Every mouth will one day declare Jesus is Lord. And this is the glory of God.

Do Everything without Whining

¹² Cowboys, y'all have always followed my lead whether I was with you or not. Now, continue to ride out your salvation with reverence and fear. You should be afraid of dishonoring the Boss. ¹³ It is this attitude God works through to give you the courage to complete his mission for your life.

¹⁴ Do everything without whining or bickering. ¹⁵ In this way, you will become strong cowboys who will be admired and imitated. You will be true children of God without fault in front of a crooked world. You will shine bright like a campfire on a bald hill on a moonless night. ¹⁶ Tie hard and fast to the word of life. Then, when Jesus comes back, I will be able to say I was proud to ride with y'all. The long miles and heartache I have suffered will then be washed away in the cool stream of his love. ¹⁷ Even if that stream runs red with my blood, poured out like a drink offering in sacrifice to God, I will do so with a smile on my face and peace in my heart. ¹⁸ You too should be happy with me.

Two Top Hands: Timothy and Epaphroditus

¹⁹ I'm hoping Jesus will let me send Timothy out to help y'all gather. This'll lift my spirits because I know y'all will be getting a lot done. ²⁰ There ain't another cowboy like young Timothy. This man truly knows how to care for others. ²¹ Most people only ride for themselves, but Timothy rides for the Lord. ²² He has proven

himself over and over. I think of him just like a son and I wouldn't be prouder of him if he was. 23 As soon as I figure out what's going to happen to me here, I'll send him your way. 24 And I'm sure I'll be right behind him if the Lord wills it.

25 But while we wait on all that, I am going to send Epaphroditus back your way. This man is my brother, pard, and fellow cowboy and has taken care of me like you asked him to. 26 He's been troubled because he misses y'all. He knew y'all had heard how sick he'd been and were worried. 27 Saying he was sick was an understatement. He had one foot in the Boothill Cemetery before God snatched him back. I thank God for saving him too. I've had sorrow after sorrow and if he'd died, I don't know how much more I could take.

28 That's why I am so eager to send him back. I know he wants to go and I know y'all want to see for yourselves that he's doing good. 29 Welcome him back with the love of God and throw him a party. Cowboys like him don't do what they do for recognition, but he deserves the honor for what he has done. 30 He risked life and limb riding for the brand. He was only here because y'all couldn't be. Remember that.

CHAPTER 3

Cowboys and Coyotes

Listen cowboys! Throw your frowns in fire and be glad about what God has done for you. I know y'all have heard it before and you'll hear it again and again. I will drill it in your heads for your own good. 2 Keep a sharp eye out for those coyotes, those charlatans, those scissor-wielding pickle-clippers. 3 True circumcision comes from worshiping God in the Spirit. That means relying on what Jesus did instead of what we can do. We have no confidence in ourselves, but all the confidence in the world in God. 4 If I wanted to rely on who I was, all I'd have to do is show y'all my pedigree. If others think they are papered well, I'm papered better—I assure you!

5 My pickle was clipped at just eight days old. I've got Hebrew on the top and bottom that goes all the way back to Benjamin. Nobody has more than that. I belonged to the Pharisees. We kept the letter of the Law better than anyone. 6 I was an ardent defender of the Law. I was a religious bully and hurt a lot of people who didn't do

things the way I did them. I justified everything I did because I felt like I was right with God because I followed rules real good.

7 What I once thought was my crowning achievement, I now think of as crap. What I can do is worthless compared to what Jesus did. 8 The only thing in life that is important is knowing Jesus Christ as my Lord. Because of him, I have left everything behind. I left my former life like garbage waiting on the fly-wagon. You have to lose everything if you are to gain Christ. 9 This is the only way to become one with him and ride for his brand. I no longer believe I am right with God because I can obey rules. I am right with God because I have faith in what Jesus did for me. Following rules won't get you right with the Boss. Only faith can do that. 10 I don't want to just ride for the Lord. I want to know him! This means experiencing the same things he did. I want to know the power of being brought back from the dead. I even want to suffer like he did so I can know the death he endured. 11 Whether it be knowing his life or knowing his death, I will know Jesus and be raised from the dead on that day. 12 Now, I ain't put a loop on all of this yet. For some of it I haven't even taken down my rope, but I'm already tied on and I've got my eye on Jesus just like he had his eye on me. 13 Listen cowboys, it's not that I don't ever miss a shot, but I'm going to be ready when Jesus calls my name. How do I get ready? I forget about all the misses I've made in the past and I focus on the next shot. 14 I'm running across God's pasture at full-stupid so that I can win the prize that is waiting for me in Christ Jesus.

Hell-Bent or Heaven Bound

15 The real cowboys will agree with me. Even if some disagree to an extent, I know God will clear things up for them in time. 16 We've worked real hard to get snubbed up next to God. We can't slip any rope now and lose the progress we've already made.

17 Saddle up and ride for the Lord the way we showed y'all. Pay attention also to others who ride the way we do. 18 It breaks my heart that many cowboys only ride for themselves. In doing so, they make themselves enemies of the cross. 19 They whip and spur, hell-bent on self-destruction. Their god is their voracious appetites for the things of this world. What they think

is their glory is the one thing that shows their shame. They point their ponies toward an easy life without realizing they're headed for the hard pits of hell. ²⁰ But our horses already have a stall in heaven waiting on us! We keep one eye on the sky as we eagerly wait for him to come riding back and save us all. ²¹ He's going to swap this frail, weak body we currently live in for one that is indestructible and will last forever. And it is with this power that he will make every knee bow down under his control.

CHAPTER 4

Y'all keep riding for the brand! Stay true to the code of Christ. I can't wait to see y'all again my friends. Y'all have proved my work was not in vain. I'm sure I'm going to get a trophy buckle in heaven for the things y'all have done on earth.

Keep on Keepin' On

² A word to Euodia and Syntyche. If y'all really ride for the Lord, then you must quit your squabblin' with each other. ³ The one reading these words or hearing them spoken, I'm asking you to be a real cowboy and step up to help settle this disagreement between these great women. They have faithfully spread the good news with me. They rode just as hard and just as far as anyone while riding with Clement and the other cowboys. All of these will surely be listed in the book of life.

⁴ Keep your chins up! Celebrate God every single day for what he has done for you. I'll say it again, get glad about what you've got! ⁵ Show kindness wherever you go. Remember, the Lord is coming back soon.

⁶ Don't fret about nothing! Instead, pray about whatever is bothering you. Pray about what you need. Pray to God and thank him for saving your sorry hide. ⁷ Only in this way will you find the peace you've been prowling the brush looking for. God's peace cannot be understood nor explained, only experienced by real hands. His peace will protect your heart and your mind as you ride for the Lord.

⁸ Finally, cowboys, whatever is sure 'nough true, whatever is just, whatever is no-nonsense, whatever is unpolluted, whatever is pretty as a newborn calf, whatever is worth admiring—if anything is worth its weight or deservin' of a smile—ponder on these things. ⁹ Keep on keepin' on with the things you heard and learned from me. That means riding for the Lord, not just walking around in your shiny boots and store-bought hat. God will ride with you and give you the peace you need.

Appreciation

¹⁰ I thank God that y'all have been worried about me. I know y'all care and you couldn't help me before because your hands were tied. ¹¹ But don't fret about that. I never really needed any real help. I've learned to live with a little or a lot. I'm content with my lot no matter what. ¹² I know how to ride with everything or nothing. I've learned the secret of life for every single trail. It doesn't matter whether your belly is full or empty. It doesn't matter if your pockets are full or empty either. ¹³ I can handle any bronc and any situation because the Lord is my strength. ¹⁴ But I do appreciate y'all snubbing for me in this latest bronc of a situation.

¹⁵ You cowboys from Philippi were the only ones to help me out financially when I brought y'all the good news. When I rode off toward Macedonia, y'all made sure I was not without. No other outfit helped me out, not one. ¹⁶ Even when I was in Thessalonica, y'all sent me some money as I gathered the lost and brought back those who'd strayed away. ¹⁷ I'm not bringing this up so y'all can send some more. I want y'all to be rewarded for what you've already done.

¹⁸ Right now my saddle bags are full. I still have much of what you sent with Epaphroditus. I know God was pleased with your offering and your sacrifice. ¹⁹ And my God will fill your life and your pastures with everything you need accordin' to everything that was given to you through Jesus. ²⁰ Glory to the Boss forever and ever!

See Y'all Later

²¹ Tell all the cowboys I said hello. The ones here with me say hello also. ²² All of God's people send their howdy, especially those in Caesar's outfit.

²³ May God's grace, which is the Lord Jesus Christ, ride with you always.

COLOSSIANS

CHAPTER 1

Howdy, boys!

This letter is written by Paul, chosen by God to ride for his outfit, and our pard, Timothy. **2** To all the cowboys riding for the Lord around Colossae, we pray your grass is green, your cattle are fat, and that all the great things of God surround you.

A Word of Thanks and Prayer

3 Y'all are always in our thoughts and prayers. Y'all give us reason upon reason to be thankful. **4** We've heard about your faith and love for all of God's herd. **5** This faith and love is being passed on through you from the hope y'all have in God. Y'all know heaven's gates will be opened to y'all when you come riding in. This is the good news y'all heard us preach about.

6 But y'all aren't keeping the good news secret—and you shouldn't! It's changing lives and hearts all across the world every single day. It did the same for y'all when you first heard about God's amazing grace. **7** Y'all heard the message from the cowboy, Epaphras, who went out for Christ in search of strays. He found y'all and you listened. **8** He came back and told me of the great love and purpose that had been awakened in y'all.

9 This is the reason we always pray for y'all. We never stop praying for y'all. We ask that God fill your hearts with knowledge, your life with wisdom, and your heads with understanding. **10** Only through these will you find your purpose and worth. The Lord himself will be pleased when you do good works, grow in the knowledge of him, **11** and by becoming strong through his mighty power resulting in great endurance and plenty of patience. **12** You will also please the Lord by being thankful for being able to ride for his outfit, to share in the inheritance of his glorious kingdom that is a ranch of a thousand hills. You are his cowboys. You are his beloved children. **13** For he has rescued us from a life of worthlessness and deemed us worthy and honorable. He did this through his Son. **14** It is through him we have found purpose for life and forgiveness for sin.

God's Son Is Now the Boss

15 Jesus is the visible image of our invisible God. Jesus is the firstborn, the heir, of all creation. **16** All things were created through him. The things of heaven and earth; the visible and invisible; no one takes a step or utters a command that wasn't first made through Him. **17** We were made with his hand and still he holds all things together. **18** And he is the boss over our outfit, which others know as the church. He is the beginning, and the first to rise from the dead. He has conquered everything—even death. **19** God was glad to hand the reins to his son and ride with him and in him. **20** It was God's plan all along to gather the strays back home through his Son. He brought us all home, not through hooves and horses, but through the blood that ran down the cross. Peace has been returned to all who wish to receive it.

21 There was a time we were all enemies of God through the evil things we did. **22** But now, God has brought you home through the only cowboy who could change our hearts. Jesus's death now presents us pure and holy, not by the things we do, but by the blood he shed. We are free from blemish and wart. But we are also free from accusation and condemnation—²³ if you stay tied on to faith, both feet in the stirrups of hope that have been delivered through the good news. This is the story of Jesus you've heard me tell around campfires and in the midst of congregations. I, Paul, am a servant to his story and slave to his name.

Paul's Long, Hard Ride

²⁴ I do not look at my suffering as part of something terrible, but as something wonderful. Jesus suffered to bring y'all back and now I get to experience that as well. ²⁵ God has given me the job and the responsibility of giving y'all the truth—the entire truth that has been hidden. ²⁶ This truth had been kept hidden since the beginning, but now it has been revealed to cowboys and cowgirls who ride for the brand. ²⁷ No longer are God's riches reserved for those who are well-papered. These wonderful riches are now available to those who are grade (unregistered, thought worthless, without pedigree). Here is the secret in black and white, Christ lives in you. And you get to share in his glory.

²⁸ So we spread the good news. We warn people about the box canyon of sin and self-dependence as well as teach with wisdom that can only come from God. We want to present all people perfect before God. The only way this happens is through Christ. ²⁹ That's why I've ridden ten thousand miles and worked so hard. I did it by depending on Christ's mighty strength that dwells within me.

CHAPTER 2

I want y'all to know how hard I'm riding for y'all and the others in Laodicea. This also includes all the cowboys who I have yet to meet personally. ² My goal for them is to be a complete crew, being able to accomplish any task God sets before them. This can only be done by loving one another. Then they can have complete confidence in understanding God's mysterious plan. This plan isn't a thing, it's a person. That person is Jesus Christ. ³ Only by riding with him will we be able to tie hard and fast to boundless wisdom and knowledge.

⁴ I'm telling you this so you won't fall prey to wolves with silver tongues. ⁵ I may not be right there with you, but my heart is. Nothing makes me happier than to hear y'all have joined this great gathering.

Quit Looking for Rules to Make You Right

⁶ Don't just ride for Jesus, you've got to learn to ride in him. Turn your toes out and take a firm seat of faith in him. Then you will be anchored in place when life starts to pitch and buck. ⁷ Hold tight to the truth and your heart will be full of thanks.

⁸ Don't let yourself get hung up in the stirrup of counterfeit words and fancy philosophy. These things don't come from Christ, but arrive from human thinking and spiritual darkness of this world. ⁹ Jesus is God in human form. One who we can talk to, listen to, and relate to. ¹⁰ Only through Christ can you become the cowboy you were meant to be. No king or ruler is above the power of Jesus. ¹¹ When you saddled up with him, your sinful nature was circumcised, not a part of your body. ¹² You rode to the grave with him in baptism and you'll ride with him in the new life you have when he brought you out of the grave just as God did for him.

¹³ You were dead in your sin, but God made you alive in Christ. ¹⁴ Through the cross, your debts were paid in full—once and for all time. No longer are you condemned in your actions, but now you are consecrated by his. ¹⁵ Jesus put a whipping on the enemies of God by his triumph on the cross.

¹⁶ Don't let anyone judge you for not following their religious rules or ceremonies. ¹⁷ These things weren't a way to live, but a shadow of the life to come that is through Jesus. ¹⁸ Don't listen to the false promises of those who insist on fake humility or the worship of angels. Just because someone says they've had a vision of these things doesn't make it the truth. They are pointing at themselves for salvation, not to Jesus. ¹⁹ They don't ride for the Lord, but for themselves. They ride for their own brand and their own agenda. Jesus is the ramrod of our crew and he holds it together with his own perfection. This is where growth and maturity come from. It doesn't come from following man-made rules.

²⁰ When you died with Christ, you were freed from religion's rules and regulations. If you are freed from them, why do you continue to follow

that trail? ²¹ They tell you, "Don't pick up that. Don't taste this. Stay away from this or that." ²² These rules are just human ways of trying to do what can only be done by riding for Christ. ²³ I know these regulations seem wise because they require strict discipline, self-denial, and much practice. But they are useless in conquering your sinful self. They actually open the door to sin, they don't close it.

CHAPTER 3

If you truly have a new life in Christ, set your thoughts on him, not rules about yourself. Jesus is riding at the right hand of God. He has offered you a place in his work, but you'll never accomplish anything by beating yourself up with rules you can never follow. ² By obeying a false code, you attempt to bring glory to yourself. By obeying Jesus, you bring glory to him. ³ You died to the past, but new life is found in the present, and the presence of God. ⁴ When Christ is revealed through you, you will share in his glory.

⁵ Ride off from all the things you used to ride for—sexual nastiness, corruption and desecration, lustful thoughts, and greed, which makes money and possessions your god. ⁶ These are the things God will destroy. Don't be one who is destroyed along with them. Make no mistake, God is coming and the things of this world will be destroyed along with all who partake in it. ⁷ These used to be your way of life, but you have a new life now. ⁸ Other things that will get you bucked off into the eternal fire are anger, rage, malice, talking crap about your neighbor, and other filthy things that come out of your mouth. ⁹ Quit lying to each other. You're not that person anymore. You are a brand-new cowboy with a new ride and purpose in life. ¹⁰ Ride in this new life and be remade in his will and way. ¹¹ In this new life, it doesn't matter if you are papered or grade, slave or free, barbaric or civilized. Jesus is all that matters and the quicker you learn that, the quicker you learn his ways.

¹² Since you've been chosen by God to ride for him, clothe yourselves with love for one another, patience, nice words and deeds, not thinking too mightily of yourself, and not jerking on the reins of anything or anyone. ¹³ Give each other a break, no matter the word or deed. Since God has given you a break for the things you've done,

do the same for others. ¹⁴ The most important thing to remember is to ride in love. It is the cinch that holds us all in the saddle. When we're all cinched down tight in love, we will be able to stay in the saddle and accomplish the task set before us. ¹⁵ Let the peace that comes from God guide your ride. All of God's cowboys are called to live in peace and always be thankful.

¹⁶ The message of Jesus should rule your lives. Mentor each other with the wisdom he gives. Let your life be the song in which you praise God with grateful hearts. ¹⁷ Whether you're in town getting supplies or out on the ranch gathering strays, remember that you represent the brand in everything you say and do. Let all your life be a way of giving thanks to God.

The Cowboy Way for Christian Homes

¹⁸ Ladies, show respect for your husbands and submit to him out of your love for the Lord.

¹⁹ Guys, love your wives and don't be mean to them. This is your way of submitting to them.

²⁰ Kids, do what your mommas and daddies tell you to. This is what makes God happy.

²¹ Dads, don't be bullies toward your kids or they'll end up hating you.

²² Day hands, do everything the wagon boss tells you to do. Do the right thing whether or not they're watching you. Make a good impression in all you do, not for them, but out of your respect for God. ²³ Whatever you do, ride with all your heart, riding for the Lord, and not for men. ²⁴ Your reward for integrity isn't waiting in a promotion or a paycheck, but in heaven as an inheritance of peace and prosperity for eternity. No matter where you are or what you are doing, remember that you ride for the Lord. ²⁵ A day hand who doesn't check the corners in a gathering will be held responsible—for God sees all. Riding for the Lord isn't an excuse to do poor work. You are held to a higher standard because you are a top hand.

CHAPTER 4

Wagon bosses, treat the day hands like they were your own precious sons. Do what is right and just. Remember, you too are just a day hand and you have a Boss in heaven.

Additional Insights

² Be diligent in prayer, thankfulness, and focus. ³ Don't forget us in your prayers as well.

Ask God to open locked gates so we may go in and gather strays and remnants who are sick and hurting. We will doctor them with the good news, which is the mystery of Jesus. It's for him that I suffer in the saddle. [4] Pray that I can make the gospel easy to understand. [5] Watch how you deal with folks who don't ride for the brand. [6] Use every interaction as an opportunity to reveal God. Be someone they can look up to. Bring value to their lives by showing them grace and mercy. These are the answers to every interaction.

Last Words

[7] Tychicus is going to fill you in on the rest of what I've been up to and how I am doing. He's a top hand for the Lord and I am so thankful for him. [8] I chose him because he's going to tell y'all the truth about what we've been going through. This message is going to encourage y'all to keep on keeping on. [9] Onesimus in going to be riding with him. He's also a top hand and one of y'all. They're going to tell y'all everything.

[10] My cellmate, Aristarchus, says to tell y'all hello. Mark, Barnabas's cousin, is also here with us. If Mark comes to see y'all, welcome him as if it were me. [11] Jesus (not the Lord, but the one we call Justus) also said to tell y'all hello. These are the only Jews who now ride for the brand of Christ who have joined me in this gathering. They have been great hands and a comfort to me on my journey.

[12] Epaphras, one of your own cowboys and a friend to us, sends greetings as well. He's constantly praying for y'all to become better and better cowboys, strong and perfect in Christ. He asks God to fill y'all with confidence in your ride with the Lord. [13] Don't let there be any doubt that he is one who is praying for y'all and all the cowboys in Laodicea and Hierapolis.

[14] Doctor Luke and Demas give their love and prayers as well. [15] Please give a hug and a handshake to the cowboys and cowgirls at Laodicea, as well as the rest of the outfit that meets at Nympha's house.

[16] After you show this letter to everyone there, send it on to Laodicea so they can take a gander at it. I'm sending a letter to them too, so get theirs and read what I wrote them.

[17] Tell Archippus I said to finish the gathering God had appointed him to.

[18] This greeting is written by me, Paul, in my own hand. Remember the chains I am in for your sake. May God's grace always be with you.

1 THESSALONIANS

CHAPTER 1

This letter is from Paul, Silas, and Timothy.

To the outfit in Thessalonica, y'all who belong to God through the grace of Jesus Christ.

Let God's amazing grace and peace rule your hearts and your ride.

The Thessalonian's Faith

² We're always thanking God for y'all and pray for you night and day. ³ While we pray, we imagine y'all out there in the pastures, whether rain or shine, wind or hail, riding for God and gathering the strays and mentoring other cowboys in the hope that y'all have in our Lord Jesus Christ.

⁴ We know y'all have been handpicked by God to cowboy for his outfit. He loves y'all more than you can ever imagine. ⁵ When we first gathered y'all in the sick pen and doctored you with the good news, he produced a healing inside each of you. It wasn't our words that did it, but the power of the Holy Ghost. We've kept a watchful eye for y'all ever since. ⁶ We told y'all when you saddled up for the Lord it wouldn't be easy. Y'all have suffered just like we said you would and you did it gladly, like top hands should. Y'all rode the way we showed ya and talked like we told ya. ⁷ And so y'all have become the top hands in all of Greece, including Macedonia and Achaia. ⁸ Folks have noticed your ride and now they are talking about it and wanting to learn. I don't have to explain that what they're seeing is your faith. ⁹ We've run into people who tell us how you ride. They tell us of your improvement. They tell us you no longer have other idols, but that you follow God and God alone. They've marveled at how you welcomed us with open arms. ¹⁰ But it's the other things that mean just as much. Things like how you are waiting on Jesus to ride back one day. When he gets here, he will rescue us from the prescribed burn that will consume all things and all people who've chosen to ride for themselves instead of God's outfit.

CHAPTER 2

Paul Remembers the Branding at Thessalonica

You cowboys and cowgirls remember that we didn't just make a social call when we came to work your pastures. ² Even though we went through hell in Philippi, we boldly told y'all the same message that caused us so much trouble there. We pulled out our running iron to change people's brands from the world to God's brand through Jesus Christ. And there were plenty of people who wanted to stop us at any cost. ³ We are not trying to change people's brand for selfish motives or personal gain. We didn't try to trick y'all like smooth talking horse traders. ⁴ We were bold and honest. God gave us a job of gathering the lost and bringing back those who strayed away. He told us to brand those who believed with the Holy Ghost. Even then, we weren't trying to be cool in people's eyes. We did this to be right with God and do the job he entrusted us with. ⁵ We didn't sugar coat the message or try to use it to get rich. God knows this to be the truth. ⁶ We didn't want you or anyone else patting us on the back or looking up to us, even though as God's chosen cowboys we could have used that authority.

⁷ Instead, we rode through your herd like little kids at their first branding. We cared for y'all with the gusto of a protective stud watching over his mares and foals. ⁸ We showed you we loved you, not with words, but with action and commitment. We shared the good news with y'all, but we also told you the hardship of the narrow trail we've ridden.

⁹ Don't you remember all our hard work? We were the first ones saddled up in the morning and the last ones to unsaddle in the evening. We even took all the night check duties so we would not be a burden and expect others to do something we wouldn't do. We preached and worked at the same time. ¹⁰ Y'all saw with your own eyes, and God was watching too, how we conducted ourselves in a manner worthy of the Lord every single day. ¹¹ We treated y'all like a loving rancher teaches his own kids how to be top hands. ¹² We encouraged y'all every single day to never give up, get back on when you were thrown, and to ride in a manner that would make God smile. Every single part of our ride should bring glory to God and his outfit.

¹³ We are so thankful you didn't turn a deaf ear to what we had to say. You didn't act like God's message was just another self-help course taught by the world. It was the word of God and you accepted it with the awe and reverence you should have. It is this power that is now available to you and at work within you whether you realize it or not.

¹⁴ Now that you are branded with the Holy Ghost, you've experienced just how hard it can be to be a real cowboy. You've had trouble from your own friends, family, and countrymen because of the cowboys you've become. You're not alone in your suffering. This is what had already happened to the outfits in Judea. Those cowboys suffered horrible things from the Jews just because they rode for the brand of Jesus. ¹⁵ The Jews have a habit of killing God's cowboys. Some of them are even responsible for the death of Jesus himself. If they did it to them, they'll do it to us. Your troubles aren't because you've done something wrong, but because you are now doing things right. We are living evidence of this fact. But make no mistake about it. God ain't pleased with them or their ways. They, and the others of the world like them, stand in the gate to the narrow trail in hopes that a little difficulty will make those destined for eternity turn around and run. ¹⁶ These Jews have parked themselves in front of the gate and try to prevent us from bringing the remnants into God's green pastures. But God isn't turning a blind eye or a deaf ear to what they are doing. He's just giving them enough rope to either hang themselves or tie hard and fast to the grace that is available to all.

Paul Can't Wait to Ride Back to the Thessalonians

¹⁷ But, just because we've been separated physically (not spiritually), that doesn't mean we don't hanker to return and ride in glory with y'all again. ¹⁸ We, especially I, Paul, have attempted to return time and time again. But that old forked-tail devil has seemed to block the way every single time. ¹⁹ But he can never succeed. Y'all will be the trophy saddle in heaven one day when we stand before the Lord at the awards ceremony. ²⁰ Y'all are our crowning achievement and the source of our joy.

CHAPTER 3

So, when we could stand it no longer, we sent Timothy to y'all. ² We created a diversion in Athens that allowed a single cowboy to get there when we all couldn't. He is young, but he is as handy a cowboy as God has ever put on this earth. He's been there for every wreck and successful branding. We sent him to y'all to show y'all the ropes. ³ He warned y'all of the trials and tribulations that come for riding for the Lord. Y'all know top hands ain't made by riding old broke nags and kid's ponies. When you ride the rough trail, you've got to be able to ride the rough stock. It's what makes you who you are. ⁴ When we were there, we told y'all you'd have to ride the rough stock to get where God wants you to be. We told y'all not to expect pony rides. And guess what? Now you realize we were telling y'all the truth. ⁵ When I couldn't stand it any longer, I sent Timothy to give y'all a hand, but also to check on y'all. I was scared the devil might have snuck in and turned you away from the life God had called y'all to. I was hoping and praying all our hard work hadn't been for nothing.

Timothy's Return Report

⁶ Timothy has made it back with nothing but good news. He's told us about your faith and love for all people. He told us y'all remember our teachings and continue to ride in the manner in which we taught you. He said y'all can't wait for us to come see y'all and we feel the same. ⁷ There were times we wanted to give up too, but Timothy's report has rejuvenated us. ⁸ Y'all are why we continue to saddle up every single day, take our running irons, and change the brand of those who believe. ⁹ We ain't got enough words to thank God for every single one of y'all cowboys. ¹⁰ Night and day we pray God will allow us to return and see y'all again; to witness your faith in action. But to also see how we can help y'all to be better cowboys.

¹¹ We've asked God continuously to pave the way back to y'all. ¹² We want God to fill y'all with such love that it overflows to everything and everyone around you. It's this type of love that produced the change in y'all. ¹³ May he give y'all the strength and courage to continue in your ride for the brand. Only then will you be allowed into the presence of God when Jesus comes riding back for the final gathering.

CHAPTER 4

As for some other things, we've taught y'all the fundamentals of how to ride for the Lord. But don't be satisfied with a little progress. Continue to grow and ride further every day. ² Y'all know everything we taught was straight from the Lord. Do it our way and you'll be doing it God's way.

³ God wants for y'all to be top hands. He wants you to be holy. They are one and the same. You can't do that if you're working for the Lord during the day and visiting the whorehouse at night. ⁴ A top hand controls his body and his desires. Be honorable and admirable in all that you do and at all times. ⁵ Don't be like those wannabe cowboys who run around with their tongue hanging out so far in lust they could accidentally zip it up in their britches. I don't care what they say, these wannabe "cowboys" don't know God and sure don't ride for the brand. ⁶ Only a wannabe cowboy would take advantage of someone and sell a lame horse. And I know you understand I ain't talking about trading horses. I'm talking about right living. Make no mistake, God is go-

ing to give out what they got coming. Take that as a warning. Don't learn this lesson the hard way when it's too late. ⁷ God did not invite us in to talk big, but to ride hard. ⁸ Anyone who scoffs at what I'm saying isn't rejecting me, but God himself. And it is the God who gives us all we need to accomplish his goals through the Holy Ghost.

⁹ I don't need to repeat myself about loving and looking out for each other. God himself is the author and giver of the love y'all have. ¹⁰ I know y'all ain't selective about who you look out for. I know you care what happens to the other cowboys riding for the brand all through Macedonia. Keep on caring. Don't give up on that. It's not a weakness, but the very strength you've been given. It doesn't keep you from being a top hand, it's what makes you into a top hand. ¹¹ Make it your top priority to lead a quiet life. You do this by minding your own business and working like a cowboy should. You've already heard this from us, so this isn't anything new. ¹² This kind of life will win the respect of those we are trying to reach. Ride into a herd this way and they'll stand quiet instead of throwing their tails up and heading for the brush. When you become this caliber of cowboy, you won't have to worry what others think.

The Cowboys Who Have Made Their Final Ride

¹³ Listen up amigos, we want ya to know the plain truth about those who have made that final ride so you won't be consumed with tears and fears like those who have no hope. ¹⁴ Here's the way it is, since Jesus died and came back, all those who've made their final ride with Christ in their hearts are going to be brought back to life. ¹⁵ According to the word of God, any of us who are alive when Jesus rides back will not get to ride in front of those who have made their final ride. We will follow them into eternity, not the other way around. ¹⁶ Jesus himself will come riding back from heaven, he will then give the loud command for the archangel to blow the trumpet of God so all those cowboys who have died will lead the charge back over the hill. ¹⁷ Those of us who will be standing there watching will then be gathered up and taken up into the air to meet the Lord. And there we will live with him forever. ¹⁸ Encourage each other with this good news.

CHAPTER 5

Now amigos, I know you're wondering when this is all gonna happen. ² But believe it or not, you know when it will happen. It'll happen when you least expect it. ³ When everyone is complacent and content with the ways of this sorry world, the fires of the prescribed burn will be lit. And just like a pregnant woman can't stop the birth, neither will the scoffers be able to escape the fire.

⁴ But you cowboys and cowgirls won't be caught flat footed when the fire is lit. Y'all will be ready and waiting. ⁵ You are children of the light, not the darkness. Only those in darkness will be destroyed. ⁶ Don't be like those who will be surprised by the Lord's return. Be ready, with both feet in the stirrups and ready to ride. ⁷ Those who are lazy won't be ready. Those who are drunk won't be able to catch their horse. It'll be too late for them. ⁸ Since we live in the light, be ready at all times to whip and spur for heaven's hills. Faith and hope will be our chaps and the hope of being saved is the hat we wear on our head for protection. ⁹ Our destiny is not for destruction in the prescribed burn, but for the endless water and grass of heaven's salvation which is Jesus Christ. ¹⁰ Christ died so he could throw open the gates of heaven so all his cowboys could ride in. Not just those who have rode over the final hill, but those who are still riding as well. One day, we'll be riding together with him. ¹¹ Encourage each other and give each other a hand, just like you've been doing.

A Final Word

¹² We ask that all y'all give respect to all those who have taught y'all how to ride for the Lord. Sometimes they encouraged you and sometimes they might have had to get on to you. ¹³ Hold them in regard for their work. Do this by avoiding petty squabbles over unimportant things. ¹⁴ We urge you to light a fire under the lazy and deal with the troublemakers. Encourage those who are trying to give up and give a leg up to those who have lost their strength. And above all, be patient with everyone. ¹⁵ Don't seek revenge on those who have wronged you, but use every last breath you have to treat everyone else in a manner that will make God smile.

¹⁶ Keep your chins up, ¹⁷ don't quit talking to God, ¹⁸ and be thankful for the hills and valleys of life; for this is what God wants from you. And the only way to accomplish any of this is through your personal ride with Christ.

¹⁹ Don't be a wet blanket for the fire God lit inside of you through the Holy Ghost. ²⁰ If someone says they have a word from God, don't dismiss it without testing it. ²¹ But at the same time, don't be gullible. If it's right, tie hard and fast to it. ²² If it's wrong, pop your dallies and ride off.

²³ Let the Lord of peace rule your ride and make you blameless for when Jesus rides back over the hill. ²⁴ The one who's called you to ride for him is faithful and never goes back on any promise he's made.

²⁵ Please remember to pray for us. ²⁶ Greet every one of God's cowboys with a hearty handshake. ²⁷ God told me to tell y'all to read this letter to every cowboy and cowgirl who rides for his brand.

²⁸ May the grace of God, who is our Lord Jesus Christ, guide you always in your ride.

2 THESSALONIANS

CHAPTER 1

Hey, boys! It's Paul, Silas, and Timothy again.

This goes out to all the cowboys and cowgirls in Thessalonica who ride for the Father, Son, and Holy Ghost.

² We are hoping and praying God is giving you the grace and mercy of our Lord Jesus Christ.

Getting Back On

³ We can't help but be proud of y'all because of your faith and love for one another. ⁴ We pass along how proud we are of you to the other outfits riding for the same brand we do. We commend y'all for always finishing what you've started and getting back on no matter how hard life has bucked you off. ⁵ And God is going to use these hard times y'all been experiencing to show his judgment on this world and that y'all are worthy of the great things he has planned for your eternity on a thousand hills. ⁶ He is a just God and will pay back all those who have hurt his kiddos. ⁷ And just when you think you can't handle any more, he's gonna come riding in and help you. He's done the same for us over and over again. You'll know when he comes to give you relief because you'll see him riding back over the hill. But he won't be alone! He'll bring with him the purifying fire and all his powerful angels. ⁸ There will be a reckoning waiting on those who have worshipped the world and its ways instead of accepting his grace and forgiveness. ⁹ They'll realize too late how much they missed when they are cut off forever from God's love as a result of their hard hearts. ¹⁰ He's coming back to prove our faith is real and to show the world who the real boss is. He will welcome you into his arms because you have seen, heard, and believed his message.

¹¹ We are always in God's ear that he will make you worthy cowboys by his power. We pray that he will make happen all the good things y'all have wanted to achieve through faith. ¹² We pray this, not so that you will be glorified, but so that he will. All the glory and respect belongs to the grace of God through Jesus Christ.

CHAPTER 2

The Devil's Son

I want to talk to y'all about the time when Jesus comes back and we finally get to ride with him in person. ² Don't let those who say Jesus has already came back get under your skin. Believe me, he's coming back to get us. ³ Don't let anyone pull the wool over your eyes. Jesus won't come riding back until the devil's son has been revealed, the one destined for destruction by God. ⁴ You'll know him because he will make himself an enemy of God by claiming he is the one who is to be worshipped. He'll even put a throne in God's house, proclaiming himself to be God.

⁵ But none of this is anything I haven't already told you. ⁶ And now you know Jesus is just waiting for the devil's son to reveal himself so God can prove who is really the boss and has the power. The time has to be right. There'll be no rushing God's plan. ⁷ But this outlaw is already at work, even if he hasn't made himself known. ⁸ One day, all these covert plans will be unveiled

and then Jesus will come back in the same manner. But the fight will have already been won. Darkness has already been defeated, whether anyone realizes it or not. Jesus will not win with a quick draw or the strength of his right arm, but with the breath of his mouth and the power of his word.

⁹ The devil's son will come to do the work of his father, Satan. He'll use sleight of hand to do miracles, signs, and wonders. But it's all counterfeit. ¹⁰ He will amaze the fools and they'll follow him like pigs to the slaughter. These pigs are those who refuse to believe the truth of who can save them. ¹¹ God won't stand in the way of their delusional fantasies. They'll believe the lies ¹² and be slaughtered for not believing the truth, but delight in wickedness.

Sit Tall in the Saddle

¹³ That's why we thank God for y'all who are cherished by God. God has chosen y'all to be the first to ride for his brand and the first to be saved by the truth. ¹⁴ He invited y'all to join his outfit through our story. But you don't just get to ride for God, you get to share in the glory of Jesus Christ and what he has done.

¹⁵ So sit tall in the saddle my friends. Tie hard and fast to the truth that we taught y'all. It doesn't matter if you heard it straight from us or by letter. The truth is the truth and you should believe it.

¹⁶ May the Lord, and his Father who loves us, give you hope and encouragement to continue your ride. ¹⁷ Keep your toes out and your chins up as you do God's good works and spread his good word.

CHAPTER 3

A Warning against Laziness

One more thing, amigos! Keep on praying that God's message through us will be heard, just as y'all heard it and believed. Pray that the gathering of the strays happens quickly and effectively. We want as many people as possible to know the truth before it's too late. ² Also pray that we will not be defeated by those unbelievers who are hell-bent on stampeding those we've gath-

ered. ³ But the Lord never goes back on his word. He'll give you the strength and be the one who watches your back when the evil one tries to attack. ⁴ We have no doubt in your ride for the Lord and that you will continue to ride in the ways we taught you. ⁵ Here's to the Lord making your trail straight to God's love and Christ's "never give up, never give in" attitude.

⁶ We aren't asking, we are telling you to steer clear of every believer who is either lazy or causes problems. If they don't do the job we gave all of you, ride off and don't look back. ⁷ Y'all know the way we taught y'all . . . so do it. We weren't lazy when we were with you, ⁸ nor did we eat anyone's grub without earning it. We worked night and day so we wouldn't be a burden on anyone. ⁹ It wasn't that we didn't have the right to accept such things, but we worked hard so y'all would see us walking the walk, not just talking the talk. ¹⁰ Y'all even heard us say, "If you ain't willing to work, then you must be willing to have an empty stomach."

¹¹ We've heard some of you have become lazy and since you didn't have anything better to do, you've started causing problems within the crew. ¹² In the name of the Lord, we're telling you to get off your butts and earn the food you eat. ¹³ For the rest of y'all who are busting your butts day in and day out, don't ever get tired of doing the right thing, no matter how hard it is.

¹⁴ Pay attention to those who roll their eyes at what we have to say in this letter. They've made their choice not to be a part of your crew so treat 'em as such. I hope they do feel ashamed and left out. ¹⁵ I'm not saying they should be treated as enemies, but let your actions be a warning to them, not because you hate them, but because you love them.

Final Words

¹⁶ May the Lord's peace overflow within you. May you ride beside him at all times through all seasons.

¹⁷ I, Paul, write this with my own hand. Don't let anyone tell you this isn't from me. Y'all know me and how I write with truth and love.

¹⁸ May the grace of God guide your hearts and minds down every trail.

I TIMOTHY

CHAPTER 1

This is from, Paul, a cowboy on a special task from God through Jesus Christ who is our hope and how we are able to hold on when life gets rank.

² To my son in faith Timothy, may you ride in peace, mercy, and grace from God as you gather the strays and remnants.

Timothy Is Told How to Handle Counterfeit Cowboys

³ Don't forget what I told you when I was going to Macedonia. I told you to stay in Ephesus to battle the counterfeit cowboys who were teaching something other than faith in Jesus. ⁴ You'll also have to contend with those who try to rebrand God's chosen people with made-up stories. Also keep a watch out for those who think they are better than everyone else because they have fancy pedigrees. Such people don't have faith, they just like to talk. Such talks lead to endless arguments that don't lead people down the narrow trail. ⁵ The goal of the new code of Christ is to love. The only way to do this is with a pure heart, a clean conscience, and an authentic faith. ⁶ Some have gone rogue and don't want to ride for the Lord, they just want to hear themselves talk. ⁷ They say they are "teachers of the Code", but they don't know anything more'n a fencepost. They talk big, but they ain't got no salt to back it up.

⁸ The code of Moses wasn't a bad thing when it was taken in context of showing people just how much we need God's help. ⁹ But it wasn't intended to bash believers with, it was to show how ornery and rebellious cowboys were by nature. No one accidentally follows God. We are all ungodly and full of sin. But these people hold nothing sacred. They'd kill their own moms and dads if it'd save their own hides. ¹⁰ The code of Moses was for them and the perverts, slave traders, liars and swindlers, and anyone else who doesn't do what they should. ¹¹ What they should do is leave their sorry ways behind and follow God. That's what God told me and so that's what I tell everyone else.

Paul Didn't Get What He Deserved

¹² I'm thankful Jesus chose me to ride for his brand. He has made me strong and trustworthy in the duties he's appointed me. ¹³ Even though I once cursed Jesus's name, in word and deed, ¹⁴ I didn't get what I deserved. Instead, Jesus poured out his grace all over me and it transformed itself within me into unending love and faith.

¹⁵ Listen to this, it's the best thing you'll hear all day, "Jesus came to save the scoundrels and outlaws." And understand, there weren't never a worse one than me. ¹⁶ But God took the worst of the worst and showed him mercy. He made me into who I am today. If he can do that for me, imagine what he could do with someone else who wasn't near as bad. Heaven wasn't made for the saints, but for every sinner who's been saved. ¹⁷ We don't brag about what we've become. We brag about what God has done. It's him who gets the credit. He is the Boss, the King Forever, the one who is never seen, but always there; he alone is God. Amen.

Timothy's Duty

18 Listen to me, my son. I'm going to give you some advice. What was spoken over you so long ago wasn't a lie. Use what was said as your strength and your shield in the battle to come. **19** Tie hard and fast to your faith in Christ. Don't do anything that will make you lose sleep at night. Some cowboys think their sorry deeds don't go unnoticed, but it weighs heavy on their hearts. They might still be in the saddle, but their faith was left for the buzzards on the trail a long way back. **20** Hymenaeus and Alexander are great examples of this. I threw them out of the crew for talking bad about the Boss. Now they ride for Satan's brand—the forked tail. I hope a minute in his crew will change their hearts.

CHAPTER 2

How to Give True Honor to God

Never give up praying for everyone, not just those you like. Only God can work a man over from the inside out. Be thankful that he never rests. **2** Pray like this for all the cow bosses, jigger bosses, and ranch managers of this world. We all long for a peaceful and quiet life. Godliness and dignity in today's world is rarer than gold. **3** These two things are what make the Boss smile. **4** God wants to save people with the truth. He's offering everything for faith. **5** The way to get it is through Jesus. He's the gate between destruction and life. **6** His death on the cross threw the gates of heaven wide open to anyone who believes. This is the message of God. It came at the right place and the right time. **7** I've been given the duty of sharing this message with the world. I was sent to the outsiders, not those of Jewish birth. I'm offering truth, faith, and eternity to anyone with the guts to ride. This ain't a tall tale. It's the truth—easy as that.

8 Where once men raised their fists in anger, I now ask them to reach out to God and be saved.

9 I don't want women to put a priority on fancy clothes, highlighted hair, and rhinestone belts. **10** They should clothe themselves in devotion to God by riding for his brand every day. This is where true beauty comes from.

11 A real lady doesn't go around bossing people around. Instead of trying to prove herself to men, she should prove her devotion to God. **12** Just because a lady has taken a few lessons doesn't mean she's ready to teach. This ain't no different for anyone. Her job is to learn quietly and practice what she learns. **13** There is a way of doing things. God made Adam first and then Eve. **14** Eve was deceived by Satan, but even though Adam knew better, she convinced him to follow. The result is the sorry world we live in. **15** But through her womb and all of her daughters, Jesus eventually came and so did the cure for what ails us. Every woman will share in the pain of childbearing, but through faith, love, and decency, she will also share in eternity with everyone else.

CHAPTER 3

Qualifications for Wagon Boss and Jigger Bosses

Don't let this go in one ear and out the other, whoever thinks they're ready to be a wagon boss on God's outfit desires a good thing, but it'll also be hard. Don't choose them based on looks. **2** A wagon boss must be well-thought-of by everyone. He needs to be faithful to his wife and family. He needs to be able to control his temper, show respect to all, open his home to anyone, and pass on his knowledge and skill. **3** He shouldn't be a drunk or a man prone to fisticuffs. His nature should be gentle but tough, not quick-tempered or money hungry. **4** If he can't run his own family and have respectable children, he ain't going to run God's outfit very long without a lot of problems. **5** If you can't run a small outfit of those who love you, you won't last long in a bigger outfit. **6** He doesn't need to be a greenhorn, or the authority will go to his head. This leads to conceit and he will fall under the same wrath the devil will get. **7** Everyone should think highly of him, not just church cowboys. Go ask about him at the sale barn and see what others have to say. Don't just talk to his friend. Find out more. Don't put him into a position to fail and fall into the devil's noose.

8 Just the same, jigger bosses (or deacons) should be well respected, honest, and not at the beer store every single day. They should never put good money ahead of good people. **9** They need to be tied hard and fast to the truths of the faith and have a clean conscience. **10** Only choose those who have proven they can ride the rough string and make hard decisions. If they practice what they preach, then let them be a jigger boss.

11 But let's not forget about the cowgirls. They should be well respected, not idle gossipers. Self-control and faithfulness should be their way.

12 A jigger boss must be faithful to his wife and be a good dad to his children. 13 Those who are good jigger bosses will be rewarded with respect from all and their trophy buckle will be a bigger faith in Jesus Christ.

The Truth about Our Ride for the Brand

14 Even though I hope to see you soon, I want you to have all this stuff in writing. 15 If I don't make it, you can read this over and over and know what to do in most situations. Teach folks how to ride for the brand in God's outfit. This outfit is what we call the church. He is a living God and he cares for all of us. This is what holds everything together.

16 I know this is hard to understand. It is the mystery of our faith—God came down from heaven so we could see him. He didn't need human acceptance. The Spirit of God was with him. The angels saw his glory. He taught the truth to the world and many believed it. And when his ride was through, he rode up to heaven in glory.

CHAPTER 4

Now the Holy Ghost has warned us. Later on, people will forsake the brand of God and follow the ways of demons instead. 2 Their teaching will come from liars who will adhere to a double standard. Their consciences will be like ash from a fire. 3 They will tell people who they can and cannot marry and convince people not to eat certain foods. Food comes from God so that we can give thanks. We who know the truth know who to believe. 4 Nothing is to be rejected if God made it and a man is thankful for the full belly. 5 God's word and a cowboy's prayer can make anything holy.

6 If you teach a cowboy the truth, you will be a good cowboy on God's outfit. A cowboy is built and made on a diet of truth, faith, and the right way to ride. 7 Don't pay any attention to old wives' tales and campfire stories that come from human lips, rather, train yourselves to ride like God wants you to. 8 Being a tough cowboy is good, but doing things God's way is even better.

Godliness has great benefit here on earth and in the eternal life to come. 9 You can believe what I say. 10 That's why we saddle up every day and ride out to spread the good news. We have faith and hope in the promises of God. He is the one who will save us all, and most importantly, those who ride for the brand.

11 These are the things I want you to teach and tell people. 12 Don't let anyone look down on you because you are young. Prove them wrong by the way you speak, act, love, and the way you prove your ride is truth. 13 Until I see you again, tell people what the Good Book says. Don't ever shy away from preaching or teaching. 14 Don't give up using the gift God gave you. This gift was revealed when the wagon bosses prayed over you and put their hands on you.

15 Don't throw a leg over the saddle horn like you've accomplished your task already. Keep both feet in the stirrups and always ready to tell someone about Jesus. People will take notice that you never give in and you never give up. 16 Practice what you preach. Never turn loose of your faith. If you stay tied on to Jesus, you will save yourself and those who hear your words about the grace of God.

CHAPTER 5

Don't jump all over an older cowboy who rides with you. Treat him as you would your own dad. Treat young men in your outfit like you would a brother. 2 Treat older women like your mother and younger cowgirls the same as your little sister. Help keep these young women pure.

3 If a widow needs a hand, be the first to offer it. 4 But don't step in to help if her family should be doing it. If they ride for the brand, let them take care of their own, tell them to do this. This is how they should honor their mothers and fathers. And plus, God likes it too. 5 If a widow truly is all by herself, I guarantee you she's relying on God to give her a hand. She's been praying every single day and every single night for help. 6 But keep a wary eye out for widows who don't really need help, but get the attention they desire with tearful sob stories. A woman who'd do that is dead already. 7 Teach people how to tell the real difference in the two. 8 Any real cowboy doesn't have to be told to take care of his family. If he doesn't, he ain't a real cowboy and is worse than an unbeliever in God's eyes.

⁹ Keep a list of the widows in need, but they need to be over sixty. They also must have been a faithful wife to their husband. ¹⁰ She must also be well respected around the area. This respect should come from her previously being a good momma, feeding hungry cowboys passing through, cleaning up those who need help, lending a hand to those who are sick, and never tiring of doing good things.

¹¹ If a young woman's husband dies, don't automatically offer her help. She'll eventually want to find another husband and her carnal desires will replace her faith. ¹² They'll soon be doing things those of the faith shouldn't do. ¹³ They'll start gossiping, being lazy, and expecting everyone else to do what they should be doing themselves. Don't enable them by doing everything for them. ¹⁴ If there is a young widow, I encourage them to find a new husband, but do it the right way. She should have children, take care of their home, and not give in to idle talk about others. These latter things just open the door to the devil to come in. ¹⁵ I know many who have quit God's outfit and traded eternity for riding for the devil.

¹⁶ If any cowgirl in the outfit has been caring for a young widow, she should continue to do so. Don't let her pass the buck to y'all. Let God's outfit care for those who really need it.

¹⁷ The cow bosses who run the outfit in a respectable manner should be treated with double respect. ¹⁸ The Good Book says, "Don't keep the draft horse from getting a bite of hay while he is pulling the swather," and "The cowboy who works deserves his pay." ¹⁹ Don't listen to someone griping about a cow boss unless they have two or three witnesses. ²⁰ But if a cow boss slips into sin, don't just correct him in private. Let everyone know you've dealt with it. That way, others will know you mean business and you don't play favorites. ²¹ I'm holding you accountable in front of God and everyone else to do what I've told you to do. Like I said, don't play favorites. Everyone must carry their own load and do what God tells them to do.

²² Don't hesitate to pray for people and lay your hands on them, but don't do what sinners do either. Keep yourself free from sin.

²³ I know your stomach causes you problems. Don't just drink water, but try a little wine and see if that helps.

²⁴ Some people's sins are as plain as the nose on their face, but others are not. ²⁵ But the same goes for good deeds. Some are real obvious, but even those nobody knows about will not go unnoticed forever.

CHAPTER 6

Anyone who is a slave should give full respect for their master. Not because of who the master is, but because of who they are. That way, God's ways are never questioned in any situation. ² Even if a slave is a believer and so is his master, that doesn't mean the slave shouldn't obey like he should. A believing slave should obey a believing master better than any other slave does.

Wannabe Cowboys and Money Hungry Horse Traders

I'm telling you these things because I want you to teach others what you've learned. ³ If anyone hears your teachings about Jesus Christ and decides to teach something different, ⁴ they are not real cowboys and know nothing. These are wannabe cowboys who are only after looking good and being admired. They'll argue with people and cause all sorts of problems like jealousy, division, and gossip, and everyone will start double-crossing everyone else. ⁵ These people are troublemakers. They have been corrupted and would trade a lame horse off as kid's horse just to turn a profit.

⁶ But those who ride with a pure heart and contentment are the real ones who will prosper. ⁷ We'll leave this world with the same amount of things we brought into the world. ⁸ If you have food in your belly and a shirt on your back, then you should be content. ⁹ Those who only want to get rich will fall into temptation and end up hung up in the stirrup of destruction. And they'll take as many people out with them as they can. ¹⁰ The love of money has caused many a great cowboy to hit the ground and never get on again. They ride off from faith, not toward it. We'll find them drug to death, run through with mesquite thorns of their own grief.

One Last Thing

¹¹ But you're a cowboy of God. Whip and spur away from all types of sin. Instead, ride straight toward a life of right living and a godly life. Ride in faith, love, perseverance, and gentleness. ¹²Be

battle tested in the fight for the true faith. Tie hard and fast to the eternity God has promised all cowboys who ride for the brand. You accepted the challenge, now finish it, and finish it well. ¹³ I'm calling you out in front of everyone, and even before Jesus Christ, who offered Pontius Pilate the grace he didn't deserve, ¹⁴ that you ride like a real cowboy should in all situations, not just the easy trails. Then, no one will be able to find fault in anything you do. Stay this way until Jesus rides back over the hill to get us all. ¹⁵ The Boss is already saddled up and ready to come get us. He won't be a minute early or a minute too late. He's going to show up right when God, the Real Boss, High King, the Almighty God tells him to. ¹⁶ He's the only one who cannot see the noose placed around his neck. The light within him shines so bright that no mortal can even look at him, much less get close to him. Every honor and glory belongs to him and him alone. Amen.

¹⁷ If a cowboy is rich, tell him not to think of himself as superior to any other cowboy. Money can come and go like a leaf in the wind. Teach him to trust only in God, not the things of this world. God will, and does, provide everything of importance we need to enjoy life. ¹⁸ Rich folks should use their money to do good things. True riches come from doing good things, not having lots of money. Tell them to be generous to those without. ¹⁹ By doing these things, they will be making deposits in heaven. Their good deeds will be the foundation of their eternal lives. It's in eternity that their true life will be revealed.

²⁰ Timothy, protect the duty God has given you. Yes, people are going to argue with you and start fights, but don't fall for the bait. They may seem smart, but their wisdom is like mud stuck in a horse's hoof. ²¹ There are many who've wandered off the trail of life by behaving like fools.

Ride with God's grace, every one of you.

2 TIMOTHY

CHAPTER 1

I, Paul, a cowboy for Christ, chosen by God, gather the lost and bring back those who have strayed away by telling others of the life promised to those who put their faith in Jesus.

² To Timothy, a man who is like a son, may you ride in grace, love in mercy, and live in peace that comes from God through Christ Jesus.

Keep Your Chin up and Your Toes Out

³ Timothy, I am more thankful to God for you than you'll ever know. I ride through this world with a clear conscience and my head held high, just like my granddaddies did. There's not a day that goes by that I don't pray for you. ⁴ I can't wait to see you again. I remember the tears we shared when we shook hands and said goodbye. That memory will stay with me until it can be replaced with another handshake when we meet again.

⁵ I recall how authentic your faith was. Your grandmother Lois and your momma, Eunice, did a good job of raising you right. Their faith continues to be strong living within you. ⁶ Don't let the fire go out by not using the gifts God gave you when I laid my hands on you. ⁷ For God did not give us the spirit of a sissy, but a spirit of strength, love, and self-control.

⁸ Don't ever be ashamed about telling someone of your love for the Lord. I ask that you not be ashamed of me either. I know what others say because I'm in prison. But I'm locked up because of my love of the Lord, not because I did something shameful. As you grow in strength, so will grow the bullseye on your back. The strength you need to endure will come from the good news, not your-

self. ⁹ God saved us and called us to ride a trail of holiness. We didn't deserve either of these, but that was his plan all along. His plan was simple—to show us grace through Christ Jesus. ¹⁰ This grace wasn't just talked about, it appeared in person as our Savior. He shattered the power of fear and death and blazed a new trail to life and immortality through the good news. ¹¹ And I was chosen to be a voice in the darkness, a teacher in times of trial and trouble, and a cowboy who gathers the lost with the good news.

¹² That's why I sit and suffer in this dark cell. But I do not hang my head in shame. I keep my chin up and my toes out as I continue to serve the Lord, regardless of my circumstance. My trust is in God and I know he is able to deliver me in life and in death as I wait upon his return.

¹³ This is the way I want you to ride. Follow this trail that I've left. It is not a trail marked by sign, but by faith and love for Christ Jesus. ¹⁴ But the power we need comes not from our own might, but by the strength of the Holy Spirit who rides with us and in us. Keep this truth locked deep in your heart.

¹⁵ You know everyone who rode with me from the province of Asia has turned tail and run, including Phygelus and Hermogenes.

¹⁶ I pray the Lord will show favor and mercy to Onesiphorus. He is one of the few who has cared for me. He never boogered at the chains on my feet or the blood on my face. ¹⁷ He even came all the way to Rome to find me. He searched every draw and coolie around until he found me. May the Lord give him a special reward for the kindness he showed, not just here in Rome, but also in Ephesus.

CHAPTER 2

Listen Timothy, you are like a son to me and you must be strong in the grace that is found in Christ Jesus. ² Teach others to ride for God the way I've taught you. Find other cowboys who can teach and show them how to truly ride.

³ When life knocks the breath out of you, suck it up just like I do. Be a great cowboy for the Boss. ⁴ Cowboys don't get messed up in city people's thoughts and desires. They only care about what the cow boss says to do. ⁵ Bronc riders won't take home a buckle if they don't get their mark out. They have to follow the rules to win. ⁶ Ranchers should enjoy a good steak they worked so hard to give others. ⁷ Think about these things and let God fill in the gaps.

⁸ Don't forget Jesus, who came from the line of cowboys from David, rode back from the dead. This is the good news I keep telling everyone about. ⁹ And because I tell others this good news, I have ended up shackled like a dog. But God's word breaks every chain. ¹⁰ This is why I never give up. I can endure anything if it helps people saddle up for eternity when they hear God's call to gather. Salvation and eternal life waits on every cowboy who rides for the brand through Christ Jesus.

¹¹ Don't forget that old cowboy saying, "Only those who die with him, live with him. ¹² If we never give up, he will give us all we ever dreamed of. If we shun him, he will shun us. ¹³ If we ride off, he will keep riding. He will not deny who he was made to be."

Dealing with Wannabe Cowboys

¹⁴ Don't let people forget who they are supposed to be. In God's name, tell them to stop bickering over words. Arguing over petty stuff never made a good cowboy, but it has ruined many who had promise. ¹⁵ Hold your head high. Make yourself the best cowboy you can be so you will never have reason to be ashamed. Speak the truth and handle it like a loaded weapon. ¹⁶ Stay away from foolish talk that leads a cowboy down the wrong trail. ¹⁷ Foolish talk is like a contagious cancer. You just have to look at Hymenaeus and Philetus to see the devastating effects of this disease. ¹⁸ They have rode off the narrow trail. They have convinced others to follow them saying there will not be a physical resurrection for the cowboys who ride for the brand.

¹⁹ But the bedrock of God's truth is inscribed with, "The Lord knows who his cowboys are," as well as, "All who ride for the brand must ride off from evil ways."

²⁰ On a nice ranch that takes care of the cowboys, some horses are good and some horses are special. The special horses are used for special occasions while the other ones are for everyday use. ²¹ Hone your skills in riding for the Lord and you will be like a special horse used for the honorable duties. Your life will be without blemish and you'll be ready for the Boss to call on you for the best jobs.

²² Whip and spur as fast as you can from anything that makes you act like a young stud with only one thing on his mind. A real stud can be ridden and used in any situation without lust grabbing ahold. This is done by living the right way, being faithful, loving others, and exhibiting peace in all you are and do. Ride with other cowboys who ride in a manner worthy of the Lord's service.

²³ How many times do I have to say it? Stay away from petty arguments that only bring quarreling and bickering. ²⁴ A real cowboy doesn't engage fools, but is kind to all, able to instruct, and patient—especially with difficult people. ²⁵ Be gentle with those who deny the truth. Only God can convince an unbeliever. Hopefully, they will tie hard and fast to the truth before it's too late. ²⁶ The truth is the only thing that can get them out of the devil's snare. Until then, they are his slaves to do whatever he wishes with them.

CHAPTER 3

The Hard Trail Ahead

Know this, Timothy! When the end is near, the trail will be very difficult. ² People's priorities will only be money and themselves. They will be arrogant and proud. Not only will they scoff at God, but their parents as well. They won't have a grateful bone in their body. Nothing will be sacred. ³ Their saddlebags will be filled with hate and unforgiveness. They'll be slaves to lust and slander. Cruelty will mark their trail and they will hate anything that is good. ⁴ They'll stab their friends in the back for a buck and puff their chests out in pride for what they've done. Their pleasure will be other's pain and they will not know God. ⁵ They will act religious, but deny the power that could change their lives into something special. Steer clear of cowboys like that.

[6] These cowboys are really snakes that slither into vulnerable women's homes with empty promises and lustful desires. [7] Vulnerable women will believe any new teaching that promises them a better life than the one they have. They will be unable to see the truth. [8] These wannabe cowboys are counterfeits. They are like Jannes and Jambres who went up against Moses. [9] But they won't get away with their falsehoods for long. Every fool will one day get what's coming to them and others will see them for who they really are.

Timothy's Final Order

[10] Timothy, you've seen how I ride and how I live. You've seen my purpose and know I've held fast. You've seen my faith, my patience, and my never-give-in attitude. [11] You've seen all the troubles I've gone through in my ride for Christ. You know all about my persecution in Antioch, Iconium, and Lystra. But remember, God got me through all of it. [12] Every cowboy who rides for the brand will suffer at the hands of the unbelievers. [13] These wannabe cowboys will ride a trail from debauchery to depravity and take many people with them.

[14] But you must remain faithful to the brand. You know the truth and you know you can trust what we say. [15] You've believed what the Good Book says and it has guided you to the salvation of Christ Jesus. [16] The Good Book is written by God to show us the trails to take and the ones to stay away from. It points out our wrongs and helps us to live right. [17] It's God's voice in the darkness that prepares his cowboys for the gathering and doctoring of the herd.

CHAPTER 4

I urge you in the name of God and Christ Jesus, who will one day give everyone what's coming to them, [2] to spread the word of God. Keep both feet in the stirrups and always be ready, no matter the season or circumstance. Never shy away from correcting or encouraging, but do both with patience and careful teaching.

[3] A time is coming when people will turn a deaf ear to the truth. They'll follow their own lustful desires and only listen to those who tell them what they want to hear. [4] They'll trade the truth for lies. [5] Keep yourself under control at all times. Don't be afraid of taking a hit for the Lord. Spread the good news and ride in the way God has called each of us to.

[6] My life is slipping away faster and faster. The time is near and my sacrifice is nearly complete. [7] I have fought the good fight. I have finished the drive. I have been, and continue to be, faithful until the end. [8] Waiting for me at the end is the trophy buckle of righteousness. The Most Righteous, Christ Jesus, will present it to me on that day. But there's not just one. One is waiting for all who've longed to meet him face to face and receive the reward for their ride.

Last Words

[9] Strike a long trot and try to get here quickly. [10] Crescens had pressing matters in Galatia. I had to send Titus to Dalmatia. But Demas just quit me flat-out. He started longing for the world's ways and rode off to Thessalonica in search of worldly pleasure. [11] Luke is here though. He hasn't given up. Find Mark and bring him with you. I have some things I need to tell him. [12] I've sent Tychicus to Ephesus. [13] When you ride through Troas, stop and get my cloak I left with Carpus. While you're there, get my writing materials and the things I've written.

[14] Alexander the metalworker did a number on me. The Lord knows his sins and he will get what's coming to him, of that I am positive. [15] If you run across him, be wary. He opposed our message and he is a strong adversary.

[16] When I was on public display against him, nobody stood up and helped me. The silence of the supporters hurt worse than anything, but I pray nothing is held against them. Fear drives people to silence, but I will not be silent. [17] But even though others deserted me, God did not. He gave me the strength to speak the good news of love, grace, and forgiveness so the outsiders would hear it. I was saved from the lion's teeth. [18] The Lord is my protector and will deliver me from every evil attack and deliver me safely to his side in his heavenly kingdom. To God be the glory forever. Amen.

Adios, Amigos

[19] Say hello to Priscilla, Aquila, and Onesiphorus and all his family. [20] Erastus stayed in Corinth to continue the gather and Trophimus was ill in Miletus last I heard. [21] Try to get here before the snow flies. Eubulus says, "Howdy!" and so does Pudens, Linus, Claudia, and all the other cowboys and cowgirls.

[22] May the Lord fill your spirit. And may his grace rule in you all.

TITUS

CHAPTER 1

Howdy boys, it's Paul again. I've given my life to God and I ride for the brand of Jesus Christ. I've been tasked with taking the outside and gathering those who want to ride for the truth and want to learn how to live for God. ² The truth I have is a guarantee of eternal life. God don't lie and that's what he's promised to those who ride for his outfit. ³ God has revealed this wonderful truth at just the right time. It's our job to spread this good news. The Boss sent me out to tell it to others and that's what I'll do with every last breath I have. He gave me a job to do and I ain't gonna let him down.

⁴ This letter is for my pard, Titus. He's like a son to me through the trails we ride and the faith we share.

I ask God now to send you grace that you don't deserve and peace that you ain't got.

The Crete Gatherin'

⁵ I left you in Crete to finish the gathering we had started. I asked you to find some cowboys who could lead other men in riding for the brand. ⁶ These ramrods, if you will, should be upstanding cowboys and have good reputations. He must be a faithful husband to his wife and his kids should believe in God without being rebellious and wild. ⁷ A ramrod is a church leader who takes care of God's outfit. That's why he should be a stand-up kind of cowboy. He shouldn't be a braggart or a hothead. He shouldn't be prone to too much whiskey, too much fighting, or a crooked horse trader. ⁸ Instead, he should enjoy having cowboys over for dinner and have a great love for do-ing the right thing. He needs to be very self-controlled and live like God has commanded us to live. ⁹ He has to believe wholeheartedly in the truth that comes from God. That way, he can teach others the truth and be able to stand up to those who are wrong.

¹⁰ There are a lot of gunsels who all they do is talk and try to lie to others. The one's I'm referring to right now are those who insist you have to have your pickle clipped in order to make it to heaven. ¹¹ These people need to have their mouths shut because they are driving people away from God with their foolish talk. Pickle clipping and selling salvation is big money and that is their god. ¹² Even one of their own men, one who could be considered a prophet in Crete, has said about them, "The people of Crete are lazy, backstabbing, no-accounts." ¹³ I haven't seen anything to change my view of this. So, don't be afraid to speak to them frankly, without any sugarcoating. It's better to hurt their feelings and bring them to faith than not say anything and let them find out how hot hell is. ¹⁴ They are like cows on loco weed. They've developed a taste for Jewish myths and old wives' tales of other people and it's killing them.

¹⁵ Good hay comes from good pastures and bad hay can only come from bad pastures. Same goes for the heart of a man. ¹⁶ There'll be many a cowboy and cowgirl who wear the cross and claim to know God, but the way they ride says something completely different. They deny God with their actions while claiming him with their words. These are charlatans, rustlers, and liars. I'd call them coyotes, but that would be too good for them.

CHAPTER 2

The Mark of a Real Man

Titus, you focus on teaching people how to ride for the brand, not just talk about the brand. [2] Teach the older cowboys how to control their temper, be respectable in all ways, and to live wisely. Their faith needs to be sound. A faith is lame without patience and love.

[3] Likewise, show the older ladies how to live a life that is honorable toward God. Their tongues shouldn't wag and they need to lay off the sauce. Instead, they should be helping each other know what is right and good. [4] These older ladies should be an example to the younger ones. They need to show them how to love their husbands and their kids. [5] They should teach them how to be wise and live without a cause for blame. Other things they should teach them are to keep busy in their homes, do good things, and to trust their husbands and take care of them as the husbands are taking care of them. This is the way God wants it and it will keep them from any shame.

[6] And we ain't done yet! Teach them younger cowboys to be responsible and wise. [7] You be the example for them by doing good things and riding like God told you to. Let every action show integrity and strength that will back up your good teaching. [8] Teach nothing except the truth and then, even when you are criticized, your critics won't have a leg to stand on. They'll end up making fools of themselves when they fall.

[9] Day hands must do what their boss tells them to do whether they like it or not. They shouldn't talk back or mumble under their breath when given something to do. [10] Tell them not to steal and instead show themselves completely trustworthy. This will make more of an impression for God on others than blowing up and acting like a tough guy.

[11] God didn't give us what we deserved, but showed his grace by allowing anyone to be able to come and ride for his brand. [12] We do this by turning away from sinful pleasures and living a life worthy of the gift God gave us. Sure, we ride through sorry pastures, but we can do so with wisdom, right living, and obedience to the Boss. [13] We all keep one eye on the horizon as we wait for our great God and Savior, Jesus Christ, to come riding back over the hill to get us. [14] He died so that we could be freed from the hobbles of sin, be cleansed from the rankness that permeated our lives, and to make us cowboys of his very own, totally committed to riding for him and gathering the lost and bringing back those who've strayed away.

[15] Teach these things! Pat them on the back when they do good and don't be afraid of chewing someone's butt for not doing what they are supposed to. Don't let anyone talk down to you as you try to raise them up right.

CHAPTER 3

Make the Good Ride

Remind the cowboys to respect the government and its authorities. Be respectful at all times and always be ready to ride for the good. [2] They shouldn't be trash-talkers and should stay a far piece from any sort of quarreling. Show them how to be humble, gentle, and kind at all times, not just when it's convenient.

[3] There was a time when we were all troublemakers. We thought we were tough, but we were merely slaves to sin, lust, and personal pleasures. Our lives were guided by our own opinions filled with evil, lust, and jealousy. It's no wonder we squabbled with everyone over everything. [4] But everything changed for us when Jesus came. [5] He saved us, not because we'd done something good, but because he did it all perfect and had mercy on our souls. He took the tally book of our sins and erased it once and for all through our new birth and new ride through the Holy Ghost. [6] God doused us with his power through Jesus Christ who saved us. [7] This is God's grace that has made us right in his sight. We are absolutely certain heaven waits on Jesus's cowboys.

[8] Don't forget any of this. Drill it into people's heads so they will saddle up every single day and ride for Jesus. There's nothing we've said that won't show people the right way, even if it seems hard.

[9] Don't get your thumb caught in the dally of silly arguments about pedigrees or whether we should follow Jewish customs. These talks are absolutely useless and a complete waste of time. [10] If someone starts causing trouble, warn them a couple of times. Everyone gets caught up sometimes and makes a mistake. But if they

continue, show them their walking papers, and have nothing to do with them. ¹¹ Don't let people who've turned away from the truth split the herd. They'll get what's coming to them.

The Final Adios

¹² I'm thinking about sending either Artemas or Tychicus your way. When one of them gets there, meet them at Nicopolis. That's where I plan on wintering. ¹³ Do anything you can to help that lawyer Zenas, as well as Apollos, with the trip they are going to make. ¹⁴ Our cowboys must learn to fill the gap. There's always something to do to help someone else. We want them to make a hand, not sit on them.

¹⁵ Everyone here says hello. Tell all the cowboys there that I'm thinking about them and I love them.

Grace to y'all.

PHILEMON

CHAPTER 1

Howdy, amigos! This is from Paul, a cowboy for Jesus Christ who is gathering the lost and the strays by telling the good news to all folks. Timothy is here with me and says hello as well.

This letter is for Philemon, a cowboy for Christ, ² as well for Apphia and Archippus. It's also for all the cowboys and cowgirls who meet in your house to learn about riding for the Lord.

³ I pray God and our Lord Jesus Christ give you grace and peace.

Saying Thanks

⁴ Philemon, I always thank God for you in my prayers. ⁵ Over and over I have heard about your faith in Jesus and your love for God's cowboys. ⁶ My prayer is that your faith will result in generosity that comes from understanding and seeing first hand all the great things we have in Jesus. ⁷ The love and comfort you've shown me has helped me and countless others.

Paul Asks a Favor for Onesimus

⁸ I write to you to ask you a favor. I could make a demand of you because it is the right thing to do in God's eyes, ⁹ but I'd rather show you the same kind of love you've shown me and just simply ask you. Consider it a simple request from a friend. I'm just an old friend who is out riding pastures and looking for strays for the sake of Christ.

¹⁰ I want you to give Onesimus a break. I have become like a father to him while locked up for my work. ¹¹ Onesimus has been of little value to you in the past, but now he has become something great for the both of us. ¹² I'm sending him back to you and my heart comes with him.

¹³ I really wanted to keep him here to help me while I'm locked up. Because he belongs to you, it would be as if you yourself were here helping me. ¹⁴ But I didn't ask you first so I'm sending him back. I really do want your help, but not if you didn't have a choice in the matter. ¹⁵ He was a slave who ran away, but now he's coming back as one of Jesus's cowboys. You lost him for a while, but now you're getting him back for good. ¹⁶ I don't want you to look at him like a slave anymore, but rather a brother like he is to me. You have not lost anything by this, but gained so much more because now you have a cowboy who rides for the Lord.

¹⁷ If you consider us pards, welcome him home just like you would me. ¹⁸ If he has a debt to you, charge me for it. ¹⁹ I, Paul, write this with my own hand: I will assume all of his debt. I won't even mention that you owe me much more for bringing you the word that saved your soul.

²⁰ This is the favor that I ask, brother. Do it for the Lord's sake. Don't let my heart be heavy in this matter.

²¹ As I write, I'm fully confident that you will do this and even more. ²² If I may be so bold as to ask for one more thing—make a room for me when I come visit. I'm hoping that your prayer for my visit will be answered very soon. I can't wait to see you, cowboy.

A Final Adios

²³ Epaphrus, a fellow cowboy in Christ, is here with me and says to tell you hello. ²⁴ Mark, Aristarchus, Demas, and Luke all send their regards as well.

²⁵ May you be filled with God's grace my friend. Adios.

HEBREWS

CHAPTER 1

Jesus: The Word and Son of God

In the old days, God used to speak to us through cowboys who were called prophets. ² But now God has chosen to speak directly to us through his Son, who he has given all things and all authority to. It is also through his Son that all the universe was formed. ³ The Son is the visible sight of God. He is the nature and character of God himself and through him everything is sustained by the power of his Word. When the Son had erased our tally book of sin, he sat down at the right hand of God in heaven. ⁴ This makes him far above any angel and his name is greater than all their names combined.

The Angels Don't Hold a Candle to Jesus

⁵ God never said to any angel the things he said to Jesus, "You are my son and today I have become your Father."

Again, God said, "I will be his Daddy and he will be my Son."

⁶ And when he'd brought his firstborn Son into the world, he said, "All my angels will bow down and worship him."

⁷ And speaking of angels, he said, "He sends his angels on the winds; his servants are like the flames of fire."

⁸ But when speaking of his Son he says, "Your throne will last forever. With justice you rule. ⁹ You love justice and deplore evil. God, your God, has lifted you higher than all others and anointed you with the oil of pure joy."

¹⁰ He also says, "You laid the foundations of the earth and the heavens are your handiwork.

¹¹ Even though all of these will fall, you will be forever. They will eventually wear out like old britches. ¹² You will fold them and throw them away for the old things they are, but you will always be the same, forever and ever."

¹³ God never said to the angels, "Sit at my right hand and take up the honor that is yours. Sit here until I conquer your enemies and make them a bench to rest your feet upon."

¹⁴ That's why I'm telling you angels are just day hands in the kingdom of Heaven compared to Jesus. They are sent here and there to tend the herd until they inherit eternal life.

CHAPTER 2

Keep Both Feet in the Stirrups

We must pay attention to the truth we have heard. We must keep both feet in the stirrups or we will become lazy and fall off or drift away. ² If the old message that the angels delivered from God made all be held accountable for the things they did, ³ do you suppose we can ignore the message delivered by someone far greater, that being Jesus Christ himself? ⁴ God proved Jesus's message true by doing miraculous things and by giving the gift of the Holy Spirit to those who he's chosen.

Jesus Was a Man

⁵ In addition, let us not think it is the angels who are in control of the future. ⁶ The Good Book did say, "Why do you bother with mere cowboys and cowgirls? Why do you even glance their way? ⁷ You made them less than angels, but still they were given honor and glory. ⁸ You gave them authority over all things."

When God said "all things", he meant all things. But this hasn't come to pass yet. ⁹ But what has come to pass is that Jesus, who was a man and a little lower than the angels for a time, is now crowned with God's glory and honor. Jesus was God's grace for us by suffering the death that should have been ours. ¹⁰ God's plan all along was to bring his kids to him by the way of suffering. But it is not through our suffering that this plan of eternal life was enacted, but through the suffering of Christ—the perfect Boss.

¹¹ So now Jesus vouches for us before his Father. Jesus makes us holy and gives us the same Father he has. This is why Jesus calls us brothers and sisters. ¹² Jesus told his Dad, "I will tell my brothers and sisters who you are. I will worship you and my cowboys will do the same."

¹³ He also said, "My life is lived trusting in God. The cowboys God gives me will do the same."

¹⁴ Because God's kids are flesh and blood, Jesus was also made flesh and blood. Only as a human could Jesus suffer death. And only through dying could he defeat the devil, who has the power of death. ¹⁵ Jesus died for us and so has freed us from the power of fear of dying. No longer are we afraid to die because Jesus did it for us.

¹⁶ Make no mistake, Jesus didn't come and do all he did to save angels. He did it all to save us, the children of Abraham. ¹⁷ In every way Jesus was like us so he could represent us on the cross. He is our high priest vouching for us before the throne of God. It was only in this way could he offer up a sacrifice that would take our place and take away our sin once and for all. ¹⁸ Since he suffered everything we have and more, he is able to lead us through temptation.

CHAPTER 3

Jesus Is More Than Moses

And since Jesus is our ramrod in heaven and God's own messenger, we must acknowledge who he really is. ² Jesus is the key to everything. He was faithful in everything God told him to do. Moses also did what God told him to, ³ but Jesus deserves much more credit. The horse trainer is worth more than the horse. ⁴ The trainer can make more, and the one who made everything is God.

⁵ Moses was most certainly a top hand for God. His work showed what God would do in the future. He took good care of God's outfit for a while. ⁶ But Christ, the Son of God, is in charge of God's outfit for all time. We are God's outfit if we stay brave and stay confident in our hope of what Jesus did for us.

⁷ The Holy Ghost says to us, "Don't turn a deaf ear to God's word. ⁸ Don't let your hearts turn to stone like Israel did when they turned their backs on me in the wilderness. ⁹ Your granddaddies tested and tried me. They saw miracle after miracle for forty years, but still looked the other way. ¹⁰ So, I got mad at them and said, 'Their hearts have forgotten me. They refuse to ride for me like I told them to.' ¹¹ That's when I decided 'They won't come through the gate to get rest or grub from my table.'"

¹² So, watch out for yourselves, cowboys. Make sure your hearts are not turning away from God and the way he told you to ride. ¹³ Open your eyes and help each other. Don't let one another be deceived by sin and turn away from God. ¹⁴ If we can stay in the saddle until our ride is over, believing and trusting in God the way we did at first, we will share in all the things that belong to Jesus. ¹⁵ Don't forget it has been said, "Today is the day you ride for him and listen to his voice. Don't harden your hearts and become rebels like Israel did long ago."

¹⁶ Think about it. Who was it who turned their backs on God even though they clearly heard his voice? It was the very people Moses gathered up out of Egypt. ¹⁷ And wasn't it them who made God mad those forty years in the wilderness? It was these sinners whose bodies still lay in the desert. ¹⁸ Who do you think God was talking about when he said they wouldn't come through his gate for rest or grub? It was the people who refused to ride for him and chose to ride for themselves. ¹⁹ It was this choice they made for themselves that kept them from God, his rest, and his grub.

CHAPTER 4

The Promise of Rest

Now listen, we've still got that promise from God. We can still have the rest he promised us, but you've got to be careful you ain't left in the dust. ² We've got the same good news as they had, but they didn't listen. Be sure you do. You do that by having faith in what you hear and then doing it. ³ Those who believe get the rest that was promised, just like God said, "I made them a promise when they made me mad, 'They won't ever get any rest.'"

God's work is done. It has been since the seventh day after he'd made it all. ⁴ He already told us this when the Good Book said, "On the seventh day, God sat down and rested because he was done." ⁵ But remember he warned, "Those who don't believe won't get any of my rest."

⁶ This all means some will still get the rest they're looking for, and others who've heard the good news and didn't trust in it, did not and will not. It ain't because God don't love them. It's because they don't love God. ⁷ He told us what day the rest was available. The day he named was "today." This happened when he talked to us through David and said, "Today, if you hear his word, don't turn a deaf ear."

⁸ The rest didn't happen when Joshua led them into the promised land. The rest is still promised to us today. ⁹ There's another rest coming. A much better one for those who ride for God! ¹⁰ All those cowboys who have finished the drive have been able to experience this rest, just like God did after creating the world. ¹¹ Set your eyes and hearts on this, cowboys. But you won't get there riding for yourself. If you do, you'll be left in the desert just like they were to rot.

¹² God's word is real. He means what he says. It is sharper than a straight edge razor. His word cuts right in between the soul and the spirit, through doubts and desires. His word lays bare who we really are. ¹³ Nothing can hide from God. Everything is naked and exposed. We will all answer to him one day and give account of the ride we made.

Jesus Is Our Trail Guide

¹⁴ Look at is this way, since our trail guide has found his way to heaven, let us follow him there through our faith. Tie hard and fast to it and don't let go or look away. ¹⁵ We ain't got a trail guide who merely met us at the end. He rode every mile just like he asks us to. He knows how hard it is and the trials and trails we will have to take. He took 'em too. But remember, he never made a wrong turn. ¹⁶ Because of this, we know that our wrong turns won't be held against us in front of God. We can go right up to him and know he sees his son's ride and not our own. This gives us the confidence we need to finish it out when the trail turns rank.

CHAPTER 5

Every trail guide who's ever been was a man chosen to lead the cowboys to God. A trail guide offers God all his sacrifices as gifts for his mistakes. ² But a trail guide needs to be understanding of the hardships of the trail because he followed the same one. ³ The trail guides before had to offer their own sacrifices for the mistakes they made as well.

⁴ No one can be a trail guide because he wants the notoriety. He must be called by God just like Aaron was. ⁵ Jesus didn't even ask to be the trail guide. He was chosen by God himself when he said, "You are my boy. Today, I have become your Dad."

⁶ Another time God said, "You are the last trail guide. You'll finish what Melchizedek started."

⁷ While Jesus still rode on this earth, he offered up tears and groans to the only one who could rescue him from the outlaw called death. And because of his faithfulness, God listened. ⁸ But just because he was God's Son, Jesus still learned what it meant to obey God. He didn't learn obedience through anything more than the hard trail he rode. ⁹ Because of this, God made him the last trail guide. The trail Jesus forged became the way to heaven for all those who ride with him. ¹⁰ God made him the last trail guide on the trail that Melchizedek started.

Don't Fall Off

¹¹ Now there's a whole bunch left to say on this subject, but I'll let it go for now. It's hard to explain and some of y'all are still greenhorns. Not because you don't know how to ride, but because you don't know how to listen or believe. ¹² You've been riding long enough now you should be teaching others how to, but you still need us to tell you to keep your butt down, toes out, and your head up. We shouldn't have to be telling y'all this over and over. This is basic stuff on riding for God. ¹³ If you ain't got out of the round pen yet, you don't know how to take on the tough trails of a ride with God. ¹⁴ Taking the outside in God's gathering is only for top hands, who've given God everything and ride for him every stinkin' day.

CHAPTER 6

So, listen up, cowboys. We've got to head out. We can't keep going talking about the basics over and over and over. You've got to get out of the round pen to become top hands. We can't get caught up again with the simple things like trusting God and staying away from sin. **²** You've heard what we've said about getting baptized, hands-on praying, resurrection of the dead, and the eternal judgment that will come. If you ain't got it by now, you probably ain't going to, **³** but we're moving out.

⁴ There ain't nothing we can do for those who have ridden for God and then gone back to the ways of the world. **⁵** They've seen what God can do and they just don't want it. **⁶** These cowboys have turned their backs on God and his grace and mercy. You just can't fix these boys. They are nailing him to the cross once again with their treachery.

⁷ When a calf crop is a hundred percent, you keep all of 'em back. **⁸** But if a herd does nothing except eat and take all the good without giving anything back, the rancher will send 'em all to the sale.

⁹ Now, we ain't saying any of this applies to you. We think God has great things in store for you. We know it! **¹⁰** God ain't wishy-washy. He has seen you ride and how hard you've worked. You cared for the sick and tended the herd like you was supposed to. We know you are still riding the pastures as we speak. **¹¹** What we are hoping for is that you will continue on the trail marked out for you. **¹²** If you do, you'll avoid the canyons that lead to indifference and thick-headedness. Instead, you'll follow the trail of those who have gone on before you. They've reached the end and have received the promises of God, just like you can. You just got to keep going and never give up or give in.

God's Promises Are Guaranteed

¹³ We ain't talking about fairy tales. Remember the promise God made to Abe? God made a promise on his own name (there is nothing greater to swear by), **¹⁴** saying, "I'm going to bless you and grow your herd bigger than any number."

¹⁵ All Abe had to do was wait on God and then get what he'd promised.

¹⁶ When people make a promise, they call on someone greater than themselves to hold them to it. A promise made like this can't be broken. **¹⁷** God made a promise on himself so

that it would guarantee what he said was true. He ain't going to crawfish on his word. **¹⁸** God made an oath and a promise. These two things are guaranteed because God can't lie. Those of us who've fled to the shelter underneath him are guaranteed what he promised. **¹⁹** Our hope is strong and we now have an anchor in the storm. We have a back cinch to keep our saddle flat when the world yanks us around. This promise leads us through the pain and straight to him. **²⁰** Jesus has marked the trail and become the last trail guide that old Mel had started.

CHAPTER 7

Old Mel, a Great Man of God

Old Mel, or Melchizedek, was the king of Salem and a great preacher who rode for the True God. When Abraham was returning to his own ranch after winning a big battle against some powerful rulers, he stopped by Mel's place and Mel blessed him. **²** Abraham was so moved by the blessing that he gave Mel ten percent of all the plunder he'd taken from the outlaw rulers. The very name, Melchizedek, means "king of justice" and Salem means "king of peace." **³** Since we have no papers to show where he came from or where he went, he resembles Jesus in that he has always and will always rule.

⁴ Now, old Mel was a great cowboy and y'all need to chew on this for a minute. Even Abraham, God's chosen man to be the first of his people, saw how great Mel was and showed his respect by giving him ten percent of the plunder he'd won. **⁵** The Code makes a ten percent tithe mandatory and all the priests descending from Levi collect it because God said to. **⁶** But Mel wasn't a descendant of Levi and he got a tenth from Abe. But it wasn't just one-sided. Because Abraham gave, Mel blessed his socks right off. **⁷** So if you're following along, consider this, the one who does the blessing is greater than the one who gets the blessing.

⁸ All those descendants of Levi who collected the tithes for the church are dead and gone. Rumor has it old Mel is still around somewhere. **⁹** You could even say those Levites who collected the tithes were kind of paying Mel a tithe because Abraham did. **¹⁰** Even though Levi hadn't been born yet, he was inside Abraham when he paid the tithe to Mel.

¹¹ So the Levites were the preachers of the Code of the Law, but obviously this code didn't make anyone perfect. That's why God came along and took us down the trail to perfection that Mel had started instead of continuing to follow the one that Levi and Aaron took.

¹² So if the trail has changed, the Law must also be changed to allow it. ¹³ The trail we follow now never came from the line of Levi. ¹⁴ Jesus came from the line of Judah, not Levi. Moses never mentioned those from Judah as being priests who showed others the trail to follow.

Jesus Is Like Mel

¹⁵ I mentioned that the trail had changed. That's because there is a new trail boss, one who closely resembled old Mel. ¹⁶ Jesus is the trail boss now. It's not because he was papered a certain way, it's because he has the power of everlasting life. ¹⁷ Even in the Psalms it talks about this when it says, "You will forever be the trail boss who leads us down the trail like Mel did."

¹⁸ All the old Code of the Law, or the old trail, was abandoned because it couldn't save people's souls. ¹⁹ The Law never made anything perfect. But now we are confident this new trail leads us straight to God.

²⁰ This new trail was blazed through the world with a solemn oath. Aaron's people never made an oath to become priests. ²¹ But God made an oath about Jesus when God said, "The Lord has made a promise and it won't ever be broken—you are the trail boss forever."

²² Because of this promise, Jesus is the one who guarantees to lead us straight to God.

²³ Every other priest and trail guide along the old trail has died. ²⁴ But since Jesus lives forever, his position as priest and trail boss lasts forever also. ²⁵ Because of this, Jesus is the only one who can save us by leading us straight to God. Jesus lives forever in order to show us the trail that leads to God. Not only does he lead us to God, but he vouches for us when we get there.

²⁶ He is the trail boss we all need. He never strayed, never wandered from the trail. He never sinned. That's why he has a place in heaven reserved only for him. ²⁷ Unlike the old trail, sacrifices are no longer needed every day. The sacrifices on the old trail were for the trail bosses' sin first, and the followers second. But Jesus didn't need to offer a sacrifice for his sin because there was none. However, he did offer himself as the sacrifice for us because we are sinful. ²⁸ The Law made men high priests, but they were still weak. But now, after the promise God made, Jesus is our priest and trail guide who absolutely leads us to perfection.

CHAPTER 8

Jesus Is Our New Trail Boss

Now we are getting to the meat of the matter. We have a trail boss who has a spot reserved for him in heaven at the right hand of the Almighty God. ² From his spot, he leads the worship in the true house of God, not one built by human hands, but built by God himself.

³ Every trail boss was supposed to offer gifts and sacrifices to God and our new trail boss does too. ⁴ If Jesus was on earth, he wouldn't even be a trail boss. There are plenty who can give gifts and make sacrifices according the old code. ⁵ They serve in a house of God that is just a fuzzy copy of the real one in heaven. This is why Moses was given instructions to build God's worship tent in a very specific way.

⁶ So you see how Jesus, our trail boss, has a ministry that far surpasses the old way. He vouches for us based on a better agreement and a better promise.

⁷ I mean, if that first agreement between God and his people was perfect, then there wouldn't be a need for another agreement. ⁸ But God knew his people wouldn't be able to follow the old trail, and really, that was the whole point. That's why he said, "There's a day coming when I'll shake hands with the people of Israel and Judah and show them a new trail. ⁹ This new agreement and new trail won't be like the old one I made with their forefathers who I led out of Egypt. They didn't stay on the trail like I told them so I let them wander away from me. ¹⁰ But this is the new agreement I'm going to make with Israel and Judah. I'll write my code on their hearts and brand it into their brains. I'm going to be their God and they're going to be my cowboys. ¹¹ They won't need to teach their neighbors or their kin. They won't have to say, 'Know God.' There'll never be another excuse for not knowing me. Everyone from top hands to wannabes will know me already. ¹² And I'm

going to erase their tally book of sins and forgive all their wickedness."

¹³ When God says he made a new agreement, it means the old one has been replaced, not added to. It has served its purpose and will soon disappear like an old trail nobody walks anymore.

CHAPTER 9

A Better and Final Sacrifice

The first agreement was full of rules and regulations on how to do things in the holiest place on earth at the time. ² One of these things regarded the way God's tent was set up. The first part of the tent was called the Holy Place. In here was a lamp, table, and some special made bread. ³ The second and innermost part of the tent was the Most Holy Place. ⁴ In here was a golden smoker and chest of God. The chest was covered in gold and inside was a jar of angel food (manna), Aaron's staff that had flowers sprouting from it, and the stone tablets that had the agreement written on them. ⁵ Watching over the ark were some angels with their wings covering the place of mercy. But listen, all of this has been lost now and so we can't go into more detail than that.

⁶ The first part of the tent was for religious ceremonies. ⁷ The holiest part of the tent was reserved for the high priest, and he only went in there once a year. When he did, he made a sacrifice for his sins and the people's sins they committed out of ignorance, not choice. ⁸ The Holy Spirit did this to show that this method was only going to be used temporarily until the perfect sacrifice could be made.

⁹ We can still see some remnants of the old way in the first part of the tent. People bring their offerings and sacrifices, but it never cleanses their guilt or their soul. ¹⁰ These things were just used in various religious ceremonies for purification and stuff. God chose this way until his true plan was set into action.

¹¹ But Christ came riding in as the last high priest, the final trail boss. His way is good and better for all of us. He didn't go through a tent to get to God, he was one with God. ¹² Jesus didn't use the blood of animals to forgive sin, he used his own blood. Since it was perfect, there never needs to be another sacrifice for those who believe in him.

¹³ The blood and ashes of animals could cleanse someone's body, but not their soul. ¹⁴ But the blood of Christ washes us all clean, inside and out. By the power of the Holy Ghost, Jesus offered himself up as the final sacrifice and cleansed our consciences from the sorry deeds we've done. Now that we are free and pure, we can ride for the living God.

¹⁵ Because of Christ's sacrifice, he pulled the new agreement out of his saddle bags and gives it freely to anyone who wants it, even those who were under the first agreement.

¹⁶ A last will and testament has no power until that person is proven dead. ¹⁷ Only after death is the will of the departed put into effect.

¹⁸ It was the death and blood of animals that put into effect the first agreement. ¹⁹ Moses passed along every command God had given him to the people. After that, he took the blood of goats and cows and sprinkled it on the book to seal the agreement. ²⁰ He said, "The blood seals the deal between God and his people." ²¹ Even after this, blood was always sprinkled on everything used in worship according to the first agreement. ²² Moses taught us that blood could cleanse nearly anything. But the wage of sin was death and something had to die to take the sinner's place in death. Without blood, there can be no forgiveness of sin.

²³ Now the things down here were just copies of what was really happening in heaven. But the real deal in heaven couldn't be cleansed with animal blood. A better sacrifice was needed. ²⁴ Jesus didn't walk into a holy place made from human hands, he went to the real deal in heaven so he could vouch for us once and for all in front of God. ²⁵ The high priest had to offer sacrifices every single year with blood that was not his. But Christ didn't have to go into heaven every single year and offer himself as a sacrifice again and again. ²⁶ He didn't have to because the sacrifice he made once was perfect and will last for all time. ²⁷ Everyone dies once and then they are judged. ²⁸ Jesus died once and then took away the sins of the world. No need to do it again if it was perfect the first time. Jesus is going to come riding back, but it won't be to save us from sin, he already did that. He will come riding over the hill again to take his cowboys who have been watching for him back home with him forever.

CHAPTER 10

Christ's Job Is Done

That old agreement between God and his people was just the shadow on the ground of the real thing to come. Every single year, every sacrifice had to be made again and again. Animal blood just couldn't get the job done for very long. The cleaning it gave just wasn't pure. Following rules and sacrificing animals couldn't make anyone perfect. **²** If it could've made someone perfect, then there wouldn't by any need for more sacrifices. There'd have been no feeling guilty for anyone. **³** Quite the contrary, those animal sacrifices did nothing except to remind the people of their sins every year. **⁴** You've heard us say it and we'll say it again, the blood of bulls and goats doesn't take away sin. **⁵** That was Christ's job. He even said to God, "You didn't want more animal sacrifices or more sin offerings. You've given me a body to use as a sacrifice. **⁶** Burnt offerings or otherwise were not good enough. **⁷** Then I said, 'I'm here to do the job you sent me to do just like the Good Book said.'"

⁸ Let's look at this. First, Christ said, "You didn't want more animal sacrifices or more sin offerings. You didn't want a burnt offering or any other kind because they couldn't get the job done." They were still required by the code of Moses, but that was just to hold down the fort until Jesus could come in and save the day. **⁹** Then Christ said, "I'm here to do the job you sent me to do." He cancels out the need for the first code in order to make mandatory the second code (agreement). **¹⁰** It was God's plan all along to make us holy by the sacrifice of Jesus Christ once and for all—no if's, and's, or but's.

¹¹ Under the old code, a man of God would stand before the altar and do the same thing again and again and again, but it never took away one sin. **¹²** But our Man of God, Jesus, gave himself as an offering to God one time and it took sins away for all time. When his job was done, he got to sit down at the right hand of God who is on the throne of thrones. **¹³** Jesus waits as his enemies are humbled and become a footstool under his feet. **¹⁴** His one sacrifice made perfect all those who are being made holy by riding for his brand every day.

¹⁵ The Holy Ghost agrees when he says, **¹⁶** "This is the new code for my people says the Lord, it's not written on stone this time, but in their hearts and on their minds." **¹⁷** Then he says, "I have forgotten their sins and sorry deeds forever."

¹⁸ Since there is no more sin to be forgiven, there is no more need for animal sacrifices.

Getting up Close to God

¹⁹ So, here's the deal now, we can walk right into the throne room of God because of what Jesus did for us. **²⁰** His death threw open the gate to God's ranch and the throne room where he resides. **²¹** Since Jesus runs God's house now, **²²** we can walk right in because we ride for him. We no longer feel guilty or ashamed because we have been washed clean by the blood of Christ.

²³ Let us tie hard and fast to the hope we've been given. God don't crawfish on his promises. **²⁴** We need to ponder on ways to encourage one another to love others and do great things. **²⁵** Don't forget, as some have the habit of doing, that it's important to sit around the campfire and share each other's company. Give encouragement and spur each other on to good deeds—more and more as you see the Day comin' fast.

²⁶ Listen cowboys, if you continue to live sinfully after you've been forgiven, you're digging your own grave. No sacrifice will cover that. **²⁷** The only thing you'll have to look forward to is the last few breaths you have. God's judgment and a raging fire is what waits for you. **²⁸** If anyone disobeyed the code of Moses, they were put to death if there were two or three witnesses. **²⁹** It'll be so much worse now. To continue to sin after you've been forgiven is like walking over the body of Jesus like a doormat, wiping your feet off on him. Do you really think God is going to be okay with that? That is blasphemy of the Holy Spirit and God will not have mercy on the cowboy who does it. **³⁰** We weren't deaf when we heard him say, "I'm on my way and I will have my revenge." He also said, "The Lord's going to judge his riders."

³¹ Listen, you'd better get your heart right. It won't be pretty to fall into the hands of the living God.

³² Think back when you first saddled up with Christ. Even through hard times, you kept the faith back then. **³³** You lost friends and jobs, but you still found time to help others who were suffering. **³⁴** Shoot, you suffered right along with them and were thrown into jail. When everything was taken from you, you didn't bat an eye. You even called it joy. You knew there was something better waiting on you in the next life. The next life will be forever and perfect.

35 So don't throw all that away. Keep trusting in God and having the confidence you once had in Him. There's a great reward waiting on the faithful. **36** You just keep on keeping on. Keep on riding for him and everything will be fine, but not easy. Only then will you get what you've been promised.

37 "It won't be long before the one who is coming back will ride over the hill. He won't be late. **38** My cowboys will ride by faith, but I won't tolerate anyone who drinks from my well and turns his back on me."

39 But we aren't like the ones who've turned their backs on the Lord. They will suffer for their actions. We are the faithful. We will be saved.

CHAPTER 11

A Heapin' of Faith

Now faith is being full of hope and plumb certain of what lies over the hill that we cannot see. **2** Back in the old days, this is what people lived by and that brought a smile to God's face.

3 It's faith that helps us see that God made everything in the universe and we don't need more explanation than that.

4 It was Abel's heapin' of faith that helped him bring a sacrifice to God that was worthy of what it was supposed to be. Cain's was not. Abel's sacrifice showed his faith in God and God showed his approval. Even though Abel has long been in the grave, his example still speaks.

5 It was because Enoch had a heapin' of faith that he was taken up to heaven without dying. Before he left, he had a reputation as being someone God admired. **6** You can't please the Boss without a heapin' of faith, because in order to knock on his door you must believe that he's there and he surely gives favors to those who know where to look and who to ask.

7 It was by a heapin' of faith that Noah built him a big boat for his family to ride out the storm that wiped everyone else out. It was as simple as listening to God and doing what he said—even though no one had even heard of such a thing happening before. Noah's faith was the dividing line between who was saved and who was lost.

8 It was by a heapin' of faith that Abraham saddled up and rode off to new country like God told him to. God said there was a great inheritance waitin' on him. He rode off without a clue as to where he was going. **9** Even when he rode in to the new country, he lived there purely by faith in their cowboy teepees. Same goes for his kids, Isaac and Jake. They received the same promise their daddy had. **10** But what ol' Abe was really waiting on was a city with foundations that would last forever built by God's own hands.

11 It was by a heapin' of faith that Abe's wife Sarah was able to have a kid. She was way too long in the tooth and she was dry to boot. A child had to come from God and she believed that God keeps his word. **12** A whole new nation came from one old cowboy with one foot in the grave. This new people, God's own people, numbered more than the rocks in the rivers and the stars in the sky. You couldn't have counted them any easier than counting every blade of grass in a hundred years' worth of hay bales.

13 All of them died, but they died with God's promise of a better life on their lips. They didn't get it in their lifetime, but they got to see it and it made them glad. They knew they were just day hands on this earth and that their home was in the next life. **14** It's obvious these day hands were looking forward to a ranch they could call their own. **15** If they hadn't, they'd have ridden back to the sorry ranch they came from and forgot all about what was to come. **16** But no, they set their eyes on something bigger and better that was just over the final hill—their forever home in heaven. And it is there that God is waiting on his hands. He ain't ashamed to call them his crew and he has something amazing waiting on them.

17 It was a whole heapin' of faith that allowed Abe to offer up his only boy Isaac as a sacrifice. God wasn't really going to let him do it. With great promises come great tests. **18** Abe knew God had promised him that through Isaac he would have descendants. **19** You ain't got to understand everything to have a heapin' of faith. If Isaac did die, Abe knew God had the power to bring him back. And in a way, that's what happened.

20 It was through a heapin' of faith that Isaac blessed his sons, Jake and Esau.

21 It was because of a heapin' of faith that in Jake's last days, he blessed each of his grandsons while worshiping God and leaning on his sortin' stick.

²² It was by a heapin' of faith that during Joseph's last days on earth, he knew for certain all his people would leave Egypt. He even told them to take him back and bury his bones in the land that had been promised.

²³ It was by a heapin' of faith that Moses's momma hid him in the brush for three months after he was born. They knew Moses was a gift from God and was something special so they defied the king's order.

²⁴ It was by a heapin' of faith that Moses didn't want to be known as the son of the Pharaoh's daughter. ²⁵ He chose to share the burden of his own kin instead of the pleasures of sin. He figured it was better to ride hard for the Lord rather than take it easy with the gold and sin of Egypt. ²⁶ He swapped the glamorous trinkets of Egypt for the suffering of Christ. The easy way down here leads to a box canyon while the hard trail leads to life everlasting. ²⁷ It was a heapin' of faith that helped Moses ride away from Egypt without giving a second thought to what the king would say about it. Faith helps you keep an eye on the one who cannot be seen. ²⁸ It was a heapin' of faith that helped Moses command all the cowboys and cowgirls of Israel to put blood on the doorposts so the assassin angel wouldn't get their firstborn boys.

²⁹ It was by a heapin' of faith that the cowboys and cowgirls of Israel rode right through the Red Sea like they were on a dry trail. When the Egyptians tried to follow, they were swallowed up and drowned.

³⁰ It was by a heapin' of faith that the cowboys and cowgirls rode around Jericho for a week and then the walls of the town crumbled.

³¹ It was by a heapin' of faith that a whore named Rahab helped two Israelite spies and in return she was allowed to escape the calamity that fell on the city. All those who didn't trust in God were destroyed.

³² What more can I say? We don't even have time to talk about the faith of Gideon, Barak, Samson, Jephthah, David, Samuel, and all the rest of God's cowboys. ³³ It was a heapin' of faith that made them overthrow kings, lead with justice, and receive God's promises. The mouths of lions were closed, ³⁴ flames of fire were put out,

and the edge of the sword bore no harm. Weaknesses became strengths and the strengths won battles and scourged entire armies. ³⁵ Cowboys who were thought dead even rode back to the gals who were waiting on them.

But not everyone fared so well. Some were killed because they wouldn't turn their backs on God. They could have lived, but they chose to receive the reward that's waiting in the next life instead of the continued pain of this one. ³⁶ Many cowboys and cowgirls were made fun of and ridiculed. Their backs were torn to ribbons by the whip while others wasted away in chains. ³⁷ Others were killed by stones or pulled in half, while many died by the sword. Some had only animal skins for clothes and wandered the land as outcasts without friends or family. ³⁸ These folks were too good for this world even though they had to live in holes in the mountains and deserts.

³⁹ These cowboys and cowgirls were never able to tie on fully to the promise of God. ⁴⁰ God had something better in mind. He had them wait for us so we could all unite in faith together to receive the blessing together as one.

CHAPTER 12

Since there are so many cowboys and cowgirls around, let's cut the hobbles of sin that are keepin' us tied down. Let us ride with strength and power in the gatherin' we've been called to. ² Never take your eyes off of Jesus, the founder of our faith, who gave everything up and took himself to the cross and didn't care about the shame it caused him, and then hunkered down at God's right hand. ³ Think of how bad people treated him in the end and you won't be feeling so sorry for yourself and start giving up. ⁴ Sure, your struggle with sin is rough, but in reality, it is just a little crow-hop compared to the broncs others have rode.

⁵ Don't forget the teachin' God gave you as his kids. He said, "Listen, son. Take your butt chewin's like a man and don't swell up and pout when the Lord gets on to you. ⁶ The Lord corrects those he loves and he will even lay out some punishment that is good for his children."

⁷ If you're going through God's guidance, remember he's treating you like one of his kids. No father worth his salt would let his kids do

whatever they wanted. **8** If God doesn't discipline you then it means you are a bastard and don't have a father. **9** We all had fathers, or men in that role, who corrected us and we showed them respect. Do the same with God.

10 Our earthly fathers tried to discipline us and do a good job. But God's discipline is always perfect and always right and always good for us. This is how he teaches us to be holy. **11** No one likes a butt chewin' while it's happening, but if we will listen and do what God says we will be riding better than we were the day before.

12 So stack another dally on the horn and lift your chin up in order to strengthen those weak knees. **13** Keep your eyes on the trail so you will not wander off like a weakling into the brush, briars, and box canyons.

Listen and Do What Is Right

14 Get along to the best of your ability with everyone and don't give up riding for the Lord. Those who don't ride for him won't see him. **15** Keep an eye on your pards so they don't slip and fall out of the saddle and become trampled. Don't hold grudges. You can't ride for God toting a grudge. The worst part is that they are contagious. **16** Don't let anyone fall into immorality and sexual sin. Don't let anyone act a fool like Esau did. He traded his birthright for a bowl of stew. **17** Later, he wanted his dad to bless him, but he was rejected because of that one stupid choice. Not even the bitter tears could take back what he'd willfully done.

18 You haven't come to a mountain full of fire, wind, and brimstone like the Israelites did at Mount Sinai. **19** When God spoke, it was too terrible for them and they begged him to stop. **20** When they heard God say that if even an animal steps foot on the mountain it must be killed, they quaked in their boots. **21** Even Moses was shaking as he said, "I am terrified."

22 No, you have come to another mountain—Mount Zion. This is the city of the living God. In Jerusalem, angels have gathered together to worship and fill the city with joy. **23** This is where God's firstborn kids have gathered. Each of their names is written in heaven. You have come before God himself, the righteous Judge over all things. Here is gathered all the good people who have been made perfect. **24** You have come before Jesus himself, the one who ushered in the new code of God, the new agreement between him and his cowboys. This is where the blood of Christ offers forgiveness instead of vengeance like the blood of Abel did.

25 You'd best listen when God is speaking to you. If the Israelites were not cut any slack for not listening to God through Moses, then we will surely be held more accountable when God is speaking directly to us from heaven! **26** God's voice shook the earth when he spoke from Mount Sinai. But now God speaks of another promise, "Once more I will shake the earth with my voice, but also that of heaven." **27** This means that one day everything will be shaken and destroyed. Only unshakeable things will be left.

28 We have been given a spot in the kingdom that is unshakeable. Let us ride for him and his kingdom by being thankful and worshiping him with fear and respect. **29** God is a fire that can cleanse or destroy.

CHAPTER 13

Keep on loving others as if they were your own brother or sister. **2** Open up your ranch gates to others. Some have been hospitable to angels and didn't even know it. **3** Don't forget those who've been thrown into prison. Pray for them as if you were right there with 'em. Don't forget those who are riding the roughest trails. Remember them as if you were suffering right alongside them.

4 Marriage should be held in the highest regard. The marital bed must be kept pure. It is just the husband and wife and no one else. God will judge those who are immoral and those who cheat on a marriage.

5 Don't have a hankerin' for money. Be glad about what ya got, because the Big Boss has said, "I ain't never gonna leave ya, nor forsake ya."

6 So we are more'n confident when we say, "The Lord rides beside me. I ain't afraid of nothing. People don't scare me at all. What could they do?"

7 Remember your teachers, leaders, and mentors who taught ya how to ride for the Lord. Remember how they lived and ride like they did.

8 Jesus ain't changing a lick. He's the same every day. **9** Don't listen to those selling new ideas. God's grace is what makes you strong, not following rules about food.

[10] We have a sacrifice religious folks can't eat from. [11] Under the old code, priests brought the blood into the Holy Place, but left the bodies outside. [12] Jesus suffered and died outside the gates as well. His blood made his cowboys holy. [13] Let us not be afraid to venture outside the gates and suffer as he did. [14] Do not think this shell and this dirt is our forever home. We look forward to a new place that is perfect and without fault. A home that is to come.

[15] Because of all this, we should offer a sacrifice of continuing thankfulness to God. We should steel ourselves to ride for him every single day. [16] Ride hard, help others, and share what you have. These are the kinds of sacrifices that make God smile.

[17] Listen to those who God has appointed to lead you. Do what they say to do. They are held accountable to God for your guidance. Their work should be rewarding so don't make things hard on them. They shouldn't be filled with sorrow for their great works. Nothing good will come from you treating them ill.

[18] Pray for us. We hold our heads high and live the lives God has commanded us to. [19] Pray that I can ride back and see y'all soon.

[20] I pray that the God of peace, who raised Jesus from the dead, the great cowboy, the originator of the new code, [21] may he give you everything you need to ride for him. May he make you into the cowboy or cowgirl, through the power of Jesus Christ, he has called you to be that is pleasing to him. All honor and glory to him forever, amen.

[22] I can't stress enough to y'all how much you should listen to the things I've written here for you. [23] Timothy has been let out of jail. If he comes here, we will ride over together to see y'all.

[24] Say hello to everyone for me. The cowboys from Italy send their regards.

[25] God's grace rides with you.

JAMES

CHAPTER 1

My name is James and I ride for, and only for Jesus Christ. I'm writing to the twelve outfits of Israel and I offer a heartfelt handshake to all of 'em!

Be Happy Even during the Hard Stuff

² Listen up cowboys, don't sweat it when you go through the rough and rank patches of life. Shoot, you ought to be glad you go through them because it's these things that'll sure enough make a man out of ya. These times will knock the quit right out of ya and your ³ faith will be ever the stronger because of what ya went through. ⁴ And if you keep on keepin' on, you'll make a top hand yet. There won't be nothin' you won't be able to tackle or ride. ⁵ But don't forget about being smart in the ways of God. If you lack the knack of wisdom, just ask the Boss for it and he'll give it to ya. ⁶ You've got to truly believe he's gonna give ya what ya ask for. If you're a doubter, you ain't no more solid than rollin' paper blown away by the wind. ⁷ The Boss ain't gonna give a saddle to the fella who can't decide if he wants to walk or ride. ⁸ Them double-minded folks ain't no more stable than a one-legged eatin' table.

⁹ Now the lowly cowboy should be happy in his high position. ¹⁰ But them rich folks better have a humble air about 'em because they ain't no different in the grand scheme of things than any other blade of grass by the pond. ¹¹ That old sun can dry up the deepest of water holes and then every blade of grass withers away. Same thing goes for the rich folks ridin' down the trail; they will waste away. ¹² That fella who keeps on ridin', even when it's hard, he will prove he is authentic and get the great things the Boss has planned for those who love him like a dad they never had. ¹³ Don't ever catch yourself thinkin' or sayin' God's trying to get you to ride somewhere or do somethin' that ain't right. The Boss can't be seduced by such things and he ain't gonna do that to you either. ¹⁴ We all go the bad way, not because of anything God does or doesn't do, but just because we have a natural desire for the wrong ways. ¹⁵ Then when desire calves out, it gives birth to sin, and when sin comes to full weight, it turns right into death. ¹⁶ Don't go chasin' them foolish notions, cowboys. ¹⁷ All good things and good horses come from the Boss, who don't ever change or falter. ¹⁸ He had the old trail marked out with truth since the beginning. We are, out of everything on his ranch, his favorite accomplishment.

Walk the Walk

¹⁹ Don't let your dally slip on this next part! Be quick to lend an ear, slower'n molasses in winter to open your mouth, and chain up your temper and lock it up tight. ²⁰ Livin' and ridin' right don't include a quick fuse or sharp tongue. ²¹ Unload all the filth you've been carryin' around and listen to the word that can save your sorry souls. ²² You best walk the walk and not just spin a good yarn. Doin' so is just lyin' to yourself. ²³ Just listenin' and not doin' is like someone lookin' at themselves in a reflection. ²⁴ If someone just listens to something from God and doesn't act on it, it's like lookin' at your own reflection and then ridin' off and forgettin' what you look like.

²⁵ But the cowboy who focuses on what God says, and doesn't go off and forget it, he will be looked after favorably. ²⁶ If someone thinks he is followin' the right trail, but shoots his mouth off at every occasion, he has lied to himself and he may be sittin' tall in the saddle, but he ain't got a horse to ride or an honest leg to stand on. ²⁷ If you want to follow the true and perfect trail, this is what the Boss says to do—care for kids without mommas or daddies, look out for widows who are having a hard time, and don't live like those no-account counterfeits who do what everyone else is doing.

CHAPTER 2

If you're ridin' for the Lord, don't go to shunnin' some folks and favorin' others. ² If one fella comes in with boots and a hat, and another walks in with raggedy short britches and worn out toe-thong sandals, ³ do you shake the cowboy's hand and ignore the other guy? ⁴ If you do, then you are judgin' wrongly and you ain't no better'n a coyote. ⁵ Listen up cowboys! Didn't the Boss choose the poor and ragtag to be rich in faith and in line for the ultimate inheritance for those who love to ride for him? ⁶ But you've been lookin' down your nose at those less fortunate. Are they the ones takin' people to court and makin' life hard for people or is it the rich? ⁷ Aren't the rich the ones who are ridin' down the wrong road and talkin' crap about the Boss? ⁸ But if you uphold the highest standard in the Good Book, "Take care of your neighbor as good as you take care of yourself," you are ridin' the right trail. ⁹ But if all you do is ride by those less fortunate than you or who are different than you, then it is you who is the scoundrel and will be treated as such. ¹⁰ You can't pick and choose which of the Boss's standards you want to follow. If you willingly ignore one, then you might as well ignore 'em all. ¹¹ The Boss has already told us, "Don't jack with another man's Jenny," and he also said, "Don't dare commit murder." If you've done one, then you've done the other in the Boss's eyes. ¹² Walk and talk like a cowboy who will be judged by the standard that sets men free. ¹³ There will be no mercy waitin' on a cowboy who never showed anyone else such a thing. But mercy trumps judgment every single time.

Faith and Works Go Hand in Hand

¹⁴ What good is a faith that only goes as far as their lips? Is a person a cowboy if he claims to have a saddle, but it's never seen a set of pockets or a mount? Can faith that is never used actually save someone? ¹⁵ If a guy or gal only has rags to wear and not enough food for every day, ¹⁶ and a cowboy says to them, "Ride tall in the saddle my friend and stay warm and eat well," but doesn't offer to help them, what good is it to say such things? ¹⁷ Faith without works is like a saddle without a horse. ¹⁸ Now some folks will mouth-off and say that if they have faith, they don't have to do anything. But I say that a saddle ain't nothin' but a decoration if it ain't on a horse and being used. Same goes for faith and works. ¹⁹ Do you want a cookie for saying the Boss is real? Shoot, even demons know that—and crap their pants in fear.

²⁰ So you want me to prove that like a saddle without a horse is useless, so faith without works is the same? ²¹ Wasn't the great cowboy Abraham right in God's eyes because he came within an instant of sacrificing his boy Isaac? ²² His faith was workin' and it was by these works that his faith was perfected. ²³ And the good words from the Good Book were proven true when it said, "Abraham trusted God with his faith and actions and this made him right in the Boss's eyes," and he was called the Boss's pard. ²⁴ A cowboy is made right with God by putting his faith to work, not just by talkin' about it. ²⁵ Even Rahab the hooker was made right in the Boss's eyes because she helped out the Israelite spies and kept them safe. ²⁶ A body without its soul is dead, and faith without works is also deader'n a doornail.

CHAPTER 3

Bridle Your Tongue

Ain't many of you will be called to teach others how to ride for the Boss's outfit because you know these cowboys will be judged more strictly. ² Many of us have fallen off in many ways. Only someone who is perfect has stayed in the saddle in every situation, and is able to control every part of their body without ever losing a stirrup or their deep seat. ³ You know that a bit in a horse's mouth can control his whole body. ⁴ Even a big ship is controlled by a tiny rudder. ⁵ So too is the tongue a small part of the body that can have a big impact on a life. Even a small spark can start a brush fire. [6] The tongue is like a raging fire. Thousands of people set fire to the world with tongues they do not try to control. No wonder this world has gone to hell.

[7] There ain't nothing in the world that hasn't been tamed by man. [8] Well, nothing except the tongue; it is an evil bronc that can't be rode, full of malice and might. [9] We pray to God with one side and then turn right around and talk crap about those who were made in his very image. [10] Ain't no reason in the world why blessings and curses should come out of the same hole in your face. [11] A windmill don't pump good water one minute and sewer water the next, does it? [12] Can you get a filly from a cow or a heifer from a mare? Salt water doesn't become fresh by putting it in a clean cup.

A Real Ride Starts with Wisdom

[13] Who among you cowboys rides with wisdom and understanding? Good manners and honest ways, with a gentle countenance, mark the ride of a wise cowboy. [14] But if your way is riddled with bitter jealousy and always lookin' out only for yourself, don't go around braggin' and lyin' about who you really are. [15] This ain't wisdom. It's nothin' but evil and worldly . . . even demonic. [16] Where there's a cowboy ridin' in selfishness and jealousy, there's a cougar in the calvin' pen. [17] You'll know cowboys who are ridin' with wisdom because they'll leave a trail of peace, mercy, justice, gentleness, good deeds, hospitality, and no ounce of hypocrisy. [18] These peacemakers will plant seeds of goodness and get a bumper crop of right living.

CHAPTER 4

The Good and the Bad

Why are all y'all squabblin' about everyone and everything? Is it not because you have a battle goin' on inside you? [2] You want and want, yet do not have; you slay and lust, but you cannot get; you start fights and argue over everything. You don't have what you really need because you don't ask for it. [3] You don't get what you ask for because the things you are asking for come from your evil desires and lustful passions.

[4] You double-crossers, do you not realize that by making friends with the world you are making an enemy of the Boss? [5] Did you think God was just listening to himself talk when he said, "The spirit I gave you don't take kindly to fence jumpers"? [6] But the Boss is above and beyond generous. That's why the Good Book says, "God shuns the proud, but always makes a spot for the humble." [7] So ride in the way the Boss has told you to. Turn your back on the devil and he will hightail it away from you. [8] Spread your bedroll next to the Boss and he will keep the fire warm and the wolves away. Wash your hands of the filth you've been living in and quit ridin' for the Boss during the day and the devil by night. [9] The way you've been living should break your heart. Them old ways you used to love ought to bring you pain. [10] Be willing to do anything and everything for the outfit without complaint or grumble and the Boss will make you a top hand.

[11] Don't stab other cowboys in the back. Anyone who speaks against a fellow cowboy speaks against what God has to say. If you speak against what God has to say then you are placing yourself above Him. [12] There is only One cowboy whose word is true and he is able to save or destroy. So let's just ask the question, who do you think you are?

[13] Here's somethin' for all who go around saying stuff like, "Today I'm gonna ride into town and tomorrow I'm gonna start breakin' horses and start my own business." [14] What do you know of tomorrow? You think so mighty of yourself that you can predict your own future? Cowboy, you ain't nothing more than smoke off a calf's branded hide. You are here for a second and then you're gone. [15] If you had any brains and were of a mind to listen, this is what you'd say instead, "I'm gonna check with the Boss before I do anything." [16] But no, you've got everything figured out and you're expecting God just to go along with whatever you want to do. There ain't nothin' right about doing things that way. [17] So let this be a warning, whoever knows the way they should do something and they do it otherwise, they are guilty of sin.

CHAPTER 5

If You're Rich, You Better Watch Out

Take a deep seat all you who are rich. You think you've got it easy, but there's a mess of trouble headed your way. ² Your money will rot and moths will eat your best clothes. ³ Even your gold and silver has corroded with rust and it will be this rust that will testify against what you've done with your money. That rust is gonna spread across you like a burning range fire. You have hoarded your treasure and it has nailed you to the stake. ⁴ You haven't even paid the cowboys who gathered your pastures or the good, hard-working folks who put up your hay. They've spoke words against you to the Lord and the Lord is listening. ⁵ You're full of pleasure and plenty, but all this is just like grain you've been feeding yourself for the slaughter to come. ⁶ You've thrown the weight of your money around and it has crushed those who were living right and working hard.

Patient Suffering

⁷ So be patient cowboys. It's just like a rancher who patiently waits on the spring and fall rains that grow the grass his cows eat. In his patience, he watches his herd grow fat and hearty. ⁸ Park your horse under a strong cedar and have courage as you wait on the Lord to come ridin' back . . . and he ain't far off now. ⁹ Don't moan and complain about what others do and you won't be judged; and the Judge is standing at the gate. ¹⁰ If you want to see what patience and riding the hard trail looks like, all you have to do is peek in at those cowboys who are often called prophets. ¹¹ To ride further and harder than anyone else is an honor. A man don't make a name for himself by sitting around twiddlin' his thumbs. Think about that Job fellow. His life and the trail he rode proved the Lord looks after and cares for those who ride for Him. ¹² And one last thing, pards. Don't be swearing you'll do this or that. Just let your yes mean yes and your no mean no.

Hit Your Knees and Pray

¹³ Have any of you felt like life has bucked you off and stomped a mud hole in you? That fellow should pray. Is anyone feeling mighty blessed? Let loose in song! ¹⁴ Is anybody feeling poorly? He should ask the leaders of the church to pray for him and they will rub some oil on his head in the name of the Lord. ¹⁵ No sickness can stand against a faithful prayer. The Lord will then sit 'em tall in the saddle, ready to ride. The Lord is so good that even if that guy has been sinning, all of those sins will be thrown in the brush and forgotten. ¹⁶ So if you've done some things you ain't proud of, go to another cowboy and tell 'em about it and your heart will no longer be heavy. A fellow who rides hard and straight, his prayers are strong and they get the job done. ¹⁷ Shoot! Even Elijah was just a cowboy like us and he prayed God would stove-up the rains and it didn't rain for three and a half years. ¹⁸ Then he hit his knees and prayed and God turned the water back on. Them dry pastures drank deeply and grew once again.

¹⁹ Listen cowboys, if any fellow strays from the narrow trail and someone brings him back, ²⁰ he should know that he has saved him from being drug to the fire. There ain't nothing better you can do for a man than to bring him back to the One who does the forgivin' of sins.

1 PETER

CHAPTER 1

Howdy, boys! It's me, Pete, a ramrod in the outfit of Jesus Christ.

I'm sending out this message to all the day trash who were driven out and scattered across the mountains and the prairies. ² God planned all along to make y'all his cowboys, his holy people, which is the work of the Holy Ghost. God wanted y'all to ride for him and him alone and to be washed in the blood of his Son's sacrifice.

May your ride with God be filled with grace and peace.

A New Ride of Hope

³ God is good, cowboys. God's mercy gave us something to hold on to that won't ever let go of us. This is the new life we've been given. It's full of hope and wonder through Jesus's ride back from death. ⁴ Now we are just waiting to receive the full amount of blessings God has promised to his kids. These blessings are waiting on you in heaven where they can't be chewed on by mice or ruined by moths.

⁵ God has your back because of your faith in him. He'll keep you until the day you'll join him over the final hill. Your salvation is just waiting on you, cowboy. ⁶ I know you're excited about the great things to come, even though you know the brush and hell you'll have to ride through to get there. But in the end, it'll all be worth it. ⁷ These troubles make your faith stronger and make you authentic. Faith like this is worth more than all the cash and cattle in the world. Gold can be made pure through fire, but pure gold can ruin a man. Your faith will not.

⁸ Even though you haven't seen Jesus, you still love him. You can't see him with your eyes, but you believe in him with your heart. You have a joy inside of you that cannot be explained. ⁹ Your ride with God is not aimless. You have a destination in mind and that is your salvation and coming home to God.

¹⁰ The old cowboys who rode for God studied hard and tried to figure out the grace that was coming. ¹¹ Jesus's Spirit was with them and whispered of his sufferings and how you would benefit from them. Those old cowboys desperately wanted to know what this new ride of hope would look like. And now you get to ride it.

¹² Everything these old cowboys did was not for themselves. They were looking out for you when they told of what God had showed them about the future. You have heard about the future they were shown when those you know shared with you the good news of Jesus Christ through the Holy Spirit. Shoot, even the angels long to know more about these things you were told.

A Holy Ride

¹³ Get your minds wrapped around being a servant because that's what you've been called to be. Be self-controlled and ride with hope in the grace that is yours when Jesus comes riding back to get us. ¹⁴ Before, you only rode for yourself and did whatever you wanted to do. But now you are children of God and we ride for him and do whatever he wants us to. ¹⁵ Do the right thing in all you do. This is the way to ride for God and he chose you. ¹⁶ Don't forget what the Good Book says, "Be holy because I am holy."

[17] You talk to God and call him your Father, but he ain't going to cut you no slack. Everyone will answer for the lives they live. So, while your time on earth is short, make it a good ride. Ride with respect toward God and all he has done for you. [18] The way you used to live is useless to you now. You didn't know any better so you just did what everyone else was doing. But you have a new boss now who is showing you a better way. You were purchased from death at a terrible price that was not silver or gold. [19] The currency used to buy you was the blood of Jesus. He was the only one pure and perfect enough to be the sacrifice that took away your sins. [20] He was chosen for this ride before the world was made, but now you have had the opportunity to witness it. [21] It is through Jesus that you have faith in God. And it is this God who raised Jesus from the dead and will raise you too if you believe and hope in Him.

[22] Now that you have been made pure through doing what God has told you to do, you will be able to love others like you're supposed to. Love each other with all you've got—hold nothing back. [23] You have been made new! This new life isn't made from something perishable, but imperishable. You were made new through the good news that lasts forever and ever. [24] The Good Book says, "Our lives are like the grass in the spring, and any honor we enjoy is like the flowers in the field; though the grass and flowers will fade and die, [25] the word of the Lord lasts forever."

And this is the word that was given to you.

CHAPTER 2

So, pop your dallies on all malcontent behavior. Shuck yourself loose from all deceitful horse tradin', two-faced actions, jealousy, and all manner of negative talk. [2] Like a new foal, you must have a desire for the milk that will help you grow and be strong in your new salvation. Don't let nothing get in the way of heavenly nourishment. [3] Soon, you will have a taste for God's love and kindness.

The Rock in the Corner

[4] You are riding toward Christ, who is the rock in the corner of God's house. He was thrown out by his own people, but chosen by God to do great things and have great honor.

[5] And you are also living rocks God will use to construct a spiritual sanctuary. Not only that, but each of you cowboys are his holy men spreading his message. Your sacrifice will not be in blood, but in the life you give to God through Jesus Christ. [6] The Good Book says, "I'm putting a rock in the corner of Jerusalem. He is chosen for a great honor and anyone who rides for him will never be turned away."

[7] Y'all know what I'm talking about. Y'all who ride for him have seen the glory given to him by God. But for those who turn away from him, the Good Book says, "The rock the builders found unworthy has now become the cornerstone."

[8] It also says, "He is the rock that knocks them down."

They will get knocked down because they do not do what God says to do. When you don't do what God says and let him save you, you'll get what's coming to ya.

[9] But y'all ain't like that. No sir! Y'all are God's chosen cowboys. You are holy men, in a holy crew, belonging and riding only for God. This is why we must show others how to ride for him. He's called us out of the brush and into green pastures.

[10] There was a time you didn't know who you were or what you were supposed to do. Now you ride for God because he has shown you great mercy in allowing you to do so.

[11] Cowboys, your ride through this world is temporary. You're like an outcast in the world now. Stay away from the things of the world that will entangle you and stick to you like cockleburs. These things can destroy your soul. [12] Ride properly when you are around unbelievers. If you ride right, then even if they accuse you of something bad, no one will believe them. You'll honor God in this way.

Respect Those in Authority

[13] If you want to honor the Lord, do what those in authority on earth tell you to do. I don't care if he is a king, a governor, [14] or an elected official. The king has sent them to dole out punishment on those who do wrong and give a pat on the back to those who do right.

[15] God's plan is to shut up those who are ignorant and make false accusations against you. [16] You are free, but at the same time you have chosen to ride for God and do whatever he says to do. Don't use your freedom to do bad things.

¹⁷ Show respect to everyone and love others, especially the crew who rides for God. Respect God and respect the king.

Slaves

¹⁸ Y'all slaves must show respect to your earthly masters. Do what they tell you, even if they are unkind. ¹⁹ God smiles when you ride for him and go through unjust treatment. ²⁰ Unjust treatment doesn't include getting whipped for something you did wrong. But if you suffer for doing what is right, God will smile down upon you.

²¹ God has called you to do the right thing, regardless of the consequences. That's what Jesus did and you should follow his example.

²² He never sinned one time, nor did he mislead a single soul. ²³ He kept his mouth shut when he was insulted and didn't threaten revenge when he suffered. He left everything up to God, who is always just and judges everyone fairly. ²⁴ Jesus became our sin that was nailed to the cross. We are dead to sin and now can ride for what is right. By his injuries we are healed. ²⁵ You were once like fence-jumping cattle that had run off. But now you have been gathered by the Top Hand, who is the protector of your soul.

CHAPTER 3

Married Folk

Ladies, you need to respect your husbands in the same way. Even if some of them ain't riding for the Lord, your godly living will speak words that mouths cannot. Your right living will win 'em over. ² They will see how pure and reverent you are.

³ Don't worry about your outward appearance. Fancy hairstyles, big jewelry, and beautiful clothes don't make you beautiful. ⁴ Clothe yourself with the kind of gorgeous that can only come from inside of you. I'm talking about a gentle and quiet presence about you. These are the things that are precious to the Lord. ⁵ This is how the old-time women acted and why they seemed so regal. They trusted God and put themselves under the authority of their husbands. ⁶ Do you remember Sarah? She obeyed Abraham and even called him master. You ladies are like daughters of Sarah when you do what is right without worrying about what your husbands might do.

Husbands

⁷ Y'all ain't off the hook either, husbands. You should honor your wives. Understand that she is a precious gift as you live together. She may not be as physically strong as you, but she is equal in your new life that God has given you. Treat her right so your prayers will be heard.

Everyone

⁸ Finally, y'all should all be like-minded. Take care of each other. Be humble and tender. ⁹ Don't retaliate against each other or trade insults like uppercuts. If someone hurts you, bless them. Pay them back with prayer. This is the kind of life God has called you to. You live like this and God's blessings will overflow. ¹⁰ The Good Book says, "If you want to enjoy the life you have, keep your tongue from speaking ill and your lips from telling lies. ¹¹ Turn your back on all this world's sorry ways. Snake out a loop and keep an eye out for peace. When you see it, rope it and tie off hard. ¹² The Lord is watching over everyone who does what is right. He listens to these cowboy's prayers. But the Lord will turn his back on those whose ways are belligerent."

Good Suffering

¹³ Who is really going to want to harm a man for doing something good? ¹⁴ But even if it happens, God will reward you for your right doing and the pain you suffer. Don't fret about their threats. ¹⁵ Instead of worrying and frettin', ride with God every single day and be ready to introduce everyone you know to the one you follow. ¹⁶ But whatever you do, be gentle and respectful. Do things the right way so your conscience is always clear. This way, when people speak ill of you to others, it will be the slanderer who is shamed because of your good conduct. ¹⁷ Think about it, if you have to suffer, do it for the right reasons, not the wrong ones.

¹⁸ Don't you remember Christ was nailed to a tree in suffering once and for all time? He never messed up—not once! But he died like a sinner in your place, so you too could have a place in heaven. Even though he died a physical death, he was brought back from the grave in the Spirit.

¹⁹ While in this spiritual state, Jesus went and preached the good news to those in prison. ²⁰ I'm talking about those who scoffed at Noah while he built his boat. Only eight folks survived the

flood and the rest drowned like rats. ²¹ But don't miss the point of all of this. Noah was saved from the water, but now we are saved by the water. The waters of the baptism don't wash away the dirt from your skin, but by washing away the sins from your soul by symbolically following Jesus through his death, burial, and resurrection.

²² Now Jesus is in heaven. He has taken his place at the right hand of God and has all the authority of all of creation under God.

CHAPTER 4

Cowboys Know How to Suffer

Don't you remember that Jesus suffered physically? If it happened to him it will happen to you so be ready. If you suffer for the same reasons Jesus suffered then that proves you are done with sin. ² This is good news because you will no longer be chasing your tails, but will be ready to ride for the Lord. ³ You've had your fill of living a sorry life with its lust, sex parties, drunken stupors, and worshiping man-made things. ⁴ And now, all those you used to run around with are surprised you no longer do these things. Don't worry when they call you mean things. ⁵ But one day, they will give account of their lives to God and it sure ain't going to pretty. ⁶ That is why the good news was preached to those who have already died. Since they heard the message and believed, they will share in the same things as those of us who will still be alive when Christ comes riding back.

Use What You've Got for God

⁷ The end of the trail is right around the corner. Keep your wits about you and pay attention to your prayers. ⁸ Don't ever give up on loving folks. A little bit of love covers a bunch of sin. ⁹ Invite folks into your bunkhouse if they need a cup of coffee or a cot. ¹⁰ You've each been given some special abilities so use them for the good of others. ¹¹ If you talk good, talk about God and his grace. If you're a hard worker, work hard for others and God. Do these things so God will get the glory. Amen.

More on Suffering

¹² Don't wig out when you suffer for the sake of Christ. It don't mean you're doing something wrong. It means you're doing something right. ¹³ Be glad you get to share the same trail Jesus

followed. It means you're on the right track. ¹⁴ If you get insulted because you ride for Jesus, take it as a compliment. This means God is riding with you. ¹⁵ Now, I ain't talking about suffering because you did something wrong. ¹⁶ I'm talking about suffering for doing something right. Don't be ashamed or hard on yourself. Give thanks to God for making you stronger.

¹⁷ It's time for a reckoning, and God's cowboys will be reckoned first. If we who ride for him are reckoned first, how terrible it will be for those who come after and don't believe. ¹⁸ The Good Book even says, "It's hard for a good cowboy to be saved. How much harder is it for godless sinners and no-accounts?"

¹⁹ So, if you're suffering for doing good, then that means God is on your side and will keep his promise of the reward you will get.

CHAPTER 5

A Little Advice for Jigger Bosses and Young Cowboys

I've got a little advice for the jigger bosses of the church like me. I've seen what Christ suffered for and I'll get the reward he has set aside for that. I'm seriously asking you ² to look after the herd God has trusted you with. Do your jobs because you want to, not because you have to. Don't even do it for the reward, do it because you want to please God. ³ Don't ask anyone to do something you're not willing to do or haven't done. Be a good example of what a top hand looks like. ⁴ And when the best Top Hand comes back, you will get your trophy buckle for the work you've done.

⁵ Now, let me speak to the young hands. Do what the jigger bosses tell you to. If they want your opinion, they will ask. Keep yourself humble and help each other out. The Good Book says, "God turns his back on the proud, but gives grace to the humble." ⁶ So be humble and God's powerful hand will lift you up in good time. ⁷ Leave all your frettin' in God's tack room because he loves you and doesn't want you packin' it around.

⁸ Keep your head on a swivel and pay attention. The outlaw, the devil, stalks you every minute of every day like a hungry lion. ⁹ Keep both feet in the stirrups of faith and don't turn your back on him. Everyone who rides for Jesus has

to deal with the devil, too. [10] But don't think the suffering will last forever. God's grace is going to make you eternal, perfect, stout, strong, and with a solid foundation that cannot be knocked down. [11] This is God's power forever! Amen.

A Final Adios

[12] Silas helped me write this little letter to y'all. He's a good pard and faithful to Christ. I hope this encourages you and all I've written is true. Believe it.

[13] God's outfit in Babylon says to tell y'all hello and so does Mark. [14] Give everyone a hearty handshake to show God's love for each other.

May you in ride in peace and for the brand of Christ.

2 PETER

CHAPTER 1

Hey, pards! This is Pete again, a hand for Christ.

I'm writing to all the cowboys who ride the rough trail of righteousness for the sake of Jesus Christ, our God and Lord. This faith you ride in is the code of justice and fairness that comes straight from the Boss.

² Here's hopin' God is going to dole out more and more grace and peace on ya as you grow through ridin' for his brand.

The Faith Feed Yard

³ We don't lack nothin' because God has given us everything we're needin' to ride for him. By giving us everything we need, God is letting us share in his glory and greatness. ⁴ It's by these two things that he gives us his word that we will share in his divine nature and escape the thick brush that is the world's corruption of lust and the allure of a lazy life.

⁵ Because of this, don't be lazy in responding to God's promises. Throw in a heaping of goodness on top of your faith. To your goodness, add a bunch of wisdom. ⁶ To your wisdom, pile on self-mastery. To self-mastery, add in endurance. To that throw in a feed sack full of godliness, ⁷ and to godliness, don't forget about being a pard. But don't just be a pard to a few, love 'em all.

⁸ This is the feed yard of faith. Feeding on stuff like this will make you productive and useful to God. In other words, it'll make you handy. ⁹ But those who jump the fence and chase after other things will become blind as a cancer-eyed cow.

They will no longer be able to see that their sins have been forgiven.

¹⁰ So, cowboys and cowgirls, ride hard and prove you belong to the brand. Do these things I've told you and you won't fall off. ¹¹ When your time comes, God will open the gate wide and give you a place on his spread.

¹² That's why I'm going to keep repeating myself even though you've heard all this before. ¹³ I won't ever stop reminding you that you don't live for yourself, but you ride for the brand. ¹⁴ Jesus has made it apparent to me that I won't be riding these old trails much longer. ¹⁵ But with the time I have left in the saddle, I'll make sure you don't forget who you're supposed to be and what you're supposed to be doing.

¹⁶ We didn't make up a bunch of cowboy stories around a campfire about how Jesus came to earth and did what he did. We are first-hand witnesses to all the things he did. ¹⁷ We were there when God blessed him. We heard with our own ears when God said, "This is my boy and he makes me happy." ¹⁸ We ourselves were sitting slack-jawed on that holy mountain when we heard it.

¹⁹ Because of that and other things we've seen and heard, we know the things those old prophets were talking about were true. Pay attention to what they wrote. Their words are like a warm campfire on a cold, dark night. Their words will keep you out of the dark and warm until the morning star, Jesus Christ, shines in your hearts. ²⁰ Don't forget, them prophets didn't write those things from their own understanding. ²¹ It wasn't human inspired or initiated at all. It was all the Holy Spirit talking through 'em.

CHAPTER 2

Counterfeit Cowboys

Pretender prophets swindled people in the past and counterfeit cowboys will ride through your gates. They'll fill you full of lies and tell you things contrary to what the Boss said. They'll get what's coming to them in the end, but they can sure wreak havoc before that happens. **2** There will be many a cowboy who will leave the narrow trail and follow the immoral highway. Their lives will seem so much better on the outside, therefore many will shun the authentic cowboy way. **3** These counterfeit cowboy's will sell their fabulous stories for a profit made off of your soul. The noose is ready for the counterfeit cowboys. Their judge has already slammed the gavel down on their destruction.

4 Think about it, God didn't even spare the angels who'd sinned against him. He threw them in the branding fire, chained and bound to await their day of sentencing. **5** God got so fed up with our ancient ancestors that he destroyed the whole world with a flood. Only Noah and seven others were saved. Noah was a cowboy who urged righteous living and practiced what he preached. **6** Sodom and Gomorrah were two outfits that got what was coming to them. They were utterly destroyed with fire and brimstone as an example to what happens to people living godless and shameless lives. **7** Lot lived there, but was rescued because he didn't like what was going on around him and didn't conduct his business in the same way those heathens did. **8** Lot was a good hombre, but it pained him every day to see that lawlessness around him. **9** God knows who is good among you and who is counterfeit. He will rescue his real cowboys from their trials, but he will hold the counterfeit in chains to await their day of sentencing. **10** This is especially true of those who travel down the trail of lust and shun God's authority in their lives.

These counterfeit cowboys are bold and show-offs. They show no respect for the glorious creatures of heaven, but instead make fun of everything that is holy. **11** Even angels, with all their might and power, do not condemn or make fun of anyone before God—not even the counterfeit cowboys. That's because the angels are smart and the counterfeits are not. **12** These types of folks are like badgers. They live only by instinct and base emotions. They live their lives like they are born to be captured or killed. They attack anything they don't understand or agree upon with insults and vile sarcasm. They will be destroyed as surely as a wolf preying upon the shepherd's flock. **13** Their punishment will be the suffering they caused paid back in kind. They love to shock others in broad daylight with satisfaction of the lustful, bodily hungers. They disgrace your table when you let them join you in a meal. Especially when you delight in the sinful ways. **14** They eat you up with their adulterous eyes and their sinful desires are never satisfied or satiated. The weak among you fall into their devilish traps and snares. They are well-trained and practiced in greed—masters of the trade. Despite it all, they live under the curse of God. **15** They have left the narrow trail and wander lost in the abyss. They have followed the trail of Balaam, who traded what was right for what was profitable. **16** It was so bad that he was rebuked by his donkey who spoke with a human voice and stopped him from becoming completely insane in his greed.

17 These people are like dried up dirt tanks. They drift away like the clouds after a storm. They have a place in the forever-dark prepared for them by God. **18** They yell loudly and make ignorant statements about anything and everything. They use their bodies to trap people in lust. They prey upon the weak of body and mind. I'm talking about those who are trying to get away from that kind of life, but continue to go back again and again to sin. **19** They promise freedom, but really offer slavery to sin and corruption. You are a slave to whatever controls you. **20** Anyone who takes Jesus's hand to escape a life of sin and returns to it after being saved is worse off than he was in the first place. **21** It would have been better to have never seen righteousness than to experience it and throw it in the dirt. We are commanded to live holy lives, and it's worth it. **22** There is truth in the old saying, "A dog goes back to its own vomit." Another old saying that is true is, "A clean pig will return to the mud at the first opportunity."

CHAPTER 3

Jesus Will Ride Back

Cowboys, this is the second letter I've sent y'all. Both times I've aimed for getting you to see the truth of the right way to think and act. ² Don't forget what the old cowboys of God told us, as well as the commands of Jesus himself given by his twelve cowboys. ³ First off, there will come a day when people make fun of God in broad daylight and do nothing except worship their own lustful wants and needs. They'll laugh in your face for riding for Jesus ⁴ and will ask, "Where is this cowboy who said he would come and save you? I don't see him! Show him to us. All of our ancestors have died and nothing has changed since the world began."

⁵ They've heard the truth, but chosen to ignore it. With a word, God created all the heavens and earth. The land was brought up out of the water, ⁶ and it was this same water that God used to destroy the land in the great flood. ⁷ By the same word, God is now preserving the earth and heavens for the day they will all be destroyed, not by water again, but this time by fire. The current heaven and earth are waiting on the day when all godless people will be destroyed in the fire to come.

⁸ I think it's important for you to understand time isn't the same for us as it is for God. To him, a thousand years is like a day and a day is like a thousand years. One is the same as the other to him. ⁹ The Lord isn't slow-bucking his promises to us. He is being patient with all of us so that all who can be will be saved. He wants everyone to turn from their sins and ride for him. He's going to wait as long as he can because he doesn't want anyone to be destroyed. He's waiting for everyone to turn loose of their sins.

¹⁰ But the day of execution will come like a horse thief at night. When that day comes, the sky will collapse with a wail. Everything we can see in the sky will be destroyed in fire. Everything on earth will vanish in ash. ¹¹ Now that you know all of this, what kind of cowboy do you want to be? Ride with God in reverence and obedience. ¹² Those of us who ride for God eagerly await this time when everything will be consumed in fire. Everything except us. ¹³ We wait for God to come through on his word; he promised us a new heaven and a new earth where his cowboys will ride in stirrup-high green grass and sit beside crystal-clear waters forever.

¹⁴ Until this time comes, ride with your head held high and your back straight. Be pure and faultless in God's sight and be at peace by riding only for him. ¹⁵ This waiting we endure is not a punishment, but an opportunity to get better. Paul talked to you a lot about this through the wisdom that came from God, not himself. ¹⁶ He talks all about getting better and how to be saved. A lot of what he says can be misconstrued by the weak of heart and mind. These types of people take what Paul says and twist it to their own opinion, just like they do with the rest of the scriptures. This doesn't change the truth, it signs their death warrants.

¹⁷ But I know I'm just explaining cattle to cowboys. Y'all already know all of this. Keep an eye on the horizon so you will not be lured away by lawless vagabonds and lustful temptresses. Stay close to God and stick to the narrow trail and you'll be safe. ¹⁸ But don't use your sense of safety to stagnate. Use it to grow closer to Jesus and get to know him better and better. Make him your best pard and you'll be amazed by the outcome. God gets the glory, now and forever.

1 JOHN

CHAPTER 1

The Life of the Word

We are here to tell you the story of the Word of Life. It existed when nothing existed. We've seen it with our own eyes, heard it with our own ears, and touched it with our own hands. ² When this life showed itself to the world, we were right there. We were eyewitnesses to the glory, not bards or poets with fantastical tales of whim and fancy. We are here to tell you about the eternal life which is offered by the Father and made known to us. ³ We tell you what we have seen and heard so that you will join us in the crew that rides for the Father and his Son, Jesus Christ. ⁴ This is what your life has longed for and your participation is what our life longs for.

The Light

⁵ This is what the Son told us about his Father. God is light and there is no darkness in him at all. ⁶ So then, if we say we ride in his crew, but we ride in darkness, then we are counterfeits in word and deed. ⁷ But if we ride in the light, because he is the light, then we all belong to the same crew with one another. The blood of the Son unites and cleanses us all of our sins.

⁸ If we say we don't have any sin, then we are nothing but liars and no truth resides in us at all. ⁹ But if we admit our sins to God, he will do what he said he would and forgive us and pardon us of all wrongdoing. ¹⁰ If we claim we have not sinned, then we are calling God a liar because he said we are all sinners. To make this claim proves we do not ride for Him.

CHAPTER 2

The point of this letter is so you will turn loose of your sins. But just in case we fall off and do sin, we have someone who is pleading our case on our behalf before God. That man is Jesus Christ, the only perfect man to ever live—and he is on our side! ² Jesus is the reason our sins can be forgiven. And it's not just our sins, but everyone's.

³ The one way to know for sure you ride for the brand is if you obey God's commands. ⁴ If we say we ride for him, but we don't do what he says, then we are counterfeits and fakes and there is no truth in us at all. ⁵ But if we conduct our lives like God says to, that means we love him. This is how to know if you are really riding for him or not: ⁶ if you ride for God, ride the way Jesus did.

A New Directive

⁷ Cowboys, this directive I am writing to you is not a new one. It's the old one you've heard from the beginning of your ride—love each other and have each other's backs. You already know it. ⁸ But I write to you now about a new one. Or maybe I should say it is the old one made new. Jesus was the embodiment of the command, and so are you who live in him. The darkness is dying away and the light has begun to shine on the horizon.

⁹ If we say we ride in the light, but hate others, we are liars in darkness. ¹⁰ Living in the light boils down to loving others. We love others in such a way as to lift them up and never cause them to sin. ¹¹ Hate lives in the darkness and so do we if it has a place in our hearts. Hate blinds

us and we know not which way to turn or what to do. It blinds us to the light.

¹² I write to tell you kids that your sins are forgiven because of Christ. ¹³ I write to you fathers because you ride in faith and know Jesus, who has been there since the beginning. I am writing to you young people to let you know the devil has been defeated.

¹⁴ I write to you kids because you know the Boss. I write to you fathers because you know the one who was there in the beginning. I write to you young people because you are tough. The word of God rides with you and in you, and you have defeated the devil.

¹⁵ Don't love anything in the world or that comes from it. You have to choose between loving the world and what it has to offer or loving God and what he has to offer. ¹⁶ All this stuff most people cherish and hold on to—sinful desires, material things, and everything else like fame, fortune, and pride—none of it comes from God. Those are all worldly things and will get you destroyed. ¹⁷ This entire world is gripped in the throes of death. This world's desires are passing away like paper in a fire. But those who ride for God will live forever.

Jesus's Nemesis

¹⁸ Cowboys, the end is so close you can nearly touch it. You were told Jesus's nemesis would come. Many of his enemies have already come and gone, so we know the time of the end is close. ¹⁹ These folks didn't belong in our crew. That's why they left. If they had belonged with us, they would have stayed. This is just proof they didn't belong with us.

²⁰ But all of y'all are here because Jesus gave y'all the Holy Spirit and you all know the truth. ²¹ I'm not writing you to tell you some truth you don't know. I'm writing to you because you do know the truth. It ain't hard to understand that no lies come from the truth.

²² Then where do the lies come from? The lies come from those who say Jesus is not who he says he is. These people are the real enemies of Christ. They spit in the face of God and the Son with their lies. ²³ You can't ride for God while rejecting his Son. You don't get one without the other.

²⁴ Hold on to the truth that you've heard from the start. If you keep that truth near and dear

to your hearts you will always ride with the Father and the Son. ²⁵ And this is what Jesus has promised his hands who ride for him—perfect, eternal life.

²⁶ I'm writing you to warn you about those who are lying to you about the truth. ²⁷ I know y'all have the Holy Spirit and don't need anyone else's help. The Holy Ghost will explain what is true and what is not. Listen to him and keep riding for Christ.

²⁸ Don't let up and keep going. Keep riding for him as long as your heart beats. Those who ride for him will not want to hide themselves in shame and will be full of courage when he comes riding back over the hill. ²⁹ You know Jesus rides the right way and all his hands do the same as he does.

CHAPTER 3

God has showered us with his love like a spring rain on dry ground. He loves us so much he calls us his own kids. And if God says it, it is so. That's why the world treats us like it does. The world doesn't know God and doesn't know us. ² Listen up, cowboys. We've been adopted by God himself, but we don't know just what this entails yet. But we do know this, when Jesus comes riding back, we will be made like him. We'll see him for who he really is and we will see ourselves as we were meant to be, not as we were. ³ This is why we stay away from things that will cast a foul light upon our souls. We keep ourselves pure for the one who is pure.

⁴ Sin is just a word we use for doing anything that goes against what the Boss told us to do. ⁵ Jesus came to save us from our sins. He was the only one who could because he never sinned himself. ⁶ If you ride for Jesus, you don't ride in sin. It's that simple. But those who continue to choose sin over Jesus do not ride for him or know him.

⁷ Don't let anyone pull the wool over your eyes! If you do what is right then you are right, just like Jesus is. ⁸ Those who continue to sin ride for the devil. The devil has sinned from the beginning and teaches others to do the same. Jesus came to defeat what the devil and sin have done in the world.

⁹ Those who ride for God don't continue to sin intentionally. If you ride for God, then you

become like God because he is your Boss. God doesn't sin and neither should you. ¹⁰ This is the truth about those who ride for God and those who ride for the Devil. Those who do not do what is right or love others do not ride for God.

Lovin' Each Other

¹¹ The message that has been stuck on repeat is this—love each other. ¹² Don't be like Cain, who rode for the devil and killed his own brother, Abel. Why did Cain kill his own brother? Because Cain did wrong things and Abel did right things.

¹³ So, in light of this, why does it surprise you that the world, who does wrong things, hates you for doing right things? ¹⁴ We have already died and come back to life because we love others. Those who hate are still under the curse of death. ¹⁵ Haters don't have life in them. They are murderers and murderers don't live forever. ¹⁶ This is the definition of love: Christ gave his life for us. We ought to do the same for others. ¹⁷ If we are rich and see someone in need, but do not help, how can we say we love God? ¹⁸ A cowboy's love isn't all talk and no walk. Our love is true and can be seen in everything we do.

Confidence before God

¹⁹ What we do will show the truth of our ride. When we stand before God, we will be confident in our ride with Jesus. ²⁰ Even if we might feel guilty, God is bigger than our feelings because he knows everything.

²¹ Cowboys, guilt keeps us away from God. You can't be bold and feel guilty at the same time. ²² Our prayers will be answered because we ride the way he says to ride and we do things he likes. ²³ This is what God has told us to do—believe in his son, Jesus, and love each other. ²⁴ Do these and you will ride with him and he will ride with you. And we know he is riding with us because the Spirit he sent rides with us twenty-four seven.

CHAPTER 4

The Authenticity Test

Listen, cowboys. Just because some hombre rides up claiming to have the Spirit in his life don't make it so. There's been a ton of counterfeit cowboys who have made the same claim. ² If you ain't sure whether or not someone really has the Holy Ghost, just put 'em through the authenticity test. Ask them if they have faith that Jesus was God and came to earth as a real person. ³ Those who deny it are counterfeit cowboys. They don't have the Holy Ghost, but the devil's spirit of lies inside 'em. You've heard that the Antichrist would come, but he is already here in many ways.

⁴ But don't fret none, cowboys. You ride for God and have already defeated all these counterfeit cowboys. The Holy Ghost inside you is vastly more powerful than the lies in them. ⁵ These counterfeit cowboys talk only of things in this world and how to get them. That's because they are slaves to this world, not God. ⁶ But we are God's very own crew. Those who want to know him listen to us. Those who don't want to know him shun us. It's as simple as that. This is how we can tell the difference between authentic cowboys and counterfeit ones.

Tie Hard and Fast to Love

⁷ Cowboys, we've got to love one another. God loves us and we pay it forward to others. Whoever loves another rides for God and knows Him. ⁸ Those who don't love don't ride for the brand. ⁹ God showed us his love by sending his only Boy to give us life. ¹⁰ This is what tying hard and fast to love looks like. It's ain't about how much we love God, but about how much he loved us by sending his Son in order to forgive our sins.

¹¹ Pards, if this is how much God loves us, then we should pay that love forward to others. ¹² Ain't no one ever laid eyes on God, but when we love others, he rides with us and we ride with him. His love makes us complete and authentic.

¹³ We're certain we ride for him and he rides for us because of the presence of the Holy Ghost in our lives. ¹⁴ While we haven't seen God, we did see his Son who he sent to be the rescuer of the world. ¹⁵ If we live in the truth that Jesus Christ is the Son of God, we ride for him and he rides with us. ¹⁶ Like I've said, we know and believe just how much God loves us.

God is love and those who love others ride for his outfit. ¹⁷ That love we have of his grows in us each and every day so that on the day of reckoning, we will be able to have courage and confidence. Jesus wouldn't be worried about that day and since we ride for him, we won't worry about it either. ¹⁸ Real love has no fear. Perfect love like God's drives away all fear.

A person who is afraid doesn't realize how much God loves them. Fear comes from being afraid of punishment and we are destined for glory, not punishment.

¹⁹ We love because God loved us first and best. ²⁰ If we say we love God, but hate others, that makes us liars. You cannot love God, who you have not seen, without loving those who you have seen. ²¹ It all boils down to what Jesus told us, if you love God then you'll love others.

CHAPTER 5

Anyone who believes Jesus is the one who was sent to save us all gets the right to be children of God. If you love a father, then you also love his son. ² We can know we love God's kids if we love God and do what he says to do. ³ Of course we love God. And if we love him, we are going to obey him just like we would any great father. What he asks us to do is not too hard. ⁴ Shoot, we're just glad that because we are God's kids, we can defeat the world and its ways. We do this by our faith in him. ⁵ Who can defeat the whole world? The cowboy who believes Jesus Christ is the Son of God.

⁶ Jesus proved who he was when he was baptized in water and shed his blood on the cross. Not just one or the other, but by both. The Holy Ghost confirms that this is true. ⁷ There are three witnesses to who Jesus was: ⁸ the Holy Ghost, the water, and the blood that was shed. ⁹ If three witnesses on earth would validate a truth, then these three witnesses confirm the truth of who Jesus is. But really, we have only to listen to God, because he told us himself that Jesus was his Son. ¹⁰ Anyone who believes in Jesus knows this to be true. Those who don't believe in Jesus are just calling God a liar.

¹¹ This is what God said, he has given us eternal life and it is only found in his Son. ¹² If you ride with the Son, you will ride forever. If you don't, then you won't.

The Forever Ride

¹³ I'm telling you all this so you can be sure you have eternal life by your ride with Jesus. ¹⁴ We are courageous when we come before God because we know he loves us and listens to our needs. We know he will take care of us. ¹⁵ If he hears us and listens to us, then we know he will give us what we ask of him.

¹⁶ If you see a fellow cowboy doing something he shouldn't, you should pray for him and God will hear the prayer and bring him back. That's not to say there is a possibility someone could do something so heinous that God would turn their back on them. Possibly something as bad as turning their backs on God. Praying for that guy probably wouldn't do a lot of good. ¹⁷ Listen, we are all going to mess up and that is what it means to sin. But God is better at saving than we are at sinning . . . to an extent.

¹⁸ Anyone who truly rides for God as one of his kids doesn't keep on intentionally sinning. Jesus keeps them safe from the devil.

¹⁹ We know we ride for God even though everyone else rides for the devil.

²⁰ We know Jesus came to show us who his Father is. We ride for him every day because we know him and he knows us. This is what it means to have eternal life.

²¹ Cowboys, keep a far distance from anything that looks like a false god.

2 JOHN

This letter is to my crew and their families from your jigger boss, John. I think the world of all of you. And it's not just me. Anyone who knows what truth really means knows who y'all are. ² This is one of our goals, to know the truth and ride in it always.

³ Here's hoping the Boss and his Son will shell out mercy, grace, peace, love, and truth on us all.

The Truth

⁴ It means the world to me that many of y'all are willing to ride in the truth just like the Boss told us to. ⁵ If we do that, then I know we are taking care of each other. This isn't some shocking new revelation. It's been part of our code since the beginning. ⁶ Taking care of each other means we are doing what God said. He's repeated himself over and over and over. Look out for each other and watch each other's backs.

⁷ There's been a lot of counterfeit cowboys passing through claiming that Jesus wasn't a real man. Don't listen to these fools. They are enemies of Christ. ⁸ Watch your backs so that you don't get bushwhacked by silly notions and foolish opinions. Don't lose what you've ridden so hard to get.

⁹ You've got to stay right with Jesus. Many people get excited and start adding stuff to what he said. These people are riding in front of the Boss and it ain't going to be pretty when they are called out on it. You stay right with the Boss and his Son and they'll stay right there with you. ¹⁰ If someone comes through your gate with a message other than the Father and the Son, send them packing. Don't even wish them well as they go. ¹¹ Anyone who wishes someone well that spreads lies becomes an accessory to the evil they do.

Last Words

¹² I've got a lot more to say, but I don't want to do it with a pen. I hope soon to see y'all in person. We'll all look forward to that.

¹³ All your neighbors here said to tell y'all hello.

3 JOHN

From John, the jigger boss—

To Gaius, my pard, who I've ridden the hard trail with.

² Hey, cowboy! I hope all is well with ya. I pray that you ain't caught the consumption and that you are fit as a fiddle. I know your soul is good and I pray your health is the same. ³ I sure was glad when some of the boys showed up and told me about how faithful you'd been to the truth. ⁴ It sure didn't surprise me any, but I was glad about it nonetheless.

Taking Care of God's Hands

⁵ Listen, my friend. I want to thank you for taking such good care of the other cowboys, even if you don't know them. ⁶ They came here and told us how you treated them. Keep on helping them all like this. If they are riding for the Lord, then send them away with enough that they can keep spreading the word. God likes that. ⁷ They rode out to gather the wild ones without any help from unbelievers. ⁸ Listen, here's a code to live by, if you ain't riding out to spread the good news, then help those who are.

⁹ I wrote a short note to the outfit there, but Diotrephes, who likes to think of himself as some sort of ramrod, would not listen to what I had to say. ¹⁰ When I make it over to y'all, I'm going to spill the beans about what he's been doing and saying. If lying wasn't enough, he won't lift a hand to help any of the boys riding for God. Get this, he even keeps others from helping them too. He tells our boys to hit the road and don't come back.

¹¹ I don't think I have to say this, but don't act like that. Be better than that. Those who do good belong to God and those who act like Diotrephes, don't. Simple as that.

¹² But, everyone I've seen speaks well of Demetrius. The truth speaks for itself, but it's nice to hear from others about the good things some people are doing.

So Long

¹³ I've got a lot more to say, but I'm tired of writing it. ¹⁴ I hope to saddle up and see y'all in person soon.

¹⁵ Keep your chin up and your toes out.

JUDE

This letter is from Jude, a cowboy of Christ and James's brother.

To all those who've been called to ride for the brand with the love and protection of Jesus Christ.

² Here's hoping that God is going to overload you with grace, mercy, and love.

Counterfeit Cowboys

³ Listen, pards, I wanted to write to you about this great salvation we share, but something else has come up. I feel like I need to warn you about the fight you're fixing to find yourself in. ⁴ There are counterfeit cowboys springing up out of the brush everywhere and trying to undermine the truth of what Jesus said and did. The Good Book said long ago that fire waits on these no-account curs.

⁵ You already know this, but let me say it again. You remember that the Lord saved everyone from Israel who was held hostage in Egypt. After they'd all escaped, the Lord decimated the unbelievers. ⁶ Also remember those angels who didn't do what God had said. They are now locked in chains in the forever dark below. God is making them wait for his Day of Sentencing. They'll get what's coming to them. ⁷ Don't forget about Sodom and Gomorrah. Their people acted like those angels. They all indulged in sexual immorality and perversion. Those cities and their peoples were destroyed. Think of it like a warning shot from God for all of us not to ride those trails.

⁸ There are some people who claim to have dreams that come from some god. They live lustful lives, scoff at authority, and insult the angels and such. ⁹ But even Michael, one of the strongest of God's angels, didn't dare to even condemn the devil (a one-time angel himself) with harsh words. When they were arguing over the body of Moses, Michael just said, "It ain't happening. God's gonna give you what you've got coming, Lucifer." ¹⁰ But people like this attack anything they don't understand with venomous insults. They are like snakes that don't know anything except to bite. The trouble is, venomous snakes that try to bite get their heads chopped off. ¹¹ Honestly, it's sad. They have chosen the trail of Cain. For no more reason than money, they've chosen to turn from the Lord like Balaam did. They've gone off the deep end like Korah did and rebelled against God. And just like him, they are destroyed. ¹² With the way they holler and lustfully carouse around, they are like a venereal disease running through the registered herd. They are like cowardly cowboys who only take care of themselves, not the herd. They are like black clouds that don't offer a drop of rain or fruit trees that bear no fruit and have been pulled up by the roots. ¹³ The deeds of their lust lie on the beach like foam after a churning sea. They are like comets shining bright, but headed for a black hole.

¹⁴ It was Enoch, seven generations removed from Adam, who told the truth about these counterfeit cowboys, "The Lord will ride in with thousands of his angels behind him ¹⁵ to bring judgment on all of them for the godless lives and immoral acts they did. Those who stand in judgment will come to regret the godless words they used to insult the Lord."

¹⁶ This type of person is always complaining about this or that and blaming others for everything. They follow their own evil ways and brag about all they are and all they've done. They flatter others with lies so they can rob them blind.

Watch Out!

¹⁷ But don't forget what Jesus's twelve cowboys told y'all. ¹⁸ They said, "When the end gets near, people will laugh at you and follow their own godless ways." ¹⁹ These are the folks who split herds. They aren't controlled by God, but by their own evil desires. The Holy Ghost ain't in them. ²⁰ But you cowboys, y'all keep riding in faith. Pray with the power of the Holy Ghost. ²¹ Stay saddled up with the love of God as you wait for Jesus to come riding back over the hill to get us and take us home.

²² When someone is having a hard time and having doubts, don't kick them when they're down. ²³ Snatch them up quick before they land in the fire. Go easy on people, but not on sin.

Final Prayer

²⁴ To him who is able to keep you in the saddle and present you as faultless before God—²⁵ to our one and only God, our only savior, Jesus Christ, let there by glory, majesty, might, and authority, forever and ever, amen.

REVELATION

CHAPTER 1

This is what's to come. It comes straight from Jesus Christ so all those who ride for him will know what will happen. He sent an angel to deliver it to John, a cowboy for Christ. ² John has written down everything he saw—which is Jesus Christ, the full revelation of God. ³ Blessings await those cowboys who read these words aloud around a campfire. These same blessings are for those who take these words to heart. The time is drawing near!

John Greets the Seven Churches

⁴ This letter is written to the seven churches in the Asia province. Sit tall in grace and ride in courage with the one who was, is, and always will be. Ride with the seven spirits who stand at the throne, ⁵ and with Jesus Christ, the one who's seen it all, who rose from the grave, and rules over all kings.

All the honor goes to Christ who has set us free from our sins with his own blood. ⁶ We are now a priestly outfit in the kingdom of God. Power and glory to him for all time! Amen.

⁷ "Look over there! He rides the clouds of heaven and everyone is a witness to his glory—even those who killed him. The nations will wail and moan for him." This will happen, amen!

⁸ "I am the Alpha and the Omega—I ride point and drag," says the Lord. "I am the one who was, is, and will always be. I am the Almighty."

John's Vision

⁹ I, John, am your pard and brother in the suffering of the trail. I have been patient and endured for Jesus on the island of Patmos. I was banished for preaching the truth of Christ. ¹⁰ It was a Sunday and I was worshiping God when I heard a voice behind me that sounded like a trumpet. ¹¹ The voice said, "Write down all you see and send it to the seven churches: Ephesus, Smyrna, Pergamum, Thyatira, Sardis, Philadelphia, and Laodicea."

¹² I turned to see where the sound was coming from and saw seven torches sitting in golden stands. ¹³ There among them was a man who looked like Jesus, dressed in a poncho that reached his feet. Around him was a golden belt. ¹⁴ His hair was exquisitely white and his eyes blazed brighter than the sun. ¹⁵ His feet glowed like metal out of the blacksmith's furnace. His voice was like the sound of a rushing river. ¹⁶ He held seven stars in his right hand and out of his mouth came a deadly-sharp sword. His face shone with the brilliance of a thousand suns.

¹⁷ When my eyes fell on him, I dropped to the ground at his feet like a dead man. He reached down with his right hand and said, "Do not fear. I am the first and the last. ¹⁸ I am the living one even though I died. Look at me. I am alive and will always be. I hold the keys of the dead and Hell itself.

¹⁹ "Write down what you see. It will be things that have happened as well as things that are to come. ²⁰ Let me tell you what you've seen so far. The seven stars are the angels who guard the seven churches. The seven torches are these seven churches.

CHAPTER 2

A Letter to the Outfit in Ephesus

"To the angel of the outfit in Ephesus write this:

I am the one who holds the seven stars in his right hand. I walk among the seven torches.

2 I've been watching you. There's nothing I haven't seen. Don't think I didn't see the hard rides and the patience through all the rough times. I saw you had nothing to do with wicked folks—the ones who claimed to ride for me, but didn't. You tested them and found them wanting. 3 You suffered greatly for me without quitting.

4 But I do hold this one thing against you, you don't love me or each other like you did when you first saddled up. 5 Look how far you've slid down the mountain. Cinch back up and ride hard to get to where you were before. If you don't change your ways, I will take your torch away. 6 But don't get too discouraged. I will give you credit though, you don't like the sorry ways of the Nicolaitans any more than I do.

7 Open your ears and pay attention to what the Spirit has to say to the seven outfits. To those who finish their hard ride for me, I will give freely to them the fruit from the tree of life that sits in the middle of paradise.

A Letter to the Outfit in Smyrna

8 "To the angel of the outfit in Smyrna, write these words:

These are the very words of him who was first and is last—the one who died, but is no longer dead. 9 I know your terrible struggles and the poverty in which you've lived. Your poverty has made you rich with me. I have heard all the sorry things that have been said of you. They claim to be Jews, but their church belongs to Satan, not God. 10 Don't fret over the suffering that will happen soon. The devil will throw some of y'all in prison to test your courage.

You will suffer for ten days, but if you remain faithful in the face of death, you will get the trophy buckle of life.

11 Open up your ears and listen to the what the Spirit says to the outfits of God. The one who remains in the saddle all the way until the end will not be hurt at all by the second death.

A Letter to the Outfit in Pergamum

12 "To the angel of the outfit in Pergamum, write these words:

This is the letter from the one who wields the deadly-sharp sword. 13 I know you live in the area where Satan has his throne, but you have remained loyal to my brand. None of you denied riding for me, even when Antipas, my trusted cowboy, was killed where Satan resides.

14 But don't go patting yourselves on the back just yet. You say nothing even though some around you teach things like Balaam did. He showed Balak how to get the people of Israel bucked off. He told them it was okay to eat food sacrificed to idols. He said there was nothing wrong with committing sexual sins. 15 Y'all have some Nicolaitans around y'all doing these same things. 16 Quit keeping your mouth shut. I've about had enough of them. If they don't stop it, I will put them to the sword of my word.

17 Open up your ears and listen to the what the Spirit says to the outfits of God. To the one who stays in the saddle until the end, I will give the manna of heaven. I will also hand them a white stone with a new name inscribed on it that only they will understand.

A Letter to the Outfit in Thyatira

18 "To the angel of the outfit in Thyatira, write these words:

This is I, God's Son, whose eyes shine like the sun and whose feet are like furnace-fired metal. 19 I have seen the great things you've done. I've seen your love and faith, service and fortitude. You are doing more now than you did in the beginning. That's riding for me!

²⁰ But there is one thing I need to point out, you've let Jezebel have free rein. She calls herself a prophet and teaches my cowboys to have nasty sexual relations and even eat food that was sacrificed to false gods. ²¹ I've given her enough rope to get herself out of her sin, but she refuses. She's going to use it to hang herself with. ²² The adulterous bed she lies in will become her suffering. Even those who come to her bed will suffer unless they turn from their sorry ways first. ²³ Her children won't even survive. This will be a sign to all the outfits that I know the hearts and minds of all. Nothing is hidden from me and each will get what they deserve.

²⁴ To the rest of y'all in Thyatira who've not fallen for her treachery and the devil's lies, I'm not going to make things any harder on y'all. ²⁵ Y'all just take a deep seat and screw your hat down until I get back.

²⁶ To all who finish the long ride with me, I will make them straw bosses over all the nations. ²⁷ They will rule with a metal-handled quirt and smash them like glass jars.

²⁸ They will have the same power as I got from my Dad and I will even give them the morning star. If you've got ears, listen to what the Spirit is telling you.

CHAPTER 3

A Letter to the Outfit in Sardis

"To the angel of the outfit in Sardis, write these words:

This letter is from the one who can hold the seven spirits of God in one hand and seven stars in the other.

I can see through your charade. You talk big, but you walk small. You put on big airs, but you are dead to me. ² But I'm telling you to get up! Get back in the saddle before I change my mind. You've got a lot to do and little time to do it. ³ Do the things you did at first when you started riding for me. You've gotten lazy and now it's time to come back. If you don't get back on track, I'll come like a horse thief in the night and you won't even know what hit you.

⁴ Yet, there are a few top hands left in Sardis. They will wear white pearl snap shirts. They will walk with me and ride by my side for they are worthy. ⁵ The one who is victorious over death will also be in white. I will not erase top hand's names from the Life Book. Even more than that, I will say that cowboy's name personally, with honor, to my Father and the angels when the time comes to stand before the throne.

⁶ If you've got ears, you best be listening to what the Spirit is saying to the outfits.

A Letter to the Outfit in Philadelphia

⁷ "To the angel of the outfit in Philadelphia, write these words:

The one who holds the key of David is the one speaking. What he locks stays locked and what he wants opened gets opened. ⁸ I have seen what happened to you. I can tell you are completely spent and worn out. I have opened a door for you that no one can close. You have been loyal to my brand and never denied me. ⁹ I will make those who ride for the devil, even though they call themselves real cowboys, come and bow down before you and acknowledge that y'all are the real hands who I love. ¹⁰ Since you did what I said and rode the tough trail to the end, I will keep you from the time of testing that the rest of the world will have to endure.

¹¹ I'm riding back soon. Don't let up or someone else might steal your prize. ¹² All who finish their ride, I will make them a pillar in the house of God. Their spot will forever be theirs. I will write on them the name of God, his city, and my new name that no one knows. ¹³ If you've got ears, use them to hear what the Spirit says to the outfits.

A Letter to the Outfit in Laodicea

¹⁴ "To the angel of the outfit in Laodicea, write these words:

These are the words of the first and last amen, the one who saw and revealed, the ramrod over God's pastures. ¹⁵ I know what you've done. I know you are neither hot nor cold. You can't rope or ride. I wish you could at least do one. ¹⁶ I'm fixing to spit you out like a bad taste in my mouth. ¹⁷ You think you are rich and don't need anything else. But what you don't understand is you are actually poorer than dirt, blind, and naked. ¹⁸ You should listen to me and I'll show you real wealth. What I have has been proven on the tough trails. I have clothes that are white to cover your shame. I have medicine for your eyes to make you see the truth.

¹⁹ Listen, if I didn't care, I wouldn't be hard on you. Stand up and be a man and turn your back on the sorry ways that got you into this mess. ²⁰ Look at me! I stand on your porch and knock at your door. Anyone who hears me and invites me in, I will sup with them and them with me.

²¹ To the one who rides to the end, they will sit on the throne with me. I rode to the end and was invited to sit on the throne with my Father.

²² If you've got ears, you best be listening to what the Spirit is saying to the outfits."

CHAPTER 4

A Look into the Big House

I turned around and saw right into heaven through a door that had been opened. The same voice that had first spoke to me like a trumpet spoke to me again and said, "Come on in. I'm going to show you what happens next." ² Then the Holy Ghost showed me someone sitting on the throne in heaven. ³ This someone shone like they were made of precious gems. An emerald rainbow circled the throne. ⁴ Around this throne were twenty-four more thrones. Seated on them were the twenty-four old bosses. They were dressed in white shirts with shining buckles on their belts. ⁵ Thunder and lightning rolled from the throne down to the seven torches that were blazing bright. ⁶ The area in front of the throne was like a river of glass and crystal.

Now, around the throne were four critters. They were covered in eyes from the front to the back. ⁷ The first critter looked like a lion, the second like a cow, the third looked like a man, and the fourth was like an eagle. ⁸ Every one of these critters had six wings each. Each wing was covered in eyes on top and bottom. All I saw them do, day and night, was sing, "Holy, holy, holy is the Almighty—who is, was, and will be."

⁹ When they would sing and honor the Forever One on the throne, ¹⁰ the twenty-four old bosses would hit their knees to honor him, too. They would offer their buckles that had been given to them to the throne and say, ¹¹ "Only you are worthy of honor, our Lord. All of creation takes a knee before you because you made all of it."

CHAPTER 5

A Lion and a Lamb

Then the one on the throne had a scroll in his right hand. It was sealed with seven seals and had writing on the inside and out from what I could tell. ² Just then a mighty angel roared, "Who is worthy to open the scroll?" ³ But no one in heaven or earth was able to open it and read what it said.

⁴ Tears formed in my eyes because there was no one good enough to break the seals and see what the scroll said. ⁵ One of the twenty-four old bosses turned to me and said, "Quit your snivelin'! Look there, the Lion of the tribe of Judah has won and is worthy to open the scroll."

⁶ But when I turned to look, I saw a Lamb that had been slaughtered. It was standing in front of the throne and all the others gathered there. The Lamb had seven horns and seven eyes, which somehow, I knew was the sevenfold Spirit of God that is sent to all corners of the earth. ⁷ The slaughtered Lamb stepped forward and took the scroll from the right hand of the Mighty One who sat on the throne. ⁸ When he'd taken it, all the old bosses and animals circling the throne fell down before the Lamb. All of them had a harp and bowls filled with prayers to God that smelled like incense. ⁹ A new song began, "You alone are worthy to open the seals. Your blood was used to purchase every person from every tribe and every nation. Your sacrifice was enough! ¹⁰ They are now a kingdom of priests that serve God and God alone, and they will rule the earth."

[11] I looked again and saw millions of angels around the throne and around those gathered there. [12] They sang in a loud voice, "The Lamb that was slaughtered has been found worthy—power, wealth, wisdom, strength, honor, glory, and praise are his!"

[13] And then all of creation itself lifted its voice to join in, "All bow down to the One on the throne and to the Lamb. Glory and honor forever!"

[14] When the song was finished, the four creatures surrounding the throne said, "Amen!" And the old bosses took a knee and worshipped again.

CHAPTER 6

I watched as the Lamb tore off the first seal. Then one of the four creatures roared, "Ride out!"

[2] What I saw was a cowboy on a white horse with a bow and a crown. He rode out to conquer the world and be triumphant in many battles.

[3] Then the Lamb tore off the second seal. The second creature roared, "Ride out!" [4] Another horse rode out. It was a sorrel horse with the deepest color of red I'd ever seen. The cowboy who rode it was given the power to wage war on earth and make people slaughter each other. He rode tall in the saddle with a large sword held in his hand.

[5] Then the Lamb tore off the third seal. The third creature roared, "Ride out!" This time the horse was midnight black. The cowboy held a set of balancing scales in his hand. [6] From among the creatures, a voice said, "A quart of wheat and three of barley for a day's wage. Take all the oil and wine you want."

[7] Then the Lamb tore off the fourth seal. The fourth creature roared, "Ride out!" [8] This horse was pale grey and its rider was called Death, and Hell was right behind him. They were given power over a quarter of the earth. They were to kill by war, famine, disease, and wild beasts.

[9] Then the Lamb tore off the fifth seal. All of a sudden, I could see underneath the throne. There were all the cowboys and cowgirls who'd been slain for riding for the Lord. [10] They all shouted out, "Mighty God! How long before you judge the earth for our deaths?" [11] Each of them were given a white shirt and told to wait a little bit longer. They had to wait until the complete number of other cowboys and cowgirls had been killed for their faith.

[12] The Lamb tore off the sixth seal. The earth shook with a violent quake and the sun went out. The moon turned blood red. [13] Stars fell from the sky like figs shaken from a tree during a storm. [14] The sky slammed shut like a big book, and every mountain and island was moved from its foundation. [15] All the people of the earth, whether powerful or weak, hid themselves in caves under rocks. [16] They all cried out, "Crush us with the weight of the world! It is better than being seen by the One on the throne and suffering the wrath of the Lamb! [17] Nobody can bear their anger."

CHAPTER 7

Then I saw four mighty angels standing at the four corners of the earth and holding back the wind. The sea didn't move and not a single leaf stirred over the whole earth. [2] Another angel came in from the east carrying the seal of the Living God. He shouted to the four angels holding the wind, [3] "Hold up! Don't harm the land or the sea until we have branded all the cowboys who ride for God."

[4] And I heard the tally of those given the brand. There were 144,000 marked with the brand of God from the twelve tribes of Israel. The tallies were: [5] Judah—12,000, Reuben—12,000, Gad—12,000, [6] Asher—12,000, Naphtali—12,000, Manasseh—12,000, [7] Simeon—12,000, Levi—12,000, Issachar—12,000, [8] Zebulun—12,000, Joseph—12,000, and Benjamin—12,000.

[9] Then an enormous crowd appeared. There were more people than a cattle buyer could count. They were from every nation, every breed, and every color. They stood in front of the Lamb with white shirts and holding an olive branches in their hands. [10] They all cried out in unison, "God is the only one who can save us! There is only God who sits on the throne and his Lamb!"

[11] All the angels, the four living creatures, and the old bosses all threw themselves on the ground in front of the throne and worshiped God. [12] They all said, "Amen! Praise, glory, wisdom, thankfulness, honor, power, and strength belong solely to God forever and ever! Amen."

[13] One of the old bosses turned to me and asked, "Who are these dressed in white shirts and where do the hail from?"

[14] "I ain't quite sure, sir, but I bet you have a notion," I answered.

He said, "These are the ones who've come through the terrible ride. They were washed in the blood of the Lamb and were made white. [15] That is why they stand before the throne and worship God day and night. He who sits on the throne protects them with his presence. [16] Never again will they experience hunger or thirst. Never again will the sun burn down on them. [17] The Lamb, who is in the center of the throne, is their shepherd. He guides them to the springs of eternal life. God will wipe away every tear from their eyes for all time."

CHAPTER 8

The Lamb Tears Open the Seventh Seal

When the Lamb tore open the seventh seal, there was silence in heaven for about thirty minutes. [2] Seven angels of the Lord were given seven bugles.

[3] Another angel had what looked like a lantern with smoldering coals in it. He strode up to the throne and was given something to add to the smoldering fire within the lantern. [4] The smoke started to rise from the golden lantern and it wafted along with the prayers from all of God's cowboys that other angels delivered to the throne. [5] Then the angel with the golden lantern filled it with fresh fire from the altar and slung it down upon the earth. Thunder crashed and lightning flashed as the ground shook.

The Bugles

[6] Then the seven angels with the seven bugles took a deep breath.

[7] The first angel blew his bugle. Hail and fire made of blood struck the earth. A third of everything on the earth perished.

[8] Then the second angel blew his bugle. A huge mountain of flame descended from the heavens and struck the ocean. [9] A third of the sea was turned to blood and the fire killed a third of the inhabitants who lived there. One out of three ships on the oceans were destroyed instantly.

[10] Then the third angel took his turn. Something like a star dropped out of the sky and struck a third of the rivers and springs. [11] The star was called Bitterness. A third of the rivers and springs became unusable and unable to sustain life. The waters turned bitter and people died from drinking it.

[12] Then the fourth angel let loose his bugle call. A third of the sun, moon, and stars went dark. There was no light for a third of the day and a third of the night.

[13] Then I spotted an eagle on the wing. It flew high and mighty and cried out in a loud voice, "Doom! Pain! Horror! How terrible it will be for all who ride when the last three angels let loose their bugle cry!"

CHAPTER 9

The Terror of the Fifth

Then the fifth angel blew his bugle. I saw a star that had crashed to the earth. It had the key to the well of the bottomless sinkhole. [2] The star unlocked the sinkhole and smoke billowed forth as if from the fire of a blacksmith's forge. The smoke blotted out what was left of the light of the sun and clogged most of the air over the entire earth. [3] Locusts appeared out of the smoke with tails like scorpions. [4] They only targeted and tormented those without the brand of Christ on the foreheads. [5] The terrible locusts were not allowed to kill the unbranded, but only to inflict tremendous torture on them for five months. [6] During those five months, people will look for death to ease the pain, but be unable to find it.

[7] The locusts were like battle-ready horses lined up across the fields. They had crowns on their heads with faces of men. [8] Their hair was long like a woman's, but their teeth were those of lions. [9] They had iron breastplates of armor and their wings sounded like chariots racing across the battlefield in pursuit of another victim. [10] Their tails were like scorpions with needles like swords, ready to inflict pain and suffering as quickly as a rattlesnake's strike. For five months they will ravage the lives of the unbranded. [11] They have a ruler—the angel in charge of the abyss. His Hebrew name is Abaddon, or in Greek they call him, Apollyon (meaning "The Destroyer").

[12] After this first horror is complete, there are still two more to come.

[13] The sixth angel blew his bugle. I heard a loud voice coming from the four corners of the altar of God. [14] The voice said to the angel, "Release

the four angels bound at the Euphrates Creek!" [15] These four angel's shackles were cut loose. It is their day. It is their hour. It is the minute they were made for. Their mission, their only mission, is to kill a third of the human race. [16] These four angels took the form of two hundred million horses and their riders. Their breastplates shone like hot iron, blue as sapphire and yellow like glowing sulfur.

[17] The horses had heads like lions. Fire, smoke, and sulfur poured out of their mouths like deadly exhaust. [18] One out of every three people on earth were killed by these three plagues—fire, smoke, and sulfur which came out of the horse's mouths. [19] The horse's strength wasn't confined to their mouth. They had tails like venomous vipers that struck and killed with deadly quickness and precision.

[20] But still, even those who weren't killed did not turn away from their lust after materialistic idols. They didn't stop worshiping demons, idols of gold, stone, wood, and bronze. [21] They didn't repent of evil ways such as murder, witchcraft, sexual immorality, or thieving.

CHAPTER 10

The Angel with the Little Scroll

Then another mighty angel appeared out of heaven. He wore a cloud and a rainbow for a crown. His face was as bright as the sun and his legs were pillars of molten fire. [2] He had a little scroll open in his hand. He placed one mighty leg on the sea and the other on the land. [3] He called out in a thunderous voice that sounded like a million lions. His call was answered by the seven thunders. [4] I was about to write down what they said, but a voice told me, "Keep that part to yourself. Do not write it down."

[5] The mighty angel standing on the land and the sea raised his right hand to the sky and [6] made a promise in the name of God who is eternal, who is the creator of heaven and earth and everything in between. The angel said, "Now is the time! [7] When the seventh bugle has been sounded, God's secret plan will be revealed. This secret is known to his cowboys and the old hands who rode for him."

[8] The voice from heaven spoke to me again and said, "Go take the little scroll from the angel standing on the land and sea."

[9] I did as instructed and the angel said, "Eat it. It will be like honey in your mouth, but your stomach will sour."

[10] I took the scroll and ate it. Sure enough, it tasted sweeter than the sweetest honey. But my stomach instantly turned over when I swallowed. [11] Then the voice said, "Once again you must ride out and tell of God's work to all men and all nations, sparing no king or peasant."

CHAPTER 11

The Two Cowboys

I was then given a staff with measurements on it. I was told, "Go and measure the house of God and its altar. Take a tally of those worshiping there. [2] Do not bother measuring the outer court because it has been handed over to the Outlaws. They will trample the Holy City for forty-two months. [3] I will send my two cowboys to preach the message for 1,260 days."

[4] The two cowboys are the two olive trees and the two lanterns that stand before the Lord of the earth. [5] Those who try to harm them will be consumed by fire that comes out of the two cowboy's mouths. Everyone who tries to harm them will be utterly consumed in brimstone. [6] These two hands will have the power to stop the rain during the time they preach the good news. They will be able to turn springs into blood and strike the earth with any plague they wish as often as they want.

[7] When their preaching is done, the foul beast will come up out of the abyss and fight them. The battle will be fierce and the cowboys will be killed. [8] Their bodies will lie like dead dogs in same streets where Jesus was crucified. Jerusalem will become like Sodom or Egypt. [9] People from all nations, tribes, crews, languages, and races will walk past their bodies for three and half days. They will keep the bodies from being buried. [10] There will be dancing and celebrating in the streets because these two cowboys were defeated. They will have blamed them for all the suffering the earth had endured.

[11] After the three and a half days were up, the breath of God came down and the cowboys stood back up. People ran for their lives and were terrified. [12] Then the two cowboys heard a voice from heaven that said, "Get up here!" As their enemies watched, the two cowboys rode right into heaven in a cloud.

[13] When they had gone, a mighty earthquake shook the foundations of the earth and a tenth of Jerusalem was destroyed along with seven thousand people. The ones left alive started praising the greatness and might of the God of Heaven. [14] The second horror had come to completion, but the third was saddling up.

The Seventh Bugle

[15] Then the seventh angel sounded his bugle. Loud voices rang out in heaven saying, "The power to rule the world has now returned to God and his Messiah. He will rule forever and ever!" [16] The twenty-four old bosses, who sit on their thrones in front of God threw themselves down upon their faces and worshiped God saying, [17] "Almighty God! The one who is and who was. Thankfully, the time has come for you to reveal your power and regain your rule over the earth! [18] The angry nations now get to taste your wrath and power. The time has come for the dead to be judged. The time of reward has come for your cowboys, those who rode for you, served you, revered you, and trusted you. The time has come to bring destruction to the destroyers."

[19] The doors of God's house in heaven were thrown open and the Ark of the Covenant was there for all to see. Lightning flashed, thunder roared, earthquakes shook, and hail filled the skies.

CHAPTER 12

The Lady and the Dragon

Then an amazing sight was seen in the sky. A lady with a dress like the sun was standing on top of the moon with a crown of twelve stars. [2] She cried out with the pain of childbirth as her time was near.

[3] Another amazing sight appeared in the sky. A monstrous red dragon took flight. It had seven heads and ten Watusi horns. Each head wore its own crown. [4] The dragon's tail swept one third of the stars out of the sky and flung them to the earth. It stood in front of the woman with saliva falling out of its mouth waiting to devour her child the second it was born. [5] The lady gave birth to a king. This king will rule forever with an iron rod. Before the dragon could devour the boy, he was taken quickly to the throne of God. [6] The lady was secreted away to a place in the desert that God had prepared for her. She will stay there and be guarded for 1,260 days.

[7] Then war broke out in heaven. The boss angel, Michael, along with his angels, battled against the dragon and its angels. [8] The dragon was defeated and it was kicked out of heaven with the other angels who had fought at its side. [9] The huge dragon was thrown out. You know the dragon as that ancient snake, the devil, or Satan, the deceiver of the world. He was thrown down to earth and all his angels fell with him.

[10] Then a booming voice from heaven said, "Salvation and power has come! God has shown his power as King and the authority of his Messiah. The accuser of man has been cast down out of heaven. [11] The battle was won by the power of the blood of the Lamb and the power of the good news the cowboys taught. And lastly, they didn't pause while looking death in the face. They were willing to die for the truth. [12] Heaven can rejoice now that the dragon is no longer there, but that cannot be said for the earth and sea. For the devil is now with you and he is enraged at his defeat. He knows there is little time left for him to destroy man."

[13] When the dragon woke up and realized where he was, he took flight to look for the lady. [14] She was given wings like a great eagle to fly her to the place in the desert. There she will stay for three and half years, safe from the dragon's insatiable appetite. [15] The dragon's mouth spit forth a flood of water in hopes of killing the lady. [16] But the earth came to her rescue and swallowed up all the water. [17] When that didn't work, the dragon waged war on her descendants, who are all of those who ride for the brand. [18] The dragon perched on the seashore and waited.

CHAPTER 13

The Beasts

Then I noticed a great beast coming out of the sea. It also had seven heads and ten horns with ten crowns. Each head had a name written on it that blasphemed God. [2] The beast looked like a leopard with bear's feet and a lion's mouth. The dragon gave its strength and power to the beast, as well as its throne and its dominating authority. [3] One of the heads looked like it had been wounded, but it had healed. The whole earth was enamored by the beast and fell in love with it. [4] The world worshiped the dragon because of the power it had given the leopard. They also worshiped the beast saying things like, "The beast is all powerful and not even God can stand against it."

[5] The beast bellowed its proud claims of invincibility and continually hurled insults at God. It was allowed to strut its pride for forty-two months. [6] It cursed God, his name, his home in heaven, and all those who reside there. [7] It was allowed to fight against God's cowboys and win. It was also allowed to have authority over every nation, tribe, race, and language. [8] Everyone living on earth worshiped the beast, except for those whose name was in the brand registry. This book belongs to the Lamb of God that was slain.

[9] Open your ears if you've got 'em! [10] All who are meant to be captured will be. All who are meant to die by the sword will. If you ride for the Lord, ride tall with courage, honor, and faith.

[11] Then another beast was seen coming up out of the ground. It had two horns like a lamb, but it spoke like a dragon. [12] It was like a puppet of the leopard. It made everyone worship the first beast that had been healed of a deathly strike. [13] This second beast performed many miracles. It called down fire from the skies for everyone to see. [14] It deceived all the people of the earth with these miracles it was granted to perform while with the first beast. The second beast commanded idols to be made and worshiped of the leopard (which had been mortally wounded by a sword, but still lived). [15] The second beast had been given the power to bring the first back like a zombie to be worshiped. The first beast was made to talk and walk. It could even kill those who didn't worship it. [16] The beast forced all people, big or small, rich or poor, slave or free, to have a mark placed on their right hand or forehead. [17] You couldn't buy or sell without this mark—the beast's brand, which is his name or number that means his name.

[18] This will take a whole bunch of wisdom to figure out the meaning of the number of the beast. The number stands for the name of someone. The number is 666.

CHAPTER 14

The Lamb and the 144,000

Then I saw the Lamb standing on Zion Mountain. He was surrounded by 144,000 cowboys who had his brand on their foreheads. [2] I heard a sound coming from heaven that sounded like thunder mixed with powerful ocean waves breaking against a rocky shore. At the same time, it sounded like a million stringed instruments playing in unison.

[3] A great ensemble of cowboys sang a wonderful new song in front of the throne of God, the twenty-four old bosses and the four living creatures. No one knew the song except for the 144,000. [4] They have kept themselves pure as virgins, riding for the Lord down every trail he went. This great host of cowboys was purchased from all the inhabitants of the earth as a special offering to God and to the Lamb. [5] These cowboys have told no lies and are without blame.

Tres Angels

[6] Then I saw a great angel flying in the air. He told the good news to the whole world. [7] "Do not cower or be afraid!" he shouted. "Give glory to God, for the time has arrived for him to sit and judge the world. Worship the one who made it all."

[8] A second angel followed the first saying, "She's been yard-darted! The great Babylon has been bucked off and rises no more. She was a whore who intoxicated mankind with her passions."

[9] A third angel appeared behind the other two, trumpeting with a loud voice, "Those with the brand of the beast on their hand or forehead [10] will drink the hard liquor of God's fury, which is his anger against those he did so much for, but was repaid with evil. Those with the brand of the beast will suffer in fire and sulfur before the angels and the Lamb. [11] The smoke from that fire never goes out or loses its heat. There will be no relief, day or night for those who worship the beast and its image."

[12] Meanwhile, God's cowboys stand patient and steadfast, continuing to follow and worship the word of God and riding for Jesus.

[13] Then a voice from heaven said, "Write this down: 'Great rewards for those who die from here on out in service of the Lord.'"

"It's true!" answers the Holy Spirit. "They will enjoy rest from the hard ride because what they have reaped, they will now sow forever in perfection."

A Time of Harvest

¹⁴ Then I saw a cowboy sitting on a white cloud. He had a crown on his head and a sickle in his hand. ¹⁵ Another angel came from God's house and said to the one on the cloud, "Use your sickle and reap the harvest. The time has come to harvest the earth!" ¹⁶ The cowboy rose up and used the tool, and the earth's harvest was gathered.

¹⁷ Then another angel appeared with his own sharp sickle.

¹⁸ Still another angel appeared. He was the one in charge of the fire of the altar. His voice boomed as he said to the angel with the sharp sickle, "Use your tool and cut the grapes from the vines of the earth. They are ripe and ready for harvest." ¹⁹ So the angel swung his sickle on the earth, and all the grapes were thrown into the distillery of God's furious anger. ²⁰ The grapes were squeezed out in the press outside the city and blood flowed for two hundred miles at five feet deep.

CHAPTER 15

Angels of the Last Plague

Just when I thought I'd seen it all, there were seven more angels carrying seven more plagues. These were the last ones because they were the final outpouring of God's anger.

² Then I saw something that was like a sea of glass and fire. Standing on the sea of glass were those who had fiddles. These were the ones who had won victory over the two beasts and the one with a number for a name. ³ They played the song of Moses on their fiddles and the lyrics of the Lamb, "Our mighty God, you are triumphant and good! You are the King of all nations and rule in honor and righteousness. ⁴ Who doesn't look at you with wonder? Who will say you are not great? You are the one, the only one who is true. All countries bow before you, because your good deeds are seen by all."

⁵ Then I saw the gates of heaven thrown open wide and the sacred teepee was there. ⁶ The seven angels came out of it carrying the seven plagues. They wore solid white shirts with gold ties. ⁷ One of the four living creatures gave the seven angels seven gold bowls that contained all of God's anger. ⁸ The house of God was filled with smoke and the glory of the one who makes his home there. No one could enter until the seven bowls had been emptied out.

CHAPTER 16

Then a voice echoed throughout heaven and said, "Release God's anger on the earth!"

² The first angel flung the contents of his bowl on the earth like someone throwing out dirty dishwater. Suddenly, those with the brand of the beast got sores all over the bodies. These people wailed and cried at the pain inflicted by the contents of the bowl.

³ Then the second angel poured his bowl into the sea. The water became like thick, congealed blood of someone who was dead. Every living thing in the sea died.

⁴ The third angel watched all this happen and the poured out his bowl in the rivers and springs of the earth. Just like the sea, they all turned to blood. ⁵ This angel cried out, "This is right, O Holy One. Your judgments are fair and just. You are the one who is, was, and will be. ⁶ These people didn't flinch when they poured out the blood of your prophets and cowboys, so you have given them blood to drink. It is time to pay the fiddler." ⁷ Then a voice from the throne room said, "Mighty God! True and just are your judgments upon the earth."

⁸ The fourth angel stepped forth and poured his bowl upon the sun. The sun's fire intensified and ⁹ everyone with the brand of the beast was burned and scorched. They cussed God, but would not turn from their sins. They scoffed at his power and greatness.

¹⁰ The fifth angel poured his bowl upon the throne of the beast. Darkness permeated its kingdom like a living force. People bit their own tongues off from the pain of the darkness. ¹¹ Still they cussed God and didn't turn away from their sins.

¹² The sixth angel poured out his bowl upon the mighty Euphrates Creek. The creek became a dry riverbed for the kings of the East to travel down easily. ¹³ Then I saw three demons that looked like frogs come from the mouth of the

dragon, the beast, and its puppet (who is the false prophet). ¹⁴ These demons could perform miracles and they went out to the kings of the earth. They gathered them together for battle against the Lord on the day of the Almighty God and his judgement.

¹⁵ "Stay awake on night watch! I come like a thief at night. Blessed are those who stay dressed and awake. Those who don't will run around the streets naked and ashamed."

¹⁶ The demon frogs inhabiting the kings of the earth came to do battle with God at the place in Hebrew called Armageddon.

¹⁷ The seventh angel poured out his bowl upon the air. A loud voice from the throne room of God said, "The last bowl has been emptied! It is done!" ¹⁸ Earthquakes, thunder, and lightning ripped the earth apart. This was the largest earthquake since the beginning of creation. ¹⁹ The great city was torn into thirds and every city in every country was utterly destroyed. God especially remembered Babylon and made her drink directly from the bowl of his anger. ²⁰ Every mountain and island on the earth disappeared. ²¹ Hundred-pound chunks of ice fell from the sky on the people who continued to cuss God because of the plagues of his wrath.

CHAPTER 17

The Whore

One of the angels who had poured out a bowl came over and said, "Ride with me. I'm going to show you what will happen to that great whore called Babylon. ² She has intoxicated countless kings with her wine and the whole world has become enslaved to her immorality."

³ The Holy Spirit took control of me and the angel and I rode out to the desert. I saw a woman sitting on a beast that was covered in words that cussed God. This beast had seven heads and ten horns. ⁴ She wore red and purple and was covered in fancy jewelry. She held a wine glass in her hand filled with the filth of her immorality. ⁵ She had a tattoo on her forehead with a secret meaning, "Babylon the Great, mother of whores and perverts." ⁶ The whore was drunk on the blood of God's cowboys who had been killed.

I looked at her in amazement, ⁷ but the angel asked me, "Why do you look at her like that? I'll let you in on who she is and who the beast she

rides is. ⁸ The beast was alive at one time, having crawled out of the hole, but will soon go off to be destroyed. Those who are still alive who aren't written down in the tally book of life will look at the beast and be amazed. It was once alive, now dead, but it will rise again.

⁹ "This all calls for a bunch of understanding and wisdom. The seven heads are the seven hills where the whore sits. They are hills, but also kings. ¹⁰ Five of the kings are dead, one is still alive, and the other one isn't here yet. When he gets here, his time will be short. ¹¹ The beast itself might be considered an eighth king, but still one of the seven. But remember, he is headed straight to hell.

¹² "The ten horns are kings who haven't had their rule yet. They will be given one hour to rule with the beast, that is all. ¹³ These ten kings will only have one purpose—to make the beast stronger. ¹⁴ There will be a fight with the Lamb and his cowboys, but the beast and his followers will be defeated because Jesus is the Lord of lords and the King of kings."

¹⁵ The angel then said, "The waters upon which the whore sits are the nations, races, and people of the earth. ¹⁶ The ten horns and the beast will turn on the whore. They will take everything from her and leave her naked in the street to die with her flesh ripped and burned away. ¹⁷ This was God's plan all along, for everyone to give power to the beast until the word of God is complete.

¹⁸ "The woman you saw is a symbol of the city that rules the earth with fear and tyranny."

CHAPTER 18

Then I saw another angel ride out of heaven. You could tell by the way he rode that he had authority and by the way he sat, the saddle brightened the whole earth. ² He hollered out, "She's done for! The great Babylon has fallen. She camps in a ghost town of demons now. Vultures and buzzards live within her. ³ Every nation has partaken of her bittersweet wine of her immoral lust. Kings slept with her and businesses of the world grew rich off of her sexuality."

⁴ Then another voice from heaven shouted, "Pop your dallies and get away from her! Don't partake in her sins; you don't want to share in the punishment she's got comin'. ⁵ Her wrongs

are stacked against her all the way to heaven and God will not forget her wicked deeds. ⁶ Give her a taste of her own medicine. Double-cross her like she double-crossed you. Give her twice the crap she's been giving you. ⁷ Throw a trip on her like all the times she reveled in knocking you down. She thinks she's some sort of untouchable queen who will never experience hard times. ⁸ But God's going to give her what she's got coming. In just one day, she'll be afflicted with disaster—festers, failure, and famine. And then she will be thrown in the branding fire because the One who judges her is mighty and just.

⁹ "The rulers of the earth who enjoyed her so much will grovel and weep when they see her burned to the ground. ¹⁰ But they ain't stupid, they won't get too close because they don't want to get a taste of what she's going through. They will say, 'This is horrible. What a waste! In just one hour Babylon has been brought down.'

¹¹ "The businessmen of the earth will also cry out in loss. No one will buy from them anymore. ¹² No one will purchase their gold, silver, jewels, and shiny pearls. No one will buy their fine linen, purple cloth, silk, or scarlet robes, no rare woods or things made of elephant tusk, bronze, metal, or marble. ¹³ There will be no market for their cinnamon, spice, smoking incense, myrrh, or frankincense, wine or oil, flour or wheat, cattle or sheep, horses or carriages, slaves, or even human lives.

¹⁴ "The businessmen will say to her, 'Every fancy trinket you strove for is gone with your wealth and your beauty. They will never be found again.' ¹⁵ These businessmen too will stand a long way off. Neither do they want to share in her suffering. Sure, they will cry and whine ¹⁶ and say, 'This is a total waste. How terrible is this day?! She used to be the most beautiful and decorated thing on earth, ¹⁷ but in one hour she lies in ruin.'

"Others who will stand a long way off and observe the destruction are the ships' captains, their passengers, the sailors, and all who earned their living on the water. ¹⁸ They will also cry out in anguish as the flames consume her. 'She was the greatest city ever!' ¹⁹ They will paw at the dirt and cry and wail, saying, 'This is such a terrible loss. This is the worst thing that has ever happened. She made all the ships of the world rich. All of it is gone in one hour.'

²⁰ "But heaven rejoices at her destruction. God's cowboys, prophets, and apostles all let out a cheer. God has paid the whore back for all she did to God's people."

²¹ Then a huge angel picked up a boulder that looked like a millstone and threw it into the sea. He said, "This is how Babylon will be thrown down and never seen again. ²² No more music or choirs, flutes or trumpets will ever be heard from your lips again. No work or trade will ever surface around you. ²³ Never again will your lamp light the way toward sinful deeds; no more will you entice brides and grooms. Your business partners were the most powerful in the world, but now they are none. No longer will your magic influence anyone."

²⁴ Babylon was punished for the blood of God's people who were found inside her gates. Blood from every part of the earth had stained her streets.

CHAPTER 19

After this I heard a loud celebration in heaven. Everyone was shouting, "Praise God! Salvation, glory, and power are God's and God's alone. ² His rule is right and just. He has condemned the whore who condemned the earth with her immorality and wickedness. God has defeated her because she killed his cowboys."

³ Then again they shouted, "Praise God! The smoke from the fires of her destruction rises forever and ever!"

⁴ Then the twenty-four old bosses and four living creatures took a knee before God and worshiped him who was on the throne. They repeated over and over, "Amen! Praise God!"

The Wedding Fiesta and the Lamb

⁵ Then a voice from the throne came saying, "Praise God, all his cowboys and all his hands, both big and small, who honor him."

⁶ Then the sound of a crowd like a rushing waterfall or peals of thunder came. I heard them say, "Praise God! Almighty God who is our Lord! God is King! ⁷ Be happy all of you and praise God's greatness! The time of the wedding for the Lamb has come. His bride has prepared herself for this time. ⁸ She's been given white to wear

for her purity." (This stands for the good deeds of God's cowboys.)

⁹ Then the angel told me, "Jot this down: 'Happy are those who take part in the wedding fiesta of the Lamb.' These are the true words of God himself."

¹⁰ I fell on my face to worship him, but he jerked me back up and said, "No way, cowboy. I'm a servant like you and all the other cowboys who believed Jesus was the Truth. Worship God only."

For the truth Jesus proclaimed is what the prophets talked about.

¹¹ Then the gates of heaven opened onto the narrow trail and there was a cowboy, called Faithful and True, riding on a white horse. He is justice and fights with truth. ¹² His eyes were like fire and he wore many crowns. His name was written on himself, but only he knows what it means. ¹³ The clothes he wore were covered in blood. His name is the Word of God. ¹⁴ The armies of heaven rode on white horses in a jig line behind him. They were all dressed in white pearl snap shirts. ¹⁵ Out of his mouth came a sword with which he will mow down his enemies. He will rule them with an iron rod and smash his enemies like grapes in the winepress of God's fury. ¹⁶ On his shirt and on his thigh was written "King of kings and Lord of lords."

¹⁷ Then I saw an angel standing on top of the sun. He called out to all the birds of the air and said, "Come, for a great feast awaits you! ¹⁸ Eat the flesh of those who thought they were powerful—kings, generals, soldiers, prideful cowboys and their mounts, the bodies of all unbelievers, slave and free, great and small alike."

¹⁹ Then I saw the beast and the kings of the earth marshal their armies against the cowboy on the white horse and his army. ²⁰ The beast was taken prisoner along with the false prophet who had performed miracles in his presence. (It was those miracles that mesmerized those who had the brand of the beast and those who worshiped it.) The beast and the false prophet were hurled into the lake of fire that burns with the yellow glow of sulfur. ²¹ Their armies were mowed down by the sword that came from the mouth of the one riding the horse. All the birds cried out in delight at the feast of flesh they were allowed to partake of.

CHAPTER 20

A Thousand Years

Then an angel rode out of heaven carrying the key to the bottomless pit and a heavy chain. ² He grabbed the dragon, that old snake—the devil or Satan—and hog tied him for a thousand years. ³ The angel chunked him into the pit and locked it up tight. That old dragon wouldn't be able to deceive anyone for a thousand years. He'd be turned loose for a little while after that.

⁴ Then I saw a bunch of judge's chairs. Those cowboys sitting on them were given the authority to judge others. I also witnessed those who had their heads chopped off for not following the beast or taking his brand. They had told the truth about Jesus up to the very end. They were brought back to life and reigned like kings with Jesus for one thousand years. ⁵ (The rest of the dead did not come back to life until after the one thousand years were over.) This is the first raising of the dead. ⁶ There wasn't anyone who was raised to life who said it wasn't worth it. They were all happy. The second death has no power over them. They will be cowboy priests for Christ and God. They will rule for a thousand years.

Satan's Defeat

⁷ After a thousand years, Satan will be untied and dragged out of the pit. ⁸ Once again, he will be allowed to deceive the nations of the world—namely, Gog and Magog. Satan will rally the world once again and try to defeat God's people. Satan's army will number like the grains of sand on all the beaches. ⁹ They surrounded God's camp and his cowboys who he loves. But just as he was about to strike, fire came down from heaven and killed all of the devil's army. ¹⁰ Then that old snake was thrown into the lake of fire and sulfur just like the beast and false prophet were. They will be tormented day and night forever and ever.

The Last Verdict

¹¹ Then I saw the great white throne and the one who sits there. Earth and heaven disappeared in his presence and were never seen again. ¹² Everyone who had ever died now stood before the throne. Their station in life, whether great or small, didn't matter in this moment. Different books were opened and then one book was brought out, the tally book of life. The

dead were judged on how they'd lived their lives according to the deeds recorded in the books. ¹³ The dead came out of the sea as well as the ground. All were judged according to the lives they had lived. ¹⁴ Then death and hell were thrown into the lake of fire which is the second death. ¹⁵ Those whose names were not found in the tally book of life were thrown into the lake of fire.

CHAPTER 21

All of a sudden there was a new heaven and a new earth. The old ones were gone along with the sea. ² The new city of Jerusalem came down from heaven dressed like a bride ready to get hitched. ³ A loud voice from the throne said, "God has unsaddled his horse and made his home among his cowboys. He will live with them and they with him. He will be their God and they will be his hands. ⁴ He will take his neckerchief and wipe away every tear. There will be no more death, crying, or pain. Those things have disappeared."

⁵ Then God spoke from the throne and said, "I am making all things new again." He then spoke directly to me and said, "Jot this down, cowboy. My word can be trusted." ⁶ Then he said, "It's all done. I am the first and the last. I am the point rider and the drag. To anyone who is thirsty, I will give them drink from the windmill of life without charge. ⁷ Those who make it down the hard, narrow trail will get me as their God and I will love them like my own children. ⁸ But those who are lily-livered, double-crossers, perverts, killers, without morals, practicers of witchcraft, idol worshipers, and all liars will end up in the lake of fire. This will be their second death."

The New City

⁹ One of the bowl angels came up and said, "Saddle up. I'm going to take you to see the bride of the Lamb." ¹⁰ He took me in the spirit to the top of a tall mountain. He had me look at the New Jerusalem as it descended out of heaven. ¹¹ It shone with the glory of God. It looked to be made of expensive stone and was clear as crystal. ¹² It had a big wall with twelve gates. Each gate had an angel watching over it. Each gate was named after one of the twelve clans of Israel. ¹³ Three gates adorned each side. ¹⁴ The walls were built on twelve foundation rocks.

These rocks had the names of Jesus's twelve cowboys who rode with him while he was on earth. ¹⁵ The angel I was with had a golden staff with measuring marks on it. It was used to measure the walls, gates, and the city itself. ¹⁶ The town was a perfect square measuring 1,500 miles on each side. ¹⁷ He measured the wall to be 216 feet high. ¹⁸ The wall was built of jasper and the city itself was made of such pure gold that it looked like glass. ¹⁹ The foundation rocks were covered in precious jewels. The first foundation rock was jasper, the second sapphire, the third agate, the fourth emerald, ²⁰ the fifth onyx, the sixth carnelian, the seventh yellow quartz, the eighth beryl, the ninth topaz, the tenth chalcedony, the eleventh turquoise, and the twelfth amethyst. ²¹ The twelve gates were twelve pearls. Each gate was made from a single pearl. The streets were pure gold that looked like glass.

²² There was no temple because God and the Lamb are the temple. ²³ There was no need for a sun or moon. It is lit with the glory of God and the Lamb is the torch. ²⁴ The cowboys of the world will ride by its light. The rulers of the earth will bring their money and riches to the town. ²⁵ The gates will never be closed. There will be no night. ²⁶ All the nations and countries will bring their honor and glory to the town. ²⁷ Nothing vile or nasty will ever be able to enter the town, nor anyone who does shameful things or tells lies. Only those whose names are written in the tally book of life will be able to enter.

CHAPTER 22

Then the angel pointed out to me the creek of life, shining like a diamond coming from the throne of God and the Lamb. ² It flowed down the middle of the street. On each side of the street grew a tree of life that makes fruit twelve times a year. Its leaves will heal the nations.

³ No curse shall be found on anything. This is where the throne of God, the Lamb, and their cowboys are. The cowboys will worship them for all time there. ⁴ They will be able to look upon the face of God and his name will be on their foreheads. ⁵ Since there is no night, there is no need for lamps or the sun. God's glory will light everything. God and his Lamb will rule forever and ever.

⁶ Then the angel said to me, "Nothing you've seen will not happen. It's all true. The Lord God, who spoke to the prophets, has sent me to tell his cowboys what will happen in no time."

Jesus Is Riding Back

⁷ "Listen up!" Jesus said. "I am riding back soon. There won't be a single cowboy who will regret riding for my brand. They will never despair for obeying the words of this book."

⁸ I, John, heard and saw all these things. When it was all over, I fell down at the feet of the angel who had been talking to me. ⁹ He said, "Don't bow down to me. I'm just one of God's hands like you are. We obey God and do what he says to do—the way he says to do it. Bow down to God and God alone!" ¹⁰ And then he said, "Don't keep what you've seen and heard a secret. All of this will happen soon. ¹¹ Everyone will keep on with the ride they started. If they were evil, they'll continue their ride. If they were nasty, they'll keep it up. If they were good, they'll keep going. And if they're holy, they'll stay that way."

¹² "Hey!" Jesus hollered. "I'm riding back soon! I'll be bringing y'alls reward with me when I come. Each will receive a reward based on what they've done. ¹³ I am the first and the last. The point rider and the drag, the beginning and the end."

¹⁴ No one who washes their white shirts and eats from the tree of life will be disappointed. None will regret being able to walk through the gates of the town. ¹⁵ But outside the gates will be those perverts who practice magic, lie, cheat, and steal. Outside are those who worship idols and kill.

¹⁶ "I, Jesus, sent my angel to tell the churches these things I have shown you. I am an ancestor of David's family; I am the bright morning star."

¹⁷ The Holy Spirit and the bride say, "Come on!"

Everyone who hears this must also say, "Come on!"

Come on, whoever is thirsty. Drink from the windmill of life as a gift. It is yours without charge.

Finally

¹⁸ I, John, am warning anyone who listens to the words of this book that they cannot add anything to it. If they do, God will punish them like the plagues described in this book. ¹⁹ If anyone takes anything away from this book, their right to eat from the tree of life will be taken from them.

²⁰ Jesus is the author of all of this and he says, "It is true! I am riding back soon."

²¹ May the grace of Jesus be with all of y'all. Amen.

I grew up in Big Lake, Texas. Without a long and drawn out biography, I gave my heart to God as a teenager. It would be nearly two decades later that I gave my life to God. Yeah, sometimes those two things happen at once . . . sometimes they don't.

I spent my life working the big ranches in Texas. When I thought I needed more money than a cowboy could make, I even went to work for the Texas Department of Criminal Justice - Institutional Division. That's a fancy way of saying I worked for a Texas prison. I spent most of that time working horseback, guarding inmates working outside the fence.

After that played out, I went into oilfield sales and had a lucrative career. I was making six figures and had a private plane fly me around Texas. It was a pretty sweet gig. But then I got the call from God. It came after I prayed, "God, I don't know what you could do with a sorry cowboy like me, but if you'll have me in your outfit, I'll go where you want me to go, say what you want me to say, do what you want me to do, and be who you want me to be."

Little did I know that God would hold me to that prayer. After three years of preaching at a small cowboy church in Fort Stockton, Texas, God called me to Colorado. But alas, that is too long of a story for now.

I had a sweet life being a bi-vocational preacher. I was raising my kids on the family ranch and life was so good it was nearly absurd. That's when God asked me if I had meant what I said when I gave him my life. Of course, I told him yes.

I left everything behind to spread the Good News through the legacy, artistry, and traditions of the working ranch cowboy. That leaving was more than it sounds. It involves angry relatives, mad friends, and even a couple of tragedies.

But still, I persevere.

I don't know what y'all could do with a sorry cowboy like me, but if you'll have me, I'd love to come speak at your church or share a cup of coffee with you on Save the Cowboy's Long X Ranch.

For booking information, email admin@savethecowboy.com.

I'll see y'all in this life or the next. Until then . . .

Kevin Weatherby

Made in the USA
Las Vegas, NV
06 February 2025

17670210R00157